A HISTORY OF THE

BARCLAY FAMILY

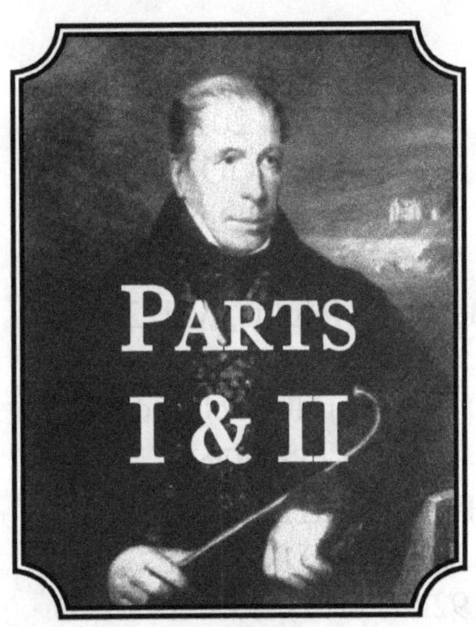
PARTS
I & II

COMPILED BY
THE REV. CHARLES W. BARCLAY &
LIEUT.-COLONEL HUBERT F. BARCLAY

HERITAGE BOOKS
2015

HERITAGE BOOKS
AN IMPRINT OF HERITAGE BOOKS, INC.

Books, CDs, and more—Worldwide

For our listing of thousands of titles see our website
at
www.HeritageBooks.com

A Facsimile Reprint
Published 2015 by
HERITAGE BOOKS, INC.
Publishing Division
5810 Ruatan Street
Berwyn Heights, Md. 20740

Originally published
LONDON
THE ST. CATHERINE PRESS
STAMFORD STREET, S.E.
1924 (Part I), 1933 (Part II)

— Publisher's Notice —
In reprints such as this, it is often not possible to remove blemishes from the original. We feel the contents of this book warrant its reissue despite these blemishes and hope you will agree and read it with pleasure.

The color plate of the tartan that appeared in the original edition has been ommitted in this edition as it was a dark rendition with the wrong coloration for the time period being discussed.

International Standard Book Numbers
Paperbound: 978-1-58549-858-1
Clothbound: 978-0-7884-6090-6

PEDIGREE
OF THE HOUSE OF BARCLAY
FROM ROGER DE BERCHELAI
1066—1924

RISSA, described in document now at Rouen as with her husband Roger being a benefactor to the Abbey of Aumâle. = ROGERIUS DE BERCHELAI, named in Domesday Book as holding the great Manor of Berchelai in 1086. Died 1093.

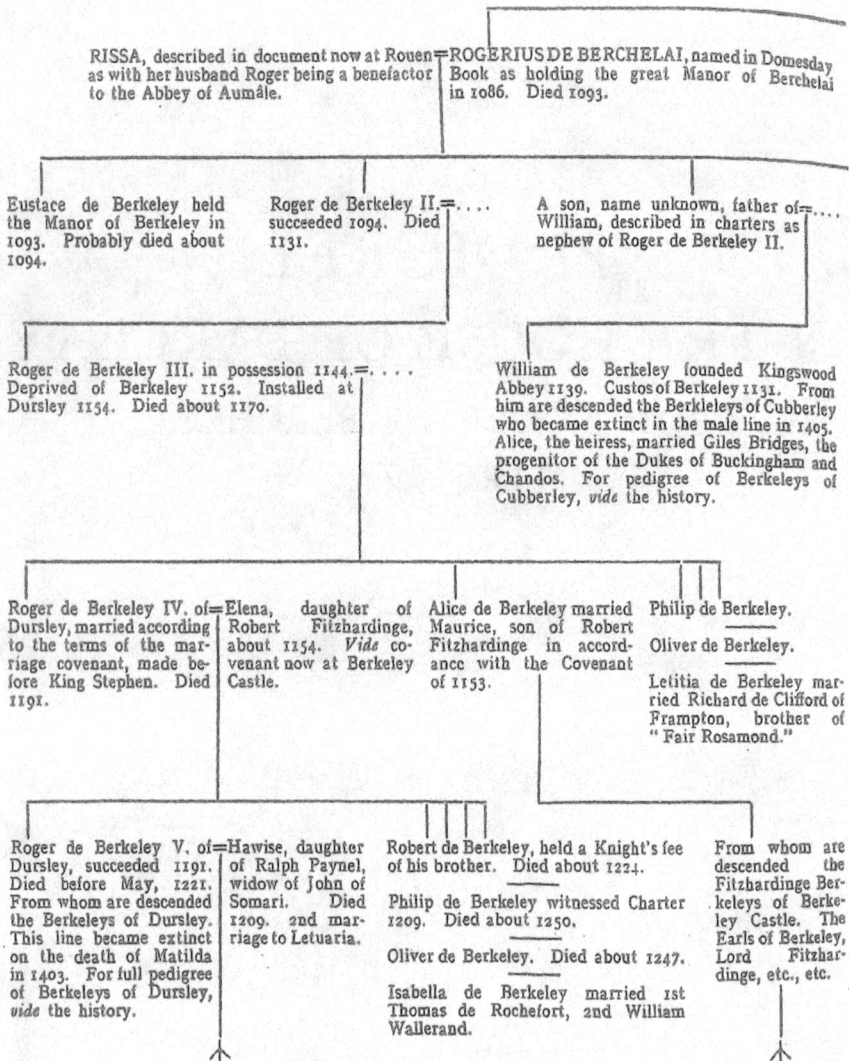

Eustace de Berkeley held the Manor of Berkeley in 1093. Probably died about 1094.

Roger de Berkeley II. = ... succeeded 1094. Died 1131.

A son, name unknown, father of = ... William, described in charters as nephew of Roger de Berkeley II.

Roger de Berkeley III. in possession 1144. = ... Deprived of Berkeley 1152. Installed at Dursley 1154. Died about 1170.

William de Berkeley founded Kingswood Abbey 1139. Custos of Berkeley 1131. From him are descended the Berkleleys of Cubberley who became extinct in the male line in 1405. Alice, the heiress, married Giles Bridges, the progenitor of the Dukes of Buckingham and Chandos. For pedigree of Berkeleys of Cubberley, *vide* the history.

Roger de Berkeley IV. of Dursley, married according to the terms of the marriage covenant, made before King Stephen. Died 1191. = Elena, daughter of Robert Fitzhardinge, about 1154. *Vide* covenant now at Berkeley Castle.

Alice de Berkeley married Maurice, son of Robert Fitzhardinge in accordance with the Covenant of 1153.

Philip de Berkeley.

Oliver de Berkeley.

Letitia de Berkeley married Richard de Clifford of Frampton, brother of "Fair Rosamond."

Roger de Berkeley V. of Dursley, succeeded 1191. Died before May, 1221. From whom are descended the Berkeleys of Dursley. This line became extinct on the death of Matilda in 1403. For full pedigree of Berkeleys of Dursley, *vide* the history. = Hawise, daughter of Ralph Paynel, widow of John of Somari. Died 1209. 2nd marriage to Letuaria.

Robert de Berkeley, held a Knight's fee of his brother. Died about 1224.

Philip de Berkeley witnessed Charter 1209. Died about 1250.

Oliver de Berkeley. Died about 1247.

Isabella de Berkeley married 1st Thomas de Rochefort, 2nd William Wallerand.

From whom are descended the Fitzhardinge Berkeleys of Berkeley Castle. The Earls of Berkeley, Lord Fitzhardinge, etc., etc.

HISTORY OF THE BARCLAY FAMILY

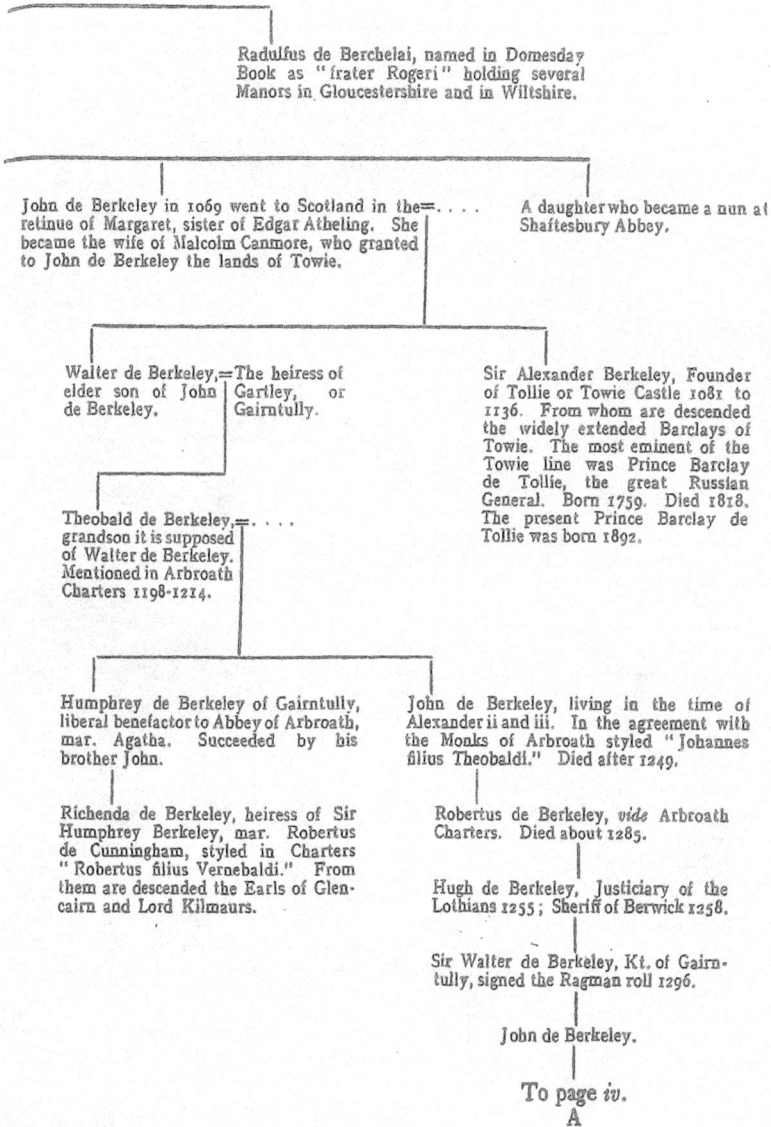

Radulfus de Berchelai, named in Domesday Book as "frater Rogeri" holding several Manors in Gloucestershire and in Wiltshire.

John de Berkeley in 1069 went to Scotland in the retinue of Margaret, sister of Edgar Atheling. She became the wife of Malcolm Canmore, who granted to John de Berkeley the lands of Towie. = ...

A daughter who became a nun at Shaftesbury Abbey.

Walter de Berkeley, elder son of John de Berkeley. = The heiress of Gartley, or Gairntully.

Sir Alexander Berkeley, Founder of Tollie or Towie Castle 1081 to 1136. From whom are descended the widely extended Barclays of Towie. The most eminent of the Towie line was Prince Barclay de Tollie, the great Russian General. Born 1759. Died 1818. The present Prince Barclay de Tollie was born 1892.

Theobald de Berkeley, grandson it is supposed of Walter de Berkeley. Mentioned in Arbroath Charters 1198-1214. = ...

Humphrey de Berkeley of Gairntully, liberal benefactor to Abbey of Arbroath, mar. Agatha. Succeeded by his brother John.

Richenda de Berkeley, heiress of Sir Humphrey Berkeley, mar. Robertus de Cunningham, styled in Charters "Robertus filius Vernebaldi." From them are descended the Earls of Glencairn and Lord Kilmaurs.

John de Berkeley, living in the time of Alexander ii and iii. In the agreement with the Monks of Arbroath styled "Johannes filius Theobaldi." Died after 1249.

Robertus de Berkeley, *vide* Arbroath Charters. Died about 1285.

Hugh de Berkeley, Justiciary of the Lothians 1255; Sheriff of Berwick 1258.

Sir Walter de Berkeley, Kt. of Gairntully, signed the Ragman roll 1296.

John de Berkeley.

To page *iv*.

A

A
From page *iii*.

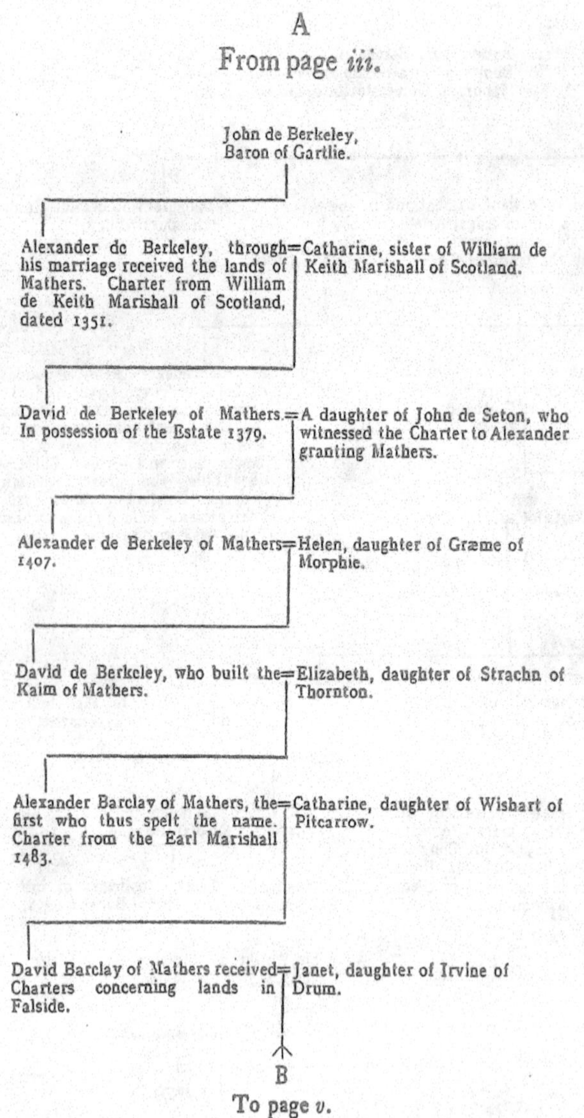
John de Berkeley,
Baron of Gartlie.
Alexander de Berkeley, through his marriage received the lands of Mathers. Charter from William de Keith Marishall of Scotland, dated 1351.
=Catharine, sister of William de Keith Marishall of Scotland.
David de Berkeley of Mathers. In possession of the Estate 1379.
=A daughter of John de Seton, who witnessed the Charter to Alexander granting Mathers.
Alexander de Berkeley of Mathers 1407.
=Helen, daughter of Græme of Morphie.
David de Berkeley, who built the Kaim of Mathers.
=Elizabeth, daughter of Strachn of Thornton.
Alexander Barclay of Mathers, the first who thus spelt the name. Charter from the Earl Marishall 1483.
=Catharine, daughter of Wishart of Pitcarrow.
David Barclay of Mathers received Charters concerning lands in Falside.
=Janet, daughter of Irvine of Drum.

B
To page *v*.

B

From page *iv.*

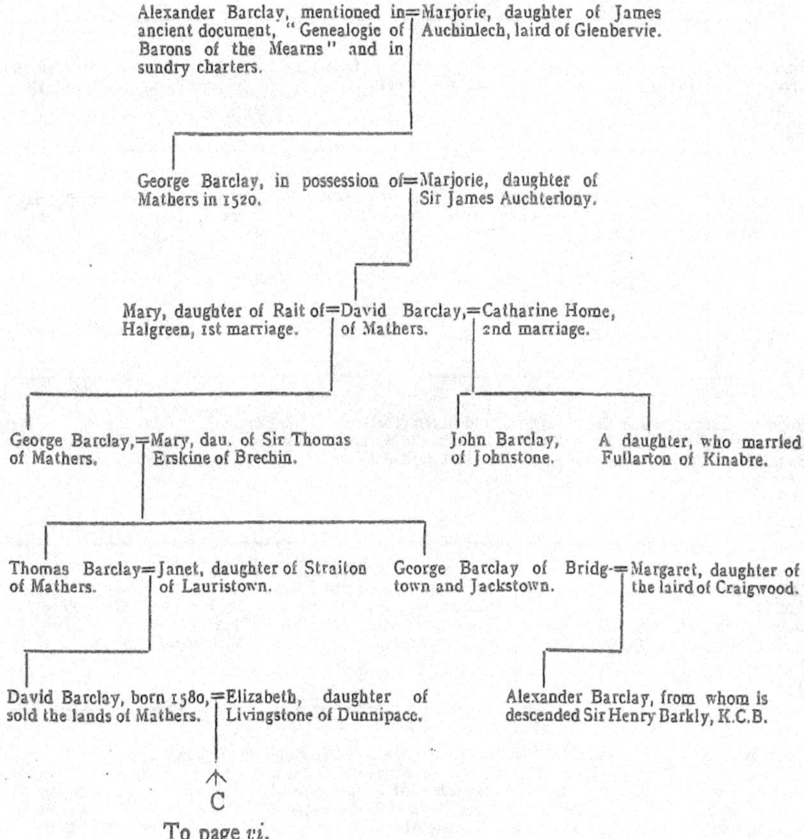
Alexander Barclay, mentioned in ancient document, "Genealogie of Barons of the Mearns" and in sundry charters.
=Marjorie, daughter of James Auchinlech, laird of Glenbervie.
George Barclay, in possession of Mathers in 1520.
=Marjorie, daughter of Sir James Auchterlony.
Mary, daughter of Rait of Halgreen, 1st marriage.
=David Barclay, of Mathers.
=Catharine Home, 2nd marriage.
George Barclay, of Mathers.
=Mary, dau. of Sir Thomas Erskine of Brechin.
John Barclay, of Johnstone.
A daughter, who married Fullarton of Kinabre.
Thomas Barclay of Mathers.
=Janet, daughter of Straiton of Lauristown.
George Barclay of Bridgtown and Jackstown.
=Margaret, daughter of the laird of Craigwood.
David Barclay, born 1580, sold the lands of Mathers.
=Elizabeth, daughter of Livingstone of Dunnipace.
Alexander Barclay, from whom is descended Sir Henry Barkly, K.C.B.
C

To page *vi.*

HISTORY OF THE BARCLAY FAMILY

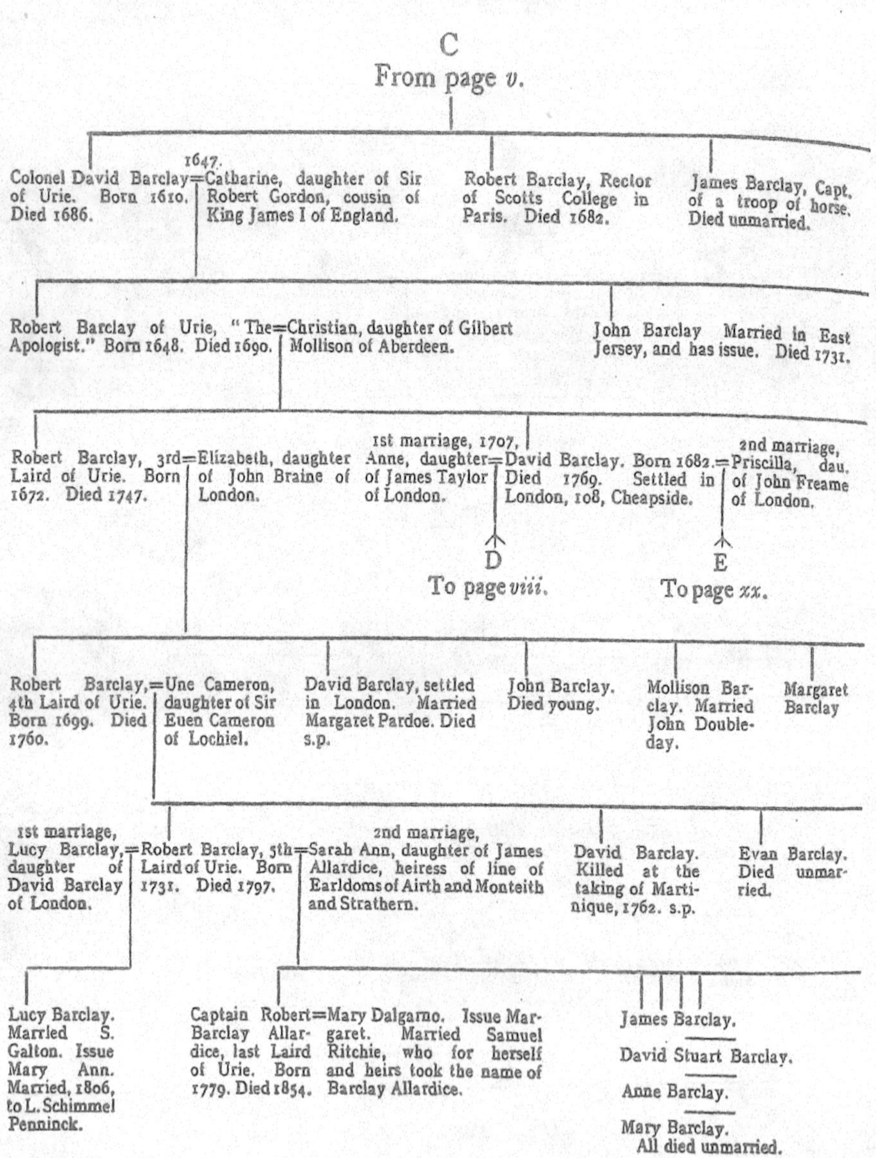
C
From page *v.*
1647.
Colonel David Barclay of Urie. Born 1610. Died 1686.
=Catharine, daughter of Sir Robert Gordon, cousin of King James I of England.
Robert Barclay, Rector of Scotts College in Paris. Died 1682.
James Barclay, Capt. of a troop of horse. Died unmarried.
Robert Barclay of Urie, "The Apologist." Born 1648. Died 1690.
=Christian, daughter of Gilbert Mollison of Aberdeen.
John Barclay Married in East Jersey, and has issue. Died 1731.
Robert Barclay, 3rd Laird of Urie. Born 1672. Died 1747.
=Elizabeth, daughter of John Braine of London.
1st marriage, 1707,
Anne, daughter of James Taylor of London.
=David Barclay. Born 1682. Died 1769. Settled in London, 108, Cheapside.
2nd marriage,
=Priscilla, dau. of John Freame of London.
D
To page *viii.*
E
To page *xx.*
Robert Barclay, 4th Laird of Urie. Born 1699. Died 1760.
=Une Cameron, daughter of Sir Euen Cameron of Lochiel.
David Barclay, settled in London. Married Margaret Pardoe. Died s.p.
John Barclay. Died young.
Mollison Barclay. Married John Doubleday.
Margaret Barclay
1st marriage,
Lucy Barclay, daughter of David Barclay of London.
=Robert Barclay, 5th Laird of Urie. Born 1731. Died 1797.
2nd marriage,
=Sarah Ann, daughter of James Allardice, heiress of line of Earldoms of Airth and Monteith and Strathern.
David Barclay. Killed at the taking of Martinique, 1762. s.p.
Evan Barclay. Died unmarried.
Lucy Barclay. Married S. Galton. Issue Mary Ann. Married, 1806, to L. Schimmel Penninck.
Captain Robert Barclay Allardice, last Laird of Urie. Born 1779. Died 1854.
=Mary Dalgarno. Issue Margaret. Married Samuel Ritchie, who for herself and heirs took the name of Barclay Allardice.
James Barclay.
David Stuart Barclay.
Anne Barclay.
Mary Barclay.
All died unmarried.

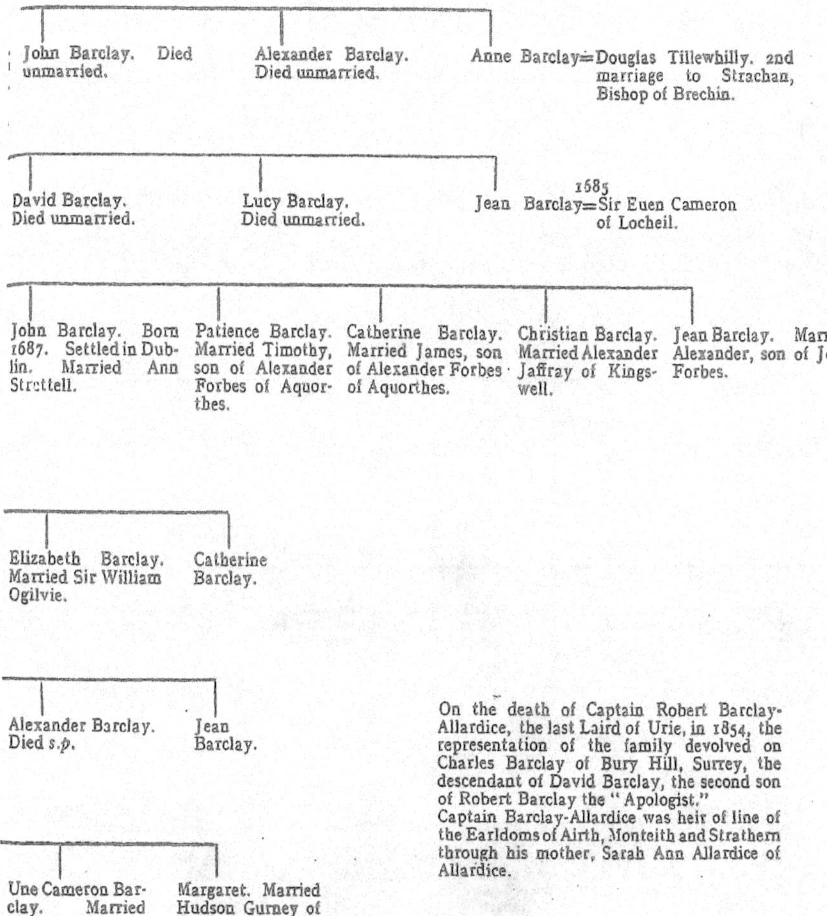
John Barclay. Died unmarried.
Alexander Barclay. Died unmarried.
Anne Barclay=Douglas Tillewhilly. 2nd marriage to Strachan, Bishop of Brechin.
David Barclay. Died unmarried.
Lucy Barclay. Died unmarried.
Jean Barclay=Sir Euen Cameron of Locheil. 1685
John Barclay. Born 1687. Settled in Dublin. Married Ann Strettell.
Patience Barclay. Married Timothy, son of Alexander Forbes of Aquorthes.
Catherine Barclay. Married James, son of Alexander Forbes of Aquorthes.
Christian Barclay. Married Alexander Jaffray of Kingswell.
Jean Barclay. Marrie Alexander, son of Job Forbes.
Elizabeth Barclay. Married Sir William Ogilvie.
Catherine Barclay.
Alexander Barclay. Died s.p.
Jean Barclay.
Une Cameron Barclay. Married John Innes.
Margaret. Married Hudson Gurney of Keswick.
See page xx.

On the death of Captain Robert Barclay-Allardice, the last Laird of Urie, in 1854, the representation of the family devolved on Charles Barclay of Bury Hill, Surrey, the descendant of David Barclay, the second son of Robert Barclay the "Apologist."
Captain Barclay-Allardice was heir of line of the Earldoms of Airth, Monteith and Strathern through his mother, Sarah Ann Allardice of Allardice.

HISTORY OF THE BARCLAY FAMILY

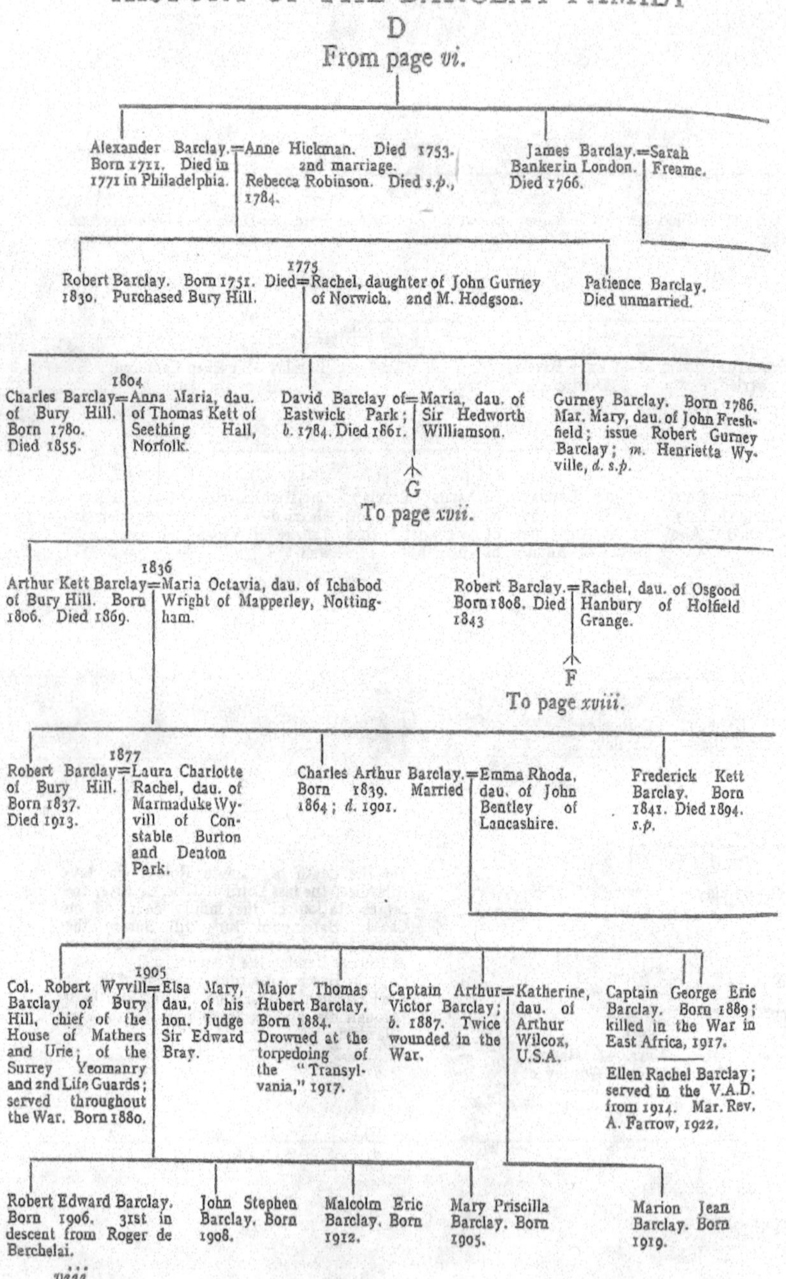
D
From page *vi.*
Alexander Barclay. = Anne Hickman. Died 1753. 2nd marriage. Rebecca Robinson. Died s.p., 1784.
Alexander Barclay. Born 1711. Died in 1771 in Philadelphia.
James Barclay. = Sarah Freame.
James Barclay. Banker in London. Died 1766.
Robert Barclay. Born 1751. Died 1830. Purchased Bury Hill. = 1775 Rachel, daughter of John Gurney of Norwich. 2nd M. Hodgson.
Patience Barclay. Died unmarried.
Charles Barclay of Bury Hill. Born 1780. Died 1855. = 1804 Anna Maria, dau. of Thomas Kett of Seething Hall, Norfolk.
David Barclay of Eastwick Park; b. 1784. Died 1861. = Maria, dau. of Sir Hedworth Williamson.
G
To page *xvii.*
Gurney Barclay. Born 1786. Mar. Mary, dau. of John Freshfield; issue Robert Gurney Barclay; m. Henrietta Wyville, d. s.p.
Arthur Kett Barclay of Bury Hill. Born 1806. Died 1869. = 1836 Maria Octavia, dau. of Ichabod Wright of Mapperley, Nottingham.
Robert Barclay. Born 1808. Died 1843 = Rachel, dau. of Osgood Hanbury of Holfield Grange.
F
To page *xviii.*
Robert Barclay of Bury Hill. Born 1837. Died 1913. = 1877 Laura Charlotte Rachel, dau. of Marmaduke Wyvill of Constable Burton and Denton Park.
Charles Arthur Barclay. Born 1839. Married 1864; d. 1901. = Emma Rhoda, dau. of John Bentley of Lancashire.
Frederick Kett Barclay. Born 1841. Died 1894. s.p.
Col. Robert Wyvill Barclay of Bury Hill, chief of the House of Mathers and Urie; of the Surrey Yeomanry and 2nd Life Guards; served throughout the War. Born 1880. = 1905 Elsa Mary, dau. of his hon. Judge Sir Edward Bray.
Major Thomas Hubert Barclay. Born 1884. Drowned at the torpedoing of the "Transylvania," 1917.
Captain Arthur Victor Barclay; b. 1887. Twice wounded in the War. = Katherine, dau. of Arthur Wilcox, U.S.A.
Captain George Eric Barclay. Born 1889; killed in the War in East Africa, 1917.
Ellen Rachel Barclay; served in the V.A.D. from 1914. Mar. Rev. A. Farrow, 1922.
Robert Edward Barclay. Born 1906. 31st in descent from Roger de Berchelai.
John Stephen Barclay. Born 1908.
Malcolm Eric Barclay. Born 1912.
Mary Priscilla Barclay. Born 1905.
Marion Jean Barclay. Born 1919.

HISTORY OF THE BARCLAY FAMILY

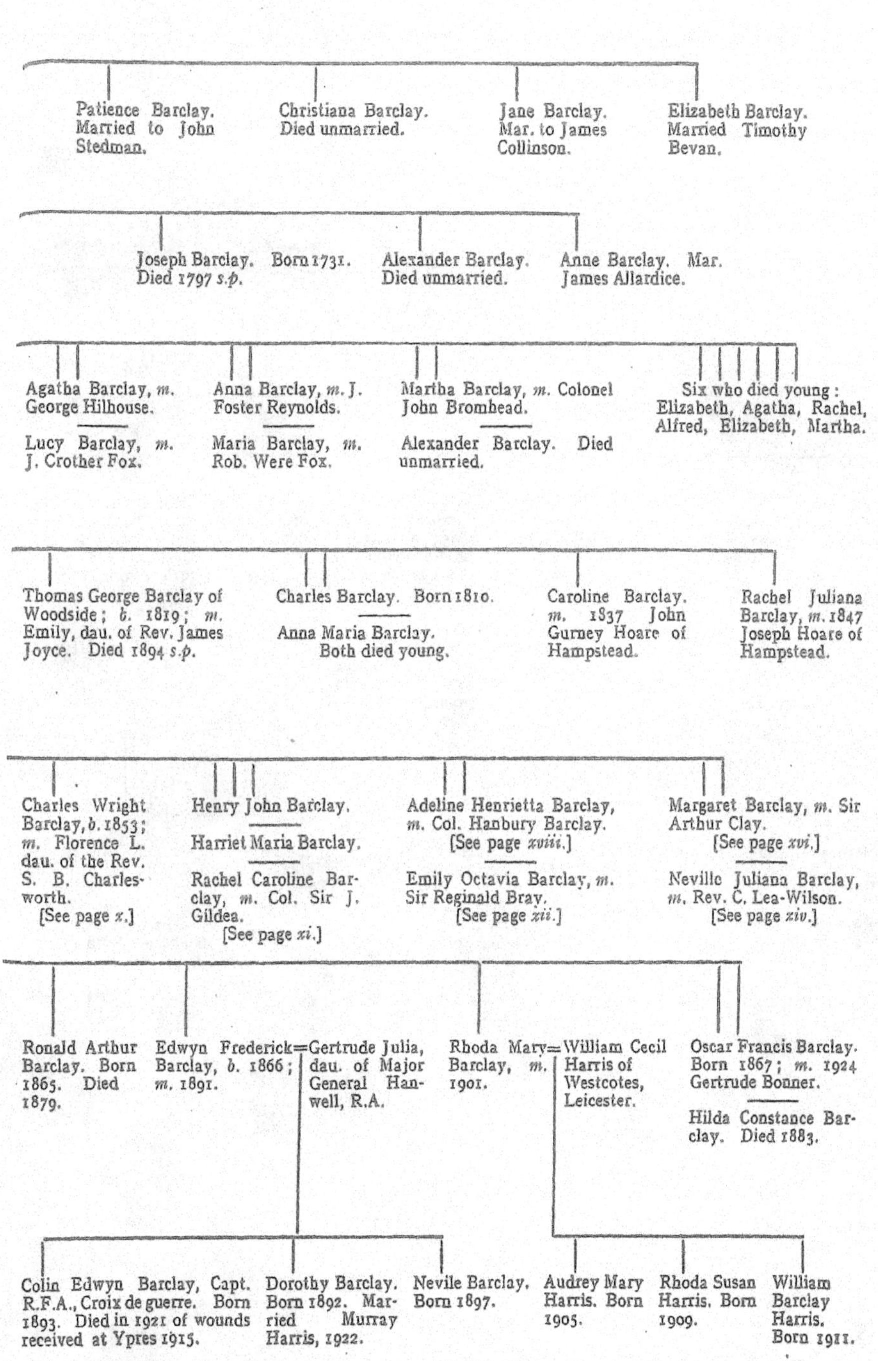

Patience Barclay. Married to John Stedman.
Christiana Barclay. Died unmarried.
Jane Barclay. Mar. to James Collinson.
Elizabeth Barclay. Married Timothy Bevan.
Joseph Barclay. Born 1731. Died 1797 *s.p.*
Alexander Barclay. Died unmarried.
Anne Barclay. Mar. James Allardice.
Agatha Barclay, *m.* George Hilhouse.
Lucy Barclay, *m.* J. Crother Fox.
Anna Barclay, *m.* J. Foster Reynolds.
Maria Barclay, *m.* Rob. Were Fox.
Martha Barclay, *m.* Colonel John Bromhead.
Alexander Barclay. Died unmarried.
Six who died young: Elizabeth, Agatha, Rachel, Alfred, Elizabeth, Martha.
Thomas George Barclay of Woodside; *b.* 1819; *m.* Emily, dau. of Rev. James Joyce. Died 1894 *s.p.*
Charles Barclay. Born 1810.
Anna Maria Barclay. Both died young.
Caroline Barclay. *m.* 1837 John Gurney Hoare of Hampstead.
Rachel Juliana Barclay, *m.* 1847 Joseph Hoare of Hampstead.
Charles Wright Barclay, *b.* 1853; *m.* Florence L. dau. of the Rev. S. B. Charlesworth. [See page *x*.]
Henry John Barclay.
Harriet Maria Barclay.
Rachel Caroline Barclay, *m.* Col. Sir J. Gildea. [See page *xi*.]
Adeline Henrietta Barclay, *m.* Col. Hanbury Barclay. [See page *xviii*.]
Emily Octavia Barclay, *m.* Sir Reginald Bray. [See page *xii*.]
Margaret Barclay, *m.* Sir Arthur Clay. [See page *xvi*.]
Neville Juliana Barclay, *m.* Rev. C. Lea-Wilson. [See page *xiv*.]
Ronald Arthur Barclay. Born 1865. Died 1879.
Edwyn Frederick Barclay, *b.* 1866; *m.* 1891. = Gertrude Julia, dau. of Major General Hanwell, R.A.
Rhoda Mary Barclay, *m.* 1901. = William Cecil Harris of Westcotes, Leicester.
Oscar Francis Barclay. Born 1867; *m.* 1924 Gertrude Bonner.
Hilda Constance Barclay. Died 1883.
Colin Edwyn Barclay, Capt. R.F.A., Croix de guerre. Born 1893. Died in 1921 of wounds received at Ypres 1915.
Dorothy Barclay. Born 1892. Married Murray Harris, 1922.
Nevile Barclay. Born 1897.
Audrey Mary Harris. Born 1905.
Rhoda Susan Harris. Born 1909.
William Barclay Harris. Born 1911.

HISTORY OF THE BARCLAY FAMILY

From page *ix*.

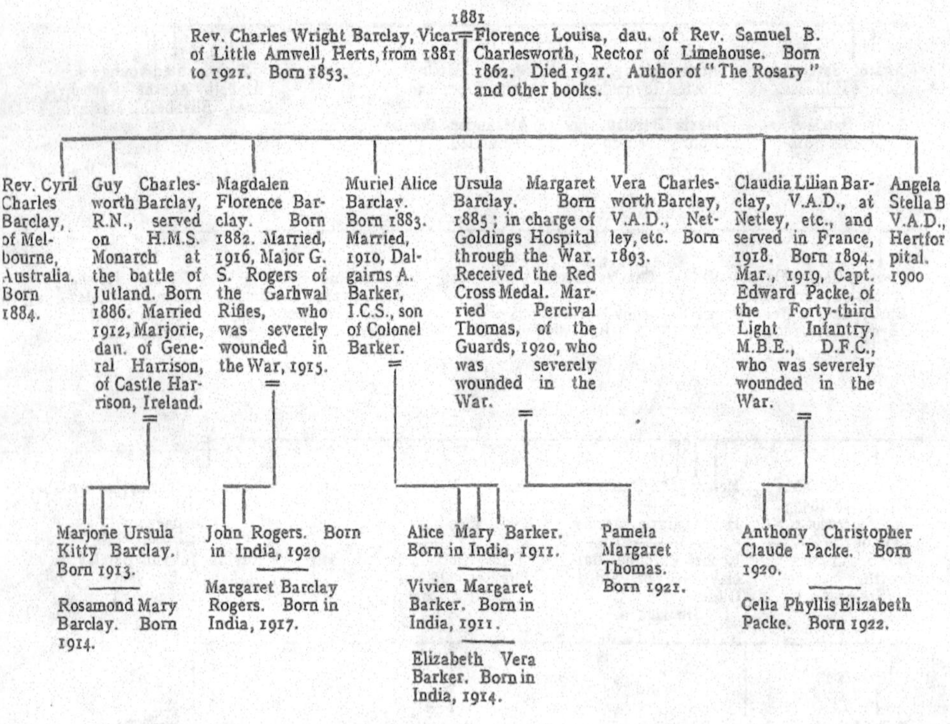

Rev. Charles Wright Barclay, Vicar of Little Amwell, Herts, from 1881 to 1921. Born 1853. = (1881) Florence Louisa, dau. of Rev. Samuel B. Charlesworth, Rector of Limehouse. Born 1862. Died 1921. Author of "The Rosary" and other books.

Children:

- Rev. Cyril Charles Barclay, of Melbourne, Australia. Born 1884.
- Guy Charlesworth Barclay, R.N., served on H.M.S. Monarch at the battle of Jutland. Born 1886. Married 1912, Marjorie, dau. of General Harrison, of Castle Harrison, Ireland. =
    - Marjorie Ursula Kitty Barclay. Born 1913.
    - Rosamond Mary Barclay. Born 1914.
- Magdalen Florence Barclay. Born 1882. Married, 1916, Major G. S. Rogers of the Garhwal Rifles, who was severely wounded in the War, 1915. =
    - John Rogers. Born in India, 1920
    - Margaret Barclay Rogers. Born in India, 1917.
- Muriel Alice Barclay. Born 1883. Married, 1910, Dalgairns A. Barker, I.C.S., son of Colonel Barker. =
    - Alice Mary Barker. Born in India, 1911.
    - Vivien Margaret Barker. Born in India, 1911.
    - Elizabeth Vera Barker. Born in India, 1914.
- Ursula Margaret Barclay. Born 1885; in charge of Goldings Hospital through the War. Received the Red Cross Medal. Married Percival Thomas, of the Guards, 1920, who was severely wounded in the War. =
    - Pamela Margaret Thomas. Born 1921.
- Vera Charlesworth Barclay, V.A.D., Netley, etc. Born 1893.
- Claudia Lilian Barclay, V.A.D., at Netley, etc., and served in France, 1918. Born 1894. Mar., 1919, Capt. Edward Packe, of the Forty-third Light Infantry, M.B.E., D.F.C., who was severely wounded in the War. =
    - Anthony Christopher Claude Packe. Born 1920.
    - Celia Phyllis Elizabeth Packe. Born 1922.
- Angela Stella B V.A.D., Hertfor pital. 1900

From page *ix*.

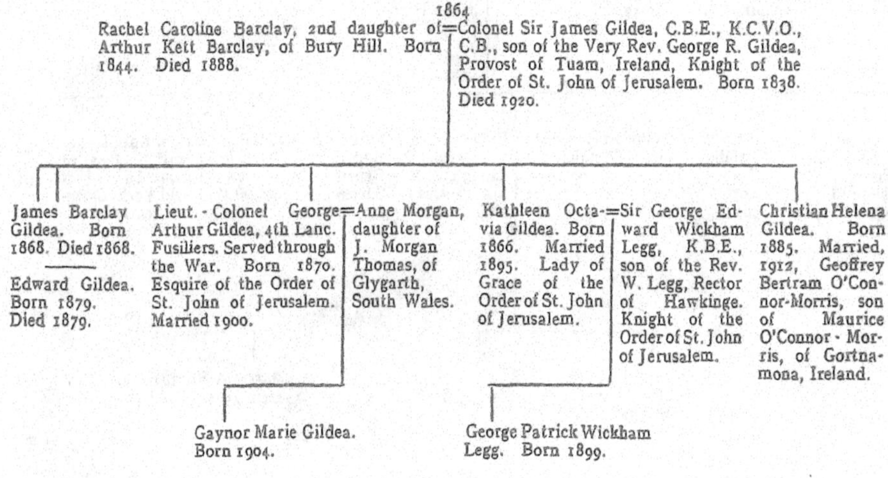
1864
Rachel Caroline Barclay, 2nd daughter of Arthur Kett Barclay, of Bury Hill. Born 1844. Died 1888.
=Colonel Sir James Gildea, C.B.E., K.C.V.O., C.B., son of the Very Rev. George R. Gildea, Provost of Tuam, Ireland, Knight of the Order of St. John of Jerusalem. Born 1838. Died 1920.
James Barclay Gildea. Born 1868. Died 1868.
Edward Gildea. Born 1879. Died 1879.
Lieut.-Colonel George Arthur Gildea, 4th Lanc. Fusiliers. Served through the War. Born 1870. Esquire of the Order of St. John of Jerusalem. Married 1900.
=Anne Morgan, daughter of J. Morgan Thomas, of Glygarth, South Wales.
Kathleen Octavia Gildea. Born 1866. Married 1895. Lady of Grace of the Order of St. John of Jerusalem.
=Sir George Edward Wickham Legg, K.B.E., son of the Rev. W. Legg, Rector of Hawkinge. Knight of the Order of St. John of Jerusalem.
Christian Helena Gildea. Born 1885. Married, 1912, Geoffrey Bertram O'Connor-Morris, son of Maurice O'Connor-Morris, of Gortnamona, Ireland.
Gaynor Marie Gildea. Born 1904.
George Patrick Wickham Legg. Born 1899.

From page *ix*.

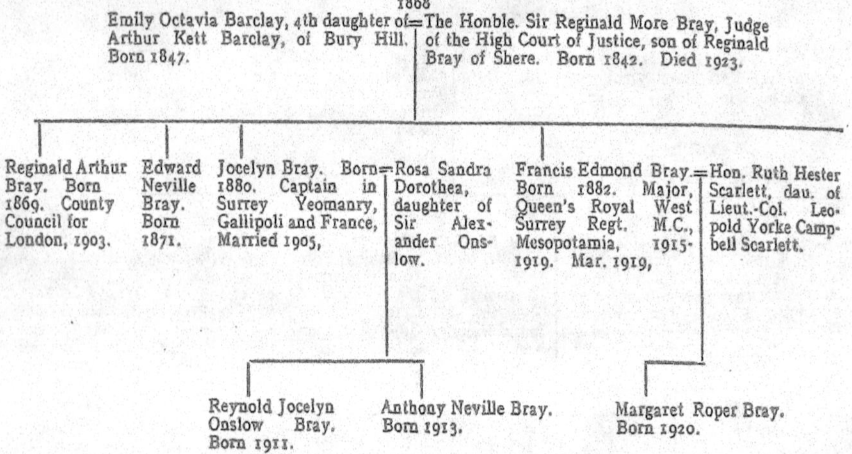
1868
Emily Octavia Barclay, 4th daughter of Arthur Kett Barclay, of Bury Hill. Born 1847.
= The Honble. Sir Reginald More Bray, Judge of the High Court of Justice, son of Reginald Bray of Shere. Born 1842. Died 1923.
Reginald Arthur Bray. Born 1869. County Council for London, 1903.
Edward Neville Bray. Born 1871.
Jocelyn Bray. Born 1880. Captain in Surrey Yeomanry, Gallipoli and France, Married 1905,
= Rosa Sandra Dorothea, daughter of Sir Alexander Onslow.
Francis Edmond Bray. Born 1882. Major, Queen's Royal West Surrey Regt. M.C., Mesopotamia, 1915-1919. Mar. 1919,
= Hon. Ruth Hester Scarlett, dau. of Lieut.-Col. Leopold Yorke Campbell Scarlett.
Reynold Jocelyn Onslow Bray. Born 1911.
Anthony Neville Bray. Born 1913.
Margaret Roper Bray. Born 1920.

HISTORY OF THE BARCLAY FAMILY

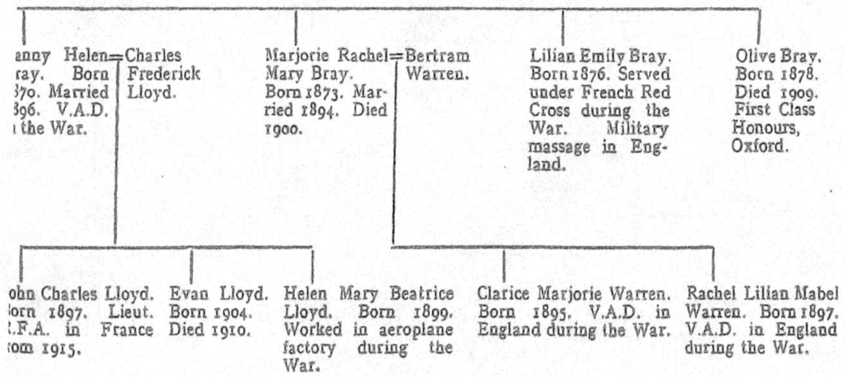
anny Helen Bray. Born 370. Married 396. V.A.D. i the War.
Charles Frederick Lloyd.
Marjorie Rachel Mary Bray. Born 1873. Married 1894. Died 1900.
Bertram Warren.
Lilian Emily Bray. Born 1876. Served under French Red Cross during the War. Military massage in England.
Olive Bray. Born 1878. Died 1909. First Class Honours, Oxford.
ohn Charles Lloyd. Born 1897. Lieut. R.F.A. in France rom 1915.
Evan Lloyd. Born 1904. Died 1910.
Helen Mary Beatrice Lloyd. Born 1899. Worked in aeroplane factory during the War.
Clarice Marjorie Warren. Born 1895. V.A.D. in England during the War.
Rachel Lilian Mabel Warren. Born 1897. V.A.D. in England during the War.

From page *ix*.

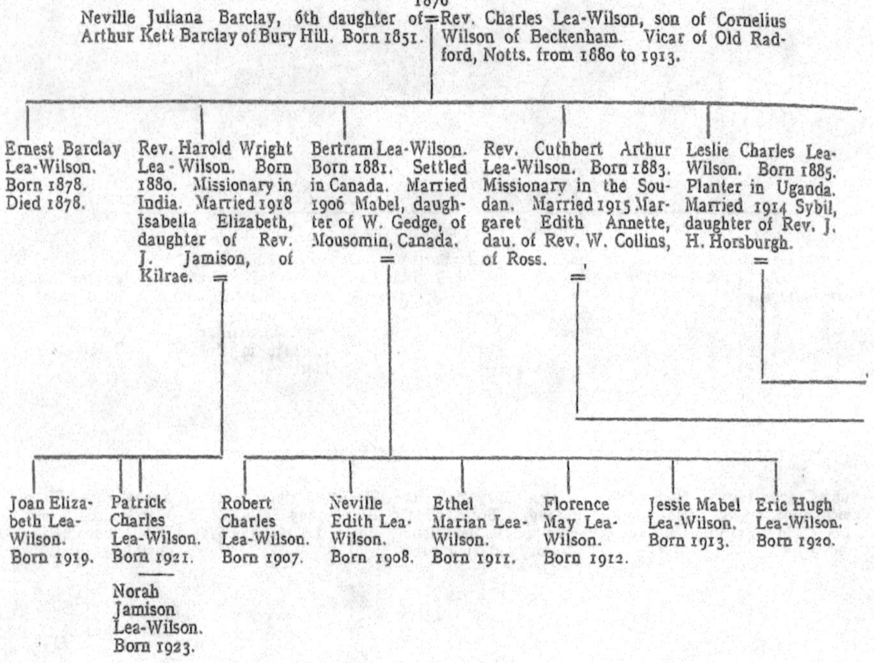
1876
Neville Juliana Barclay, 6th daughter of Arthur Kett Barclay of Bury Hill. Born 1851.
= Rev. Charles Lea-Wilson, son of Cornelius Wilson of Beckenham. Vicar of Old Radford, Notts. from 1880 to 1913.
Ernest Barclay Lea-Wilson. Born 1878. Died 1878.
Rev. Harold Wright Lea-Wilson. Born 1880. Missionary in India. Married 1918 Isabella Elizabeth, daughter of Rev. J. Jamison, of Kilrae. =
Bertram Lea-Wilson. Born 1881. Settled in Canada. Married 1906 Mabel, daughter of W. Gedge, of Mousomin, Canada. =
Rev. Cuthbert Arthur Lea-Wilson. Born 1883. Missionary in the Soudan. Married 1915 Margaret Edith Annette, dau. of Rev. W. Collins, of Ross. =
Leslie Charles Lea-Wilson. Born 1885. Planter in Uganda. Married 1914 Sybil, daughter of Rev. J. H. Horsburgh. =
Joan Elizabeth Lea-Wilson. Born 1919.
Patrick Charles Lea-Wilson. Born 1921.
Norah Jamison Lea-Wilson. Born 1923.
Robert Charles Lea-Wilson. Born 1907.
Neville Edith Lea-Wilson. Born 1908.
Ethel Marian Lea-Wilson. Born 1911.
Florence May Lea-Wilson. Born 1912.
Jessie Mabel Lea-Wilson. Born 1913.
Eric Hugh Lea-Wilson. Born 1920.

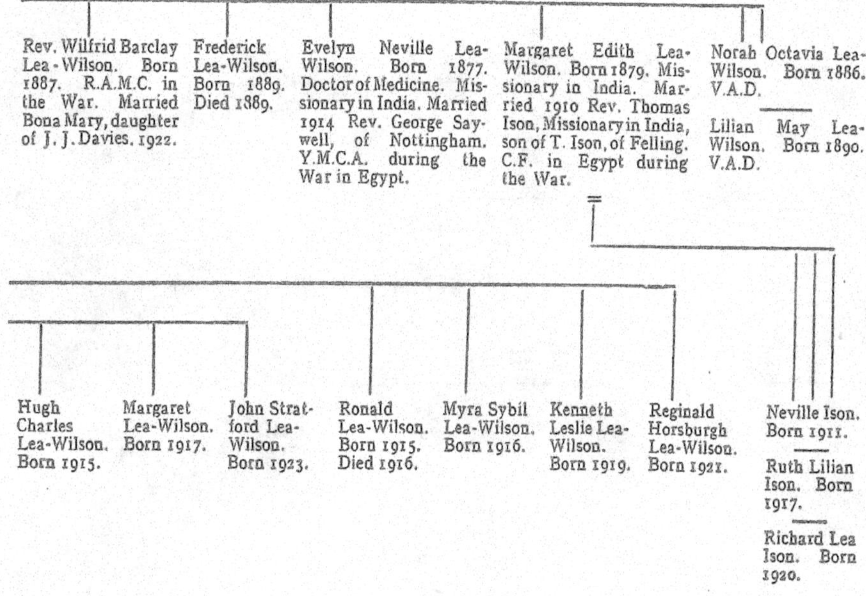
Rev. Wilfrid Barclay Lea-Wilson. Born 1887. R.A.M.C. in the War. Married Bona Mary, daughter of J. J. Davies. 1922.
Frederick Lea-Wilson. Born 1889. Died 1889.
Evelyn Neville Lea-Wilson. Born 1877. Doctor of Medicine. Missionary in India. Married 1914 Rev. George Saywell, of Nottingham. Y.M.C.A. during the War in Egypt.
Margaret Edith Lea-Wilson. Born 1879. Missionary in India. Married 1910 Rev. Thomas Ison, Missionary in India, son of T. Ison, of Felling. C.F. in Egypt during the War.
Norah Lea-Wilson. V.A.D.
Octavia Lea-Wilson. Born 1886.
Lilian May Lea-Wilson. Born 1890. V.A.D.
Hugh Charles Lea-Wilson. Born 1915.
Margaret Lea-Wilson. Born 1917.
John Stratford Lea-Wilson. Born 1923.
Ronald Lea-Wilson. Born 1915. Died 1916.
Myra Sybil Lea-Wilson. Born 1916.
Kenneth Leslie Lea-Wilson. Born 1919.
Reginald Horsburgh Lea-Wilson. Born 1921.
Neville Ison. Born 1911.
Ruth Lilian Ison. Born 1917.
Richard Lea Ison. Born 1920.

HISTORY OF THE BARCLAY FAMILY

From page *ix.*

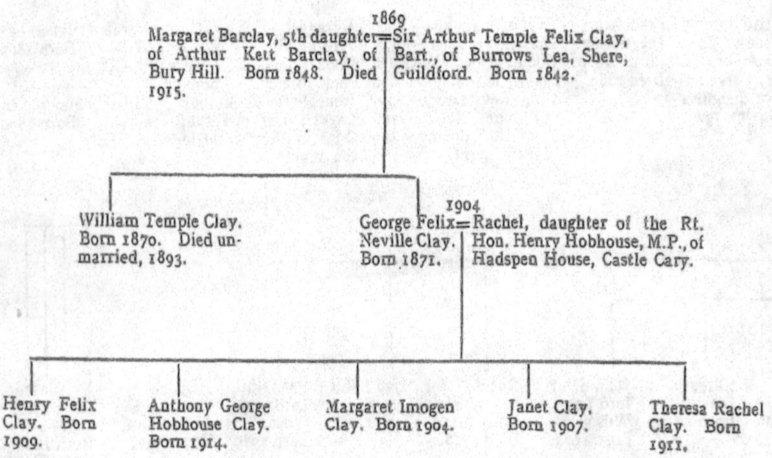
1869
Margaret Barclay, 5th daughter of Arthur Kett Barclay, of Bury Hill. Born 1848. Died 1915.
=Sir Arthur Temple Felix Clay, Bart., of Burrows Lea, Shere, Guildford. Born 1842.
William Temple Clay. Born 1870. Died unmarried, 1893.
1904
George Felix Neville Clay. Born 1871.
=Rachel, daughter of the Rt. Hon. Henry Hobhouse, M.P., of Hadspen House, Castle Cary.
Henry Felix Clay. Born 1909.
Anthony George Hobhouse Clay. Born 1914.
Margaret Imogen Clay. Born 1904.
Janet Clay. Born 1907.
Theresa Rachel Clay. Born 1911.

HISTORY OF THE BARCLAY FAMILY

G

From page *viii*.

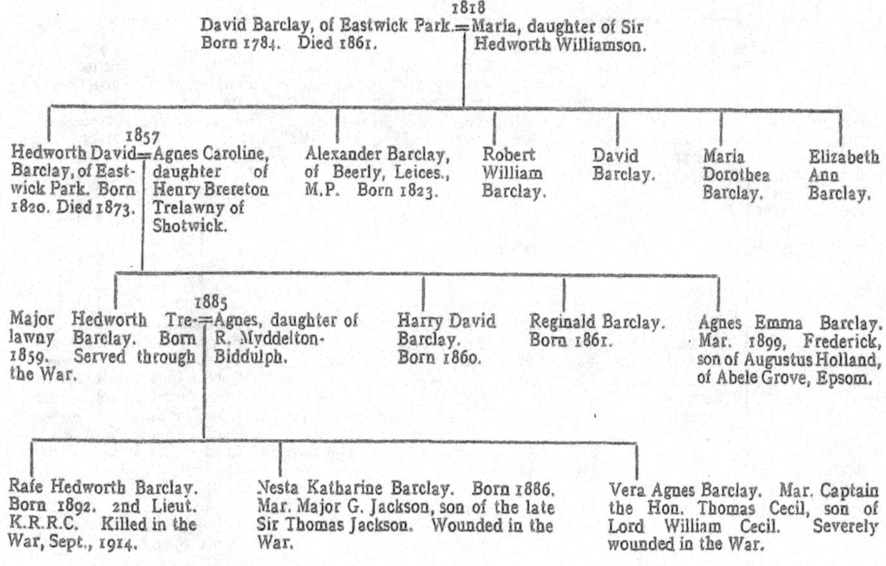
1818
David Barclay, of Eastwick Park. Born 1784. Died 1861.
Maria, daughter of Sir Hedworth Williamson.
1857
Hedworth David Barclay, of Eastwick Park. Born 1820. Died 1873.
Agnes Caroline, daughter of Henry Brereton Trelawny of Shotwick.
Alexander Barclay, of Beerly, Leices., M.P. Born 1823.
Robert William Barclay.
David Barclay.
Maria Dorothea Barclay.
Elizabeth Ann Barclay.
1885
Major Hedworth Trelawny Barclay. Born 1859. Served through the War.
Agnes, daughter of R. Myddelton-Biddulph.
Harry David Barclay. Born 1860.
Reginald Barclay. Born 1861.
Agnes Emma Barclay. Mar. 1899, Frederick, son of Augustus Holland, of Abele Grove, Epsom.
Rafe Hedworth Barclay. Born 1892. 2nd Lieut. K.R.R.C. Killed in the War, Sept., 1914.
Nesta Katharine Barclay. Born 1886. Mar. Major G. Jackson, son of the late Sir Thomas Jackson. Wounded in the War.
Vera Agnes Barclay. Mar. Captain the Hon. Thomas Cecil, son of Lord William Cecil. Severely wounded in the War.

F

From page *viii*.

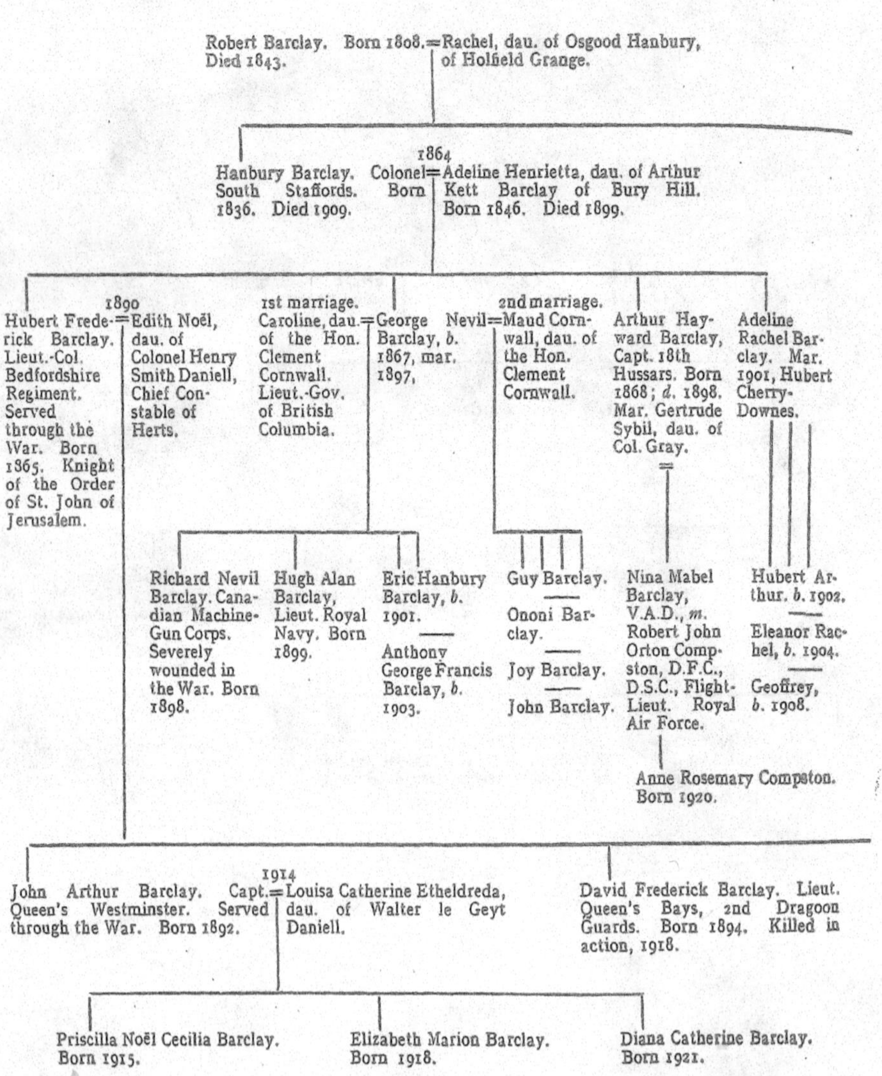
Robert Barclay. Born 1808. = Rachel, dau. of Osgood Hanbury, of Holfield Grange.
Died 1843.
1864
Hanbury Barclay. Colonel South Staffords. Born 1836. Died 1909. = Adeline Henrietta, dau. of Arthur Kett Barclay of Bury Hill. Born 1846. Died 1899.
1890
Hubert Frederick Barclay. Lieut.-Col. Bedfordshire Regiment. Served through the War. Born 1865. Knight of the Order of St. John of Jerusalem. = Edith Noël, dau. of Colonel Henry Smith Daniell, Chief Constable of Herts.
1st marriage.
Caroline, dau. of the Hon. Clement Cornwall. Lieut.-Gov. of British Columbia. = George Nevil Barclay, b. 1867, mar. 1897,
2nd marriage.
= Maud Cornwall, dau. of the Hon. Clement Cornwall.
Arthur Hayward Barclay, Capt. 18th Hussars. Born 1868; d. 1898. Mar. Gertrude Sybil, dau. of Col. Gray.
Adeline Rachel Barclay. Mar. 1901, Hubert Cherry-Downes.
Richard Nevil Barclay. Canadian Machine-Gun Corps. Severely wounded in the War. Born 1898.
Hugh Alan Barclay, Lieut. Royal Navy. Born 1899.
Eric Hanbury Barclay, b. 1901.
Anthony George Francis Barclay, b. 1903.
Guy Barclay.
Ononi Barclay.
Joy Barclay.
John Barclay.
Nina Mabel Barclay, V.A.D., m. Robert John Orton Compston, D.F.C., D.S.C., Flight-Lieut. Royal Air Force.
Anne Rosemary Compston. Born 1920.
Hubert Arthur. b. 1902.
Eleanor Rachel, b. 1904.
Geoffrey, b. 1908.
1914
John Arthur Barclay. Capt. Queen's Westminster. Served through the War. Born 1892. = Louisa Catherine Etheldreda, dau. of Walter le Geyt Daniell.
David Frederick Barclay. Lieut. Queen's Bays, 2nd Dragoon Guards. Born 1894. Killed in action, 1918.
Priscilla Noël Cecilia Barclay. Born 1915.
Elizabeth Marion Barclay. Born 1918.
Diana Catherine Barclay. Born 1921.

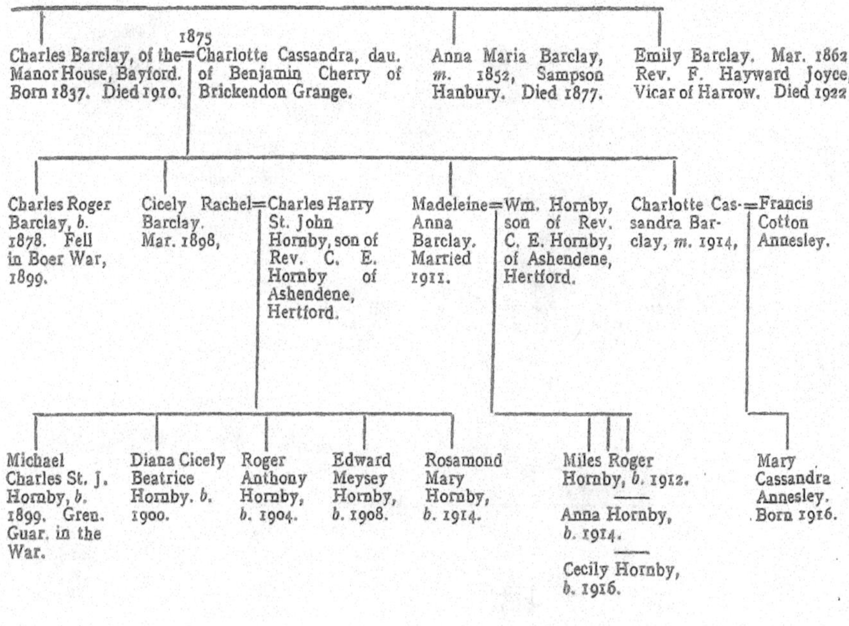
1875
Charles Barclay, of the Manor House, Bayford. Born 1837. Died 1910.
= Charlotte Cassandra, dau. of Benjamin Cherry of Brickendon Grange.
Anna Maria Barclay, m. 1852, Sampson Hanbury. Died 1877.
Emily Barclay. Mar. 1862, Rev. F. Hayward Joyce, Vicar of Harrow. Died 1922.
Charles Roger Barclay, b. 1878. Fell in Boer War, 1899.
Cicely Rachel Barclay. Mar. 1898,
= Charles Harry St. John Hornby, son of Rev. C. E. Hornby of Ashendene, Hertford.
Madeleine Anna Barclay. Married 1911.
= Wm. Hornby, son of Rev. C. E. Hornby, of Ashendene, Hertford.
Charlotte Cassandra Barclay, m. 1914,
= Francis Cotton Annesley.
Michael Charles St. J. Hornby, b. 1899. Gren. Guar. in the War.
Diana Cicely Beatrice Hornby. b. 1900.
Roger Anthony Hornby, b. 1904.
Edward Meysey Hornby, b. 1908.
Rosamond Mary Hornby, b. 1914.
Miles Roger Hornby, b. 1912.
Anna Hornby, b. 1914.
Cecily Hornby, b. 1916.
Mary Cassandra Annesley. Born 1916.

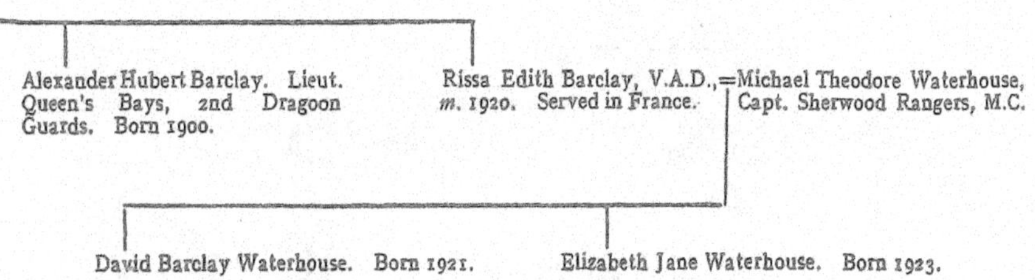
Alexander Hubert Barclay. Lieut. Queen's Bays, 2nd Dragoon Guards. Born 1900.
Rissa Edith Barclay, V.A.D., m. 1920. Served in France.
= Michael Theodore Waterhouse, Capt. Sherwood Rangers, M.C.
David Barclay Waterhouse. Born 1921.
Elizabeth Jane Waterhouse. Born 1923.

HISTORY OF THE BARCLAY FAMILY

E
From page *vi*.

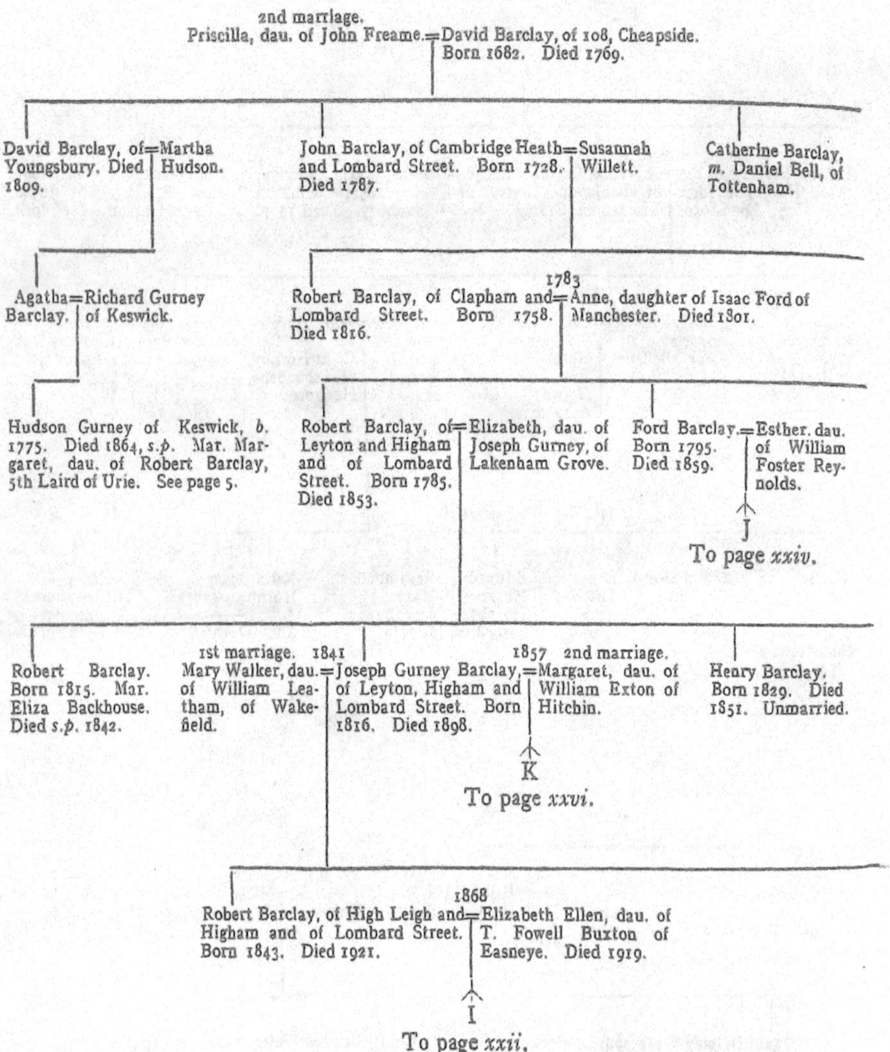

2nd marriage.
Priscilla, dau. of John Freame.=David Barclay, of 108, Cheapside. Born 1682. Died 1769.
David Barclay, of Youngsbury. Died 1809.=Martha Hudson.
John Barclay, of Cambridge Heath and Lombard Street. Born 1728. Died 1787.=Susannah Willett.
Catherine Barclay, m. Daniel Bell, of Tottenham.
Agatha Barclay.=Richard Gurney of Keswick.
1783
Robert Barclay, of Clapham and Lombard Street. Born 1758. Died 1816.=Anne, daughter of Isaac Ford of Manchester. Died 1801.
Hudson Gurney of Keswick, b. 1775. Died 1864, s.p. Mar. Margaret, dau. of Robert Barclay, 5th Laird of Urie. See page 5.
Robert Barclay, of Leyton and Higham and of Lombard Street. Born 1785. Died 1853.=Elizabeth, dau. of Joseph Gurney, of Lakenham Grove.
Ford Barclay. Born 1795. Died 1859.=Esther, dau. of William Foster Reynolds.
J
To page xxiv.
Robert Barclay. Born 1815. Mar. Eliza Backhouse. Died s.p. 1842.
1st marriage. 1841
Mary Walker, dau. of William Leatham, of Wakefield.=Joseph Gurney Barclay, of Leyton, Higham and Lombard Street. Born 1816. Died 1898.
1857 2nd marriage.
=Margaret, dau. of William Exton of Hitchin.
K
To page xxvi.
Henry Barclay. Born 1829. Died 1851. Unmarried.
1868
Robert Barclay, of High Leigh and Higham and of Lombard Street. Born 1843. Died 1921.=Elizabeth Ellen, dau. of T. Fowell Buxton of Easneye. Died 1919.
I
To page xxii.

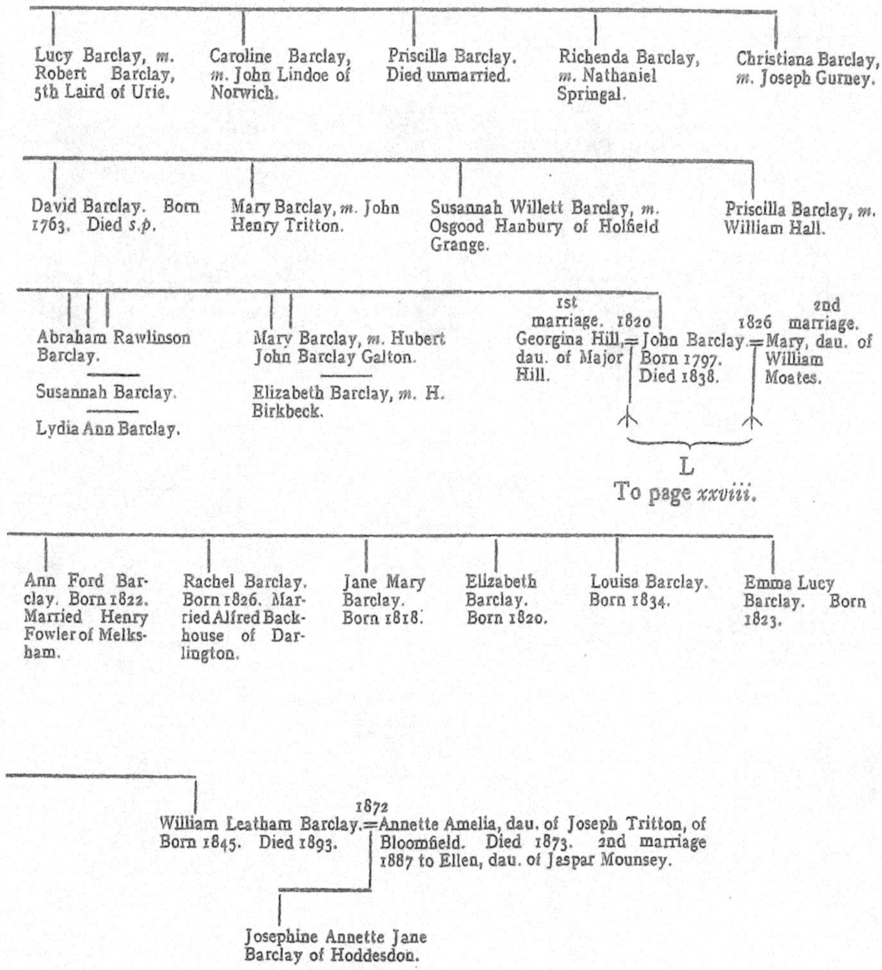
Lucy Barclay, *m.* Robert Barclay, 5th Laird of Urie.
Caroline Barclay, *m.* John Lindoe of Norwich.
Priscilla Barclay. Died unmarried.
Richenda Barclay, *m.* Nathaniel Springal.
Christiana Barclay, *m.* Joseph Gurney.
David Barclay. Born 1763. Died *s.p.*
Mary Barclay, *m.* John Henry Tritton.
Susannah Willett Barclay, *m.* Osgood Hanbury of Holfield Grange.
Priscilla Barclay, *m.* William Hall.
Abraham Rawlinson Barclay.
Susannah Barclay.
Lydia Ann Barclay.
Mary Barclay, *m.* Hubert John Barclay Galton.
Elizabeth Barclay, *m.* H. Birkbeck.
1st marriage. 1820
Georgina Hill, dau. of Major Hill.
John Barclay Born 1797. Died 1838.
1826 2nd marriage.
Mary, dau. of William Moates.
L
To page *xxviii.*
Ann Ford Barclay. Born 1822. Married Henry Fowler of Melksham.
Rachel Barclay. Born 1826. Married Alfred Backhouse of Darlington.
Jane Mary Barclay. Born 1818.
Elizabeth Barclay. Born 1820.
Louisa Barclay. Born 1834.
Emma Lucy Barclay. Born 1823.
1872
William Leatham Barclay. Born 1845. Died 1893.
Annette Amelia, dau. of Joseph Tritton, of Bloomfield. Died 1873. 2nd marriage 1887 to Ellen, dau. of Jaspar Mounsey.
Josephine Annette Jane Barclay of Hoddesdon.

HISTORY OF THE BARCLAY FAMILY

I

From page *xx.*

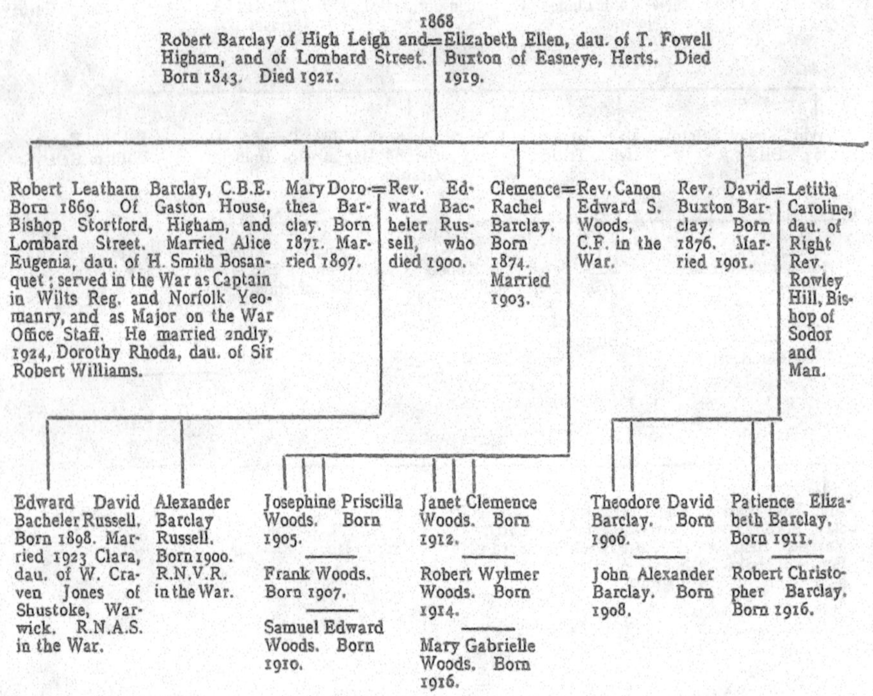

1868
Robert Barclay of High Leigh and Higham, and of Lombard Street. Born 1843. Died 1921.
= Elizabeth Ellen, dau. of T. Fowell Buxton of Easneye, Herts. Died 1919.
Robert Leatham Barclay, C.B.E. Born 1869. Of Gaston House, Bishop Stortford, Higham, and Lombard Street. Married Alice Eugenia, dau. of H. Smith Bosanquet; served in the War as Captain in Wilts Reg. and Norfolk Yeomanry, and as Major on the War Office Staff. He married 2ndly, 1924, Dorothy Rhoda, dau. of Sir Robert Williams.
Mary Dorothea Barclay. Born 1871. Married 1897.
= Rev. Edward Bacheler Russell, who died 1900.
Clemence Rachel Barclay. Born 1874. Married 1903.
= Rev. Canon Edward S. Woods, C.F. in the War.
Rev. David Buxton Barclay. Born 1876. Married 1901.
= Letitia Caroline, dau. of Right Rev. Rowley Hill, Bishop of Sodor and Man.
Edward David Bacheler Russell. Born 1898. Married 1923 Clara, dau. of W. Craven Jones of Shustoke, Warwick. R.N.A.S. in the War.
Alexander Barclay Russell. Born 1900. R.N.V.R. in the War.
Josephine Priscilla Woods. Born 1905.
Frank Woods. Born 1907.
Samuel Edward Woods. Born 1910.
Janet Clemence Woods. Born 1912.
Robert Wylmer Woods. Born 1914.
Mary Gabrielle Woods. Born 1916.
Theodore David Barclay. Born 1906.
John Alexander Barclay. Born 1908.
Patience Elizabeth Barclay. Born 1911.
Robert Christopher Barclay. Born 1916.

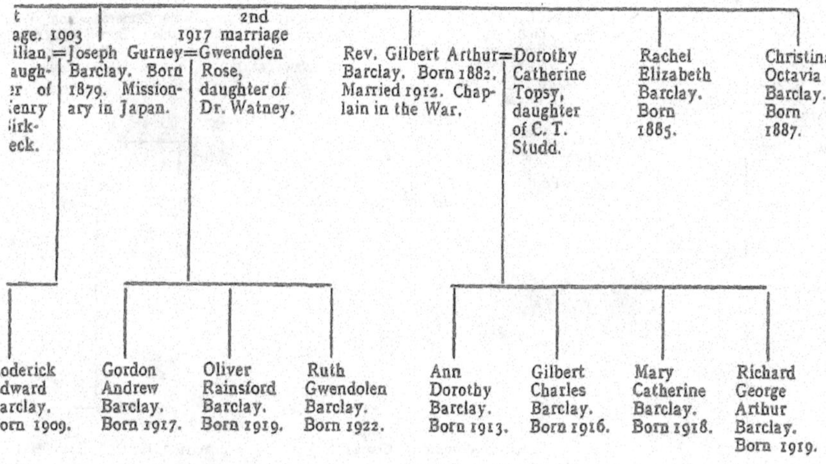
t
age. 1903
ilian,=Joseph Gurney=Gwendolen
augh-
er of
ienry
3irk-
eck.
Barclay. Born 1879. Missionary in Japan.
2nd
1917 marriage
Rose, daughter of Dr. Watney.
Rev. Gilbert Arthur=Dorothy
Barclay. Born 1882. Married 1912. Chaplain in the War.
Catherine Topsy, daughter of C. T. Studd.
Rachel Elizabeth Barclay. Born 1885.
Christina Octavia Barclay. Born 1887.
oderick
dward
arclay.
orn 1909.
Gordon Andrew Barclay. Born 1917.
Oliver Rainsford Barclay. Born 1919.
Ruth Gwendolen Barclay. Born 1922.
Ann Dorothy Barclay. Born 1913.
Gilbert Charles Barclay. Born 1916.
Mary Catherine Barclay. Born 1918.
Richard George Arthur Barclay. Born 1919.

HISTORY OF THE BARCLAY FAMILY

J

From page *xx*.

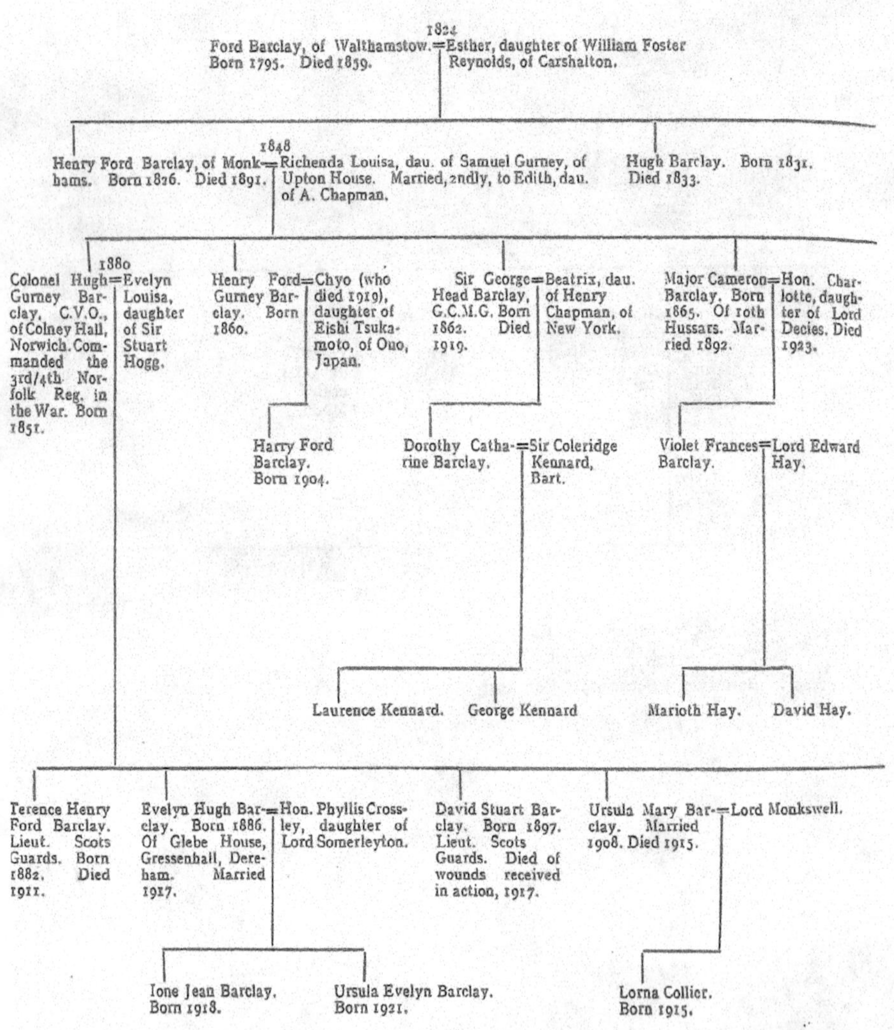
1824
Ford Barclay, of Walthamstow. Born 1795. Died 1859. = Esther, daughter of William Foster Reynolds, of Carshalton.
1848
Henry Ford Barclay, of Monkhams. Born 1826. Died 1891. = Richenda Louisa, dau. of Samuel Gurney, of Upton House. Married, 2ndly, to Edith, dau. of A. Chapman.
Hugh Barclay. Born 1831. Died 1833.
1880
Colonel Hugh Gurney Barclay, C.V.O., of Colney Hall, Norwich. Commanded the 3rd/4th Norfolk Reg. in the War. Born 1851. = Evelyn Louisa, daughter of Sir Stuart Hogg.
Henry Ford Gurney Barclay. Born 1860. = Chyo (who died 1919), daughter of Eishi Tsukamoto, of Ono, Japan.
Sir George Head Barclay, G.C.M.G. Born 1862. Died 1919. = Beatrix, dau. of Henry Chapman, of New York.
Major Cameron Barclay. Born 1865. Of 10th Hussars. Married 1892. = Hon. Charlotte, daughter of Lord Decies. Died 1923.
Harry Ford Barclay. Born 1904.
Dorothy Catharine Barclay. = Sir Coleridge Kennard, Bart.
Violet Frances Barclay. = Lord Edward Hay.
Laurence Kennard.
George Kennard
Marioth Hay.
David Hay.
Terence Henry Ford Barclay. Lieut. Scots Guards. Born 1882. Died 1911.
Evelyn Hugh Barclay. Born 1886. Of Glebe House, Gressenhall, Dereham. Married 1917. = Hon. Phyllis Crossley, daughter of Lord Somerleyton.
David Stuart Barclay. Born 1897. Lieut. Scots Guards. Died of wounds received in action, 1917.
Ursula Mary Barclay. Married 1908. Died 1915. = Lord Monkswell.
Ione Jean Barclay. Born 1918.
Ursula Evelyn Barclay. Born 1921.
Lorna Collier. Born 1915.

HISTORY OF THE BARCLAY FAMILY

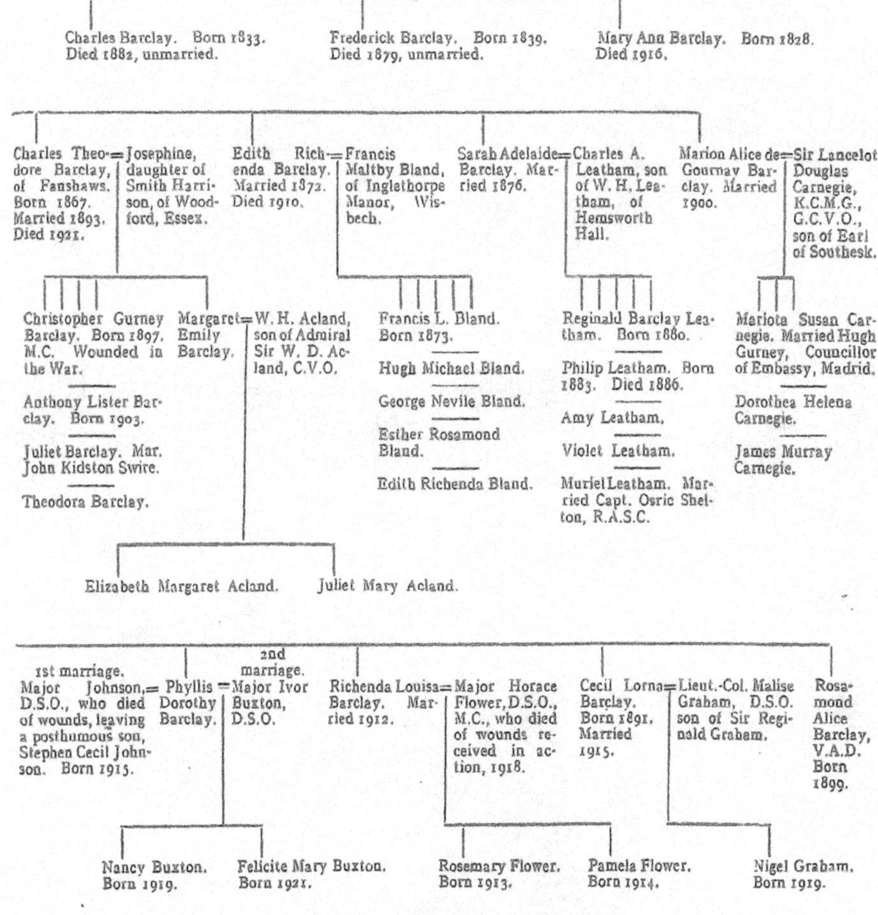
Charles Barclay. Born 1833. Died 1882, unmarried.
Frederick Barclay. Born 1839. Died 1879, unmarried.
Mary Ann Barclay. Born 1828. Died 1916.
Charles Theodore Barclay, of Fanshaws. Born 1867. Married 1893. Died 1921.
Josephine, daughter of Smith Harrison, of Woodford, Essex.
Edith Richenda Barclay. Married 1872. Died 1910.
Francis Maltby Bland, of Inglethorpe Manor, Wisbech.
Sarah Adelaide Barclay. Married 1876.
Charles A. Leatham, son of W. H. Leatham, of Hemsworth Hall.
Marion Alice de Gournay Barclay. Married 1900.
Sir Lancelot Douglas Carnegie, K.C.M.G., G.C.V.O., son of Earl of Southesk.
Christopher Gurney Barclay. Born 1897. M.C. Wounded in the War.
Anthony Lister Barclay. Born 1903.
Juliet Barclay. Mar. John Kidston Swire.
Theodora Barclay.
Margaret Emily Barclay.
W. H. Acland, son of Admiral Sir W. D. Acland, C.V.O.
Francis L. Bland. Born 1873.
Hugh Michael Bland.
George Nevile Bland.
Esther Rosamond Bland.
Edith Richenda Bland.
Reginald Barclay Leatham. Born 1880.
Philip Leatham. Born 1883. Died 1886.
Amy Leatham.
Violet Leatham.
Muriel Leatham. Married Capt. Osric Shelton, R.A.S.C.
Mariota Susan Carnegie. Married Hugh Gurney, Councillor of Embassy, Madrid.
Dorothea Helena Carnegie.
James Murray Carnegie.
Elizabeth Margaret Acland.
Juliet Mary Acland.
1st marriage. Major Johnson, D.S.O., who died of wounds, leaving a posthumous son, Stephen Cecil Johnson. Born 1915.
Phyllis Dorothy Barclay.
2nd marriage. Major Ivor Buxton, D.S.O.
Richenda Louisa Barclay. Married 1912.
Major Horace Flower, D.S.O., M.C., who died of wounds received in action, 1918.
Cecil Lorna Barclay. Born 1891. Married 1915.
Lieut.-Col. Malise Graham, D.S.O. son of Sir Reginald Graham.
Rosamond Alice Barclay, V.A.D. Born 1899.
Nancy Buxton. Born 1919.
Felicite Mary Buxton. Born 1921.
Rosemary Flower. Born 1913.
Pamela Flower. Born 1914.
Nigel Graham. Born 1919.

K

From page *xx*.

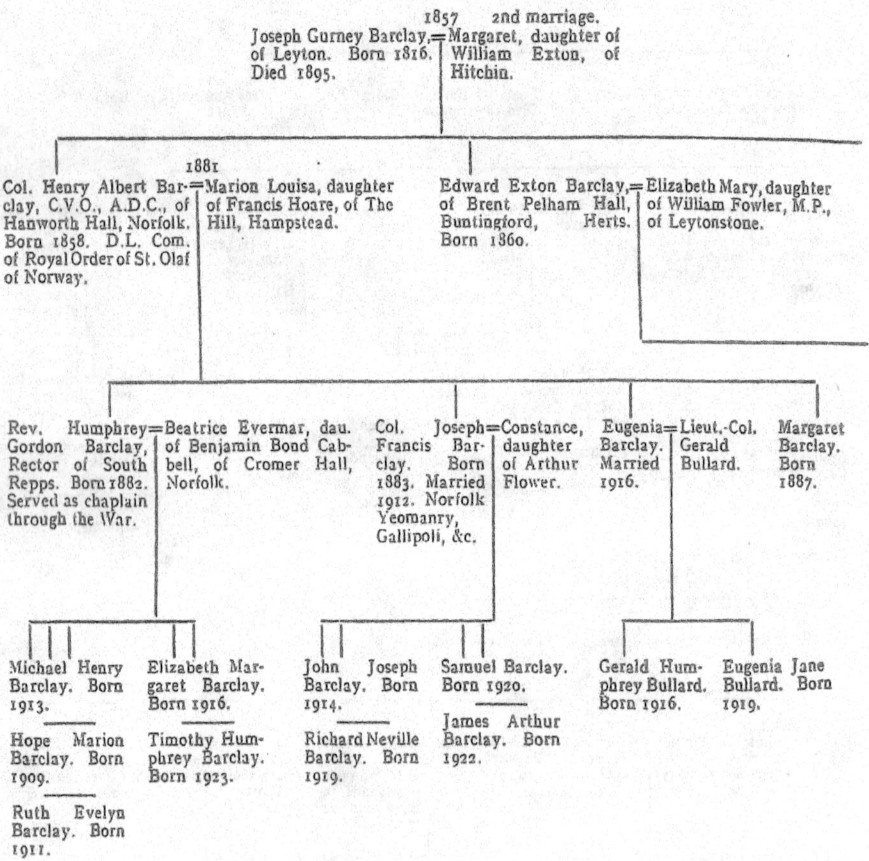
1857 2nd marriage.
Joseph Gurney Barclay, of Leyton. Born 1816. Died 1895. = Margaret, daughter of William Exton, of Hitchin.
1881
Col. Henry Albert Barclay, C.V.O., A.D.C., of Hanworth Hall, Norfolk. Born 1858. D.L. Com. of Royal Order of St. Olaf of Norway. = Marion Louisa, daughter of Francis Hoare, of The Hill, Hampstead.
Edward Exton Barclay, of Brent Pelham Hall, Buntingford, Herts. Born 1860. = Elizabeth Mary, daughter of William Fowler, M.P., of Leytonstone.
Rev. Humphrey Gordon Barclay, Rector of South Repps. Born 1882. Served as chaplain through the War. = Beatrice Evermar, dau. of Benjamin Bond Cabbell, of Cromer Hall, Norfolk.
Col. Joseph Francis Barclay. Born 1883. Married 1912. Norfolk Yeomanry, Gallipoli, &c. = Constance, daughter of Arthur Flower.
Eugenia Barclay. Married 1916. = Lieut.-Col. Gerald Bullard.
Margaret Barclay. Born 1887.
Michael Henry Barclay. Born 1913.
Hope Marion Barclay. Born 1909.
Ruth Evelyn Barclay. Born 1911.
Elizabeth Margaret Barclay. Born 1916.
Timothy Humphrey Barclay. Born 1923.
John Joseph Barclay. Born 1914.
Richard Neville Barclay. Born 1919.
Samuel Barclay. Born 1920.
James Arthur Barclay. Born 1922.
Gerald Humphrey Bullard. Born 1916.
Eugenia Jane Bullard. Born 1919.

HISTORY OF THE BARCLAY FAMILY

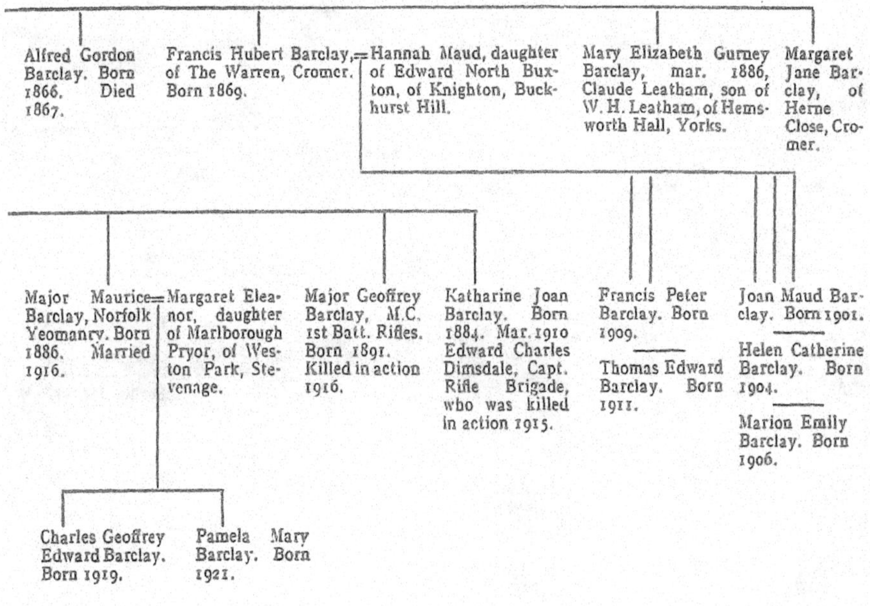

Alfred Gordon Barclay. Born 1866. Died 1867.

Francis Hubert Barclay, of The Warren, Cromer. Born 1869. = Hannah Maud, daughter of Edward North Buxton, of Knighton, Buckhurst Hill.

Mary Elizabeth Gurney Barclay, mar. 1886, Claude Leatham, son of W. H. Leatham, of Hemsworth Hall, Yorks.

Margaret Jane Barclay, of Herne Close, Cromer.

Major Maurice Barclay, Norfolk Yeomanry. Born 1886. Married 1916. = Margaret Eleanor, daughter of Marlborough Pryor, of Weston Park, Stevenage.

Major Geoffrey Barclay, M.C. 1st Batt. Rifles. Born 1891. Killed in action 1916.

Katharine Joan Barclay. Born 1884. Mar. 1910 Edward Charles Dimsdale, Capt. Rifle Brigade, who was killed in action 1915.

Francis Peter Barclay. Born 1909.

Thomas Edward Barclay. Born 1911.

Joan Maud Barclay. Born 1901.

Helen Catherine Barclay. Born 1904.

Marion Emily Barclay. Born 1906.

Charles Geoffrey Edward Barclay. Born 1919.

Pamela Mary Barclay. Born 1921.

L

From page *xxi*.

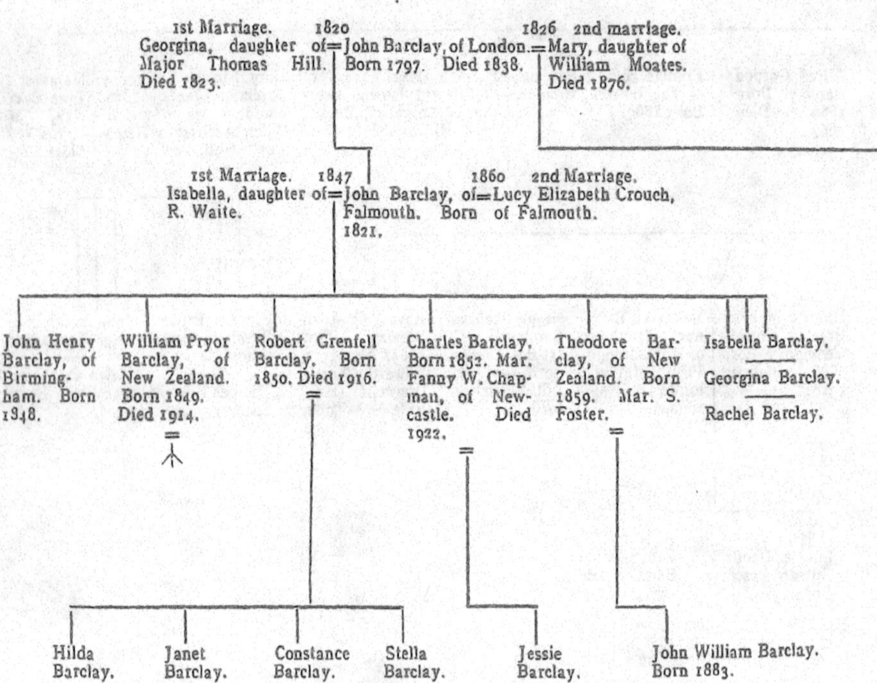
1st Marriage. 1820
Georgina, daughter of Major Thomas Hill. Died 1823.
= John Barclay, of London. Born 1797. Died 1838.
1826 2nd marriage.
= Mary, daughter of William Moates. Died 1876.
1st Marriage. 1847
Isabella, daughter of R. Waite.
= John Barclay, of Falmouth. Born 1821.
1860 2nd Marriage.
= Lucy Elizabeth Crouch, of Falmouth.
John Henry Barclay, of Birmingham. Born 1848.
William Pryor Barclay, of New Zealand. Born 1849. Died 1914.
Robert Grenfell Barclay. Born 1850. Died 1916.
Charles Barclay. Born 1852. Mar. Fanny W. Chapman, of Newcastle. Died 1922.
Theodore Barclay, of New Zealand. Born 1859. Mar. S. Foster.
Isabella Barclay.
Georgina Barclay.
Rachel Barclay.
Hilda Barclay.
Janet Barclay.
Constance Barclay.
Stella Barclay.
Jessie Barclay.
John William Barclay. Born 1883.

HISTORY OF THE BARCLAY FAMILY

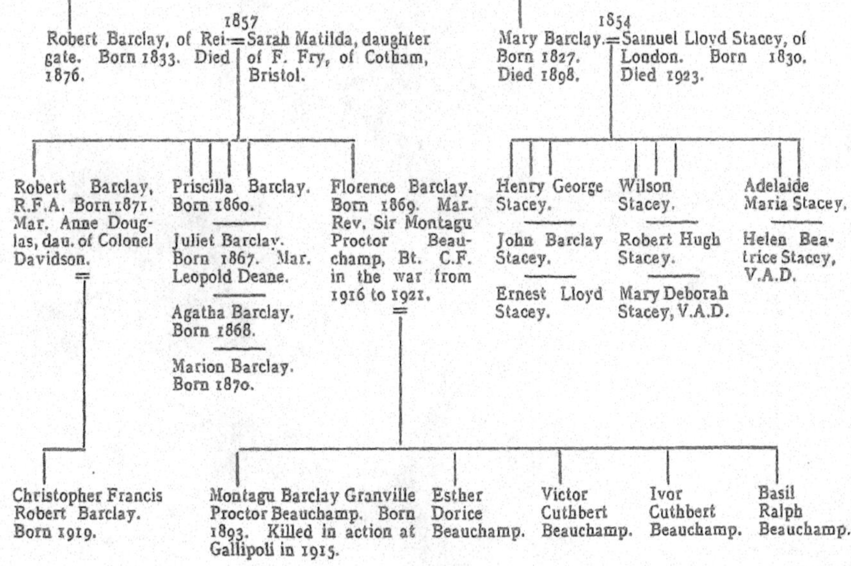

1857
Robert Barclay, of Reigate. Born 1833. Died 1876. = Sarah Matilda, daughter of F. Fry, of Cotham, Bristol.
1854
Mary Barclay. Born 1827. Died 1898. = Samuel Lloyd Stacey, of London. Born 1830. Died 1923.
Robert Barclay, R.F.A. Born 1871. Mar. Anne Douglas, dau. of Colonel Davidson.
Priscilla Barclay. Born 1860.
Juliet Barclay. Born 1867. Mar. Leopold Deane.
Agatha Barclay. Born 1868.
Marion Barclay. Born 1870.
Florence Barclay. Born 1869. Mar. Rev. Sir Montagu Proctor Beauchamp, Bt. C.F. in the war from 1916 to 1921.
Henry George Stacey.
John Barclay Stacey.
Ernest Lloyd Stacey.
Wilson Stacey.
Robert Hugh Stacey.
Mary Deborah Stacey, V.A.D.
Adelaide Maria Stacey.
Helen Beatrice Stacey, V.A.D.
Christopher Francis Robert Barclay. Born 1919.
Montagu Barclay Granville Proctor Beauchamp. Born 1893. Killed in action at Gallipoli in 1915.
Esther Dorice Beauchamp.
Victor Cuthbert Beauchamp.
Ivor Cuthbert Beauchamp.
Basil Ralph Beauchamp.

A HISTORY OF THE BARCLAY FAMILY

WITH FULL PEDIGREE FROM 1066 TO 1924

COMPILED BY

THE REV. CHARLES W. BARCLAY

ILLUSTRATED

PART I

LONDON

THE ST. CATHERINE PRESS

STAMFORD STREET, S.E.

1924

NOTE

The completion of this history has been long—far too long—delayed. Much of it was written many years ago, indeed the search for information has been carried on, intermittently, for fully fifty years.

A full pedigree from the earliest days to the present time has been compiled, but only the Gloucestershire part has been elaborated with a full history, although a mass of material has been collected for the detailed account of the Scottish and English generations.

It has been thought well to print now what has been done as Part I, leaving for a Part II the concluding portion and bringing the record of the family down to the present day, thirty-one generations from Roger de Berchelai.

The details of the later generations of the pedigree have been verified by members of the various branches of the family.

Colonel Hubert F. Barclay, owing to whose efforts this volume has been printed, has, I am glad to say, undertaken the work of preparing the second volume, which will contain a full account of the Scottish and English Barclays, and some information with respect to the American branches.

C. W. B.

CONTENTS

CONTENTS

APPENDIX

Copies of Original Documents and Charters.

LIST OF ILLUSTRATIONS

INTRODUCTION

LITTLE short of two hundred years ago a brief record of the Barclay family, entitled, *A Genealogical Account of the Barclays of Urie*, was compiled by Robert Barclay of Urie, and printed by his son in 1740. The author's quaint and simple letter to his brother David, the first of the line who settled in London, describes the anxious care with which he had searched the Registers of Scotland, and the documents preserved at Urie, for reliable data upon which to base his history. There were, however, many sources to which he had not access, from whence he might have derived important information. Clearly he had not consulted Domesday Book, then preserved in the Chapter House of Westminster Abbey. The distance of Urie from London, no doubt, also precluded any search among the English records at the Tower and elsewhere. The British Museum, now containing many works under the name of Barclay, did not exist until some years after his time; and he does not seem to have been acquainted with Dugdale's Baronage of England. His sources of information were so limited that we need not wonder if the account is somewhat meagre in detail, and occasionally incorrect as to fact, but rather be thankful that he has rescued from complete loss that which may be of consequence in the further stages of our enquiry.

The MS., dated 1730, is preserved at Bury Hill.

Letter from Robert to David Barclay at Bury Hill.

In the "Genealogical Account" the founder of the family is stated to be Theobald de Berkeley, born about 1110, and from him each successive generation is traced by means of authentic documents, many of which are still preserved at Bury Hill, the seat of Robert Wyvill Barclay, the present chief of the family. The earliest of these documents is a charter from William De Keith, Marishall of Scotland, in favour of Alexander de Berclay of Mathers, in the year 1351. Dated two years later we find a charter of David II, King of Scotland, confirming the lands of Mathers to Alexander de Berclay.

Bury Hill charters and documents.

It has remained, however, for later genealogical enquiry to

INTRODUCTION.

connect the early Scottish Berkeleys with the ancient Gloucestershire family, and to point out with assured certainty that the Berkeleys may trace their descent to neither a British, Caledonian nor Saxon origin, but to a true *Norman* stock.

The "Genealogical Account" was reprinted in the year 1812, and copies of the original edition are now of the utmost rarity.

Authorities for this history.

Only of late years has it become possible to compile a history of the earlier generations. The great interest recently taken in antiquities has called into being numerous associations for the publication of early documents, and although the transactions of the older bodies, such as the Archæological Society, the Spalding Club, the Camden Society, the Bannatyne and others, are invaluable as giving much information, it is to the later publications, such as those of the county archæological associations, the Pipe Roll Society, the published cartularies of the monasteries and the contents of private muniment rooms, to which we are most indebted for the earlier portion of the history of the Barclays. No doubt there are many other charters and documents hidden away, unknown and neglected, which in future years may see the light, perhaps to confirm, possibly to disprove, some of the surmises contained in the following pages. Frequently the links of evidence on various points are slender, a single entry of a name as a witness to some ancient charter, which we might long to confirm more fully; but it will be noticed that conjectures are always plainly stated to be so, while facts capable of proof are coupled with the authority, so that they may be verified and followed out more fully by those who desire so to do.

Occasionally it has been necessary to disprove some of that apocryphal history, which is sure to cling to an ancient family, and nothing is inserted which does not rest upon a basis more sure than that of mere tradition, which, however valuable when corroborating documentary evidence, cannot be allowed to carry weight when found to be antagonistic.

A brief account of a few of the more important sources of information will greatly add to the interest of the details as we

Domesday Book.

come to them. In the forefront we must place Domesday

Book—of which more hereafter—and Dugdale's Baronage of England, published in 1675, a work of very great accuracy. With it we may class his "Monasticon Anglicanum," a most valuable compilation embodying the cartularies of the suppressed monasteries. Many of the deeds and charters, on which much of our history is based, are taken from these works of Sir William Dugdale. From the evidence room of Berkeley Castle, however, we gather our chief store of information. The "Lives of the Berkeleys" and the "History of Berkeley," completed by John Smyth of Nibley, the steward of Berkeley, in the year 1618, but only recently printed in three sumptuous volumes, give much information also with regard to the *early* house of Berkeley. Although we cannot invariably rely upon Smyth's statements, we are greatly indebted to his patient and painstaking researches, spread over nearly fifty years of his life, and to his invariable custom of referring to, and quoting from, original authorities.

Baronage of England, by Sir William Dugdale, Norroy King of Arms. 2 vols. fo. 1675.

Dugdale's Monasticon Anglicanum.

Smyth's Lives of the Berkeleys, etc., 3 vols., 1883.

Recently another volume of great interest and service to our enquiry has seen the light, "A Descriptive Catalogue of the Charters at Berkeley Castle," compiled by Mr. Jeayes of the British Museum. Many of the charters given in the appendix are taken from this volume. Frequent quotations will be made from the Pipe Rolls and other Rolls and documents preserved in the repository of the Record Office. The Magni Rotulli Scaccarii, or Pipe Rolls as they are commonly called, are the great rolls of the Exchequer, containing the account of all sums paid into the Royal Treasury, whether rents, fines, profits on lands, or other payments. These Rolls are almost complete from the year 1155. The entries are made upon brown leather skins, and their appearance, when rolled up, has in all probability originated the name *Pipe Roll.* Other rolls, such as the "close rolls," "feet of fines," etc., from which quotations are made, will be found in the list of authorities.

Catalogue of the Muniments at Berkeley Castle, 1892. Appendix III. p. 91.

Pipe Rolls and other Rolls.

On turning from such works of ancient date to modern writings, we are able to gather much information from the invaluable publications of the Bristol and Gloucestershire Archæological Association. It is impossible to exaggerate their value. Almost every volume in the series of "Transactions"

Bristol and Gloucestershire Archæological Association.

INTRODUCTION.

contains papers which throw light upon our enquiry. Pre-eminently among them must be mentioned the papers by the late Sir Henry Barkly, K.C.B., on the earlier house of Berkeley, and on the Berkeleys of Dursley and Cubberley, besides many other most able contributions. Sir Henry had welcomed the suggestion that these papers should be made use of in the present volume. Hence lengthy extracts from his writings have been included. Indeed had his invaluable researches not been undertaken, the present account would have been shorn of its chief value and interest. But the present writer has ventured to differ on some few points. Also the publication of the Berkeley Charters has necessarily modified some of his statements. Bearing in mind this acknowledgment of the great value of Sir Henry Barkly's papers to the present work, continual reference will not be made to them in the subsequent pages. The marginal references are chiefly to original authorities.

Sir Henry Barkly, K.C.B.

Before proceeding to the detailed account, it may be well, in the interest of those who are unacquainted with the early history, to give here in brief outline, without authorities, that which will be elaborated in full as we proceed with the history.

Brief outline of the history.

Roger de Berchelai, the true founder of the family, we may infer, came over from Normandy as one of the invading army of William the Conqueror in the fateful year of 1066, for we find him placed by Earl William Fitzosborn as overlord of the great Manor of Berkeley and its adjacent territories at the very time when the country was divided up by Earl William among the Conqueror's soldiers of fortune. We have clear indications that he was in possession of estates in Normandy, though we are unable, at present, to identify their locality, for unlike many of his companions, Roger discarded his former territorial designation on becoming lord of Berkeley, possibly owing to the greater importance and extent of his English lands. Domesday Book affords full particulars of Roger and his brother Ralph's holdings, and also gives the names of the ejected Saxon owners, a fact of considerable importance. Roger de Berchelai also owned large territories held extra-manorially, both in Gloucestershire and Wiltshire.

Roger de Berchelai, founder of the Barclay family.

For full discussion of the Norman origin see hereafter, pages 13-14.

BERKELEY CASTLE

To face page xvii

In this charge he was succeeded by his sons Eustace and Roger, and his grandson, also Roger. Probably owing to the fact that this Roger III refused to join the standard of Henry II (then Duke of Normandy and Anjou) and took part with Stephen, and also that he appears to have refused to pay his yearly dues to the King, about the year 1150 the Duke made a grant of the Berkeley Manor to Robert Fitzhardinge, a wealthy merchant of Bristol; who had assisted him with pecuniary aid to a large extent. Roger being ejected from Berkeley, took up his residence at Dursley near by, but kept up an intermittent warfare against his rival. Eventually, to stay hostilities, and also because Roger was on the point of ousting Fitzhardinge, the Duke, in conjunction with King Stephen, arranged the plan of a double marriage—Roger's daughter Alice marrying Fitzhardinge's son, and Roger's son marrying Fitzhardinge's daughter. The agreement is still extant in the archives of Berkeley Castle, and will be given *in extenso*, in due course. It was now arranged that the original Berkeleys should reside at Dursley, which was formed into a Barony, while Berkeley Castle was confirmed to the Fitzhardinges, who subsequently took the name of Berkeley. The Dursley Berkeleys, together with the collateral line of the Berkeleys of Cubberley, became extinct early in the fifteenth century, and, if we may rely on the historical accuracy of a sixteenth century manuscript, the succession of the family devolved on the descendants of John de Berkeley, a younger son of the first Roger de Berkeley, who in the year 1069 went to Scotland in the suite of Margaret, sister of Edgar Atheling, and to whom the lands of Towie were granted by Malcolm Caenmoir, her husband.

INTRODUCTION.

Robert Fitzhardinge.

Marriage Covenant in Berkeley Castle.

Dursley becomes the seat of the Berkeleys.

Matthew Lumsden's "Houss of Forbes." Dated 1580.

John de Berkeley goes to Scotland 1069.

Through many centuries we find records of three main lines of Berkeleys in Scotland—of Gartlie, Towie and Mathers—who long ranked among the lairds of the counties of Banff, Aberdeen and Kincardineshire. Among other collateral lines we may mention the Berkeleys of Colairnie, Kippo, Touch, Pierston, Johnson, Balmakewan and also the Brechin Berkeleys. Much labour and care would be needed to elaborate a full history of all the branches of so widely spread a family. It will be necessary to confine our history to the *main line* from

Vide "History of the Scottish Barclays," by Leslie Barclay, 1915.

INTRODUCTION. which are descended the Barclays of Mathers and Urie, and later on the Barclays of Bury Hill and the collateral English lines as shown in the pedigree.

Towie remained a possession of the family as late as 1753. Long before this date, however, the lands of Mathers had been granted to Alexander de Berkeley by William de Keith, Marishall of Scotland, his brother-in-law, and the Castle or Kaim of Mathers had become the seat of the family.

Bury Hill Charters, 1351.

Vide pedigree.

We shall follow down through many generations to David Barclay, who in 1580 sold Mathers, and the castle and estate of Urie was purchased by his son Colonel David Barclay, the famous old soldier of Gustavus Adolphus. In later years Colonel David became a prominent Quaker, as also his still more famous son Robert Barclay "the apologist." A few more generations down the line and we reach Captain Robert Barclay-Allardice of sporting and pedestrian fame, the last laird of Urie, who died in 1854 without male issue, and the representation of the family devolved on Charles Barclay of Bury Hill, the descendant of David, second son of Robert Barclay "the apologist."

The last laird of Urie 1854.

The family thus again becomes the *English* Barclays after the long sojourn of six hundred years in Scotland. It is only necessary to trace in brief their fortunes down to the present day, having followed the long succession of generations from Roger de Berchelai of Domesday Book, down to Robert Edward Barclay, eldest son of Robert Wyvill Barclay, the thirty-first in descent from the old follower of the Conqueror.

Thirty-one generations from Roger de Berchelai.

LIST OF PRINCIPAL AUTHORITIES CONSULTED
FOR PART I

Domesday Book, Facsimile of Gloucestershire part.
" " by W. de Grey Birch, F.S.A.
" " Analysis of Gloucestershire part, by C. S. Taylor.
" " Landholders of Gloucestershire.
" " for Wiltshire, by W. H. Jones.
Lives of the Berkeleys, by John Smyth, of Nibley, written 1618.
History of Berkeley, by John Smyth, of Nibley, written 1618.
Fosbroke's Introduction to Berkeley MS.
Muniments at Berkeley Castle, Ed. by J. H. Jeayes.
Anglo-Saxon Chronicle.
William of Malmesbury's Chronicle.
Florence of Worcester's Chronicle.
Robert of Gloucester's Chronicle.
Anglia Sacra.
Hollinshed's Chronicle.
The Nuremberg Chronicle.
Gesta Stephani, Edit. Duchesne.
Camden's Britannia.
Sharon Turner's History of the Anglo-Saxons.
Robert Ricart's Kalendar, 1479 (Town Clerk of Bristol).
Pipe Rolls, Close Rolls, Feet of Fines and Others, in Record Office.
Dursley and its Neighbourhood, by Rev. F. H. Blunt.
Freeman's Norman Conquest.
Palgrave's Normandy and England.
The Conqueror and His Companions, by J. R. Planché.
Tanner's Notitia Monarchia.
Abbot Newland's Roll, MS. in Berkeley Castle.
Cartularium de Reading.
Bristol and Gloucester Archæological Society's Transactions, 45 Vols.
Gloucestershire Notes and Queries.

PRINCIPAL AUTHORITIES CONSULTED

Transactions of Archæological Society, Spalding Club, Camden, Bannatyne and other Societies.

Dugdale's Baronage of England, 2 Vols.

" Monasticon Anglicanum, 8 Vols.

Sir Robert Atkins's History of Gloucestershire.

Bigland's History of Gloucestershire.

Cartulary of Malmesbury Abbey.

Steven's Abbeys.

Dr. Seyer's History of Bristol.

Royal Commission on Historical Manuscripts.

Froissart's Chronicles.

Lyson's Gloucestershire Antiquities.

Mediæval Military Architecture, by G. T. Clark.

Memorials of Old Gloucestershire.

Cosmo Innes' Sketches of Early Scottish History.

Matthew Lumsden's Houss of Forbes, dated 1580.

Genealogical Account of the Barclays of Urie, 1730.

THE BARCLAY FAMILY

EARLY HISTORY OF BERKELEY

HISTORY OF BERKELEY. Origin of name.

The origin of the surname of Barclay may undoubtedly be traced to the district of Berkeley in Gloucestershire, the ancient domicile of the family in the time of William the Conqueror.

Saxon Chronicle.

In the *Saxon Chronicle* we find the name written Beorcenlau, a form suggesting a derivation from *beorce*, the beech tree, which grows plentifully to the present day in the vale of Berkeley. The name might, however, be traced with greater probability to the birch tree, since in Domesday Book it takes the form of Berchelai, suggestive of *berk* or birch, and *lea* the old word for meadow. It seems probable that so well watered and wooded a district might derive its name from the prevailing timber.

Domesday Book, Appendix i. page 87.

The castle to the present time stands on a wooded slope, just as in former years, when Shakespeare wrote:

> "There stands the castle by yon tufted trees."

Shakespeare, Richard II.

In early days Berkeley formed part of a petty British Kingdom. It is presumed, upon justifiable grounds by Sharon Turner, that Thornbury in the vicinity of Berkeley was a British city where resided Cyndellan, a British King who fell in 577 at the fatal battle of Dirham. In the Anglo-Saxon era we find that Beorclea signified a country of far superior extent to the Berkeley Hyrnesse, or Hundred. The Abbots of Westbury were denominated Abbots of Berkeley.

Sharon Turner's History of the Anglo-Saxons.

Anglia Sacra i., 470, 472.

Dugdale's Monasticon, i., 125.

We have evidence of a religious house there in the eighth century. Tilhere, Bishop of Worcester, in 778 seems to have been previously Abbot of Beorclea, as was Ætheldune, also his successor at Worcester, in 915. Tanner thinks the "family at Berclea" mentioned in the acts of a synod at Cloveshoe in 824 may also refer to a religious house there. An abbess, Ceolburgh by name, presided over the Abbey of Berkeley in the year 805.

Florence of Worcester's Chronicle.

Freeman's Norman Conquest, ii., 544.

William of Malmesbury, who was born 1095, gives a curious legend of the Witch of Berkeley, dating it to the time of King

William of Malmesbury's Chronicle. Bohn's Series, p. 230

HISTORY OF BERKELEY.

The Nuremberg Chronicle.

Legend of the Witch of Berkeley.

Edward the Confessor. As illustrating the superstitions of the age it may be deemed worth giving in full. A remarkable illustration may be found in the *Nuremberg Chronicle*. The legend is as follows :—

"There resided at Berkeley a woman addicted to witchcraft, as it afterwards appeared, and skilled in ancient augury: she was excessively gluttonous, perfectly lascivious, setting no bounds to her debaucheries, as she was not old, though fast declining in life. On a certain day as she was regaling, a jackdaw which was a very great favourite, chattered a little more loudly than usual. On hearing which the woman's knife fell from her hand, her countenance grew pale, and deeply groaning, 'This day,' said she, 'my plough has completed its last furrow; to-day I shall hear of, and suffer, some dreadful calamity.' While yet speaking, the messenger of her misfortunes arrived; and being asked, why he approached with so distressed an air? 'I bring news,' said he, 'from that village,' naming the place, 'of the death of your son, and of the whole family by a sudden accident.' At this intelligence, the woman sorely afflicted, immediately took to her bed, and perceiving the disorder rapidly approaching the vitals, she summoned her surviving children, a monk and a nun, by hasty letters; and when they arrived, with faltering voice, addressed them thus: 'Formerly, my children, I constantly administered to my wretched circumstances by demoniacal arts: I have been the sink of every vice, the teacher of every allurement: yet, while practising these crimes, I was accustomed to soothe my hapless soul with the hope of your piety. Despairing of myself, I rested my expectations on you; I advanced you as my defenders against evil spirits, my safeguard against my strongest foes. Now, since I have approached the end of my life, and shall have those eager to punish, who lured me to sin, I entreat you by your mother's breasts, if you have any regard, any affection, at least to endeavour to alleviate my torments; and although you cannot revoke the sentence already passed upon my soul, yet you may, perhaps, rescue my body by these means: Sew up my corpse in the skin of a stag; lay it on its back in a stone coffin; fasten down the lid with lead and iron; on this lay

On a pinnacle of Berkeley Church is a figure representing the Witch of Berkeley borne away by the Devil.

The Legend appears in the Polichronicon of Reinulph of Chester and has been made the subject of a ballad by Southey. Bris. & Glouc. Arch. Soc., vol. 28, p. 4.

a stone bound round with three iron chains of enormous weight; let there be psalms sung for fifty nights, and masses said for an equal number of days to allay the ferocious attacks of my adversaries. If I lie thus secure for three nights, on the fourth day bury your mother in the ground; although I fear lest the earth, which has been so often burdened with my crimes should refuse to receive and cherish me in her bosom.' They did their utmost to comply with her injunctions : but, alas! vain were pious tears, vows or entreaties; so great was the woman's guilt, so great the devils' violence. For on the first two nights while the choir of priests was singing psalms round the body, the devils, one by one, with the utmost ease bursting open the door of the church, though closed with an immense bolt, broke asunder the two outer chains; the middle one being more laboriously wrought, remained entire. On the third night about cock crow the whole monastery seemed to be overthrown from its very foundation by the clamour of the approaching enemy. One devil more terrible in appearance that the rest, and of loftier stature, broke the gate to shivers by the violence of his attack. The priests grew motionless with fear, their hair stood on end and they became speechless. He proceeded, as it appeared, with haughty step toward the coffin, and calling on the woman by name, commanded her to rise. She replying that she could not on account of the chains: 'You shall be loosed,' said he, 'and to your cost'; and directly he broke the chain, which had mocked the ferocity of the others, with as little exertion as though it had been made of flax. He also beat down the cover of the coffin with his foot, and taking her by the hand, before them all, he dragged her out of the church. At the doors appeared a black hörse, proudly neighing, with iron hooks projecting over his whole back; on which the wretched creature was placed, and immediately, with the whole party, vanished from the eyes of the beholders; her pitiable cries, however, for assistance were heard for nearly the space of four miles."

LEGEND OF THE WITCH OF BERKELEY.

Inventions like these were common modes of revenge among ecclesiastics, similar stories being told of the body of Charles Martell, King of France, and others. Perhaps

HISTORY OF BERKELEY.

the farce was acted by persons in disguise, for this was not unusual.

Nunnery of Berkeley.

Walter Mapes' story.

With respect to the nunnery of Berkeley before the Conquest we have no further records, till we come to the story of its dissolution, related by Walter Mapes. Earl Godwin, by means of a disgraceful ruse, managed to bring such discredit upon the abbess and the nuns, that the suppression of the nunnery became inevitable; and thereupon he begged Berkeley of King Edward the Confessor, and settled it on his wife Gueda. Of the actual buildings there are no visible remains. Very probably the present castle occupies the original site. There appears later on to have been some revival of this nunnery, or possibly some of the ejected nuns received pensions, for nearly eighty years after this transaction we find in the Pipe Roll of Henry II mention of sixty shillings for the clothing of three nuns at Berkeley. It is also worthy of note in this connection that Adeliza, Queen of Henry I, gives by charter to the Church of Reading, "Berkeley Hern, that is the church of Berkeley with its appended prebends, and the prebends of two nuns," which would appear to refer to a nunnery.

Pipe Roll 31 Hen. I. "in vestitura iii. Monalium lx. s."

Dugdale's Monasticon, iv. 42 & vi.

Cartularium de Reading MSS. Parsons in Bodlean.

The scandalous story of Walter Mapes concerning the suppression of the nunnery of Berkeley derives some support from a curious entry in Domesday Book, whence it appears that Gueda the wife of Godwin, and mother of Harold, "had Udecester near Berkeley from her husband, he having bought it from Azor, that she might live there, till she should live at Berkeley, for she was unwilling to eat anything from that manor on account of the destruction of the abbey."

Domesday Book. Woodchester.

"Nolebat enim de ipso mannerio aliquid comedere pro destructione abbatiæ."

Godwin forfeits Berkeley.

Nothing more can be ascertained concerning Berkeley, prior to the Conquest, save the one fact that Earl Godwin had forfeited the great manor, in common with all his vast property, in the year 1051, and it had become forfeit to the Crown.

The Domesday Survey.

In the year 1086 the great survey of the whole of England was made by order of the Conqueror. Its record, preserved to us in the volumes of Domesday Book, is of extreme value in any enquiry referring to these early dates. To them therefore we turn for valuable knowledge concerning the great Berkeley Manor. Domesday Book contains a vast amount of informa-

Domesday Book and the Chest in which it is Kept

DOMESDAY SURVEY, 1086.

tion, often of so quaint and curious a nature, that a brief account of it may well be given here. Gloucester was its birthplace. We are told that at Christmas, 1085, King William "Wore his crown in that city, and held deep council with his Witan." The country seems to have fallen into an utterly wretched condition. The latter part of King Edward's reign had been a time of feeble government; and that of King William a period of war, oppression and plunder. The taxes which were imposed were, in many cases, almost insupportable, especially the gheld tax of six shillings on every hide of land. This tax was not paid on the King's property; many of the religious houses were also exempt. Therefore it fell chiefly on the poor, and formed a heavy burden. The title to much of the land was uncertain and its tenure precarious; so, however much the Saxon bordars and villeins resented the apparently inquisitorial enquiry into their possession by the foreign invaders, it was of considerable benefit to them in many ways. From the *Saxon Chronicle* we may gather something of the feeling which was aroused by the survey; we there read concerning the Conqueror: "So very narrowly he caused the land to be traced out that there was not a single hide, or yard of land, not even—it is a shame to tell, though it seemed to him no shame to do,—an ox, cow or hog that was not set down." This, no doubt, was an exaggeration, but the enquiry was very full. The method adopted to obtain the information was as follows: The King sent small companies of his leading statesmen into the various parts of the country. They obtained the facts on oath from the officials of every county and hundred, and from representatives of the inhabitants of every manor in the kingdom. The names of the Commissioners for the County of Gloucester are the only ones accurately known. These were Remigius, Bishop of Lincoln, Walter Giffard, Henry de Ferrieres and Adam Fitzherbert. The subjects of enquiry are stated to have been: What is the estate named? Who held it in the time of King Edward? Who holds it now? How many hides are there? How many in *demesne?* How many in the hands of the tenants? How many villani? and many other similar questions concerning every detail of the property; also what was its value in the time of

Saxon Chronicle.

Demesne signifies those lands which the Lord of Manor has reserved for his own use.

King Edward? and what its present value? The standard date, "in the time of King Edward" is generally the day of his death, January 5th, 1066, or to use the quaint language of the record itself, "that day on which King Edward was alive and dead."

DOMESDAY SURVEY, 1086.

"ea dies qua Rex Edwardus fuit vivus et mortuus." Domesday.

Domesday Book is contained in two volumes. The report of Gloucestershire in the first, a thick folio, written on 382 double pages of vellum, in a small but plain character. Each page has a double column containing about sixty lines of writing. The names of the owners are usually in red ink, and the names of the places have a red line through them. The language is Latin abounding in contractions. The account of Gloucestershire is contained in seventeen pages and a half. A brief extract is given below, first a facsimile of the original entry, next the first part transcribed into full Latin and lastly a translation of the same portion :

Facsimile of Extract from Domesday Book. *Vide* Appendix i. No. 6, p. 88.

xlii TERRA ROGERII DE BERCHELAI. In Respigete hund.
ROGERIUS de Berchelai ten Coberleie. Ibi .x. hidæ. Dena
tenuit tem regis. E. In dnio sunt .ii. car. 7 xix. uitti 7 iiii. bord.
cu .v. car. Ibi .iiii. serui. 7 v. ac pti. Silua .iii. qz lg. 7 ii. lat.
Valuit. vii. lib. modo .viii. lib. [illegible]
Isd Rog ten [illegible] Ibi .iii. hidæ 7 ii. partes dimid hidæ.
[illegible] tenuit T.R.E. In dnio .e. i. car. 7 viii. uitti 7 iiii. bord
cu .iiii. car. Ibi .iiii. serui. 7 x. ac pti. Val 7 ualuit .iii. lib.
Isd Rog ten [illegible] Anne tenuit. [illegible]
Ibi .v. hidæ geld. In dnio sunt .ii. car. 7 viii. uitti 7 x. bord
cu .iiii. car. Ibi .iiii. serui. 7 viii. ac pti. Val 7 ualuit .c. solid.

xlii Terra Rogerii de Berchelai. In Respigete hundred Rogerius de Berchelai tenet Coberlie. Ibi x hidæ. Dena tenuit tempore regis Edvardi. In dominio sunt ii carucatæ et xix villani et iv bordarii cum v carucatæ. Ibi iv servi et v acræ prati. Silva iii quarentenis longa et ii quarentenis lata. Valuit vii libras modo viii librar, etc., etc.

The same in full Latin.

The land of Roger de Berchelai. In Respigete hundred Roger de Berchelai holds Coberlie. There are ten hides. Dena

The same translated into English.

DOMESDAY SURVEY, 1086.

held it in the time of King Edward. There are in the demesne two carucates and 4 bordars with 5 carucates. There are 4 serfs and 5 acres of meadows. The wood is three furlongs long and two furlongs broad. It was worth 7 pounds, now it is worth 8 pounds.

———

For the Domesday measures, Taylor, Birch, Ellis, Kelham, etc., may be consulted.

In many manors there would not be more than 120 acres to the hide.

The hide was a measure of value rather than of area, but on the average we are not very far wrong if we reckon a hide to be equivalent to 460 acres in the Berkeley Manor. The carucates, or plough lands, may be taken to be one-third of this amount.

Important as Domesday may be in a topographical or genealogical enquiry, yet the greater part is dry reading. However, there are not wanting flashes of life to enlighten its hard record of hides, acres and pounds. We may see how, just as at the present day, the letter W was a stumbling block to the men of Gloucestershire eight hundred years ago, for in the quotation concerning Woodchester already given we find it called Udecestre, thus showing that a wood, on the Cotswolds, was, as now, an 'ood eight centuries since. Then we have a touch of irony in the entry of the assertion of Roger Berkeley, himself provost, that Earl William Fitzosborn had committed the estates of two brothers at Cromhall to the provost of Berkeley that he might have their service—"*so Roger says.*"

" Sic dicit Rogerius."

To the great authority of Domesday we turn now for all the information we can gather concerning the lands of the lords of Berkeley, and if the quotations from the ancient record itself seem to differ from the information given in the publications and MS. genealogies of one who should be a great authority in such matters—viz., Sir Bernard Burke, Ulster King of Arms—we cannot but conclude that Domesday is right. Unfortunately his errors owing to the authority of his name and office have been widely copied, recently so in the lithographed pedigree of the Barclay family by the present writer in 1884.

Sir Bernard Burke, Ulster King of Arms.

Lithographed Pedigree of the Barclay family, 1884.

Sir Bernard Burke states that Roger de Berkeley is described in Domesday as holding land in Gloucestershire in the reign of King Edward the Confessor. The most cursory examination of Domesday makes it quite evident that this is altogether erroneous, for nowhere do we find any record whatever of the

Berkeleys holding land in the time of the Confessor. As a matter of fact the precise opposite is implied, for of the lands belonging to Roger de Berchelai, the name of the former Saxon owner in the time of King Edward is invariably given.

DOMESDAY SURVEY.

This error has been corrected in recent issues of the "Landed Gentry."

Since few readers may have the opportunity of studying Domesday for themselves, the most important entries relating to the lords of Berkeley will be given in full, a translation in the text, and facsimiles of the original in the appendix.

So also with many other ancient charters and documents. *Vide* Appendix i, page 87.

Under the heading of the King's property at Gloucester occur the entries of some cases of encroachment apparently; among others we find:

In demesne on the land of the King, Roger de Berchelai holds one house, and one fishery on the vill itself, and it is outside the possession of the King. Baldwin held this in the time of King Edward. No. 1.

The owners of the land in Wales lying between the Wye and the Usk are given under Gloucestershire. Among them:

Roger de Berchelai holds two carucates of land at Chepstowe and has there 6 bordars with one carucate. It is worth 20 shillings. No. 2.

Next occurs, under the general heading of the King's Lands, a brief entry that in the hundred of Blakeney:

Roger de Berchelai holds Etlœ.

Then follows, still under the heading of the King's Lands, the whole account of the great Manor of Berchelai, by far the largest and most important in the county. In the translation the modern names of the parishes are given. Should there be any doubt as to the accuracy of these, reference can be made to the original, printed in the appendix. The great Manor or Hundred, included a large number of lesser manors within its boundaries. The total acreage was 70,583; the number of hides being 150. The whole is under the charge of Roger de Berchelai, who renders a yearly payment of £187 10s., but of this more hereafter.

An analysis of Domesday by C. S. Taylor. 1889. Page 42, etc.

In Berchelai King Edward had five hides and in demesne five carucates and twenty villeins and five bordars with eleven carucates and nine serfs, and two mills of twelve shillings rent. There are ten Radchenisters having seven hides and seven carucates. There

No. 3. Great Manor of Berchelai.

DOMESDAY BOOK.

is one market town, in which seventeen men reside and pay a tax in ferme.

These hamlets belong to Berchelai—

In Hill 4 hides,	In Elberton 5 hides,
In Hinton 4 hides	In Cam 17 hides,
In Gossington 4 hides,	In Dursley 3 hides,
In Coaley 4 hides,	In Uley 2 hides,
In Nympsfield 3 hides,	In Wotton under Edge 15½ hides,
In Simondshale ½ hide,	In Kingscote 4½ hides,
In Beverstone 10 hides	In Ozelworth ½ hide,
In Almonsbury 2 hides,	In Horsfield 8 hides,
In King's Weston 7 hides,	In Cromhall 2 hides,
In Arlington 9 hides	In Ashelworth 3 hides

These above mentioned divisions all belong to Berchelai. There were in these hamlets in the time of King Edward in demesne forty nine and a half carucates, and two hundred and forty two villeins, and one hundred and forty two bordars with one hundred and twenty six carucates. There are one hundred and twenty seven serfs. There are nineteen freemen, Radchenisters having forty eight carucates with their men. There are twenty two soccage tenants and fifteen female serfs. There are eight mills of fifty seven shillings and six pence rent.

No. 4. The two brothers at Cromhall.

In this manor in the time of King Edward two brothers held five hides in Cromhall having in demesne two carucates and six villeins, and five bordars having six carucates. These two brothers might dispose of themselves with their land as they pleased. It was then worth four pounds, now three pounds. Earl William commended them to the Provost of Berchelai that he might have their service. So Roger says.

For this manor with all belonging to it, Roger pays a rent of one hundred and seventy pounds by weight of lawful money.

Slimbridge was given as the dower of Alice de Berkeley on her marriage with Maurice Fitzhardinge, 1154.

The same Roger holds of the land of this manor two hides in Slimbridge, one hide at Clinger, one hide at Hurst, seven hides at Newington. There are in demesne ten carucates and thirteen villeins, and twenty one bordars with twenty two carucates. There are sixteen serfs and a mill of five shillings rent. The whole in the time of King Edward was worth £9, now £11 10s.

Land of Bernard the priest. Probably the provision made for the religious needs when the manor escheated to the Crown.

The same Roger holds five hides, the land of Bernard the priest. He has there 3 carucates and two villeins and six bordars with five carucates. It is worth and was worth sixty shillings.

In Nesse there are five hides belonging to Berchelai, which Earl William set apart to make a little castle. Roger reports this."

The next entry of interest in our investigation has already

been alluded to, as affording so curious a corroboration of the story of the dissolution of the religious house at Berkeley related by Walter Mapes. It may be remembered that this entry in Domesday is made less than fifty years after the events recorded are alleged to have taken place : DOMESDAY BOOK.

Gueda the wife of Godwin and mother of Earl Harold held Udecester in Langetrev hundred. Godwin bought it from Azor and gave it to his wife, that she might live there, until she would live at Berchelai. For she was unwilling to eat anything from that manor on account of the destruction of the abbey. No. 5. *i.e.*, Woodchester.

We come now to an account of the lands held by Roger de Berchelai and his brother Ralph extra-manorially in Gloucestershire, and also an extract from the Wiltshire portion of Domesday which mentions estates held by Roger in that county :

The land of Roger de Berchelai. In Respigete Hundred Roger de Berchelai holds Coberlie. There are ten hides. Dena held it in the time of Edward. In demesne there are two carucates and nineteen villeins and four bordars with five carucates. There are four serfs and five acres of meadow. The wood is three furlongs in length and two in breadth. It was worth £7 now £8. In Hedredstan hundred the same Roger holds Dodintone. There are three hides and two parts of half a hide each. Aluin held it in the time of King Edward. In demesne there is one carucate and seven serfs and four bordars with four carucates. There are four serfs and ten acres of meadow. It is and was worth £3. No. 6. Saxon owners of Berkeley in time of King Edward.

The same Roger holds Sistone. Anne held it. In Pulcrecerce hundred there are five hides which pay gheld tax. In demesne there are two carucates and eight serfs and ten bordars with four carucates. There four serfs and eight acres of meadow. It is worth and was worth a hundred shillings. *i.e.*, Pucklechurch.

The land of Radulf de Berchelai. In Pulcrecerce hundred Radulf brother of the same Roger holds from the King Wapelie. There is one hide. Godric held it. In demesne there is one carucate and four serfs. It is worth and was worth twenty shillings. No. 7. Lands of Radulf de Berchelai

In Blacelaw hundred, the same Radulf holds Stanleye. There are four and a half hides. Godric and Wisnod had held it. Stanley St. Leonard's, which was inherited by Roger's heirs.

In demesne there are two carucates and six serfs and thirteen bordars with twelve carucates. There are five serfs and ten acres of meadow. It was worth and is worth a hundred shillings.

DOMESDAY BOOK.

Roger de Berchelai's land in Wiltshire.

The coscets were small cottagers.

Under Malmesbury this is described as "1 masuram de firma Regis."

A virgate was probably one-fourth of a hide.

Land of Roger de Berchelai. Roger de Berchelai holds Foxeledge of the King. Aldret held it in the time of King Edward, and it paid gheld for two hides. The land is four carucates. Of this there is one hide in demesne, and there are two carucates, and three serfs; and there are four villeins, and three coscets, with three carucates. There is a mill, worth seven shillings and six pence, and four acres of meadow, and eight acres of pasture, and one house in Malmesbury. It was, and is, worth forty shillings.

The same Roger holds one hide, all but half a virgate of the demesne farm of Cepeham. Celein held it in the time of King Edward, as a purpresture of Edric the sheriff.

Roger himself owns Estone. Alwi held it in the time of King Edward, and it paid gheld for three hides, all but half a virgate. The land is three carucates. Of this there are two hides in demesne, and there are two carucates, and four serfs; and there are two villeins, and three bordars with one carucate. There is a mill paying six shillings. It was worth thirty shillings; it is now worth forty shillings.

Roger de Berchelai we thus find holding upwards of 70,000 acres, nearly one-tenth of the whole shire, and undoubtedly one of the most powerful and influential men of Gloucestershire.

Earl Godwin. 1051.

We have seen that Earl Godwin held Berkeley up to 1051, when it became forfeited to the Crown. In 1086 we find Roger de Berchelai præpositus, or provost. There is strong probability that Earl William Fitzosborn, the nearest personal friend of the Conqueror, put Roger into possession of the great Manor, for Roger himself states to the Domesday Commissioners that the Earl had assigned him as provost the services of two brothers at Cromhall, and had set apart likewise five hides at Nesse for the construction of a small castle. This must have been prior to 1070, when Fitzosborn finally quitted England. Earl William Fitzosborn was one of the Conqueror's chief statesmen, and in 1067 during the King's absence from England, he was associated with Bishop Odo in the regency, with authority to erect castles at discretion in all parts of the kingdom. To him was entrusted in large measure the distribution of lands among the followers of the Conqueror, and the Domesday record makes frequent allusion to him in this capacity.

He was killed in battle in 1071 at Ravenchouen. "The Conqueror and his Companions," by J. R. Planché. 1874. Vol. i. page 179. *Idem*, page 92.

These plain statements from Domesday necessarily strike a blow at the old traditional belief that Roger de Berchelai and his ancestors before him were lords of Berkeley from time immemorial. We cannot even claim that Roger or Ralph held any land whatever in Gloucestershire during the reign of King Edward the Confessor. All this must lead us to a somewhat singular inference, but in order that it may be brought forward with greater weight, we will here allude to the existence of an ancient document now at Rouen, which, among other benefactions to the Abbey of Aumâle in Normandy, contains mention of those of Roger de Berchelaico and Rissa, his wife.

DOMESDAY BOOK.

Gloucestershire tenants of Domesday. Bris. and Glouc. Arch. Soc. Vol. iv. page 147.

Charter of Aumâle, *vide* Archælogia. Vol. xxvi. page 349. Appendix ii, page 90.

Furthermore, in the time of Stephen, a later Roger obtained from Bernard de St. Valerie for himself and for his heirs exemption from the dues of the port of St. Valerie sur Somme, which seems to imply frequent journeys to a Norman estate.

Dugdale's Monasticon. Vol. i. p. 812.

These facts must surely lead us to infer the extreme probability of a Norman origin for Roger de Berchelai. We find him put in possession as lord of the great Manor of Berkeley at the time the land was divided among the followers of the Conqueror. We find that in the case of the lands which he holds extra-manorially the name of the former Saxon owner is invariably given. If we suppose Roger de Berchelai to be of Saxon race the Conqueror's dealings with him would be quite inexplicable, and very different to his treatment of other Saxons. The *Chronicles* tell us how their estates were confiscated, how many of them fled abroad, their lands being granted to Norman nobles. We hear how King William deprived the Anglo-Saxons of *all* offices of State, and how even the Saxon monasteries were, in some cases, plundered, and the very primate, Stigand, deposed, and Lanfranc, a Milanese monk, promoted to the See of Canterbury. At such a time it is past belief that a Saxon should be promoted to power and influence from which other Saxon owners had been driven.

The Norman Descent.

Freeman in his *Norman Conquest* points out that in the generation represented by Domesday a man's name is an absolutely certain guide to his nationality. The names Roger and Ralph indicate unmistakably a Norman stock. A brief exami-

Freeman's Norman Conquest.

THE NORMAN DESCENT.

The Conqueror and his Companions, by J. R. Planché.

nation of the lists of the Conqueror's chief followers shows that no names are more frequently repeated; for instance, Raoul, son of Roger de Mortimer, Roger de Montgomeri, Roger de Beaumont, Raoul de Tœni, son of Roger de Tœni, Raoul de Gael, Roger de Mowbray and many others.

It is true that the name of Raoul was to be found in England before the Conquest, but only in the case of undoubted Normans. Moreover had Roger de Berkeley been of Saxon race we should not have expected, in those early times, to find the Norman style "de Berkeley," although later on doubtless many of the Saxons may have adopted the common usage.

We have strong additional evidence of his Norman origin in the fact that in conjunction with his wife Rissa he made a benefaction to a Norman abbey, which would have been a somewhat singular proceeding for a Saxon, at such a time, and later on we find records suggestive of his grandson possessing property in Normandy.

As opposed to all this, the arguments for the Saxon stock appear weak in the extreme. We have merely the statement of John Newland, Abbot of St. Augustine's at Bristol, in 1481, that Roger de Berkeley, a descendant of the Conqueror's provost, was "an ancient Saxon Baron of the same blood as King Edward the Confessor." What this statement may be worth, or what grounds he had for making it, we cannot now determine. No original evidence in its favour has been forthcoming.

Roll in Berkeley Castle. Printed Brist. and Glouc. Arch. Soc. Vol. xiv. page 117.

John Smyth, the historian of the Fitzhardinge family, writes of the original Berkeleys as "that ancient Saxon family." His statement, however, is no additional proof as his ideas on the subject evidently originated from the Abbot Newland's roll, from which he constantly quotes.

Smyth's Lives of the Berkeleys.

The arguments for the Saxon origin are thus manifestly slender; little more than a family tradition. We may dismiss the statement of Newland as scarcely deserving credit, it was the usual custom for the monkish historians to find royal blood in the veins of their patrons, and their unverified statements do not therefore carry much weight.

A few words on the origin of the Normans may be of interest in view of the descent of the Berkeleys from this northern race.

BERKELEY CASTLE

To face page 15

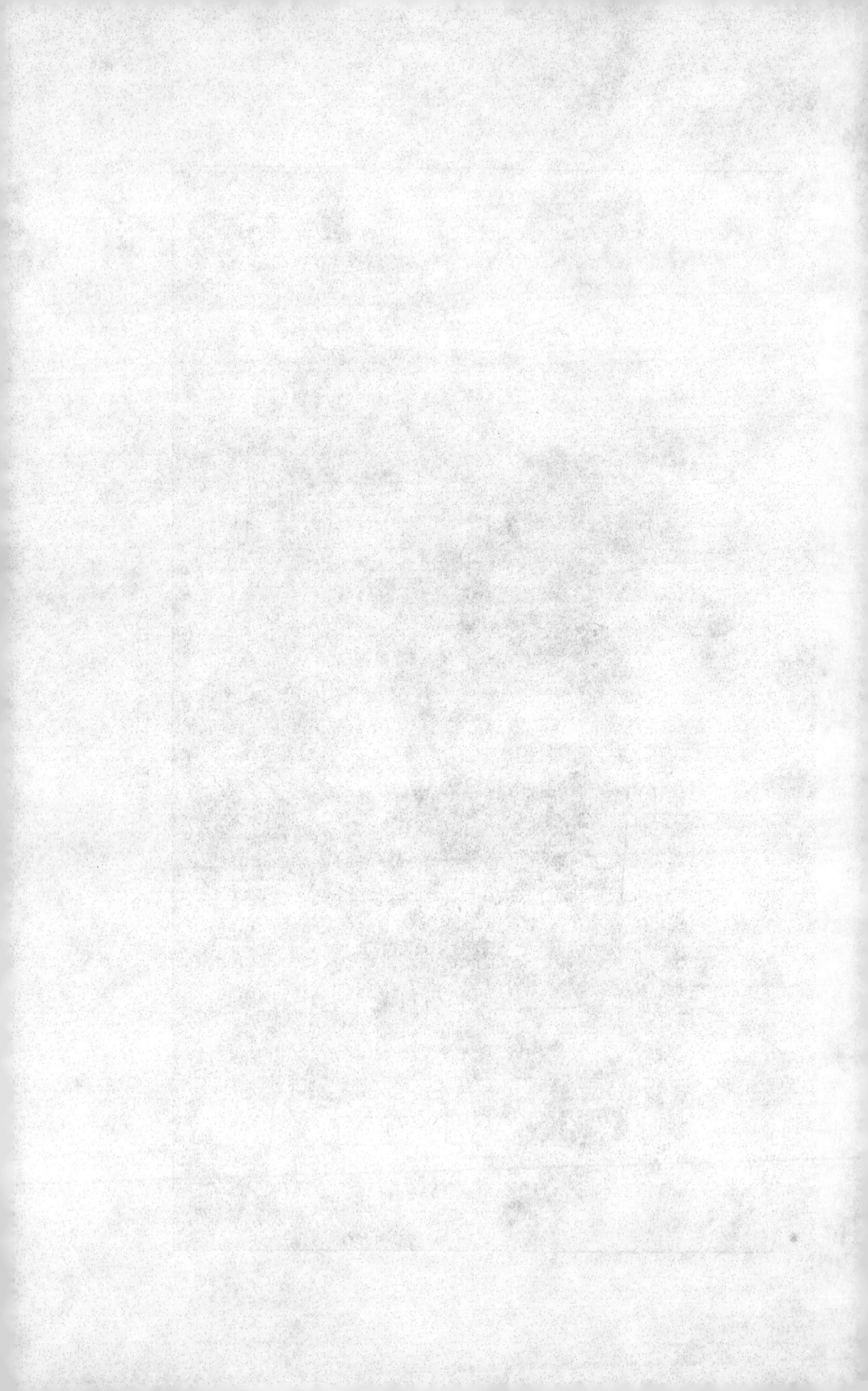

"The coasts of France had long been ravaged by the incursions of the Northmen, from Norway and Denmark, thus the way was prepared for the final subjugation of the country by Rollo, son of the Norwegian jarl Rögnwald. From Rollo, who died in 931, William the Conqueror sprung fifth in descent. The name 'Normandy,' however, does not appear until the eleventh century. The Normans when they invaded England had lost all trace of their northern origin in language and manners, yet the more essential attributes of body and mind are not so easily shaken off, and they were still distinguished from the other natives of France by *their large limbs and fair complexions*."

THE NORMAN DESCENT.

Hume's History of England.

Before turning to the genealogical details of the Berkeley family, and attempting to follow the life of each individual, it will be well to throw some light upon the much-vexed question as to the date of the building of Berkeley Castle, and whether we are correct in assigning, at any rate to some portion of it, a date prior to the Conquest. It has been frequently stated that no castle existed at Berkeley until the year 1154, for in the original Charter of Henry II (then Prince Henry, Duke of Normandy), when granting the great Manor to Robert Fitzhardinge, he undertakes to build for him a castle there, and he came to Berkeley soon afterwards to see this promise fulfilled.

Berkeley Castle.

Charter of Henry II. at Berkeley Castle. Appendix iii No. 1, p. 91.

But it appears probable that there was already an ancient castle occupying the site. We have seen how in the *Saxon Chronicle* the existence of a castle is mentioned. Henry I shortly after his marriage to Adeliza of Louvaine spent his Easter at Berkeley, probably at the castle, and the Conqueror himself had spent the Christmas of 1080 at the same place.

Saxon Chronicle.

Robert of Gloucester's Chronicle. "His Easter sooth at Berkeley."

The shell keep is the most ancient part of the building, and Lysons, no mean authority, in writing of it says: "It has been suggested to me by the learned author of the *Munimenta Antiqua* that this keep was the castle built by Earl Godwin in the time of King Edward the Confessor out of the ruins of the monastery, and not by Robert Fitzhardinge, in the reign of Stephen, as is commonly supposed, as its form does not resemble that of the other edifices known to have been erected

Lyson's Glouces. Antiquities, 1806. Page 32.

BERKELEY CASTLE.

at that time. The doorways which appear decorated like those of a later age, might have been added by Robert Fitzhardinge."

Mediæval Military Architecture, by G. T. Clark. Vol. i. page 236.

Mr. G. T. Clark, author of *Mediæval Military Architecture*, gives an interesting account of Berkeley Castle. With respect to the keep he writes: "If the masonry of Berkeley Castle were to be removed, as at Kilpeck or Ewias Harold, its remains would show a mound of earth, and attached to three sides of it a platform, the whole encircled with a ditch or scarp. It would, in fact, be a moated mound with an appended platform of a character very common in England, in the Welsh marches, and in Normandy, and would resemble such works at Tamworth and Towcester, the dates of which are given in the *Anglo-Saxon Chronicle*. The inference is, therefore, that Berkeley was the seat of an English lord. Had the fortress been an original Norman work, it is scarcely probable that a shell would have been the form of keep selected, or that, having been selected, its lower 22 feet would have been filled with earth." Thus we have good authority for believing that this castle was the stronghold of Roger de Berkeley. Possibly he may have been the builder of a portion of it himself, for the following statement in Domesday, though obscure, may point to this: "There are five hides in Nesse belonging to Berchelai, which Earl William set apart to make a little castle, so Roger reports."* By Nesse is probably meant Sharpness, a few miles from Berkeley, and as there is no record or indication of there ever having been a castle there, the Domesday entry would seem to indicate the provision which Fitzosborn made for building, or adding to the castle at Berkeley. Berkeley Castle, as it now stands, is in very perfect preservation, and although it bears the marks of many a siege and fight, it is still a noble structure. In solid, massive grandeur the old grey castle, standing out from its background of vivid green, forms a picture unequalled for beauty and interest.

Domesday Book.

The castle, church and town of Berkeley occupy rising ground about fifty feet above the meadows lying to the south

* Dr. Seyer in his history of Bristol, Vol. i, 472, translates "Misit Extra" "put outside the farm" as in many instances firmam follows misit extra. In this case it might seem Earl Fitzosborn proposed building a castle for himself, an intention never fulfilled.

FONT
IN BERKELEY CHURCH

To face page 17

and west; through them flows the little Avon, which falling into the Pill or creek of Berkeley, reaches the Severn, here expanded into a wide estuary. The southern shore is about two miles from the castle. A few yards to the north stands the parish church with its detached tower, and again a little to the north is the town which has grown up under the protection of its powerful neighbour. A deep and wholly artificial fosse intervenes between the churchyard and the castle, crosses the high ground, and isolating the latter protects it on the north and west sides. The south and east is made secure by the natural declivity, scarped and rendered steeper by art. The meadows, out of which the castle hill rises, lie but little above the Severn, and were formerly an extensive and almost impassable morass, adding much to the strength of the place. Under the skill and labour of centuries they have become grass lands of great beauty and fertility. The timber is of great size and adds much to the beauty of the scene. In the distance to the west rise the Welsh mountains, and to the east the Cotes-wold hills.

BERKELEY CASTLE.

The town and castle stand, geologically, upon the old red sandstone, which at a short distance to the east is succeeded by the Ludlow rocks.

The main approach to the castle lies through the town; on passing the gatehouse the keep is immediately before you; part of it has been removed and a large breach formed, showing that the interior is full twenty-two feet above the level of the ground outside. It is built of very rude rubble masonry. The annexed illustration gives some idea of the appearance of the fine old building. The oratory is now used as a muniment room, and is rich in ancient documents. Here are to be found many of the original charters, and ancient histories, on which the present pages are so largely based.

Appendix iii, page 91.

Berkeley is a rare example of an ancient castle inhabited for at least eight centuries, and which has descended in one family through the male line from the reign of Stephen, and in the female line from the time of the Conqueror.

Alice de Berkeley married Robert Fitzhardinge.

HISTORY OF THE BARCLAY FAMILY

ROGER DE BERCHELAI I

ROGER DE BERCHELAI I, 1066–1091.

The dates given at the head of each page give the time of succession to the time of death, some approximately.

"Prepositos."

Saxon Chronicle.

Saxon Chronicle.

Roger de Berchelai, the progenitor of the various branches of the Barclay families in England, Scotland, Ireland and America, was, as we have already shown, a man of vast wealth and territorial power in Gloucestershire, holding the position of an earl by tenure. He had been appointed provost of Berkeley shortly after the Conquest, by Earl Fitzosborn, and was confirmed in his possession by the King himself. He continued in high royal favour, and in the year 1080 we find King William spending Easter at Berkeley. To his brother Ralph the lands of Wapley and Stanley had been committed. Probably Ralph died during the lifetime of his brother, as we find Roger's son occupying the lands of Wapley and Stanley and dealing with them on the same footing as the lands which he had inherited from his father. Roger de Berchelai must have suffered severely during the struggle for the throne at the Conqueror's death: for the *Saxon Chronicle* informs us that in 1088 "all Berkeley Hernesse was waisted and the town" (one version adding "*and castle*") "burnt by the Barons in arms against William Rufus."

There is no mention of this in Domesday.

Hist. et Cart. Mon. S. Pet. Glouc. Vol. i. page 101.

For original Latin, *vide* Appendix iv.

Appendix iv. No. 5.

Hist. et Cart. S. Pet. Vol. i. 112.

Idem, page 112.

His disputes, too, with Serlo, the imperious Abbot of St. Peter's Abbey of Gloucester, must have occasioned him much trouble and anxiety. The Abbot accused him of having, at the Domesday Survey, asserted the rights of the Crown over Nymdesfeld, and of having encroached elsewhere on lands to which St. Peter's Abbey laid claim. The following is the note made in the cartulary of the Abbey: "In the year of the Lord 1087 Rogerus Senior de Berkeleye in the description of the whole of England made Nymdesfeld to be described as providing for the King's table, the Abbot Serlo not knowing." But in the end, as old age came upon him, he made peace with Serlo, and on January 17th, 1091, became a Benedictine monk under Serlo's rule, making full restitution to the Abbey by giving up the lands of Shoteshore which he had long held in possession notwithstanding the claims of the monks. The entries in the Abbey cartulary with respect to this great change of front in the sturdy provost read as follows : "Roger

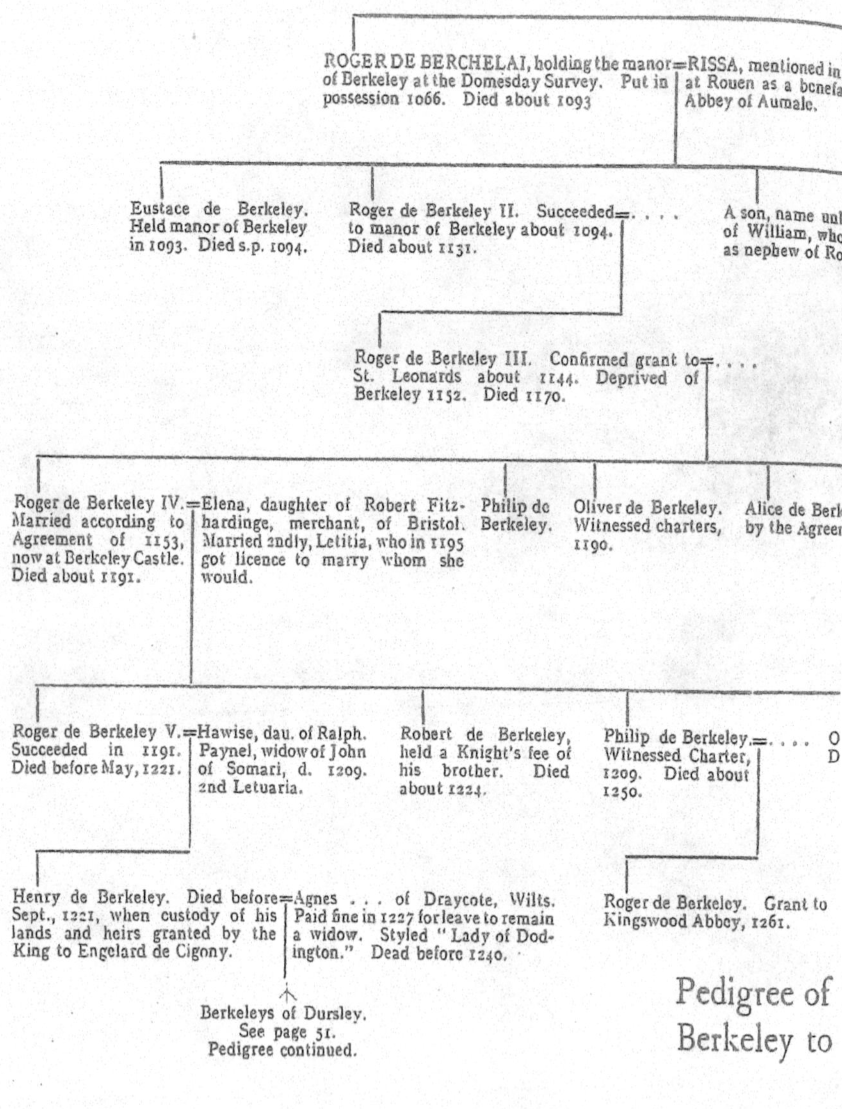
ROGER DE BERCHELAI, holding the manor of Berkeley at the Domesday Survey. Put in possession 1066. Died about 1093
=RISSA, mentioned in at Rouen as a benefa Abbey of Aumale.
Eustace de Berkeley. Held manor of Berkeley in 1093. Died s.p. 1094.
Roger de Berkeley II. Succeeded to manor of Berkeley about 1094. Died about 1131.
= . . . .
A son, name unk of William, who as nephew of Ro
Roger de Berkeley III. Confirmed grant to St. Leonards about 1144. Deprived of Berkeley 1152. Died 1170.
= . . . .
Roger de Berkeley IV. Married according to Agreement of 1153, now at Berkeley Castle. Died about 1191.
=Elena, daughter of Robert Fitz-hardinge, merchant, of Bristol. Married 2ndly, Letitia, who in 1195 got licence to marry whom she would.
Philip de Berkeley.
Oliver de Berkeley. Witnessed charters, 1190.
Alice de Berk by the Agreem
Roger de Berkeley V. Succeeded in 1191. Died before May, 1221.
=Hawise, dau. of Ralph. Paynel, widow of John of Somari, d. 1209. 2nd Letuaria.
Robert de Berkeley, held a Knight's fee of his brother. Died about 1224.
Philip de Berkeley. Witnessed Charter, 1209. Died about 1250.
= . . . .
O
D
Henry de Berkeley. Died before Sept., 1221, when custody of his lands and heirs granted by the King to Engelard de Cigony.
=Agnes . . . of Draycote, Wilts. Paid fine in 1227 for leave to remain a widow. Styled "Lady of Dodington." Dead before 1240.
Roger de Berkeley. Grant to Kingswood Abbey, 1261.
Berkeleys of Dursley.
See page 51.
Pedigree continued.

Pedigree of
Berkeley to

AY FAMILY

h de Berchelai, described
omesday as brother of
r. Died s.p.

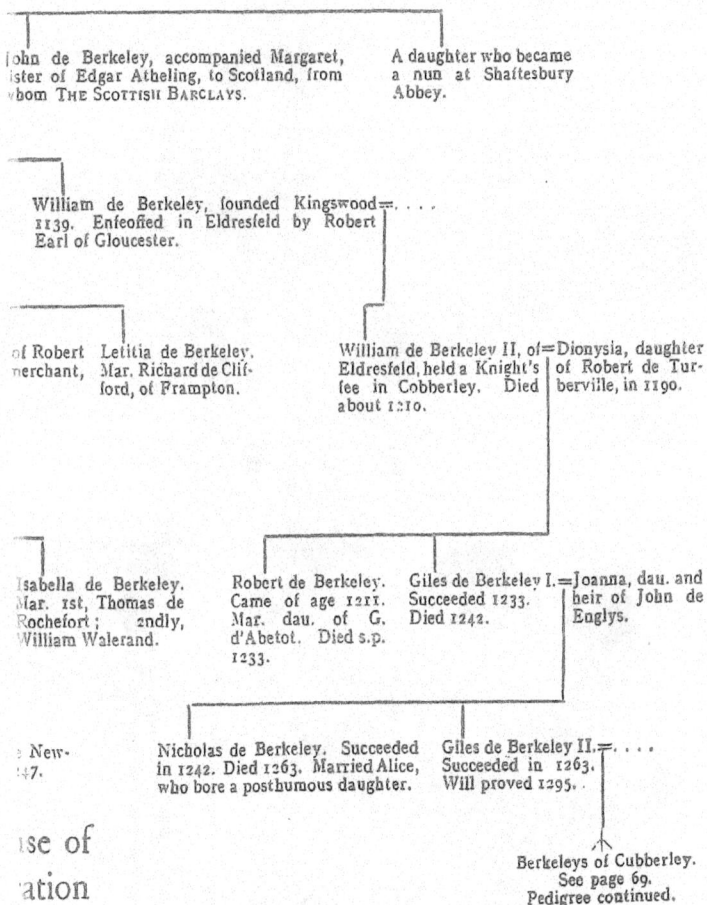

John de Berkeley, accompanied Margaret, sister of Edgar Atheling, to Scotland, from whom THE SCOTTISH BARCLAYS.

A daughter who became a nun at Shaftesbury Abbey.

William de Berkeley, founded Kingswood 1139. Enfeoffed in Eldresfeld by Robert Earl of Gloucester. = ...

of Robert
nerchant,

Letitia de Berkeley. Mar. Richard de Clifford, of Frampton.

William de Berkeley II, of Eldresfeld, held a Knight's fee in Cobberley. Died about 1210. = Dionysia, daughter of Robert de Turberville, in 1190.

Isabella de Berkeley. Mar. 1st, Thomas de Rochefort; 2ndly, William Walerand.

Robert de Berkeley. Came of age 1211. Mar. dau. of G. d'Abetot. Died s.p. 1233.

Giles de Berkeley I. Succeeded 1233. Died 1242. = Joanna, dau. and heir of John de Englys.

New-
47.

Nicholas de Berkeley. Succeeded in 1242. Died 1263. Married Alice, who bore a posthumous daughter.

Giles de Berkeley II. Succeeded in 1263. Will proved 1295. = ...

se of
ation

Berkeleys of Cubberley.
See page 69.
Pedigree continued.

de Berkeleye Senior on St. Sebastian's day being made a monk, under the rule of Serlo the Abbot, gave back to God and to St. Peters, of Gloucester, Shoteshore, freely and quietly, which he had held unjustly for a long time, King William the Elder confirming it. This was done in the year of the Lord 1091." Shoteshore was, no doubt, a place of some importance owing to its stone quarries. We may conclude that before Roger's retirement into the monastery, his wife Rissa had died; of her we know very little, but her piety and devotion to the Church are evident from the nature of their joint gift to the Abbey of Aumâle. The charter, before alluded to, is of much interest as giving the name of the wife of Roger de Berchelai, which we should not otherwise have known. Upon the suppression of the monasteries in France the contents of their muniment rooms were transferred to the public offices. Among them, those of the Abbey of St. Martin d'Auchy, commonly called the Abbey of Aumâle, were deposited in the archives of the Department of the Seine Inférieure at Rouen. The charter in question is still extant, written upon parchment; and its paleography corresponds with the date warranted by its internal evidence. It commences with these words:

ROGER DE BERCHELAI I, 1066–1091.

Archæologia. Vol. xxvi., page 351. Appendix ii, page 90.

"In the name of our Lord Jesus Christ in this charter are contained the benefices and rents hereby specified of the Church of the Mother of our Lord, the Virgin Mary, and of St. Martin the Confessor of Christ which in the time of Richard, 4th Duke of the Normans, was founded near the town of Aumâle," etc. Then follows an enumeration of gifts from various persons. The clause of special interest here is the following:

"*Rogerus de Berchelaico, with his wife Rissa, gave a cope with a pallium, a costly priestly vestment, in which not even was its girdle wanting. He gave also a silver cup, a golden cross and two bells.*"

The 4th Duke of the Normans was Richard II., who died 1096. Rissa.

It has been pointed out by Thomas Stapleton, Esq., F.S.A., that the name Rissa bespeaks her Welsh extraction, but this is certainly most unlikely. She must have been married in all probability some years before the Conquest, for her son John, as we shall presently see, accompanied Margaret, the sister of

Page 46.

ROGER DE BERCHELAI I, 1066–1091.

Edgar Atheling, to Scotland in 1069. We cannot suppose that he can have been under twenty years of age.

In forming a consecutive narrative of the early generations it is a matter of very great difficulty to ascertain without doubt the correct descents. This can cause no surprise when it is remembered that we are dealing with the history of a private family more than eight centuries ago. We shall presently enquire who succeeded the first Roger de Berchelai, as Lord of the great Manor in Gloucestershire, but before doing so, we must follow for a while the fortunes of a younger son who became the founder of the families of the Scottish Barclays, and their wide ramifications, not only in Scotland, but in England, Ireland and America. We may regret that we are not here treading upon the firm ground of original charters or contemporary documents; still the evidence cannot be rejected as altogether unworthy of credit, for it is corroborated by allusions in the pages of the Chroniclers and other writers. Our chief source of information is an extract from *A Manuscript History of the House of Forbes and Others*, written in the year 1580 by Matthew Lumsden of Tuliekerne:*

Matthew Lumsden's MS. History of the House of Forbes.

"Among those who about the year of Christ 1069 were with Margaret, the King of England's eldest sister, driven by tempest upon the coast of Scotland was John Barclay, son to the Lord Barclay in England. Malcolm Caenmoir, King of Scotland, having married the said Margaret (for her piety afterwards called St. Margaret) did bestow upon several of the English nation, both lands and titles of honour, for attending her, and her mother, brother and sister, in their voyage out of England, intending at that time for Hungarie, but were driven by providence upon Scotland. Among those of the English nation upon whom King Malcolm bestowed lands was John Barclay, son of Lord Barclay in England, upon whom the King bestowed the lands of Towie in the shire of Aberdeen. This John Barclay had many sons, the eldest of whom took to wife, —— Gartly, Heretrix of the lands of Gartly, in the shire

Edgar Atheling.

* The printed edition of this work is incomplete; where Matthew Lumsden has digressed to give accounts of other families than the Forbes, the editor has omitted the passages. Hence the annexed quotation is not printed.

also of Aberdeen, which afterwards from him were called, the lands and barony of Barclay, he having received from the King the title of Barclay of that ilke, as witnesseth the charter of the said lands, wherein the lady is always Barclay de Eodem."

ROGER DE BERCHELAI I, 1066-1091.

. . . .

"The eldest of John Barclay of Towie, his sons being advanced to ane considerable estate by his marriage with the Heretrix of Gartly and confirmed by the King's favour in the foresaid title of honour, the said John did transmit and leave to his *second* son the foresaid lands of Towie. The rest of his children by their virtue and good service to their King and Country attained to considerable fortunes, and honourable estates, for of them are descended the family of the Laird of Mathers in the shire of Mearns; the family of the Laird of Johnstone Barclay *ibidem;* likewise the family of the Laird of Collairney in the shire of Fife; and we have it also by tradition, that the Lord of Brechin, nephew to King Robert Bruce, was descended of the same race of John Barclay of Towie."

Sic.

Towie to the second son.

William of Malmesbury in his chronicle says: "Malcolm willingly received all English fugitives." Also from Cosmo Innes' sketches of early Scotch history we learn that partly on account of the marriage of Malcolm with Margaret there took place a great influx of English and Norman families who, rapidly pouring over Scotland, displaced the old inhabitants in all important posts. "They were fit," he writes, "for the society of a court, and became the chosen companions of our princes. They were men of the sword, above all servile and mechanical employments. It is astonishing with what rapidity those southern colonists spread even to the far north. From Tweed and Solway, the whole arable land may be said to be held by them. Of the race of the English colonists came Bruce, Balliol, Biset, *Berkeley*, Colville, Cumin, Douglas, Dunbar; and descended from Northumbrian princes, Fleming, Fraser, Gordon, Hamilton, Lindsay, Maule, Maxwell, Mowbray, Stewart, Sinclair, Wallace, and many others."

Wm. of Malmesbury. Edit. Giles, 1883. Page 282.

See also Hollinshed's Chronicle.

Cosmo Innes' Sketches of Early Scottish History. 1861. Pages 9 and 10.

It appears, therefore, that John, the younger son of Roger de

ROGER DE BERCHELAI I, 1066–1091.

Berchelai, went to seek his fortune in the far north, and laid the foundations of the widespread Barclay stock. Later on in this history we shall return to him and follow the line of his descendants down to the present day; but, first of all, it is necessary to come back to the main Gloucestershire line, which we must trace through many generations until its final extinction; when we shall again take up John de Berkeley, on whose descendants the representation of the family then devolves.

Roger I.'s successor.

It is no easy matter to decide who was the successor of Roger de Berchelai. Probably the descent as given in the accompanying chart is correct. We will trace it step by step.

Appendix iv. 1 and 2, p. 95.

Roger de Berchelai I is styled, as we have seen, in the cartulary of St. Peter's Abbey, Gloucester, as Rogerus de Berkeleye *Senior*, thus proving that he had a son of that name, whom we find also mentioned in the same cartulary, as Roger de Berkeleye *Junior*. Moreover from a deed in the Register of Malmesbury Abbey at a later date we find a Roger de Berkeley, who confirms to the church of St. Adhelm a hide of land in Codrington, which *Roger his grandfather and Roger his father* had granted to the church in pure alms. In its proper place the date of this deed will be considered, but there is strong probability that the document was executed by Roger III. If so we have a clear succession of three Rogers. This agrees precisely with much other evidence, though some difficulties still remain to be explained.

Cartulary of Malmesbury Abbey. Vol. i. p. 433. Appendix vi, page 102.

EUSTACE DE BERKELEY

1092–3.

"In the cartulary of St. Peter's we read, Eustace de Berkeley in the year 1093 gave back Nymdesfeld to the abbey in the time of Serlo." Who was this Eustace whom we find exercising an authority over the great Berkeley Manor? We have seen that Roger I had become a monk at the Abbey in 1091. What is more probable than that Eustace de Berkeley was his eldest son, who became provost of Berkeley on this father's retirement? But it is clear that the following year the provostship was held by Roger de Berkeley Junior, for in a list of dona-

Appendix iv. No. 3, p. 95.

tions to the Abbey we read: "Roger de Berkeleye junior in the year of the Lord 1094 gave to God and to St. Peters of Gloucester a little piece of land called Clehungre with the consent and confirmation of King William the younger, but he stole away Nymdesfeld in the time of Abbot Serlo."

EUSTACE DE BERKELEY, 1092–3.

Hist. et Cart. S. Pet. Glouc. Vol. i. page 72. Appendix iv. No. 1, p. 95.

Thus we must conclude that in all probability Eustace died within a year of his becoming provost. The only other alternative is that the intervention of Eustace in regard to Nymdesfeld was purely ministerial, in virtue possibly of an order from William Rufus, who, we read, in that very year, 1093, when he thought himself dying at Gloucester, vowed that he would make restoration of all Church lands—a vow which he forgot to keep on his recovery, calling to mind the distich:

> "The devil was sick, the devil a saint would be.
> The devil got well but devil a saint was he."

ROGER DE BERKELEY II

1094–1131.

We hear nothing more of Eustace, but we find Roger II holding the manor of Berkeley. We know that he is a son of Roger I, and therefore a younger brother of Eustace.

Nymdesfeld seems to have been a cause of frequent dispute for many a long year. The Abbot Serlo charged Roger I with giving false information about it at the Domesday Survey, and now it is given and taken back again, apparently almost at will, by the lords of Berkeley. Their conduct in this case, and also over Shoteshore, and in other instances, proves that as young men the Berkeleys were very ready to despoil the abbeys of their possessions, and in later life to make restitution, in more than one instance entering on the "religious life" themselves.

We have seen how in 1091 Roger I on becoming a monk gave back Shoteshore, which apparently he had been holding unjustly, to the abbey. Roger II acts in precisely the same way as his father, for another entry, undated, but which cannot be less than twenty years later and probably considerably more, states: "Roger de Berkeley junior gave Shoteshore to the Abbey which he had held unjustly for a long time in the time of Abbot William." It is worthy of remark that Roger con-

Appendix iv. No. 5, p. 95.

Hist. et Cart. St. Pet. Glouc. Vol. i. 112. Appendix iv. No. 6, p. 96.

ROGER DE BERKELEY II, 1094–1131.

tinues to be called junior, no doubt because his father was still living as an old man in the monastery.

Dr. Seyer's History of Bristol.

Recently Dr. Seyer in his history of Bristol started the idea that this Roger II was son of Radulfus de Berchelai, of Domesday, and identified him with "Roger the son of Ralph," the Domesday tenant of Clifton, because he considered that manor might have been given him by Roger I as a dependency of Barton of Bristol, which he is supposed to have held from the King,* *vide* Domesday. It had, however, been separated *before* the Conquest, and there is no connection traceable between the family of de Clifton, which sprang from Roger FitzRalph and the de Berkeleys. It is true that Roger II possessed the Manors of Wapley and Stanley, which had belonged to Ralph de Berkeley at the time of the survey but we may well suppose that on his death, without issue, they went to his elder brother or his heirs.

"Quod tenuit Sewin præpositos de Bristowe de rege Edwardo." Domesday.

Roger II before his death was filled with zeal for the Church, for he founded and liberally endowed the priory of St. Leonard's on his manor of Stanley. The records, however, of the early history of this collegiate foundation are scanty. He dedicated it as a small college of canons with a prior at their head in the first half of the twelfth century, and endowed it with gifts of land and gave it also the advowsons of the churches of Arlingham, Slimbridge and Uley. A deed of confirmation by Theobald, Archbishop of Canterbury, signed by him in the time of Simon, Bishop of Worcester, and therefore between the years 1130 and 1149 states that the advowsons of Eston, Arlingham, Coaley, Ouselworth and Cam, together with the prebend of Bernard the chaplain in Berkeley, had been given some time previously to the priory of St. Leonard, Stanley, and speaks of Roger de Berkeley as patron of the church. Thus Roger gives back to the church the land of Bernard the priest, which his father had wrongfully held. No

Bris. and Glouc. Arch. Soc. Vol. v. 119.

Tanner's Not. Mon. Page 147.

Dugdale Mon. Ang. i. 119; iii. 64.

Steven's Abbeys, i. 275.

Bris. and Glouc. Arch. Soc., Vol. v. p. 41.

Vide Domesday "Roger holds 5 hides the land of Bernard the priest." Appendix i No. 4.

* The Domesday entry upon which this supposition is based is a statement that "Rogerius" held Barton of Bristol from the King. But there is no reason for believing that this was Roger de Berkeley as has been frequently stated (Ellis, Bris. & Glouc. Arch. Vol 4, 146. Sir H. Barkly Vol. 8, 196, etc.). He is more probably Roger de Pistres, the Sheriff. See Taylor's *Domesday Survey of Gloucestershire*, page 199.

doubt it was an endowment for the spiritual welfare of the people on the suppression of the Berkeley nunnery.

ROGER DE BERKELEY II, 1094–1131.

The original foundation was probably one of Black or Austin Canons, who wore a black cassock, over it a white alb or surplice, and over all a black woollen cope with a hood. This dress is described by Chaucer in the prologue to the *Chanon's Yeoman:*

Bris. and Glouc. Arch. Soc., Vol. v, p. 120.

Chaucer's Chanon's Yeoman.

> "At Boughten under the blee us gan a take
> A man that clothed was in clothes blake,
> And under that he had a white surplise :
> . . . . .
> All light for sammer rode this worthy man
> And in my hearte wondren I began
> What that he was, till I understood,
> How that his cloke was sewed to his hood.
> For which when I had long avised me,
> I deemed him son chanon for to be."

Roger de Berkeley, no doubt, came to the conclusion that such a small and unimportant foundation would have no chance of security or redress in those lawless times; he, therefore, wisely placed it, with the consent of its prior, Sabrithius, and of Simon, Bishop of Worcester, under the protection of the powerful Abbey of St. Peter's, Gloucester. It continued to be a cell of that abbey until the dissolution in 1539. At the dissolution there were only three monks in residence. The ancient Collegiate Church of Stanley St. Leonard's still exists, and certain structural features about it would seem to prove conclusively that it was built by Roger de Berkeley, for there are distinct differences between the Church of a college of canons and a monastic church of whatever order.

Vide paper by J. T. Mickle-thwaite, F.S.A., in the Yorks. Arch. Soc. Trans. 1877.

Although in later times monastic and collegiate church plans, through various alterations, became very much alike, yet in early days they were perfectly distinct in form one from the other. The churches of the monks, even the earliest we are acquainted with, are large cruciform buildings *with aisles*, and this original Norman plan was generally adhered to through the many changes that took place. Canon's churches, on the other hand, took as their model the ordinary parish church—in fact, most canon's churches were parish churches. The

ROGER DE BERKELEY II, 1094–1131.

original Norman plan for a parish church, with very few exceptions, was a building *with transepts*, but never with aisles. On account, then, of the plan of the church of St. Leonard, Stanley, and without any other evidence, we might safely conclude that it was built not for a monastic but for a collegiate foundation. We have seen that Roger de Berkeley, the founder, himself changed the form of the institution from a college of canons to that of an ordinary monastic attachment to the Abbey of St. Peter. We may, therefore, conclude, as the church was evidently built before the change, that Roger himself built it. The church is cruciform with transepts, and a tower in the centre. Many of the original Norman windows remain, and there is much of interest in the fine old church, especially some fourteenth century paintings which have been lately uncovered. On the east jamb of the north-east window there is portrayed a standing figure, clad in flowing drapery, and holding in his left hand the model of a church, to which he points with his right; he has no nimbus and probably represents Roger de Berkeley the founder. This figure has been completely destroyed during a *restoration* of the church a few years since. Outside the church but little remains of the collegiate buildings. The extent of the cloister is shown by the corbels which supported its roof along the south wall of the nave. The most interesting relic of the priory is a chapel which still exists, though in a sadly mutilated and ruined state. It probably adjoined the prior's house. The chapel is now used as a cowshed, and the greater part of the churchyard, in spite of its being consecrated ground, and the property of the church it surrounds, is turned into a farm enclosure.

Painted figure of Roger de Berkeley.

Sir Robert Atkins's History of Glouc., p. 25.

Tanner's Not. Mon., etc., etc.

The tradition noted by most of the county historians and other writers, that Roger de Berkeley late in life entered the priory of Stanley St. Leonard's, is probably true, although no *ancient* authority can be found to decide the point.

Vide original Charter of Hen. I. Dug. Mon. Ang., Vol. v. page 427. Appendix v. No. 3, p. 98.

Before Roger II assumed the cowl at Stanley St. Leonard's we find records of a transaction which led to the subsequent founding of Kingswood Abbey by his nephew William de Berkeley. This is a permission from Henry I "to alienate his manor of Acholt in perpetuity for canons or monks." But

Stanley St. Leonard

ROGER DE BERKELEY II, 1094–1131.

Pipe Roll xxxi. Hen. I.

Pipe Roll 31 Hen. I. "Will. de Berckelai reddit compotum de firma de Bercklai, etc."

Idem. "Ut habeat in custodia terram et ministerium avunculi sui."

Sir Robert Atkins gives ncorrect and misleading translations of the charters. For original Latin see Appendix v. No. 3.

Roger's pious intention was stayed by his death, which happened before Michaelmas, 1131, judging from the Pipe Roll for that year. Some facts recorded in that roll tend to corroborate the tradition that he had previously become a monk in the Priory of Stanley St. Leonard's. For instance, "Sabricht the Canon," whose name in after years occurs as Prior of St. Leonard's, accounts for Roger's pecuniary transactions in a way that can hardly be explained on any other supposition. The principal representative of his estate is, however, his nephew William, who is credited with payment to the Treasury of a balance of £234 14s. 8d. on account of the ferm of Berkeley, an amount equivalent, at the Domesday rate, to sixteen months' rental, besides £61 15s. for the ferm of Roger's own lands. He is, moreover, said to render account of £190 (of which he only paid £40) "*that he may have in custody the land and office of his uncle.*" Despite this explicit statement, that this heavy fine was paid in order that he might be temporarily custos of the honour of Berkeley, and not by way of relief on succession thereto, this William de Berkeley is generally regarded as having inherited the possessions of Roger II, on the ground apparently, of his having been instrumental in carrying out his wishes as to Acholt by founding an Abbey at Kingswood. Yet a reference to its cartulary will show, beyond the possibility of a doubt, that the actual successor was no other than his son Roger III.

ROGER DE BERKELEY III

131-1169.

William de Berkeley's letter to Pope Innocent, Appendix v, No. 4. p. 98.

We find William de Berkeley administering the Manor of Berkeley at the death of the last lord, who when dying committed to him the fulfilment of his wishes as to Acholt. William appears now to act as though he were the owner of the manor, and in his own right bestows both Kingswood and Acholt on the newly introduced Cistercian order. Roger, the true heir, must have been absent at the time of the death of his father, or William would not have become acting provost. It is not likely that he was under age, for Roger II must have been over sixty when he died. It appears probable that he was absent from England, and it has been suggested with much plausibility that he had gone on the crusading pilgrimage to the Holy Land, for at a later date he bore on his seal a knight fighting with a lion, a device often assumed by Crusaders to typify their adventures in the East. This seal of Roger de Berkeley is of considerable interest, as being the earliest indication of armorial bearings of the house of Berkeley. ROGER DE BERKELEY III, 1131–1169.

SIGILLUM ROGERI DE BERCHELAIA

SEAL OF ROGER DE BERKELEY III

We must bear in mind that in those days coat armour had not become hereditary. We cannot hope to find the familiar *crosses pattee* and *chevron* of later times. This seal is attached to a deed of confirmation of certain lands, and is now preserved in the muniment room of Berkeley. It is of unusual size, of green wax, with the legend SIGILLUM ROGERI DE BERCHELAIA. The drawing is taken from two impressions of the same seal, from that at Berkeley Castle, which gives the lettering distinctly, although partially broken. The other, from a seal affixed to a charter now at Hereford Cathedral, showing the figures particularly well. The authorities at the British

Berkeley Castle charters, No. 21.

Herefordshire seal of Roger de Berkeley. British Museum personal seals.

ROGER DE BERKELEY III, 1131–1169.

Museum most courteously furnished a cast of this seal for the present work. By combining the two impressions in the drawing it is possible to reproduce both the lettering and figures in their original condition.

Dugdale's Mon. Ang. Vol. v. p. 427. Appendix v, No. 6. p. 99.

No doubt Roger de Berkeley returned to claim his inheritance before the death of Henry I, in 1135, for in his charter as to Acholt he refers to his *Lord* King Henry, an expression signifying in a feudal sense that he had performed homage to him for his lands. There is, however, much difficulty in determining the dates, owing apparently to Roger and William acting concurrently for at any rate a time, though clearly there was serious dissension between them. For although we find the above-mentioned charter of Roger which must have been executed prior to the death of King Henry on 1135, yet William founded the Abbey in 1139. It would be easy to suppose that the cartulary scribe made an error in transcribing the documents, but perhaps we are scarcely warranted in thus dealing with them. The cartularies of the monasteries, however, do not carry the weight of original charters, being merely copies made by the monkish scribe.

Idem. Kingswood Charters. Appendix v, No. 5, p. 99.

Two more charters, from the Kingswood list, throw light upon the somewhat obscure history of its founder. The first of these is fortunately dated, an unusual circumstance. Roger de Berkeley in 1148 for the souls of his father and of his ancestors confirms the whole of Kingswood to the abbots and monks : "*free from all claims which William de Berkeley used to owe me for the fee of the said abbot, the monks in their chapter acknowledging me as founder of the said place.*" This is again alluded to twenty years later in a charter from Roger de Berkeley IV, who repeats the statement as to the knight's service due by William to his uncle (Roger II) and adding that the said William was present in 1148 and consented to the transfer of the foundership.

Idem. Kingswood Charters. Appendix v, No. 7, p. 100.

Pipe Rolls 16, 17, 18, 19 Hen. II.

Entries in the Pipe Rolls of a later date seem to explain the matter to some extent. Each year from 1169 to 1172 occurs the statement "William de Berkelai owes 100 shillings for right of the knights fee which Roger de Berkelai holds."

Vide Rotullus Cancellarii 3 Joh.

Evidently William having alienated the fee without royal

permission had annually for the rest of his life to pay its value into the Exchequer.

ROGER DE BERKELEY III, 1131–1169.

Kingswood Charters.

Shortly after his foundation of Kingswood, William wrote a letter to the Pope, the object of which is evident when we have all the preceding information before us. We can see how he seeks to give a wrong impression concerning his cousin's tenure of the land, and attempts to bring any meddler, be he King or other, under the dreaded ban of Roman excommunication. How little he succeeded is shown from the Pipe Roll entries, and the fact of no recorded reply from Pope Innocent. The actual letter is quaint and curious. A translation is here appended:

LETTER OF WILLIAM DE BERKELEY TO POPE INNOCENT.

See Appendix v, No. 4, page 98.

"To the most Reverend, by Divine grace, the Lord Pope Innocent, William de Berkeley, founder of Kingswood, sendeth all reverence and obedience, and all cheerfulness due to God's high priest. The pious favour of a pastor and his affection and goodwill towards all under his care have embolden me to apply myself to the successor of St. Peter, the prince of the Apostles; your readiness to redress all complaints, and munificence in good works, assures me that I shall meet with no repulse when my requests are just; therefore that the present business may not be rendered obscure, I will upon my oath acquaint your majesty of all the particulars. Henry King of the Englishmen did for a certain price grant absolutely to my uncle Roger de Berchlai certain lands, without any other reservation only that my uncle should be obliged to settle the same on some religious persons, either monks or canons. My uncle was prevented by death, and left the estate to me, on condition to fulfil the former intentions. But lest there be any unjust demand made on those lands, he procured it to be confirmed by the charter of the said King, which is now laid before you. We, therefore, desirous to perform his will, have settled those lands descended to us from our uncle to found an abbey for monks of the Cistercian Order, which order seems to us to exceed all others in sanctity. Therefore that your authority may oblige the order to ratify and confirm the same, and that

Roger de Berkeley III, 1131–1169.

there may never be any dissolution or infringement hereof, we do humbly implore the favour of your goodwill that this foundation may be established and corroborated by your apostolical authority, that whosoever shall hereafter make any unjust exaction or injurious claim on these lands, or against this foundation, he must at the same time violate the Roman privilege, and so may desist being frightened by the sword of excommunication.

"Farewell."

Dugdale's Mon. Ang., Vol. v, 424.

The history of the foundation of Kingswood is given at length in an appendix to the Abbey register. It appears that according to the intention of Roger de Berkeley II, it was to be an abbey of Cistercian monks from Tintern, but the abbot and most of the monks were, in the latter part of the reign of King Stephen, or in the beginning of that of King Henry II, by agreement with Reginald of Saint Walery, removed to Haselden in the parish of Rodmarten, and from thence, for want of water, in a little time they went to Tettlebury, to which place Kingswood became a grange or cell, with only a monk or two to say mass. After some attempts made by the Abbot of Waverley to place a few of his monks at Kingswood, all were compromised by the concurrence of Roger de Berkeley and Bernard de St. Walery, and the abbey was once more removed to Tettlebury to a place called Mireford in Kingswood, not far from the old site, about the year 1170.

This brief explanation seems needed in order to make clear some of the charters given in appendix.

It was the duty of the præpositos or provost to make a bi-yearly account of all moneys received on behalf of the King to the Exchequer Court. The accounts were taken down by the scribe on leather skins and formed the well-known Pipe Rolls. They contain abundance of curious information, but are sometimes not easy to decipher, owing not only to the cramped court hand, but to the abundance of contractions and the unclassical Latin in vogue. A brief extract with translation is here given as a specimen:

Many of the rolls have been printed, some by the Record Commissioners, others by the Pipe Roll Society.

Extract from Pipe Roll 5 Hen. II., *i.e.*, 1159.

" Rogerꝰ de Berchet deƀ. xl. m̃i ꝑ hōīe plegiato ꝑ hōīe occiso.

Iđ vič redđ comp̃ de. L. m̃i de Dono Militṽ de Gloec̆scr̃. In tħ liƀauit. in iiii. tał. Et Quietꝰ est."

"Roger de Berkeley owes forty marks for suretyship for a man killed.*

"The same sheriff renders an account of fifty marks from the contribution of the soldiers of Gloucester. He descharged it into the treasury in four tallies, and is quit."

ROGER DE BERKELEY III, 1131–1169.

Translation of the same.

Pipe Roll 7 Hen. II.

It will be noticed that Roger de Berkeley is called Vice Comes. Originally the *Vice Comes* was the deputy of the *Comes* or Earl, to whom the counties were originally committed, but in process of time the business of the country was transferred wholly to the former. The Vice Comes or Sheriff was the first man in the county. He had large powers of jurisdiction, and preserved the rights of the Crown. He was also accounting officer to the Royal Exchequer for the revenue which passed through his hands; in early times the Sheriffs were men of high rank.

For fuller particulars, see "Introduction to the study of Pipe Rolls," 1884. Vol. iii, p. 97.

Such a one was Roger de Berkeley, but his high position, power and wealth did not free him from the grievous troubles incidental to a time of civil war. Robert Ricart states in his *Calendar* that Roger de Berkeley took part with Stephen. In this he is no doubt perfectly correct, yet Sir William Dugdale on the contrary says that "Roger adhering to Maud met a very hard fate." Dugdale gives a marginal reference at the passage to *Gesta Stephani*, but an examination of that curious volume shows that there is in reality no statement whatever as to the side to which Roger de Berkeley adhered, but there is much which leads us to infer that he cannot have been a partisan of Maud. Since the whole future of the family is so deeply involved in this question it will be well to consider the evidence and probability on either hand. Robert Ricart, writing about 1478, states clearly that Roger was a partisan of Stephen. Dugdale writing two hundred years later takes the opposite view, apparently through misunderstanding the writer of *Gesta Stephani*. Smyth, the historian of the Berkeleys, writing early in the seventeenth century, is of opinion that Roger was on the side of Stephen, but his testimony cannot be

Robert Ricart's Calendar, about 1478.

Dugdale's Baronage, Vol. i, p. 350.

Gesta Stephani Edit. Duchesne, 1846, page 119.

Appendix vii.

Smyth's Lives of the Berkeleys, Vol. i, p. 3.

* We have no information as to the occasion of Roger killing the man alluded to above, but since we find from the Pipe Roll only two years later that he is again fined for killing men, we must conclude that he was a somewhat turbulent character.

ROGER DE BERKELEY :II, :131–1169.

taken as independent since he quotes from Robert Ricart. The following extract is a translation from the passage in *Gesta Stephani* which bears upon the question:

iz. Robert Earl of Gloucester.

"Walter the brother of Milo, Earl of Hereford, in agreement with the Earl himself, treacherously seized upon Roger de Berkeley, a man not only uncondemned but also linked to them by a league of mutual peace, and united by a close blood relationship. They stripped him, exposed him to scorn, bound him with fetters and with a rope round his neck thrice drew him up at his own castle gates with threats that if he would not deliver the castle to the Earl he should suffer a miserable death, and when he was almost dead carried him to prison there to endure further tortures."

r Henry rkly, who ongly lds that ger was partisan of aud.

It has been pointed out how impossible it would have been for Roger de Berkeley to have lived in peace at Berkeley on the road between Bristol and Gloucester, the headquarters of Milo, Earl of Hereford, and Robert, Earl of Gloucester, two of Maud's chief supporters, unless he had himself joined their party. But the fact is that he did *not* live in peace, and the quotation from *Gesta Stephani* seems to emphasise the lengths to which the bitter feelings in the civil war could be carried, when "a blood relation and one linked by a league of mutual peace" could thus be treated. Philip, the Earl of Gloucester's youngest son, who married Roger de Berkeley's niece, had after his father's discomfiture at Farringdon in 1145 gone over to King Stephen with Ralph, Earl of Chester, and other leading men. This may have incensed his father and led to the indignities practised on his relative Roger de Berkeley.

it. et t. S. Pet. ouc., Vol. . 113.

Roger's captivity, however, could not have lasted long, for in 1146 we find him placing his priory of Leonard Stanley under the protection of St. Peter's Abbey, and two years later confirming the grant to Kingswood by the charter already alluded to.

As we might expect, Roger is now on good terms with King Stephen, and we may assign to this period the grant of free-warren from that monarch, which Smyth states was extant in the archives of Berkeley Castle when he wrote, and which he describes as constituting a confirmation to Roger and his

yth's es of the keleys, . i, p. 32.

heirs. A copy of this charter in a 16th century hand is now in the Library at Holkham.

ROGER DE BERKELEY III, 1131–1169.

We are now approaching an epoch in the history of the Berkeley family—their deprivation of the Castle and Barony of Berkeley, which never was regained. The cause leading to this has been often misstated. To understand it we must trace briefly the history of another family whose rise brought about the fall of the earlier line of Berkeley. Residing in the city of Bristol was a wealthy merchant, provost of the town, Robert Fitzhardinge by name. His father before him had occupied a large stone house in Baldwin Street, where Robert was born, towards the end of the reign of William the Conqueror. He was a man of position and power, but there is little reason to believe the tradition that he traced descent from the King of Denmark. It was a common weakness of family historians to find royal descents for their powerful patrons. In this case perhaps the evidence is as worthless as that which described Roger de Berkeley as being of the same blood as King Edward the Confessor. The earliest suggestion of the kind was made by John Trevisa, Vicar of Berkeley, 236 years after the supposed date of Harding's death.

Loss of Berkeley Castle.

Robert Ricart's Calendar, p. 20.

Smyth's Lives, Vol. i, p. 23.

Abbot Newland's Roll in Berkeley Castle.

Smyth's Lives, Vol. 20.

Recent genealogists state that Harding* was a son of Alnod, a horse thane or staller under King Edward the Confessor. Here, at least, the authority of the old chronicler, William of Malmesbury, brings some corroboration.

These researches le[ad] to curious results—t[he] probabilit[y] of the Fitzhardings being of Saxon orig[in] and the Be[r]keleys of Norman stock.

Robert Fitzhardinge now plays an important part in the fortunes of the Berkeley family. It will be well to let Robert Ricart tell the history in the quaint language of the Kalendar:

"King Harry Beauclerk, son of William Conqueror, hadde a doughter callid Maude, that was his heir, whiche was weddid to themperour of Alemaigne. And after the decece of the seide Emperoure King Harry sende for his doughter home into Englonde. And bicause he hadde none othir heir, he willid and desired al the barons of Englonde to de fealte vnto the seide Maude, and to admyt hir for his heir. Amongest whome the

Robert Ricart's Calendar, pp. 20, 21 and 22.

* A lengthy discussion has taken place in the pages of *Notes and Queries* on this point. Also see Eyton's *Analysis of Domesday*, and *The Dictionary of National Biography*, article 'Robert Fitzhardinge.' *Eadnoth Berkeley Family*, by W. Hunt.

ROGER DE BERKELEY III, 1131–1169.

furst that swere was Stephyn Erle of Boloigne, the Kynges nevewe. So it befille that after that, Geffrey Plantagenet, Erl of Angeon, weddid the seide Maude and begate on hur a son callid Harry, whiche afterwards was callid King Harry the second. And a non after the decece of King Harry the furst, the seide Erle Stephyn breke his othe, and toke on him the crowne of Englonde vnjustly agaynst his feithe and fealte that he had made to the seide Maude, vnto whome the Realme of right aught to be conserued. Whois son Harry grew duly unto maunes state, and came into Englonde to pursewe his modirs enherytaunce and his owne right. Vnto whome Robbert the son of Hardyng assisted bi his power, and departid largely with his golde and seluer to the susteigneng of his armes. And when Harry the secounde was Kyng he forgate not the grete kyndenesse of the seide Robbert, but for the same he gave him the Barony of Berkleys hernes whiche that Roger of Berkley lorde of Dursseley hilde to fee ferme of the Kyng. And the same the King toke fro him bicause he paide not his ferme, and also bicause he toke partie with King Stephin ayenst the Kyng. Nevir the lees the seide Kinge Harry, at the instaunce and prayer of dyuers of his lordes, he graunted vnto the seide Roger the barony of Dursseley as his enherytaunce. How be it the seide Roger vexed and troubled in many sondry wises the seide lorde Robbert, for the whiche the seide Robbert besought the Kynges gode grace to take fro him ayen the seide Barony of Berkley Hernes whiche he hadde geve him, seeng he kowde not kepe it in ease for troublyng of the seide Roger. But then the seide Kyng Harry made peace by twene Roger and Robbert, so that Roger gave his doughtir Alice to wife vnto Morice son of Robbert, and gave with hur the towne of Slymbrugge, and made double maryages bi twene their bothe children, and fynall peace bi twene them. Whiche mariages, covenaunts and peace bitwene the seide Robbert, son of Hardyng, and Roger of Berkley, lorde of Durrseley were made in the hows of the lorde Robert, son of Harding, at Bristowe, in presence of King Stephin and of the lorde Harry, Duke of Normandy, and of Gyayne and Erle of Angeo, in presence of many othirs, lordis and knyghtes spirytuall and temporall."

Hernes signifies what is obedient, a province or lordship.

Roger de Berkeley III, 1131–1169.

Two causes combined to bring about the great disaster of the loss of Berkeley. Owing to Roger's adherence to Stephen he had declined to pay his yearly dues to Maud, or to her son, Henry, Duke of Normandy; while, on the other hand, Robert Fitzhardinge, the wealthy merchant of Bristol, had largely assisted Henry with pecuniary aid. The two charters by which Roger was divested of his inheritance are still extant in the archives of Berkeley Castle. The first, although not dated, was probably granted in 1153, for Henry landed in England from Normandy on January 6th, 1153, and is known to have visited Bristol before June. It is probable that this charter was granted during that visit. By this document Henry granted to Robert Fitzhardinge the manor of Bilton, and a hundred librates of land in the Manor of Berkeley to hold by the serve of two mewed* hawks with an undertaking to build a castle at Berkeley according to the taste of the said Robert. Of this charter Smyth quaintly remarks :

Appendix iii, No. 1, p. 96.

"How great a reputation a charter of such an extrordinary quality brought to this Robert, and what an opticke glasse it remaynes to shewe the honor of his person and greatness of his purse let others observe."

Smyth's Lives of the Berkeleys, Vol. i, p. 23.

But the second deed, executed probably the same year, for Henry visited Bristol in November, 1153, is far more sweeping. He then grants to Fitzhardinge the whole of the Berkeley manor, and all Berkeley Hernes to hold in fee at the merely nominal cost of one knight's service.

The Duke, who at first had altogether dispossessed Roger de Berkeley, gave way to the wishes of his lords and permitted him to retain the Barony of Dursley, where he built a castle which for many a generation was the "caput Baroniæ" of the family. For the future he is known as Roger de Berkeley de Dursley. We cannot, however, conceive the sturdy Crusader being dispossessed so easily of his inheritance, and the few brief words of Ricart's quaint story give some indication of a long series of reprisals. We can imagine how "the seide Roger vexed and troubled in many sondry wises the seide lorde

* Hawks which had been mewed or confined for moulting operations, hence hawks which had finished their moulting and were in good condition.

ROGER DE BERKELEY III, 1131–1169.

Robbert, for the whiche the seide Robbert besought the Kynges gode grace to take fro him ayen the seide Barony of Berkley Hernes which he hadde geve hime, seeing he kowde not kepe it in ease for troublyng of the seide Roger."

Virtually, therefore, if not in act he dispossessed the Fitzhardings, and only by terms of agreement were they permitted to remain at Berkeley.

The history of this agreement is full of curious romance. In October, 1153, King Stephen and the Duke came to terms, and it was arranged Stephen should possess the crown during his lifetime, but Henry's right to dispose of the lordship of Berkeley appears to have been in some sort admitted, for King Stephen confirmed the grant by Henry, Duke of Normandy, of Almondsbury and Ashelworth, both in the honour of Berkeley, to St. Augustine's, Bristol.

Vide Report Royal Commission on Hist. MSS., Vol. iv, p. 363. Charter at Berkeley Castle.

But with respect to the lordship of the Royal Manor of Berkeley, both Henry and Stephen who came into the neighbourhood shortly after Christmas, took part. It was undoubtedly at this time that Fitzhardinge besought Henry to take back the barony of Berkeley, as the ousted Roger proved so turbulent a neighbour.

The Duke, who invited both parties to meet him at Bristol, hit upon the plan of the double marriage between the sons and daughters of the two antagonists. The marriage covenant, executed in the presence of King Stephen and Prince Henry, Duke of Normandy, is still in good preservation in Berkeley Castle. The full text in Latin is given in the appendix but a rendering into English made by the Abbot Newland about the year 1520 is here annexed; the quaint old wording of the Abbot seeming to suit the antiquity of the document better than a new translation into modern English:

Appendix iii, No. 2, p. 91. Smyth's History of the Hundred of Berkeley, p. 326.

THE MARRIAGE COVENANT

Bris. and Glouc. Arch. Soc., Vol. xiv, p. 122.

"This ben the covenantes that wer made atwixe Sir Robert fizherding Lord and Baron of Berkley and Sir Roger of Berkley lord and Baron of Dursley, in the house of Sir Robert fizherding at Bristowe. And in the presence of Kyng Stevyn and of the Harry then Duke of Normandy and Earle of Angewe and

ROGER DE BERKELEY III, 1131-1169.

The marriage covenant.

by his assent, and in the presence of many othirs bothe clerkes and Laymen. Morice the son and Eyre of Sir Robert fizherding shall take to his wife Alice the doughter of Roger of Berkley Baron or Dursley And the saide Roger shall give to the saide Morice in marriage with his saide doughter Slymbrigge whiche is of his heneritance that is to wete x[li] worthe of lande. And this Morice by consent of Sir Robert his fader hath geven un to the doughter of Roger that he shall take to wife for her dower xx[li] of lande of the fee of Berkeley bi the agreement of the foresaide lor Duke Harry And under this condicions and covenantes. That if Sir Morice the son and eyre of Sir Robert fizherding shall happe to decesse ere he shall wedde the doughter of the said Roger, that then his next brother and Eyre shall take the saide Alice to his wife according to all the foresaide convencions. And if so the second son of the saide Sir Robert fizherding shall fortune to decesse before he shall wedde the doughter of the saide Sir Roger that then who so evir of the sonnes of the sayd Sir Robert fizherding shall remayne to be his Eyre shall take to wife the doughter of the saide Roger. And of likewise if the elder doughter of the sayd Sr Roger shall fortune to decesse afore that she be weddid to Morice the son and Eyre of Sir Robert fizherding or to enyothir of his bretheren that shall remayne Eyre after him that then the elder doughter levyng and remaynyng of the saide Roger shallbe geve to wife un to the son of Sir Robert fizHerding which levith and shall remayne his eire. Furthermore the son and Eyre of Roger of Berkley Baron of Durseley shalle take to wife in like forme on of the doughters of Sir Robert fizherding. And the sayd Roger shall geve in mariage to the doughter of Sir Robert fizherding for her dowery the Manor of Siston of Bristow the which maner is of the heneritance of the saide Roger. And Sir Robert fizharding shall geve in mariage with his doughter to the son of the saide Roger x[li] and x[s] worthe of lande at Dursley And with this condicion, that if on of the doughters of Robert fizherding decesse afore she be weddid to the son and eyre of the saide Roger, that then the othir doughter of the saide Sir Robert fizHerding shallbe geven wife unto him. And if hit so shall fortune that bothe the doughters

ROGER DE BERKELEY III, 1131–1169.

The marriage covenant.

of Sir Robert fizherding decesse afore eny of them bee maried un to the Son and Eyre of the saide Roger, that then his Eyre shalle take to wife the doughter of Hew of Hasele Nece of the said Sir Robert fixHerding. Of like wise if the first goten Son and Eyre of Roger of Berkley Baron of Dursele decesse afore that he marye with eny of the doughteres of Sir Robert Fizherding or of the saide Hew of Hasele then that brothir that shall remayne to be the Eyre of the said Roger shalle take to wife on of the doughteres of the said Sir Robert fizHerding. And if thei decesse all or that eny of them shalbe maried, that then the Eyre of the saide Roger shall take to his wife the doughter of the said Hewe of Hasele nece of the saide Sir Robert fizHerding according unto all the foresaide covenantes. And all these foresaid covenantes have sworen feithfully to holde, kepe and performe without eny fraude or deceyt the foresaide Sir Robert fizherding and Roger of Berkley Baron of Durseley, and thei have putte Harry Duke of Normandy aforesaid for plegge and for juge atwixe them of all these foresaide Covenantes trewly to be performed atwixe them. To thes Covenantes wele and trewly to be observed have sworen also viij noble men of the party of Sir Robert fizHerding. And also viij noble man of the party of the saide Roger, whos names ben those of the party of the sayd Roger, William the son of Duke Harry of Normandie aforesaide, Roger of Shay, Rafe of Tweley, Walberyne, Engewald of Gosynton, Guydo of Stone, Gwafere of Planca, Hew of Planca his brothir. And of the partye of Sir Robert fizHerding these ben their names, Hew of Hasele, Nigelle fizArthure, Robert of St. Maryes, Elias the brother of Sir Robert fizHerding and Jordane his brothir, Jordane le Fayre, Richard fizRobert and David Duncepouche, And these forsayd men with all their strength shall holde and kepe the foresaide Sir Robert fizHerding and Roger in all these foresaid Covenantes trewly to be observed, that if so the foresaide Robert and Roger would go from the foresaide Covenants thei shall constrayn them with all their power and myght to hold and kepe them. And if they wulde at eny tyme dissent, these foresaide noble men of their service and love shalle reduce them therunto. And for thes Covenantes aforesaid wreten, the foresayd Roger of Berkley Baron of Durseley hathe relesid and quyete claymed al maner of chalange and right that he had in the Fee ferme of the Barony of Berkeley." ROGER DE BERKELEY III, 1131-1169.

It is strange that in the agreement the names of Roger's son and of FitzHardinge's daughter are not given, but we know from documents of which particulars will be given later that the son of Roger III was Roger IV, and that Elena was the name of his wife. The singular experiment of such a double union of the antagonistic families proved, contrary to what we might have expected, a complete success, for we find the succeeding generations living in friendship and harmony. For we find them witnessing each other's charters, and making donations to each other's Abbeys, Roger to St. Augustine's, Bristol, and the Fitzhardinges to Kingswood.

Pipe Roll, 22 Hen. II.

Vide Kingswood Cartulary, and Berkeley Charters, Nos. 26, 53, 54, 55, 56, 58, etc.

The Fitzhardinges held the Castle of Berkeley with the bulk of the Royal Manor, and eventually took the name of Berkeley, while the remainder, together with their other Gloucestershire Manors of Dodington, Cobberly, Wapley and Stanley, were erected by the King into a military fief, and held as the honour of Dursley by Roger de Berkeley and his heirs. Roger may have acquiesced in the arrangement with the less reluctance when he thought of his daughter Alice as mistress in the old home, but doubtless it was a severe blow to him to lose the Baronial Castle of Berkeley.

The Fitzhardinges take the name of Berkeley.

Testa de Neville, p. 77.

Alice de Berkeley survived her husband Maurice Fitzhardinge for many years, and we find a variety of grants executed by her. The original documents preserved at Berkeley Castle consist chiefly of grants to her sons and other persons of various lands and houses.

"Berkeley Charters," pp. 24-25.

To some of these charters her brothers Roger de Berkeley of Dursley, Philip and Oliver de Berkeley are witnesses. Her name is spelt in a variety of ways, Aaleis, Aeliz, Aelesia, etc. In one case she is described as "widow of Maurice de Berkeley." Her seal is appended to some of the deeds, usually an impression upon white wax.

Appendix iii, 5 to 10, p. 93. Charters by Aaleis de Berkeley.

Smyth observes: "Shee was a lady of great vertue, and went to her grave loaden with many good works; and among others,

Lives of the Berkeleys, Vol. i, p. 73.

ROGER DE BERKELEY III, 1131-1169.

Slimbridge had been a portion of her Dower.

to Elia the son of Toky her nurse, shee gave a messuage and half a yard land in Slimbridge in ffee simple, and to have her grist ground toll free at hir mill there next after her owne corne that then should bee upon the mill in grindinge."

She bestowed many gifts also upon the religious house, for which devotion the Abbot Newland highly commends her in the doggerel lines :

Abbot Newland's Roll.

"If weomen all were like to thee
Wee men for wives should happy be."

Roger de Berkeley lived for about sixteen years after his deprivation of Berkeley, for we find various entries of his name among the records of the Exchequer. Though deprived of Berkeley, he was still a man of great wealth and position, and Dugdale is mistaken in assuming that owing to the deprivation he ceased to hold Baronial rank for there is distinct proof that he was officially included among the King's Barons when summoned to the Great Council held by Henry II at Gloucester in 1157 to decide a dispute between the See of York and St. Peter's Abbey, Gloucester.

Testa de Neville Pipe Rolls, Liber Niger.

Dugdale's Baronage, Vol. i, p. 351.

Hist. et Cart. S. Pet. Glouc., Vol. ii, p. 106.

Roger still retained jurisdiction over a part of the hundred of Berkeley, for we find in the Pipe Rolls for 1159 and 1161 his accounts rendered.

Pipe Rolls, 507 Hen. II. Appendix.

In 1165 returns were made to the King as to the number of Knights' fees held throughout the county. These documents are preserved in the *Liber Niger* of the Exchequer, and we find that Roger was in possession of enough to constitute a fair Barony. The following is a translation of Roger's report :

Liber Niger of the Exchequer.

CERTIFICATE OF ROGER DE BERCHLEY

Bris. and Glouc. Arch. Soc., Vol. xiv, p. 299.

Let my Lord the King know, that I, Roger de Berchley, have two knight's and a half enfeoffed of the old feoffment, whereof,

1	Michael holds	1 hide
2	William son of Baldwin	2 hides
3	Helyas de Boivill	1½ hides
4	Hugh de Planta	½ hide

and from these you have an entire knight.

ROGER DE BERKELEY III, 1131–1169.

For making up the half—

5	Ralph de Yweley	½ hide
6	The wife of Ralph Cantileve	1 hide
7	Roger de Albamara	1 virgate
8	Simon de Coveley	1 virgate
9	The Prior of Stanley	1 virgate

and here you have half a knight.

For making up another knight—

10	Walter de Holecumbe holds	3½ hides
11	Gerard	3½ hides
12	Reginald de Albamara	3 hides

And so these three hold ten hides, whereof they are unwilling to do service to me except for 3 virgates—viz., each for 1 virgate and so you have two knights and a half enfeoffed.

Roger's Certificate of Knights' Fees from the Liber Niger, 1165.

No new one have I enfeoffed in my time.

If it be pleasing to your mind to hear about my demesne.

In my Manor of Cobberley I have two knights' fees.

At Stanley one knight's fee, with one hide at Codrington.

In Niveton I have one knight's fee.

In Dursele one hide

In Osleworda half a hide

In Duddinton three hides and a half.

In Slimbrigge three hides, which I with your assent gave to Maurice, son of Robert, whence I have no service.

Kingswood, the white monks, hold of the gift of William de Berckley, for which I do you an entire knight's service, although they wish to do none.

Many of the Barons in making their report address the King as their "dearest lord," or "most beloved lord," so that this brusque epistle is somewhat marked. Roger could not forget how the King had deprived him of his paternal inheritance.

With regard to the report itself we may notice that Hugh de Planca and Ralph de Uley had been among his sureties in the marriage covenant with Robert Fitzhardinge in 1153.

Liber Niger. See Bris. and Glouc. Arch. Soc., Vol. xiv, p. 317.

The mention of the gift of William de Berkeley to Kingswood will be noted, and Roger's mild protest against the en-

ROGER DE BERKELEY III, 1131–1169.

The piece of land mentioned in Domesday.

quiry into his demesne lands. Robert Fitzhardinge in his certificate at this time says : "Know ye that I owe you the service of 5 knights from Berkelai, but Roger de Berkeley holds land of the honour of Berkeley for which he does me no service, to wit Osmorde and all the fee of Bernard the Chaplain."

Roger de Berkeley admits holding two and a half fees of the old feoffment, and also of the new, five fees, together with nine hides, or close on two fees more, in demesne, making a total of nine fees. But he appears to have been dealt with leniently, for we find he had in 1168 to pay 100s, or seven and a half marks, for the aid then levied at the rate of a mark per fee. The Barony of Dursley continued to be rated at 7½ fees till the close of the century.

Registrum Malmesburieuse, Vol. i, p. 433, No. xcviii. Appendix vi.

We must here again make mention of two deeds in the Malmesbury Cartulary, since they may be assigned to his period.

They have already been quoted as affording valuable evidence in establishing the succession of the three Rogers, for we find a certain Roger de Berkeley confirms to the Church of St. Adhelm a hide of land in Cuderintone which *Roger his grandfather* and *Roger his father* had granted to the church.

Idem.

In the second charter, Roger, apparently the son of the preceding, gives and confirms to the same the hide in Cuderintone "which the monks had held of the gift of his ancestors from olden time." Though both the charters are undated, we may with strong probability assign the first to Roger III, and the second to his son Roger IV; for it is clear that the latest of the two must have been executed considerably prior to the close of Henry II's reign, because the Manor of Wapley, of which Codrington was the chief vill, had ere that time passed by marriage or escheat from the Berkeleys to Ralph Fitz-Stephen, who shortly after 1189 took it from Malmesbury, and bestowed it for the benefit of the late King's soul on the Abbey of Stanley in Wiltshire, who retained possession of it, until sold by the monks in the twenty-third year of Henry VI to John de Codrington.

i.e., forfeiture.

Atkyns's Glouc.

Dugdale's Monas., Vol. iv, p. 563.

Blunt's History of Dursley states 1170, but gives no authorities.

Roger de Berkeley's death took place about the year 1169. He was living in 1168, for his son concurred with him in that year in the transfer of Kingswood. But in 1170 we find his son Roger IV confirming grants. Thus Roger III must have died between the two dates, leaving several sons *beside his heir*.

ROGER DE BERKELEY III, 1131–1169.

ROGER DE BERKELEY IV

Roger de Berkeley, the fourth of the name, as we have already heard, played a somewhat important part in the disposal of the family estates; for by the deed of agreement entered into at Bristol in the year 1153 before King Stephen and Henry Duke of Normandy he covenanted to marry Elena, daughter of Robert Fitzhardinge. We may conclude that they were both of tender age at the time, as a special stipulation was entered into that should either of the contracting parties die before the formal espousals, his or her place is to be taken by the next brother or sister in seniority, and in case none of Elena's sisters were to be had, her place is to be filled by the daughter of Hugh de Hasele, niece of Robert Fitzhardinge. There was no need, however, to act upon this stipulation, for Elena became Roger's wife in due course.

Roger de Berkeley IV, de Dursley, 1170-1190.

The marriage covenant, p. 38, and Appendix iii, No. 2.

Shortly after Roger's succession to the lordship of Dursley we find from an entry in the Pipe Roll that he was heavily fined for a transgression of the forest code. The precise offence is not noted but we read : "Roger de Berckelai the father renders account of 40 marks of mercy, for the forest. Roger de Berckelai the son renders account of 100s. for the same." Probably they had been making too free with the King's deer, a most serious matter in those days. The slaughter of a man could be atoned for by a comparatively slight fine, whereas those accused of trespassing in the King's forest and killing his game were liable to heavy amercement.

Pipe Roll, 22 Hen. II.

This entry gives clear evidence of a 5th Roger de Berkeley.

We may here bear in mind that the cousins of Roger de Berkeley settled in Scotland had risen to positions of eminence and note. Walter de Berkeley was now Chamberlain to William the Lion, and had been taken prisoner with his Royal master at Alnwick in July 1174. During his detention in England very probably he had some communication with his Gloucestershire relatives. Some intercourse at any rate may be

Chronique de la guerre entre les Anglais et les Ecossais, par Jordan Fantome, Edit. Pellechal, Paris, 1839.

ROGER DE BERKELEY IV, DE DURSLEY, 1170–1190.

Liber S. Thomæ de Aberbrothæ. Vol. i, No. 72 (Bannatyne Club).

inferred since within two years of Walter's return to Scotland Roger is found in his company at the Scottish Court. Both appear at Perth in 1178 as witnesses to a charter of King William by which he granted the lands of Monethin to the Abbey which he had just founded at Arbroath in honour of St. Thomas a Beckett. The precedence allotted to Roger de Berkeley is such as to show that he could be no less a person than the Lord of Dursley. His name precedes that of his cousin Walter, who in virtue of his office of Chamberlain ranked next to the Earls and before all the other Barons. The name of Roger de Berkeley occurs in two other Scottish chartularies. In the *Munimenta de Melros* as a witness to a charter of Patrick de Riddell concerning a grant to that Abbey, and in the *Registrum Abbaciæ de Kelchou*, to the Charter of Alan, son of Walter, Steward of Scotland. The former may have been executed in 1178 during the visit already referred to; but the latter was certainly not at an earlier date than 1190, as it contains a clause fixing the term from which an annual rent of 20 shillings was to be paid in these words: "inceptus autem terminus ad festum Sci Martini proximum ꝑ ꝗ Phillip Rex francie et Ric Rex Anglie iuerunt ierosolinam. Q'fuit anno millesimo centesimo nonagesimo ab incarnatione Dni." It seems more probable that the witness in this case was not Roger IV but his son Roger V, who we know was absent from home about this period, for he was not a witness to his father's final charter to Kingswood.

Registrum Malmburieuse, Vol. i.

Register of Kingswood Abbey. Mon. Ang., Vol. i, p. 424.

Dugdale's Mon. Ang., Vol. vi, p. 339.

Roger de Berkeley IV soon, however, returned home from Scotland, for we find records in the Abbey Cartularies of his presence in Gloucestershire. He confirms his father's gifts to Malmesbury Abbey, and ratifies the agreement with Bernard de St. Walery as to land for rebuilding Kingswood. He, moreover, gives several small plots of ground at Doddingtone and elsewhere to the Black Canons of Bradenstoke Priory, Wilts, founded by Walter de Evreux in 1142, and further did his best to settle a dispute between the Abbeys of Gloucester, Reading and Bristol as to the Churches of Berkeley Hernesse.

At a later period of his life Roger renewed in the fullest terms and in the presence of several members of his family the grant to the monks of Kingswood, originally made by William de Berkeley half a century earlier. The witnesses include Robert de Berkeley his nephew, Philip and Oliver his brothers, and William his son. The nephew, who thus occupies the place of honour was, it need hardly be said, his sister Alice's eldest son by her husband Maurice Fitzhardinge, who had a few years prior to his death in June, 1190, assumed the surname of "de Berkeley." This assumption appears to have met with no severe protest from the ancient possessors of the name, and clearly in no way disturbed the peace of the family. This is evident not only from the charter alluded to above, but also from another whereby Robert de Berkeley confirmed a gift to the Abbey of Kingswood, the first witness to which is described as "Roger de Berkeley my uncle."

ROGER DE BERKELEY IV, DE DURSLEY, 1170–1190.

Fosbroke's Lives of the Berkeleys. He cites the Register of St. Augustine's, sub anno 1175.

Register of Kingswood Abbey. Appendix v.

The Fitzhardinges assume the name "de Berkeley." *Vide* Pipe Roll 33, Hen. II. *i.e.* (1187).

Elena the wife of Roger de Berkeley is stated by Smyth to have lived till 1209. But it is difficult to assent to this in view of an entry in one of the Kingswood Charters. Roger speaks of the souls of his wives, clearly showing that he had been twice married.

Vide Charter in 5th Report Royal Commission on Hist. MSS.

There is strong probability, almost amounting to certainty, as we shall presently see, that he died before 1191. Smyth must therefore be incorrect in his statement, for the other alternative is certainly inadmissible—viz., that he was a widower when he wedded Elena. The language of the marriage contract precludes such an idea.

Smyth's Lives of the Berkeleys, Vol. i, p. 56.

Kingswood Charter, No. xii.

Very little is known of the brothers of Roger de Berkeley. No doubt Philip de Berkeli, whose name appears in the charters * of Kingswood Abbey as father of a Roger and grandfather of a Nicholas, who under the designation of de

Sir Robert Atkyns, to avoid the difficulty, translates "uxorum mearum," my wife.

* These *original* charters were offered for sale a few years since by Quaritch of Piccadilly. The present writer made an attempt to purchase them in 1895, but the price demanded was excessive. The collection consisted of 48 original charters and other documents, commencing with a grant of Isobel de Longchamp in 1225 and ending with a rent roll of the abbey of 1444. They formed part of a larger collection brought from Condover, the seat of Mr. Cholmondeley, the lineal descendant of John Smyth, and doubtless had been in his possession. Quaritch's list gives a brief account of each charter with its import and the names of the witnesses. We find Oliver de Berkeley repeatedly as witness, also Philip de Berkeley and his son Roger of Newentun and *his* son Nicholas of Newentune. Vide appendix V.

These charters are printed in full in Bris. and Glouc. Arch. Soc., Vol. xxii, p. 179.

Roger de Berkeley IV, de Dursley, 1170–1190.

Newington, were benefactors to Kingswood during the first half of the thirteenth century.

5th Report of Royal Commission on Hist. MSS.

Rotuli Cancellarii. Rolls Series.

Eyton's Shropshire Antiquities, Vol. v, p. 346.

Oliver de Berkeley was the Oliver who likewise witnessed his nephew Robert de Berkeley's (Fitzhardinge) charter, and was Deputy Constable of Bristol under him in 1202. He appeared at Westminster Hall at Easter term in 1200 as "essoniator" for Richard de Clifford, in his suit with his eldest brother Walter de Clifford. The former was married to Letitia, a daughter of Roger III, and as these Cliffords were fair Rosamund's brothers, this connection perhaps accounts for favour shown by Henry II to the Dursley line early in his reign. One other son, William by name, is mentioned in the Kingswood Charter, and described by Roger IV as "my son."

Pipe Roll, 2 Ric. I. *i.e.*, 1191.

From the Pipe Roll of the second year of Richard I a payment of 100 marks as "Relief" is accounted for by a Roger de Berkeley. Doubtless this was the payment for succession by Roger V, the son of Roger IV, and therefore fixes the date of the latter's death as prior to 1191. We know from the entry on the Pipe Roll concerning the forest fines that the son of Roger IV was named Roger, and hence we are warranted in naming him as successor to the lordship of Dursley.

Pipe Roll, 22 Hen. II.

ROGER DE BERKELEY V

1191-1220.

Roger V, as shown by the Pipe Roll already mentioned, succeeded his father about the close of the year 1190 or the beginning of 1191. We must therefore assign as relating to him several references in the subsequent rolls. In 1195 he paid 40 marks as scutage for not attending the King in Normandy. In 1197 he gave 60 marks for licence to marry "Hawise Paynel the mother of Ralph de Somery."

Pipe Roll, 2 Ric. I.

Pipe Roll, 6 Ric. I.

Pipe Roll, 8 Ric. I.

In 1199 he paid 40 marks for eight knights' fees, which he held in demesne, that he might not be compelled to go beyond the sea with horse and arms.

Pipe Roll, 1 John.

Pipe Roll, 13 John.

In 1212 he paid £7 10s. on levying a scutage for Scotland, and 15 marks for that of Wales, and about the same time it was certified that there belonged six knights' fees and a half to his honour of Dursley. We thus see how his property had decreased, possibly owing to extravagance. He had not, indeed, inherited the whole of his father's lands. We find that Robert, a younger brother of Roger V, held a knight's fee of the honour of Dursley *in capite*, and that he likewise was so well off as to be able to settle the annual revenue of £4 derived therefrom upon his sister Isabella on her marrying Thomas de Rochford, confirming the gift on her remarriage with William Walerand about 1206. This fee, however, was ordered by the Sheriff to be restored to the Berkeleys of Dursley eighteen years later.

ROGER DE BERKELEY V, DE DURSLEY, 1191–1220

Close Rolls, 8 Hen. III. printed 1833–4.

He was no doubt the Robert de Berkeley who held lands in Frampton under Richard de Clifford. Cart. St. Pet. Glouc.

Roger V appears to have become involved in serious pecuniary difficulties for his manors of Dursley, Stanley and Dodington were heavily mortgaged to the Jews of Bristol and Gloucester. In 1208 he paid 60 marks to the King for an enquiry to ascertain their yearly value, which he agreed on the lands being restored to him to pay so long as his debt remained unliquidated. Evidently he was in no haste to pay his debt for seven years later a Royal Mandate is put forth as to a sum of 200 marks which Robert de Berkeley had paid to the King on account of his brother Roger's debts to the Jews. We have no clue as to the origin of these debts. Many of the Barons of that day had pledged their lands in order to raise funds for equipping themselves and their retainers for the Crusades, and we may not unnaturally suppose Roger may have been of the number as he was evidently absent from Gloucestershire in 1190, or his name would no doubt have been included with his father and brothers in the Kingswood Charters. Roger's name, moreover, does not figure in the Gloucestershire Scutage Roll of that date, which looks as if he had assumed the Cross, since it is hard otherwise to imagine how he could possibly be entitled to exemption. Nor does it appear again until 1195, after the King had been ransomed from captivity, when Roger gave 40 marks for not attending him into Normandy. Whether he served under Richard Cœur de Lion in Palestine or not, he appears to have been in Royal favour, for two years later he obtained for a very moderate consideration licence to marry Hawise* the widow of John de Someri, the

Roll of Oblations and fines, 9 John. Also see Madox, History of the Exchequer.

Close Roll, 16 John.

Kingswood Charters, Appendix v.

Fosbroke's Gloucestershire, Vol. i, p. 14.

Pipe Roll, 6 Ric. I.

* Smythe makes a very remarkable blunder in stating that this very Hawise married Roger son of Nicholas, son of Robert Fitzhardinge.

ROGER DE BERKELEY V, DE DURSLEY, 1191–1220.

representative in the female line of the great house of Paganel or Paynel. It may seem strange at first sight that Roger's pecuniary difficulties did not disappear on his making so splendid an alliance, but it may be that he was obliged to adopt a more expensive style of living. The greater part of John de Someri's property went to his son, but Hawise acquired a life interest in the Barony of Newport Pagnel and other lands, which were shared by her husband. She speaks of Roger in a charter still extant, with every token of respect, but he evidently retained no interest in her property after her death, which took place in 1209.*

Lipscombe's History of Bucks. Tykeford Priory in Dugdale's Monasticon.

After the death of Hawise Paynel Roger de Berkeley married a lady of the singular name of Letuaria, but Henry, who succeeded him, was his son by Hawise, or possibly by a former wife, as Hawise must have been forty by the time he married her.

Feet of Fines, Octave of S. Mark. 5 Hen. III.

We learn from a charter of Robert de Berkeley (Fitzhardinge), of which more hereafter, that Roger V had, like his father, two brothers named Philip and Oliver, for they sign as witnesses. The latter is also found attesting Kingswood Charters down to 1243, when the preceding bearer of the name would have been a hundred years old.

5th Report Royal Commission on Hist. MSS. *Ibidem.*

Roger's death occurred prior to May 4th, 1220, for at that date we find his son Henry in possession of the Dursley Barony.

Rot. Litt. Clausarum. 5 Hen. III.

HENRY DE BERKELEY DE DURSLEY

1220–1221.

We have now traced the Berkeley family through five generations from Roger de Berchelai of Domesday Book, with a minuteness of detail which may well occasion surprise when we remember that we are dealing with the history of a private family of eight hundred years ago. It will be sufficient in tracing the succeeding generations, until the final extinction of this early line in the fifteenth century, merely to give a brief sketch

* "Sciant tam presentes gnam futuri gnod ego Hawis Paynel, consilio et voluntate domini mei Rogeri de Berkele dedi Deo etc." In a previous charter she speaks of John de Someri as only "Vir Meus."

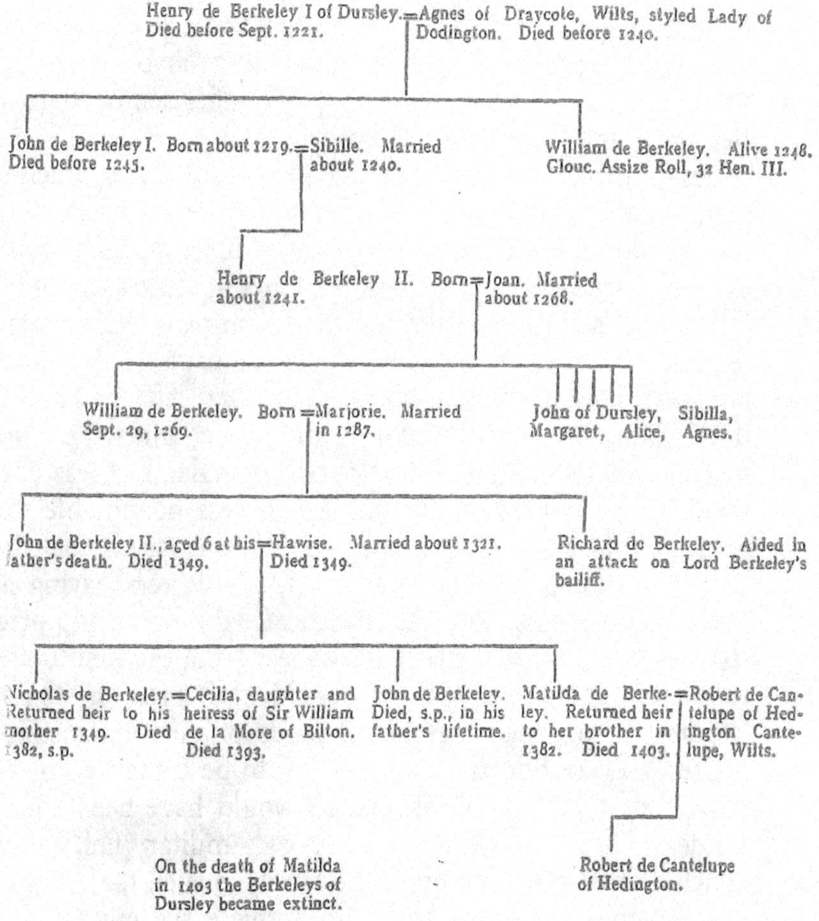
Continued from Pedigree facing page 18.
Henry de Berkeley I of Dursley. Died before Sept. 1221.
Agnes of Draycote, Wilts, styled Lady of Dodington. Died before 1240.
John de Berkeley I. Born about 1219. Died before 1245.
Sibille. Married about 1240.
William de Berkeley. Alive 1248. Glouc. Assize Roll, 32 Hen. III.
Henry de Berkeley II. Born about 1241.
Joan. Married about 1268.
William de Berkeley. Born Sept. 29, 1269.
Marjorie. Married in 1287.
John of Dursley, Sibilla, Margaret, Alice, Agnes.
John de Berkeley II., aged 6 at his father's death. Died 1349.
Hawise. Married about 1321. Died 1349.
Richard de Berkeley. Aided in an attack on Lord Berkeley's bailiff.
Nicholas de Berkeley. Returned heir to his mother 1349. Died 1382, s.p.
Cecilia, daughter and heiress of Sir William de la More of Bilton. Died 1393.
John de Berkeley. Died, s.p., in his father's lifetime.
Matilda de Berkeley. Returned heir to her brother in 1382. Died 1403.
Robert de Cantelupe of Hedington Cantelupe, Wilts.
On the death of Matilda in 1403 the Berkeleys of Dursley became extinct.
Robert de Cantelupe of Hedington.

PEDIGREE OF THE BERKELEYS OF DURSLEY

HENRY DE BERKELEY I, DE DURSLEY, 1220–1221.

of their history, although we have materials collected and at hand for an even more detailed account than has been given of the five successive Rogers. This method of treatment will undoubtedly be the more satisfactory, since it will avoid an elaboration which might prove tedious, and of no special value, when we remember that the Scottish and English Barclays of modern times do not trace their descent through the Berkeleys of Dursley or Cubberley, but that in all probability they are descended from John de Berkeley, a younger son of Roger de Berchelai, the founder of the family.

Before turning to the successive generations with which we have to deal it will be a matter of some interest to examine the social status of these De Berkeleys. We must remember that in theory all lands were held from the Crown, some as a military fief, others, such as Berkeley, on a fee farm rent. This mode of tenure, which was that by which the domains of the Crown had been held under the Saxon Kings, was left unaltered by the Conqueror, and although in after days, when the feudal system had become fully developed in England, it was characterised by writers on the subject as less honourable than tenure by the sword, there is no proof that it was originally regarded so, some of William's principal followers having accepted large grants under it. Practically the rights and privileges exercised by the Berkeleys appear from the first to have differed in no respect from those incidental to military tenure. We find them making grants of lands to different monastic houses. These donations had indeed to be confirmed by the King, but the Royal Confirmation would have been equally needed if the Manor had been held as a military fief, and we conclude that the position of the family is such that Dugdale was not mistaken when he included this early house of Berkeley in the English Baronage, and if he erred at all, did so in assuming that on forfeiting the Barony of Berkeley they ceased at once and altogether to hold baronial rank. Playfair, in his *British Family Antiquity*, says that they were in the position of Earls. There is proof that the third Roger was officially included among the King's Barons when summoned to the Great Council held by Henry II at Gloucester, three years

e.g., Roger de Ivry and Roger d'Oilly in Gloucestershire, *vide* Domesday.

Dugdale's Baronage.

Playfair's British Family Antiquity.

after his accession, to decide a dispute between the See of York and St. Peter's Abbey, Gloucester. It must also be an assured fact that the kinsmen of Milo, Earl of Hereford, heriditary Constable of England, and of Robert, Earl of Gloucester, the most powerful subject in the kingdom, were men who held a high and influential position in the county.

HENRY DE BERKELEY I, DE DURSLEY, 1220–1221.

The son of Robert, Earl of Gloucester married a niece of Roger de Berkeley.

It is a matter of interest to find among the Gloucester Corporation records a dedication of certain lands to charitable purposes by Henry de Berkeley of Dursley, date 1220. To this deed is appended a small seal impressed on dark green wax. It bears the figure of a mounted knight in full armour

Gloucester Corporation Records.

SEAL OF HENRY DE BERKELEY

brandishing his sword, his charger, which is galloping, being caparisoned as if for a tournament. His housings are embroidered with armorial bearings, *two lions passant.* The legend in the broad garter encircling the design is somewhat roughly cut, and the lettering interrupted by the hoofs of the horse. It reads S HENRICI DE BERKELEYE. There were two Lords of Dursley who bore the name of Henry. The first died in 1221. The second Henry, his grandson, came of age in 1262 and held the lordship till his death in 1287. It is clear that the grantor of the Charter was the earlier, since the name of the Sheriff is given, whose date is known.

Later on the Berkeleys of Dursley are stated by many authorities to have borne—*Azure three lions passant guardant or.*

Vide Burke, etc., etc.

Henry de Berkeley I, de Dursley, 1220–1221.

Possibly these three golden lions grew out of the lion rampant on the seal of Roger de Berkeley III, and the two lions of

Arms of the Berkeleys of Dursley

See p. 53. Henry de Berkeley. Many later writers have taken for granted that the arms of the Berkeleys of Dursley were—*Argent a fess* See p. 74. *between three martlets sable*, which were, as we shall see, undoubtedly the arms of Berkeleys of Cubberley.

We have already noted that on the death of Roger de Berkeley V about the year 1220, he was succeeded by Henry de Berkeley. A dispute which he had with his stepmother Letuaria, with regard to her claim for dower, was settled the following year by an agreement confirmed by the judges at Westminster on May 2nd. (Pedes Finium, 5 Hen. III.)

Henry de Berkeley's name occurs in a variety of legal and other documents, particularly with respect to his father's debts to Jewish moneylenders, in order to pay which Henry appears to have sold some of the Dursley property. (Rot. Litt. Clausarum, 16 John.) He enjoyed the possession of the Barony, however, for but a brief period. Barely more than a year after his father's death, at a Council held in the Tower of London on September 24th, 1221, the custody of the lands and heirs of Henry de Berkeley *deceased* was granted to Engelard de Cigony. (Rot. Litt. Clausarum, 5 Hen. III.) Since we have evidence, only a brief time before, of his taking part in public affairs, we may perhaps presume that he met with a violent death, possibly in the campaign against the Welsh under Llewellyn ap Jorwult, to which, the King having taken the field in person, he was sure, as holding by military tenure, to have been summoned.

The selection of such a guardian as Engelard was an evil omen for the widow, Agnes de Berkeley and her infant children. He had been one of the chief instruments of King John's tyranny, and was so much hated by the Barons that he was named in Magna Charta as one of the foreign mercenaries who were to be removed from office and expelled the kingdom. Instead of this he had been made Governor of Windsor Castle and entrusted with valuable appointments. In the matter of the management of Dursley he was aided by his son Oliver, to whom Henry de Berkeley's lands and heirs were committed in 1225.

HENRY DE BERKELEY I, DE DURSLEY, 1220-1221.

We do not know what the circumstances which led to her action may have been, but it is somewhat remarkable that in 1227, six years after her husband's death, Agnes de Berkeley went to the trouble and expense of obtaining the King's mandate enjoining on the Sheriff of Gloucestershire "that she was not to be vexed or molested so long as she did not marry without the leave of Engelard." Probably the eighteen long years of minority of the heir, during which time the lands of Dursley were in the charge of Engelard, was an anxious and bitter time for Agnes de Berkeley. So fully does Engelard, for the time at any rate, appear to have appropriated the estates that he is actually described by the collector of aids for Gloucestershire as "the Honour of Engelard de Dursley." However Henry de Berkeley's son on coming of age appears to have inherited the lands of Dursley without any diminution in extent.

Testa de Nevill.

His mother, Agnes de Berkeley, retired to the Dower House of Dodington, and in a later year was known as the "lady of Dodington."

Testa de Nevill.

JOHN DE BERKELEY DE DURSLEY

1221-1245.

John de Berkeley clearly attained his majority before the summer of 1241, for he was then called on to confirm several donations made by his ancestors to the Church. It appears evident that while careful to fulfil all these ecclesiastical duties, he was unable through ill-health to take part in active work.

Pedes Finium, Glouc. 25 Hen. III.

JOHN DE BERKELEY, DE DURSLEY, 1221-1245.

Rot. Litt. Clausarum. 26 Hen. III. *Ibid.* Rot. Litt. Clausarum. 29 Hen. III. Rot. Litt. Clausarum. 30 Hen. III. Rot. Lit. Pat. 30 Hen. III. Assize Roll. 32 Hen. III. Assize Roll. 32 Hen. III.

Early in the year 1243 exemption from service as a knight had been granted him by the King, and in the month of May he was excused from taking up arms. Two years later he died, and the Honour of Dursley for a second time was exposed to the disadvantages of a long minority. The first intimation of his death that we find is a writ dated May 13th, 1245, directing the Sheriff of Gloucestershire to assign reasonable dower to Sybil, who was wife of John de Berkeley, "taking security that" as soon as she shall have brought forth and recovered her strength "she will come unto the King and do fealty." In the succeeding year the Sheriff is ordered to deliver up her Manor House to her, as she has taken oath not to marry without the King's licence. This is followed by a grant to Richard de Clifford of the custody of John's lands and heirs, and the Sheriff of Gloucester is charged to have regard to her dowry. Notwithstanding the consideration shown by the Crown, she appears to have experienced great difficulty—judging from the proceedings before the Justices Itinerant at Gloucester in 1248—in obtaining recognition of her claims. Possibly she was a woman of excitable temperament, since we find her so frequently involved in law. She brought charges of robbery against various persons, but was not prepared to follow them up. Then again she brought actions against the Abbots of Gloucester and of Kingswood for her thirds from the lands of Newyngton Baggepath, and she calls her little son Henry, of only seven years old, as witness, and when the proceedings are adjourned, her little son is taken out of her charge and given to Chacepot, one of the officials, and all are charged to attend at Michaelmas Assize at Hereford. The result cannot be traced, as the Assize Rolls for Hereford for 32 Henry II are not extant.

HENRY DE BERKELEY II DE DURSLEY

1245-1286.

Inquisition post mortem Richard Earl of Gloucester.

Henry de Berkeley evidently came of age, and entered into possession of the Dursley inheritance before July, 1262, since his name is specified as holding two fees in Dodington under Richard, Earl of Gloucester, who died in France in that year.

We also find an agreement dated 1263 between Henry de Berkeley and Sampson, Abbot of Kingswood, which shows that he was in full possession of the honour.

HENRY DE BERKELEY II, DE DURSLEY, 1245–1286.

Henry de Berkeley is twice mentioned as a juror at Gloucester in the year 1269, and a little later we find him in litigation against the Abbot of Kingswood and Letuaria, widow of Thomas de Rochford. In succeeding years he is involved in other lawsuits, chiefly, it must be acknowledged, with the dignitaries of the Church which his ancestors had so liberally enriched.

Feet of Fines, Glouc. 47 Hen. III. Assize Roll, Glouc. 53 Hen. III.

In 1272 he is engaged in a dispute with the Abbot of St. Peter's, Gloucester, with regard to pasturage rights in Stanley, and four years later he has an action against the Abbot of Stanley.

Cal. Pat. Rolls. 1 Ed. I.

Since we derive the greater part of our information with regard to the Berkeleys of Dursley from legal documents and records of suits-at-law we may be inclined to unduly emphasise this litigious disposition; whereas had we more information of their private character and pursuits we could better judge what manner of men they were.

Henry de Berkeley now becomes involved in a dispute with his cousins of Berkeley Castle, which has a lasting effect upon that status of the family. The harmony which had existed for more than a hundred years is broken, at any rate, for a time. Maurice de Berkeley II of Berkeley Castle, even on Smyth's showing, was of an exacting disposition and impatient of the exercise of any authority, save his own, within the limits of the Hundred of Berkeley. Smyth in his quaint language says: "He was a Lord who would make way for his will, which was often the rule whereby he walked; breake hee might, bend hee would not." He had attempted to make another of his cousins, Nicholas, do him "suit and service" for the lands of Hill and Nymdesfeld, although held by Crown charter. For this and other high-handed proceedings the grand jury for the Hundred of Berkeley presented him before the Judges Itinerant at Gloucester in 1274; the jurors in other hundreds making similar complaints against his exactions. It appears that King Edward I so soon as he was firmly established on the throne,

Smyth's Lives of the Berkeleys, Vol. i, p. 151.

Ibid. Vol. i, p. 128.

HENRY DE BERKELEY II, DE DURSLEY, 1245-1286.

adopted measures to recover the rights and privileges usurped by the Barons under the weak administration of his father.

The Hundred Rolls.

The preliminary enquiries which were made at this time as a basis for the statute *a quo warranto* are embodied in the "Hundred Rolls." They must have revived many controversies. For instance, in the Hundred of Berkeley, the jury report that Maurice de Berkeley *and* Henry de Berkeley claim "Return of writs, Assize of Bread and of Ale, right to erect gallows, and to punish by the cucking stool."

Hundred Roll, 4 Ed. I.

Clearly each sought to exercise independent jurisdiction within his own lordship; and as the boundaries of their possessions had been in dispute ever since the partition in the days of Roger III, there was a fruitful source for the clash of authority. To diminish the risk of such conflicts in the future, about two years later, viz., in 1278, this Lord Maurice (to quote Smyth's words) "out of a faithful care to leave his estates and Barony to his son and his posterity free from all manner of question, gave 300 marks to have a deed and a fine from Henry de Berkeley, Lord of Dursley, of grant and release of all his right in the Manor of Berkeley or Berkeley Hernesse, and in the Barony of Berkeley, and in the Manor of Wotton, and the market and fair there; and in the Manor and Advowson of Slimbridge." The agreement of Maurice de Berkeley to give the 300 marks to Henry is alluded to in the Close Rolls, where also we find record of a singular transaction which does not appear very intelligible. Maurice is mentioned as covenanting to pay 50 marks, a part of the 300, to Sibilla de Berkeley, the daughter of Henry—viz., 30 marks to procure his discharge from the effect of a vow which her father had made on the occasion of his marriage, that one of his daughters should become a nun; and 20 marks toward her wedding portion. Also in the same Close Roll it is stated that Maurice has bound himself to pay Henry 78 marks at Whitsuntide, and 30 marks on All Saints' Day. This accounts for rather more than half, but there is no record as to when the rest was paid. Thus harmony was restored between the Castles of Dursley and Berkeley. But, unfortunately, three years later, in 1281, Maurice died, and the quarrel broke out more vehemently than ever with his

Vide Returns of Robert Fitzhardinge and Roger de Berkeley in the Liber Niger.

Smyth's Lives of the Berkeleys, Vol. i, p. 143.

Berkeley Charters, No. 456.

Close Rolls, 6 Ed. I.

Smyth's Lives of the Berkeleys, Vol. i, p. 191.

son Thomas, who claimed certain rights in the Manor of Dursley. Henry resisted the claim for four years, but when the question came at length to trial before the Justices Itinerant at Gloucester, the decision was given against him, the jury finding "that the ancestors of this Lord Thomas in the time of Henry II used, if any thieves were taken, either in the court or town of Dursley, to bring them to the castle of Berkeley, and to have justice executed on them there." Such an arrangement had probably for the sake of convenience been acquiesced in by the former Lords of Dursley, in the days of close friendship; but now that these rights of jurisdiction are formally taken away, a blow is struck at the dignity of the Dursley family, which little by little has been ousted from its rights by the Fitzhardinges. First the Castle and Barony of Berkeley is wrested away; now the authority of the Lords of Dursley is undermined; and half a century later we shall find the Lords of Berkeley attempting to bring about the complete subordination of the Manor of Dursley to the jurisdiction of the Court Leet of Berkeley.

HENRY DE BERKELEY II, DE DURSLEY, 1245–1286.

Assize Roll, quoted by Smyth, not now extant.

Henry de Berkeley, though he had been in possession of the estates for nearly twenty-five years, was little more than forty-five at the time of his death. The fortunes of the house had not prospered under his tenure. This appears to have been his misfortune rather than his fault. The actual alienation of property during his time was not important. He parted with lands in Cam, and also sold his rights as the Lord of the Manor of Oselworth, to the Abbot of Kingswood for 80 marks ; a very considerable sum in those days. The value of the estates, however, was greatly depreciated, and at the time of his death their owner had sunk almost to the rank of a county knight. The "Barony" of Dursley is still, indeed, officially mentioned; but Henry's interest in it had dwindled down to four somewhat heavily burdened manors. The inquisition at his death gives "the site of the mansion with garden of herbage as being of the value of 13s. 4d. per annum. Whether the building had been destroyed by accident or design we do not know. The moated castle mentioned by Leland as having fallen into decay and been removed before the date of his visit in 1540, must have

Feet of Fines, Glouc., 13 Ed. I.

Inq. post mortem, 15 Ed. I, No. 18.

Leland's Itinerary, Vol. viii.

HENRY DE BERKELEY II, DE DURSLEY, 1245-1286.

been of later erection. Henry de Berkeley before his death had settled the Manor of Dodington upon his eldest son William and his bride Marjorie. This became the cause of much trouble in future years; for the total value of the three remaining manors was returned as only £27 13s. 2d. per annum, one-third of which was due to Joan, Henry's widow, as "reasonable dower." To provide for this Stanley St. Leonard's was assigned to her, subject to the annual payment of £1 19s. 7¼d. by which sum its valuation was in excess of her claim. With this, however, she was not satisfied, apparently in consequence of not receiving the Manor of Dodington, which had already been settled on William and Marjorie. Joan accordingly brought an action in the Court of King's Bench—not merely against the heir, his brother John, and his three sisters, Margaret, Agnes and Alice, but against some twenty other individuals having an interest in the property. The full list of all these, with their holdings in the Manor, is given in the De Banco Roll, from which we learn of this colossal lawsuit. It is not easy to understand how she can have had any claim against these various tenants, or indeed have had any claim at all in respect of land settled by her husband upon his son. Possibly Henry de Berkeley may have been unable, legally, to make the settlement without her consent; for we find that she won her case; and we learn from the Fine Roll of five years later that the Sheriff of Gloucestershire, Geoffrey de Sandiacre, was at once directed to assign to her lands of the annual value of £10 15s. 6¾d. (in lieu of £9 4s. 5d. as before) and that he put her in possession of the Manor of Newington with rent charges on Dursley and on Stanley St. Leonard's sufficient to make up the amount. The De Banco Roll shows that Henry de Berkeley left to his younger son John the water mill at Dursley; and to each of his daughters a rent charge of 12s. per annum on that Manor.

(Roll of Fines, 15 Ed. I.) (De Banco Roll, 16 Ed. I, Rot. 42.) (Roll of Fines, 21 Ed. I.) (De Banco Roll, 16 Ed. I, Rot. 42.)

WILLIAM DE BERKELEY DE DURSLEY

1286-1300.

William de Berkeley is described in the inquisition taken on the death of his father as being at that date, 1286, eighteen

(Inquis. post mort., 15 Ed. I.)

years of age; and it states that he was born on Michaelmas Day 1269. Probably his marriage with Marjorie had been hurried on by his father when he felt his end approaching, in order to avoid the troubles incidental to wardship. We know that he marries, at this early age, with his father's approval, for we have seen how Henry made provision for his son's settlement. It appears, however, that he could not altogether prevent guardianship; for, although in the King's writ to the Escheator the custody of the heir is not provided for, yet in the proceedings of 1287 it is distinctly stated that his person is in charge of Richard de la Ryvere; also his lands, among which are mentioned those of Dodington, which his father had settled on him. It is not clear how long the wardship continued. He did not obtain full possession of his property till several months after he came of age, the King not having received his homage till February 8th, 1291, at Eynsham.

William, de Berkeley, de Dursley, 1286–1300.

Roll of Fines, 15 Ed. I.

De Banco Roll, 16 Ed. I, Hillary Roll 42.

Close Roll, 19 Ed. I., 9.

We find brief notices with respect to William de Berkeley in the writs of military service. The series is incomplete, and it is uncertain whether he accompanied King Edward on his first invasion of Scotland in 1296, and crossed swords with his Scottish kinsmen at Dunbar. But on the 30th March, 1298, he was ordered to be at York on May 25th, to serve against the Scots; and he obeyed. On January 24th, 1300, he was again summoned to perform knight's service, and to be at Berwick-on-Tweed by June 24th. However, he did not take part in this expedition, for he died, as we learn from the Fine Rolls, before April 30th in that same year, when rather more than thirty years of age. It is probable that Marjorie his wife did not long survive him; for, in a Subsidy Roll for the County of Gloucester dated the same year we find John de la Ryvere returned as holding Dodington as half a knight's fee "of the inheritance of John de Berkeley who is in the King's hands," and nothing is said as to her interest in it. He is set down likewise as holding half a knight's fee in Frampton Cotel of the inheritance of the same heir, and it has been suggested that Marjorie may have been of the Cotel family, since William de Berkeley inherited no part of that Manor from his father.

Writs of military service, Ed. I and II. Pub. by Record Commission

Fine Roll, 28 Ed. I.

In the same roll John Botetourte is said to hold Dursley by

WILLIAM DE BERKELEY, DE DURSLEY, 1286-1300.

King's commission, and we know from other sources that he had paid £60 for its custody "till the heir should be of legal age."

JOHN DE BERKELEY II DE DURSLEY

1300-1349.

John de Berkeley was left an orphan at the early age of six. We find little about him except casual mention of his name in connection with the patronage of certain churches, until he did homage for his father's lands on August 15th, 1314. The day is noteworthy as that on which Edward II opened a Parliament at York, where he had retired after being routed at Bannockburn on Midsummer Day. Possibly the young Lord of Dursley had been in the fight with his guardian, Sir John Botetourt, who took part in it. In 1317 John de Berkeley must have married, since he conveyed his Manor of Dodington to Anselm de Gurnay, who thereupon resettled it on John and Hawise his wife, and on their issue, whom failing on John's heirs. Possibly this Hawise may have been Hawise de Tyneworth, heiress of Bratton, near Okehampton, Devon, who married a John de Berkeley. Whether it was John de Berkeley of Dursley or John de Berkeley of the Fitzhardinge line cannot now be determined with any certainty.

Vide Bigland's Gloucestershire Collections.

Palgrave's parliamentary writs, Roll Marescal, 8 Ed. II.

Feet of Fines, Glouc., p. 152.

Feet of Fines, 7 Ed. II.

In the year 1323 John de Berkeley was summoned to be at Newcastle-on-Tyne on August 2nd to proceed against Robert Bruce, King of Scotland, but his former experiences in that country must have disinclined him for the duty, as he offered a substitute properly equipped and mounted. During the next three years we hear nothing of John de Berkeley; but at a later date we find that the ill-feeling between the Dursley and the Fitzhardinge Berkeleys had become still more accentuated.

Smyth in his history enters somewhat fully into these disputes, and especially charges John de Berkeley as acting in an unneighbourly manner in making petition to Edward III with regard to Lord Thomas de Berkeley's encroachments on his rights, at a time when that lord was on trial for his life for conniving at the murder of King Edward II at Berkeley Castle. This petition by Sir John Berkeley, as he is now styled, com-

Petitions in Parliament. 4 Ed. III.

plains "that this lord by duresse and by colour of a new purchase which of late he hath made, and by aid and countenance of Sir Roger Mortimer, late one of the King's Councillors, had obtained return of writs and all other royal franchises within this Hundred of Berkeley which before was gildable, and would incroach to him the attendance and seigneury of him the said John to his disinherison and to the damage of the King." No doubt Sir John de Berkeley must have bitterly felt the indignity of being called on to do suit of service in the Hundred Court for his Manors of Dursley and Newington, wherein, as he informs the King in a subsequent petition, "he and his ancestors, time out of mind, had used to have service of all manner of summonses, distresses and attachments, so that (save on default) neither the Sheriff of Gloucestershire nor his bayleys might enter in execution of anything to his office appertaining." We might have supposed that this would have been an opportune time for obtaining a fair hearing, since Sir John had been loyal throughout to the unfortunate sovereign whose enemies had, to say the least, been aided and abetted by the Lords of Berkeley. But the resentment of Edward III against those implicated in the murder of his father was neither deep nor lasting, for we find Thomas Fitzhardinge, the Baron, undergoing the merest semblance of a trial before a jury of Gloucestershire knights, instead of by his Peers, and restored to the full enjoyment of the Royal favour. Sir John de Berkeley obtained no redress against so powerful a lord as Baron Thomas Fitzhardinge had now become; and he had to submit to still further indignities from his overbearing neighbour. Six of Sir John's oxen were seized; whereupon he, with his brother Richard, Nicholas his son, then a boy of eleven, and a party of his retainers rescued his oxen by force, carrying off besides goods to the value of £40 and wounding a bailiff. On a subsequent occasion he went further still, preventing, by violence, the arrest and committal to Berkeley Castle of a man charged with felony. In both cases judges were appointed to try the actions brought against him, and damages awarded; but though worsted on all points, the ruling passion of his life seems to have been to recover and maintain his independence, and he

JOHN DE BERKELEY II, DE DURSLEY, 1300–1349.

Roger de Mortimer had already been condemned and executed.

Smyth's reference for this is: "Brevia Regis 10 Ed. III bundellum in turre Lond."

Murder of Edward II at Berkeley Castle with the connivance of the Fitzhardinge family.

Patent Roll, 6 Ed. III, Part 2.

Rott. in Banco Regis. 20 Ed. III. Smyth I, p. 332.

Smyth's Hundred of Berkeley, p. 175.

JOHN DE BERKELEY II, DE DURSLEY, 1300-1349.

must have been to some extent successful, as the Lords of Dursley retained their own Court Leet down to Smyth's day.

Owing no doubt to the antagonism of Baron Thomas Fitzhardinge de Berkeley he was excluded from every post of honour and trust in the county. This must have been the more annoying as Sir Thomas Berkeley, the head of the junior branch of Cubberley, held all in turn, from Sheriff, Custos of the Peace, Collector of Subsidies, etc. He was, however, returned as Member of Parliament in 1340.

Returns of Members from Earliest Date. Pub. 1878.

It does not appear that he was out of favour at Court, since in matters other than his dispute with the Fitzhardinge Berkeleys full justice was done him. In 1346 he applied for the King's permission to make grants for life of small allotments of land in his Manor of Durseley and elsewhere to no less than a dozen of his dependants. Probably these plots had previously been held by those to whom he granted them; but Sir John had to pay heavily for Royal licence to make them tenancies for life, free of all rent, or the customary services. It was a free gift to his dependants, and such an act of liberality comes as a surprise from a feudal landowner in the fourteenth century.

Inquisition post. mort. 19 Ed. III, 2nd, No. 24.

It is clear that Sir John de Berkeley, if hot tempered, was kind hearted. He was ready to speak out plainly and to take the law into his own hands regardless of consequences, if unable otherwise to get his own way. Perhaps he differed far less than we might suppose from the type of English country gentlemen who flourished four or five centuries after him.

He died in 1349 in the fifty-sixth year of his life, his wife Hawise, to whom he had been united for thirty-two years, followed him, in less than four months, to the grave. Some time before his death he had conveyed all his estates to his wife and heirs, so that he held nothing in his own right "on the day that he died." This is certified to have been February 3rd, and Hawise passed away on May 25th. Beside his two sons he left a daughter Matilda, who became the wife of Robert de Cantelupe.

Inq. post mort. 23 Ed. III, Part 1, No. 18.

SIR NICHOLAS DE BERKELEY DE DURSLEY

Sir Nicholas de Berkeley, de Dursley, 1349–1382.

Nicholas de Berkeley, who succeeded his mother, by virtue of the entail, in the family estates, is stated in the Inquisition on her death to be twenty-eight years of age. He had now considerable difficulty in establishing his claim to the Manor of Dodington, owing to counterclaims, into which it is scarcely necessary to enter here at length. The whole story may be gathered from the later Inquisitions. Nicholas was compelled to petition the King in Parliament for recognition of his rights and a commission was issued. The jury report cannot have given much satisfaction to Nicholas; for although he obtains the holding of the Manor, he is stated to hold it from Ralph, Earl of Stafford, doing homage to him and paying 100s. for the relief.

Inq. post mortem. 23 Ed. III.

Inq. post mortem. 25 Ed. III, etc., etc.

Inq. p.m. as above.

As the Commissioners on this assize were tenants of the Fitzhardinge Berkeleys, and it was held at Wotton-under-Edge, one of their principal seats, the result probably convinced Nicholas that the influence of his kinsmen was sure to turn the scale against those who were not of their party, and thus induced him to depart from the course his father had pursued, and in which he had shared as a boy. At all events there appears no more discord; he lives on the best terms with his neighbours of Berkeley Castle and a few years later accompanies them throughout the military campaigns in France. Smyth's words are: "And now (July, 1356) went also in company together, Maurice, eldest son of Thomas, Lord Berkeley, Sir Thomas Berkeley of Uley his cousin german, *Sir Nicholas Berkeley of Dursley*, Sir Peter de Veel of Tortworth, and divers others of these parts."

Smyth's Lives of the Berkeleys, Vol. i, p. 257.

This account is corroborated by the Gascon roll of that year, on which it stands recorded that Letters of Protection were granted by the King at Westminster on June 28th to "Nicholas de Berkeley de Dursley who is about to set out in the retinue of Edward, Prince of Wales, for the parts of Gascony."

Rot. Vasconiæ. 29 Ed. III. Membr. 8.

There can be no question, therefore, that Sir Nicholas de Berkeley formed one of the band of heroes who on Monday, September 19th, 1356, at Poitiers "gained the most extra-

SIR NICHOLAS DE BERKELEY, DE DURSLEY, 1349–1382.

Life of Edward the Black Prince, by G. R. P. James, who follows Froissart.

Froissart's Chronicles.

ordinary victory that the annals of the world can produce" over a force which at the lowest estimate outnumbered them by eight to one. Sir Nicholas fought no doubt side by side with Sir Maurice, who is described as having been "together with his kinsmen for two hours in the fore part of the battle," but following too hotly in pursuit of the retreating enemy was taken prisoner and not ransomed for some years afterwards. Froissart in his *Chronicle* gives the following description of the capture of Sir Maurice. The name, in the account, however, is given in error as that of his father, Lord Thomas, who certainly was not present at the battle. Froissart writes: "It happened that, in the midst of the general pursuit, a squire from Picardy, named John de Helennes, had quitted the King's division, and meeting his page with a fresh horse, had mounted him, and made off as fast as he could. At that time there was near to him the Lord of Berkeley, a young knight, who, for the first time, had that day displayed his banner: he immediately set out in pursuit of him. When the Lord of Berkeley had followed him for some time, John de Helennes turned about, put his sword under his arm in the manner of a lance, and thus advanced upon the Lord Berkeley, who taking his sword by the handle, flourished it, and lifted up his arm in order to strike the squire as he passed. John de Helennes, seeing the intended stroke, avoided it, but did not miss his own; for as they passed each other, by a blow on the arm he made Lord Berkeley's sword fall to the ground. When the knight found that he had lost his sword, and that the squire had his, he dismounted, and made for the place where his sword lay; but he could not get there before the squire gave him a violent thrust which passed through both his thighs, so that, not being able to help himself, he fell to the ground. John upon this dismounted, and, seizing the sword of the knight, advanced up to him and asked him if he were willing to surrender. The knight required his name: 'I am called John de Helennes,' said he, 'What is your name?' 'In truth, companion,' replied the knight, 'my name is Thomas, and I am Lord of Berkeley, a very handsome castle situated on the river Severn, on the borders of Wales.' 'Lord of Berkeley,' said the squire, 'you shall be my prisoner: I will place you in safety, and take care you are healed, for you appear to be badly wounded.' The knight answered, 'I surrender myself willingly, for you have loyally conquered me.' He gave him his word that he would be his prisoner, rescued or not. John then drew his sword out of the knight's thighs and the wounds remained open; but he bound them up tightly, and, placing him on his horse, led him a foot pace to Châtelheraut. He continued there, out of friendship to him, for fifteen days, and had medecines administered to him. When the knight was a little recovered, he had him placed in a litter, and conducted him safe to his house in Picardy; where he remained more than a year before he was quite cured, though he continued lame; and when he departed, he paid for his ransom six thousand nobles, so that this squire became a knight by the great profit he got from the Lord of Berkeley."

Sir Nicholas de Berkeley, de Dursley, 1349–1382.

Sir Nicholas de Berkeley de Dursley was more fortunate, however, for he appears to have got safely back to England with the Black Prince, who landed there in May, 1357; for we find him at Sandwich in Kent, in September, 1359, among those about to set out again for France with the King himself, being this time in the retinue of Sir Edward de Despencer, a Baron holding large estates in Gloucestershire.

Rot. Franciæ. 33 Ed. III, Par. 2, m. 14.

Sir Nicholas was home again by 1363, for in the month of October he was returned as one of the knights of the shire for his native county. The date of his marriage with Cecilia, daughter and heiress of Sir William de la More, is uncertain. With her he received half the Manor of Bitton, as well as lands in Wiltshire and Somersetshire. Later in life, in the year 1375, he filled the office of High Sheriff of Gloucestershire, and he appears to have been held a man of much account, for we find him appointed one of the trustees of the settlement made on the remarriage of Alicia, widow of Sir John Beauchamp of Hache, with Sir Matthew de Gournay in 1374.

Return of Members. Pub. 1878.

MS. list of Sheriffs.

In July, 1377, having been married many years and having no children, Sir Nicholas obtained leave to resettle this Manor on himself and his wife with remainder to his heirs. Five years later, in 1382, he died, having just completed his sixtieth year, and was succeeded, in virtue of the entail above referred to, by

Inquis. ad quod damnum. 1 Rich. II, No. 113.

Sir Nicholas de Berkeley, de Dursley, 1349-1382.

his sister Matilda, widow of Robert Cantelupe, Dodington and Stanley St. Leonard's remaining subject, as usual, to the claims of the widow Cecilia, who, as we have seen, was also an heiress in her own right.

Extinction of the Berkeleys of Dursley.

With the death of Sir Nicholas the whole male line of the Berkeleys of Dursley becomes extinct.

For upwards of three hundred years, from the time of the Conquest, had they held the property, at first as lords of the whole Honour of Berkeley; but, even after their deprivation of the lordship, they remained men of wealth and note in the county.

There still remained the kindred line of the Berkeleys of Cubberley, descended also from Roger de Berchelai of the Conqueror's time; and it is singular to find that this branch of the family died out within a few years of the elder. Sir Nicholas, the last of the Dursley line, died in 1382, and in 1405 occurred the death of Sir Thomas Berkeley of Cubberley. To this line we shall now turn, and trace in order each successive generation.

WILLIAM DE BERKELEY I DE CUBBERLEY

1139.

In attempting to trace the descent of the collateral line of the Berkeleys of Cubberley we are faced by some difficulties which future investigations may possibly remove; and we can only suggest as probable that which fuller information may either confirm or disprove. We are less willing to ignore this branch of the Berkeley family because it contains men of note, and also because it is well to show the extinction of all the original lines of Berkeleys descended from the Conqueror's provost.

Smyth's Lives of the Berkeleys, Vol. I.

Smyth in his quaint phraseology writes of the Cubberley line as "that antient younger branch of the Berkeleys of Dursley who long continued in great reputacyon and remarkableness in the county of Gloucester and Worcester."

This is an error of Smyth's. The Cubberley line is distinct from the Dursley.

Cubberley, which lies about three miles from Cheltenham on the top of the Cotswold Hills, is described in the Domesday Survey as one of the Manors held by the first Roger de Berchelai *in capite*, containing ten hides of land and then valued at £8 a year.

Domesday Book.

i.e, about 1,600 acres.

Continued from Pedigree
facing page 18.

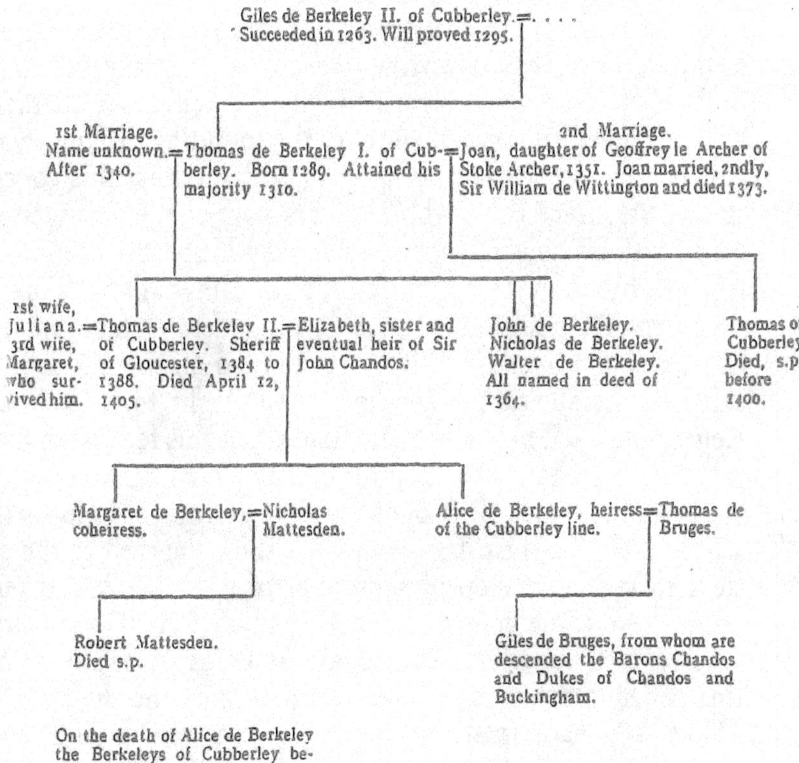
Giles de Berkeley II. of Cubberley.=. . . .
Succeeded in 1263. Will proved 1295.
1st Marriage.
Name unknown.=Thomas de Berkeley I. of Cubberley. Born 1289. Attained his majority 1310.
After 1340.
2nd Marriage.
=Joan, daughter of Geoffrey le Archer of Stoke Archer, 1351. Joan married, 2ndly, Sir William de Wittington and died 1373.
1st wife, Juliana.=Thomas de Berkeley II. of Cubberley. Sheriff of Gloucester, 1384 to 1388. Died April 12, 1405.
3rd wife, Margaret, who survived him.
=Elizabeth, sister and eventual heir of Sir John Chandos.
John de Berkeley.
Nicholas de Berkeley.
Walter de Berkeley.
All named in deed of 1364.
Thomas of Cubberley Died, s.p. before 1400.
Margaret de Berkeley, coheiress.=Nicholas Mattesden.
Alice de Berkeley, heiress of the Cubberley line.=Thomas de Bruges.
Robert Mattesden. Died s.p.
Giles de Bruges, from whom are descended the Barons Chandos and Dukes of Chandos and Buckingham.
On the death of Alice de Berkeley the Berkeleys of Cubberley became extinct.

PEDIGREE OF THE BERKELEYS OF CUBBERLEY

WILLIAM DE BERKELEY I, DE CUBBERLEY, 1139.

Dugdale's Monasticon, Vol. iv, p. 470.

See p. 43.

See pp. 30-1.

From the time of the Great Survey down to the year 1144 we find no records concerning Cubberley, but in that year Roger de Berkeley III confirms the gift of its church to the Priory of Stanley St. Leonard's, founded by his father.

Twenty-two years later, in 1166, this same Roger III in the certificate of his knight's fees addressed to King Henry II, states that he has two *in demesne* in his Manor of Cubberley. A few years later, however, we find a part of the Manor in the hands of William de Berkeley. Who this William actually was cannot at present be shown with absolute certainty; but, in all probability, he may be identified with the William de Berkeley with whom the disagreement over the founding of Kingswood Abbey had taken place. It appears probable that this concession of an interest in Cubberley was part of the arrangement made with his cousin Roger de Berkeley III on the relinquishment of his claim to be the founder of Kingswood. This relinquishment is related in the Abbey register. At all events, on the death of Roger III William is debited on the Gloucestershire Pipe Roll 100s. "for having the right to a fee which Roger holds." There can be no doubt that this fee was in Cubberley; for, in 1182, William de Berkeley compromised a lawsuit with the monks of Gloucester as to pasturage in Cubberley where they, too, held lands; and in 1188 he agreed to the settlement by the Bishop of Worcester of a further controversy with these same monks as to the advowson of the Parish Church of Cubberley. As William de Berkeley had been distinguished in the wars between King Stephen and the Empress Maud, and had, many years before, received from Robert, Earl of Gloucester, the Manor of Eldersfield in Worcestershire, and from Ranulf, Earl of Chester, the Manor of Chilcote in Derbyshire, his position was very superior to that which a mere cadet of Dursley could have occupied, and explains perhaps how his descendants rose to a position of greater power and influence than the representatives of the parent house.

Register of Kingswood Abbey. Dugdale's Monasticon, Vol. v.

Pipe Roll, Glouc. 16, 17, 18 and 19 Hen. II.

Chartulary of Monastery of St. Peter's, Glouc. Vol. i, pp. 234-5.

Calendar of Charters in the Bodleian Lib., Oxford. Pub. 1878.

Patent Roll, 3 Ed. IV.

Dugdale's Baronage, Vol. i.

The name of William de Berkeley's father we do not know. He is described as a nephew of Roger de Berkeley II. Sir Henry Barkly considered him to have been the son of Eustace; but this seems improbable, as we have seen that there are substantial grounds for believing Eustace to have been the eldest son of Roger de Berchelai, the founder, and that, dying without issue, he was succeeded by his brother Roger II. The year of William de Berkeley's death is not known; but there is no doubt that he was succeeded by his son William de Berkeley II of Cubberley.

WILLIAM DE BERKELEY I, DE CUBBERLEY, 1139.

WILLIAM DE BERKELEY II DE CUBBERLEY 1189.

The earliest evidence of William de Berkeley's possession of his father's inheritance is a charter by which Prince John (who received the Honour of Gloucester, through marriage, before King Henry's death in 1189) confirmed Eldersfield to William, son of William de Berkeley. Later when Prince John was deprived of that Honour by Richard I, William de Berkeley had to pay the King 30 marks for a fresh confirmation to Eldersfield. Notwithstanding this, as soon as John succeeded to the throne, William hastened to Normandy and procured from him a fresh confirmation for which he had to give 15 marks and a palfrey, which he had to break in himself. In 1203 he had to pay one mark for not having followed the army. William had still further difficulties in establishing his claim to Chilcote. The contest at law was long, and he must eventually have been worsted; for he is charged in 1205 with having taken possession forcibly; but in the end he triumphed and his posterity possessed the place.

See Nash's Worcestershire.

Worcestershire Pipe Roll, 7 Ric. I.

Rotulli Charterum, 28.

Worcestershire Pipe Roll, 5 John.

Rot. de oblatis et finibus, 7 John, Derbyshire.

With respect to the lands of Cubberley William de Berkeley appears to have obtained control of the whole Manor, for he rented the interest which the Berkeleys of Dursley still retained, and came to an arrangement with the monks of St. Peter's, Gloucester, as to the lands of Little Cubberley. Sir Robert Atkins indeed states that a portion of Cubberley Manor House was built upon the Abbey lands.

Pipe Roll, Glouc.

Hist. of Glouc. by Sir R. Atkins.

The wife of William de Berkeley was Dionisia, daughter of Robert de Turville, who brought as her dowry the Manor of Saltford. Her marriage must have taken place nearly twenty years before her husband's death, which occurred in 1208, for an arrangement had been entered into by him for the betrothal of

Pipe Roll, 10 John, Glouc.

WILLIAM DE BERKELEY II, DE CUBBERLEY, 1189.

their eldest son, John, to one of the daughters of Geoffrey de Abetot, a Worcestershire knight, and the youth attained his majority before 1212. In that year Dionisia was called on to pay 100 marks for having her dower in Cubberley; but as only two-thirds of the amount had been paid off by the end of five years, when she apparently died, the balance was debited to her heir.

Pipe Roll, 14 John. Pipe Roll, 19 John.

1208-1233.

ROBERT DE BERKELEY DE CUBBERLEY

Robert de Berkeley is always styled on the Pipe Rolls as son of William de Berkeley, to distinguish him, no doubt, from Robert, younger son of the fourth Roger de Berkeley, and also from Robert de Berkeley of Berkeley Castle. He is charged with the debt of 200 marks for succession to his father's lands; it was, indeed, a heavy demand, and though paid by instalments, and helped by loans from friends, he was barely free from the debt by the time of his death, in 1233, when little over forty years of age.

Pipe Roll, 14 John. Pipe Rolls, 9, 10, 11 Hen. III, etc.

As he left no children he was succeeded by his brother Giles.

1233-1242.

GILES DE BERKELEY I DE CUBBERLEY

Not many records of Giles de Berkeley are extant. He married before 1236 Johanna, daughter and heiress of John le Engleys, of Woollaston, Shropshire, which Manor he was holding in that year in right of his wife.

Eyton's Salop, Vol. vi, p. 373. Close Roll, 21 Hen. III.

In 1238 he purchased the Manor of Quedgeley, near Gloucester, of Humphrey de Bohun.

Feet of Fines, Glouc. 225-226. Hen. III.

In 1240 he was in possession of rights over the mill and other interests in the Manor of Doddenham, in Knightwicke Parish, for which the Prior of St. Mary's, Worcester, had to pay him ten shillings a year. Throughout the entries in the Parish Register he is described as "Dominus Egidius de Berkele, showing him to have been by then a knight.

Registrum Prioratus beatæ Mariæ Wigornensis (1285). Pub. by Camden Soc. 1865.

Giles was evidently a man of note in the county, for he was

appointed by the King one of the Commissioners to report as to the repairs needed by the Royal Castles in Gloucestershire. His death occurs two years later, for in 1242 the custody of the Manor of Eldersfield is given to William de Cantelupe, who was directed to assign reasonable dower to Johanna, *widow* of Giles de Berkeley. The inquisition as to the Manor of Saltford, is dated April 25th, 1243. He left two sons of tender age.

GILES DE BERKELEY I, DE CUBBERLEY, 1233–1242.

Rot. Litt. Claus., 27 Hen. III.

Idem.

NICHOLAS DE BERKELEY DE CUBBERLEY 1242–1263.

Nicholas de Berkeley, the elder of the two sons of Giles, inherited his father's possessions in all five counties of Gloucester, Oxford, Worcester, Shropshire, and Derby, on coming of age in 1257. Before long we find him engaged in a suit against the Prior of Worcester as to Doddenham; which was not finally confirmed to him until 1260. He had, moreover, to pay half a mark before his right to Chilcote was acknowledged. In 1262, though only twenty-five years of age, he was nominated Custos of the Honour of Gloucester, on the sudden death of Earl Richard de Clare; but did not live long to perform the duties of his high office. The following year he died. In the inquisition at his death, held on January 12th, 1263, the Jurors state that he died in possession of a knight's fee in Eldersfield, held from the late Earl of Gloucester, and that his nearest heir was his brother Giles, who was twenty-two years of age on the previous Midsummer day.

Rot. Litt. Patent, 42 Hen. III.

Idem, 45 Hen. III.

Idem, 42 Hen. III.

Atkins's Gloucestershire.

Inq. post mortem No. 8, 47 Hen. III.

GILES DE BERKELEY II DE CUBBERLEY 1263–1294.

Giles de Berkeley on succeeding his brother Nicholas paid 100s. for relief in Eldersfield on February 10th, and no doubt also obtained possession of the rest of his brother's lands. But in the month of August a difficulty arises, for seven months after the death of Nicholas, his widow, Alice, bore a daughter. Giles objected to surrendering the property to this posthumous child, but the widow, who had married Walter de Heliun, had her dower and many friends to help her on recourse to

Fine Roll, 47 Hen. III.

Pipe Roll, 5 Ed. I.

Assize Roll, Glouc., 53 Hen. III.

GILES DE BERKELEY II, DE CUBBERLEY, 1263-1294.

Idem and Inq. post mort., 1 Ed. I, No. 6.

law, and Giles was soon ejected from the Honour of Eldersfield. Whether he managed to retain the other manors we do not know, but evidently he secured Cubberley as shown by several of the rolls. He cannot, however, have had full possession of all the lands until the death of his niece Margaret in 1277, at the age of fourteen. The difficulties with regard to his property had not, however, hindered him from making his way in the world. He had won his spurs at the very commencement of his career, for his name and blazon appear on the earliest extant Roll of Arms, usually attributed to the reign of Henry III. The entry runs: "Giles de Berkel, *quarterly or and azure,*

Roll F, Harleian MSS., Brit. Mus.

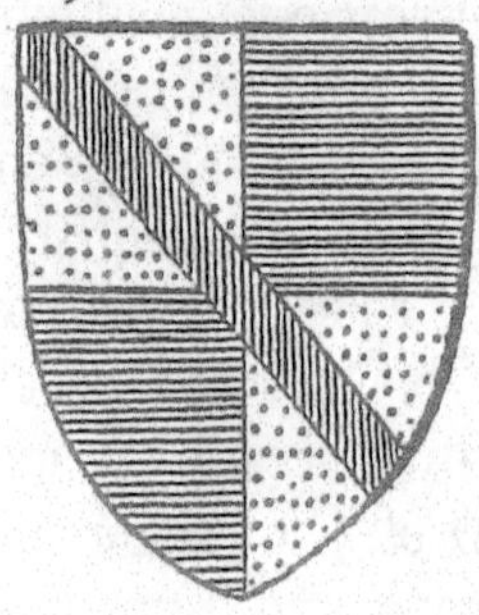

a baston gules." In these early days armorial bearings had not become hereditary, and we find his son, Sir Thomas, adopted: "*Argent, a fess sable between three martlets of the last,*" as shown in Cubberley Church, and this coat must have been adhered to by the second Sir Thomas, for it was quartered by

Cubberley Church.

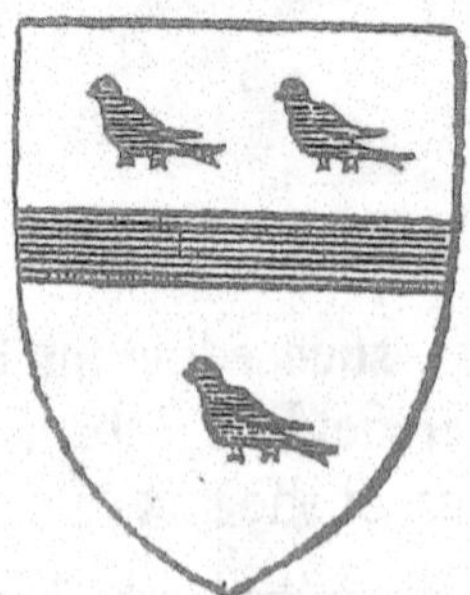

the Brydges family as descended from his daughter and heiress Alice de Berkeley. They likewise assumed in right of her mother's representation of the Chandos line—"*Or, a pile gules*"—its armorial bearings, and still borne as one of the quarterings by the present ducal family of Buckingham and Chandos.

GILES DE BERKELEY II, DE CUBBERLEY, 1263–1294.

Very probably Sir Giles de Berkeley was among the number who accompanied Prince Edward to the Holy Land in 1270, which would explain his subsequent rise to high royal favour. However this may be, he was present in Gloucestershire in 1273. This is clear from an incident recorded on the Gloucestershire Assize Rolls, which notes his complaint as to the abstraction of certain charters and £70 in money from a chest, which he had deposited in charge of one of the monks of St. Peter's, Gloucester, under St. Paul's Altar about the festival of Ascension, the guilty parties, who were servants in the Monastery, having absconded.

Assize Roll No. 5, 2 Ed. I.

Introd. to Hist. and Cart. St. Peter's, Glouc., III, 90.

In 1275 Sir Giles is appointed Sheriff of the County of Hereford, and constable of its castle, posts of dignity and importance, which are entrusted to him for the next five years. But the most striking proof of the King's favour and confidence is shown by Edward I making the Manor House of Cubberley one of his halting places after holding a Parliament at Gloucester in the autumn of 1278. The King wrote a letter with his own hand, dated Cubberley, October 17th, 1278, to King Alexander III of Scotland, saying he would receive his homage at Westminster on October 27th.

Roll original, 3 Ed. I, No. 36.

Letter from Ed. I to Alexander III of Scotland. See Robertson's Celtic Scotland.

Sir Giles sold the lands of Wollaston, which came to him on his mother's death, to Robert Burnell, Bishop of Bath and Wells, whose Manor of Acton Burnell was close to Wollaston. Sir Giles' aptitude for business must have been highly thought of, since he was frequently nominated to take special assizes and State enquiries, and he is associated with many eminent in these duties, which are spread over the period of ten years, and it is noteworthy that in one year, as we learnt from the Patent Roll, he was nominated to no less than 127 such special assizes. In the year 1283 Sir Giles was summoned, with five other judges, to sit with the Barons in Parliament at Shrewsbury to try the Welsh Prince David. In 1290 he was returned as one of the knights of the shire to Parliament. We find his name repeatedly in the Rolls as taking part in important investigations and inquisitions.

Close Roll, 1 Ed. I.

Patent Roll, 8 Ed. I.

Parliamentary Writs, Palgrave, i, 465.

Placita de quo warrando. 20 Ed. I, etc., etc., etc.

GILES DE BERKELEY II, DE CUBBERLEY, 1263–1294.
Register of See of Worcester. Fine Roll, 28 Ed. I. "Probatio æt." at the Record Office, shows him to have been born 1289. Memor. Roll, 28 and 29 Ed. I.

Toward the close of 1294 he made a will disposing of his goods and directing that his body should be buried before the image of St. Giles in the Church of Little Malvern, but his heart to be deposited in the chancel of his church of St. Giles at Cubberley. His death evidently occurred soon after, for on November 22nd his executors got leave to administer his estate. He had married in all probability only a few years previously, for his eldest son is proved to have been born in 1289. A long minority must have ensued, and as regards Cubberley, Humphrey de Waldeden and John de Crokesle had custody till September, 1299, when it was transferred to Thomas de Bottiler, "till the heir came of age."

1294–1365.

THOMAS DE BERKELEY I DE CUBBERLEY

Pipe Roll, Glouc., 30 Ed. I, and 7 Ed. II.

Thomas de Berkeley came of age in June 1310, but it was not until February 10th of the following year that orders were addressed to the *Escheator* "to deliver to Thomas, son and heir of Giles de Berkeley, as he had proved his age, the lands which the latter had held by knight's service of the heir of Robert Walrand."

Calendar of Close Rolls, 1311.

Nomina Villarum. Record Commission.

Chartulary of St. Peter's, Glouc., Vol. ii.

For the next few years we find no certain records concerning him, although the rolls abound with entries concerning a Thomas de Berkeley, the greater part of these, however, clearly refer to members of the Fitzhardinge family of the same name. In March, 1316, an Act was passed at the Parliament of Lincoln, with a view to raising a force to avenge the disastrous defeat of Bannockburn, requiring every *vill* to furnish a man at arms. In the return sent in for Gloucestershire we find, "Villa de Coberley, et Thomas de Berkeley est Dominas ejusdem villæ." This must have been his usual designation, for on January 26th, 1316, his attestation appears to a grant made by his neighbour John Giffard of Brimpsfield to the Abbey of Gloucester as "Thomas de Berkeley dominus de Cubberley."

Although made to contribute to the Scottish wars, it is evident that the Lord of Cubberley shared in the growing discontent of the nation at the weakness of the King, for a few years afterwards, when disputes in Gloucestershire came to a head, he joined the barons and knights who ravaged the manors of the Le Despencers. For this outrage the castles of Baron Maurice de Berkeley (Fitzhardinge), of the Giffards and others were seized by the King's orders in 1321, Thomas de Berkeley's participation being proved by a special writ dated at Gloucester on February 16th, 1322, sequestrating his lands and chattels and ordering his rents to be paid in to the Treasury. However, he made his submission with no great delay, for on the Close Roll of the same year writs are issued to the Sheriffs of Worcestershire and Gloucestershire directing his lands to be restored. He thus escaped the fate of his friend John Giffard, who was executed, and of others who, in the words of the writ of August 3rd, 1323, were obliged to pay heavy fines "for saving their lives and lands." By way, no doubt, of evincing his loyalty, Thomas de Berkeley volunteered after his pardon to furnish a man at arms with a horse to serve the King for forty days. On March 16th, 1322, he took part in the battle of Boroughbridge, his name occurring in the Boroughbridge roll of arms, a list of persons who took part in that engagement. In this roll his armorial bearings are set forth in the Norman French then in vogue, as *Gules, queyntee de la mermoude*, and he is styled Sir Thomas de Berkele. The blazon is very obscure. Mr. Walford Selby, formerly of the Public Record Office, is unable to explain it, and later examination by the present writer of various glossaries of Norman French has failed to throw any light upon the expressions *mermoude* or *queyntee*. It is possible the mermoude may be a term for mermaid, not infrequently a charge on coats of arms, and in this connection it may be noted that at a later period for a short time the Fitzhardinge Berkeleys bore mermaids as their supporters. *Queyntises* is employed in Chaucer's *Romance of the Rose* as apparently signifying quaint or strange.* It is note-

THOMAS DE BERKELEY I, DE CUBBERLEY, 1294–1365.

Fine Rolls, 15 and 16 Ed. II, "Et Thome fil Egidii de Berkeley de Cubburley."

Close Roll, 15 Ed. II, Memb. 18.

Close Roll, *Idem.*

Marshall's Roll, 16 Ed. II.

The Borobridge Roll of Arms, given in the "Genealogist," Vol. i, p. 51.

* We must leave to a future page the difficult question of the origin of the arms as borne by later generations in Scotland viz., *Azure, a chevron and three crosses pattee in chief argent*, and the similarity of this coat to the bearings of the Fitzhardinge Berkeleys—*Gules, a chevron between ten crosses pattee argent*. These arms are stated by Smyth of Nibley to have been first used in 1201, as shown by the effigies in Bristol Cathedral.

THOMAS DE BERKELEY I, DE CUBBERLEY, 1294–1365.

Miscellaneous Rolls, No. 175, 19 Ed. II, in Record Office.

worthy that he is here styled as a knight, but it was not till some years later that he obtained this distinction.

The next notice that we find of him is his inclusion in a writ issued under the Statute of Winchester, 19 Edward II, against those who "having 40 librates of land ought to be knights, but were not knights," and liable therefore "to be distrained on without delay." This omission he clearly soon rectified for early in the reign of Edward III he is styled in official documents "Chivaler and Miles."

Soon after the accession of Edward III appointments of various kinds were conferred on Sir Thomas. In 1330 he was made Sheriff of Gloucestershire. It is somewhat singular that the appointment should have been given to one who was of the same name as, although no near relation of, the Baron of Berkeley Castle, Thomas Lord Berkeley, who was so deeply involved in the murder of Edward II, and Sir Thomas Berkeley of Cubberley had a difficult task to perform with respect to the matter, for the King was determined that the actual perpetrators of the crime should be punished, and Sir Thomas, as Sheriff, was ordered to seize their goods and chattels wheresoever found; a duty which he appears to have performed for two years, since besides paying into the Treasury £20 5s. 8d., realised by sales, there is an entry in the Pipe Roll of 1332, as to two mares for breeding warhorses which had belonged to "John Maltravers an outlaw," delivered to Maurice de Berkeley by Thomas de Berkeley of Cubberley, late Sheriff. The latter words show that he had ceased to execute the office prior to Michaelmas that year, and this is corroborated by an entry on the Pipe Roll of the following year—viz., a letter from the King allowing him to employ a deputy, and excusing him from rendering his accounts in person. During the years 1331 and 1332 he sat as one of the Justices of Assize at Gloucester, and in the latter year was made "Commissioner of Array," in which capacity it became his duty to select and equip archers for service abroad. Numerous entries on the rolls are clear evidence that this appointment was no sinecure; he may well, therefore, have desired to escape the onerous duties of Sheriff. The first entry that we find is a command from the King to

Pipe Roll, 6 Ed. III, Glouc.

Pipe Roll, 7 Ed. III, Glouc.

send him 100 archers for his Irish service; nor were his duties confined to supplying men, for he and William Tracey were directed by another writ to provide ships for the King's passage and the conveyance of victuals to Ireland, when he went there at Michaelmas to restore order. Then, again, on April 25th, 1333, he was ordered to select 500 men whereof the greater part should be archers from the Forest of Dean, and to bring them to Newcastle to serve with the King against the Scots, and again, on March 27th, 1335, to send thither 100 foot soldiers and 40 Gloucestershire archers.

THOMAS DE BERKELEY I, DE CUBBERLEY, 1294–1365.

Patent Roll, 6 Ed. III.

Rot. Scotiæ, 7 Ed. III.

Rot. Scotiæ, 9 Ed. III.

On June 12th following the King addressed a special writ from York directing "his beloved and faithful Thomas de Berkeley of Cubberley" to array and lead to Newcastle-on-Tyne, 200 archers as quickly as he could, and it is clear that he complied with this order, at least as far as going to York, for on June 25th he passed a Fine before the judges in that city whereby he alienated certain messuages and lands in Wolverthorpe and Heyhamstead near Gloucester to Andrew le Walshe and Isabella his wife, possibly to obtain funds for his journey. In August of 1337 we find that he sat as Member of Parliament at Westminster. At the close of the session he once more became Sheriff, and it is worthy of note that this was the precise date at which Edward III is reported to have conceded the right of electing that officer to the Freeholders. He continued to hold the office in 1338 and 1339, but ceased to do so in 1340 when this privilege was withdrawn by Act of Parliament, nor was he reappointed by the Crown till after a lapse of fifteen years. We find many references to him in the rolls, showing how closely he was identified with all the prominent business of the county. In 1339 for a second time he sat as Justice of Assize at Bristol, and took part in commissions for the preservation of the peace in Gloucestershire, and for the protection of the sea coast of the county, which was issued by the King in 1344 and 1346. It was about this time that Sir Thomas Berkeley found leisure to complete arrangements for Cubberley Church, which he had been rebuilding. In 1344 an enquiry was directed as to "whether it would be to the damage of the King or anybody else" if Sir Thomas de Berkeley gave certain lands in Cub-

Idem.

Pedes Finium, 9 Ed. III. Glouc.

House of Commons Blue Book, 1890.

Assize Roll, 13 Ed. III, Glouc.

Bigland's Gloucestershire.

Fosbroke's Gloucestershire.

THOMAS DE BERKELEY I, DE CUBBERLEY, 1294-1365.

berley for the endowment of a chantry in that church. The report was favourable and the amounts of cash, land and wood are very exactly specified. Three chaplains are to be supported. In the *inq. ad quod damnum* Sir John Berkeley of Dursley, his overlord, is referred to by the jurors as a consenting party. The deeds recite that the grant is intended to secure the celebration of daily prayers for his own health so long as he lived and for that of his soul "when he shall have migrated from this sublunary sphere," and also for the souls of his ancestors, and of all the faithful dead in the church of St. Giles of Cubberley. It is somewhat singular that no mention is here made of his wife, nor of his children, although it is certain that he had married prior to that date.

Inq. ad quod damnum, 18 Ed. III, No. 26.

The war with France was now about to commence, and in the autumn of 1345 six knights from each county were told off to cross the Channel with the King; among those from Gloucestershire is included the name Thomas de Berkele Cuberle. There is but little doubt that he took part in the famous battle of Crecy, which was fought in August the following year. It is uncertain whether he remained in France during the long siege of Calais, but we know that some of the Gloucestershire knights visited England and returned again to France. This may possibly account for the payments made by him as Sheriff during this period, or on the other hand the payments may have been made in his name by a deputy whom he must certainly have left in charge during his absence. In the account of the collectors of the Aid in November, 1346, "for making the Black Prince a knight," we find under Gloucestershire, "Thomas son and heir of Giles de Berkeley of Cubberley" rated at forty shillings for his fee there, and the same amount for his fee in Eldersfield in Worcestershire, and also twenty shillings in Derbyshire for the "half fee which had belonged to Giles de Berkeley his grandfather."

French Roll, 19 Ed. III.

Pipe Rolls, various.

The Book of Aids, Record Office.

There is no mention now of Sir Thomas in the public records for two or three years, from which we may infer that he was absent in France. But at the close of this period he took a step which looks as though he determined to give up military service in a foreign land and settle down, for at an age of

Inquisitio post mortem, 24 Ed. III.

nearly three score he married for a second time a young lady of the age of only twenty, Johanna (Joan), daughter of Geoffrey le Archer, of Stoke Archer in Cleeve Hundred. Geoffrey had no son to succeed him, and perhaps planned this alliance with an old comrade to secure a protector for his heiress, for he himself died at Michaelmas of the year of the marriage. Sir Thomas Berkeley did homage for his wife's lands in the year 1350. In the year following, probably on the birth of his son, he conveyed to trustees a part of the lands of Archerstole, the King's permission having been obtained for the sub-enfeoffment, for the eventual benefit of the joint heir of himself and Johanna, whom failing to her right heirs. It is a little singular that seven years later he repeats this transaction, apparently settling again the same lands on the same trusts. After his marriage Sir Thomas resumes the leading position he had previously held, both in the civil and military affairs in the county. On May 23rd, 1352, he was ordered to array 200 archers in Gloucestershire for France, and though during the same year a letter of exoneration from such functions "for certain causes" was issued to him, he was only temporarily excused. Possibly the reason may have been that other duties were imposed upon him as one of the Justiciaries appointed under the Statute of Labourers passed in 1351 in consequence of effects of the Black Death, to enquire as to the rate of wages to be assigned, he himself drawing, by the by, six shillings and eight pence a day for pains.

THOMAS DE BERKELEY I, DE CUBBERLEY, 1294–1365.

Rot. Fin., 24 Ed. III.

Rot. Fin., 25 Ed. III.

Inq. ad quod damnum, 25 Ed. III.

Ped. Fin., 32 Ed. III, Glouc.

Rymer's Fœdera, Vol. iii, p. 243.

Rot. Claus., 26 Ed. III.

In 1355–56 we again find him appointed by the King to be Sheriff of Gloucestershire and also Escheator for that county and the Marches of Wales. In 1358 he is again one of the knights of the shire in Parliament, and in 1359 as Commissioner to preserve peace during the absence of the King he was ordered to array the men of Gloucestershire and later on exhorted in still more emphatic language to "save the kingdom." Sir Thomas now appears to have retired into private life, as no further entries can be found respecting him on the public records. He lived, however, at least five years longer, as it was not till Michaelmas, 1364, when he had attained the good age of seventy-five that he conveyed his paternal estates to trus-

Return of Members of Parliament, 1876.

Rymer's Fœdera, Vol. iii.

THOMAS DE BERKELEY I, DE CUBBERLEY, 1294-1365.

Fines, divers counties, Ed. III. to Hen. VI, Record Office.

tees for resettlement on his sons by his first marriage. Two fines were at that time passed before the judges at Westminster; the first between Thomas de Berkeley de Cubberley, Chivaler, querent, and Edmund de Brugge and others, deforciants, after reserving a life interest to the former in his Manors of Cubberley and Eldersfeld, settling these on his death upon his eldest son Thomas, and Juliana his wife, and the heirs of their bodies, or if they should die without heirs, then, after the decease of both of them on his younger sons, John, Nicholas and Walter and their heirs successively. The second fine between Thomas, son of Thomas de Berkeley, Chivaler, and Juliana his wife, querents, and the same trustees, deforciants of the Manor of Childcote, to be held by Thomas (II) and Juliana, and the heirs of their bodies, whom failing the manor to revert to his father, Sir Thomas I for life, and after him to each of Thomas's three younger brothers in succession or to their respective heirs; the said Thomas, son of Thomas and his wife Juliana, giving to Edmund de Brugge and his co-trustees for this concession 200 marks of silver. This sum was probably for the benefit of Sir Thomas's younger children of the first marriage, his second wife and her boy having been provided for by the entail of Stoke Archer. She remarried shortly after Sir Thomas's death, which happened about 1365, William de Whytington, whom some of the Gloucestershire historians have confused with the famous Lord Mayor, loading her, in consequence, with undeserved obloquy as the cruel stepmother through whose ill-treatment Dick ran away to London. The dates, however, must dispel this notion. Sir William de Whittington of Pauntley, Dick's father, after being outlawed for debt, died as shown by the writ of "*diem clausam*" in October 1359, six years before Joan le Archer became a widow; while, on the other hand, the William de Whytington whom the latter married survived her and actually held Stoke Archer for a short time after her death in 1369. Possibly he was Sir Richard Whittington's elder brother. The inquisition on the death of Joan was not taken until her son

Lyson's Gloucestershire and others.

Dick Whittington.

Inq. post mort., 33 Ed. III.

THOMAS OF CUBBERLEY

THOMAS OF CUBBERLEY, Born 1351.

came of age in 1372, his "proof of age" showing that he was born at Cubberley on the day of St. Dionysius—October 9th—in 1351. With respect to this Thomas of Cubberley, who is nowhere designated of Berkeley, there appears some confusion in the minds of the Gloucestershire historians. Some consider that he succeeded on the death of his half-brother, the second Sir Thomas de Berkeley, to Cubberley, and the other manors, because the third and last Sir Thomas de Berkeley of Cubberley died there in 1405, having in possession Stoke Archer, leaving his two daughters as co-heiresses. But this view is scarcely tenable in view of the settlement of 1364 already referred to, which shows that if his half-brother Thomas had died without issue, there were three other half-brothers to succeed before Thomas de Cubberley. As a matter of fact, Nicholas, the second of these, certainly did survive the eldest and was also executor of his will. Still there appears to be no record of the death of Thomas de Cubberley or Thomas de Berkeley de Cubberley between 1364 and 1405, which is strange since Stoke Archer was held from the Crown. Taking, however, all the facts into consideration it appears probable that Thomas of Cubberley died without issue during the fourteenth century, bequeathing Stoke Archer to his half-brother, the second and last Sir Thomas de Berkeley of Cubberley.

Lyson's Gloucestershire.

It is certain that Thomas of Cubberley died before 1402, for in that year "Sir Thomas Berkeley de Coburleye" had evidently been in possession for some years. The existing monuments in Cubberley Church afford a certain amount of corroboration of this surmise that Thomas of Cubberley died soon after coming of age, for there is a monumental effigy of a youth in civilian costume, which very probably was erected to him. Mr. J. H. Middleton describes it as of late fourteenth century style and Mr. A. Hartshorne, F.S.A., in a paper on the monuments in Cubberley Church, considers it to be in the style of Edward III's reign, and both agree in referring it to one of the Berkeley lords. It cannot represent the first Sir Thomas Berkeley, who was seventy-five when he died in 1365,

Inq. post mort., 3 Hen. IV.

Bris. and Glouc. Arch. Soc., Vol. iii.

Archæological Journal, June, 1889.

THOMAS OF CUBBERLEY, Born 1351.

Monuments in Cubberley Church.

Sir Giles de Berkeley.

nor the second Sir Thomas, who was over sixty at the time of his death in 1405. With regard to the other monuments in Cubberley Church, there is not very much room for doubt. The curious "heart monument" in the chancel has already been mentioned as, no doubt, in memory of Sir Giles de Berkeley, who bequeathed his heart to be placed there in 1294. The recumbent life-sized figures of a knight and lady originally within the altar rails, must be those of Sir Thomas Berkeley, who may be called the second founder of the church, and of his *first* wife, who died while the work of enlarging the building was in progress. The small effigy of a girl in hood and gown is most likely that of a daughter of the first Sir Thomas. The absence of any monument to the second Sir Thomas, who left directions that he was to be buried in Cubberley Church, may be accounted for by the destructive treatment to which the interior of the building has been subjected. Bigland, writing in 1790, speaks of many mutilated fragments, and slabs robbed of their brasses.

Bigland's Gloucestershire.

SIR THOMAS DE BERKELEY II DE CUBBERLEY

1365-1405

The precise date of the birth of the second Sir Thomas de Berkeley cannot be ascertained, but there can be very little doubt that it was about the year 1340. He inherited the Manor of Cubberley in 1365, but he appears to have held no official position in Gloucestershire for at least fifteen years, possibly owing to having continued to reside at Chilcote in Derbyshire. From 1380, however, he was constantly employed in his native county on very much the same lines as his father, but his life proved to be much less eventful. He was named as one of the knights of the shire of Gloucester, and was also appointed collector of the subsidy there. He also served as Sheriff in the eighth, ninth and eleventh and twelfth years of Richard II. In 1390 he was again in Parliament, and in the following year was put on a Royal Commission "to enquire as to the Insurrection," which appears to have been his last public service. The only insurrection which the *Chronicles* mention in that year was in Kent. Perhaps the Gloucestershire

Return of Members of Parliament, 1876.

Rot. Fin., 4 Ric. II.

Rot. Litt. Clausa, 15 Ric. II.

EFFIGIES OF SIR HENRY BERKELEY AND HIS WIFE IN COBERLEY CHURCH

To face page 84

knight was sent there owing to his impartiality. In 1402, in an inquisition preserved at the Record Office, as to those liable to pay the aid for marrying Blanche, the King's eldest daughter, we find : "Item dicunt quod Thomas Berkeley de Coburleye tenet de Do Rege, sine medio, quandam terr et tenem apud Stoke in eodem hundredo," which carries on his possession of that manor for some years. He was married three times; Juliana whose surname is not recorded, died without issue before 1375, for his eldest daughter by his second wife, Elizabeth Chandos, was born in 1376. After the death of Elizabeth he was married to a third, named Margareta, whom he appointed executor of his will. She survived him little over a year, dying in April, 1406. The inquisitions taken on her death relate solely to her right of dower in Stoke Archer, Cubberley, Eldresfeld and Chilcote, and show clearly that her "thirds" reverted to Margaret and Alice, the daughters and co-heiresses of the late Thomas de Berkeley of Cubberley, by a former wife, and that she herself had no children, since her nearest heir is declared to be Pabenham, aged thirty. These details are given because the Peerages assert that this Margareta was the sister of Sir John Chandos, and mother of Sir Thomas Berkeley's daughters, which is not only disproved as above, but also by the inquisition on Sir John's death in which his sister Elizabeth is twice mentioned.

THOMAS DE BERKELEY II, DE CUBBERLEY, 1365-1405.

Inquisition at Record Office, 3 Hen. IV.

Inq. post mort., 7 Hen. IV.

Idem.

Inq. post mort., 23 Hen. VI.

Sir Thomas Berkeley on March 29th, 1405, feeling, as he says in the preamble, the hand of death imminent, made his will, desiring his body to be buried in the Church of St. Giles at Cubberley, leaving various small legacies to that and other churches in the towns of Worcester, Gloucester and Cirencester, and devising the rest of his personalty to his executors, who included his wife and his brother, to be disposed of as they should deem best. He died on Palm Sunday following April 12th, his writ of "diem clausit" being tested by the King at Westminster on the 20th of that month. The inquisition under it sets forth the various manors he had held, and states that his heirs were his two daughters Margaret and Alice, aged respectively thirty and twenty-six years. Margaret, the elder, is stated to be the wife of Nicholas Mattesden, and Alice,

This will, written in Latin, is one of the earliest on record at Somerset House.

Inq. post mort., 6 Hen. IV.

THOMAS DE BERKELEY II, DE CUBBERLEY, 1365–1405.

Inq. post mort., 7 Hen. IV.

Inq. post mortem, 36 Hen. VI.

the younger, wife of Thomas de Brugge. The husbands of these ladies entered into an arrangement with Margaret for a surrender of her territorial rights in consideration of an annuity which she did not live to enjoy, and then divided the estates between them. Curiously enough Margaret died also on Palm Sunday, only one year later than her husband, Sir Thomas, on that same day. The division of the property was confirmed by the Crown, but its effects were not destined to be of long duration, for on the death of Robert, son of Nicholas, and Margaret Mattesden, in 1468, his share of the estates passed to the son of Alice, the other coheiress, Giles Brydges, whose posterity were created in 1554 Barons Chandos of Sudeley and eventually Dukes of Chandos.

Thus we have traced the old line of Berkeley in Gloucestershire to the extinction as territorial magnates. We do not, indeed, know whether the younger sons of the first Sir Thomas long survived their elder brother or themselves left any posterity. But we may infer that this was not the case, as we find none of the name inheriting any lands or holding any position in the county.

APPENDIX I

No. 1

In dnica terra regis ten' Rogeri de berchelai una domu
7 una piscaria in ipsa uilla. 7 est extra manu regis.
Hanc Balduin tenuit. T.R.E.

No. 2

Rogeri de Berchelai ten. ii. car' tre ad Surgoiels
7 ibi hnt. vi. bord cu. i. car. Val xx. sol.

No. 3

In Berchelai habuit. E. rex. v. hid. 7 in dnio. v. car.
7 xx. uitti 7 v. bord cu. xi. car. 7 ix. serui. 7 ii. molini
de. xii. solid. Ibi. x. radchenistres. hntes. vii. hid. 7 vii. car.
Ibi un foru in quo manent. xvii. hoes. 7 reddt censu in firma.
Hg Berewic ptin ad Berchelai.
In hilla. iiii. hide. In Almintune. iiii. hide. In hinetune.
iiii. hide. In Camma. vi. hide. 7 alie. xi. hide. In Gosintune
iiii. hide. In Derslege. iii. hide. In Couelege. iiii. hide.
In Euuelege. ii. hide. In Nimdesfelle. iii. hide. In Wotune
xv. hide 7 dimid. v. In Simondeshale dimid hida.
In Chingescote. iiii. hide 7 dimid. In Beurestane. x. hide.
In Olleuuorde dimid hida. In Almodesberie. ii. hide.
In horefelle. viii. hide. In Westone. vii. hide 7 una v.
In Eldbertone. v. hide. In Cromale. ii. hide. In Erlingehā
xi. hide. In Esceleuuorde. iii. hide.
Hec supdicta mebra oma ptinent ad Berchelai.
Int totu.
In hs. T.R.E. in dnio. xl ix. car 7 dimid. 7 cc. xl. ii. uitti.
7 c xl. ii. bord. cu. c. xx vi. car. Ibi. c xx. vii. serui.
Ibi. xix. libi hoes Radchenist. hntes. xl viii. car. cu suis hoib.
Ibi xxii. colibti. 7 xv. ancille.
Ibi. viii. molini de. l. vii. sol 7 vi. denar.

Extracts from Domesday Book relating to Berkeley, or the Berkeley family

For translations see pages 9 to 12

APPENDIX I.

No. 4

In isto m tenuer .ii. frs T.R.E. in ~~Cromhal~~. v. hidas
hntes in dnio .ii. car. 7 vi. uillt. 7 v. bord hntes .vi. car.
Hi .ii. frs cu tra sua se poterant uertere quo uolebant.
Tc valeb .iiii. lib. m .iii. lib. Hos .W. com comdauit
pposito de berchelai ut eis habet seruitu. Sic dic Rogeri.
De hoc m cu omib ad eu ptinentib, redd Rogeri
ad firma .c lxx. lib. arsas 7 pensatas.
Ipse Rogeri ht de tra hui m in hessinbruge .ii. hid.
Ad Claenhangare .i. hid. Ad hirslege .i. hid. Ad Neueton
vii. hid. Ibi sunt in dnio .x. car. 7 xiii. uilli 7 xxi. bord.
cu .xx ii. car. Ibi .xvi. serui. 7 Molin de .v. solid.
Tot T.R.E. ualb .xx. lib. Modo .xx. lib 7 .x. solid.
Isd Rogeri ten tra Bernardi pbri. v. hid. Ibi ht .iii. car.
7 ii. uillos. 7 vi. bord. cu .v. car. Val 7 ualuit .lx. sol.
In ~~Hesse~~ sunt .v. hide ptinent ad Berchelai. qs
W. com misit ext ad faciendu un castellulu. h Roger

No. 5

Gueda mat comit heraldi tenuit ~~Voccestre~~. ~~In Langebrige hd.~~
Goduin eam emit, ab Azor 7 ded sue uxori. ut inde uiueret donec
ad Berchelai maneret. Nolebat eni de ipso m aliqd comedere.
p destructione abbatie.

No. 6

xlii TERRA ROGERII DE BERCHELAI. ~~In Respigete hund.~~
~~ROGERIUS~~ de Berchelai ten ~~Cosseleie~~. Ibi .x. hide. Dena
tenuit ~~tenuit~~ regi. E. In dnio sunt .ii. car. 7 xix. uilli 7 iiii. bord
cu .v. car. Ibi .iiii. serui. 7 v. ac pti. Silua .iii. qx lg 7 ii. lat.
Valuit .vii. lib. modo .viii. lib. ~~In Hedredestan hd.~~
Isd Rog ten ~~Dodintone~~. Ibi .iii. hide 7 ii. partes dimid hide.
Aluuin tenuit T.R.E. In dnio .e. i. car. 7 vii. uilli 7 iiii. bord
cu .iiii. car. Ibi .iiii. serui. 7 x. ac pti. Val 7 ualuit .iii. lib
Isd Rog ten ~~Sistone~~ Anne tenuit. ~~In Pulcrecerce hd.~~
Ibi .v. hide geld. In dnio sunt .ii. car 7 viii. uilli 7 x. bord
cu .iiii. car. Ibi .iiii. serui. 7 viii. ac pti. Val 7 ualuit .c. solid.

Extracts from Domesday Book

For translations see pages 9 to 12

No. 7

APPENDIX I.

xliiii. TERRA RADULFI DE BERCHELAI. In Folchecerce hd.
Radulfus fr ipsius Rogerii ten Doregge Wapelie.
Ibi .i. hida. Godric tenuit. In dnio e una car 7 iiii servi.
Val 7 valuit .xx. solid. In Blachelew hd.
Isd Rad ten Sewelsee. Ibi .iiii. hide 7 dim. Godric
7 Wlnod tenuer p .ii. m. In dnio sunt .ii. car 7 vi. villi
7 xiiii. bord cu xii. car. Ibi .v. servi. 7 x. ac pti.
Valuit 7 val. c. solid.

Extract from Domesday Book

For translation see page 11

APPENDIX II

Extracts from a charter formerly among the muniments of the Abbey of St. Martin d'Auchy, near Aumâle, and now in the archives of the Seine Inférieure at Rouen.

Translation.

"In the name of our Lord Jesus Christ, in this charter are contained the benefices and rents hereby specified, of the Church of the Mother of the Lord, the Virgin Mary, and of St. Martin the Confessor of Christ, which in the time of Richard, fourth Duke of the Normans, was founded near the town of Aumâle in the vill which is called Auchy, by a certain personage, to wit Guerinfridus, who was also the founder of the castle which is called Albamarla upon the river which is called Eu, in that part where it divides the province of Amiens from the land of the Normans; and the same personage, to wit the venerable Guerinfridus established in the above mentioned church six canons to serve the Lord, and endowed it according to his means with lands and rents, tithes and advowsons wherewith the clerks who ministered in the church might be supported; all which we have been careful to set down below by order of the Count Enquerrand, who was the son of Berta, daughter of Guerinfridus, named above, and of the Countess Adelidis his wife, sister to wit of William, King of the English, who wishes them to be authenticated by writing, to the intent that none of the benefices of the church should be taken away by posterity."

Then follows at length various regulations and lists of benefactions, among others the gifts of the Countess Adelidis, the sister of William the Conqueror, and her daughter, Countess Judith, and immediately following them the donations of *Roger de Berkeley* and *Rissa* his wife, as given on page 19. In the original Latin the record of their donation reads:

" Rursus *Rogerus de Berchelaico* cum uxore sua *Rissa* dedit cappam unam de pallio, nec minus quoddam preciosum vestimentum sacerdotale in quo nec cingulum defuit, dedit idem et calicem argenteum, crucem auream et duas campanas."

APPENDIX III

Charters in the Muniment Room of Berkeley Castle

1

Grant from Henry, Duke of Normandy, Count of Anjou, to Robert Fitzharding, of certain land in the Manor of Berkeley, with an undertaking to build a castle at Berkeley. Dated at Bristol in the year 1153.

2

Marriage contract between Rodbert Fitzharding and Roger de Berckele, made in the house of the said Rodbert at Bristol, in the presence of Henry, Duke of Normandy, whereby it is covenanted that Maurice, son of Rodbert Fitzharding, shall take in marriage the daughter of Roger de Berckele, with Slimbridge as her portion, and that Roger, the son and heir of Roger de Berckele, shall take in marriage the daughter of the said Rodbert Fitzharding with the manor of Siston for dowry. Date about November, 1153.

Copy of the Actual Charter.

(Translation on page 38)

Iste sunt pactiones que facte fuerunt inter Rodbertum filium Hardingi et Rogerum de Berckel' in domo Rodberti filii Hardingi apud Bristou in presentia domini Henrici ducis Normannorum et Aquitanie et comitis Andegavie ejusdem assensu et in presentia multorum aliorum clericorum et laicorum.

Mauricius filius Rodberti filii hardingi cepit filiam Rogeri de Berckel' in uxorem ita quod Rogerus dedit Mauricio cum filia sua in matrimonio Slimbrugiam que est de sua hereditate, hoc est decem libratas terre, et Mauricius concessu patris sui Rodberti filii Hardingi dedit filie Rogeri quam ipse cepit uxorem in dotem xx libratas terre de feudo de Berckel' assensu domini Henrici ducis. Tali conventione quod si Mauricius filius Rodberti moreretur antequam cepisset filiam Rogeri uxorem: frater ejus post eum primogenitus acciperet eam uxorem per supradictas conventiones. Et si etiam ille alter filius Rodberti moreretur ante sponsalia filie Rogeri: quisquis de filiis Rodberti post illum heres remaneret filiam Rogeri uxorem acciperet. Similiter si filia Rogeri antequam desponsaretur Mauricio filio Rodberti moreretur, secunda post ipsam Mauricio daretur in uxorem vel cuilibet fratrum suorum qui heres remaneret post Mauricium. Ita et de ceteris filiabus Rogeri si primogenite morerentur illa que remaneret post ipsas daretur illi de filiis Rodberti filii Hardingi qui heres ejus remaneret, sicut superius prelocutum est. Preterea filius Rogeri de berckel' qui heres ejus est debet accipere uxorem unam de filiabus Rodberti filii Hardingi et Rogerius de Berckelai debet illi filie Rodberti dare in dotem manerium Sistone prope Bristou quod manerium est de hereditate Rogeri. Et Rodbertus filius Hardingi debet dare in matrimonium cum filia sua filio Rogeri x librates et x solidatas terre apud Derselegam eo pacto quod si una de filiabus Rodberti filii Hardingi moreretur antequam filius Rogeri eam acciperet uxorem: altera filia Rodberti daretur illi. Et si utraque filia Rodberti ante sponsalia moreretur: filius Rogeri qui heres ejus esset acciperet uxorem filiam hugonis de Hasele neptim Rodberti filii hardingi. Similiter si primogenitus Rogeri de berckel' moreretur ante supradicta sponsalia ille de fratribus suis qui remaneret post ipsum primogenitus et heres acciperet uxorem unam de filiabus Rodberti filii Hardingi que domi sunt vel si utraque ante sponsalia moreretur, filiam Hugonis de Hasele per supradictas pactiones. Has pactiones affidaverunt Rodbertus filius Hardingi et Rogerus de Berckelai tenere et servare sine fallacia et dolo et posuerunt Dominum Henricum ducem obsidem et justiciam inter se de servandis his pactionibus. Hoc etiam affidaverunt viii probi viri ex parte Rodberti et alii viii ex parte Rogeri quorum nomina hec sunt. Ex parte Rogeri Willelmus filius Henrici, Rogerus de Sckai, Radulphus de Huelega, Walkelinus, Engebaldus de Gosintunia, Guido de Rupe, Gwaiferus de Planca, Hugo de Planca frater ejus. De parte Roberti, Hugo de Hasela, Nigellus filius Arthuri, Robertus de Saltemareis, Helyas frater Rodberti filii Hardingi, Jordanus frater ejus, Jordanus le Warre, Nicholaus filius Rodberti, David

Duncepucke. Et isti viri Rodbertum et Rogerum in his pactionibus servandis totis juribus tenebunt. Quodsi Rodbertus et Rogerus de his pactionibus vellent exire, isti cogent eos pactiones tenere quantum poterint. Et si ipsi adquiescere noluerint, isti viri de servicio et amore eorum recedent. Et propter has supradictas pactiones Rogerus de Berkele clamavit quietum totum chalangium suum et quicquid juris habebat in firma de Berkalai.

The translation on page 38 made by the Abbot Newland in 1520 does not fully correspond with the above. Possibly it may have been made from another copy.

CHARTERS AT BERKELEY CASTLE

3

A confirmation by Roger de Berkeley to Maurice, the son of Nigel of sundry lands [1170].

In Latin, with large seal of green wax, representing man with shield, etc., in combat with a lion.

4

A grant from Roger de Berkeley, son of Roger de Berkeley, to Reginald Mazoni, of certain lands in Dursley. Latin, time of Henry II.

5

Grant from Aaleis de Berkeley to William, her son, of her burgage in Berkeley. Latin, 1190, with small white seal.

6

Grant from Aaleis de Berkele to Guy, son of Roger de Vilers, of land in Slimbridge, rent a pair of gilt spurs. Latin, late 12th century.

N.B.—This Aaleis de Berkeley was the daughter of Roger de Berkeley III, and the wife of Maurice Fitzhardinge, married after the Covenant before King Henry at Berkeley.

Appendix III.

7

Grant from Aaleis de Berkele on the request and with the consent of her son, Robert de Berkele, to Elias, son of Toke, her nurse and servant, of land in Slimbridge. Latin, late 12th century.

8

Grant from Aeliz, widow of Maurice de Berkeley, to Thomas of her land in Bristol. Witnesses: Roger de Berkeley, Philip and Oliver, his brothers, etc., etc. Latin, 12th century, with seal.

9

Grant from Aleis de Berkele to Thomas, her son, of all her lands in Berkeley. Witnesses, among others: Maurice and Henry de Berkeley, her sons. About 1200, Latin.

10

Grant from Aelesia de Berkelai to St. Augustine's Abbey, Bristol, of a house in Redclive Street, Bristol. She makes this for her soul's health. Witnesses: Robert de Berkelai, Philip de Berkelai. 12th century, Latin, with seal.

APPENDIX IV

From the Chartulary of the Monastery of St. Peter's, Gloucester

1

List of donations to the monastery : Rogerus de Berkeleye junior anno Domini Millesimo nonagesimo quarto dedit Deo et Sancto Petro Gloucestriæ quandam terrulam Clehangre nomine consensu et confirmatione regis Willelmi junioris: abstutit vero Nyndesfeld tempore Serlonis abbatis.

2

Anno domini millesimo octogesimo septimo, Rogerus senior de Berkelee in discriptione totius Angliæ fecit Nymdesfeld describi ad mensam regis, abbate Serlone nesciente.

3

Anno Domini Millesimo nonagesimo tertio, Eustachius de Berkeleyee reddidit Deo et Sancto Petro Gloucestriæ, Nymdesfeld tempore Serlonis abbatis.

4

Rogerus de Berkeleya ecclesiam de Oselworthe didit prioratui de Stanleye Ecclesiam de Coveleye Ecclesiam de Erlyngham Ecclesiam de Slymbrugge Ecclesiam de Uleye cum decimis et terris et omnibus rebus ad eas pertinentibus.

5

Rogerus de Berkeleye senior in die sancti Sebastiani sub domno Serlone abbate monarchus effectus reddidit Deo et Sancto Petro Gloucestriæ Shoteshore liberam et quietam, quam diu injuste tennerat, rege Willelmo Seniore confirmante. Hoc factum et anno Domini Millesimo nonagesimo primo.

Appendix IV.

6

Rogerus de Berkeleye junior reddidit Deo et Sancto Petro Gloucestriæ Shoteshore quam diu injuste tennerat, liberam et quietam, sicut eam ipsi monarchi præstiterunt tempore Willelmi abbatis.

7

Anno Domini Millesimo centesimo quadragesimo sexto Rogerus de Berkele dedic Deo et Conventui Santi Petri Gloucestriæ Ecclesiam sancti Leonardi de Stanleye cum omnibus pertinentiis suis assensu Tabrithri prioris et fratrum ejusdem loci, per manum domini Symonis Wygorniensis Episcopi. Idem Rogerus dedit Ecclesiam de Osleworthe prioratui de Stanleye et Ecclesiam de Coveley, et Ecclesiam de Erlyngham et ecclesiam de Slymbrugge, et ecclesiam de Uleye cum decimis, terris et omnibus rebus ad eam pertinentibus, tempore Gilberti abbatis.

8

List of donations to the monastery :

Rogerus senior de Berkeleye monarchus factus reddidit Schotteshore.

Rogerus de Berkeleye junior dedit Clehonger.

APPENDIX V

Charters from the Chartulary of the Abbey of Kingswood, Wiltshire

1

Carta R. de Berckley

Notum sit fidelibus omnibus quod ego R. de Berckley concessu regis et rogatu, sed et petitione capituli Cistercii consensu quoque conjugis meæ et hæredis mei, concessi monarchis de Kingswode Misertus paupertatis eorum, transferre abbatiam suam de fœdo meo quam antecessores mei fundaverunt; hoc tenore, ut manerium illud, scilicet Kingeswode remaneat illis liberum et quietum ab omnibus serviciis secularibus et querelis sicut prius fuit, stante ibi abbatia.

Ita tamen, ut ibi ab uno sacerdote monarcho missa continue privatim celebretur, simque particeps omnium beneficiorum translatæ abbatiœ tanquam fundator, et omnium abbatiarum Cisterciensis ordinis, tam ego quam conjux mea et hæres meus cum antecessoribus et successoribus meis. Ipsi autem monarchi ut meliorem gratiam invenirent apud me, dederunt mihi viginti septem marcas et dimidiam, et filio meo unum cacorem vel unam marcam, et manutenebo eos pro posse meo sicut fundator. Et si forte quolibet modo redierint, reddam eis quantum dederunt ad suum placitum. Hanc pactionem me servaturum fide firma, Testes, etc.

2

Carta R. de Berckley

R. de Berckley omnibus fidelibus qui literas istas inspexerint salutem. Notum sib vobis quod Willielmus de Berckley dedit abbaciæ de Tynterna, pro salute anima Henrici regis Angliæ et suæ, totum Kingeswode cum omnibus pertinensiis suis ad construendam ibi abbatiam de ordine Cisterciensi, et pater meus illud gratum habuit et ratum tenuit. Et postquam abbatia de Kingeswode translata erat ad Tettebiriam, consensu patris mei R. de Berckley, ipse pater meus consensu et voluntate mea dedit et concessit Bernardo de Sancto Walerico quadraginta acras apud Mureford ad removendam illuc abbatiam suam quæ fuit prius apud Tettebiriam. His testibus.

3

Carta Hen. I Regis Angliæ

H. Rex Angliæ S. Wigorn Episcopo et N. Gloucestriæ omnibusque baronibus suis et fidelibus suis Francis et Anglis de Gloucestreschire salutem. Sciatis me concessisse *Rogero de Berchley* quod det Acheolt in perpetuam elemosinam canonicis vel monarchis pro animabus nostris et antecessorum nostrorum. Quare volo et firmita præcipio quod prædicta terra sit ita libera et quieta ex omnibus servitiis et querelis et consuetudinibus sicut ego ipse melius et liberius tenebam in meo dominio. Testibus W. Camerario de Tancervill et M. Gloucestriæ, et Pagano filio Johannis, apud Elingas.

4

Letter of William de Berkeley to Pope Innocent

Reverendissimo Dei gratia domino Papæ Innocencio Willielmus de Berkeley et fundator Kingswode reverentiam cum fide et . . . hillaritate summo pontifici debitam. Pia pastoris gratia subditos affectio votum beati Petri apostolorum principis successorem interpellare pusillanimitati nostræ ausum dedit. Præterea dextra in sublevando sedula in dando munifica omnem in desiderio sancto querulam excludit repulsam; inde ne in hoc negotio ulla tumultuetur opacitas, rem ex integra magestati vestræ intimari juravimus. Henricus Rex Anglorum patruo nostro *Rogero de Berkeley* certi pretii taxatione terram quandam absque calumpnia sibimet reservatam dedit, condicione tali quatenus eam religioni horum alteri profitenti monachatum, scilicet seu canonicatum sanciret. Sed quoniam hic idem morte præventus est, memor tum propositi, illam nobis condicione præfata legavit. Et ne inde ulla inposterum exactio violens posset inferri regis præfati munimento, præsentiæ vestræ delato confirmavit. Nos itaque voluntate ejus supplentes ordini Cisterciensi, quia cœteris in sanctitate preponderare nobis visus est, terram illam ab patruo scilicet hoc sine vobis legatam ad abbatiam fundandam concessimus. Proinde vestra eidem ordini anctoritas moderetur cantelam, quatenus idem ratam habeatur et constans et ne ejus rei ulla possit dissolusio uspiam inveniri, precamur benevolenciæ vestræ gratiam, quatenus auctortitate apostolica corroboretur, ut siquis exactionis cujuslibet, aut etiam detrimenti calumpnia molitus Romano, insuper privilegio versuciam conetur inferre, anathematis gladio repercussus absistat. Valete.

A translation of the above letter will be found on page 31.

5

Carta Rogeri de Berkley de Kingswode cum pertinentiis

[Dated 1148]

Simoni Episcopo Wigorn et omnibus fidelibus *Rogerus de Berkeley* salutem. Notum vobis sit quod ego Rogerus de Berkeley pro me ipso et uxore mea, et liberis meis et pro anima patris mei et antecessorum meorum, concedo et confirmo abbati et monarchis de Kingeswode totam terram de Kingeswode, tam nemus quam culturas et prata et quicquid ad ipsam pertinet liberam et quietam ab omnibus querelis et nominatim a servitio unius militis, quod *Willielmus de Berkley* pro feudo ipsius abbatis mihi debebat. Ipsi vero monarchi in capitulo eorum receperunt me prædicti loci fundatorem. Datum apud Chiveleiam sexto idus martii anno ab incarnatione *millesimo centesimo quadragesimo ovtavo*. Testes sunt Simon Episcopus Wigorn. Willielmus abbas de Margan, et Gervasius Archidiaconus, Hugo monarchus de Truarcho, Hugo decanus, Johannes Papa, Willielmus de Winton et alii.

6

Carta *Rogeri de Berkley* senioris de Acholt

Sciant præsentes et futuri quod ego Rogerus de Berkeleya pro Deo et salute animæ domini mei Henrici regis et animæ meæ et animarum hæredum meorum et omniam antecessorum

APPENDIX V.

et successorum meorum dedi, concessi et hac præsenti carta mea confirmavi Deo et Ecclesiæ beatæ Mariæ de Kingeswode et monarchis ibidem Deo servientibus totum manerium meum de Acholte, cum omnibus pertenentibus suis in liberam puram et perpetuam elemosinam tenendum et habendum omnia prædicta, Ecclesiæ suæ prædictæ et monarchis ibidem Deo servientibus et eorum successoribus libere et quiete ab omnibus exactionibus secularibus sicut libera et pura elemosina liberius et purius haberi et teneri et excogitari poterit imperpetuum. Et ego prædictus Rogerus et hæredes mei warantizabimus prædictum manerium de Acholte cum omnibus quibuscumque pertinentiis suis prædictæ ecclesiæ de Kingeswode et monarchis ibidem Deo servientibus et eorum successoribus sicut liberam et puram et perpetuam elemosinam et acquietabimus eos et defendemus ab omnibus quæ unquam inde aliquo modo poterint contra omnes mortales imperpetuum. Et ut hæc mea donacio concessio et præsentis cartæ meæ confirmatio rata et stabilis imperpetuum permaneat, eandem sigilli mei munimine robaravi. Hiis testibus Simone Episcopo Wigorn, abbate santi Augustini de Bristol, abbate de Tynterna Roberto filio Hardyngi, Henrico Lovel et aliis.

7

Confirmatio *Rogeri de Berkeley* junioris de Manerio de Kingeswode.

Universis Christi fidelibus ad quos præseus carta pervenerit. Rogerus de Berkley, æternam in Domino salutem. Noverit universitas vestra me caritatis intuitu, pro animabus patris et matris meæ, et animabus antecessorum et hæredum meorum et uxorum mearum consilio et assensu hæredum meorum, concessisse et confirmasse Deo et ecclesiæ beatæ Mariæ de Kingeswode et monarchis ibidem Deo servientibus in perpetuam et puram elemosinam, totum manerium de Kingeswode quod præfati monarchi ejusdem loci tenuerunt *de Rogero patre meo* et me tenendum et habendum de me et hæredibus meis, in bosco et plano culturis et pasturis, aquis et pratis, viis et semitis, liberum et quietum ab omnibus querelis et exactionibus et nominatim a servicio unius militis quod *Willielmus de Berkley* pro feudo ipsius abbathiæ patri meo debebat. Prædicti vero monarchi in capitulo eorum receperunt prænominatum R. patrem meum et hæredes ipsius, prædicto *Willielmo de Berkley* annuente et consentiente suœ domus fundatore. Hiis testibus Roberto de Berkleya, nepote meo, *Philippo et Olivero fratribus meis*, et Willielmo filio meo magistro Richardo de Rorestan et Benedicto capellano fratre Richardo de Bradeleya et aliis.

APPENDIX VI

From the Register of Charters of Malmesbury Abbey. Preserved at the Public Record Office

Cap. xcviii. De una hida terræ in Chotherintone. Sciant omnes tam præsentes quam futuri quod ego *Rogerus de Berkelay* divinæ pietatis intuitu, et pro salute animæ meæ et antecessorum et successorum meorum, dediet consessi et hac carta mea confirmavi Deo et Ecclesiæ Sancti Aldhelmi de Malmesburia, unam hidam terræ, de feodo meo in Cuderintone, ad vestituram monarchorum ibidem Deo servientium, in puram et perpetuam elemosinam, liberam et quietam ab omni regali militari et seculari servicio. Quam videlicet hydam *Rogerus avus meus et Rogerus pater meus*, eidem, ecclesiæ dederant et concesserant in puram et perpetuam elemosinam pro salute antecessorum et successorum suorum ut mererentur participes fieri omnium bonorum orationum et elemosinarum, etc., etc. His Testibus.

This is a charter by Roger III. In it he mentions Roger I and Roger II. The next charter is by Roger IV, and in almost identical terms.

APPENDIX VII

From "Gesta Stephani" by an Ecclesiastic, a Contemporaneous writer of whom nothing is known. He was clearly a Partisan of King Stephen

Circa idem quoque tempus Walterius quidam frater comitis Herefordiæ, assensu, ut aiebant ipsius comitis, cepit *Rogerium de Berchelai*, insidiis prætensis circumventum; virum indemnem nec solum amicitia, et alternæ pacis fœdere sibi astrictum, sed et germana contribulis sanguinis cognatione propinquum; vestibusque tandem nudatum, et ludibriis expositum, sed et vinculis arctissime mancipatum, ante suum, quod in vicino habuerat castellum, tribus vicibus, loro collo innexo, suspenderunt, et tertio, laxatis vinculis, ad ima dismiserunt; talibusque indecentibus modis interitum viro minitantes, immo eum, nisi castellum suum comiti committeret, ad interneciem dirissime compellentes inexanditi postremo discessere, miserumque seminecis *Rogerii* cadaver, quia tennis adhuc vitalis animæ spiritus in vexato corpore palpitabat secum ferentes, ad carceris perferenda supplicia diutius reservarunt, etc., etc.

APPENDIX VIII

Various Ways in which the Name of Barclay is Spelt

1. *Beorcenlau:* in the Saxon Chronicle.
2. Rogerius de *Berchelai:* Domesday Book, 1086.
3. Rogerias de *Berchelaico:* Aumâle Charter, before 1096.
4. Rogerius de *Berchelaia:* Roger II's seal.
5. *Beorkenlai:* Florence of Worcester's Chronicle.
6. Johan *Barclaye:* List of Friars, Gloucester Records.
7. Philip of *Berkeli:* Kingswood Charter, 1250.
8. *Berkely:* Kingswood Charter, 1275.
9. *Berkelegh:* Kingswood Charter, 1309.
10. Oliver de *Berkelay:* Kingswood Charter, 1243.
11. Rogerus de *Berkley:* Kingswood Charter.
12. Rogerus de *Berchley:* Kingswood Charter.
13. Robertus de *Berkleya:* Kingswood Charter.
14. Rogerus de *Bercheley:* Kingswood Charter.
15. Rogerus de *Berckle:* Kingswood Charter.
16. Roger de *Berckale:* Pipe Roll, 1159.
17. Rogerias de *Berckley:* Liber Niger scaccarii.
18. Roger de *Berkelai:* Pipe Roll, Gloucester.
19. Rogerius de *Berkele:* Pipe Roll, 9 John.
20. *Birecleia:* History of St. Peter's Abbey.
21. Rogerius de *Berkeleye:* Cartulary, St. Peter's, Gloucester.
22. Rog. de *Berchelei:* Cartulary, St. Peter's, Gloucester.
23. Eustachius de *Berkeleyee:* Cartulary, St. Peter's, Gloucester.
24. Rogerus senior de *Berkelee:* Cartulary, St. Peter's, Gloucester.
25. Rog. de *Berchele:* Cartulary, St. Peter's, Gloucester.
26. *Berkeleye:* Cartulary, St. Peter's, Gloucester.
27. *Birchlega:* Cartulary, St. Peter's, Gloucester.
28. Will[s] de *Berckelai:* Magnus Rot. scarc. xxi Hen. I.
29. *Berckalai:* Magnus Rot. scarc. xxi Hen. I.
30. *Barkeley:* Gloucester Records.
31. Henricus *Berkel:* Book of Knights' Fees, Ed. i.
32. *Bearkley:* Dursley Papers.

33. Johanne de *Bercle* de Dursele: Exchequer Books of Aids. APPENDIX VIII.
34. *Berkel'*: Feet of Fines.
35. *Bercleg'*: Feet of Fines.
36. *Berkleg'*: Feet of Fines.
37. *Berchela*: Cottonian MS., about 1100 A.D.
38. *Berchele*: Berkeley Charters at Berkeley Castle.
39. *Berclea*: Acts of Sinod at Cloveshoe, 824 A.D.
40. *Berckel'*: Marriage Covenant of Roger III.
41. *Berkelei*: Smyth's Lives of the Berkeleys.
42. *Bercley*: Spalding Club Papers.
43. Syr Alex. *Barklaye*: Translation of Saluste, 1451.
44. Walterus *Berclai* de Tolli : Charter of 1457.
45. Alexander *Berclay*: Dom. de Kerkow, 1400.
46. Valterus *Barculay* de Towie: Charter 1512.
47. Alexander de *Berklay*: Charter of Mathers, 1353.
48. Dame Isbel *Barkley*: Dun Papers, 1539.
49. *Barcley*: Burke's Armory, Devon.
50. *Barkele*: Burke's Armory, Cornwall.
51. *Barkeley*: Burke's Armory, Cornwall.
52. *Barkley*: Burke's Armory, Leicester.
53. *Barclei*, in Orlando Furioso.
54. Alexander *Barcklaye*: British Museum Catalogue.
55. *Barckley*: British Museum Catalogue.
56. *Barclæus*: British Museum Catalogue.
57. *Barclai*: British Museum Catalogue.
58. *Barclaius*: British Museum Catalogue.
59. *Bercley*: British Museum Catalogue.
60. *Barklay*: British Museum Catalogue.
61. *Barklai*: British Museum Catalogue.
62. *Berkelius*: British Museum Catalogue.
63. Robert de *Bercl'*: Charter of King Malcolm.
64. *Berkeley*: Modern spelling.
65. *Barkly*: Modern spelling.
66. *Barclay*: Modern spelling.

A HISTORY OF THE BARCLAY FAMILY

WITH PEDIGREES FROM 1067 TO 1933

PART II

THE BARCLAYS IN SCOTLAND FROM 1067 TO 1660

COMPILED BY
LIEUT.-COLONEL HUBERT F. BARCLAY

LONDON
THE ST. CATHERINE PRESS
STAMFORD STREET, S.E.
1933

FOREWORD TO PART II

My uncle the Rev. Charles Wright Barclay, compiler of Part I of this History, died in 1926, having dealt with the Gloucestershire section. He laid upon me the duty of continuing his work.

Sources of information unknown to previous genealogists have become available in recent years, necessitating a careful examination of the mass of material covering a period of eight centuries. I have been fortunate in obtaining the co-operation of Miss M. E. Simkins of the Victoria History, whose masterly research I most gratefully acknowledge.

My thanks are due to all who have assisted me, especially Captain Leslie Barclay of the Pierston Line, compiler of *History of the Scottish Barclays*, published in 1915, and Mr. Charles Herbert Barclay of the Towie Line for the valuable information collected by him over a long period and generously placed at my disposal. The manuscript notes of the late Sir Henry Barkly, K.C.B., G.C.M.G., one of the Barclays of Bridgeton, a branch of the Mathers Line, and the Press articles of the late Captain Douglas Wimberley, were of great interest.

I desire to record my deep gratitude to my wife, without whose co-operation and constant encouragement this work could not have been completed.

H. F. B.

Orchards,
Letty Green,
Hertford.
August 1933.

CONTENTS

CONTENTS

LIST OF ILLUSTRATIONS

LIST OF PRINCIPAL AUTHORITIES CONSULTED FOR PART II

MSS. History of the House of Forbes and Others. Matthew Lumsden.

Place Names in Strathbogie, with notes. James Macdonald, F.S.A.Scot.

Cuninghame, topographised by Timothy Pont (1604—1608). James Dobie of Crammock.

Chambers's Biographical Dictionary.

Lives and Characters of the Officers of the Crown and of the State in Scotland. George Crawfurd.

A System of Heraldry. Alexander Nisbet.

Chronicles of the War between England and Scotland (1173–1174), Surtees edition. Jordan Fantosme.

Annals of the reigns of Malcolm and William, Kings of Scotland (1153–1214). Sir Archibald Campbell Lawrie, LL.D.

Rotuli Scaccarii Regum Scottorum (1264–1359). (Exchequer Rolls.) John Stuart and George Burnett.

Scotland under the Early Kings. William Robertson.

Gesta Henrici Secundi. Richard Fitz Neal. (1198.)

The Encyclopædia Britannica. Eleventh Edition.

Scottish Annals from English Chronicles. David Nutt.

Scotichronicon. John Fordun, died c. 1384. Walter Bower, Abbot of the Monastery of Inchcolm (–1437).

Polichronicon. James Fraser. (Seventeenth Century.)

Chronica Majora. Matthew Paris.

Register of the Honour of Morton. Bannatyne Club.

Charters of the Abbey of Kelso.

Registrum de Panmure. Edward John Stuart.

The Douglas Book. Sir William Fraser.

Register of Glasgow. Registrum Episcopatus Glasgoensis.

Memorie of the Somervills.

Bridgwater MSS. Historical MSS. Commission Report.

Mr. Macdonald's Notes in the Lyon Office.

PRINCIPAL AUTHORITIES CONSULTED

Chancery Miscellaneous Bundles.
Close Rolls.
Roll of the Comptroller of the Prince of Wales's Household.
Accounts of the Great Chamberlain. Bannatyne Club.
History of Scots Affairs. James Gordon, parson of Rothiemay.
Index of Missing Charters. Robertson.
Murray Charters. Hist. MSS. Commission. Bannatyne Club.
Documents and Records of Scotland. Sir F. Palgrave.
Barbour's "The Brus." Spalding Club.
Chancery Portfolios (Scotland).
Orygynale Cronykil of Scotland. Andrew de Wyntoun. 1350.
Balmerino Charters.
Family of Wemyss.
Hamilton Charters.
Report of the Mar case. Hist. MSS. Commission.
Rotuli Scotiæ in Turri Londiniensi.
The Book of Pluscarden. Liber Pluscardensis.
Calendar of Papal Registers. Vatican Transcripts.
Exchequer, Scots Documents. Box 2.
Collections of Aberdeen and Banff. Spalding Club.
Land of the Lindsays. Andrew Jervise.
Miscellanies. Spalding Club.
The Family of Leslie.
The History of the Garioch. Davidson.
Records of Aboyne. Spalding Club.
Domestic Annals of Scotland.
Accounts of the Lord High Treasurer of Scotland.
Retours Special of Aberdeenshire. Inquisitionum Retornatorum Abbreviatis.
The Barclays of Barclay, Grantuly or Gartly and Towie. Captain Douglas Wimberley.
Diurnall of Remarkable Occurrants in Scotland. Maitland Club.
Chiefs of Grant.
Family of Forbes.
History of the Scottish Barclays. Captain Leslie Barclay.
Memoirs of the Affairs of Scotland. David Crawfurd. 1753.
Historie of Scotland from the Slauchter of King James I. R. Lindsay of Pitscottie.

PRINCIPAL AUTHORITIES CONSULTED

Peerage of Scotland. 1815. Sir Robert Douglas. (John Philip Wood.)
Peerage and Baronetage. Sir Bernard Burke.
Landed Gentry. Sir Bernard Burke.
Register of the Privy Council of Scotland. (Series 1, 2, 3.)
Bury Hill Deeds and Charters.
British Family Antiquity. Playfair.
Border Minstrelsy. Sir Walter Scott.
Sculptured Stones of Scotland.
The Baronage of Angus and Mearns. David MacGregor Peter.
Genealogical Collections of Scotland. Walter Macfarlane.
Acta Dominorum Concilii.
Acta Dominorum Auditorum Regni Scotiæ.
Irvine of Drum. Leslie.
Royal Commission on Historical Manuscripts Reports.
G.E.C. Peerage.
G.E.C. Baronetage.
Ancient Criminal Trials in Scotland. Robert Pitcairn.
A Short History of Scotland. Charles Sanford Terry.
A History of Scotland. Margaret MacArthur.
Armorial Seals. MacDonald.
Burgesses and Guild Brethren of Glasgow. Scot. Hist. Soc.
Kirtounhill Writs.
History of the Parish of Laurencekirk. William R. Fraser.
The Public Records of Scotland. J. Maitland Thomson.
Kincardineshire Sasines.
Cartulary of the Abbey of Lindores. (Scot. Hist. Soc.) The Right Rev. John Dowden, D.D.
Monasticon Anglicanum. 1664. Sir William Dugdale.
Liber Sancte Marie de Melrose. Bannatyne Club.
Acta Parliamentorum Regni Scotiæ.
Charters of Inchaffray Abbey. Scot. Hist. Soc.
Liber S. Thome de Aberbrothoc. Registrum Vetus. Bannatyne Club.
Scalacronica. (Maitland Club.) Sir Thomas Grey of Heton, Kt. 1536.
Registrum Ste. Marie de Newbottle.
Registrum Episcopatus Brechinensis.

PRINCIPAL AUTHORITIES CONSULTED

Scottish Parliament. Rait.
Registrum Magni Sigilli Regum Scotorum. (Register of the Great Seal.)
Tytler's History of Scotland. Sir Archibald Alison.
Fœdera, Conventiones. Thomas Rymer. (1704.)
The Red Book of Grantully. Sir William Fraser.
Liber Sancti Andrie. (Charters of St. Andrews Abbey.)
Genealogical Account of the Barclays of Urie. Robert Barclay.
Liber Ecclesia de Scon. Charters of the Abbey of Scone.
Calendar of Scottish Documents.
Acts and Decreets.
Registrum Episcopatus Aberdonensis. Spalding Club.
Towie Evidences. Gordon's College, Aberdeen.
Troubles. Spalding.
Sheriff's Clerk's Records. Aberdeen.
Collairnie Evidences.
Statistical Account of Scotland.
Charters of Dunfermline Abbey.
Calendar of the Laing Charters. The Rev. John Anderson.
Genealogical Deduction . . . Rose of Kilravock. Sir Robert Gordon of Lochinvar.
Ane Account of the Family of Innes.
Registrum Episcopatus Moraviensis.
Extracts from the Council Register of Aberdeen.
Memories of the Arbuthnots. A. J. Arbuthnot.
Memorials of the Montgomeries Earls of Wintoun.
The Red Book of Menteith.
The Barclays of New York, who they are and who they are not. Burnham Moffat.
Scottish Record Society. Gavin Ross.

PEDIGREE I.

The Barclay Tradition

[Non-proven.]

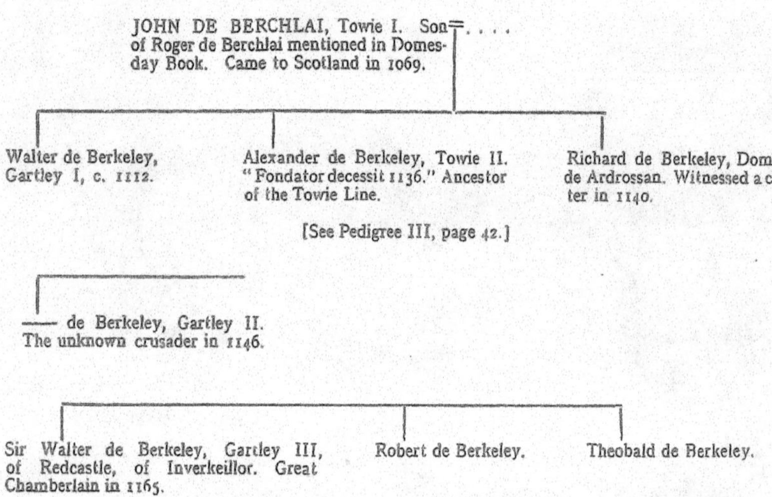
JOHN DE BERCHLAI, Towie I. Son of Roger de Berchlai mentioned in Domesday Book. Came to Scotland in 1069. = ...
Walter de Berkeley, Gartley I, c. 1112.
Alexander de Berkeley, Towie II. "Fondator decessit 1136." Ancestor of the Towie Line.
Richard de Berkeley, Dominus de Ardrossan. Witnessed a charter in 1140.
[See Pedigree III, page 42.]
—— de Berkeley, Gartley II. The unknown crusader in 1146.
Sir Walter de Berkeley, Gartley III, of Redcastle, of Inverkeillor. Great Chamberlain in 1165.
Robert de Berkeley.
Theobald de Berkeley.

[See Fedigree II, page 10.]

THE BARCLAY FAMILY

THE BARCLAY TRADITION

The tradition of the migration of the Barclays to Scotland may be read in the original manuscript of *Genealogy of the House of Forbes and Others*, by Matthew Lumsden, now in the possession of Sir Charles Forbes of Newe and Edenglassie. This work has been printed and also included by Macfarlane in his Genealogical Collections, but the printed versions do not include any reference to the Barclays.

JOHN DE BERKELEY, c. 1069, Towie I.

(It should be noted that the Forbes family in question were also of " Towie," but not the Towie connected with the Barclays. The Towie Castle which was in the possession of the Forbes from the late fifteenth century was situated on the banks of the Don, opposite the mighty Bruce Castle of Kildrummy.)

Matthew Lumsden thus gives the Barclay story :—

" Among those who about the year of Christ 1069 were, with Margaret the King of England's sister, driven by tempest upon the coasts of Scotland, was John Barclay, son to Lord Berchlai in England. Malcolm Caenmoir, King of Scotland, having married the said Margaret (for her piety afterwards called St. Margaret) did bestow upon several of the English nation both lands and titles of honour, for attending her and her mother, brother and sister, in their voyage and flight from the rage of William the Conqueror, out of England, intending at that time for Hungary, but were driven by Providence upon Scotland.

" Among those of the English nation upon whom King Malcolm bestowed lands was John Barclay, son of Lord Berchlai in England ; upon whom the King bestowed the lands of Towie in the shire of Aberdeen.

" This John Barclay had many sons, the elder of whom took to wife . . . . . . , heritrix of the lands of Gartley, in the shire of Aberdeen, which afterwards from him were called the lands and barony of Barclay.

" He received the title from the King, of Barclay of that Ilk, as witnesseth the charter of the said lands, wherein the lady is always ' Barclay de eodem.'

" The elder of John Barclay of Towie his sons, being advanced to ane considerable estate by his marriage with the heritrix of

JOHN DE BERKELEY, c. 1069, Towie I.

Gartley, and confirmed by the King's favour in the foresaid title of honour, the said John did transmit to his second son the foresaid lands of Towie.

"The rest of his children, by virtue and good service to the King and country attained to considerable fortunes and honourable estates, for of them are descended the family of the Laird of Mathers, in the shire of Mearns, the family of the Laird of Johnstone-Barclay, *ibidem*; likewise the family of the Laird of Collairnie in the shire of Fife, and we have it by tradition that the Lord of Brechin, nephew to King Robert Bruce, was descended from the same race of John Barclay of Towie."

Matthew Lumsden's MSS.

Matthew Lumsden wrote in 1580 of a tradition already five hundred years old, but that distance in time, when history was handed down in song and story, would be very different from five hundred years in later days.

The Towie in question is in the parish of Turriff, in Aberdeen, and came to be known as Towie-Barclay from the family association with it. The Gartley which the Barclays received by marriage with the heiress, and which later gave them their territorial designation, lies partly in the district of Strathbogie in the county of Aberdeen and partly in the county of Banff, about fifteen miles north-east of Towie.

Macdonald's Place Names, page 82.

The name is spelt in various ways, Garentulach, Grandtully, Garitolly, Gairtly, Garlies, Grintuy and Grantly. The Gaelic-speaking people give as the original form, Carntulaich, "the cairn of the knoll," and point out the knoll with the cairn as proving this derivation. Mr. Macdonald is disposed to think that these names have the same origin, and that the Gaelic form is Garadh-an-tulaich (*dh* mute), which means "the enclosure on the knoll." This is the literal meaning, but, like many similar words, "garadh" also denotes what is enclosed, as a garden, a dwelling or town, so that Garntuly may be fairly translated "the town of the knoll" or, as we now say, the Hilltown, and we have evidence that the name was so understood.

Grandtully is the form retained by another Gartley on Tayside in the county of Perth, near Kinclaven, with which the Barclays were also connected. The history of this Grandtully in Perthshire has been written by Sir William Fraser, whose account, *The Red Book of Grandtully*, begins at the end of the fourteenth century, when the property came into the possession of a branch of the Stewart family. He gives a warning against confusing the two Gartleys. JOHN DE BERKELEY, c. 1069, Towie I.

Robert Barclay of Urie, son of the Quaker Apologist, writing in 1740, appears to attach little importance to Matthew Lumsden's story of the Barclays. He declares his disbelief in a Norman origin for his family on the grounds that such an important post as that of Great Chamberlain to King William the Lion, held by Walter de Berkeley in 1165–89, would only have been bestowed upon one whose family had been more than a century in Scotland.

In the present day we possess more information than was available to Robert Barclay of Urie. In studying contemporary history we find that precisely such an influx of Englishmen and Normans as that described by Matthew Lumsden did actually follow the marriage of the saintly Margaret of England to Malcolm Caenmoir, the Scottish King.

The story at this stage must remain legendary, and it is not clear how the incident of John de Berkeley journeying to Scotland in the retinue of Princess Margaret fits in with our knowledge of the Gloucestershire Berkeleys of the time. The Queen's marriage took place in 1067 or 1068, and it was between 1068 and 1071 that Earl William Fitz-Osborn, to whom Berkeley had been granted after the Conquest, made Roger I provost of the manor of Berkeley from which he took Part i, p. 18. his name, and which was confirmed to him by the Conqueror *circa* 1080. Even if we assume that he had been established in the manor at the shortest possible time after the Conquest, it does not give him long to acquire a territorial designation, which his son would have used.

This, coupled with the fact that Berkeley had been the property of Earl Godwin and an escheat of the Crown after his forfeiture in 1051, and that Godwin's son Tostig helped Malcolm to win the Scottish kingdom, may have led Robert Barclay of Urie to believe in a pre-Conquest settlement of his ancestors in Scotland.

Although this earliest chapter of Scottish Barclay history

JOHN DE BERKELEY, c. 1069, Towie I.

cannot be based on charters and other authentic records, it must be recognised that it is strictly in accordance with probabilities, since it is clear that the family were not of Celtic origin. If absolute precision as to date is impossible, lack of it does not weaken the essential point. We may accept that it was in the company of the English Royal Family, or at their summons, that the Barclays first came to Scotland, and the attractive picture of John de Berchlai accompanying the future Queen agrees with the appearance of his kinsfolk in Scotland, in the enjoyment of wealth and position, by the middle of the next century.

Many races played their part in the history of this island, both north and south, during the early centuries and the changing fortunes of warring kings.

Edgar Atheling and his sisters had been born in Hungary, where their father, Edward the Exile, son of the English Edmund Ironside and of his Danish wife, had found a refuge at a friendly court. Their mother was a Hungarian princess.

The England to which Edward the Confessor intended to make his nephew, the Atheling, heir was Danish as well as English before its destiny was decided by the visit to him of the Norman William, and the subsequent Conquest.

King Malcolm, who was a widower when he wedded the English Margaret, had married his first wife Ingelborg, widow of the Norwegian Earl Thorfinn, for the assistance such a match would contribute towards obtaining control of the northern extremity of our island, which Thorfinn then held.

Malcolm had spent his boyhood in Cumbria, and his youth at the court of Edward the Confessor, who had himself been educated in exile at the court of Normandy. Malcolm was only half Celt, his father, Shakespeare's "gentle Duncan," having married an Anglo-Dane, the daughter of the Northumbrian Earl Siward. Tostig, son of Godwin the great Earl of the West Saxons, who had become Earl of Northumberland, assisted Malcolm to gain the victory over Macbeth, Shakespeare's Macbeth, which won him his kingdom in 1057.

Godwin, who had married his daughter Edith to Edward the Confessor and procured the latter his peaceful accession, had headed the national party against the Norman favourites of the Confessor long before his own son Harold was elected to the throne. He was outlawed in consequence of his opposition to the Norman in 1051, together with his sons.

JOHN DE BERKELEY, c. 1069, Towie I.

It was then that he took refuge with Baldwin, Count of Flanders, father-in-law to his son Tostig, until he returned in the long boats, which carried him to the Isle of Wight and up the Thames, to win back, with the support of the southern counties, the favour of Edward the Confessor, at whose table he expired of apoplexy at Winchester in 1053.

It is easy to understand that when Edgar Atheling and his mother and three sisters were cast upon the shores of Scotland they received a warm welcome from a king whose reign is remarkable as the epoch in which Norman and English influences began to bring civilisation to the Scottish Celtic Kingdom. They would bring with them a higher culture.

The marriage of Margaret was followed by the establishment of Norman and English settlers, and Flemish followed soon after.

Although there is no documentary mention before the fourteenth century of the properties of Gartley and Towie being in the possession of the Barclay family, indications abound to make it possible to connect with one or the other branch members who make their appearance in contemporary records.

We can visualise them during the hundred years after the Conquest as dim warrior figures, employed near the person of the sovereign and taking their part in such few scenes as have not been quite lost to posterity. We can imagine them present when William the Conqueror invaded Scotland in 1072, when Malcolm Caenmoir came to Abernethy, on the Tay, to do homage, and in the expeditions into England undertaken by Malcolm on behalf of his brother-in-law, the Atheling.

Tradition has yet another contribution to make to our story of these early days. A valuable pedigree of the Barclays of Towie (or Tollie) was arranged by John Peter and the Rev. George Peter in 1877 from writings of various dates in the possession of that line of the Barclay family. The

JOHN DE BERKELEY, c. 1069, Towie I.

compilers differ from Matthew Lumsden in that they state that it was John de Berkeley himself who married the heritrix of Gartley and not his eldest son, to whom they give the name of Walter. They also give the name of Alexander to his second son, to whom were transmitted the lands of Towie. Presumably it was this Alexander who, as we shall see, is commemorated as the founder of the castle of Towie and as dying in 1136.

The first documentary evidence of the presence of the Barclays in Scotland is a charter dated 1140, which gives the name of Richard de Berkeley, Dominus de Ardrossan, as witness to a grant by Richard de Morville of the Cuninghame.

Pont's Cuninghame, page 58.

The existence of this charter supports the Barclay tradition, as quoted by Matthew Lumsden, namely, that John de Berchlai came to Scotland from Gloucestershire about the year 1069, and "had many sons." He tells us that the eldest son married the heiress of Gartley, and that the second son succeeded his father in the estates of Towie. The Berkeleys of Berkeley Castle were only granted the great Manor of Berkeley after the Conquest, and they were the first to take as surname that territorial designation. We may therefore presume that Richard de Berkeley, Dominus de Ardrossan, was a younger son of John and brother to Gartley and Towie.

The first notable personage of this early line is a certain Walter de Berkeley, who held the office of Chamberlain to King William the Lion in 1165, but a consideration of dates seems to preclude the theory that he was a son of the first Walter, and to suggest an intervening generation.

There is a legend in the North that one of the Barclays of Gartley went to the Holy Land, leading with him five hundred claymores and returning with only ten. Assuming that Walter, Gartley I, had a son, it might well be this nameless laird of Gartley to whom this legend refers. He would have been contemporary with Roger de Berkeley (III) of Gloucestershire, and it has been suggested by the writer of Part I of this History that as Roger (III) was absent from England at the time of his succession to the Manor of Berkeley, he might have been engaged with his legendary Scottish kinsman in the second Crusade, preached by St. Bernard in 1146.

JOHN DE BERKELEY, c. 1069, Towie I.

Walter, the Chamberlain, and his two brothers, Robert and Theobald, were thus either grandsons or great-grandsons of John de Berchlai.

The Gartley line now emerges from the mists of tradition and we may follow it on the firmer ground of contemporary documents.

PEDIGREE II.

The Gartley Line

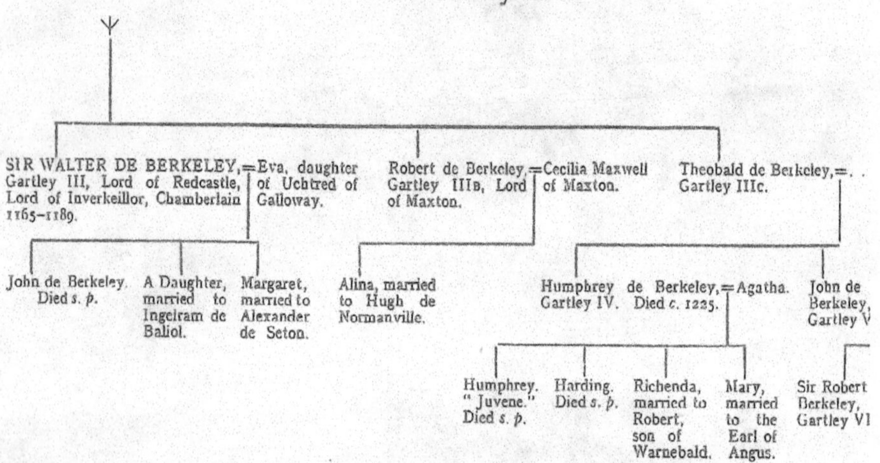
SIR WALTER DE BERKELEY, = Eva, daughter of Uchtred of Galloway.
Gartley III, Lord of Redcastle, Lord of Inverkeillor, Chamberlain 1165–1189.
Robert de Berkeley, = Cecilia Maxwell of Maxton.
Gartley IIIB, Lord of Maxton.
Theobald de Berkeley, = . .
Gartley IIIc.
John de Berkeley. Died s. p.
A Daughter, married to Ingelram de Baliol.
Margaret, married to Alexander de Seton.
Alina, married to Hugh de Normanville.
Humphrey de Berkeley, = Agatha.
Gartley IV. Died c. 1225.
John de Berkeley, Gartley V
Humphrey. "Juvene." Died s. p.
Harding. Died s. p.
Richenda, married to Robert, son of Warnebald.
Mary, married to the Earl of Angus.
Sir Robert Berkeley, Gartley VI

[See Pedigree V, page 96.]

The Gartley Line

SIR WALTER DE BERKELEY, THE CHAMBERLAIN

Sir Walter de Berkeley, 1127–1190, Gartley III.

The reign of Malcolm Caenmoir ended in 1093.

William Rufus summoned him to Gloucester to do homage. He replied by setting out to harry Northumberland, and at Alnwick he was entrapped, and he and his eldest son Edward were slain.

Queen Margaret died three days later at Edinburgh Castle, which was already besieged by Donald Bane, the King's brother. Secretly and through the enshrouding mists her body was conveyed to Dunfermline for burial in the stately church that she had founded. Lovely, learned and pious, she had done much to civilise the northern kingdom, and still more to assimilate the Celtic Church to the rest of Christendom. She was canonised by Pope Innocent IV in 1250.

Chambers's Biographical Dictionary.

The Celtic law of Tanistry (succession to a dead chief by that member of the family elected as fittest) led to warfare which lasted for six years, and only ended when Edgar Atheling, now reconciled to the Normans, led an army into Scotland on behalf of his eldest nephew Edgar and, after much fighting, secured for him his father's throne.

Three sons of Malcolm and Margaret reigned in succession: Edgar 1098-1107, Alexander I 1107-1124, and David 1124-1153.

They were worthy heirs of the culture and saintly character of their mother and of the courage of King Malcolm. Both Alexander and David were brought up in England, and the alliance of their sister Edith (or Matilda) with King Henry I was the first of those marriages which were to unite, in ever closer kinship, the two Royal Houses.

When his elder brother, Alexander, succeeded to the throne of Scotland in 1107, David became Prince of Cumbria, a territory which, besides part of Cumberland, included all southern Scotland, except the Lothians. By his marriage with Matilda, widow of the Norman Earl of Northampton and

SIR WALTER DE BERKELEY, 1127-1190, Gartley III.

sister of the Saxon Earl of Northumbria, he became Earl of Huntingdon. He succeeded his brother on the throne of Scotland in 1124, and in 1127 took oath with other great Barons of England to maintain the right of his niece, Matilda (or Maud), to the English Crown. When Stephen seized the throne, he took up arms on her behalf, and penetrated as far as Durham, where peace was purchased by the confirmation of the Earldom of Huntingdon to his son Henry, and the promise of that of Northumberland. In 1138, however, war was renewed, and King David suffered defeat at the battle of the Standard, near Northampton.

The rest of his reign was devoted to the welding of the different races of Scotland into one nation, and the civilisation of the people. It marks the end of the Celtic and the beginning of the Feudal period in Scotland. Though never formally canonised, he was often called St. David, and his name was inserted in the calendar prefixed to Laud's Prayer Book for Scotland in 1637.

King David died at Carlisle in 1153, and as his only son, Henry, had predeceased him, the throne passed to his grandson, Malcolm.

Malcolm IV, known as Malcolm the Maiden, reigned only twelve years. He accompanied Henry II on an expedition to Toulouse, and was knighted by him at Tours, but the English King appears to have taken advantage of his youth to procure from him the cession of Northumberland and Cumberland. This roused the Earl of Strathearn and five other chiefs to a revolt which Malcolm successfully quelled on his return from France. His short life ended at Jedburgh in 1165. He was succeeded by his brother William, known as the Lion (or Lyon).

During the years thus briefly surveyed English customs pervaded Scotland, and a sojourn at the English Court became usual with the Scottish nobility. Tenure by charter had been growing common before the close of the reign of King David, though only a few examples survive from the reigns of Edgar and Alexander.

In virtue of his combination of offices, the Chamberlain in

[Photograph by Valentine and Sons, Limited

the thirteenth and fourteenth centuries was one of the most important and influential of the great officers of the Scottish Crown. He was at once the collector and the disburser of the Royal revenue, he exercised a jurisdiction over burgs, and from the funds under his control he met all public expenditure, including the charges of the Royal Household, and to a certain extent military expenses.

SIR WALTER DE BERKELEY, 1127-1190, Gartley III.

Exchequer Rolls, Vol. i, xxxiii.

The first layman to hold this high office was Walter de Berkeley, Lord of Reidcastle (or Redcastle). "He was preferred to the Chamberlain's place in 1165, when Nicolaus, his predecessor in the office, was made Chancellor." He is described as being possessed of good estates in Forfarshire, the "Barony of Innerkillour," which he had from King William. The chronicles show that he was senior in position to other Barclays who appear as witnesses, and there is no doubt that he was connected with them, but there is no direct evidence that he was connected with Gartley.

Crawfurd's Officers of State, p. 253.

He bore, however, the same coat-of-arms as that borne by the Barclays of Mathers, the Barclays of Brechin and their acknowledged cadets, and by no other Barclays—viz. Tincture of the field Azure and the crosses Argent—and our assumption that he was head of the House of Gartley is strengthened by the general indication of the records.

Nisbet's Heraldry, Vol. ii, p. 236.

From various chronicles and official records and charters much of the career of Sir Walter de Berkeley, the Chamberlain, may be traced. The duties of his high office would have kept him in close attendance upon the person of his Royal master, William the Lion, in those historic scenes which come before us with the clear outline and vivid colouring of an illuminated manuscript.

In 1166 the Scottish King went to the Court of Henry II at Windsor, where he received back the Honour of Huntingdon and did homage for it, but did not obtain the return of the Earldom of Northumberland for which he had hoped. Later he accompanied King Henry to France, as vassal in the fief of Huntingdon.

At Easter 1170 the Lion was once more at Windsor, and this time accompanied by his heir presumptive, designated in

SIR WALTER DE BERKELEY, 1127-1190, Gartley III.

his frequent appearances as "David the King's brother," upon whom King William bestowed the fief of Huntingdon, presumably by the process of subinfeudation. They both did homage to Henry's son Henry at the latter's coronation, which it will be remembered took place during the lifetime of his father.

King William the Lion, tempted by the recently crowned Henry's grant of the Earldom of Northumberland, entered into an alliance with the rebel Princes, and wasted the English borders. At first he was successful and obtained a truce which enabled him to send assistance to his brother, David Earl of Huntingdon, who was aiding Robert de Beaumont at Leicester against Henry II, and to invade Northumberland. But his good fortune did not last, for the truce came to an end after Easter 1173.

The story of the campaign may be read in the Chronicle of Jordan Fantosme, Spiritual Chancellor of the Diocese of Winchester. He is thought to have been a Scoto-Norman of the twelfth century, and from the brilliance of his descriptive writing may well have been an eye-witness of the events he has preserved for us. He tells of the harrying of the North of England, and of the approach to Wark Castle, when part of the Scottish army was sent to Besford and Bamborough.

Jordan Fantosme (Surtees Soc.), p. 63.

"Very great was the booty which the King's men carry away
They came to (Newcastle)-on-Tyne to their lodgings,
They have joy for that and much amusement,
For they are rich in cattle, oxen and horses,
In clothes and money, in jewels and rings.
Then the King of Scotland sent for his knights,
The Earls of his land, all the best warriors,
Through good advisors he wished to besiege Wark;
He wished to take the castle by means of Flemings and archers,
By good stone bows (perieres), by his very strong engines
And by his slingers and his cross-bow men."

Lawrie's Annals of King William, p. 157.

The assault lasted long, but King William "ceased not to lose." The siege of Wark was abandoned and he marched away to besiege Carlisle.

"Away goes King William with his great gathered host
Towards Carlisle the fair the strong garrisoned city;

Lord Roger de Mowbray and his chivalry,
And lord Adam de Port joins his Border men;
The Earls of Scotland lead the hated people,
Who never had any repugnance to do fiendish things.
They so perform their march . . .
That they could see Carlisle filled with beauty,
The sun lights up the walls and turrets . . .
Lord Robert de Vaux gently begs men
Not to be alarmed nor play the coward;
For if God keeps his life safe and sound
He by no means fears this host nor the King of Albany.
The King summons Roger and Adam to his council,
Walter de Berkeley, who was one of his liegemen:
'Now behold noble knights, a very grand array,
You cannot count the white or the red,
There are so many banners against the sun;
Go for me to Robert, say that I summon him
To surrender the Castle this very moment.'

SIR WALTER DE BERKELEY, 1127-1190, Gartley III.

* * *

They go to Robert de Vaux . . .
He was dressed in a breastplate, leaning on a battlement,
And held in his hand a sharp sword
With a keen edge, he handled it gently . . ."

Lawrie's Annals of King William, p. 161.

The messengers threaten him that "he will have no succour from any living man, and the King of England will never more be his defender, without instant surrender." Surrender was refused, but the reply was couched in such diplomatic, if somewhat contemptuous language that the King of Scotland left Carlisle and proceeded with his host to Appleby, where he found the town undefended and took it.

The upshot of the campaign, however, justified the chronicler in his opinion that those who advised the war against England were "evil councillors of the King of Scotland," though he expressed a high opinion of the fighting qualities of David, the King's brother, who "warred very well."

William the Lion, with a small band of followers, among whom was his Chamberlain, Sir Walter de Berkeley, was ambushed while riding near Alnwick, in July, 1174. The capture was effected by a band of Yorkshire Barons, and we learn from the account of one of the party, the great lawyer-

Sir Walter de Berkeley, 1127-1190, Gartley III.

warrior Ranulf de Glanville, keeper of the Honour of Richmond, that the value of the Chamberlain, when he came to be assessed for ransom later, was 28 marks.

The Scottish King was hurried ignominiously to Henry at Northampton, with his legs hobbled under his horse's belly, and on August 8th Henry sailed for Normandy, taking with him his illustrious captive.

It is suggested by the Editor of the *Calendar of Scottish Documents*, as there is no special entry in regard to so notable a prisoner as the Great Chamberlain, that Walter de Berkeley's passage to Normandy was probably included in the freight of 40 vessels which conveyed Earl William de Mandeville and the King's retinue, with the widowed Countess of Brittany, sister to William the Lion, and other prisoners of high degree in Porchester Castle. They sailed from Southampton to Rouen on August 10th, 1174.

Negotiations between the two kings proceeded slowly during the following months, first at Caen and later at Falaise. We are told that the Scottish King, "all loaded with chains," was visited by numerous friends, this "consolation" being allowed him on the grounds that their presence was necessary to the discussion of terms of peace.

Greatly as William desired freedom, it was not until five months had passed that he submitted to the humiliating terms dictated by the rapacity of Henry.

On December 11th the Treaty of Falaise was signed and William the Lion became the liegeman of the English King, together with his brother, his Barons, the clergy and all his vassals. The castles of Berwick, Roxburgh, Jedburgh, Stirling and Edinburgh were delivered to English garrisons at Scottish expense. The Scottish Church surrendered to the supremacy of the Church of England.

Three days after signing the treaty the Lion sailed for England, leaving behind him his brother and twenty-two Scottish nobles, among whom was Sir Walter de Berkeley, as hostages, until the castles had been duly handed over. Each of these noblemen was further required, after his release, to give a son or next heir in pledge for the terms of the treaty.

The actual Homage of Scotland did not take place until a year later, 1175, and is vividly described in *Gesta of Henry II* by Richard FitzNeal.

SIR WALTER DE BERKELEY, 1127-1190, Gartley III.

"And . . . King Henry went to York and came thither on the feast of St. Lawrence (10 August); and he had there to meet him William, King of Scotland, who had brought with him all the Bishops and Earls and Barons, Knights and Freeholders of his land, from the greatest to the least, to do there homage and allegiance and fealty to the King of England and his heirs forever, against all men, as had been agreed between them at Falaise in Normandy, before the King of Scotland went out from his prison. . . .

This order, always observed, indicated the precedence given to the ecclesiastics.

"When therefore all were assembled in the Church of St. Peter of York, William, King of Scotland, commanded the Earls and Barons to do allegiance and fealty and homage to Henry, King of England, son of Maud the Empress and to King Henry his son; and so it was done.

"At first the King of Scotland himself and David his brother became the vassals of the aforesaid King for all their holdings; and especially for Scotland and Galloway. And touching the sacred Evangels, they swore to him fealty and allegiance against all men; and afterwards became the vassals of the King his son, and swore to him fealty, saving fealty to his father.

"Then similarly, by command of the King of Scotland . . . the Bishops, Abbots, Earls and Barons . . . and they swore that if the King of Scotland drew back from the aforesaid agreement, they would hold with the King of England against him until he came to befitting satisfaction and to do the will of the King.

"And then in the presence of all, the King of England caused to be read and to be confirmed by the King of Scotland and David his brother, the following agreement, which had been made between him and the King of Scotland. . . .

"This is the agreement and the compact which William, King of Scotland, has made with the Lord Henry, King of England, son of Maud, the Empress.

"William, King of Scotland, has become the liegeman of the Lord King against every man, for Scotland and for all his other lands, and has done him fealty as to his liege Lord, as his other vassals were accustomed to do to him. Similarly he has done homage to his son, and fealty, saving his faith to the Lord King his father. . . .

"Moreover the vassals of the Lord King shall hold the lands which they had, and ought to have, of the Lord King, and of the King of Scotland and of his vassals. And the vassals of the King

SIR WALTER DE BERKELEY, 1127-1190, Gartley III.

of Scotland shall hold their lands which they had and ought to have, of the Lord King and his vassals.

"And in token to the Lord King and Henry, his son, and to his heirs, of the sure observance by the King of Scotland and his heirs of this agreement and compact, the King of Scotland has delivered to the Lord King the castle of Roxburgh, and the castle of Berwick, and the castle of Jedburgh, and the castle of Maidens (Edinburgh) and the castle of Stirling. . . .

"Moreover in token of the fulfilment of the aforesaid agreement and compact, the King of Scotland has delivered up to the Lord King his brother, David, as hostage, and Earl Duncan and Earl Waldeve, and Earl Gilchrist, and the Earl of Angus, and Richard de Morville the Constable . . . and Walter de Berkeley and . . .

"When therefore this had taken place at York, immediately the King of Scotland with his household went back to Scotland from York."

We may presume that Walter de Berkeley was present in the Minster for the homage, as was David the King's brother, and that the deliverance of the hostages like that of the surrender of the castles refers to what had already taken place.

It is evident that King William the Lion, during the long months of negotiation, had considerable difficulty in persuading his nobles to submit to the terms of this ignominious treaty, forced upon him by conquest and capture. Many proud Scottish hearts bitterly disagreed with it, not a few rebelled openly.

Numerous Scottish families received grants of land from King William and became vassals for fresh estates at this date, among them cadet Barclays.

We read in the *Scalacronica* of the disputes which arose in consequence of the treaty as follows :

"pur quoi il emprit od ly en Escoce plusours des fitz pusnes der seynours D'Engleterre qi ly estoient beinvoillauntz, at lour dona lez terres dez authres l'y ly estoient rebells. Si estoint Claude des Balliols, de Bruys, de Soulis, et de Moubray et les Saynclers ; les Hayes, les Giffards, les Ramesays, et Laundels, les Biseys, les Berkeleys, les Walenges, les Boyfis, les Montgomeries, les Vaus, les Colevyles, les Frysers, les Grames, les Gourlays, et plusours autres."

The *Scalacronica* is not contemporary testimony. It was written by Sir Thomas de Gray during his imprisonment in Edinburgh, 1355–1356 ; it cannot be taken too literally, as it relates incorrectly the sequence of events, but doubtless it represents the facts in stating that because these families accepted the agreement with England, their cadets or " pusnes " were enriched by the lands of those who did not, and that they returned home to Scotland in the King's train.

SIR WALTER DE BERKELEY, 1127-1190, Gartley III.

During the next fifteen years animosity between the Kings seems to have lessened, for the Vassal William repeatedly attended the English Court, and in 1186 he married a cousin of Henry II, Ermingarde, daughter of the Viscount of Beaumont. But it was not until the accession of Richard I that the wound to Scottish pride was healed, and that only at a price. Richard needed funds to equip his Crusade, and for the sum of 10,000 merks he was willing to surrender all claim of superiority over Scotland.

The work of collecting the good red gold could only have been carried out to the tune of murmurings and discontent, but it was accomplished, and the Treaty of Falaise revoked by the Treaty of Canterbury, on December 5th, 1189. Peace between England and Scotland was now secured for a century.

King William did not resemble his grandfather, King David, who was jestingly nicknamed by one of his successors, James I, " a sair Sanct for the Croon," by reason of the lavish grants of royal property with which he endowed numerous religious houses, for the Abbey of Arbroath was the only personal foundation of " the Lion."

He bestowed upon it thirty-two parish churches, land from Forth to Tay, and the sacred banner of St. Columba.

Founded in 1178, its consecration was delayed until 1197, and it became one of the richest abbeys in Scotland.

Immediately north of Arbroath is Inverkeillor, or Inverkileder, in which lordship, granted to Walter de Berkeley by King William, stood Redcastle. It is reported to have been built by the Chamberlain, and was described by Lewis, as late as 1849, as

" one of the oldest castellated ruins in Angus, small but some of it still immovably strong, with a considerable rampart, rising from the sheer rock almost perpendicular from the sea, and commanding the whole bay of Lunan, at the mouth of the river Lunan."

Sir Walter de Berkeley, 1127-1190, Gartley III.

Near by is the Court Hill, where the Lord of Redcastle held his courts, and two castles, Tappy and Fast, once stood on Court Hill Farm. Fast Castle is said to have been the lord's prison house. There are witch pools in Lunan Water, and the names of Hawk Hill and Gallows Hill, near by, show to what use those spots were severally devoted.

We are told by James Fraser, author of *Polichronicon* in the seventeenth century, that King William lived with his family "at Redcastle in Angus, near the shore," during the years when he was building the Abbey of Arbroath. Walter de Berkeley, generally described as "of Redcastle," would assuredly have been in attendance as Chamberlain if, indeed, he was not at that time the host of the King.

The dedication of the Abbey of Arbroath to St. Thomas of Canterbury has sometimes been held to be an act of direct defiance to the King of England, but that opinion seems hardly justified.

William the Lion and Becket had been well acquainted at the English Court, where indeed the Archbishop had been especially commended to the Prince by the Pope. Canterbury and its shrine was fast becoming the greatest centre of pilgrimage in Christendom. Its proximity to the port of Dover, with all the coming and going for war and crusade, increased its popularity, and King William, in his assiduous cultivation of trade and traffic with the Continent, may well have desired to have a similar centre of attraction in his own kingdom. In his zeal for the Abbey of Arbroath he enlisted the practical interest of his entourage, and among them the Berkeleys.

Lindores Abbey was founded about the same time. Earl David of Huntingdon, "the King's brother," owned the castle adjacent to it. The two abbeys were not far apart, for Arbroath (Aberbrothock) is situated in Forfar, where the river Brothoc falls into the North Sea, while Lindores is in Fife, looking over the Firth of Tay, on the opposite side of which, and midway between the two abbeys, is Dundee.

Lindores Castle is said to have been the property of Duncan Macduff, first thane of Fife. In the woods to the west of it are the remains of an ancient cross, that of Magdrum, and about a mile further south, on the confines of Stratherne, is Macduff's cross, the pedestal of which is still to be seen. A legend tells that after the defeat of the usurper Macbeth in 1057, and the succession of Malcolm Caenmoir to the Scottish throne, Macduff, as a reward for his assistance, was granted special privileges for his kinsmen. Clansmen within the ninth degree of relationship could, on reaching the cross, claim remission of the capital sentence by paying the fine for homicide, nine kye (cows) and a colpindash (young cow). It will be seen later that the Barclays of Mathers had occasion to claim the privilege of Clan Macduff, and obtained pardon for the murder of the sheriff of the Mearns in 1421.

SIR WALTER DE BERKELEY, 1127-1190, Gartley III.

Encyclo. Brit. Vol. xxiv, p. 129.

Lindores has many interesting associations for the Barclays. The Castle was hèld by them through marriage with the Brechin descendants of Earl David, and passed from them to the Earl of Atholl, who was executed in 1437. Chiefs of the Brechin line of Berkeleys were styled "Lord of Lindores," and the Barclays of Collairnie, whose castle was near by, were hereditary Bailies of Lindores from February 20th, 1563, until that office was abolished in 1747.

David "the King's brother" is a romantic figure round whom many legends have gathered. James Fraser tells a picturesque story of the foundation of Lindores Abbey.

"At this time, David Earl of Huntingdon, son to King David, and brother to Malcolm IV, a famous worthy and a great souldier, returned from the Holy Land, and in great danger upon the seas, arrived at length in the Tay, without rudder or tackle, Providence putting him in at Electon, now called Dundee, Aelly in Irish, a rocky place, and now Dune Tay. It is said that in gratitude, he built the famous steeple and church of Dundee and the Abbey of Lindores."

Polichronicon, by James Fraser

If indeed the founding of Lindores was in fulfilment of a vow made in peril at sea, it is strange that there is no allusion to the fact in the foundation charter. A few scattered vestiges are all that exist to-day to show the ancient splendour of the abbey which Earl David so generously endowed with twenty-two churches and many lands.

* * *

When it is realised that we are dealing with the history of a man who lived eight hundred years ago, we count ourselves

Sir Walter de Berkeley, 1127-1190, Gartley III.

fortunate in being able to trace not only his many journeyings but not a little of the private life of Walter de Berkeley the Chamberlain.

Something of an itinerary could be drawn from the long list of places at which he and his kinsmen attested charters, mostly for King William, and the names of his co-witnesses are so often repeated that they constitute a list of those who must have been his close friends. David, "the King's brother," Earls Waldeve and Duncan, Malise, Gillechrist, Gilbert, Richard de Morville the Constable, Roger de Quincey, Richard and William Comyn, William de Laceles (Leslie), Walter and David de Lindeseia (Lindsay), Walter Olifard (Oliphant), Philip de Valoynes and a host of others too numerous to mention.

Sir Walter de Berkeley married the Lady Eva, daughter of Uchtred of Galloway, and had one son and two daughters. He was a man of great possessions, holding land in different parts of the country.

It is recited in a Bull of Pope Alexander III (1175) that he made a grant of land to the Abbey of Holmcultram, in Cumberland.

> "Haec omnia dedi pro animabus Dom mei Reg
> Scocie et pro animabus omn antecessorum
> meorum et meae et sposae meae . . ."

He may have held this land through his wife, or possibly the interest of the Lady Eva in the Abbey led to the benefaction. The grant is confirmed by her brother Roland, son of Uchtred, as overlord.

Dugdale's Monasticon, Vol. v, p. 615.

The people of Galloway were among the most turbulent of the Scottish vassals, but the allegiance of their Lords seems to have been secured later, as we find both Roland and his son, Alan, in the Royal service.

John son of Walter de Berkeley is distinguished by being so described in two instances. In a charter by Alan, son of Walter the Steward of the King of Scotland, the name, partially obliterated "JOA . . . filio Walteri de Berkeley" is followed by that of Robert de Berkeley, David, "the King's brother," Gilbert, Earl of Stratherne, William de

Liber de Melros, Vol. i, p. 84. Acts of Parl. Scotland, Vol. i, p. 388b.

Morev(ille) the King's Constable, and other highly placed witnesses.

Sir Walter de Berkeley, 1127-1190, Gartley III.

Among those present " in curia regis " in Edinburgh (1189-1196) we find " John, son of Walter de Berkeley." His name also occurs in a grant made by his mother, the Lady Eva. It is evident that he predeceased his father.

Walter de Berkeley's eldest daughter succeeded to his estates. Her name has not come down to us, but his "heiress" married Ingelram de Baliol of Barnard Castle in Durham. Her son Henry was, like his grandfather, Lord High Chamberlain. It is said by Crawfurd, the historian, that the family of de Baliol, one of whom afterwards became King of Scotland, gained their first footing in that country by the marriage with the heiress of Sir Walter de Berkeley, Lord of Redcastle.

Crawfurd's Lives, p. 253.

His younger daughter, Margaret, married Sir Alexander de Seton and was ancestress of the Earls of Eglinton and Winton. Sir Alexander de Seton witnesses a donation for Saher de Quincey, Earl of Winchester, to the Abbey of Dunfermline before 1223. He had one son, Secher de Seton.

Sir Walter de Berkeley's wife, the Lady Eva, survived him and married his old friend and co-witness to many documents, Robert de Quincey, a Northamptonshire Baron. Robert de Quincey had been previously married to Orabilis, daughter of William of Ness, who brought him vast estates in Scotland; by her he had one son, Saher de Quincey, afterwards Earl of Winchester. The date of his second marriage cannot be ascertained. He was Justiciar *c.* 1175 and went to Jerusalem 1191, when King William remitted part of a debt due by him to Aaron the Jew of Lincoln. Mr. Lindsay was of opinion that he never returned from the Holy Land, but the Northamptonshire Pipe Rolls for 1198 show that he was in England in that year. He was also one of the witnesses to the foundation charter of Inchaffray.

Scot. Hist. Soc. Inchaffray Charters, p. 8.

His wife, the Lady Eva, was once more a widow before the close of the reign of William the Lion, in 1214, as is shown by the following grant, which is of peculiar interest as giving the names of both her husbands, her son, her brother and sister.

[Photograph by the Rev. Charles W. Barclay

THE RUINS OF THE ABBEY OF ARBROATH

the Abbey of Arbroath by Hugh, the Chancellor, of a toft in the borough of Forfar describes it as near the toft of Walter de Berkeley.

SIR WALTER DE BERKELEY, 1127-1190, Gartley III.

It was while he was Chamberlain that Walter de Berkeley received from the King a grant of Newton, afterwards to be known as Chamberlain Newton, to hold by the service of half a knight.

Arbroath Charters, Vol. i, pp. 13, 329.

King William the Lion founded the Abbey of Arbroath in 1178, and his Chamberlain bestowed upon that foundation a considerable benefaction, namely the church of St. Macconoc of Inverkileder. He granted to the said church and Master Henry, the parson, "the King's clerk and mine," the "grescanum" and all the service which the land of the said church and the men dwelling on the said land were wont to do to the thanes of Inverkileder and "afterwards to me": Henry and the men dwelling on the said lands to be quit of all "canum" and rent belonging to us or to any other lay person, and they were to have common of pasture "with me and all my men in all my land of Inverkileder."

Ibid. Vol. i, p. 39.

Ibid. Vol. i, p. 37.

A renewal of this benefaction is found later, when Ingelram de Baliol, then Lord of Redcastle and Inverkileder, through his wife, the daughter of Walter de Berkeley, adds to it the "Tithes of my Mill," in those days a valuable addition.

Ibid. Vol. i, p. 38.

In the Cartulary of Arbroath we find a particularly interesting document. It is a grant of William the Lion of one carucate of land in Monethin to the Abbey, signed at Perth 1178-80, and among the witnesses it bears the names of Roger de Berkeley and Walter de Berkeley "Camerario." Charles Wright Barclay, writer of the first part of this history, was of the opinion that this record referred to the head of the Gloucestershire line, Roger IV of Dursley, at that time paying a visit to his Scottish kinsman, the Chamberlain.

Ibid. Vol. i, p. 64.

Part I, p. 45.

This is the only reference to a Roger de Berkeley in this generation in Scotland, though the name appears some years later.

The charters witnessed by Sir Walter de Berkeley are too numerous to mention in detail. They are to be found in the Cartularies of Kelso (1177-82), Melrose (1171-77),

SIR WALTER DE BERKELEY, 1127-1190, Gartley III.

Arbroath (1177-82), Glasgow (1182-90), Dunfermline (1182 or later) and others.

The isolated instance which appears in the Cartulary of Cupar Abbey of "William de Berkeley, Chamberlain," points to a clerical error, Walter de Berkeley being intended. Crawfurd, in his *Lives of the Officers of the Crown*, does not allude to him, and in the Preface to the extracts of the Exchequer Rolls of Scotland, by John Stewart and George Burnett, they state that they do not believe that William de Berkeley, Chamberlain, ever existed.

Exchequer Rolls, Vol. ii, p. cxix.

ROBERT DE BERKELEY

ROBERT DE BERKELEY, Gartley IIIB.

It is evident from the records that Walter de Berkeley had two brothers, Robert and Theobald.

Robert de Berkeley's name appears in numerous records and so frequently as witness to Royal Charters in the reigns of David I, Malcolm IV and William the Lion that it seems likely that he held some Court appointment.

He married Cecilia, daughter of Liulph, son of Maccus, and through his marriage became possessed of the Maccus town lands, in Roxburgh, which had been granted by King David to Maccus (Maxwell).

Before the year 1200 Sir Hugh de Normanville and Alina, his wife, were in possession of this Manor of Maccustoun, so we may presume that Alina was daughter and heiress of Robert de Berkeley.

Reg. Mag. Sig. 1424-1513, 804.

In a charter of King David to the burgesses of Inverness, granting quitclaims of customs of all his lands, we find the name of Robert de Berkeley as witness. This must have been previous to 1153.

Robert de Berkeley and Cecilia, his wife, and his heir (probably daughter) granted to the Abbey of Melrose a carucate of land in Maxton, "east of Derestrete," with rights of pasture for 100 sheep, 12 oxen, 6 kine, 3 horses and one sow with their fodder, wherever the donor's own animals or those of his men, in the said vill, had theirs. The gift also included stone from his quarry at Alwerdene for the building of the Abbey: "ad sufficienciam ad edificia domus de Melros."

Liber de Melros, Vol. i, No. 90.

This grant was made for the souls of King David and King Malcolm, of Earl Henry, and for the salvation of King William and David his brother, as well as of Robert and Cecilia, the donors. It is a complete memorial to the Scottish Royal family, evidently made before the marriage of King William to Ermengarde, his Queen, in 1198. Walter, the Chamberlain, is among the witnesses to its confirmation, and to mark the benefaction the monks of Melrose set up a great stone as one of their boundaries, " magnam petram in testimonium erexerunt."

ROBERT DE BERKELEY, Gartley IIIB.

Liber de Melros, Vol. i, p. xix, note.

Hugh de Normanville and his wife Alina later granted to the Abbey lands called Kelvesete and Fanlawe, in exchange for those given by Robert and Cecilia, in Maxton "east of Derestrete."

Ibid. No. 92.

In the Kambuskenneth Cartulary we find Robert de Berkeley witnessing, *c.* 1165, the grant of King William of a full toft in his new burg of Perth to St. Mary of Kambuskenneth, and the same cartulary contains one of the numerous examples of Robert and Walter de Berkeley acting as co-witnesses, of which the spelling is interesting :

" Waltero de Barkillie camarario, Roberto de Berkele.
—Stirling 1180."

Robert de Berkeley's name also appears as a witness to the charter of Alan, son of Walter, previously referred to, immediately following that of " JOA . . . filio Walteri de Berkeley."

Liber de Melros, No. 97.

THEOBALD DE BERKELEY

THEOBALD DE BERKELEY, Gartley IIIC.

Of Theobald de Berkeley we know nothing, except that he was the father of two sons, Humphrey and John.

Unlike his brothers, he granted no benefactions and witnessed no charters.

These were the days when the interest of all Christendom centred in Jerusalem. The crosses patées in the armorial bearings of the Barclay family point to participation in the Crusades, and if Theobald was one of those who " put on the Cross " it would account for the absence of his name in

THEOBALD DE BERKELEY, Gartley IIIc.

the various records with which others of his generation were associated.

We have, however, two authorities to prove his existence, and genealogists agree that he was of the house of Gartley.

His name appears in a charter made in 1242 between the Abbot of Arbroath and John Wishard concerning the lands of Conveth, Halton and Scottiston. It is herein stated that the said lands were granted by King William to "Umfrido de Berkeley filio Theobaldi."

Arbroath Charters, Vol. i, p. 206.

Also in an agreement between the Abbot of Arbroath and John de Berkeley (Gartley V), the said John is referred to as "Filio Theobaldi."

SIR HUMPHREY DE BERKELEY

Sir Humphrey de Berkeley, 1160-1226, Gartley IV.

The name of Sir Humphrey de Berkeley occurs in a number of documents, but there does not appear to be one in existence bearing his territorial designation. Three authorities, however, Sir Robert Douglas in his *Peerage* (1794), Mr. Wood in his later edition of the same work (1813) and Mr. Anderson in his *Scottish Nation*, style him "Sir Humphrey de Berkeley of Gartley," and his descendants, the Barclays of Mathers, many years later, possessed the same property held by him in the Mearns in 1198.

The records indicate that Sir Walter de Berkeley the Chamberlain, as head of the family, granted Gartley to his nephew Humphrey and secured it to the male line, when by the death of his son John he was left without heirs male.

Sir Humphrey de Berkeley was a man of high position, and in great favour with King William the Lion, who bestowed upon him and his heirs, "for homage and services rendered," two extensive properties, the lands of Balfeith, and the lands of Conveth, Halton and Scottiston, in the Mearns.

Arbroath Charters, Vol. i, p. 206.

By his wife Agatha he had two daughters, Richenda and Maud (or Mary).

Playfair states that he had two sons, and in his transcript of a charter in the Cartulary of Arbroath he gives their names as "et Umfredi et Harduini nostrorum filiorum." Mr. Innes and Mr. Chalmers in their work for the Bannatyne Club quote the same charter in the original Latin, which reads "et heredum meorum," no names being given, but the name of "Umfredi juvene" is found among the witnesses. The point is of small importance as, if sons he had, it is evident that they predeceased their father, for the two daughters of Sir Humphrey are described as wealthy heiresses.

Arbroath Charters, Vol. i, p. 60.

Richenda married Robert, son of Warnebald, ancestor of the Cunningham family, and Maud (or Mary) married Duncan, Earl of Angus, son of her father's close associate and constant co-witness, Gilchrist, Earl of Angus.

Sir Humphrey de Berkeley, 1160-1226, Gartley IV.

The first mention of Humphrey de Berkeley is found in a deed, previously quoted as bearing the names of Roger de Berkeley (of Dursley) and Walter de Berkeley, the Chamberlain, whereby King William grants to the Abbey of Arbroath one carucate of land in Monethin. The land in question is described as having been measured by Humphrey de Berkeley, with certain other "probi homines" of the King, in Angus and Mearns. This points to his holding some official position. The term "probi homines" is probably a description of the smaller tenants in chief. Although included among them at this time, it is evident that acquisitions of property raised Humphrey above that status later. He appears as a witness to the King's grant of lands in Strathaven to William Giffard, and also to two confirmations of Turpin, Bishop of Brechin (1178–98). He is also a witness at Montrose with Robert de Berkeley, his uncle, to the grant of King William of the church of Agilgirg to the Abbey of St. Andrews, to which Abbey a general confirmation records that Humphrey granted the church and tithes of Conveth (Laurencekirk).

Rait's Scottish Parliament, p. 15.

Newbottle Register, p. 288. Reg. Brechin, p. 257.

Reg. St. Andrews, p. 229. *Ibid.* 231.

Sir Humphrey de Berkeley granted to the Abbey of Arbroath certain lands in Balfeith, which he had received at the hands of his Sovereign Lord, King William. The date of this grant would be between 1198 and 1211, as the young Prince Alexander is included in the list of the members of the royal family for the welfare of whose souls the gift was made.

Arbroath Charters, Vol. i, p. 206.

The deed has many interesting points. The property is described as having been perambulated according to an assize of the Kingdom, in the presence of Matthew Bishop of Aberdeen and Gilbert of Strathearn, by Angus McDuncan and other "probi homines" of the King in Angus and Mearns. The boundaries are precisely set down "inter rivulum de Munbedachyn et acquam de Bervyn," and the rights include peatery and pasture from Humphrey's "feu of Kinkell and Conveth." The monks were to have common right of pasture in Humphrey's wood adjoining the monastery buildings, grazing for a hundred beasts, as many swine, and as numerous a breed of horses as they might choose to have, in Tuberlach, Crospath and Glenferyn, also the right to build a mill.

Among the witnesses are "Agatha sposa mea" and "Umfredi juvene," and to the confirmation of this donation by King Alexander II Robert de Berkeley, uncle to the donor, is a witness.

SIR HUMPHREY DE BERKELEY, 1160-1226, Gartley IV.

Sir Humphrey de Berkeley was succeeded in the estates of Gartley by his brother John.

JOHN DE BERKELEY

John de Berkeley, c. 1226, Gartley V.

John de Berkeley (Gartley V) witnessed on two occasions for Roger Bishop of St. Andrews. One charter is undated, but the other was executed "in the year of the birth of Alexander, son of the illustrious William, King of Scotland," 1198.

Arbroath Charters, Vol. i, pp. 101, 103.

After the death of his brother Sir Humphrey, and at some date previous to the year 1226, John de Berkeley appears to have disputed the legality of the grant by Humphrey, of the lands of Balfeith and the rights over Kinkell and Conveth, to the Abbey of Arbroath, presumably upon the ground that the said property had been bestowed by King William upon Humphrey *and his heirs*.

Robert Barclay (Urie III) states that John de Berkeley

> " turned the Abbot and Monks out of all their possessions in the lands ; but was obliged with the consent of his son and heir, Robert de Berkeley, to come to an agreement with them to pay to him and his heirs, in all time coming, the sum of thirteen merks of silver yearly."

Genealogical Account, p. 8.

Further, Robert Barclay states that the agreement of John de Berkeley and its subsequent confirmation by King Alexander II were among documents "registrate in the ancient cartulary of Aberbrothwick in the Advocates Library in Edinburgh," whence they were extracted by him. Neither are included in the printed list of that cartulary, but transcripts (1740) are in the possession of the family, and read as follows :

Bury Hill Papers.

An Agreement made between the Abbot and the monks of Arbroath of the one part and John de Berkeley and his son Robert of the other.

This is an agreement made between the Abbot and monks of St. Thomas the Martyr of the one part, John, the son of Theobald, and Robert his heir of the other, with the consent and approbation of our Sovereign Lord King Alexander. To wit the said John, the son of Theobald, and Robert his heir have given for them and their heirs to God and the blessed St. Thomas, the Martyr, in Arbroath, and the monks there serving God, in free pure and perpetual alms, all the right they had or should have to the lands and heritages formerly belonging to Humphrey, brother to the aforesaid John, in Scotland, with whatever justly pertained thereto for the soul of good memory of William illustrious King of Scotland, and for the soul of the aforesaid Humphrey and for the souls of his ancestors and successors.

JOHN DE BERKELEY, c. 1226, Gartley V.

Yet so that the said John retain and keep possession of the said lands and heritage in feu and vassalage of the forenamed Abbot and monks paying them yearly one pound of incense at the Feast of the Translation of St. Thomas, the Martyr, reserving always to the said Abbot and monks for ever the Mill of Conveth with full appurtenances thereof out of which they shall pay yearly to the said John and his son Robert thirteen merks of silver at two terms of the year to wit one half at Whitsunday, the other half at Martinmas in winter. The said John and his heirs being fully to answer to all services due to the said lands to our Sovereign Lord the King, but the Abbot and monks shall acquit and defend the said John and his heirs at the King's hands of any failure or deficiency that shall happen in the service and shall make them up themselves, and it is understood that neither the said John nor any of his heirs shall either divide, give away or diminish the same. The advice, assent or liberty of the said Abbot or monks for themselves on the one part and John, the son of Theobald, and Robert his heir for them and their heirs on the other part do solemnly vow and swear that they shall never contradict this agreement nor in any way presume to try and evade or shun it and for the better certainty and security in all times coming both parties affix their seals to one anothers doubles and also have appointed the seals of these honourable men

G. Lord Bishop of Brechin.
Lord William de Bosco, Chancellor of our Lord the King.
Lord Robert de Lundun, brother to the illustrious King Alexander.

Witnesses. William, chaplain to the Lord Bishop of Brechin.
Magister Rudolph de Hart.
Mag Andrew de Perth.
Mag Hugh de Melburn.
Richard, clerk to the Lord Chancellor, and many others.

CONFIRMATION of the above agreement by King Alexander II.

Alexander by the grace of God King of Scots to all honest men within his dominions both clergy and laity Greeting.

Know ye all by these presents that we have granted and confirmed that agreement made between the Abbot and the monks of St. Thomas, the Martyr, in Arbroath, of the one part and John, son of Theobald, and Robert his heir of the other part concerning a

JOHN DE BERKELEY, c. 1226, Gartley V.

donation which the said John and Robert his heir have made to God and the Blessed St. Thomas, the Martyr, of Arbroath, and the monks serving or who shall serve there in pure free and perpetual charity of all the right they had or could have in all the lands and heritage that belonged to Humphrey de Berkeley, brother to the said John, in Scotland, with everything justly pertaining thereto and of the whole Mill of Conveth with all its privileges : firmly and inviolably keep for ever as is concerted in writing, reserving always what services are due to us.

Witnesses. Gregory, Bishop of Brechin.
William de Bosco, our Chancellor.
Robert de Lunde, our brother.
Henry Lundie and Mag Adam, our chaplains.
Hugh Cameron. Thomas Stibbin and Richard clerk.
At Dundee. 1 January.

Robert de Lunde or Lundun was a natural son of King William the Lion.

Robert Barclay asserts that this agreement was made after the death of Richenda, daughter and heiress of Humphrey, but that is clearly an error. William de Bosco, whose name appears in both agreement and confirmation, was Chancellor to Alexander II from the commencement of his reign until the year 1226, when

Crawfurd's Lives, p. 11.

"being worn out with age and unable to undergo the fatigue of the place, he quit the great seal to the Archdeacon of Glasgow Mr. Sterling."

It is clear that Richenda, daughter of Humphrey, had inherited from her father some property closely adjacent to the lands over which her uncle, John de Berkeley, was thus concerned to safeguard his overlordship, for in 1238 we find Robert, son of Warnebald, and Richenda his wife granting to the Abbey of Arbroath their fee in the parish of Fordun, in the Mearns, namely the "two Tubertachthas and Glenferkeryn and Kynkell and Kulbak and Monbodachyn." The gift is made for the souls of our ancestors and successors "in this our extreme affliction," and the confirmation of King Alexander II in the same year repeats this phrase as to their affliction.

Arbroath Charters, Vol. i, p. 198.

Ibid. Vol. i, pp. 198, 199.

In 1245 Richenda confirms, as a widow, the gift she had made with her late husband "in their great affliction," and the

King's confirmation in the following year styles her Richenda daughter and heiress of Humphrey de Berkeley and Agatha his wife, and again refers to her sorrow and grievous losses. There is nothing to indicate the nature of the affliction thus pathetically recorded.

JOHN DE BERKELEY, c. 1226, Gartley V.

In the second year of Alexander III (1251), we find the confirmation of another grant made by Richenda in her widowhood. With the consent of the Abbot and monks of Arbroath, to whom she refers as "our lords," she granted to Roger Wyrfant the land which Hugh, son of Waldeve, had held of her in Conveth, "to be held of her and her heirs at a peppercorn rent."

St. Andrews Charters, p. 285.

The lands of Conveth (now Laurencekirk), in the Howe of the Mearns, were the subject of many deeds and, it would seem, not a little controversy. Humphrey de Berkeley had granted the church and tithes of Conveth to the Abbey of St. Andrews. When granting Balfeith to the Abbey of Arbroath he had included certain rights in the fee of Conveth, but retained the mill, in those days a valuable property. John de Berkeley surrendered it to the monks, as we have seen in the Agreement. The mill is omitted from the grant of Richenda and her husband, but included in the final confirmation of her grant, as a widow, by King Alexander II in 1245.

The small number of signatures in existence of John de Berkeley and his son, Robert, suggests that they spent their days withdrawn from public affairs. Gartley, being in Banffshire, would be at a remote distance from the Scottish Court.

SIR ROBERT DE BERKELEY

SIR ROBERT DE BERKELEY, 1226-1262, Gartley VI.

Sir Robert de Berkeley (Gartley VI), already mentioned as concurring in his father's agreement with the monks of Arbroath, witnesses at Scone, in 1247, the grant of a gift of land, in Kyntulach, by Orabilis de Say, sister and heir of Lord Hugh de Say, formerly the wife of Reginald de Warrenne. His co-witness was Malise, Earl of Stratherne.

Scone Charters, p. 56.

His name also occurs in the report of an inquisition, held by Sir Albert Uviet, Sheriff of Lanark, on 5th March 1262–3, to decide a matter concerning a grant of the lands of Sornefaloch, Hayfurst and Drumgran, by Henry de Wiston to Hugh de Moravia (Moray). The list of jurors is headed by Sir Robert de Berkeley, and their verdict records that Henry de Wiston was coerced by violence and fear and imprisonment.

Cal. Scot. Doc. Vol. i, p. 555, No. 2677.

In thus tracing the distinguished personages in the Barclay line at this period, it should be realised that behind them must have stood many cadet families, of whom no record remains. Under the feudal system only those who held lands were of importance, in that they were in a position to provide men for military service. Cases are recorded of younger sons in these days working as labourers on the paternal estates and only when the elder line failed and succession devolved on him as heir male did a cadet assume importance.

In the reign of Alexander II we find in the Cartulary of Melrose an isolated mention of a Laurence de Berkeley who witnessed a charter of Aufrida, daughter of Edgard, but there is no clue to his connection with others of his name.

Melrose Charters, Vol. i, p. 83, No. 201.

During the lives of Humphrey de Berkeley and his brother changes on the throne of Scotland and England had each in turn imperilled the amity between the two countries.

On the accession of King John, King William the Lion did homage to him at Lincoln for his English possessions, but there was no kindly feeling between the two monarchs.

Open rupture was narrowly averted when the English King tried to build a castle at Tweedmouth and thus ruin the trade of Berwick, at that time the most important commercial city in Scotland. The Scots drove away the builders and levelled the castle, and for some time both kings kept threatening armies on the Border.

Sir Robert de Berkeley, 1226-1262, Gartley VI.

David, Earl of Huntingdon, "the King's brother," allied himself with the English Barons in their struggle against John's injustice and extortion, and in 1212 the English King demanded of him not only the person of his son John, known as "le Scot," as hostage for his fidelity, but also the instant surrender of Earl David's castle of Fotheringhay, in Northamptonshire, threatening to take it by force if his order was not instantly obeyed.

The illness and death of William the Lion at Stirling, in December 1214, brought Earl David to Scotland, for chroniclers relate how he met the body of his brother, at the Bridge of Perth, and dismounting from his horse, though "now beset with age and infirmities," insisted on lifting one arm of the bier upon his shoulder and acting for a while as bearer. He accompanied the funeral cortège to the place of sepulture, in the church of the Abbey of Arbroath, and stood by the grave, "lamenting as became a brother."

He survived William only four years, but he lived to participate in one of the greatest events in the constitutional history of the English people. The Barons, among whom his name is recorded, at length brought King John to bay, and on 15th June 1215 the great charter of liberties, "Magna Carta," was sealed at Runnymede. Less than a week later King John ordered the release of Earl David's son and other hostages, and the restoration of his castle of Fotheringhay.

Considerable social progress marked the reign of William the Lion, who extended the influence of civilisation by holding his courts in such remote places as Elgin, Nairn and Inverness. Many important towns in Scotland date their charters from his reign. In spite of constant risings in various parts, there was great increase of commerce, fostered in the towns of the North by a similar league to the great continental "Hansa" which united for mutual trade and support the cities of the Baltic.

Alexander II, the son of King William's old age, was only

Sir Robert de Berkeley, 1226-1262, Gartley VI.

seventeen years old when he was crowned at Scone, on 10th December 1214.

In the hope of gaining Northumberland, he entered into league with the English Barons and, crossing the Tweed with a strong force, laid siege to Norham.

King John, enraged by this action of the youth, whom he scornfully dubbed "the little red fox," marched north with a host of savage mercenaries, and wasted the countryside with fire and sword. He crossed into Lothian, and destroyed Haddington and Dunbar. Alexander retreated to Edinburgh and John followed, but finding that the country could not support his troops, he returned to England, sacking and plundering. The men of Galloway, always conspicuous for their barbarities, were dismissed from his following for having, among many outrages, burned the Monastery of Holmcultram in Cumberland.

The Scottish King was present at the signing of Magna Carta and subsequently did homage, at Dover, to Louis of France, who came at the invitation of the Barons to assume the crown of England.

The death of King John and the victory of his son, Henry III, at Lincoln changed the whole state of affairs, and in 1217 Alexander did homage to Henry and was invested with the Honour of Huntingdon. Four years later the bond between them was drawn closer by his marriage with Princess Joan, eldest sister of Henry III, and peace followed, though Alexander still claimed Northumberland, and Henry upheld the right of the Archbishop of Canterbury to supremacy over the Scottish Church.

Alexander II early displayed that wisdom and strength of character in virtue of which he holds so high a position among the Scottish kings, but his authority over the kingdom was but imperfectly established, and insurrections were frequent, both in the North and South of Scotland.

In order to follow the course of events during this century, it should be borne in mind that there were seven great Scottish earldoms among whose Earls or Mormaers the King of Scotland was originally *primus inter pares*: Angus—now the

Sir Robert de Berkeley, 1226-1262, Gartley VI.

county of Forfar, with Mearns—now the county of Kincardine; Athole, with Gowrie—now the north and east of Perthshire; Caithness, with Sutherland; Moray, with Ross; Fife, with Fortreve—now County Fife; Mar, with Buchan—now the counties of Aberdeen and Banff; and Stratherne, with Monteith—now the southern part of Perthshire.

The rigorous exaction of tithes and other ecclesiastical dues excited a violent outbreak in Caithness, resulting in the murder of the Bishop, who was burned alive in his palace, in 1222.

Alexander put to death no fewer than four hundred persons who were implicated, and the Earl of Orkney and Caithness was punished for his connivance in the murder by the forfeiture of his estates, which he was afterwards permitted to redeem. In 1231 the Earl was murdered and burnt in his own castle, out of revenge, it is said, for his share in the death of the Bishop.

A still more formidable commotion broke out in Galloway in 1233, which may be recorded as instancing the turbulent state of the country, and having a bearing on subsequent events.

Alan, Lord of Galloway, Lord High Constable of Scotland and the most powerful subject in the kingdom, died without male issue. He was son of Roland, who rendered important service to King William the Lion, and was nephew, it will be remembered, to the Lady Eva, wife of Sir Walter de Berkeley, the Chamberlain. Alan of Galloway had been twice married. He left three daughters, to whom he bequeathed his vast territories. His only daughter by his first wife married Roger de Quincey, Earl of Winchester, who in her right claimed the office of Constable.

Alan's second wife was Margaret, the eldest daughter of David, Earl of Huntingdon, brother to William the Lion. By her Alan had two daughters—Christian, who married the son of the Earl of Albemarle and died childless; and Devorguila, who became the wife of John de Baliol of Barnard Castle, grandson of Walter de Berkeley, the Chamberlain. This Devorguila was the mother of John Baliol, presently to be seen as successful competitor for the Scottish crown, and remembered as the founder of Balliol College, Oxford.

SIR ROBERT DE BERKELEY, 1226-1262, Gartley VI.

The Galwegians, upon the death of Earl Alan, refused to submit to the partition of their country among the daughters and took up arms in support of the claim of Thomas, Alan's natural son. Aided by an Irish chief, Gilderoy, they ravaged the adjacent districts with barbarous severity, and placed the King himself in imminent peril, from which he was with difficulty extricated by the Earl of Ross. The war was carried on for several years, but in the end the leaders submitted to the King's mercy and were pardoned.

In consequence of dissensions between the Scottish and the English Kings, a conference was held at York, in September 1237, and it was agreed that certain land in Northumberland and Cumberland should be given to Alexander in full satisfaction of all his demands.

Joan, Queen of Scotland, sister to King Henry, died childless in 1238, and the marriage of Alexander the following year to Mary de Couci, daughter of a great Baron of Picardy, probably helped to weaken the bond between the Kings, but they still continued on friendly terms, for when Henry planned an expedition to France in 1242 he entrusted the Border provinces to the charge of Alexander.

In the same year an incident occurred which nearly plunged the two countries into war. Walter Bysset, a member of a great Norman house, which held extensive possessions near Loch Ness, was unhorsed at a tournament at Haddington by the Earl of Athole. A day or two later the Earl, a young nobleman distinguished for his knightly accomplishments, was murdered and the house where he lodged burnt to the ground. Suspicion fell upon the Byssets, and popular clamour was directed against the uncle of Walter Bysset, head of the family, as instigator of the crime. The King and Queen exerted themselves to protect the Byssets, but public feeling was so strong that their estates were forfeited and they were further compelled to take oath that they would undertake a pilgrimage to Jerusalem, and there, for the rest of their lives, pray for the soul of the murdered Earl. Walter Bysset, however, fled to England, where he found refuge at the Court of Henry III. There he represented that Alexander, being a vassal of England, had no right to inflict such a punishment on his nobles without permission of his liege Lord, and further he seems to have inflamed the anger of Henry by declaring that Scotland was an asylum for the enemies of the English King.

SIR ROBERT DE BERKELEY, 1226-1262, Gartley VI.

Henry thereupon assembled an army, composed mainly of Flemish auxiliaries and men from Ireland, and marched North, threatening to invade Scotland. Alexander mustered a great force to resist the invasion, and an English contemporary records that

> "the Scottish cavalry were brave and well mounted, although their horses were neither of the Spanish nor the Italian breed, and the horsemen were clothed in armour of iron network. The infantry approached to one hundred thousand, all animated by the exhortations of their clergy and by confession, courageously to fight and resolutely to die in the just defence of their native land."

Hostilities were averted, for Alexander was well liked by the English nobles, who came to the war with little enthusiasm, and through the exertions of Richard, Earl of Cornwall, brother of King Henry, and the Archbishop of York, a treaty was concluded in 1244 by which, among other agreements, a marriage was arranged between the young son of the Scottish King and the daughter of Henry III. Alan Durward, the "most accomplished knight and the best military leader in Scotland," Henry de Baliol and David de Lindsay, with other knights and prelates swore on the soul of their Lord the King that the treaty should be kept inviolate by him and his heirs.

There is no record that Berkeleys took part in this crisis, but the names of the "Bissets and the Berkeleys" so frequently appear together in ancient ballads that there seems no doubt that the two families were closely associated.

In 1249 Alexander II undertook an expedition against Angus, Lord of the Isles and of Argyle, but he was seized with a fever when the royal fleet was at Kerrara, opposite the Bay of Oban, and died on the 9th of July.

He was succeeded by his son Alexander, a child of eight years old, whose accession was the signal for plot and counterplot, and in the stirring events which followed Berkeleys both of Gartley and of Towie had their share.

PEDIGREE III.

The Towie Line

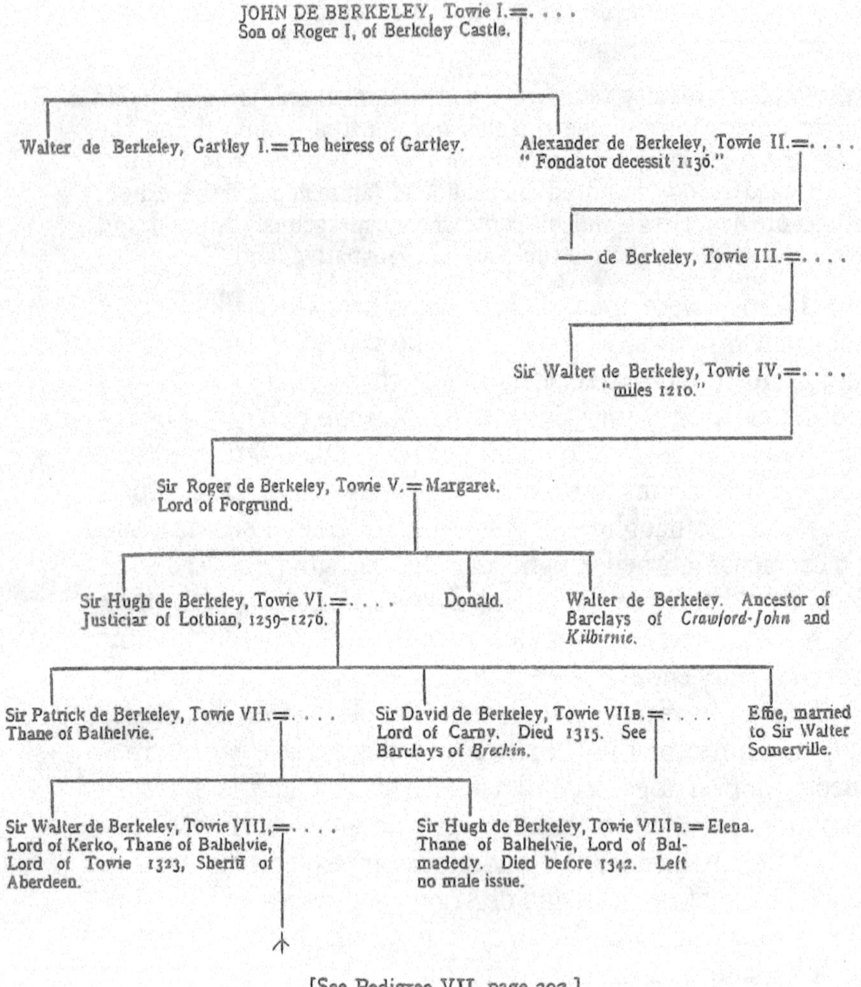
JOHN DE BERKELEY, Towie I.=. . . .
Son of Roger I, of Berkeley Castle.
Walter de Berkeley, Gartley I.=The heiress of Gartley.
Alexander de Berkeley, Towie II.=. . . .
" Fondator decessit 1136."
—— de Berkeley, Towie III.=. . . .
Sir Walter de Berkeley, Towie IV,=. . . .
"miles 1210."
Sir Roger de Berkeley, Towie V.=Margaret.
Lord of Forgrund.
Sir Hugh de Berkeley, Towie VI.=. . . .
Justiciar of Lothian, 1259–1276.
Donald.
Walter de Berkeley. Ancestor of Barclays of *Crawford-John* and *Kilbirnie*.
Sir Patrick de Berkeley, Towie VII.=. . . .
Thane of Balhelvie.
Sir David de Berkeley, Towie VIIB.=. . . .
Lord of Carny. Died 1315. See Barclays of *Brechin*.
Effie, married to Sir Walter Somerville.
Sir Walter de Berkeley, Towie VIII,=. . . .
Lord of Kerko, Thane of Balbelvie, Lord of Towie 1323, Sheriff of Aberdeen.
Sir Hugh de Berkeley, Towie VIIIB.=Elena.
Thane of Balhelvie, Lord of Balmadedy. Died before 1342. Left no male issue.

[See Pedigree VII, page 202.]

The Towie Line

The notable member of the Berkeley family in the reign of Alexander III is Sir Hugh de Berkeley, and we now arrive at a point in our history where the examination of chronicles and documents not available to previous genealogists compels departure from their conclusions.

John de Berkeley, c. 1069, Towie I.

Robert Barclay of Urie and Nisbet in his almost identical statements give only one generation between John de Berkeley (Gartley V) and his son Robert (Gartley VI), who made the agreement with the monks of Arbroath, previous to 1226, and Alexander de Berkeley (Gartley XB) and his wife Catherine Keith, to whom Mathers was granted in 1351. They name as successor to Sir Robert de Berkeley (Gartley VI) "Hugh de Berkeley of Gartley, who obtained a grant of the lands of Westerton from King Robert Bruce." Comparison of dates proves this erroneous, and the grant to Hugh de Berkeley refers, as we shall see, to a later Hugh, who was not of Gartley but of Towie (VIIIB).

Genealogical Account, p. 10.

Nisbet's Heraldry, Vol. ii, p. 238.

Modern research reveals members of both lines who took their part in the troubles in Scotland during the next hundred years.

In the reign of Alexander II, and previous to the year 1226, we find record of a Roger de Berkeley, undoubtedly a man of great importance and property in Scotland. He is described as a knight and, judging by the imposing retainers who witness to his benefactions, lived in considerable state. Sir Roger de Berkeley was a contemporary of Sir Robert de Berkeley (Gartley VI), and although it is not so stated, it seems clear that he was head of the Towie line.

It has already been related that John de Berkeley (Towie I), who arrived in Scotland in the retinue of Margaret, the King of England's sister, received from Malcolm Caenmoir the lands of Towie, and that when the eldest son obtained the lands of Gartley by marriage, the said John bestowed his estate of Towie upon his second son, Alexander.

Alexander de Berkeley, . . . -1136, Towie II.

It is said that the Berkeleys of Towie originally lived at the

ALEXANDER DE BERKELEY, . . .-1136, Towie II.

castle of Cullen, near Auldhaven in Banffshire, but no vestige of it remains, and its exact site is uncertain. It was probably a type of castle not uncommon along the coasts of Kincardine, Aberdeen and Banff, of simple construction, and designed for defence rather than comfort.

The castle of Towie, near Turriff, in Aberdeenshire, was built or rebuilt in the sixteenth century, and some stones more ancient than the edifice, but of uncertain date, were set over the doorway. One of these stones bears the inscription " Sir Alexander Barclay of Tolly foundator decessit A.D. 1136." This is doubtless a pious commemoration of the first of the Towie line, second son of the original John de Berkeley. The other stone reads as follows: " Sir Walter Barclay of Tolly miles foundit 1210."

SIR WALTER DE BERKELEY, C. 1210, Towie IV.

The carved stones may have come from earlier buildings, but the form of the inscriptions precludes either belonging to the twelfth or thirteenth centuries, as Arabic figures were not then in common use.

Sir Walter de Berkeley was presumably grandson of Sir Alexander (Towie II), but no record exists of the generation which must have intervened between the two builders.

SIR ROGER DE BERKELEY

Sir Walter de Berkeley (Towie IV) was followed by his son, Roger, who by these premises would have been fifth of the Towie line.

SIR ROGER DE BERKELEY, c. 1226, Towie V.

Sir Roger de Berkeley had three sons by Margaret his wife, Hugh, Donald and Walter.

He was closely associated with the sons of David, Earl of Huntingdon, brother to King William the Lion, and was a benefactor to the Abbey of Lindores.

This information was not available to the earlier genealogists, for it was only in 1886 that the Cartulary of Lindores Abbey came to light among the possessions of the family of Cunninghame of Caprington. Dr. Dickson writes in his preface :—

> " The volume consists of eighty-six leaves of vellum, measuring seven and a half inches. Its ancient binding is now so dilapidated that only part of one of the oak boards remains attached to it, and their leather covering has disappeared with the exception of a minute fragment, only sufficient to show that the colour was red. Still the stout leather bands and the strong sewing are unbroken, and the book remains firm and well preserved."

Scot. Hist. Society. Cartulary of Lindores, p. xc.

Sir Roger de Berkeley witnessed a grant of Malcolm, Earl of Fife, which was confirmed by King Alexander II, at Stirling. To the subsequent confirmation of this grant by the King, " William de Bosco, Cancellario meo," and Alexander Viscount of Stirling are witnesses, *inter alios*. The name of William de Bosco once more enables us to date this record as previous to the year 1226. .

Register Hon. de Morton. Bannatyne Club, p. xxxiii.

He witnessed also with John de Huntingdon, Earl David's legitimate son, and others a grant of Patrick de Ridal to the church and monks of Melrose,* and the confirmation of an agreement between the monks of Kelso and the men of Inverwick.

Melrose Charters, Vol. i, p. 143. Kelso Charters, p. 206.

His name, as " Dominus Rogero de Berkeley," is among the knights in a list of witnesses to a deed in which Gilbert de Hay

* In Part I (p. 45) this record is erroneously assigned to Roger of Dursley (IV).

SIR ROGER DE BERKELEY, c. 1226, Towie V. confirms to the Abbey of Lindores a grant made by his father of :—

Cartulary of Lindores, p. 84, No. 78.

"a third part of his draw nets on the sands of Glesbanyn and on the sands of Rugesablum over against Coleric."

Sir Roger de Berkeley bestowed two benefactions on the Abbey of Lindores, and it is in the record of these that we learn the names of his wife, his sons and his chief retainers. He grants :—

Cartulary of Lindores, p. 74, No. 68.

"for the weal of his soul, and the soul of Margaret his wife, and the souls of his ancestors and successors one oxgate of land in his manor of Forgrund. . . ."

The list of witnesses to this deed commences with the name of Sir Henry of Stirling, a natural son of David, Earl of Huntingdon, and concludes with the retainers of the benefactor : "Randulpho my seneschal, Postoyle my marus, and Alwin my servant." The marus was the official who executed the summons of his lord's court.

Sir Roger de Berkeley also granted to Lindores

"half a stone of wax, to be received yearly out of the rent which Robert Hernys held of him in Forgrund, to be delivered as free, pure and perpetual alms at the Assumption of the Blessed Mary" [August 15th].

The witnesses to this grant are :—

Cartulary of Lindores, p. 75, No. 69.

"Dominis Patricio vicario de Forgrund, Hugone, Dovenaldo, Waltero, filiis meis, Randulpho seneschaldo meo, Postoyle maro meo, Alwin serviente meo, et multis aliis."

The name of "Towie" does not appear to have been used as a territorial designation by Barclays of this line earlier than 1321, and this grant is of supreme interest in proving that one of this family was holding lands in that district in these early days.

Forgrund, now Forglen, was situated in the thanage of Balhelvie, and closely adjacent to the estates which were later known as "Towie-Barclay."

Of Hugh de Berkeley and his brother Walter, sons of Sir Roger, there is much to be related, but the name of Donald does not appear again.

SIR HUGH DE BERKELEY, JUSTICIAR OF LOTHIAN

Sir Hugh de Berkeley, 1246-1298, Towie VI.

Sir Hugh de Berkeley is witness to a charter at Edinburgh, 9th August, 1248, in which Robert de Brus confirms to the Abbey of Lindores the donation made by his mother, Ysabella de Brus, of her whole messuage of Cragyn.

Witnesses :—Alexander Comyn, Earl of Buchan,
Domino William de Brechin,
Gilbert de Hay,
Humphrey de Kirkpatrick,
Ingram de Monceus,
Hugh de Mauleverer,
Hugone de Berkeley,
Hugh de Beaumys,
Militibus.

Cartulary of Lindores, p. 42, No. 41.

The list of witnesses is extremely interesting, in showing not only that Hugh de Berkeley continued his father's interest in Lindores, but also his association with the Comyns, in whose political machinations he was to be so closely concerned. Alexander Comyn was the second Comyn Earl, and Constable of Scotland. William de Brechin was son of Henry de Brechin, natural son of Earl David of Huntingdon. He held lands and a castle at Lindores and had married a daughter of William Comyn, first Earl of Buchan, and was therefore brother-in-law to Alexander Comyn.

Ibid. p. 248.

There were at this time in Scotland three powerful earls and thirty-two knights of the name of Comyn, and to follow the doings of their factions and the connection of the Berkeleys therewith we must remind ourselves of the history of the early years of the reign of Alexander III.

Alexander III was only eight years old when he ascended the throne of Scotland, and immediately a struggle for the regency began between those nobles who favoured the English influence, headed by Alan Durward, the great Justiciar, and those who formed a Scottish national party, of whom the leader was Walter Comyn, Earl of Menteith.

The coronation of the boy King at Scone in 1249 was an

Sir Hugh de Berkeley, 1246-1298, Towie VI.

occasion for conflict. The Bishops of St. Andrews and Dunkeld, with the Abbot of Scone, attended to officiate, but Alan Durward attempted to delay, on the pretext that Alexander was not yet a knight. The Earl of Menteith countered by proposing that the Bishop of St. Andrews should perform both ceremonies, and urged the danger of delay. Fortunately his arguments prevailed, as Henry III had sent a messenger to the Pope, representing Scotland as a fief of England, and asking that the coronation should be interdicted until Alexander had obtained leave of his feudal superior.

Tytler's History of Scotland.

We read how the Bishop of St. Andrews girded the King with the belt of knighthood, and then conducted him to the regal chair, or sacred stone of Scone. The crown was placed on his head, he was invested with the royal mantle, and the nobility, kneeling in homage, threw their robes beneath his feet. A highland sennachy or bard, of great age, clad in a scarlet mantle, with hair venerably white, then advanced from the crowd and, bending before the throne, repeated in his native tongue the genealogy of the King, deducing his descent from the fabulous Gathelus.

Henry III had resolved on an expedition to the Holy Land and, in order to assure peace with Scotland, the marriage of his daughter Margaret with the young Alexander III, which had been arranged seven years before, was solemnised at York, at Christmas 1252.

The great event was the scene of another clash between opposing factions, although to avoid more serious disaster the wedding service was performed secretly early in the morning. The guests at the bridal were the King and Queen of England and Mary de Couci, Queen dowager of Scotland, who had come from France with a great retinue, nobility and clergy of both countries, with a great number of vassals in their suite. In the *Chronica Majora* of Matthew Paris we have a graphic description of the occasion. He tells of the crowding of the city by English, French and Scots, of the extravagant attire of the nobles, the princely hospitality of the Archbishop, of the unsuccessful endeavours of Henry III to persuade his youthful son-in-law to do homage for his kingdom as well as for his English lands, and the diplomatic reply, with which the boy had been prepared by his councillors.

SIR HUGH DE BERKELEY, 1246-1298, Towie VI.

"But when they were all come to York, those who had come with the King of Scotland were for precaution lodged in one street without admixture of others. . . . And while certain of the nobles' officials were providing lodging for their Lords, they came to blows, first with fists, then with their mails, and finally with their cudgels. And some were seriously hurt, one fell slain, others wounded never afterwards recovered.

"But the Kings through the guardians they had there, discreet and moderate, prudently restrained the dissensions of both lords and servants. The Archbishop's men, moreover, provided accommodation sufficient, considering the time, for all, although they exceeded number, lest the scarcity of lodging should provoke strife.

"And on the morrow of Christmas, the King of Scotland married the daughter of the King of England. . . .

"There were indeed so many diversities of people, so many numerous hosts of nobles of English, French, and Scots, so many large troops also of knights adorned with wanton robes, vain in their silks and changing adornments. . . .

"For a thousand knights and more appeared there on behalf of the English King at the wedding, clothed in silk and to speak in the vulgar tongue in 'cointises,' and on the morrow they threw all these aside and presented themselves at court in new robes . . . and on behalf of the King of Scots sixty knights and more and many the equivalent of knights with sufficient appropriateness, presented themselves to the gaze of all . . . and they all dined for several days with the Archbishop, who was as a northern prince and the cheerful host of all."

Space forbids further description of the entertainment, but Scottish documents provide a very complete picture, even such details as the food and clothing being given.

The precautions of the worthy Archbishop were unsuccessful in preventing trouble, for in the midst of the festival Walter Comyn, Earl of Menteith, accused Alan Durward, who, as High Justiciar, was chief adviser of the young King, of designs against the crown of Scotland. Alan Durward had married a natural daughter of Alexander II, and the ground of the accusation was his attempt, with the connivance of the Scottish Chancellor, to procure from Rome the legitimation of

SIR HUGH DE BERKELEY, 1246-1298, Towie VI.

his wife, in order, said his accusers, that his children should succeed to the throne, if the King died childless. It is possible that there was some foundation for the charge, as certain of the accused fled, and Henry appointed new guardians to the young King, chief among whom were the Earls of Menteith, Mar and Buchan. After the return of the wedded children to Scotland, it is evident that they were used as pawns in the struggle between the National and the English parties.

Allied to the National party and the Comyns were Robert de Ross " of stainless and blameless repute," John Baliol and many friends, among whom were the brothers Hugh and Walter de Berkeley. Their growing power was further augmented by the arrival in Scotland of the Queen Mother and her second husband, John de Brienne, whose adherents were known as " the Queen's gainsayers." The English party came to be termed " the King's friends." Alan Durward secured restoration to the favour of Henry III, who further inflamed bad feeling by sending unpopular English nobles as successive guardians to the young King. In 1255 " the King's friends " seized Alexander and his little Queen and carried them from Edinburgh to Roxburgh Castle. King Henry summoned his army to the Scottish border, and the King and Queen of Scots were brought to him at the castle of Robert de Ross at Wark, where a great number of both factions assembled.

A regency was appointed, which included all the clergy and nobility favourable to England ; and the Comyns with Bishop Gamelin, the Earls of Mar and Ross, John Baliol, and their chief followers were deprived of all share in the government. Alexander and his Queen now went to Edinburgh, and Henry, after having attempted to replenish his exhausted coffers by selling a pardon to John Baliol and confiscating the estates of the Earl of Ross, returned home. The year following Alexander and his Queen went to England, where they were entertained with great magnificence in London, Oxford, Windsor and Woodstock.

Meanwhile Scotland was torn with disorder and violence and the National party gained ground. The Bishop of

St. Andrews prevailed upon the Pope to excommunicate Durward and the councillors of the King. The ceremony was performed by the Bishop of Dunblane and the Abbots of Jedburgh and Melrose, and repeated "with bell, book and candle in every chapel in the kingdom."

Upon the return of the King and Queen the Comyns gathered their forces, proclaiming that the government was mismanaged and the King detained in the hands of excommunicate and accursed persons. Under cover of night, they and their friends, among whom was Hugh de Berkeley, attacked the Court, which was then at Kinross, seized the King and carried him and the Queen to Stirling. John of Fordun in his *Chronicle* says poignantly "Woe unto the kingdom where the King is a boy," and gives a graphic account of the raid of Kinross, though his English sympathies evidently colour his description of the Comyns and their friends :—

> "They took council together and with one accord seized the King by night while he was asleep in bed at Kinross, and before dawn carried him off with them to Stirling the day after St. Simon and St. Jude, 1257, taking away also by force the great seal. . . . The ringleaders in this kidnapping were Walter Comyn, Earl of Menteith, Alexander Comyn, Earl of Buchan, William, Earl of Mar, a man of great shrewdness in evil deeds, John Comyn, a man prone to robbery and violence, Hugh de Abernethy, David of Lochore, Hugh of Berkeley and a great many other hangers on of these disaffected men, who did all they pleased and nought that was lawful, and reigned over the people right or wrong. And thus the last going astray was worse than the first. Thenceforth there arose much persecution and distress among the Scots lords . . . and such grinding of the poor and robbing of churches as have not been seen in our day."

This successful coup of the National party dispersed their opponents, and after a year of plotting and violence a compromise was arrived at, and a new regency appointed, which included the Queen Mother and her husband de Brienne, Alan Durward, Walter Comyn, Earl of Menteith, and supporters of both parties.

The Comyns, however, sought by every means to strengthen their cause, and on March 18th, 1258, entered into a bond of

SIR HUGH DE BERKELEY, 1246-1298, Towie VI.

mutual alliance and friendship with Lewelin, son of Griffin, Prince of Wales, and David, his brother uterine, and others, that, without mutual consent, they will make neither peace nor truce with the English King, each saving his allegiance to the King of Scotland, as sworn on the holy Evangels.

Fœdera, Vol. i, p. 370.

Cal. Scot. Doc. Vol. i, p. 421, No. 2155.

CONVENTIS mutuæ confederatio niis et amicitiæ inter magnates Scotiæ et Balliol; quod non facient pacem cum rege Angliæ sine mutuo consensu omnibus et

Walt. Cumin Comes de Menteith.
Alex. Cumin Comes de Buchan, Justiciar Scotiæ.
Willelmus Comes de Ros.
Willelmus Comes de Mar.
John Comyn, Justiciar Galwediæ.
Amerus de Makeswell, Camerarius Scotiæ.
Freskmus de Moravia.
Hugh et Walter de Berkeley, Fratres.
Reginaldus Cheyn . . . etc., etc.

The signatories to this bond were all of the triumphant National party.

The Comyn faction now held the chief offices of the Crown, and they did not fail to reward the followers who assisted them to power. In 1259 we find Hugh de Berkeley occupying the important office of Justiciar of Lothian, under which designation he signs a confirmation by King Alexander III of a grant made by Roger de Quincey, Earl of Winchester and Constable of Scotland.

Scone Charters, p. 73.

In spite, however, of holding this high office, Hugh de Berkeley was yet to be concerned in a further deed of violence with the Comyns.

In 1261 Walter Comyn, Earl of Menteith, died suddenly in suspicious circumstances. His wife, the Lady Isabella, was accused of having been a party to his death, and her hasty marriage to an English knight, Sir John Russell, strengthened the anger of the Comyns against her. The magnates of Scotland bitterly resented the marriage, and there were many claimants for the Earldom and its vast estates. In one period in the long struggle which followed, a party of the Comyns and their friends, among whom was Hugh de Berkeley, seized John Russell and his wife, the Countess Isabella, and, holding them captive, forced them to yield the Earldom and its estates to John Comyn, who did not long enjoy possession, as they were wrested from him by Walter the Steward. The feud was not finally settled until 1285, when King Alexander at his Parliament at Scone divided the Earldom into two portions, Walter Steward retaining the title and castle, and the free barony going to William Comyn, in right of his wife, the daughter of the murdered man.

Sir Hugh de Berkeley, 1246-1298, Towie VI.

The death of Walter Comyn, Earl of Menteith, gave the young King the opportunity to assume the reins of government, which he did with great firmness, though not yet of age. He attended the coronation of his brother-in-law, Edward I, at Westminster in 1272, and six years later did homage through the lips of Bruce, Earl of Carrick. The words of the homage were designedly very vague, "for the lands he holds of the English King," or, according to the Scottish version, "saving my own kingdom."

Intermittent encroachments of the Norwegians, who were masters of the Outer Isles, were successfully quelled, and in 1281 Alexander gave his only daughter, Margaret, in marriage to the King of Norway. She died in 1283, leaving an infant daughter, known to history as "the Maid of Norway," who, upon the death of the Prince of Scotland, only surviving son of Alexander III, a few months later, became heiress to the Scottish throne.

At a meeting of the Estates of the Realm, held at Scone on February 5th, 1283-4, the Barons of Scotland bound themselves to acknowledge the infant Margaret of Norway as their sovereign, should Alexander have no other child. The King, greatly desirous of an heir, now married Joleta, daughter of the Count de Dreux, at Jedburgh. The chronicler Fordun describes how, in the middle of the wedding ceremonies, a strange masque was exhibited, in which a fearful spectre like death glided among the guests, and quickly vanished. This he held to be a supernatural foreshadowing of misfortune for the Kingdom, and the portent was remembered when, three years later, the King was killed by a fall from his horse, when riding at night near Kinghorn.

SIR HUGH DE BERKELEY, 1246-1298, Towie VI.

Alexander III was a wise and able sovereign. His personal character and courage kept his nobles in check, and his death was the great calamity of Scotland.

The grief of his people is well described in a fragment of early Scottish verse :—

" Quhen Alyssandyr, oure Kyng wes dede
That Scotland led in luwe and le
Away wes sons of ale and brede
Of wyne and wax, of gamyn and gle.
Our gold was changyd to lede . . .
Christ born in-to virgunyte,
Succour Scotland and remede,
That stad is in perplexyte."

(luwe=love. le=tranquillity.)

Sir Hugh de Berkeley discharged the duties of Justiciar of Lothian for seventeen years, 1259-1276, and we shall not underrate the responsibilities of that office if we realise that Lothian, the ancient province of Laodinia, although reduced from its original extent, still denoted the whole of Scotland south of the two Firths. The Exchequer Rolls 1264-66 show that he was Sheriff of the border county of Berwick.

Exchequer Rolls, Vol. i, p. 126A.

In 1262 he witnesses, as Justiciar, an enrolment by Sir Gilbert de Ruthven, at Scone, and among his co-witnesses is his brother, Walter de Berkeley. With the exception of the Welsh Bond of Alliance this is the only instance in which the names of the brothers occur together.

Reg. de Panmure, No. 83.

Attestations by Sir Hugh, as Justiciar, are to be found in the registers of the Abbeys of Newbottle, Kelso, Soltre, Lindores, Coldstream and elsewhere. Sir William Fraser gives two charters of Hugh of Abernethy, witnessed by him as Justiciar, and a third in which he signs " tunc Justiciar et vicecomite."

Douglas Book.

The *Calendar* for the years 1264-1339 (pp. 2, 22, 27) contains accounts of payments and receipts by him from 1264-66 as Sheriff of Berwick. They include payments to him by the Sheriff of Perth of his fee of £40 per annum, and a request for 20 merks allowed to him yearly from the Lordship of Berwick by grace of the King, as well as statements of his expenses as Sheriff.

Exchequer Rolls.

A glimpse of Hugh the Justiciar in his official life, "in full court . . . with many worthy men," is to be found in a reproduction of a fine thirteenth-century deed in Sir William Fraser's *Book of Carlaverock, or Memoirs of the Maxwells, Earls of Nithsdale, Lords of Maxwell and Herries*, of which 150 copies were privately printed for William, Lord Herries, in 1873. It is a charter recording a grant by John of Pencateland to Herbert of Maxwell of land and the advowson of Pencateland church. This grant was made on May 18th, 1276, in the castle of Maidens (Edinburgh), in the presence of the Justiciar, whose seal was affixed at the grantor's petition, as his own, he considered, was not sufficiently well known. SIR HUGH DE BERKELEY, 1246-1298, Towie VI.

The confirmation by Alexander III dated at Berwick 1268 of a grant by William Cunyburg to Herbert de Maxwell is of peculiar interest. It is witnessed by Hugh de Berkeley, Justiciar of Lothian, and others, among whom is Patrick de Berkeley.

This is the first time that the name of Sir Patrick de Berkeley appears, and although it is not stated, later evidence makes it clear that he was the son of Sir Hugh, the Justiciar.

The grant of John of Pencateland, previously alluded to, is the last signed by Sir Hugh as Justiciar, but on May 18th, 1277, he witnesses at Haddington a grant of Devorguila de Baliol. His name is recorded as Hugone de Berkeley, and among his co-witnesses is William de Soules, who succeeded him as Justiciar of Lothian, but neither are so designated. Devorguila de Baliol was daughter and heiress of Alan of Galloway and mother of John de Baliol, presently to be King of Scotland. Reg. Glasgow, p. 193.

Sir Hugh de Berkeley was by this time a man of advanced years, but, as we shall see, he was yet to take his part in the troubles of his country and to live to a great age.

In spite of the fact that Margaret, daughter of the King of Norway, and granddaughter of Alexander III, was the last of the legitimate descendants of King William the Lion, and that she had been formally recognised by the Parliament of Scotland as heiress to the throne, a strong party was formed against her, headed by Robert Bruce. Others of the nobility

SIR HUGH DE BERKELEY, 1246-1298, Towie VI.

negotiated secretly with King Edward of England, whose main desire was to add the realm of Scotland to his own Kingdom. He planned to arrange a marriage between his son, Prince Edward, and the Maid of Norway, but her father was loath to entrust his little daughter to Scotland, for the country was in a state of civil war between opposing factions, in particular those of Bruce and Baliol, both of whom had designs upon the throne. An agreement was finally reached and a ship sent by Edward to fetch the little Maid, but she did not survive the voyage and died in the Orkneys in September, 1290.

The death of Margaret placed the succession to the throne of Scotland in serious dispute. Many claimants arose, chief among whom were the direct descendants of the three daughters of David, Earl of Huntingdon, brother of King William the Lion. John Baliol, grandson of Margaret, Robert Bruce, known as "Le Viell," son of Isabella, who, being an old man, renounced his claim in favour of his son, Robert "Le Jeune," whose son Robert was later to be King of Scotland, and John Hastings, son of Ada, the third daughter.

The Regents of Scotland appealed to King Edward I to settle the matter.

The English King held a council at Norham in June, 1291, where each of the competitors personally presented his claim.

It was not, however, until November in the following year, at Berwick, that Edward gave his judgment in favour of John Baliol.

This decision, though just, because Baliol represented the elder daughter of David, Earl of Huntingdon, was a bad one for Scotland, for Robert Bruce was the better man with the strongest following.

The humiliating terms imposed by England were weakly accepted by Baliol, and in the presence of the assemblage the Great Seal of Scotland was broken into four parts, which were deposited in the treasury of King Edward, in token of his sovereignty over Scotland.

On the following day John Baliol swore fealty to Edward, and on St. Andrew's Day, 1292, was crowned at Scone, amid cries of dissent. He again did homage to Edward on the day after Christmas, but it was not long before the English King, who had purposed to rule the northern kingdom through a submissive vassal, found King John "contumacious."

SIR HUGH DE BERKELEY, 1246-1298, Towie VI.

Tytler's History of Scotland.

In 1294 war broke out between France and England, and when the Scottish King and his nobles entered into a treaty with Eric, King of Norway, and Philip, King of France, against England, Patrick de Berkeley (Towie VII) was among the nobles therewith concerned.

In compliance with this treaty a Scottish army crossed the Border and wasted the northern counties.

Thereupon Edward proceeded north and destroyed Berwick, then the finest city and trading centre of Scotland. Meanwhile a party of Scottish nobles, determined to secure the independence of their country, seized Baliol and forced him to send a formal renunciation of his fealty to the English King.

Having totally reduced Berwick, Edward fought a victorious battle at Dunbar on April 12th, 1296, and marched on to Edinburgh, where he occupied the palace then known as Holirudhuis. Having laid successful siege to the castle, he captured the crown jewels, and passed on to Stirling and Perth. He removed the sacred Stone of Destiny from Scone and the Fragments of the True Cross and the sacred "Holy Rood" of St. Margaret, and finally returned to Berwick, after a triumphant campaign of twenty-two weeks.

The Scottish forces, rent by bitter contention between the factions of Bruce and Baliol, were incapable of serious opposition.

At Berwick, King Edward convened a parliament of the two realms, and summoned the nobles to make submission to him and to do homage for their estates. The list of these submissions and others which had been rendered at various stages of his progress through the country constitute what is known as "The Ragman Roll." The derivation of the word "Ragman" has never been satisfactorily explained, but it

Sir Hugh de Berkeley, 1246-1298, Towie VI.

survives in the colloquial "rigmarole," "a rambling and incoherent statement."

Nearly two thousand names are entered in this invaluable record of the landowners of Scotland. Ninety Scottish magnates appear as doing homage on March 14th at Wark, this probably being homage rendered personally to King Edward, who crossed the Tweed in that month: and a more general homage was performed on August 28th at Berwick, when earls, barons, knights, burgesses, churchmen and *probi homines* of the kingdom took the oath of fealty.

Sir Patrick de Berkeley made his submission, and others of his Gartley kinsfolk, as we shall see, but his father, the old Justiciar, never "came to his peace" with the King of England. It is easy to imagine that the destruction of the beautiful city of Berwick, where he had held public office for so many years, added fuel to the flame of his lifelong hatred of the English. As an adherent of John Baliol, he may have been among those who, like Sir William Wallace, held on through that autumn and winter fighting a forlorn hope on behalf of an unworthy King, or we can picture him a worn and battle-scarred old man, spending his last days in retirement at his castle of Cullen, staunch and stubborn to the end.

He lived for two years after the parliament at Berwick, as we know from entries in the Acts of Parliament of Scotland, which are exceedingly interesting, as supporting the theory of the connection of the Scottish Barclays with their namesakes in Gloucestershire.

In 1298 Edward I issued writs both in England and Scotland directing that all lands held by adherents of John Baliol, late King of Scotland, should be taken into the hands of the Crown.

Cal. Scot. Doc. Vol. ii, No. 736.

The Sheriff of Gloucester, in reply to the King's command, stated that no such person held lands in his jurisdiction, but that a rent at Camme was held by Sir Hugh de Berkeley, knight, a follower of the said John Baliol.

This property at Camme, here referred to, was held (as overlords) by the Fitzharding de Berkeleys, and the rent of two merks paid by the tenants, an English family named de Draycote.

Sir Hugh de Berkeley presumably forfeited this rent, but the Fitzharding de Berkeleys, as overlords, must have re-granted it to the Scottish de Berkeleys as soon as the latter had adjusted their allegiance. A later enquiry held at Gloucester in 1335 shows that the rent of the two virgates in Camme, still held by the de Draycotes, had been granted to David de Berkeley (Towie VIIB, second son of Hugh de Berkeley, the Justiciar), and had passed by hereditary succession to John de Soules, by whom it had been forfeited in the reign of Edward II.

SIR HUGH DE BERKELEY, 1246-1298, Towie VI.

It is worthy of note that Camme is in the parish of Dursley, in Gloucestershire, and it would appear that this small holding had remained in the Towie line, as part of the original property of their family in that county.

In addition to Sir Patrick already mentioned as witnessing with his father at Berwick in 1268, Sir Hugh de Berkeley had a younger son, David, the progenitor of the Berkeleys of the Brechin and Collairnie lines, who will be dealt with later, and a daughter Effie, who married Walter de Somervill.

"Memorie of the Somervills."

Of Walter de Berkeley, brother to Sir Hugh the Justiciar, who was associated with him in the Bond with the Welsh Princes in 1258, nothing further is recorded, but the tradition in the Towie line has always been that he remained in the West Country and was the ancestor of the Barclays of Crawford-John and Kilbirnie.

Sir Patrick de Berkeley, 1268-1296, Towie VII.

SIR PATRICK DE BERKELEY, THE CHAMBERLAIN

Something of the activities of Sir Patrick de Berkeley, son of Sir Hugh, the Justiciar, may be traced before he took part in the stirring events of the war of independence, in addition to his appearing as witness, with his father, to the grant by William de Cunyburg, already quoted.

He witnessed at Cupar a grant by King Alexander III on November 13th, 1280, to the Abbey of Arbroath, of 100 shillings, for the sustenance of thirteen poor persons, when his co-witnesses included Walter Steward, Earl of Menteith, the Seneschal, and Lord William de Brechin.

Arbroath Charters, Vol. i, p. 201.

At about this time he held the office of High Chamberlain of Scotland to Alexander III, and, although not mentioned by Crawfurd in his *Lives of the Great Officers of State*, he is included in the list of Chamberlains given in the Calendar of the Scottish Exchequer Rolls, and confirmation of this may be found in an account of expenses and receipts of Sir Andrew de Moray, Sheriff of Ayr. In this document reference is made to the difference between a certain valuation made in the time of Patrick de Berkeley and another made by Weland, the late Chamberlain. Weland is entered after Patrick in the above list, as preceding in that office Alexander de Baliol, son of Henry de Baliol, who was Chamberlain from 1287 to 1294. Unfortunately the Rolls have not survived in sufficient completeness to give information about Sir Patrick de Berkeley and Weland during their tenure.

Exchequer Rolls, Vol. ii, p. cxxii. *Ibid.* Vol. i, pp. 37, 38.

It is clear, however, that Sir Patrick did not hold office for long, for in 1285 he witnesses at Scone a charter of King Alexander to John de Lyndesay of lands in Wauchope and Stabilgorton, where his name appears simply as Patrick de Berkeley, Knight, and not as Chamberlain.

Reg. Morton, ii, p. 7.

On May 30th in the same year he again witnesses for the King at Glenluce a grant to the Priory of Whithern (Candida Casa) of the advowson of the Church of the Holy Trinity at Ramsay.

Hist. MSS. Comm. Report, xi, Bridgewater MSS.

Sir Patrick is first described as " fermor " of the Thanage of Balhelvie in June 1292, when John de Gilforde acknowledges receipt of his fee as custodian of the Castle of Aberdeen in the following terms :—

Sir Patrick de Berkeley, 1268-1296, Towie VII.

"To all whom these letters shall see or hear John de Gilforde of the Castle of Aberdeen greeting in the Lord. Know ye that I, on Sunday the feast of Holy Trinity in the year of grace 1292 at Aberdeen, have received by Peter the Clerk to the Sheriff of Aberdeen, for Sir Patrick de Berkeley, Fermor of the Thanage of Balhelvie for my fee for the custody of the Castle of Aberdeen, twelve pounds and twelve pence sterling."

Cal. Scot. Doc. Box 100, No. 189.

There had been a Royal residence at Aberdeen as early as the reign of William the Lion, and its Castle, as well as that of Banff, had been erected by Alexander III as a defence against the Scandinavians. John de Gilforde would have been an Englishman, as, pending King Edward's decision as to the succession to the throne, all important Scottish castles were in English custody, though at Scottish expense.

The hour of Scotland's humiliation was drawing near and, only four years later, Sir Patrick de Berkeley is among those who signed the Ragman Roll on July 17th, 1296, with the burgesses and community of Aberdeen. It is recorded that he of his own free will renounced the league with the King of France and swore fealty, kissing the holy Evangels. It would seem that his lands were already forfeited under writs of King Edward, who directed all Sheriffs to retain in hand the lands of John Baliol, late King, and other magnates in prison, or not yet come to the King's Peace.

Cal. Scot. Doc. Vol. ii, p. 195.

Sir Patrick de Berkeley is among the few whose submissions are recorded as having been rendered in more than one place, for on August 21st he took the oath of fealty again at Berwick, presumably for other of his property, as he is entered as Patrick de Berkeley of the county of Lanark. Only ten days later, by the King's "special grace," and on the score that he is now "powerless," all his lands were restored to him.

The explanation would seem to be that Sir Patrick, who was hardly likely to have capitulated without a struggle, had been grievously wounded before the surrender of Aberdeen.

Sir Patrick de Berkeley, 1268-1296, Towie VII.

As a prominent Scottish noble, he would have been among those who attended the councils of Norham, in 1291, and Berwick, in 1292, and must have been personally known to King Edward. Did the recollection of some past incident incline him to favour the Scotsman, or was it that the great Plantagenet felt it politic to show special clemency to this gallant enemy now utterly broken? We cannot tell, but the record is clear. On September 8th writs were issued to the Sheriffs of Aberdeen, Forfar and Lanark in the following terms :—

"For as much as Patrick de Berkeley being our tenant, in our peace, has sworn fealty to us, and wishing to do special grace unto the same Patrick, on account of his impotence, we command you that you take all the lands and tenements of the same Patrick, and cause them to be rendered to the same Patrick, without delay, provided that the same Patrick do us the same services thereof due and customary.

Cal. Scot. Doc. Vol. ii, p. 224.

"Witness the King at Berwick-on-Tweed,
"8th day of September."

Exchequer Misc. Rolls, i, No. 10.

There is also a record of a similar writ issued under the King's seal to the Sheriff of Edinburgh on the same day, concerning lands which Sir Patrick held there under Sir John de Cambron. It will be seen that in every case his rank was omitted, since he was a rebel.

In the *Calendar of Scottish Documents* are plates of a few seals of the homages of 1296, among them those of Sir Walter de Berkeley (Gartley VIII) and of Sir Patrick. The Editor explains that all these seals are not armorial, but merely represent some device, as we shall see in the case of Gartley.

The seal of Sir Patrick de Berkeley has been described as—

Mr. R. Macdonald's Notes, in Lyon Office, 18.12.25.

"a chevron, no other charges visible, within a pointed and rounded trefoil diapered. Legend . . . S. . . PATRICII DE BERK . . . Y Milit. Inner border carved, outer beaded.

"Diametre $1\frac{1}{10}$ inch."

Sir Patrick de Berkeley's name is not mentioned again after the signing of the Ragman Roll, and the date of his death is unknown.

He had two sons, Sir Walter and Sir Hugh.

Our justification for asserting that Sir Patrick was Lord of Towie lies in the fact that his sons were in possession not only of Balhelvie but of Towie in 1322. Also his younger brother, Sir David (Towie VIIB), is definitely named as being of the Towie family.

He was afterwards known as Sir David de Berkeley of Carny, and was the progenitor of the Barclays of Brechin and Collairnie, an account of whom will be given later.

SIR PATRICK DE BERKELEY, 1268-1296, Towie VII.

"Memorie of the Somervills," Vol. i, p. 74.

SIR WALTER DE BERKELEY, LORD OF KERKO

SIR WALTER DE BERKELEY, 1296-1324, Towie VIII.

Chancery Misc. Bundle 22, file 3 (1).

Sir Walter de Berkeley, son of Patrick, fought in the battle of Dunbar and was taken prisoner by the English at the storming of the Castle, on April 13th, 1296. No fewer than 130 prisoners were of sufficient note to be despatched south in the following month to be confined in various places. Sir Walter de Berkeley and Sir William de Hay were among those incarcerated in the Castle of Berkhampstead in Hertfordshire, and the accounts of the Sheriff of Bedford and Buckingham show that they arrived there on the Thursday after St. Augustine's Day, May 31st, 1296.

Close Roll, 25 Edward I, m. 6.

The prisoners are clearly described as knights, enemies of the King, taken captive at the Castle of Dunbar. The charge for the maintenance of each knight was four pence *per diem*, and the total sum for a period of one hundred and twenty-two days amounted to 75s.

Close Roll, 25 Edward I, m. 8, dorso.

On August 1st Sir Walter de Berkeley and Sir William de Hay were liberated on undertaking to join the forces of King Edward then fighting against France in Flanders, and with four Scottish knights similarly liberated from other prisons and thirteen shieldbearers, proceeded to Sandwich, expecting to embark in six days. They were still waiting on September 14th, having been joined by Sir Edmund Comyn, Sir John de Cambron and others, until their number had grown to ten knights, twenty-four "scutiferi" and armoured horses.

John, Earl of Atholl, another "Dunbar knight," had evidently secured release and restoration to the King's favour, for during this time he signs, at Winchelsea, his personal guarantee for the fidelity to the King of England of certain Scottish knights, including "Sir Wautier de Berkeley and sixteen valets" (who are named) to serve in the realm of France or elsewhere. The band of knights with their servitors, being without any means of their own while awaiting embarkation, received an allowance of 12d. *per diem* each, and each shieldbearer "if without horse" 6d. The date of their departure is not recorded.

It is interesting to note that Sandwich was one of the ports from which men and material were shipped to the war in Flanders six hundred years later.

SIR WALTER DE BERKELEY, 1296-1324, Towie VIII.

John Baliol, King of Scotland, called by the English "the Vassal King" and by the Scots "Toom Tabard" or "Empty Jacket," made his renunciation on July 7th at the hour of Vespers in the churchyard of Stracathro, and, confessing his sins against his liege lord, desired to be reconciled. Three days later at Brechin Castle, of his own free will, he formally resigned his kingdom, his royal dignity, his lands and goods, homages and rights, saving only incarceration, into the hands of the King of England, together with his Royal Seal. He was confined for three years in Hertford Castle and the Tower of London, and then permitted to retire to his estates in Normandy, where he died at Château Gaillard in 1315.

Even this abject surrender of their sovereign did not entirely destroy the loyalty of the Scots, especially in the south, and although Edward took care that all strongholds were commanded and garrisoned by Englishmen, and through his appointed guardians of Scotland took measures for the maintenance of peace, disaffection grew among the people.

The standard of revolt was raised by William Wallace, a gentleman of Clydesdale who had never sworn fealty to King Edward I. The nobles took little or no share in this rising, which was mainly confined to the people, and an army under Lord Percy was sent to quell it. A little later, while Edward was in Flanders, Wallace made himself master of the fortresses in the district north of the Tay. He defeated the English by superior strategy at the battle of Stirling, September 11th, 1297, and after this victory by common consent constituted himself Guardian of the Kingdom for King John.

Edward hastened back from Flanders and himself led a rabble army for the suppression of Wallace's rebellion, and won the battle of Falkirk on July 22nd, 1298. Wallace's force was almost entirely made up of men on foot, whose value as soldiers then counted for little. His military genius,

SIR WALTER DE BERKELEY, 1296-1324, Towie VIII.

which had been so clearly displayed by his choice of position at Stirling, was shown at Falkirk by his use of his men. He disposed them in circular formation, the spearmen kneeling and the bowmen standing behind them, a foreshadowing of the famous British square. The numerical strength of the English, however, defeated the gallantry of Wallace's small force, and he was compelled to escape from the field of battle, where, it is stated, 40,000 men lay slain.

Edward now held the country south of the Forth, but was obliged again to bring an army for the subjection of Scotland in 1303, when his son Edward, Prince of Wales, accompanied his force "to win his spurs."

We find Sir Walter de Berkeley once more in Scotland and allied to the patriotic party, with Sir John Comyn of Badenach, when engaged in negotiations with Edward's general, Aymer de Valence, which concluded in the capitulation of Strathorde, on February 9th, 1303. His name is mentioned among those knights who with Sir John Comyn and his retinue dined with the Prince of Wales on Saturday, February 22nd. The Roll of the Comptroller of the Household of the Prince of Wales records the supplies provided for the occasion. It was Lenten fare: "1,500 herrings, 52 stockfishe, 1 quart of oil, 1 bushel of peas, ½ bushel of salt, 1 quart of vinagre, 1 quart of verjus, bread 4s., wine 68 sesterces."

Cal. Scot. Doc. Vol. ii, No. 1741.

Ibid. No. 1516. Roll of the Comptroller of Prince of Wales's Household.

In the following year Wallace returned to Scotland from France, where he had been trying to gain support. He was betrayed by his servant, Jack Short, to Sir John Menteith, governor, for the English, of Dumbarton Castle, and despatched to London, where he was condemned for treason. He was hanged, drawn and quartered, his head displayed on London Bridge and his quarters at Newcastle, Berwick, Stirling and Perth.

It would appear that in spite of Sir Walter de Berkeley having taken the oath of fealty to Edward at the time of the capitulation of Strathorde, his lands were forfeited, as we find a certain Gilbert de Peche making request for them to the English King in 1306. They were not granted to him, for he obtained, in lieu, a £100 grant of land elsewhere.

Docs. Scot. Box 1, No. 1.

Sir Walter de Berkeley, 1296-1324, Towie VIII.

Edward continued to make strenuous attempts to bring about the union of the two realms and to win over the nobles, but in spite of all his efforts for the pacification of Scotland, the Scots rose in Ayr under Robert Bruce, Lord of Annandale and Earl of Carrick, grandson and heir of the rival competitor of John Baliol.

Robert Bruce had fought with Wallace, and had since been very active on the side of the English, but always with designs of obtaining the crown of Scotland for himself. By the infamous murder of John Comyn of Badenach, known as the Red Comyn, in the church of Dumfries, he made himself heir to the Crown, after the sons of Baliol.

A man of notable personality and daring, he won popular favour and was crowned at Scone on March 22nd, 1306, with ceremony only faintly resembling the splendid ritual of earlier days. The actual crowning was done by Isabella, Countess of Buchan, wife of Robert Bruce's keenest enemy. Though her husband was a Comyn, she came secretly to insist upon the hereditary right of her family, Macduff, to place the crown upon the head of the Scottish king.

At this ceremony Sir David de Berkeley, Lord of Carny (Towie VIIB), was present.

Measures of the most extreme severity were now adopted by Edward. All who were concerned in the murder of the Red Comyn were declared traitors, the Countess of Buchan and the sister of Robert Bruce were confined in cages in the Castle of Berwick, while Bruce's brother, Nigel, and his brother-in-law, Christopher Seton, were captured and suffered as traitors.

The English army was swelled by all classes from his dominions, but the King died at Burgh-on-Sands on July 30th, and his son Edward II did not continue effective measures against the rebel Scots. The chief fortresses, however, remained in English hands, and for some years Bruce went in peril of his life.

His party increased gradually, until in 1314 all Scottish strongholds, with the exception of Stirling, were in his possession. The English, in fear of losing this important

Sir Walter de Berkeley, 1296-1324, Towie VIII.

fortress, marched to relieve it under Edward II; they were entirely routed by the Scots on the field of Bannockburn, and it is said that the King and 500 knights never drew rein in their flight until they reached Dunbar and embarked for Berwick.

It is clear that Sir Walter de Berkeley did not long maintain the fealty to the English monarch imposed on him at Strathorde, for after the coronation of Bruce we find him in his service, engaged with his uncle, Sir David de Berkeley of Carny (Towie VIIb), in an expedition to compel the submission of the Earl of Ross, in 1309.

During the following years there was constant fighting on the Border, for the English refused to acknowledge the independence of Scotland which had been won at Bannockburn.

Robert Bruce appointed his supporters to the high offices in his arrangements for the peaceful government of his kingdom, and Sir Walter de Berkeley next appears as Sheriff of Aberdeen. In the accounts of this burgh he is posted as a burgess absent from the country, among those owing amercements, notified at the court held at Michaelmas in 1317.

Three years later King Robert held a parliament at Scone, known as the Black Parliament, where the name of Walter de Berkeley, Vicecomes Aberdeenia, is included in the list of those tried for high treason. The Countess of Strathearn, Lord William de Soules and Lord David de Brechin were accused of having plotted with the English, and we learn from Boece that "Walter de Berkeley of Aberdeen was Sheriffis in that day," and accused of complicity. The outcome of this plot against the King's person, known as "the de Soules conspiracy," was that the Countess and de Soules were sentenced to perpetual imprisonment and David de Brechin was among those who paid the penalty of treason with their lives. Walter de Berkeley seems to have been completely exonerated.

Fordun, Lib. iii, cap. 2.

The years of the war of independence, with its many forfeitures, changes of ownership and loss of documents, doubtless led to confusion in the ownership of property, and it may have been this fact which led Sir Walter to obtain grants or regrants of his estates from King Robert Bruce in 1322–23. In the *List of Missing Charters* is recorded one to Sir Walter de Berkeley of Kerko, Burgess of Perth, of the lands of Tollie, and another of lands in the thanage of Balhelvie. Kerko or Kerkow is situated in the parish of Kinclaven, in the Carse of Gowrie, close to Perth.

SIR WALTER DE BERKELEY, 1296-1324, Towie VIII.

By a charter dated September 25th, 1323, the King granted freedom to the burgesses and community of Aberdeen from all manner of customs duty on ale and fish (red and white) under the special reservation that they should pay and fully account for the said duty to Walter de Berkeley, knight, our present Sheriff, so long as he shall continue to be our Sheriff in Aberdeen.

Reg. Mag. Sig. Vol. i, p. 461.

Sir Walter resigned his right to these customs on the Monday preceding Christmas Day 1324, and apparently at the same time resigned the office of Sheriff, as John Drimming is recorded as holding it the following year.

Scots Affairs. Introduction, p. xvii.

The name of the wife of Sir Walter de Berkeley of Kerko has not come down to us, but he was succeeded in the Barony of Towie by William de Berkeley (Towie IX), whom we may presume to be his son.

SIR HUGH DE BERKELEY

SIR HUGH DE BERKELEY, 1296-1329, Towie VIIIB.

Sir Hugh de Berkeley (Towie VIIIB) we assume to have been the younger of the two sons of Sir Patrick de Berkeley (Towie VII), on the ground that the family estates of Towie were held by his brother Sir Walter.

Sir Hugh, with his kinsmen of the Gartley line, was among those who performed homage to King Edward I on March 14th, 1295–6. We have no further record of him for many years, but it is clear that he allied himself to the patriotic party in Scotland, and that he married the "Lady Elena" at some date previous to 1323.

On September 14th in that year King Robert Bruce confirmed to—

"Our well beloved and faithful Sir Hugh de Berkeley and his

SIR HUGH DE BERKELEY, 1296-1329, Towie VIIIB.

wife Elena and heirs born to them, to hold of the King for homage and service, a vill of the thanage of Balhelvie and the lands of greater and lesser Westerton and Egi, all within the said Lordship of Balhelvie, with the multure of these lands, brewhouse, office of smithy, office of sergeant, and 'cam' of the land of the church, a £40 land to hold in one free Barony by the said Hugh and his wife Elena and their heirs . . . with all rights belonging to a free Barony, doing three chief pleas at our court in the Sheriffdom of Aberdeen. . . . The same land to revert to the King should Sir Hugh and Lady Elena die childless."

Reg. Mag. Sig. 1304-1424, p. 427.

It will be remembered that in this year King Robert I also granted rights in the thanage of Balhelvie to Sir Hugh's brother, Sir Walter (Towie VIII).

Exchequer Rolls, Vol. i, p. clxxxi.

By the title of one of the "Missing Charters" we learn that King Robert also granted to Sir Hugh de Berkeley lands of Fyntrie Gask and Balmadedy in Buchan Ward, Banffshire.

Robertson's Index, 2.

In 1328 the name of Sir Hugh appears in connection with the payment of the second tithe of land in the thanage of Balhelvie, amounting to the sum of 26s. 8d.

Exchequer Rolls, Vol. i, p. clxxxi.

It is evident that both Sir Hugh de Berkeley and the Lady Elena were in close attendance upon Queen Isabel of Scotland, second wife of King Robert I. This royal lady died in November, 1327, and was buried in Dunfermline Abbey. She left in her will a bequest to Sir Hugh, and the sum of £30 16s. 8d. was paid to him from the King's exchequer in the following year to complete the legacy due to him.

Ibid. Vol. i, p. 90.

Two pounds of wax for the making of a frontal were granted to the Lady Elena in 1329, and the sum of 100 shillings is entered in the accounts for the same year for a frontal given by the Queen to the Abbey of Dunfermline.

Accounts of the Great Chamberlains. Bannatyne Club, p. 211.

Since the Queen had been buried in the Abbey two years previously, we must suppose that she and her ladies had been engaged upon the making of the frontal at the time of her death, and that Lady Elena de Berkeley was responsible for the completion of the work.

The records show that the lands of Balhelvie, granted to Hugh de Berkeley, were in other hands before the close of 1329,

Exchequer Rolls, Vol. i, p. 510.

which points to his death as being previous to that year. He left no male issue.

The Lady Elena survived him, for in 1342 we find that a remission was made to her of £13 6s. 8d. due for the lands of Balmadedy.

The heir male of the Berkeleys of the Towie line was William, son of Sir Walter (Towie VIII), with whom we shall deal later.

SIR HUGH DE BERKELEY, 1296-1329, Towie VIIIB.

Accounts of the Great Chamberlains. Bannatyne Club, Vol. i, p. 510.

PEDIGREE IV.

The Brechin Line

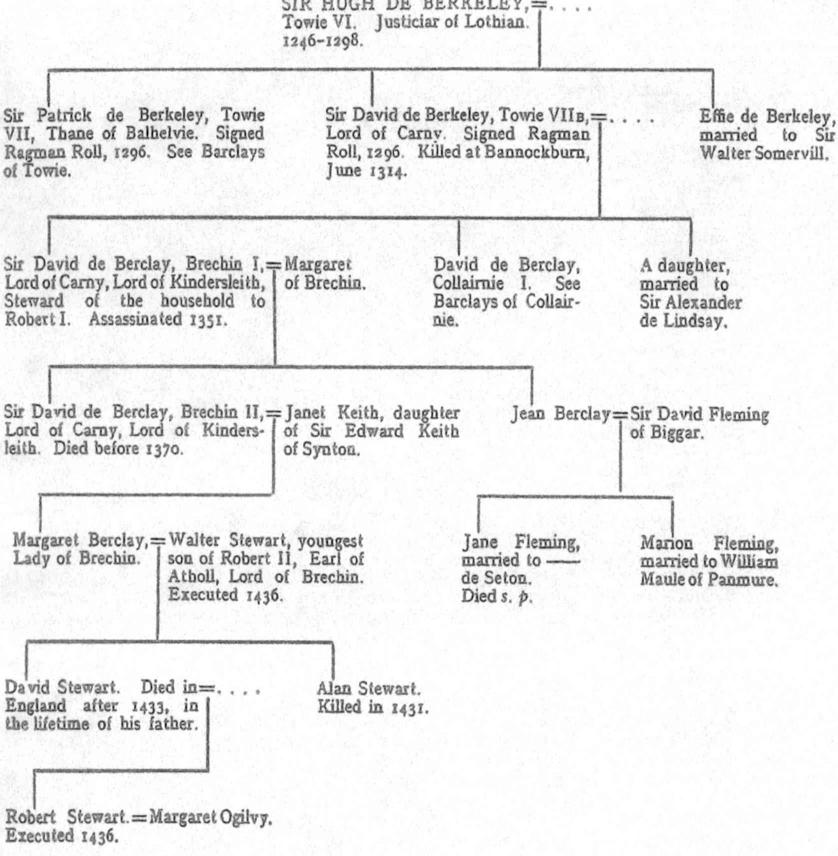

SIR HUGH DE BERKELEY, = ...
Towie VI. Justiciar of Lothian. 1246–1298.
Sir Patrick de Berkeley, Towie VII, Thane of Balhelvie. Signed Ragman Roll, 1296. See Barclays of Towie.
Sir David de Berkeley, Towie VIIB, = ...
Lord of Carny. Signed Ragman Roll, 1296. Killed at Bannockburn, June 1314.
Effie de Berkeley, married to Sir Walter Somervill.
Sir David de Berclay, Brechin I, = Margaret of Brechin.
Lord of Carny, Lord of Kindersleith, Steward of the household to Robert I. Assassinated 1351.
David de Berclay, Collairnie I. See Barclays of Collairnie.
A daughter, married to Sir Alexander de Lindsay.
Sir David de Berclay, Brechin II, = Janet Keith, daughter of Sir Edward Keith of Synton.
Lord of Carny, Lord of Kindersleith. Died before 1370.
Jean Berclay = Sir David Fleming of Biggar.
Margaret Berclay, = Walter Stewart, youngest son of Robert II, Earl of Atholl, Lord of Brechin. Executed 1436.
Lady of Brechin.
Jane Fleming, married to —— de Seton. Died s. p.
Marion Fleming, married to William Maule of Panmure.
David Stewart. Died in = ...
England after 1433, in the lifetime of his father.
Alan Stewart. Killed in 1431.
Robert Stewart. = Margaret Ogilvy.
Executed 1436.

The Brechin Line

SIR DAVID DE BERKELEY OF CARNY

Sir David de Berkeley, 1282–1314, Towie VIIb.

Sir David de Berkeley of Carny was the younger son of Sir Hugh, the Justiciar, and brother of Sir Patrick (Towie VII). He was a knight of renown before the close of the thirteenth century, a friend of Wallace and of Robert Bruce, and one of the heroes of Scottish romance.

He has always been known as Sir David de Berkeley of Carny, but the only documentary evidence of his holding that property is found when, in the next generation, his son is referred to as succeeding to Carny and Old Lindores, as his "paternal estates." Nisbet's Heraldry, Vol. ii, p. 78.

We have interesting proof that Sir David was of the Towie line through the marriage of his sister with Sir Walter of Newbigging. In the *Memorie of the Somervills* it is related that after the festivities attendant on the marriage of the young Prince Alexander, son of Alexander III,

"Sir Walter (Somervill) retourns to the tour of Lintourne, then his ordinary residence, untill the king's goeing north, and then attended his majestie in that progresse, whereby he had the acquaintance of Sir David Barclay, whose sister, Effie Barclay, he in the same year marryed in anno 1282; as may be conjectured from a band of mandrey [manrent]—(for a contract of marriage, or any other evidence relating to this affair, we have non extant) betwixt Sir Walter and Sir David, wherein, besydes ther ordinarie designatione of Newbigging and Towie, they are called bretheren in law. It is from the mutuall band, or contract, or mandrey, that we have any light either of the person to whom, or the tyme about which Sir Walter of Newbigging was marryed, therefore I think it not amisse to insert the same in this gentleman's memorie because of its antiquitie." Memorie of the Somervills, Vol. i, p. 74.

The band is as follows :—

"Be it kend till all men by thir present letters, me Sir Walter of Newbigging, and me Sir David of Towie, for all the dayes of our lyves to be obliged and bound be the faith of our bodies and thir present letters in mandred, and sworne counsell as brothers in law, to be with one another in all actiones, causes, and quarrills pertaine- Ibid. p. 76.

Sir David de Berkeley, 1282–1314, Towie VIIb.

ing to us, both in peace and in warr, against all that lyves and dyes, excepting our alleadgeance to our soveraigne lord the king.

"In witness of the whilk thing, and of ther present letters, wee have hung to our sealles att Aberdeen, the twentieth day of Apryle, the year of God, 1281, before thes witnesses, William Somervill, our brother, and John Somervill and Thomas Stelfeir."

Sir James Somervill wrote this Memorie of his family by way of an epistle to his "sones," anno 1679. It will be noted that Sir David is specially designated as of Towie.

Sir Henry Barkly in his "unpublished notes" states that Sir David de Berkeley was also at a tournament held at Roxburgh Castle in 1283.

Hist. MSS. Comm. Bannatyne Club, Murray Charters, No. 16.

In 1290 he was witness to a charter of Malcolm de Moray, and five years later to one granting Delravach to Sir William de Murray, who was one of the knights taken in the following year at Dunbar and consigned to prison in the Tower of London.

Sir David de Berkeley was among those who did homage at Wark on March 14th, 1295-6, as his name appears in the Ragman Roll as David de Berkeley of the county of Fife, but it is clear that he was soon fighting actively on the side of the patriot Wallace. He was among the Scottish knights who, at Beg, in Aberdeen, captured a convoy of stores designed for the English garrison of Ayr.

Constable's Life of Wallace.

Documents of Scotland, Sir F. Palgrave, p. 195.

The name of Sir David is found with those magnates of Scotland who performed homage to Edward I on his second invasion in 1303-4, but in spite of this he was one of the first to rally to Bruce's standard so soon as it was raised, in company with his brother-in-law, Sir Walter Somervill.

"Twa Erles alsua with hym war,
Of Lenyvax and Atholl war thai ;
Edouard the Brwyse was thar alsa,
Thomas Randall, and Hew de le Hay,
And Schyr David the Berclay,
Fresale, Summerwile, and Inchmertyn ;"

Barbour's "The Brus," ii, line 225.

Both were taken prisoners at the battle of Methven Wood, near Perth, where Bruce suffered defeat on June 19th, 1306.

"Schyr Thomas Randall thair wis tane,
That then wis a young bacheler ;
And Schyr Alexander Fraseyr ;
And Schyr David the Berclay,

Ibid. line 405.

Inchmartyn, and Hew de le Hay,
And Somirwell and othyr ma."

Sir David de Berkeley, 1282–1314, Towie VIIb.

King Edward, on being informed of the victory, commanded the execution of the prisoners, but the order was not immediately carried out, and Sir David de Berkeley must have been among those who were ransomed, as, shortly afterwards, he and his nephew, Sir Walter de Berkeley of Kerko (Towie VIII), were sent by King Robert Bruce on an expedition (1309) to compel the submission of the Earl of Ross, which entails some explanation.

Chancery Portfolios (Scotland), No. 41, p. 191.

The lands of Avoch, originally belonging to the de Morays, had been granted by King Edward I to Hugh de Ross. Afterwards, at the request of Hugh de Ross, they had been granted to David de Berkeley, no doubt for assistance rendered at the time when the latter was serving the English. When Sir Hugh's father, William de Moray, secured his release from the Tower of London, he delivered to Edward, after Bruce's coronation, the ladies of Bruce's family, who had taken refuge in the sanctuary known as the Girth of St. Duthace, within the dominions of the Earl of Ross. After their sanctuary was thus violated, it will be remembered that the ladies were confined in cages in the Castle of Berwick. After the death of Edward I, Hugh de Ross, representing that Sir David de Berkeley had now allied himself to Bruce, petitioned Edward II that the said lands forfeited by Sir David might revert to himself—

" qui est ore reverte a Sire Robert de Bruce
contre le fey notre Seigneur le Roi."

Cal. Scot. Doc. Vol. iv, Append., p. 400.

This petition is dated 1307-8.

Bruce had evidently neither forgotten nor forgiven the treachery of William, Earl of Ross, for in 1309 he sent emissaries to compel the Earl of Ross and his son Hugh to make submission. Among those thus despatched were Sir David de Berkeley and his nephew, Sir Walter de Berkeley of Kerko. The deed of submission, executed at Auldearn, in Moray, on October 31st, 1309, is published in Latin and *in extenso* in the Notes to the sixth canto of *The Lord of the Isles*, by Sir Walter

Sir David de Berkeley, 1282-1314, Towie VIIb.

Scott. It is there stated that the deed of submission of the potent Earl of Ross was never before published, and that the copy was supplied by the author's friend Mr. Thompson, Deputy Registrar of Scotland, "whose researches into our ancient records are daily throwing new and important light upon the history of our country."

Between November and March, Bruce subdued Argyle, then in English hands, while his brother Edward secured Galloway, and on March 16th, 1309, he held his first parliament at St. Andrews. Three great Celtic earls were present in person, the Earls of Ross and Lennox and Sutherland, and specially mentioned among others are Robert de Keith, Marshal of Scotland, Thomas Randolf, William Wiseman and David de Berkeley.

Acts of Parl., Scotland, Vol. i, folio 459a.

David de Berkeley was among those who, upon this occasion, concurred with the nobles in a letter to Philip, King of France, who had accepted the office of mediator between Edward II and Bruce. He is cited as having been witness in the fourth year of the reign of Robert I (1310) to the confirmation of a charter of 1265.

Sir David de Berkeley was the owner of vast properties, which were inherited by his two sons, both of whom bore the name of David. A careful comparison of records and dates indicates that the younger was issue of his second marriage, but the name of his wife, or wives, is unknown. It was not unusual for two brothers to bear the same name, the designation of their estates, by which they were called, being sufficient to identify them in those days, but the fact that there were three Davids of the Berkeley family appearing at the same time makes it well-nigh impossible to be sure to which some of the records refer.

Sir David of Carny's eldest son possessed in 1315, as his paternal estates, the lands of Cairny, Old Lindores, Kindersleith, Carny Berclay, Carny Murthac, Urchtirmonesy, Thorr, Edalston and Hindeford. By his marriage with the heiress of Brechin he became fifth Lord Brechin, as we shall see presently.

Sir David's younger son received from his father the lands

of Colcarny, in the county of Kinross. His daughter married Sir Alexander de Lyndsay. Sir David de Berkeley, 1282–1314, Towie VIIb.

Tradition has always maintained that Sir David de Berkeley of Carny was killed at the battle of Bannockburn on June 24th, 1314. This is supported in two ways. First, that although he was the devoted ally and friend of Robert Bruce, his name does not appear on the long list of those whom the King lavishly rewarded after that great victory; secondly, his eldest son was in possession of his estates in the following year.

Before tracing the line of the Berclays of Brechin through the eldest son of Sir David de Berkeley of Carny, we shall deal shortly with his younger son, David of Colcarny, who was the progenitor of the Barclays of Collairnie. It is easy to follow the gradual emergence of the place-name: Carny—Col Carny (Hill of Carny) to Collairnie.

DAVID DE BERCLAY OF COLCARNY

David de Berclay, died 1372, Collairnie I.

David de Berclay of Colcarny and Kilmarron was twice married. The name of his first wife does not appear, but he married, secondly, in 1358, Elizabeth Ramsay, daughter of Sir William Ramsay of Colluthie, who, in right of his second marriage with Isabella, was Earl of Fife.

The following extract from the Papal Registers gives her father's petition for special dispensation for the alliance :—

> "William Earl of Fife; whereas between him and David de Berclay, donsel of the diocese of Brechin, and their relations and friends, there have been killings and woundings, and in order to still the discords, they have made a treaty of marriage between David and Elizabeth, daughter of the said Earl, who was related in the fourth degree of kindred, prays for dispensation." Cal. Pap. Reg. July 1358, Vol. i, 351.

David de Berclay was Collector in Fife in the following year and witnessed the third marriage of his wife's stepmother, Isabella, Countess of Fife, in 1363, to Sir Thomas Biset of Upseclyntone. Reg. Mag. Sig. 1306–1424, p. 71, No. 331.

The lands of Colcarny, which he had received from his father, Sir David de Berkeley of Carny, he resigned in 1370

DAVID DE BERCLAY, died 1372, Collairnie I.

to his eldest son, John, by the following deed, in which it will be noted that the spelling of the name of Berkeley was gradually changing :—

Reg. Mag. Sig. p. 126, No. 361.

"Grant to John de Berclay, son of David de Berclay, of all that part of Colcarny, county Kynross, which belonged to David his father and was surrendered by him."

David de Berclay's name appears once more in a list of payments in the Exchequer Rolls of Scotland under date 1372, where it is recorded that, as Deputy Sheriff of Fife, he received the sum of £6 13s. 4d. for expenses incurred at Lindores on the late King's birthday.

His younger son, Hugh, received later a grant of the lands of Kindersleith from his cousin, David, 6th Lord of Brechin (Brechin II).

The further history of the Barclays of Collairnie is dealt with elsewhere.

SIR DAVID DE BERCLAY, LORD OF BRECHIN I

Sir David de Berclay, 1314-1351, Brechin I.

Sir David de Berclay was the eldest son of Sir David de Berkeley of Carny (Towie VIIB). He owned lands in Fife previous to 1315, when he succeeded to his paternal estates of Carny Berclay, Carny Murthac, Old Lindores, Kindersleith, Urchtirmonesy, Thorr, Edalston and Hindeford.

Nisbet's Heraldry, Vol. ii, p. 76.

Like his father, "Gude Schir Davie the Berkeley," he was a staunch adherent of Sir Robert Bruce, and is stated by tradition to have fought at Bannockburn. He married, in 1315, Margaret de Brechin, niece of King Robert, and it has been suggested that the hand of this lady was bestowed upon him as a signal honour for faithful service rendered and gallantry displayed on that victorious field.

Sir David de Berclay settled upon Margaret of Brechin at the time of the marriage, as dower for her life, all his lands of Carny Berclay, Carny Murthac, Old Lindores, Kindersleith, Urchtirmonesy, Thorr, Edalston and Hindeford.

The family of Brechin were descended from that great personage Earl David of Huntingdon, "the King's brother," with whom we were familiar in the time of Sir Walter de Berkeley (Gartley III), Chamberlain to King William the Lion.

Henry of Brechin, first Lord of Brechin, was a natural son of Earl David and succeeded to his father's lands and Castle of Lindores.

Sir William, his son and second Lord of Brechin, married a daughter of Sir Alexander Comyn, Earl of Buchan. He was co-witness with his father-in-law, and with Sir Hugh de Berkeley, the Justiciar (Towie VI), to the charter confirming the donation of Isabella de Brus to the Abbey of Lindores on August 9th, 1248.

Wyntoun, Vol. ii, p. 55.

Although Sir William de Brechin was among those nobles who, at the parliament at Scone on February 5th, 1283-4, bound themselves to acknowledge the Maid of Norway as Queen of Scotland on the death of her grandfather, Alexander III, he was prominent later with the Comyns and the National party.

Sir David de Berclay, 1314–1351, Brechin I.

His son Sir David, third Lord of Brechin, signed the Ragman Roll in 1296, and thereafter for some years maintained his allegiance to the English King. It was in his Castle of Brechin that King John Baliol, on July 10th in the same year, surrendered his kingdom and all that he possessed into the hands of Edward I. Sir David de Brechin fought on the English side at the battle of Methven Wood, June 19th, 1306, where the Scots were surprised and defeated, but after the battle of Inverury he came to his peace with King Robert Bruce. Thereafter he continued eminently loyal, and ultimately married the King's sister. By her he had two sons and one daughter, Margaret, who, as already stated, married David de Berclay.

His eldest son, Sir David, fourth Lord of Brechin, was popularly known as "The Flower of Chivalry." He went to the Holy Land and distinguished himself fighting against the Saracens, but in 1320 he was accused and found guilty of complicity in the plot known as "the de Soules conspiracy." Sir Walter de Berkeley of Kerko (Towie VIII) was also accused and exonerated, as we have seen, but Sir David de Brechin suffered the extreme penalty of treason. After his death, his brother, Thomas of Lumquhat, being also forfeited with him, King Robert Bruce bestowed upon Sir David de Berclay, husband of his niece, Margaret of Brechin, the vast estates of Brechin, and in right of his wife Sir David de Berclay became fifth Lord of Brechin.

Robertson's Index, 33.

With the consent of his wife, Sir David de Berclay, Lord of Brechin, granted to the monks of Balmerino his fishing in the Tay, in Angus, called "le Crachue," between Partincrag and Dundee.

Balmerino Charters, p. 34.

Sir David de Berclay became Sheriff of Fife previous to the year 1317, when we find him instructed to preserve the marches of the convent lands of Dunfermline, and in the following years he was witness to numerous charters at Dunfermline, Arbroath, Scone and elsewhere.

Family of Wemyss, Vol. i, p. 74.

In 1327 he appears as Comptroller of the Household of the Earl of Carrick, King Robert's little son, and renders his accounts in detail.

The following year the King of Scotland successfully arrived at an agreement with the King of England, then Edward III, whose father had been deposed and subsequently murdered at Berkeley Castle, in Gloucestershire. The claims of Robert I had been acknowledged by the Pope and other powers, and the English, however reluctant, could no longer deny them. By the treaty of Northampton in 1328 it was laid down that the Kings of England and Scotland should be allied in friendship, while maintaining the independence of Scotland.

SIR DAVID DE BERCLAY, 1314–1351, Brechin I.

As a mark of amity, Joan, sister of Edward III, was betrothed to David, King Robert's little son.

Although by this treaty the Kingdom of Scotland gained her independence, the hatred of the English engendered in the Scottish people by long years of conflict drove them to a friendship with France, and the French influence can be clearly traced in the subsequent laws, architecture and modes of Scotland.

The health of King Robert was failing fast, and it is said that he had become a leper. He spent his last year mostly in his favourite home of Cardross, on the Clyde, and the Exchequer Rolls give many particulars, in detail, of expenses. There was a park at Cardross, and a park-keeper, gardeners' wages and seeds appear in the accounts, together with charges for window glazing and a coat for the King's fool.

Sir David de Berclay was much concerned in the preparation for the wedding of the Royal children, and two missions were sent to the Continent to procure furnishings for their home. Silks from Antioch and France, spices, wines, a bed-cover of miniver, goldsmith's work, and other delights are specially mentioned. Delicacies for the wedding feast had to be provided. The land itself furnished the customary capons, ducks and pheasants, hares and peacocks. Bills were paid for chalders of wheat and thousands of fish and so forth, and Sir David's own contributions include marts and haddocks, beeves and jars of wine. His accounts for the stewardship of the young Earl of Carrick's household include large purchases of wardrobe articles, and we read that the Prince had a clerk of

Sir David de Berclay, 1314–1351, Brechin I.

Audit, a clerk of Liverance and a clerk of Wardrobe of his own. Walter, Steward of Scotland, and Lady Margery his wife, Lady Burga de Vaux and five ladies (domicelles) were in attendance upon the little Countess, and the young couple had in addition a train of nine chaplains and clerics, thirty-eight esquires, four boys, three laundresses, thirty-six sergeants, two gardeners, twenty sumpter grooms, and a page for the Countess.

Exchequer Rolls, Preface.

At the time of the marriage Sir David de Berclay received a gift of £20 from the King, and there is a further entry of 100 shillings paid to him for a robe, which he evidently did not receive, because it has been carefully cancelled in the original.

The wedding was celebrated with great rejoicing at Berwick in the end of the year, but King Robert was too ill to attend. He lived only for a few months and died on June 7th, 1329, deeply mourned by his people. In fulfilment of his last wish, his devoted friends Sir James Douglas and Sir William Keith of Galston made an unsuccessful attempt to carry his heart to the Holy Sepulchre ; Douglas fell fighting with the Moors, and Sir William alone survived to bring back to Melrose the relic of a gallant King.

In addition to his Sheriffdom of Fife and his office of Steward to the Prince, Sir David de Berclay discharged the important function of auditor of accounts at Dumbarton in 1328 and Scone in 1329. He was responsible for the arrangements of the King's funeral, and was " Purveyor " for all that was required on the occasion.

The close of the year 1331 witnessed the coronation of the ten-year-old King and his Queen at Scone, when David II was the first King of Scots to be anointed, the special right of independent sovereigns only. Fifteen tuns of old wine, a great quantity of marts, wild boars, cranes, wild and domestic geese, rabbits, capons, etc., appear in the accounts for the celebrations, which lasted for thirty-nine days.

Randolph, who had been appointed Regent before the death of the late King, assumed the reins of government, but the country was plunged into civil warfare by those nobles who possessed estates both in England and Scotland. An Act had been passed in the previous reign against absentees, and they were forced to decide which of their possessions they would retain. These malcontents gathered round Edward Baliol, son of King John Baliol, a tool in the hands of Edward III, whose ambitions could not even spare his own sister. An invasion of Scotland was undertaken in July 1332, and Baliol sailed from the Humber and landed on the coast of Fife. Randolph died suddenly, and Donald, Earl of Mar, was chosen to succeed him as Regent, but he fell with 15,000 Scotsmen at the battle of Dupplin, in Strathearn, where the invaders were victorious. Edward Baliol was crowned at Scone before the year was out and acknowledged himself the vassal of Edward III, but the latter took no part in the struggle until the Scots made incessant trouble on the Border.

In the following year the English King invaded Berwick, and the Scots raised an army to relieve it, but they were totally routed at the battle of Halidon Hill; Sir Archibald Douglas, then Regent, the Earls of Ross, Sutherland, Menteith, Lennox and Atholl were among the many left on the field, and only the loyalty of Sir Malcolm Fleming saved the young King David. Escaping from Halidon Hill, Sir Malcolm fortified Dumbarton Castle, of which he was keeper, and there defended the Royal household until he could arrange their journey to safety in France.

The young King and Queen arrived at Boulogne on May 14th, 1334. The King of France, who had sent a gift for the cost of necessaries, victualling and boats, welcomed them with great ceremonial in Paris, from whence they proceeded to Château Gaillard. In this historic castle built by Richard Cœur de Lion, the splendid ruins of which still command the quiet reaches of the Seine, the boy who was King of Scotland kept his Court for seven years.

After the disaster to the Scots at the battle of Halidon Hill, many of the Scottish nobility transferred their allegiance to the victorious English, and among these we find Sir David de Berclay. The country near the Border was in a constant state

SIR DAVID DE BERCLAY, 1314–1351, Brechin I.

of warfare. Most of the castles were in English hands, and Berwick had been surrendered by Edward Baliol, but the Chronicles relate how gradually the Scots came rallying back to the support of the Regent, Sir Andrew Moray. Some, like young Robert Steward, son of Bruce's daughter Marjory, came out of hiding, and the National party gained in strength.

We read of one dangerous exploit after another, and how after the death of Moray and Robert "the Steward" became Regent, William of Douglas fought "ane fayre jeopardy" with Lord Berkeley (of Gloucestershire) on into the night until the light was gone, at Blackburn in 1338, and of the attempt to besiege "Saynt Jhonystone in 1339," when we hear of Sir David de Berclay being within the town. The Chronicles are a curious admixture of tragedy and lightheartedness, and they talk of desperate fights and tourneys and joustings, which, fought with all courtesy and formality, but often to the death, relieved the time between the more serious operations of war.

Fordun.

On this occasion Wyntoun writes that in 1338 William of Douglas had passed secretly to Gaillard to the King, and made his homage there, and on his return brought with him two French esquires. At the request of David de Berclay these esquires and three Scottish champions were pitted against each other in the jousting :—

"Dawy the Berclay that was then
within the town as Inglisman
Askyd at Jhon de Brus justyng
Off were, and he for-owt gruchying
Delyveryt hym off coursis thre,
Fayre hale justyng men mycht se:
Bot nane wes hurt thare, as thai say."

Soon afterwards Baliol left the country and, Edward III being occupied with wars in France, the tide began to turn.

In 1341 King David returned to Scotland to take his place upon the throne. Sir David de Berclay once more changed his allegiance, and we find him in the service of the King of Scotland.

Hamilton Charters, No. 124.

In 1342 Sir David de Berclay, Lord of Brechin, was witness on May 22nd, at Edinburgh, with Dom Bullock, Chamberlain of Scotland, to a charter of Hugh, Lord of Douglas, and Sir William Douglas of Liddesdale. In the same year Sir David is commanded by the King to take in charge and hold in custody at Malimore the said Dom Bullock, Chamberlain. Sir David's changes of allegiance are no more surprising than those of this "Lord William Bullock," a chaplain, who had been Chamberlain on behalf of Edward Baliol and Lieutenant and Treasurer for the English. He surrendered to Robert Steward at Perth, became King David's liegeman and was once more made Chamberlain. After amassing great wealth in various high offices he was suspected of treason and imprisoned.

Sir David de Berclay, 1314–1351, Brechin I.

About this time (*circa* 1340) Jean, daughter of Sir David de Berclay, married Sir David Fleming of Hatyrwick, son of Sir Malcolm Fleming of Biggar. Her father settled on her as dower the estate of Lochland within the grantor's Barony of Brechin, and three merks of silver yearly from his lands of Balbreny and others within the said Barony, to be held of the grantor and his heirs for ever, by rendering to the King the service belonging to the said land. The family of Fleming had always remained conspicuously loyal to the Bruces and given devoted service. Sir David Fleming's grandfather, Sir Robert, had been with Bruce when he stabbed the Red Comyn in the church of Dumfries, and is said to have cut off his head with the famous "mak siccar" argument. The wife of Sir Malcolm Fleming of Cumbernauld, saviour of the King after Halidon Hill, was King David's nurse, and her husband was later made Earl of Wigtown. Later still his grandson was to lose lands and earldom to Archibald Douglas, Earl of Galloway, but at this period we find the families of Douglas, de Berclay, Keith Marshal and the notorious Dom Bullock signing deeds together.

Hamilton Charters.

Comparative peace followed the return of the young King David, save for certain fighting on the Border.

In 1346, King Edward being engaged with the siege of Calais, King David, encouraged by his alliance with the French, broke the truce between Scotland and England with an invading army. He was made prisoner by the Archbishop

SIR DAVID DE BERCLAY, 1314–1351, Brechin I.

of York, at the battle of Neville's Cross in Durham, and remained in captivity for eleven years, while Robert Steward governed Scotland as Regent.

Arbroath Charters.

We find Sir David de Berclay acting as Deputy for William, Earl of Ross, the "Justiciar North of Fife," in a case heard at Forfar in 1348.

Brechin Charters.

He now appears to have become embroiled in a feud with the Douglas family, for we read that Sir James Douglas, a grave and gallant man who had given signal proofs of his loyalty to King David II, by whom he was made Captain of the Castle of Lochleven, was slain in a private quarrel by Sir David de Berclay at Haywood in 1350. Other versions state that Sir David was merely present on the occasion. Sir David de Berclay, Lord of Brechin, in the following year granted some arable land in the western part of Brechin to one Thomas called Schenyl, but the Douglas had neither forgotten nor forgiven, and his end came by the assassin's dagger. Macfarlane writes :—

Fordun, Vol. ii, p. 348.

> "This Sir David Berclay was killed in Aberdeen by John of St. Michael or Carmichael and his accomplices upon Fasten's Eve (Shrove Tuesday) Anno 1351, in the reign of King David Bruce (by the instigation of William, Lord Douglas, Lord of Liddesdale, then a prisoner in England) for the slaughter of John Douglas of Dalkeith, where Sir David Berclay was present."

Writing elsewhere, Macfarlane varies his account and states that Sir John Douglas was slain in a private quarrel by Sir David de Berclay.

Sir John of Fordun adds that not one of the abettors in Sir David's murder escaped death: all were destroyed by the sword of vengeance. The Berclays and their friends never rested until the crime was punished, and as late as 1389 the Moray register shows that at one of those reconciliations after arbitration by which official authority endeavoured to put an end to these feuds, the Bishop of Moray, for the satisfaction of the Earl of Moray, had to purge himself of any responsibility for the slaying of Sir David de Berclay. Fordun, writing of the slaying of Sir William Douglas by William de Douglas, afterwards Earl Douglas, while out hunting in Ettrick Forest, unsuspicious of evil, says :—

" he was thus put to death in revenge for the death of Alexander de Ramsay and Lord David de Berclay and because also of a great many other causes of unfriendliness and many a grudge stirred up between the Douglases by their thirst for power."

Sir David de Berclay had one daughter, who, as we have seen, married Sir David Fleming of Biggar, and one son, David, who succeeded him.

SIR DAVID DE BERCLAY, LORD OF BRECHIN II

SIR DAVID DE BERCLAY, 1351–1368, Brechin II.

Sir David de Berclay, sixth Lord of Brechin, married Janet Keith, daughter of Sir Edward Keith of Synton, and had one daughter Margaret.

Circa 1353 David de Berclay, Lord of Brechin, granted to his cousin Hugh, son of "our uncle David" (of Colcarny, Collairnie I), in memory of his, the grantor's, father, the upper and lower vill of Kindersleith, for a rent of one pair of gilt spurs yearly, to be paid at "our Manor of Lindores."

This grant was confirmed by Isabella Countess of Fife as overlord, and the witnesses to the confirmation were :—

Registrum de Panmure, Vol. ii, p. 322.

William, Bishop of St Andrews,
William, Abbot of Lindores,
Sir William de Ramsay, knight,
Alexander de Ramsay.

As we have seen, Sir William de Ramsay married as his second wife the said Countess Isabella in 1357 and died soon after. His daughter, it will be remembered, was wife to David de Berclay of Colcarny.

In 1356 David de Berclay, Lord of Brechin and Lord of Lindores, confirmed a grant of Dunmore and its appurtenances, in the Barony of Lindores, made by Mariota de Dunmore, sister and heir of Henry of Dunmore. This confirmation was witnessed at Edinburgh on October 9th, 1363, by the Bishops of Dunkeld and Dunblane, the Abbots of Scone and Lindores, and by Lord Robert de Erskyne,
Ibid. p. 231.
Chamberlain of Scotland, David de Grame, David de Fleming, knights, Alexander de Lyndesay and David de Berclay "our uncles," Michaele de Balfour, Adam de Moncur and many others. Of these witnesses David de Fleming was brother-in-law of David de Berclay, Alexander de Lyndesay had married his father's sister, and David de Berclay (of Colcarny, Collairnie I) was his father's brother.

In the same year (1363) we find that King Edward III granted a safe conduct to Sir David de Berclay and others to pass through his dominions attended by twelve esquires with horses and servants, to go to the wars in Prussia. It is probable that he did not return from this expedition, as his wife, Janet (or Jean) de Berclay, *née* Keith, signed a charter on September 8th, 1368, as a widow, and in April 1370 married Thomas de Erskine, stepson of her own mother, Christina de Keith, who married secondly Sir Robert de Erskine.

Sir David de Berclay, 1351–1368, Brechin II.

Hist. MSS. Com. Report, on the Mar Case, p. 9.

Margaret de Berclay, only child of Sir David de Berclay (Brechin II), sixth Lord of Brechin, succeeded to his title and estates.

Meanwhile negotiations by Robert Steward with Edward III of England for the ransom of King David II were not brought to a successful conclusion until 1357. 100,000 merks sterling were to be paid in ten years, during which time there was to be a truce between the two countries, and in addition twenty hostages, sons of Scottish nobility, were to be surrendered as pledges for payment. Among those hostages, as we shall see, was John de Berclay (Gartley XIB).

David II died childless in 1370, and was succeeded by his nephew Robert, the Steward of the Kingdom. This office was hereditary and gradually passed into the surname of the family, and was the designation of the line of Stewart Kings, of whom Robert II was the first.

Robert II, son of Marjory, daughter of King Robert Bruce, had been twice married, first to Elizabeth Mure, by whom he had four sons and six daughters, and secondly to Euphemia, daughter of the Earl of Ross, by whom he had two sons and four daughters. The turbulence of his sons and their friction with the nobles, notably the family of Douglas, caused much strife, and the Erskines, who were active partisans of the King, became objects of envy, not only for the marriage of Sir Thomas with the widow of the Lord of Brechin but also because the said Sir Thomas was guardian of the rich heiress Margaret de Berclay, Lady of Brechin.

It was the right of the King to dispose of the hand of such important young ladies and their estates, and the arrangement of marriages, both in this and the following century, was usually a matter of considerable financial gain to the guardians. We read of a final payment of £265 13s. 4d. by the King in

MARGARET DE BERCLAY, Lady of Brechin, 1370–1404.

1373 to the said Lord Thomas de Erskine to have the wardship and marriage of the daughter and heir of the late Sir David de Berclay, of Brechin.

This was evidently the last state of the negotiations prior to the marriage of Margaret, Lady of Brechin and ward of Sir Thomas, with Walter Stewart, youngest son of Robert II by Queen Euphemia. The couple were married under age, as we learn from a charter confirmed in full parliament at Scone on October 19th, 1378 :—

"Walter Stewart, son of the magnificent Prince the Lord Robert by Divine Grace Illustrious King of the Scots, as Lord of the Barony of Brechin within the county of Forfar, together with Margaret his wife, daughter and heir of the late David de Berclay, Lord of the said Barony, married under age, and therefore seized of the Barony by authority and dispensation Royal to Thomas de Rait of Wres, a grant of lands at Arroth."

Reg. Mag. Sig. Vol. i, p. 237, No. 652.

Appended to the deed were the seals of the couple and the seals of "My Lady the Queen Euphemia and of the Magnificent Lord, my brother, John Earl of Carrick, and Steward of Scotland."

Margaret, Lady of Brechin, died previous to 1404, having had issue two sons, David and Alan Stewart. David was a hostage in England in 1430 for the ransom of James I. On November 8th of that year we find a safe conduct issued for "Patrick Berclay and Thomas Mathewson, servants of David Stewart, Master of Atholl, to travel to their Lord, a hostage in England." In the following year, February 10th, 1431, there was a similar safe conduct for "two servants of the son of the Earl of Atholl, to travel together or separately with one servant in their company, and gold jewels and other things for the expenses of the said hostage in England."

Rot. Scot. in Turr. Lond. Vol. ii, p. 271.

David Stewart died while still a hostage in England *circa* 1433, leaving one son, Robert, of whom more later. Patrick Berclay, thus found in the service of his kinsman, was a cadet of the Mathers line. Alan Stewart was killed in 1431.

The reign of Robert II saw constant raids and counter-raids on the Border. Richard II of England invaded Scotland with an army of 70,000 men and marched to the Forth, but the country had been so wasted before him that all he could do was to destroy Melrose Abbey and retire. The Scots with their French allies harried the northern counties. These were the days of Douglas and Hotspur, of Otterburn and Chevy Chase, but a truce was made between England and France in 1389, with Scotland as an ally of the latter.

John, eldest son of Robert II, was created Earl of Carrick in 1368, and held various offices in the kingdom until he was disabled by the kick of a horse in 1387. Two years later, on the score of the King's age and infirmity, the Estates appointed as guardian of Scotland, not the Crown Prince, but the younger brother, Robert Stewart, later to be known as the Duke of Albany, who played so prominent and infamous a part in the history of his time.

Robert II died in 1390, and was succeeded by the aforesaid John, Earl of Carrick, but the name of John had been made unpopular and he was crowned under the name of Robert.

Scotland was sunk in chaos at this period. The nobles, lacking the accustomed martial occupation of attacking England, attacked their neighbours and oppressed all and sundry.

Robert III was too feeble to check them, and his power passed into the hands of his eldest son, David, Duke of Rothesay, who was arrested through the jealousy of the Duke of Albany in 1400 and died shortly after, it is said by starvation, in the castle of Falkland.

King Robert III, in his distrust of his brother Albany, endeavoured to send his youngest son, Prince James, to France for education and for safety. Sir David Fleming, husband of Jean Berclay, was the King's confidential agent in arranging the escape. He saw the Prince safely on board, but the ship was captured at sea by an English vessel and the boy committed to the Tower. Sir David Fleming was waylaid on his return and murdered by James, son of the Earl of Douglas, as an act of private revenge.

The "gentle and pious King" Robert III died in 1406, of grief, it is said, for the fate of his sons.

The English were glad enough to have so important a

hostage for Scotland's good behaviour as the young King James I. He was first confined in the Tower, where his cousin Murdach, son of his uncle Albany, and Griffin, son of Owen Glendower, were with him, but one of the first acts of Henry V, after his accession in 1413, was to order the removal of the prisoners to Windsor. James, attaining his majority, was given a governor and allowed more liberty of movement. He accompanied the English King to France, and Henry did all he could to attach him to himself, but James would consent to nothing likely to compromise the independence of Scotland.

Murdach was exchanged in 1416, and after the death of his father became Duke of Albany and Regent of Scotland, but it was not until 1424 that the Scottish King's return was arranged. A ransom could not be asked as he was taken in time of peace, but the English demanded forty thousand pounds to pay for "the expenses of his education," and the Scottish nobles were required to furnish twenty-eight hostages.

Before leaving England James I married the young daughter of the Duke of Somerset, at the church of St. Mary Overy, in Southwark. His devotion to her ceased only with his life. On May 21st, 1424, James I and his Queen were crowned at Scone; Murdach, Duke of Albany and Earl of Fife, placed the King upon his throne, and in the same year the first of the parliaments, which hereafter were held annually, was called by the King.

It may be that King James had learned in England the advisability of such an assembly, to deal with nobles who considered themselves petty kings, but he bided his time, and it was not until 1425 that he dealt summarily with those who had so long kept him out of his kingdom. He ordered the arrest of Albany, his two sons and twenty-six other nobles, who were afterwards executed at Stirling.

Then followed ten arduous and difficult years, at the end of which the only great earldoms not in the hands of the Crown were Atholl, Douglas, Crawford and Moray, but there was growing discontent among the nobility. In 1425 Sir Robert Graham seized the King in the presence of the assembled parliament, declaring that he arrested him in the name of the three Estates for cruel and illegal acts done to bring his nobles into subjection. The Lords who had promised their support to Graham quailed in the King's presence and the attempt failed.

MARGARET DE BERCLAY, Lady of Brechin, 1370–1404.

During the years thus briefly dealt with there is little that concerns our story to record of Walter Stewart, seventh Lord Brechin in the right of his wife Margaret de Berclay. He was created Earl of Caithness in 1402, and Earl of Atholl in 1404. In that year he obtained a safe conduct to go on pilgrimage to Canterbury, attended by a train of 100 horsemen, and in August he received dispensation to marry Elizabeth, daughter of William Graham, of Kincardine. This marriage did not take place, as the lady married his half-brother, John Stewart of Dundonald.

It would seem that he stood high in favour of James I in 1427, when the King took from Malise Graham his Earldom of Strathearne, which he had inherited from his mother, on the ground that it was a male fief, and transferred it to Walter Stewart, Earl of Atholl, grand-uncle of Graham and only surviving son of Robert II. Nevertheless, he joined a few years later in a conspiracy against King James, which was designed to place upon the throne Robert Stewart, his own grandson, son of David Stewart, his eldest son.

The leader of the plot was Sir Robert Graham, uncle of Malise, who had been banished for denouncing the King's action in parliament.

Through Robert Stewart, who by the King's favour was Chamberlain at the time, the conspirators gained entrance to the monastery of the Black Friars in Perth, where the King and his Court were keeping Christmas, and there in the night they treacherously murdered him. The Book of Pluscarden tells how " the King, the parting cup drunk and his gentlemen dismissed for the night, was alone with the Queen and her ladies." At the approach of footsteps and the clang of arms treason was instantly suspected, and it was found that the fastenings of the doors had been tampered with. One of the ladies, the heroic Catherine Douglas, thrust her arm through

MARGARET DE BERCLAY, Lady of Brechin, 1370-1404.

the staple to do its poor duty for a bolt, while the King leapt down into a small chamber below the floor.

From this chamber there had existed a channel, used for cleaning the apartment, leading into the outer court and wide enough to have afforded an escape for the King, but by his own direction it had been built up only three days before, as the balls from the tennis court near by were frequently lost in the aperture. Discovered by Graham and his band, James was dispatched "with wounds beyond counting." Some of the murderers escaped, but all were finally taken and put to death with horrible tortures, including young "Robin Stewart," who on the scaffold courageously acknowledged that he had his deserts.

In the list of those implicated were included "two brothers german," Barclays of Tentismuir. They succeeded in fleeing the country, but were captured in France and handed over to the Duke of Brittany, and suffered death in the same horrible manner as their fellow conspirators. It seems clear that these brothers were Barclays of the Kippo line.

We read in *Macfarlane's Collections* of the remarkable steps taken by the Maules to secure from "that old serpent of ancient and evil days," the Earl of Atholl, in his last hours, an acknowledgment of their right to half the Barony of Brechin, as sole surviving heirs with the Setons, through Sir David de Berclay's sister, the wife of Sir David Fleming of Biggar.

Book of Pluscarden.

"It was upon the 28th March 1437, about three hours of afternoon" that Sir Thomas Maule, along with Sir John Sandilands of Calder, Sir Andrew Ogilvy of Inchmartine, Thomas Fotheringham of Baluny, Thomas de Cranston, Sheriff's Deputy of Edinburgh, and Robert Logy visited the Earl in prison in the Tolbooth, "the day he was first put to the torment," to obtain from him an instrument to that end. "Immediately after securing it he was brought out thereof and carried through the streets of Edinburgh, for he had been convicted and condemned before." By "this instrument" the Earl of his own free will asserted and swore that the lands of the Barony of Brechin-Berclay, which he resigned into the King's hands, were possessed by him after the death of

Margaret de Berclay, his wife, simply of the courtesy of Scotland, and that David Stewart, his son and heir, never was in fee of the Barony of Berclay.

MARGARET DE BERCLAY, Lady of Brechin, 1370–1404

Thus ended in treason and disaster the line of the Barclays of Brechin. Half the property was secured by the Maule family, who later obtained the other moiety by purchase, and continue to hold it to the present time.

PEDIGREE V.

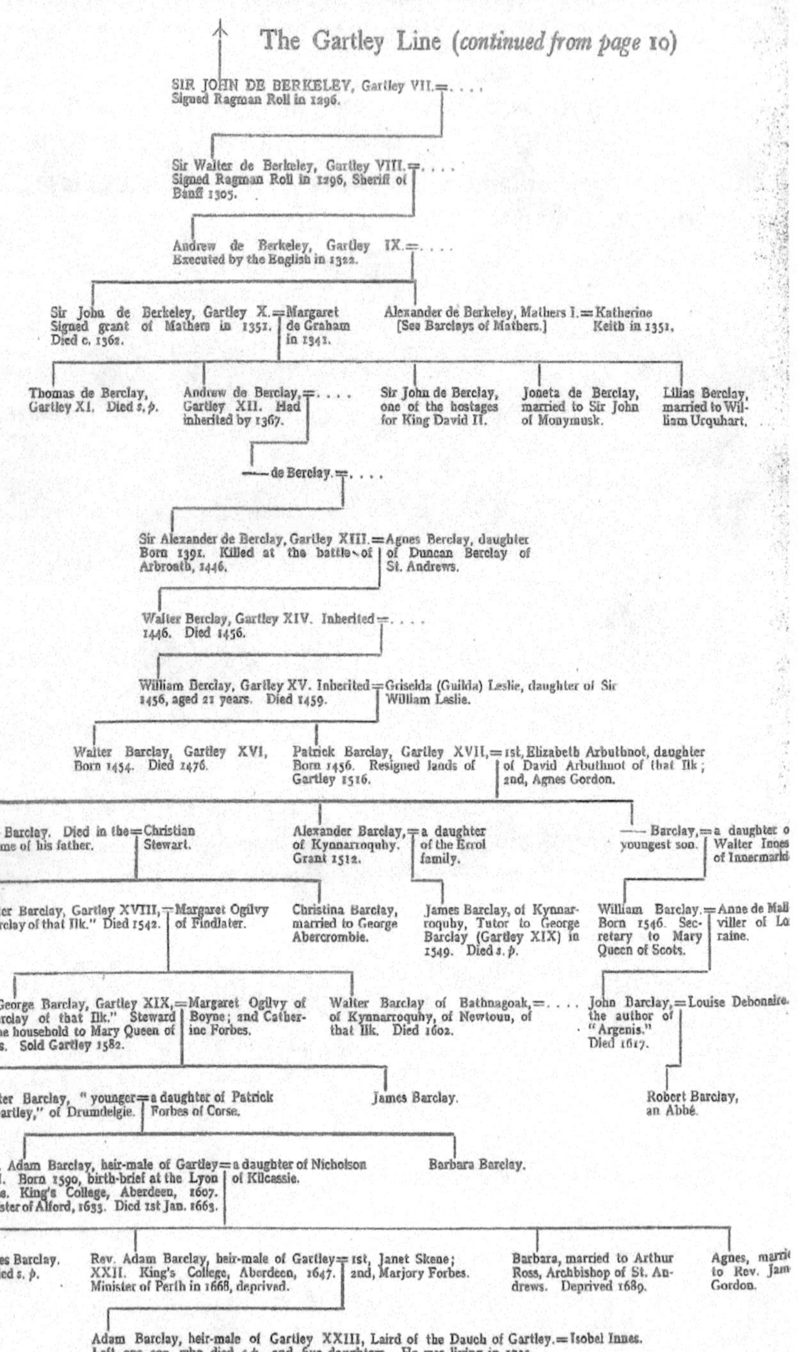

The Gartley Line (*continued from page 10*)

SIR JOHN DE BERKELEY, Gartley VII. = ...
Signed Ragman Roll in 1296.

Sir Walter de Berkeley, Gartley VIII. = ...
Signed Ragman Roll in 1296, Sheriff of Banff 1305.

Andrew de Berkeley, Gartley IX. = ...
Executed by the English in 1322.

Sir John de Berkeley, Gartley X. = Margaret de Graham in 1341.
Signed grant of Mathers in 1351. Died c. 1362.

Alexander de Berkeley, Mathers I. = Katherine Keith in 1351.
[See Barclays of Mathers.]

Thomas de Berclay, Gartley XI. Died *s. p.*

Andrew de Berclay, Gartley XII. Had inherited by 1367. = ...

Sir John de Berclay, one of the hostages for King David II.

Joneta de Berclay, married to Sir John of Monymusk.

Lilias Berclay, married to William Urquhart.

—— de Berclay. = ...

Sir Alexander de Berclay, Gartley XIII. = Agnes Berclay, daughter of Duncan Berclay of St. Andrews.
Born 1391. Killed at the battle of Arbroath, 1446.

Walter Berclay, Gartley XIV. Inherited 1446. Died 1456. = ...

William Berclay, Gartley XV. Inherited 1456, aged 21 years. Died 1459. = Griselda (Guilda) Leslie, daughter of Sir William Leslie.

Walter Barclay, Gartley XVI, Born 1454. Died 1476.

Patrick Barclay, Gartley XVII, = 1st, Elizabeth Arbuthnot, daughter of David Arbuthnot of that Ilk; 2nd, Agnes Gordon.
Born 1456. Resigned lands of Gartley 1516.

—— Barclay. Died in the lifetime of his father. = Christian Stewart.

Alexander Barclay, of Kynnarroquhy. Grant 1512. = a daughter of the Errol family.

—— Barclay, youngest son. = a daughter of Walter Innes of Innermarki[e].

Walter Barclay, Gartley XVIII, "Barclay of that Ilk." Died 1542. = Margaret Ogilvy of Findlater.

Christina Barclay, married to George Abercrombie.

James Barclay, of Kynnarroquhy, Tutor to George Barclay (Gartley XIX) in 1549. Died *s. p.*

William Barclay. Born 1546. Secretary to Mary Queen of Scots. = Anne de Malleviller of Lo[r]raine.

Sir George Barclay, Gartley XIX, "Barclay of that Ilk." Steward of the household to Mary Queen of Scots. Sold Gartley 1582. = Margaret Ogilvy of Boyne; 2nd Catherine Forbes.

Walter Barclay of Bathnagoak, of Kynnarroquhy, of Newtoun, of that Ilk. Died 1602. = ...

John Barclay, the author of "Argenis." Died 1617. = Louise Debonaire.

Walter Barclay, "younger of Gartley," of Drumdelgie. = a daughter of Patrick Forbes of Corse.

James Barclay.

Robert Barclay, an Abbé.

Rev. Adam Barclay, heir-male of Gartley XXI. Born 1590, birth-brief at the Lyon Office. King's College, Aberdeen, 1607. Minister of Alford, 1633. Died 1st Jan. 1663. = a daughter of Nicholson of Kilcassie.

Barbara Barclay.

James Barclay. Died *s. p.*

Rev. Adam Barclay, heir-male of Gartley XXII. King's College, Aberdeen, 1647. Minister of Perth in 1668, deprived. = 1st, Janet Skene; 2nd, Marjory Forbes.

Barbara, married to Arthur Ross, Archbishop of St. Andrews. Deprived 1689.

Agnes, marri[ed] to Rev. Jam[es] Gordon.

Adam Barclay, heir-male of Gartley XXIII, Laird of the Dauch of Gartley. = Isobel Innes.
Left one son, who died *s.p.*, and five daughters. He was living in 1735.

The Gartley Line

CONTINUED

SIR JOHN DE BERKELEY

Sir John de Berkeley, c. 1296, Gartley VII.

Although the Berkeleys of the Gartley line do not appear to have been so prominent in the history of the dramatic years through which we have followed their kinsmen of the Towie and the Brechin lines, we are able to trace not a little of their story.

We return to take up the tale from the son and successor of Sir Robert de Berkeley (Gartley VI).

The name of Sir John de Berkeley is to be found in the Ragman Roll, as recording his homage to Edward I at Wark on March 14th, 1295–6, together with his son, Walter de Berkeley, and his kinsman Sir David de Berkeley of Carny (Towie VIIB). He did not join in the great act of fealty at Berwick in August of that year, and we have no further knowledge of him.

Exchequer, Scots Docts., Box 4, No. 10.

SIR WALTER DE BERKELEY

SIR WALTER DE BERKELEY, 1296–1305, Gartley VIII.

The son of Sir John not only signed the Ragman Roll at the same time as his father, as just stated, but he is found among the Edinburgh homagers at Berwick on August 28th, 1296.

The seal of Sir Walter de Berkeley is one of those which have survived appended to the deed of homage, together, as we have noted, with that of Sir Patrick de Berkeley (Towie VII). The name, though much damaged, is unmistakable :—

"S WAL R D KELAY"

Introduction Exchequer Rolls.

but he was among those nobles who did not use their armorial seals for this enforced homage, but adopted a "device" which, in the case of Sir Walter, is described as "a rude squirrel."

Whether or not Sir Walter de Berkeley had been actively allied with the Scottish National party previous to his act of fealty in 1296, it is clear that thereafter he was allied with those who were of the English party.

Arbroath Charters, Vol. i, p. 165.

At the beginning of the Lent term, 1299–1300, we find him in Aberdeen, when John Comyn, Earl of Buchan, then Justiciar of Scotland, was holding pleas in his office "near the castle of Aberdeen, in a place called Castlesyd." Among the notables present Sir Walter appears with the Bishop of Aberdeen, John Earl of Atholl, then Sheriff, and others, taking second place in a list of eight knights. His attendance is also recorded in a note of this same occasion, in the Cartulary of Arbroath, when a question in regard to the regality of the Abbey was dealt with.

Acts of Parl. Scot., Vol. i, f. 121.

Rolls of Parl. i, p. 267, Appen. Claims, Ed. I.

Five years later he was definitely in the service of Edward I. At a parliament held at Westminster in September, 1305, to deal with the settlement of Scotland, it was laid down that none should be appointed Sheriffs save "the most sufficient men and most profitable for the King and people, and the maintenance of peace." By the same ordinance Sir Walter de Berkeley was appointed Sheriff of Banff.

Gartley is situated in a narrow peninsula of Banffshire

which juts into Aberdeenshire, and tradition accuses Sir Walter of having, during his tenure of office, altered the boundaries of Banffshire so as to include his estates in his own jurisdiction. It is further alleged that the Berkeleys of Gartley were hereditary Sheriffs of Banff, but no documentary corroboration of this statement can be traced.

SIR WALTER DE BERKELEY, 1296–1305, Gartley VIII.

Like so many others in these years, when first one party and then another were victorious, Sir Walter de Berkeley forsook his allegiance to King Edward so soon as the star of Bruce was in the ascendant. He hailed the deliverer of Scotland, and became a staunch adherent of King Robert I.

ANDREW DE BERKELEY

Andrew de Berkeley, 1322, Gartley IX.

Andrew de Berkeley, son of Sir Walter (Gartley VIII), was active on the side of Bruce, and met his death in the Scottish cause.

Edward III had succeeded to the throne of England, and in spite of short-lived truces and treaties there was constant warfare on the Border. In the autumn of 1322 the Scots made one of their periodic incursions into England and met with such success that the English King narrowly escaped capture at York. John of Fordun, writing of it, ends thus:—

> "Thus the King of Scotland, having gained a gladsome victory, went home again with his men in great joy and honour. The same year, on the first October, Andrew of Berkeley was taken and having been convicted of treachery underwent capital punishment."

For all its success, some members of the raid did not escape the enemy, and Andrew de Berkeley's capture meant prompt execution for treason, at the hands of north country officials, who would have known the record of his family's loyalty. Since his name never appears as having sworn fealty to England, he could with perfect justice, though with small hope of success, have defended himself with the plea used by the patriot Wallace, namely, that he might be put to death as an enemy, but never as a traitor, though all who fought against their King were traitor to the English.

Andrew de Berkeley had two sons, John, who succeeded him, and Alexander (Mathers I).

SIR JOHN DE BERKELEY

Sir John de Berkeley, 1338–1362, Gartley X.

The name of John de Berkeley is first found as witness to the confirmation of a charter of Alexander, Earl of Ross, prior to 1338.

The early death of his father and a long minority for John may account for the fact that no renewals of charters were obtained from King Robert I for Gartley, such as Walter de Berkeley of Kerko wisely secured for Towie and Balhelvie. This omission had evidently been rectified in the reign of David II, when we find John de Berkeley signing as "of Gartley."

Wyntoun, in his Chronicle, relates how, after the death of the Regent, Andrew de Moray, in 1338, a band of young men rallied to the rescue of Scotland, under his successor, Robert the Steward, and William Douglas, knight of Liddesdale. Among those young champions, whose valour regained the strongholds of Scotland, were John de Berkeley and William, son of Earl Hugh de Ross, who had fallen at Halidon Hill in 1333.

> "The land that tyme was all on ware (war)
> And in ryot as it were ere
> And yhwng men that in the land . . .
> And for the freedom of the land
> Rycht hardy thyngis tul on hand."

In 1341 John de Berkeley married Margaret de Graham, daughter of Sir John de Graham of Old Montrose, widow of Hugh, Earl of Ross, and mother of the William with whom he had fought side by side three years before.

We find in the Papal Registers a mandate, issued at Avignon, to the Bishop of Ross granting dispensation for the marriage. This dispensation had been sought because the couple were related within the third degree of affinity, and also because the alliance was considered desirable to bring peace and concord where there existed "great wars and grave enmities among relations."

Calendar Papal Registers, Vol. ii, p. 553.

Margaret, Countess of Ross, had also by her first husband a daughter, Euphemia, who married, first, John, Earl of Moray,

SIR JOHN DE BERKELEY, 1338–1362, Gartley X.

and, secondly, Robert the Steward, afterwards King Robert II. It thus followed that John de Berkeley, Lord of Gartley, was stepfather to the Queen of Scotland. His marriage seems to have been that of a young husband with a more mature wife.

The settlement of family feuds and quarrels was a reason frequently given in applying for a dispensation for marriage. It was the case when a marriage was arranged in 1350 between Euphemia, then widowed Countess of Moray, and Robert the Steward, the particular "enmity" being between her brother William, Earl of Ross, and her prospective husband.

Robertson's Index, 100 (1A).

John de Berkeley is among the witnesses to the confirmation by David II of a charter by William, Earl of Ross, to Reginald, son of Roderick of the Isles, dated July 4th, 1342. This confirmation is undated and John de Berkeley's name is not among the knights. From one deed, in 1374, it appears that he was knighted later.

Fœdera, Vol. iii (2), pp. 10-14.

The Chronicles have still something to tell us of John de Berkeley, Lord of Gartley, for Wyntoun relates the story of a serious quarrel in which he was concerned.

Sir William de Douglas was at this time custodian of Roxburgh, to which office his family considered they had hereditary right. The position of the castle rendered it highly important and its security could only be entrusted to men of proven valour and loyalty.

Shortly after the return of King David from France, and in one of the "grave wars" which were so unceasingly waged among the turbulent lords, Sir Alexander de Ramsay attacked the castle and took it by escalade. The King thereupon appointed him custodian of Roxburgh and Sheriff of Teviotdale in lieu of Sir William Douglas, who promptly retaliated by capturing the gallant Sir Alexander and starving him to death at Hermitage. David II, sincerely grieved at the death of Ramsay and greatly enraged, appointed John de Berkeley custodian of the Castle. Both Sir Alexander Ramsay and Sir William Douglas had been constant in their allegiance, and rendered noble service to the Scottish crown, and Robert the Steward, realising the danger of estranging such a man as Douglas and driving him into the hands of "Inglishmen," persuaded the King to pardon and reinstate him.

Sir John de Berkeley, 1338–1362, Gartley X.

Although John de Berkeley had fought under Sir William Douglas in the campaign of 1338, there was never good feeling between their families. We have already recorded how Sir William fought "ane fayre jeopardy" with another de Berkeley some years before, and there is no doubt that this incident of the custodianship of Roxburgh in 1343 contributed to that enmity which finally resulted in the assassination of Sir David de Berkeley of Brechin.

It was on the advice of Sir William Douglas that David II broke truce and invaded England three years later. He was captured at the battle of Neville's Cross, and "our King Dawy that weis yhong stout and joly" rode through the streets of London at the head of a train of prisoners, on his way to the Tower. Eleven years later the young son of John de Berkeley was to be one of the hostages for his release.

In 1351 "John de Berkeley of Grantoly" was witness to a deed granting the lands of Mathers to his brother Alexander and Katherine Keith, his wife. This is the first time the territorial designation appears in the Gartley line.

Original Document at Bury Hill.

Alexander, brother of John de Berkeley, was the progenitor of the Barclays of Mathers and Urie, and will be dealt with later.

John de Berkeley was also witness about 1357 to a grant for Thomas, Earl of Mar, in which he is described "Johanne de Garintuly, consanguineo nostro."

Coll. Aberd. and Banff, Spalding Club, Vol. i, p. 618.

He died previous to 1362, leaving, as we shall see, a legacy of difficulties to his family. He had issue three sons, Thomas, Andrew and John, and two daughters, Joneta (or Jonet), who married first Sir John de Monymusk, and secondly Sir Alexander de Moray, and Lilias, who married William Urquhart, Sheriff of Cromartie.

The two elder sons of John de Berkeley succeeded him in turn, but before continuing with the line we have to record the history of his younger son John.

SIR JOHN DE BERCLAY (GARTLEY XIB)

Sir John de Berclay, 1352–1374, Gartley XIb.

As the marriage of John de Berkeley, Lord of Gartlie, with Margaret, widowed Countess of Ross, took place in 1341, and this John de Berclay was the youngest of their three sons, he must have been quite a child when in 1352 we find mention of him and his wife, Christina. An indult is recorded in the Papal Calendar, under date of February of that year, that confessors should be chosen for John de Berclay and Christina, his wife, of the diocese of Moray, " who shall give them, being penitent, plenary remission at the hour of death, with the usual safeguards." It may be that this child-marriage had been arranged in view of the destiny which awaited the boy John.

During the last years of the imprisonment of King David II in England, the young King was himself employed by his captors to negotiate the terms of his ransom, which was finally agreed at the sum of 100,000 merks. In addition twenty hostages, youths of noble birth, were demanded to ensure payment of the same, and among them was John de Berclay.

A convention met at Newcastle to deliberate on the matter, and an indenture was drawn up " faite a Noefchastell sur Tyne le 13 jour de Jhyl 1354 " between the Bishop of Durham, William de Bohun, Earl of Northumberland and Constable of England, Gilbert D'Umfraville, Earl of Angus, Lords Percy and Neville, Henry de Sorrye and others of the one part, and the Bishops of St. Andrews and Brechin, Patrick de Dunbar, Earl of March, Abbot of Dunfermline, Robert de Erskyne and others of the second part. It was agreed for the payment of the said sum of silver, Monsieur David de Bruys will deliver twenty hostages. The next clause of the agreement laid down that they would be treated courteously at the " suitable charge of those who delivered them." It was not required that all the hostages should remain until the entire ransom was paid, but completion made of each 10,000 merks, exchanges might be made with " the best hostages, sons and heirs of the gentlemen of the greatest sufficiency who might be found within the country of Scotland."

Exchequer, Scots Docts., Box 2, No. 36.

Of the twenty entries in the list of noble youths, sixteen are "sons and heirs," two are heirs, one is "son of," but in the last case the entry is "one of the sons" of John de Berkeley. Why John, Lord of Gartley, was thus spared the parting from his son and heir we have no means of deducing. The record of a later convention, at Berwick in 1357, gives us not only the names of the hostages, but the men into whose charge they were to be handed. John, son and heir of the Steward of Scotland, and Humphrey, son and heir of Roger de Kirkpatrick, were delivered to Lord Percy, who would hardly have supposed that one of his young charges was to be King of Scotland as Robert III. Ronald, son and heir of Sir William More, Gilbert, son and heir of Sir John Kennedy, and John, son of John de Berkeley, were delivered to Alan de Strother, late Sheriff of Northumberland. The following year Alan de Strother, late Sheriff, had orders to deliver his hostages to his successor and take a receipt for Thomas Fleming, son of the Earl of Wigtown, Ronald More, Gilbert Kennedy, John de Berclay, David Wemyss and John de Valance.

Sir John de Berclay, 1352–1374, Gartley XIb.

Exchequer, Scots Docts., Box 2, No. 38.

By the time the final settlement was made "three great lords" were required in addition to the youths; among them was Sir Thomas de Erskine, second husband of Janet Berclay, widow of Sir David de Berclay (Brechin II), and the payment of the ransom was not completed until 1383, twenty-six years after David II was set free. The raising of the great sum of money was a fruitful cause of dissension among the Scottish nobles.

On March 17th, 1370–1, John de Berclay appears among certain Scotsmen who received safe conducts from Edward III, granted at Westminster, to travel "in our kingdom of France and England," but there is no record of when he ceased to be held hostage. There is no reason to suppose that his life in this capacity was irksome. Even prisoners were often permitted freedom to embark on warlike expeditions on behalf of their captors, and hostages would have been granted considerable liberty on parole.

This period was, nominally at least, a time of peace between Scotland and England, and in 1374 Sir William de Keith,

Sir John de Berclay, 1352–1374, Gartley XIb.

Fœdera, Vol. iii (2), pp. 10, 14.

Marischal of Scotland, received a safe conduct to go, for a year or two, beyond the seas with his son-in-law, Edmund de Mortimer, Earl of March. They went in the service of the English King, and with them went Sir John de Berclay, Chevaler, son of Sir John de Berkele, Chevaler. It may be that he received the honour of knighthood in return for his services as hostage to David II.

THOMAS DE BERCLAY

Thomas de Berclay succeeded his father, Sir John de Berkeley (Gartley X), in the year 1362. He was a young man, barely twenty years of age, when he came to his inheritance. He held the estates for less than five years, as we find his brother Andrew in possession in 1367.

THOMAS DE BERCLAY, 1362–1367, Gartley XI.

There is an entry regarding Thomas de Berclay in the records, in which he is called " Thomas de Berclay Dominus de Grantlye " (Gartley).

The entry is in the Urquhart Charters, and this fact is interesting as it strengthens the assertion in Douglas and Wood's *Peerage* that Lilias, the younger daughter of Sir John de Berkeley, and sister of Thomas, married William Urquhart of Cromartie.

The appearance of the name of Thomas is in a grant made by his half-brother, William Earl of Ross, of the burg of Cromartie to his cousin Alexander de Urquhart. The deed is undated, but as the name of John, Bishop of Murray, who died in 1362, is included among the witnesses, it fixes the date.

Scottish History Society, Vol. ii, p. 372.

The charter is as follows :—

" Charter by William, Earl of Ross, Lord of Sky, son and heir of Lord Hugh, late Earl of Ross, to Alexander de Urquhart and his heirs . . . Totum Burgum nostrum de Crommathye cum annuali redditu. . . . Witnesses Alexander Bishop of Ross, John Bishop of Murray, Donald Abbot of Novae Fermicoe, Lord Robert of Lauder, and Oliver de St. Clare, knights, Thomas de Berclay Dominus de Grantlye, Hugh de Ross, my brother and many others."

ANDREW DE BERCLAY

ANDREW DE BERCLAY, 1367–1404, Gartley XII.

Andrew de Berclay inherited the lands of Gartley from his brother Thomas (Gartley XI). He witnesses in 1367 the homage of Hugh de Fraser, Lord of Lovat, portioner of Ard, rendered to Alexander Bishop of Moray. Among those present were: Sir William de Keith, Marischal of Scotland, Thomas, Prior of Pluscarden, and Andrew Berclay, "Lord of Garntully." In an instrument dated December 12th of the same year, recording the above, William de Keith is styled "Deputy of the Lord Earl of Moray," and Andrew de Berclay as of "Grantoly and Birkynhill" (in Strathbogie).

Register of Moray, pp. 368–9.

Andrew de Berclay succeeded to burdened estates. Many of the Scottish nobles had been ruined by incessant warfare and consequent devastation, and ten years previously it had already been recorded in the Exchequer Rolls that "the hostilagio de Berclay," among many other lands, had returned no dues, "lying wasted."

On June 15th Andrew de Berclay granted to William de Leth, burgess of Aberdeen, all his lands of Drumrossy in the regality of Garioch, to hold by doing forensic service due from them to the overlord, and payment to himself and his heirs of a silver penny to be paid at Drumrossy, and blanchferm. The burgess had advanced the money for the payment of the debts of Andrew's father, John, and himself, and Andrew stated that both were heavily involved.

He was evidently responsible for legacies under his father's estate, for he grants to his sister, Joneta, relict of Sir John de Monymusk, and to Mariota and Elizabeth, her daughters by the said Sir John, and the survivor and heirs of each, all his lands of Melrose, in the county of Banff, together with the mill, in satisfaction of any claim she had or might have in the lands of John de Berkeley, her father, at the rent of one silver penny to be paid at Doune at Whitsuntide, the said land to be free of annual rent of £10 and 4 chalders of wheat to the King. The witnesses were Sir Alexander Fraser, Sheriff of Aberdeen, Master Reginald de Ogiston, Rector of Turref, William de Berclay, of Towie (IX), Lord of Kerko, and many others.

Reg. Epis. Aberdeen, Spalding Club, Vol. ii, p. 281.

Melrose in Banffshire, being Graham land, had probably been the dower of his mother, Margaret. It adjoins Cullen, which, it will be remembered, was the property of the Barclays of Towie.

ANDREW DE BERCLAY, 1367–1404, Gartley XII.

The Lady Joneta (or Jonet) of Monymusk had difficulty in obtaining her inheritance in her father's impoverished estates, and her half-sister, Queen Euphemia, interested herself in the matter. It will be remembered that Euphemia had been the wife of Sir John de Moray before she married Robert the Steward, later King Robert II, and in 1375 she arranged a double marriage between two of her Moray kinsmen and Lady Joneta and her daughter Elizabeth of Monymusk.

An indenture was executed at Perth on November 24th, 1375, between Queen Euphemia and her son Earl David, of the one part, and Alexander de Moray of Drumsegarth, of the other part, whereby it was agreed that Sir Alexander de Moray should marry Lady Joneta de Monymusk, sister of the Queen. Queen Euphemia and her son undertook to assist Sir Alexander in recovering the inheritance of Joneta, and further it was agreed that Walter de Moray, brother to Alexander, should, if he so pleased, marry Elizabeth de Monymusk, elder daughter of the Lady Joneta.

Douglas's Peerage, Vol. vii, p. 235.

We have no record of the marriage of Andrew de Berclay, who died previous to 1405.

He was succeeded by Sir Alexander de Berclay, but from the records it is evident that he was a minor and not son, but grandson of Andrew.

It should be noticed that the three lines, Gartley, Towie and Bourty, each have a nameless heir at this time. It seems probable that these three young Berclays were among those who fell at the Harlaw, in which fierce struggle their families must undoubtedly have been involved.

SIR ALEXANDER DE BERCLAY

SIR ALEXANDER DE BERCLAY, 1391–1446, Gartley XIII.

Sir Alexander de Berclay was born in 1391, and succeeded to the estates of his grandfather, Andrew de Berclay, in early childhood. He was ward of Sir Walter de Tulach and his wife Lady Agnes. After the death of Sir Walter, Lady Agnes in 1405, as surviving guardian, received payment of a rent due to Alexander de Berclay of Gartley from the customs of Aberdeen. The rent is paid to the young Alexander as "one of the heirs of Richard Ranulphi, his co-heir being Thomas Wright." Ranulphi is the early form of the Randolphs, Earls of Moray.

Exchequer Rolls, Vol. iii, p. 639.

The accounts of the Great Chamberlain record constant payments on behalf of Alexander de Berclay of his half-share in an annuity of £10, until 1412, when he draws it himself.

Accounts of Gt. Chamb., Vol. iii, p. 169.

In 1413 Alexander de Berclay, having attained his majority the previous year, is witness to a charter from Sir Alexander de Keith, granting to his son-in-law, Patrick de Ogilvy and his wife, Christian, daughter of the grantor, the Baronies of Doune and Grandoun.

Collections Aberd. and Banff, Spalding Club, Vol. iii, p. 166.

Alexander married Agnes, daughter of Duncan Berclay. The Vatican transcripts record the commission by the Pope on February 12th, 1414-15, to the Bishop of St. Andrews to grant dispensation for the marriage of Alexander de "Burchle" and Agnes Berclay, a daughter of the deceased "Duncany" Berclay, a damsel in the diocese of St. Andrews, who desired with the consent of their parents and friends to contract marriage, but were related in the fourth degree. We have no information of this Duncan Berclay.

Vatican Transcripts.

Alexander de Berclay was knighted before the year 1434, when we find him acting as Attorney of the Queen, Joan, wife of James I, and taking sasine of her pension of £100 from the great customs of the burgh of Aberdeen.

Accounts of Gt. Chamb., Bannatyne Club, Vol. iii, p. 226.

In 1438 he appears in the Exchequer Rolls as accounting for the rents of the demesne land of Kildrummy, and was auditor of accounts sent in by the grangers of Kildrummy and Durnoschetis. He owned a house in Aberdeen, for in the

Cartulary of St. Nicholas of Aberdeen there is the record of an endowment made in 1446, the year of his death, which refers to the croft at the end of the street which belonged to the heirs of Sir Alexander Berclay, as well as to the lands of Andrew Wright.

SIR ALEXANDER DE BERCLAY, 1391–1446, Gartley XIII.

On July 2nd, 1443, Sir Alexander de Berclay of Gartley witnessed a deed relating to a contract of marriage between the son of Sir Andrew Ogilvy of Inchmartin and Euphemia, daughter of David de Wemyss.

Wemyss Memoirs, Vol. ii, p. 65.

Sir Alexander met his death in a conflict known as the battle of Arbroath in 1446. The occasion was a violent clash of arms in a quarrel between the families of Ogilvy and Lindsay, concerning the office of Justiciar of the Abbey of Arbroath. Alexander de Lindsay had been removed from this office, which had been bestowed by the Abbot on Alexander Ogilvy of Inverquharitie.

When the Earl of Crawford, formerly ally of Alexander Ogilvy, heard that his son, Alexander Lindsay, assisted by the Hamiltons, had gathered in force, and that Alexander Ogilvy had done the same, he hastened to the spot to prevent mischief, but he was killed by a common soldier, who fell upon him and speared him through the mouth. The Earl's followers fell into a frenzy and many were slain in the violent fight that ensued.

Jervise's Land of the Lindsays, p. 143.

It is said that Sir Alexander de Berclay was only embroiled in the affair, because having spent the previous night with his kinsmen the Ogilvies, the laws of hospitality compelled him to ride into battle in their quarrel on the morn.

He was grievously wounded in the thigh and died the next day.

He was succeeded by his son, Walter Berclay, and it should be noted that the name now drops the " de."

WALTER BERCLAY

Walter Berclay, 1446–1456, Gartley XIV.

Walter Berclay, Lord of Grantuly, son of Sir Alexander de Berclay (Gartley XIII), received through William Schrare, burgess of Aberdeen, his deputy, the pension which had belonged to his father from the customs of Aberdeen. This payment recurs in 1448, and in 1451 it is received by his proctor, Patrick de Baidyenagh.

Exchequer Rolls, Vol. i, pp. 322, 455.

By an interesting charter of May 31st, 1449, confirmed by James II at Edinburgh on August 5th, 1452, we learn that he received in pledge from his cousin, John of St. Michael, Lord of Quhichester, the lands of Crechie at Bothelny, in the sheriffdom of Aberdeen, for which Walter Berclay paid the sum of £45 13s. 4d. The lands were to be held by Walter Berclay until repayment of the said sum had been made to him, or his heirs and assigns, "between the rising and the setting of the sun of one day on the kirk of Bothelny, on the high altar of the same by the said John, fruits and dues &c., to be lifted by the said Walter in the meantime." Quhichester is probably Whichester in Northumberland.

Reg. Mag. Sig., Vol. ii, p. 589.

In 1455 Walter Berclay signs as of "Grantuly" and "Chanon of Murra" (Moray) in witness of a Contract Matrimonial between George, Master of Huntly, and Elizabeth, Countess of Murray—Murray being a version of "Moray" which was now coming into use.

Miscellanies, Spalding Club, Vol. iv, Gordon Papers.

The exact date of the death of Walter Berclay is uncertain. He is found as the member of a Jury summoned for an Inquisition concerning the lands of Forglen, at Aberdeen, on November 3rd, 1457, but this record does not accord with an entry in the Exchequer Rolls which states that the annuity from the burgh of Aberdeen was paid to the Procurator of the deceased Walter Berclay in 1456. It seems that the date of the Jury is erroneous, as his heir was in possession of Gartley in 1456.

Collections of Aberdeen and Banff, Spalding Club, Vol. i.

Exchequer Rolls, Vol. iv, p. 41.

The name of the wife of Walter Berclay, Lord of Gartley, has not come down to us, but he was succeeded by his eldest son William, who at the date of his father's death was still under twenty-one years of age.

WILLIAM BERCLAY

WILLIAM BERCLAY, 1456–1459, Gartley XV.

William Berclay succeeded his father, Walter, in the estates of Gartley, but held them only a short time.

He received the annuity from the customs of Aberdeen through Alexander Leslie, who is described as "Tutor and Attorney for the laird of Grantuly."

Captain Douglas Wimberley was of the opinion that he succeeded as a minor, but the records indicate that William reached his majority the year that he inherited.

Alexander Leslie was evidently man of business to more than one owner of Gartley lands, for we find him also tutor to William's little son.

William Berclay received sasine of the lands of Gartley, and paid £4 as duplicand to King James II in 1456, and in the same year got sasine of the lands of Crechie. Exchequer Rolls, Vol. vi, p. 157.

He married Griselda (Guilda) Leslie, daughter of Sir William Leslie, fourth Baron of Balquhain, by his wife Elizabeth Fraser, the daughter of Hugh, first Lord Lovat, and Janet Fentoun, whose marriage had taken place in 1416. Leslie Family.

By his wife Guilda Leslie, William left two infant sons, Walter and Patrick, both of whom in their turn succeeded to his property of Gartley.

He died in 1459, in the twenty-fourth year of his age.

WALTER BERCLAY

Walter Berclay, 1459-1476, Gartley XVI.

Walter Berclay succeeded his father, William, in 1459. Alexander Leslie, as "tutor to Walter Berclay of Grantuly," received annual payment from the customs of Aberdeen until 1471, after which it was paid to Gilbert Kintore until 1475. Payment for two years was paid to "Walter Berclay himself, £5 yearly." In the same year, 1475, payment for "Walter Berclay of Grantuly" was received by his procurator, David Colison.

Exchequer Rolls, Vol. viii, p. 325.

He died in the following year, 1476, and was succeeded by his young brother Patrick.

PATRICK BARCLAY

PATRICK BARCLAY, 1476–1516, Gartley XVII.

Patrick Barclay succeeded to the estates of his brother Walter in 1476, and it may be noted that the change in the spelling of the surname took place about this date.

The reign of James II had passed in ceaseless strife between his nobles, most potent among whom were the Earls of Douglas, who constituted a menace to the throne of Scotland, and the King's anger had culminated in the stabbing of Earl William when under safe conduct.

This act of treachery had thrown the country into a state of civil war, for the Earl's brother and successor made open defiance, and the King, too feeble to break the strength of the Douglas faction, used the feuds of the nobles for his own ends.

This course only served to place power in different hands, and led to further trouble with those who thus gained the ascendancy.

James appointed the chief of the House of Gordon to command his forces in the north.

The Earl of Angus, Head of the Red Douglas, was commanding in the south, and was successful in overcoming the faction of the Black Douglas, the senior branch of his family, whose fall was completed by their defeat at Arkinholm in 1454.

Henry VI of England being occupied in the struggle between the parties of York and Lancaster, James saw his opportunity of regaining the towns still held by the English in Scotland, but in an attack on Roxburgh he was killed by the bursting of a cannon in 1460.

His son James III was no more successful than his father in controlling the turbulence of his nobility, with whom he was personally unpopular. Edward IV of England appeared friendly during the early years of the Scottish King's reign, but secretly plotted with disaffected nobles in the north, and finally entered into an agreement to place Alexander, Duke of Albany, brother of James III, on the throne of Scotland.

James mustered an army to invade England, but his nobles

PATRICK BARCLAY, 1476–1516, Gartley XVII.

revolted, and when he reached Lauder Bridge carried him back to Edinburgh. The north of the country was loyal, and when a confederacy of the lords south of the Forth claimed to have deposed him in favour of his son the Prince of Scotland, James III raised an army and met his opponents at Sauchieburn in 1488. Threatened with defeat, the King fled from the field, and in his flight was thrown from his horse and carried into a mill on the Bannockburn, where he was attacked and murdered.

It is recorded that Patrick Barclay of Gartley (XVII) was loyal to King James III in his struggle with the nobles. We have no evidence of his participation in the fighting, but the fact that the Earl of Huntly was both friend and neighbour must have made it almost impossible for him to stand aside.

It would appear that the Gartley estates had been well nursed during the tenure of the four generations which had held it so quickly in succession, for Patrick Barclay was a man of wealth and able to add considerably to his possessions.

He was twice married. His first wife was Elizabeth, daughter of David Arbuthnot of that Ilk. She bore him three sons and two daughters—Elizabeth, who married her kinsman, Patrick Barclay of Towie (Towie XIV), and ——, who married James Johnston of that Ilk and Caskiben. The name of Patrick Barclay's eldest son is unknown. He married Christian Stewart, and died in the lifetime of his father, possibly at the battle of Flodden Field. He left a son, Walter (Gartley XVIII), and a daughter, Christina. Patrick's second son was Alexander. By a charter confirmed at Edinburgh in November 1512 he granted to Alexander the lands of Kynnarroquhy:—

History of The Garioch.

"to Mr. Alexander Barclay in life-rent, the lands of Kynnarroquhy, in the sheriffdom of Aberdeen, and moreover, for good service, he granted to the said Alexander, that so long as it should so happen, that the said lands should lapse into the hands of the King, the lands should be free of any claim of the King."

Reg. Mag. Sig. Vol. ii, No. 3782.

Alexander married a member of the family of Errol, kinswoman of the Earl of Errol, and had one son, James Barclay of Kynnarroquhy, who is mentioned in the records as guardian to his young cousin, George Barclay (Gartley XIX), in 1551. On the death of James Barclay without issue the property of Kynnarroquhy passed to Walter Barclay of Bathnagoak, the brother of Sir George Barclay (Gartley XIX).

PATRICK BARCLAY, 1476–1516, Gartley XVII.

The name of the third son of Patrick Barclay and his wife Elizabeth Arbuthnot has not been recovered. He was born considerably later than his brothers and had a son, William Barclay, a man of some note, with whom we shall deal presently.

Previous to the year 1517 Patrick Barclay married, as his second wife, Agnes Gordon, but to which branch of that family she belonged cannot be ascertained.

The annuity from the customs of Aberdeen was paid to Patrick Barclay in 1476. The following year it was paid to his procurator, David Colison, and again to Patrick himself in 1479. In 1491 this pension, so long enjoyed by the Lords of Gartley, was resigned, and granted by King James IV to the Cathedral of Aberdeen.

Exchequer Rolls, Vol. viii, pp. 400, 640.

Reg. Mag. Sig. Vol. ii, No. 2032.

The name of Patrick Barclay of Grantuly appears among the witnesses to a charter granted by George, second Earl of Huntly, in favour of his natural son, Adam de Gordoun, of the Barony of Scheves, in the Sheriffdom of Aberdeen, signed at Edinburgh, 8th October 1479, and confirmed in the following year.

Ibid, No. 1438.

From this time onward the records show a close association between the families of Gordon and Barclay, until a century later, by the wreck of the Barclay fortunes, what remained of the estate of Gartley passed by sale into the hands of Sir Patrick Gordon of Auchindoun, seventh son of George, fourth Earl of Huntly.

For some years after 1480 Patrick Barclay added to his ancestral estates. In 1487 he acquired lands in Drumblade from John Langlands of Cullace, and again in 1491 and 1493 he increased his property in the vicinity.

Reg. Mag. Sig. Vol. ii, Nos. 2055, 2152.

In 1493 he and his kinsman Walter Berclay of Towie were concerned with others in an action at law, and were ordered to pay one hundred merks next Midsummer Day and another one hundred merks at the later Marymas next thereafter satisfation for "dampnage, scathis and spuilyeis com-

Acts of Council, p. 266.

PATRICK BARCLAY, 1476–1516. Gartley XVII.

mitted by the said persons or their accomplices on the land of Andrew, Lord Grey." This is the first of the two occasions on which the name of Patrick of Gartley appears with that of his kinsman of Towie and is interesting as showing the association between them.

We find Patrick acting as witness to several charters about this time. King James IV was liked by his nobles, and his rigorous maintenance of justice and his encouragement of commerce and agriculture won the good feeling of the commons. Scotland enjoyed greater peace and prosperity than had been her lot for years, and many records of buying and selling of land indicate that the nobility had leisure to pursue their private affairs.

In 1501 Patrick of Gartley was ordered by the King's auditors to pay to James Turing, burgess of Edinburgh, as assignee of the Master of Huntly

Records of Aboyne, p. 418.

"A last of salmon full red and swet on the bynd of Banff guid merchant ware salted with salt"

and at Edinburgh, 8th January 1505-6, King James IV confirmed to Patrick Barclay and Elizabeth Arbuthnot, his spouse,

Reg. Mag. Sig. Vol. ii, No. 2907.

"The half of the lands of Moncoffer, with the fishing in the waters of Dovern, in the Barony of Kynedward" (King Edward).

On September 9th, 1513, the disaster of Flodden Field struck Scotland to the heart. A truce with Henry VII had been concluded in 1497, and the two Kings further allied by the marriage of James IV with Margaret Tudor, daughter of the English monarch, in 1502, but differences arose, and when war was declared between England and France, Scotland took the side of the French. James himself led an army across the Border, only to meet with utter defeat and death. It is said that twelve Earls and thirteen Barons fell dead round him on the battlefield.

In 1514 Patrick Barclay sold to Sir Patrick Grantullie, Rector of Glas, his lands of Fowlisse, Corskquhie and Goveny, in the Barony of Kynedward, Sheriffdom of Aberdeen, and among the witnesses to his charter we find James Gordon, Patrick Barclay son and apparent heir of Walter Barclay of

Reg. Mag. Sig. Vol. iii, No. 17.

Tolly (Towie XIII) and James Barclay. Patrick Barclay of Towie was son-in-law, and James Barclay (of Kynnarroquhy) grandson of the vendor. Captain Douglas Wimberley states that Fowlisse is evidently what is now called Foulzie, nearly north of the church of King Edward and Corskquhie, probably the Corskie nearly opposite Duff House. The same writer is of opinion that James Gordon who appears as witness was James of Culquhodilstane, afterwards of Lesmoir.

PATRICK BARCLAY, 1476–1516, Gartley XVII.

Patrick Barclay as an old man resigned his vast possessions into the King's hands in favour of his grandson, Walter. The confirmation of his resignation is dated at Edinburgh, February 27th, 1516-17, and by it King James V, for good service, incorporated his estates into one free Barony. The designation of the head of the Barclays of Gartley thus became "Barclay of Barclay" or "de eodem" (of that ilk). The long and imposing list of the properties enumerated in detail in the deed commences with "The lands of Grantuly and the tower, fortalices, pendicles and pertinets." The free tenement is reserved to the said Patrick and a reasonable terce to Agnes Gordon, his spouse. Also a portion is noted as having been resigned by Christian Stewart, with consent of her husband, Edward Bruce; hence it is assumed that this Christian Stewart had been the wife of Patrick's eldest son, and was mother to his heir, Walter, and his granddaughter, Christina.

Reg. Mag. Sig. Vol. iii, No. 129.

It is not known how long Patrick Barclay lived after his resignation in favour of his grandson. During his tenure of the Gartley estates the fortunes of the family were at their highest, but after his death they gradually declined. Only two holders of the free Barony were destined to come after him.

WILLIAM BARCLAY

William Barclay, grandson of Patrick (Gartley XVII) and his wife, Elizabeth Arbuthnot, must not be confused with his contemporary William Barclay, M.D., of the Towie line (Towie XVIIb).

He was born in Aberdeenshire in 1546 and educated at the University of Aberdeen. He was a very accomplished young

PATRICK BARCLAY, 1476–1516, Gartley XVII.

man and a fine scholar, and was attached to the Court of Mary Queen of Scots, at Holyrood, in the capacity of secretary. A racy account of a " Royal Hunting," written by him, remains to us.

At the beginning of the month of August 1564 Queen Mary paid a visit of pleasure to the Highlands of Perthshire, where the Earl of Atholl was her entertainer. Robert Chambers, in his *Domestic Annals of Scotland from the Reformation to the Revolution*, tells us that "Glen Tilt was the scene of a great Hunt, in the characteristic style of the country, at which the Queen was present, and of which an account has been preserved to us by a scholarly personage who was in the Royal Train.

"In the year 1563," says he (mistaking the year), "the Earl of Athole, a Prince of the blood-Royal, had with much trouble and vast expense, a hunting match for the entertainment of our most illustrious and gracious Queen. Our people call this a Royal Hunting. I was then," says William Barclay, "a young man and was present on the occasion.

"Two thousand Highlanders, of wild Scotch, as you call them here, were employed to drive to the hunting ground all the deer from the woods and hills of Athole, Badenoch, Mar, Murray and counties about. As these Highlanders use light dress and are very swift of foot, they went up and down so nimbly that in less than two months time they brought together 2000 deer, besides roes and fallow deer. The Queen, the great men and others were in a Glen when all the deer were brought before them. Believe me! the whole body of them moved forward in something like battle order. This sight still strikes me, and ever will, for they had a leader whom they followed close wherever he moved. The leader was a very fine stag, with a very high head. This sight delighted the Queen very much; but she soon had occasion for fear, upon the Earl (who was accustomed to such sights) addressing her thus: 'Do you observe that stag who is foremost of the herd? there is danger from that stag; for if either fear or rage should force him from the ridge of that hill, let everyone look to himself, for none of us will be out of the way of harm, for the rest will follow that one, and having thrown us under foot, they will open a passage to this hill behind us.' PATRICK BARCLAY, 1476–1516, Gartley XVII.

"What happens a moment after confirmed this opinion, for the Queen ordered one of the best dogs to be let loose upon a wolf; this the dog pursued, the leading stag was frightened, he flies by the same way he had come there, and the rest rush after him, and break out where the thickest body of the Highlanders was. They had nothing for it but to throw themselves flat on the heath, and to allow the deer to pass over them. It was told the Queen that several of the Highlanders had been wounded, and that two or three had been killed outright; and the whole body had got off, had not the Highlanders by their skill in hunting, fallen upon a stratagem to cut off the rear from the main body. It was of those that had been separated that the Queen's dogs and those of the nobility made slaughter. There were killed that day three hundred deer, with five wolves and some roe." Domestic Annals of Scotland, Vol. i, p. 30.

William Barclay went to France in 1573. The cause of his Royal mistress was lost, and her chief adherents, among them, as we shall see, Sir George Barclay of that Ilk (Gartley XIX), and George, fifth Earl of Huntly, had accepted pacification and made submission to the Regent Morton in 1572. Protestantism was firmly assured, and William Barclay, a staunch servant of the Roman Catholic Church, went, as did many other young Scotsmen at that time, to continue his studies on the Continent. He sought and found shelter at the Court of Lorraine and obtained a degree of Doctor of Laws at the University of Bourges. He became "Maître de Requêtes" to Charles, Duke of Lorraine, was appointed Professor of Civil Law at the newly founded University of Pont-à-Mousson in 1578, and subsequently held other important offices.

William Barclay paid his addresses to a young lady of the Court, Anne de Malleviller, but before he was permitted to marry her was obliged to prove his descent from an ancient and noble family. At the petition of his friends in Scotland, King James VI indited a letter to the Duke of Lorraine testifying to the high birth and honourable affinities of William Barclay. This document is quoted in the original Latin in

PATRICK BARCLAY, 1476–1516, Gartley XVII.

the Introduction of *Argenis*, by John Barclay, son of William, published in Leyden in 1695.

It may be translated as follows :—

" James by the Grace of God King of Scotland unto all to whom this letter may be brought wishes safety.

It having been made known to us by our dearly loved kinsman George Earl of Huntly and also by our dear friend Lord Patrick Gordon of Auchindoun, Lord Walter Ogilvie of Findlater, GOLDEN KNIGHTS, John Leslie Lord and Baron of Balguane, John Gordon Lord and Baron of Pitlurgi, Walter Barclay Lord and Baron of Towie, etc. and by David Barclay Lord and Baron of Colairnie, etc. and other nobles of the first rank in our realm, that William Barclay a most illustrious kinsman of their own, having emigrated to France some years ago, has now established himself under the jurisdiction of our dearly loved friend and brother and relation in Lorraine, and there formed a connection not unworthy of his family and education ; and they have requested us to testify by our own hand to foreign nations concerning the ancient and noble rank of this man, but chiefly to inform our dearest brother and relation, the illustrious Duke of Lorraine, and all others among whom the aforesaid William Barclay may henceforth live that concerning his nobility he has said nothing untrue (as we are told people of low and obscure birth sometimes do) but that he is descended from the most ancient families of our Kingdom by a long series of ancestors. And having found by diligent search into the whole matter that that what the aforesaid illustrious men have told us is true, we grant cheerfully the prayer of their petition as it seems most just and inform by this most ample testimony both our dear brother and relation and all others whom it may concern to know it that the aforesaid William Barclay is lineally descended from an ancient and noble illustrious family many of whom we have been informed by good authority have been chained knights (equites torquati) for many ages back.

The which may be more evident to our aforesaid brother and relation and all others, we have ordered this testimony of our authority signed by ourselves to be sealed with our great seal.

" Given at Edinburgh on the ninth day of March in the year of our Lord one thousand five hundred and eighty-two and in the sixteenth of our reign.

James King of Scotland,
with the great seal of the Kingdom."

King James VI was related to the reigning house of Lorraine through his grandmother, Mary of Guise.

Barclay de Gairtlie
DOMINVS PROTECTOR VITÆ MEÆ
Innes de Ennermarke
Arbuthnat
Gordonne de Petlurgue
GVIL. BARCLAIVS. I. C. ANNO ÆTATIS. LIII. IN CARN DOM M.D.I.C.
Leslie de Balquhan
Ogilbie de Findlater
Durham de Grange
Pettindreich
Stemmata quid faciunt? faciunt te sanguine clarum.
At magis ingenij nobilitate micas.

WILLIAM BARCLAY

Secretary to Mary Queen of Scots, 1566

From frontispiece to Barclay's "De Regno"

British Museum Engraved Portraits

The omission of the name of Sir George Barclay, Baron of Barclay and head of the House of Gartley, from this petition is noticeable, but, as we shall see, ill fortune had by this time overwhelmed him. His old friends the Gordons rallied to do service to this cadet of his line, as did his kinsmen of Towie and Collairnie.

PATRICK BARCLAY, 1476–1516, Gartley XVII.

William Barclay was the author of some controversial works, written in Latin, one being a treatise on regal power, in which he upholds the divine right of kings. The earliest edition of this book, published in 1599, which is seldom found complete, contains his portrait (see illustration), surrounded by eight coats of arms of the families from which he claimed his descent. These coats of arms are of great genealogical value, and were without doubt appended to the birth-brief sent to the Duke of Lorraine by King James VI in 1582.

Reading the shields in the correct manner, they prove that William's father (Left I) was the son of Patrick Barclay and his wife, Elizabeth Arbuthnot (Left II), his paternal great-grandmothers being Guilda Leslie (Left III) and a daughter of Durham of Grange (Left IV), the mother of Elizabeth Arbuthnot.

On the right side of the portrait are the arms of William's mother (Right I), a daughter of Walter Innes of Innermarkie, and his wife, Christine Gordon of Pitlurg (Right II), his maternal great-grandmothers being a daughter of Ogilvy of Findlater (Right III) and a daughter of Meldrum of Pettindreich (Right IV), the mother of Christine Gordon.

William Barclay's other well-known work was *De Regno et Regali Potestate*, in which he deals with the power of the Pope so far as it is related to Kings and secular Princes.

A conflict of opinion with the Jesuits brought upon Barclay the disfavour of the Duke and he resigned his position and quitted Lorraine.

Subsequently he became a Professor of Civil Law at the University of Angers, where he died in 1608.

Encyclopædia Britannica, Vol. iii, p. 395.

His portrait hangs in the Hôtel de Ville at Nancy.

He had one son.

PATRICK BARCLAY, 1476–1516, Gartley XVII.

JOHN BARCLAY, AUTHOR OF *ARGENIS*

John Barclay, son of William Barclay, and great-grandson of Patrick Barclay (Gartley XVII), was born at Pont-à-Mousson, in Lorraine, and was author of the celebrated romance of *Argenis*. He was educated at the College of the Jesuits in his native town, and at the age of nineteen he wrote a Commentary on the *Thebaïd* of Statius. He was also well known as a poet and satirist.

Owing, it is said, to persecution by the Jesuits, he came to London with his father about 1603, and there published the first portion of his *Euphormionis Satyricon*, a severe satire on the Order. He did not remain in England long, for in 1603 he was in Paris, having married a French poetess, Louise Debonaire. He returned to London in 1606 with his wife and published *Sylvae*, a collection of Latin poems. In the following year the second part of the *Satyricon* appeared in Paris.

John Barclay remained in London until 1616. In 1609 he edited *Potestate Papæ*, an antipapal treatise by his father, and in 1611 he issued an *Apologia*, or third part of the *Satyricon*, in answer to the attacks of the Jesuits. A so-called fourth part, under the title of *Icon Animorum*, appeared in 1614.

Two years later he went to Rome and resided there until his death in 1617. He appears to have been on better terms with the Church, and notably with Bellarmine, for in 1617 he issued from a press in Cologne *Parænesis ad Sectarios*, an attack on the position of Protestantism. His next known work, *Argenis*, was completed about a fortnight before his death, which is said to have been hastened by poison.

Encyclopædia Britannica, Vol. iii, p. 394.

The record of John Barclay as a contemporary writer was of the highest.

He left one son, Robert Barclay, an Abbé.

JOHN BARCLAY, the author of "Argenis"
Cadet of Gartley

WALTER BARCLAY OF THAT ILK

WALTER BARCLAY, 1517–1542, Gartley XVIII.

Walter Barclay, Lord of the Barony of Barclay, received the lands and heritage of Gartley by resignation from his grandfather, Patrick, in the year 1517.

He married Margaret Ogilvy, daughter of Alexander of Findlater, and had two sons, George, who succeeded him, and Walter Barclay of Bathnagoak, who married Jonet Forbes.

Walter Barclay entered into his property three years after the defeat of Flodden Field had plunged Scotland into woe. The infant King was only two years old when he was crowned at Stirling, and the heir-apparent was John, Duke of Albany, son of the traitor Albany of the reign of James III, a naturalised Frenchman who could speak no other tongue. The next heir was the Earl of Arran, chief of the house of Hamilton.

The speedy marriage of the Queen Mother, Margaret Tudor, who had been appointed Regent, to the Earl of Angus (Douglas) made matters worse. In 1514 the Estates summoned Albany, who landed in the following year, secretly equipped and supported by France.

The two little children of James IV alone stood between him and the Crown of Scotland, and possession of the person of the young sovereign was necessary to his plans. As Regent, Albany appointed four peers, into whose hands Margaret was required to place her children, but she refused to obey until compelled to surrender to the forces of Albany, in August 1515, at Stirling Castle. The Queen Mother, with her husband, rode to the Border, where she gave birth tc a daughter, who was later to be the mother of Darnley and grandmother of James VI.

Angus deserted his wife within the year, and his chief fortress, Hamilton Castle, fell into Albany's hands. English plots were rife, and in 1517 Albany, anxious to obtain further support from France, sailed for that country, undertaking to return shortly. He remained away for five years, during which feuds were incessant between Angus and Arran and their factions of Hamilton and Douglas, even in the streets of Edinburgh. The famous encounter between them known as

WALTER BARCLAY, 1517–1542, Gartley XVIII.

"Clear the Causeway" took place in 1520, when Angus was victorious and Arran barely escaped with his life.

When Albany returned in November 1521, Henry VIII, on the brink of war with France, demanded his dismissal and the cessation of French influence. The Estates repudiated Henry's attempted interference, and when in 1522 the English army had crossed to France, Albany at the head of a large force threatened Carlisle. His expedition was fruitless, as he was ill supported, and accepting a month's truce he disbanded his army and returned to France, leaving the Earls of Huntly, Argyle and Arran to act as a Council of Regency.

Early in 1523 Henry VIII offered peace to Scotland, with the hand of his daughter Mary for the young King, but the Estates declined. Thereupon the English King sent the Earl of Surrey, son of the victor of Flodden, to harry the Border. Albany hurried back with foreign auxiliaries and artillery and summoned the nobles to arms, but once again his force melted away, and in the following year he left Scotland for good, taking his foreigners with him.

The English party were now in the ascendant. Henry VIII sent money and an English guard of two hundred men to replace the royal bodyguard. Through his counsellor Wolsey he made every effort to cause strife between Scotland and France. Angus, returning, supported the English interest, and though repulsed by the Queen Mother in a raid upon Edinburgh in the hope of abducting the King, in November 1524, he succeeded in joining the Council of Regency.

James V, when twelve years old, was set up to rule in his own name, with Arran as head of the government, and two years later the young King chose the Earls of Errol, Argyle and Angus to be his guardians, each to have the care of him for the period of three months. He soon found himself a prisoner in the hands of Angus, and it was not until two years had passed that he was able to escape from Falkland Castle disguised as a groom. Angus was subsequently compelled to flee to England, and the overthrow of the Red Douglas was completed.

Need for reform in the Church was openly discussed in the Scottish Parliament, but though Henry VIII repeatedly pressed his nephew to adopt the principles of the Reformation and break with Rome, the decision of James V to marry Marie of Bourbon definitely bound him to the French and Catholic interests. WALTER BARCLAY, 1517–1542, Gartley XVIII.

He sailed for France to bring home his bride, but finding that she was humpbacked did not pursue his errand. He went on to Paris, and there fell in love with the beautiful daughter of Francis I. He made her his Queen, but she survived her arrival in Scotland for only two months. The following year he married Mary of Lorraine, daughter of Duke Claude of Guise, a woman of great intelligence and determined will, and an implacable foe of the Reformed Church.

The dominating personality of his Queen and Cardinal Beaton, who was preferred to the see of St. Andrews, incited the King to action against the Protestants, and with burnings and persecution a great effort was made to root them out. Henry VIII tried vainly to come to an agreement with the Scottish King in order to bring about the dismissal of Cardinal Beaton, an enemy to England, and finally, when he revived the old claim of suzerainty over Scotland, war inevitably resulted.

In October 1542 an English army crossed the Border. James desired to invade England, but his nobles were unwilling, and therefore, as a counterstroke, he resolved to raid the debatable lands. In November a Scottish force marched forward devastating the countryside, and they were pressed by the English into an awkward position between the Solway and the Esk.

The battle of Solway Moss was another catastrophe for Scotland. We read that two earls, five barons, five hundred lairds and gentlemen, twenty pieces of ordnance and thirty standards fell into the hands of the English, who on their part lost only seven English lives.

The news of this shameful defeat reached James V at the same time as the tidings that his wife had borne him a daughter. His two sons had died in infancy, and the King, overwhelmed

WALTER BARCLAY, 1517–1542, Gartley XVIII.

with grief and disappointment, "turned his back to his lords and his face to the wall and died a week later."

Though we have no evidence that Walter Lord of Barclay was embroiled in the troubles of his time, it seems that his affairs did not prosper, for he was forced to sell parts of his estates.

Reg. Mag. Sig. Vol. iii, No. 1211.

Reg. Mag. Sig. Vol. iii, No. 1269.

In 1533 he sold to James Gordon of Culquhodilestane his lands of Crechties, etc., and the following year he resigned what interest he had in part of the lands of Auchlossin, in the parish of Lumphanan, in the Barony of Barclay.

Reg. Mag. Sig. Vol. iii, No. 1622.

Walter Barclay was among the witnesses to a charter confirmed at Stirling on August 20th, 1536, anent the sale of the lands of Fortrie by Sir Walter Ogilvy of Dunlugas, and within a few days Walter Barclay himself sold his lands in the same district.

It is clear that the family friendship with the Gordons continued, and Walter Barclay was intimate with George, fourth Earl of Huntly, for he witnessed for him on several occasions about this time. The Earl was one of the Regents of Scotland appointed by Royal Commission during the absence of King James V in France in 1536, and was now Lieutenant-General of the North. A few years later he was to command the Scottish forces which completely defeated the English at Haddenrigg, on August 24th, 1542, and do other notable services in battle.

Records of Aboyne, p. 198.

In 1540 King James confirmed at Edinburgh, on February 27th, to " Walter Barclay de eodem and Margaret Ogilvy his spouse, the half of the lands of Kirktoun of Drumblat, the third part of Garry, the lands of Newtoun de Garrye with the croft and ailhouse of the same in the Barony of Barclay," etc.

Reg. Mag. Sig. Vol. iii, No. 2364.

On May 20th, 1541, Walter Barclay was witness to a charter of Alexander Ogilvy de eodem, signed at Huntlie, and confirmed at Stirling on June 8th.

Records of Aboyne, p. 414.

In the following year, Walter Barclay de eodem and Margaret Ogilvy his spouse are purchasers of lands from John Ogilvy of Durn, by a charter signed at Fyndlater on May 3rd, 1542.

" Moreover for good service and a composition paid the King united the said lands to the lands and Barony of Barclay."

Walter Barclay appears to have died soon after this purchase. His wife, Margaret Ogilvy, became the wife of James Gordon of Lesmoir, retaining the title of "Lady of Gartlie."

WALTER BARCLAY, 1517–1542, Gartley XVIII.

King James V had six natural sons, three of whom bore the name of James Stewart.

James Stewart, Secundus, born in 1531, whose mother was Margaret Erskine, is well known to history as the Earl of Moray, Regent in the reign of his half-sister, Mary Queen of Scots.

James Stewart, Tertius, was the son of Christina Barclay, sister of Walter, Baron of Barclay (Gartley XVIII), who was the wife of George Abercrombie of Patmedane.

In the accounts of the Lord High Treasurer for the year 1527 is recorded a payment to her of £20. In 1531 there is an entry of "Claithis gevin at the King's command to getill women" under which £9 15s. 9d. is on behalf of Christiane Barclayis.

Accounts High Treasurer, pp. 287, 433.

In "the King's expenses," November 1533, we find

"Item. To ane coit to the King's son with Christiane Barclay 4 elnis tanny velvet, price of the elne £3 : 10 : 0. summa £14."

and in the following year in August is entered

"To ane coit to the King's son with Mistress Barclay 5 elnis blak chamlet, price of the elne 13/4 £3 : 5 : 8½."

James Stewart, Tertius, died without issue.

SIR GEORGE BARCLAY OF THAT ILK

Sir George Barclay, 1543-1602, Gartley XIX.

George Barclay succeeded his father, Walter Barclay of that Ilk, in 1543. He married, first, Margaret Ogilvy, daughter of Sir Walter Ogilvy of Boyne, widow of John, Master of Buchane, and second, Catherine, daughter of the seventh Lord Forbes.

George Barclay received sasine of the family estates in 1543, but his service in respect of portions of the property does not appear to have been completed until six years later. A retour is recorded on October 1st, 1549, to George Barclay, heir of Walter Barclay de eodem, in the half of the lands of Moncoffer, etc.

Retours Special, Aberdeenshire.

By a charter signed at Craigbogie on December 16th, 1549, and confirmed in the name of the Queen (Mary) at Edinburgh on June 27th, 1551, " George Barclay de eodem " with the consent of his curators, Mr. James Barclay of Kynnarroquhy and Mr. Alexander Barclay, Burgess of Aberdeen, " for his special love " and " especially for favours done and sums of money paid to him by Sir Walter Ogilvy of Boyne, granted to Margaret Ogilvy, relict of John Stewart, Master of Boquhane, in her pure widowhood, in liferent only, the lands and mains of Grantuly with the Tower, fortalice and messuages of the same," etc., etc. John, Master of Buchan had fallen at the battle of Pinkie on September 19th, 1547, and his widow, who received a life interest in Gartley, became the wife of George Barclay before October 14th, 1556, when we find the Bishop and Chapter of Moray granting a " tack of the teind sheaves of the parishes of Grantuly and Drumdelgie " to George Barclay de eodem and Margaret Ogilvy his spouse.

Antiquities of Aberdeen and Banff, Vol. ii, p. 173.

George Barclay entered into his inheritance in troublous times. The death of the King and the utter defeat of Solway Moss had crushed the hopes of the Scots. James Hamilton, Earl of Arran, next heir to the throne, was Regent, and the baby Queen in the care of the Queen Mother, Mary of Lorraine.

King Henry VIII of England made every effort to obtain possession of Scotland, but his endeavours to arrange a marriage between the little Queen and his son Edward, Prince of Wales, came to nothing, and after treaty upon treaty had been drawn up, only to be cast aside by the Estates, an English herald was despatched by Henry to declare war in the Scottish capital in 1544.

SIR GEORGE BARCLAY, 1543–1602, Gartley XIX.

An army under Edward Seymour, Earl of Hertford, landed at Granton, destroyed Leith and marched south, spreading ruin in its path.

In the following year Seymour returned again, sacking and burning religious houses, razing towns to the ground, and some of Scotland's most beautiful abbeys were reduced to smouldering ruins at this time.

Two years later Seymour, now Duke of Somerset and Lord Protector during the minority of Edward VI, made a third invasion, and the Regent Arran mustered a strong force against him, but the Scots were defeated at the battle of Pinkie on September 10th, 1547.

Henry II, King of France, and his Guise advisers were determined to prevent Scotland from following England into heresy, and possession of the Scottish Queen being vital to their plans, they sent a request for her marriage with the Dauphin, and her instant passage to France. As most of the strongholds were in the hands of the English, the Estates of Scotland deemed it wise to accept the proposal, which insured the safety of their Queen, who sailed from Dumbarton in 1548. Her next ten years were spent at the French Court, and in 1558 she was married to the Dauphin, Francis.

Meanwhile the influence of France was paramount in Scotland. The Earl of Arran resigned the Regency and returned to that country in 1554, when the French created him Duke of Châtelherault. The Queen Mother, Mary of Lorraine, succeeded him as Regent, but she and her French followers were unpopular with the nobles and she soon met with angry opposition.

In 1557 Mary Tudor, Queen of England, declared war upon France, and the Regent Queen Mother of Scotland called upon the leading nobles to retaliate by declaring war upon England. Her demand was refused. The Earls of Huntly and Argyle

Sir George Barclay, 1543–1602, Gartley XIX.

with the other leading nobles expressed themselves willing to defend their country, but not to attack England.

In this year we find George Barclay selling a portion of his property, the first of the series of similar transactions which were to culminate later in the sale of Gartley itself. He now sold to George Baird in Auchmedden his sunny half of Auchnagorth in the sheriffdom of Aberdeen, although the charter was not confirmed until many years later.

Wimberley, p. 24.

The Reformation was quickly gaining adherents in Scotland. The first Covenant, signed in December 1557, pledged the signatories " to maintain, set forward and establish the most blessed word of God," and " the Congregation of Jesus Christ," as the association of nobles openly identified with the Protestant movement came to be called, demanded immediate reform of the Church, and liberty to worship publicly in accordance with its ritual.

On the death of Mary Tudor, Mary Queen of Scots and her young husband, the Dauphin of France, ill-advisedly assumed the arms of England and Ireland, an action which Elizabeth of England never forgave. The English Queen saw her throne endangered by the rivalry of Mary of Scots, and increasingly so when, by the death of the French King, Mary and her husband were raised to the throne of France, in July 1559, and France and Scotland united under one crown.

Elizabeth did not scruple to use the nearest weapon to her hand, Scotland's Protestant revolt. The party of the Reformation gained strength, and when open conflict with the Regent followed, Scotland, burying the age-long hatred, turned to an English alliance.

Francis sent a contingent to aid the Regent, and Elizabeth, who preferred promises to action, was forced to assist the Congregation. In the last days of December 1559 the Duke of Norfolk reached the Border, preparing for war, but in February of the following year he signed an agreement with the Protestant lords at Berwick which placed Scotland, her liberties and her rights under English protection. The Regent, Mary of Lorraine, took refuge in Edinburgh Castle, where she died June 11th, 1560, and three weeks afterwards the

Sir George Barclay, 1543-1602, Gartley XIX.

treaty of Edinburgh was negotiated by the Minister of Elizabeth with the French. It dismissed them from Scotland, and assured Protestantism not only in that country but in Western Europe.

The dramatic swiftness of events at this time has seldom been surpassed in history. The Estates assembled to formulate a statement of Protestantism, prepared by John Knox, and by three successive Acts swept away the Church of the past, the authority of the Pope, the jurisdiction of all Catholic Prelates, and prohibited the Mass.

Mary Stewart, the widowed Queen, returned to her kingdom of Scotland in August 1561, after thirteen years' absence, to find the influence of France entirely set aside and herself ruler over a country officially pledged to Protestantism. Whilst Knox preached with violent threatenings from his pulpit in Edinburgh, Mary heard Mass in her private chapel at Holyrood on the first Sunday after her arrival. Religious feeling ran high, and as a Catholic she would do no more than pledge herself to uphold the law of the country in regard to religious observances, while firmly maintaining her own personal liberty of action in the matter. She showed no favour to her co-religionists, being anxious by her tolerance of the Reformed Church to placate Elizabeth, whose recognition of her right of succession to the throne of England was Mary's most ardent desire.

Her first clash came with her chief Catholic subject, George, fourth Earl of Huntly. This nobleman had twice held the office of Chancellor of the realm, first under the Regent Arran in 1546, and again under the Queen Mother. One of the chief commanders at the battle of Pinkie, he had been taken prisoner, but effected his escape from Morpeth. He had immense possessions and dominated a vast tract of country, which included the seaport of Aberdeen.

Some time previously the Earl had offered his services to the Queen against the Reformers, an offer which had not been accepted.

In February 1562 Mary conferred upon her half-brother and chief adviser, James Stewart, Prior of St. Andrews, the

Sir George Barclay, 1543–1602, Gartley XIX.

Earldoms of Mar and Moray, with the estates attached thereto. The Earl of Huntly had long enjoyed these estates and resented not only their loss, but the encroachment of James Stewart, leader of the Protestant party, into the heart of his territory.

While his anger was smouldering, his third son, Sir John Gordon of Findlater, was concerned in a brawl with the family of Ogilvy in the streets of Edinburgh, on June 27th. Findlater was Ogilvy property and had been bequeathed to John Gordon in the place of a disinherited son, to the intense dissatisfaction of the Ogilvy clan. In the fighting Lord Ogilvy was dangerously wounded, and John Gordon in consequence was sent to prison. He made his escape and, returning home, complained loudly of the indignity to which he had been subjected.

At the instigation, it is said, of her half-brother, Queen Mary made a progress into the north in August, when the Countess of Huntly, herself Elizabeth Keith, sister of William, fourth Earl Marischal, pleaded before her in person for pardon for her son. Mary required that he should deliver himself into the hands of justice and rely upon her clemency, but John Gordon escaped from the guards who were conducting him to Stirling Castle and returned to take command of his followers who were rising under arms. Hearing of his flight and rebellion, Mary refused to enter his father's house and Huntly openly revolted.

He advanced with a considerable body of men towards Aberdeen and met the Queen's forces under James Stewart, Earl of Moray, at Corrichie on October 28th. His forces were defeated and he himself trampled to death in the pursuit. John Gordon was beheaded at Aberdeen two days later, Adam being pardoned on the score of his youth. The Earl's body was carried from Aberdeen to Edinburgh and there exposed for treason, and his estates were forfeited.

In spite of the severity of their punishment, two of the Gordons became devoted adherents of the Queen. George, fifth Earl of Huntly, was convicted of treason and sentenced to be executed, but being set at liberty he regained the Queen's favour and was, as we shall see, henceforward her faithful servant. Sir Adam Gordon of Auchindoun became a notable soldier, and fought valiantly for the Queen in the hour of her greatest need.

Sir George Barclay, 1543-1602, Gartley XIX.

His sister, Lady Jean Gordon, was married, by the Queen's wish it is said, to James Hepburn, Earl of Bothwell, in January 1566, but the marriage was annulled in the following year to make way for the disastrous alliance of Bothwell with the Queen herself.

We have already noted the relationship and close friendship which existed between the Gordons of Huntly and Strathbogie and the Barclays of Gartley in previous generations, and it is clear that this friendship continued. The appearance of the name "George," always a Gordon name, in the Gartley line at this time, and the name "Adam" in succeeding generations, also suggests close association.

We have no evidence that George Barclay was implicated in the rebellion of the Gordons and the disaster of Corrichie, though we know that his kinsman William Barclay (Towie XVID) was a supporter of the Earl of Huntly, and George himself could hardly have avoided being concerned in some degree with this crisis in the affairs of his intimate neighbours; nor can we trace the date upon which he entered the personal service of Queen Mary.

It may be that when George, fifth Earl of Huntly, regained the Royal favour, he brought with him to Court his friend the Lord of Gartley, for it is clear that George Barclay was personally known to Queen Mary in the year 1564, when she stayed at Gartley Castle. From thence she indited a letter to Elizabeth of England, dated August 24th, 1564, requesting safe conduct

> "for her servitor, James Murray, son of umquhile William of Tullibardine and four in company to buy goods in England for one year Your right gud sister and cusignes Mary R."

In March of the following year the Earl of Huntly was made Chancellor of Scotland, and he figures prominently in the months which followed the Queen's ill-fated marriage to Henry Lord Darnley, on July 29th, 1565.

SIR GEORGE BARCLAY, 1543–1602, Gartley XIX.

The murder of her Italian favourite, Rizzio, her infatuation for the miscreant Bothwell, the tragic end of Darnley in Kirk o' Field, Bothwell's mock trial and acquittal, followed within a month by his marriage to the Queen, his speedy desertion on her surrender to her opposing nobles at Carberry Hill on June 15th, 1567, and her incarceration at Lochleven are matters of history too familar to need recounting here.

During the Queen's imprisonment the Earl of Huntly signed a bond supporting the authority of her son, James VI, in whose favour she abdicated on June 23rd, 1567, and he carried the sceptre at the first Parliament of the Regent Moray, but immediately upon the escape of Mary from Lochleven Castle on May 2nd, 1568, he joined the "Association" of her supporters when they rallied with six thousand men at Hamilton.

Cal. Scot. Doc. Vol. ii, p. 404.

It is at this time that George Barclay is mentioned as a member of the Queen's household. That he was a marked man to the English is certain, for in a document relating to the "Association" at Hamilton, and endorsed by Cecil, May 8th, 1568, his name appears as "Gairtlie" in the list of adherents of Queen Mary, where nine earls, including Archibald, Earl of Angus, and George, Earl of Huntly, nine bishops, eighteen lords and others are enumerated.

Huntly hastened to the north to raise forces, but the disastrous defeat of the Queen's army by the Regent Moray, with two thousand five hundred men at Langside, on May 13th, crushed all the hopes of her followers.

After three days of flight and hardship, Mary Queen of Scots crossed the Solway and threw herself upon the mercy of Elizabeth of England. George Barclay, Lord of Gartley, did not accompany her in her flight, and from the records it would appear that he stayed to procure funds before rejoining his Queen.

Reg. Mag. Sig. Vol. v, No. 339.

In the previous August, by a contract dated at Rothiemay, he had sold to Alexander, Lord of Saltoun, the superiority of the barony and lands of Lessindrum, with the mill and multures thereof in the sheriffdom of Aberdeen, and now again we find him parting with property. At Drum, on May 25th, 1568, only nine days after the flight of his Royal mistress, he sold to Alexander Irvine of Drum his lands of Moncoffer and Gownis, with the mill and salmon fishing in the waters of Dovern, etc. Among the witnesses to this sale were Walter Barclay of Sleaucht, Mr. George Barclay and Mr. William Davidson. SIR GEORGE BARCLAY, 1543–1602, Gartley XIX. Reg. Mag. Sig. Vol. iv, No. 2118.

Upon her arrival in England, Queen Mary had received a welcome from leading Catholic families in the neighbourhood of Carlisle, but on July 15th she was removed to Bolton Castle in Yorkshire, where a conference was held between her commissioners and those of Elizabeth. On October 2nd the conference was transferred to London, and George Barclay, "Gartulie Barclay," is recorded as acting for the Queen of Scots.

On January 26th, 1569, Mary was transferred from Bolton Castle to Tutbury, in Staffordshire, and we find a record dated the following month giving the names of her servitors there. The list begins :— Diurnall of Occurrants in Scotland, Maitland Club, p. 139.

"Chief men . . . Ten.
Belton. Master of Household.
Levison. Master of Horse.
Bortyque. Master of the Pantry.
The Laird of Gartley" (no office mentioned). Cal. Scot. Doc. p. 617, No. 987.

Plots were rife for the Queen's liberation, and she entrusted George Barclay with various missions on her behalf. We find him arriving on February 11th at Raderham (Rotherham), in Yorkshire, and being arrested with his party by the Bailie of the town under Lord Sussex's orders to stop all Scotsmen.

A letter from Master Alexander Leslie to Mary's firm supporter, the Bishop of Ross, tells us that the Bailie took their "Mailis and locked them in a Kist giving the key to the Laird of Gartlie," and wrote to Sussex for further orders.

"Not suffering one of our company to go back to Tutbury, but sent Gartlie's writing to the Queen and this of mine to your Lordship. *Ibid.* Papers ii, p. 620, No. 996.

SIR GEORGE BARCLAY, 1543–1602, Gartley XIX.

Lord Herries we hear is stayed and passed to York. Referring the rest to your wisdom.

"Rotherame. This Saturday by ane of the clock."

A subsequent letter dated February 13th gives us the sequel. From Alexander Leslie to the Bishop of Ross :—

Cal. Scot. Doc. Papers ii, p. 620, No. 999.

"This Sunday at thre houris efternoon a command came by post to the Bailie of Raderame to let all Scotsmen pass freely. Whereupon incontinent the Laird of Gartlie took journey for Scotland."

This detention of her messenger is protested against in a memorial presented by the Bishop of Ross to the Queen of England in the name of his Mistress, and the English Queen replies that she shall send for Lord Scrope and write to Lord Hunsdon on the matter.

Ibid. p. 645, No. 1053.

In the same memorial the Bishop declares the great sickness of the Queen of Scots and desires two physicians. This request is endorsed "granted."

On the outbreak of an insurrection in Scotland, Queen Mary was removed to Coventry on the advice of Lord Hunsdon, when a body of her followers riding to her deliverance was within a day's ride of Tutbury.

The assassination of the Regent Earl of Moray on January 20th, 1570, incited the Queen's party to still greater efforts. A convention of nobles, "being all of one factione to have the Queene's Grace regnand," met at Edinburgh, but failed to achieve any useful purpose by reason of their dissensions.

We find George Barclay again an envoy for his Queen.

"Upon the 25th day of the said month (March) 1570, the Laird of Gairtullie come from Ingland, fra the Queenis Grace of Scotland, to my Lord of Mar and Otheris Lordis, for reteining and keiping of hir sone in Scotland, and to adheyir to hir and hir assistaris within this realme and assurit thame gif thai wald nocht, that the King of France and hir friendis wald revenge hir caus, and put hir in hir awne auctoritis in contrair thair myndis and willis, and that soner nor thay belevit."

Diurnall of Remarkable Occurrants, p. 166.

In May, George Barclay, now designated "Sir" George, went to France to negotiate a Treaty arranged by the French

Ambassador and the Bishop of Ross with the Lords of Queen Elizabeth's Council, but while this treaty was in hand the English Queen learned that the articles therein contained had been privately communicated to the Pope, the King of France and the Duke of Alva, and

SIR GEORGE BARCLAY, 1543-1602, Gartley XIX.

"that there were sent to the French King, Sir George Bartley, to the Duke of Alva Mr. John Hamilton, and to the Pope Mr. Henry Keare, all to crave succour for the Scottish Queen against the Queen of England."

Cal. Scot. Doc. Papers vii, pp. 423, 424.

The treaty was broken off.

Among the letters of Sir Francis Englefield we find an interesting passage which indicates that Sir George was not the only member of his family engaged in missions for the Queen of Scots. Sir Francis, writing on May 17th, 1570, from Flanders, where the Duke of Alva was Governor of the Low Countries, to a lady in the service of the Duchess of Feria, in Spain, says :—

"Tell her Grace that another brother of the Barclays has passed this way towards Milan. I do not think he will come into Spain. Within these four or five months twenty-five or thirty persons have come out of England on pretence of the Spa waters and we daily look for more. . . ."

Meanwhile, the Earl of Huntly, who now held Queen Mary's commission as Lieutenant-General of Scotland, was actively in arms on her behalf. He was proclaimed traitor by the Regent, and with him "Found guilty and dome of forfeiture pronounced" were James, Duke of Châtelherault, and George Barclay of that Ilk. By the end of August 1571 the Queen's party were in possession of Edinburgh Castle, and when the Regent Lennox summoned a Parliament at Stirling, the Earl of Huntly surprised the assemblage by a sudden sortie from Edinburgh, in which the Regent was mortally wounded.

John Erskine was appointed to succeed him and at once attacked Edinburgh and open war followed. The Eastern Lowlands were for the King, and looked to England for help, which they did not obtain; the West, the North and the

Sir George Barclay, 1543–1602, Gartley XIX.

Border were for the Queen, and appealed to France with little better success. After much useless bloodshed a truce was agreed on. Châtelherault and Huntly had suffered long and inexpressible hardships, and Châtelherault was worn out with long fatigue and old age. The Earl of Morton, who held the Regency, proposed terms of peace and they submitted.

The document known as the Pacification of Perth was drawn up on February 3rd, 1572-3, between Archibald, Earl of Argyll, and the King's commissioners on the one part, and George, Earl of Huntly, Lord Gordon and Badenoch, for himself, his kin and partakers . . . Lord John Hamilton, Abbot of Arbroath, for his father the Duke of Châtelherault and the House of Hamilton, for the other part.

Among the many kinsmen and friends for whom the Earl of Huntly stood surety and whose sentences of forfeiture were rescinded, were his brother, Sir Adam Gordon of Auchindoun, and Sir George Barclay of that Ilk.

The first clause in the document lays down that all persons who would claim the benefits of this Pacification . . .

"shall acknowledge and confess the religion now publicly preached and professed within this Realm established by Laws and Acts of Parliament the first year of our Sovereign Lord's reign."

The Earl was begged by the Regent Morton to stop the "impetuous course of his brother's arms," for Adam Gordon, that notable and gallant fighter, had by no means despaired of yet winning Scotland for the Queen. But money and strength were at an end. Her cause was irretrievably lost and Protestantism firmly assured. George, Earl of Huntly, retired to Strathbogie, where he died four years later.

One pathetic record remains to us. In 1573 Queen Mary, then imprisoned at Sheffield Manor under the charge of the Earl of Shrewsbury and his wife, the sharp-tongued "Bess of Hardwicke," wrote to

"Sir George Barclay Knight, one of her Masters of Household, wishing him to be with her and for that purpose she has written to the Earl of Leicester and Lord Treasurer."

Sir George Barclay, 1543-1602, Gartley XIX.

The letter is endorsed

"Conteyned in the Scottish Queen's packet directed to the French Ambassador, Monsieur de la Mothe."

Cal. Scot. Doc. Papers iv, p. 365.

Did it ever reach the Lord of Gartley? Apparently not, since it is preserved among Government papers.

Sir George Barclay endeavoured to avert the financial ruin which threatened him. In 1577, with the consent of Walter Barclay, his son and apparent heir, he sold a further portion of his estates, the lands of Foulsie, to Alexander Irvine of Drum. The witnesses to the transaction, which is dated Banff, January 6th, and confirmed at Haliruidhous, February 24th, 1580-1, included Robert, Earl of Buchan, and Alexander Ogilvy of Boyne.

Reg. Mag. Sig. Vol. v, No. 118.

In the summer of the same year, 1577, George Barclay appears to have been involved in some serious trouble, though its nature is not recorded, for he was in ward in Blakness, and by a bond subscribed August 30th, and endorsed at Holyroodhuis on September 8th, we find his kinsman, Walter Barclay of Towie (Towie XVI), acting as surety for him, that if freed he should enter again in the said castle when required. Among the witnesses to this bond are William Stewart, servant to the Laird of Towie, James Barclay, and Gilbert Barclay, servitor of the Laird of Gartley.

Register of the Privy Council, Vol. ii, No. 632.

In 1577, by two charters and with the consent of "Walter Barclay, his eldest son and apparent heir," Sir George Barclay sold very considerable properties in the Sheriffdom of Banff to his brother Walter Barclay of Bathnagoak and Jonet Forbes, his spouse. From the fact that the first charter is dated from Blakness on September 11th, it would seem that Sir George had either not been freed or had been called upon to return to ward, but the second charter is dated from Leyth only three days later, September 14th, and both were confirmed at Stirling on September 20th in the same year.

Reg. Mag. Sig. Vol. iv, No. 2799.

Sir George Barclay, 1543–1602, Gartley XIX.

This disposal of property seems to have been the cause of trouble between the brothers, for a violent quarrel took place between them within the year. Walter Barclay of Bathnagoak lodged a complaint before the Privy Council against George Barclay of Garntulie and his servant Johnne Murray for trespass on the lands so recently purchased, and assaulting one of his tenants and chasing his oxen, also for coming by night on another occasion and assaulting two other tenants, and transporting them, with a third, to the " toure and fortalice of Gartulie and there detaining them prisoners." Walter Barclay appeared in person, but " the saidis George Barclay and Johnne Murray being ofttyme callit and non compearant, the Lords direct letters simpliciter to denounce the saidis personis and to escheat etc."

Register of Privy Council, Vol. iii, p. 50.

The tide of ill fortune reached its flood four years later when Sir George Barclay of that Ilk was compelled to sell what remained of the once extensive Barony of Barclay. The purchaser was Sir Patrick Gordon, brother of his old friend, George, fifth Earl of Huntly, and now of Auchindoun, through the death of Sir Adam Gordon in 1580.

The charter of sale is dated Linlithgow, 2nd April, 1582, and was confirmed at " Haliruidhuis," 24th December. The property sold is specified as "The Barony of Barclay," namely, the Manor of Barclay called the Hiltoun (Haltoun) with the castle (turre), and included in the list of lands is the Barkelyhill, or Birkenhill.

Reg. Mag. Sig. Vol. v, No. 494.

Five years afterwards doom fell on the unfortunate Mary Queen of Scots, and the final tragedy was enacted at Fotheringhay on February 8th, 1587.

Sir George Barclay, later in his life, became possessed of property which may have afforded him comfort in his old age. On November 1st, 1602, he was retoured heir to his brother, Walter Barclay of Bathnagoak and Newtoun, in the lands of Kynnarroquhy, and salmon fishings in the water of Ithin, in the Barony of Barclay. These estates had passed to Walter on the death of his cousin, James Barclay of Kynnarroquhy.

Retours Special, Aberdeenshire.

We find no mention of Sir George Barclay (Gartley XIX)

after the year 1602, and with him passed the greatness of the Barclays of Gartley.

Sir George Barclay, 1543–1602, Gartley XIX.

WALTER BARCLAY OF BATHNAGOAK

Walter Barclay of Bathnagoak (Gartley XIXB) was the second son of Walter Barclay (Gartley XVIII) and brother of Sir George. He was known as "of Bathnagoak," and also of Kynnarroquhy, and appears often in the records under both designations.

In September 1577, as we have already seen, he purchased from his brother, Sir George, a large part of the Gartley estates. Sir George granted these lands, "with the consent of Walter Barclay, his eldest son and apparent heir, to Walter Barclay of Bathnagoak, his own brother, and Jonet Forbes, his spouse."

Reg. Mag. Sig. Vol. iv, No. 2799.

Having purchased these extensive estates, Walter Barclay gave the land thus acquired the name of Newtoun, and we find the tithes of the parish of Gartley leased in 1580 by the Bishop of "Murray" to Walter Barclay of Newtoun. The above record mentioning the Barony of Barclay, and the fact that his son and grandson, as we shall see, were styled of "Newtoun and of that Ilk," indicates that he obtained the erection of his estates into a new Barony of Barclay.

The old Barony of Barclay had been specified as sold to Sir Patrick Gordon of Auchindoun in 1582, but that property continued to be known by the old name of the Barony of Gartley. Upon the death of Sir Patrick Gordon, who was killed at the battle of Glenlivet, on October 3rd, 1594, Gartley passed to the Huntly family and we find it included as "the Barony of Gartley" in the "Rental of the Lordship of Huntly" for 1600.

Walter Barclay of Bathnagoak and Newtoun was evidently a somewhat turbulent person, for, in addition to his quarrel with his brother, of which he seems to have repented, we find that in 1590 Sir Patrick Gordon of Auchindoun gave a Bond of Caution for £500 for him, "that he will not harm John Lyon of Colnagy, his bairns or his dependants." Subscribed at Gartley, 23rd April, before George

Register of Privy Council, Vol. iv, p. 477.

Sir George Barclay, 1543–1602, Gartley XIX.

Gordon, James Abernethy and Patrick Barclay (probably Towie XIX).

Walter Barclay of Bathnagoak was succeeded by his son, GEORGE BARCLAY, who was retoured heir to him as "de eodem" in 1602.

Douglas Wimberley, p. 30.

He was an advocate in Aberdeen and a burgess of that city. He also appears as Sheriff's clerk of Banff in the year 1590. His name is found in many deeds in the Register of the Great Seal, Volume v, where he is always called "George Barclay Advocate" or "Burgess of Aberdeen."

In 1581 Alexander Cheyne, Canon of King's College, Aberdeen, Prebendary of Snaw, with consent of the Principal and others, granted a charter by which he demitted in feu ferme to Mr. George Barclay, Burgess of Aberdeen, and Marjorie Cheyne, his spouse, the tenement, place and manse of Snaw, etc., lying to the west of old Aberdeen, beyond the Powis Burne, between the cemetery of Snaw Kirk and the lands held by Walter Barclay of Kynnarroquhy. Confirmed at Edinburgh 19th August, 1585.

Reg. Mag. Sig. Vol. v, p. 881.

Included in the same confirmation is a further acquisition by George Barclay and his wife, Marjorie Cheyne, of another tenement, place and manse, granted by John Elphinstone, Rector of Invernochty. As the precept of sasine in both cases is given to Walter Barclay of Kynnarroquhy, it would seem that the purchases were a marriage settlement on George Barclay and Marjorie Cheyne.

Marjorie Cheyne was the daughter of Thomas Cheyne, ninth of Esslemont. By her George Barclay of Newtoun had at least two sons. WILLIAM BARCLAY, the elder, who succeeded him, was known as "of Newtoun and of that Ilk." Like his father, he was also an advocate in Aberdeen and Procurator Fiscal from 1594 to 1631. He married Agnes Hay, and died after July 7th, 1631, leaving issue James, who was living in 1622, and who probably died without issue in the lifetime of his father, as the younger brother, CAPTAIN ALEXANDER BARCLAY, was retoured heir.

Douglas Wimberley, p. 30.

Mr. George Barclay's younger son was the REV. ALEXANDER BARCLAY, Minister of Drumblade from 1598 to 1608. He married Elizabeth, daughter of John Duncan of Sandargue, and left three sons. Of his eldest son no record has been found. His two younger sons were James, who went from Aberdeen in his eighteenth year and settled at Memle in Spruis, in the year 1635, and William, who went to "Dutchylie in Spruis," in 1643, at the age of seventeen.

Sir George Barclay, 1543–1602, Gartley XIX. Miscellany, Spalding Club, Vol. v, p. 339.

No further records of the descendants of Walter Barclay of Bathnagoak can be discovered and it is probable that the branch ceased to exist.

WALTER BARCLAY

WALTER BARCLAY, of Drumdelgie, Heir-male of Gartley XX, 1571–1598.

The eldest son of Sir George Barclay (Gartley XIX) was known as "younger of Gartley." Previous to the sale of estate, in 1577 and 1582, he was referred to in the deeds as "apparent of Gartley."

After Gartley had passed into other hands, Walter Barclay "younger of Gartley" seems to have resided at Drumdelgie, as in the next year, 1583, he appears with that territorial designation.

In 1571 he is witness as "apparent of Grantulie" to a charter granted by Robert, Earl of Buchan, and Christiana, his spouse, in favour of George Ogilvy of Dunlugas, and to another between the same parties, dated 1574. Both signed at Forglen, and confirmed at Dalkeith, May 10th and 18th, 1581.

Reg. Mag. Sig. Vol. v, No. 176.

He is mentioned, as we have already noted, as consenting with his father, Sir George, in the sale of the lands of Foulsie to Alexander Irvine of Drum in 1577, and again as consenting to the sales of the property to his uncle, Walter Barclay of Bathnagoak, in 1578, but it is noticeable that he is not named as consenting to the final sale of Gartley to Sir Patrick Gordon in 1582.

Ibid. No. 118

In 1583 Walter Barclay of Drumdelgie was a member of a Commission of Justiciary, with John, Earl of Atholl, Lord of Balveny, the Sheriffs of Banff, Elgin and Fores, and their substitutes, Thomas Ord of Fyndachtie, and Mr. John Duff of Muldavit, to apprehend and bring to trial Andrew Laggan at the mill of Balveny, his brothers and others, suspected and delated of incendiarism and burning the granaries and growing crops of Plewlands on April 6th last past.

Exchequer Rolls, Vol. xxi, p. 494.

In 1591 he was a witness with others to a bond between Sir Patrick Gordon of Auchindoun and the Gordons, and John Grant of Freuchie and Lachlan McIntosh of Dunnachtoun, for friendship between the latter and the Earl of Huntly.

Chiefs of Grant, Vol. iii, p. 181.

In 1593 Walter Barclay of Drumdelgie was surety along with William Gordon of Knockaspect, as principal, in 500

Register of Privy Council.

merks among "Northland men," bound not to assist the Earls of Huntly and Errol.

WALTER BARCLAY, of Drumdelgie, Heir-male of Gartley XX, 1571-1598.

In 1594 Walter Barclay of Drumdelgie with George Barclay, Sheriff of Banff (his cousin), was a witness to a charter of confirmation of Francis, Earl of Errol, in favour of Sir Walter Ogilvy.

Reg. Mag. Sig. Vol. vi, p. 332.

Walter Barclay was a witness to a charter of George, Earl of Huntly, in 1596, in which he granted in feu ferme to Patrick Murray, King's servitor, the lands of Kirknie, with the ailhouse, etc., in the Barony of Strathbogie, parish of Gartley, sheriffdom of Aberdeen, dated at Gartley, November 30th.

Ibid. p. 303.

Walter Barclay of Drumdelgie married the fourth daughter of Patrick Forbes of Corse and his wife, Marjorie Lumsden, daughter of Robert Lumsden of Maidler-Cushnie, and had issue one son, Adam, and a daughter, Barbara.

Family of Forbes, p. 24.

THE REV. ADAM BARCLAY, 1590–1663, Heir-male of Gartley XXI.

THE REV. ADAM BARCLAY I

The Rev. Adam Barclay was born about the year 1590. No doubt he received the name of Adam in consequence of the long connection between the Barclays of Gartley and the Gordons of Huntly, in whose family, as we have seen, the name frequently occurs.

Adam was educated at King's College, Aberdeen, and appears on the roll in 1603, graduating M.A. in the year 1607.

He became Minister of Leochel in 1616, and in 1622 King James VI presented him with the living of Monymusk. In 1630 he was Minister of Fintray, and in 1631 became Minister of Alford, which he held until the year 1651. His name appears in 1633 as Minister in connection with "the constant provision of ane schoole at the Kirk of Alford."

Antiquities, Spalding Club, Vol. iv, p. 136.

In 1634 he was appointed a Justice of the Peace for Aberdeenshire.

Scottish Barclays, p. 12.

In 1642 Adam Barclay became Professor of Divinity in King's College, Aberdeen.

He married a daughter of Nicholson of Kilcassie, and by her he had issue James, of whom we have no record, and Adam, who succeeded him as heir-male of Gartley; Barbara, who married the Right Rev. Arthur Ross, Archbishop of St. Andrews from 1684 to 1689, when he was deprived; and Agnes, who married the Rev. James Gordon.

The Rev. Adam Barclay I died January 1st, 1663.

THE REV. ADAM BARCLAY II

THE REV. ADAM BARCLAY, Heir-male of Gartley XXII, 1663- ?

was the son of the Rev. Adam Barclay I; he became heir-male of Gartley on the death of his father in 1663. He was on the roll of King's College, Aberdeen, in 1647, and, like his father, graduated M.A.

In the same year he became Minister of Towie, Strathdon, and at this time sasine was granted to him and his spouse "in meal and beare" from the Barony of Skene.

He was Minister of Keig from July 10th, 1666, to 1681, when he was deprived for refusing to take the Test. He was Minister of Perth (Eastchurch), May 1668, and was again deprived in 1689 as Non-Juror.

Adam Barclay II was twice married, firstly to Janet Skene, the daughter of Alexander Skene, thirteenth Laird and of that Ilk. The marriage took place December 26th, 1648. By her he had issue Adam, who succeeded him as heir-male of Gartley, of whom later.

He married, secondly, Marjory, daughter of John Forbes of Ashloune, son of Duncan Forbes of Lethendy, third son of William Forbes, first Laird of Monymusk. By her he had issue Barbara, married to the Rev. William Mair (died 1742), Minister of Kincardine O'Neill in 1709, and also of Tough.

ADAM BARCLAY

ADAM BARCLAY, Heir-male of Gartley XXIII, ?–1735.

Adam Barclay, son of the Rev. Adam Barclay II, was the last of the direct line of the Barclays of Gartley.

He is described in an old letter in the possession of Mr. James Alexander Beattie as follows :—

> "Adam Barclay, laird of the Dauch of Gartley, of the most ancient family of Gartley. He married Isobel Innes, and had one son and five daughters. They were all alive in 1696, when he lived at Bridgeford of Premnay, and maintained himself after his misfortunes by practising as a Notary Public."

Mr. Beattie says: "He was my direct ancestor by my maternal grandmother. I fancy that he is the Adam Barclay, laird of Acknowe and Piketillum." He received sasine of these estates in 1676. They were in the parish of Glass.

Douglas Wimberley, p. 31.

In 1687 Adam Barclay, Notary Public, is mentioned as being present at the Court of the Barony of Whitehaugh, held within the Hall of Whitehaugh by Patrick Reid of Haughton, bailie to Leith of Whitehaugh.

Miscellany, Spalding Club, Vol. v, p. 236.

Adam Barclay of Bridgeford is said to have lived until the year 1735.

After much diligent search no male representative of the Barclays of Gartley can be discovered.

For information concerning the last three generations of the Gartley line, in the heirs-male, we are indebted to Mr. Harry Pirie-Gordon, D.S.C., a descendant of Gartley through the cadet branch of the Barclays of Cairness, Jamaica. An account of this branch is given fully in Burke's *Landed Gentry* under "Gordon of Cairness." They are descended from a Rev. Alexander Barclay, whose name is entered on the roll of King's College, Aberdeen, in 1668, Minister of Auchterless in 1674 and Peterhead from 1682 to 1696. Family tradition holds that he was a cadet of Gartley. The Barclays of Cairness died out in 1765 on the death of James Barclay, who was succeeded by his sister Mary, third Lady of Cairness, who married John Gordon, sixth Laird of Buthlaw. On her death without issue the estate passed to her sister Jean, married to Thomas Gordon, brother of the above.

Many Barclays are mentioned in Scottish records of the sixteenth century, but there is no evidence to show to which family they belonged.

ADAM BARCLAY, Heir-male of Gartley XXIII, ?–1735.

Notable among these is Alexander Barclay, poet and prose writer. He is stated to have been born about 1475, to have travelled on the continent, and at some time before 1508 to have been appointed Priest of Ottery St. Mary, in Devonshire. About 1511 he became a monk of the Benedictine order of the Monastery of Ely, and later assumed the Franciscan habit at Canterbury. He died at Croydon in 1552, six months after obtaining the Rectory of All Hallows, London.

His famous poem *The Shyp of Folys of the Worlde* was written in 1509. He also published *The Castell of Labore* and *Egloges*, a translation of Sallust's *Jugurthine War*.

From the end of the Gartley line we must now return to Alexander de Berkeley of the Mearns (Mathers I), second son of Andrew de Berkeley (Gartley IX), to trace the descent in heirs-male, of the senior line, to Colonel Robert Wyvill Barclay of Bury Hill, the present Chief of Mathers and Urie.

PEDIGREE VI.

The Mathers Line

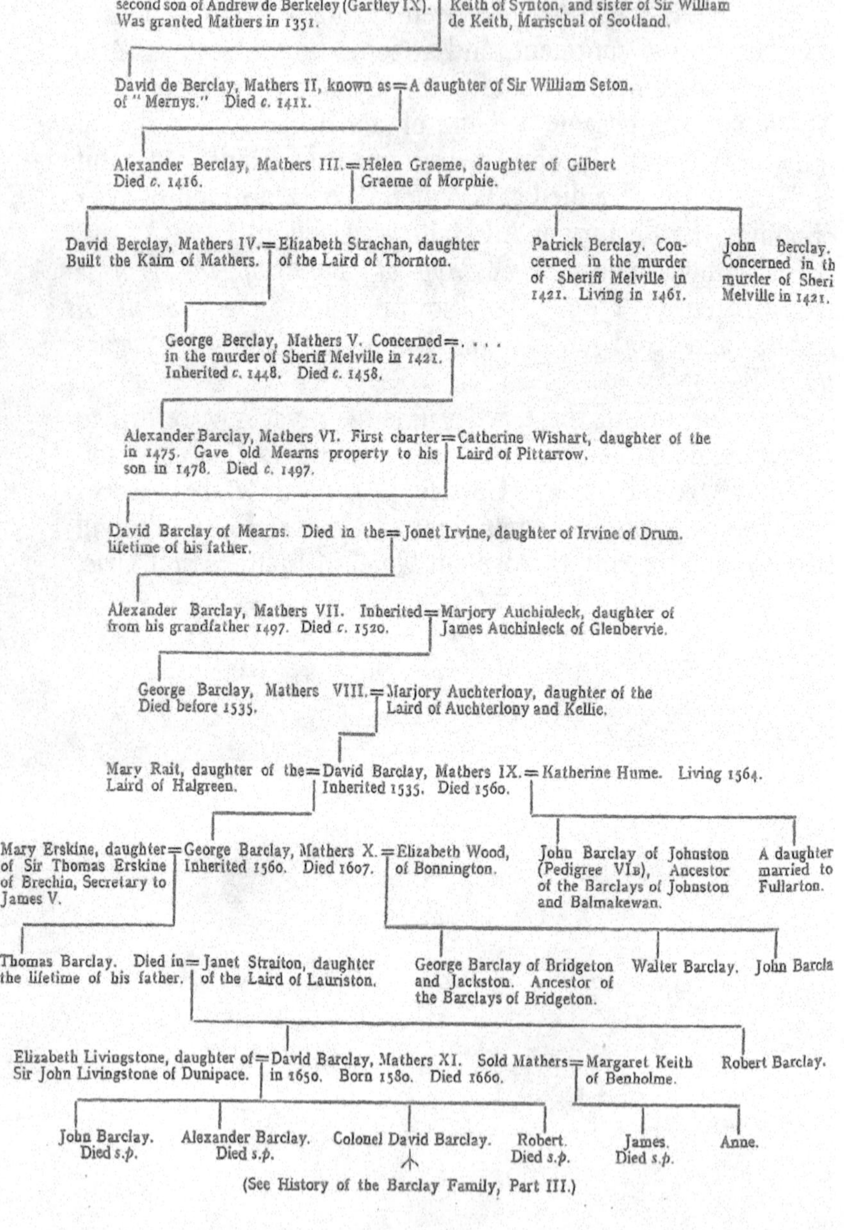
ALEXANDER DE BERKELEY, Mathers I, second son of Andrew de Berkeley (Gartley IX). Was granted Mathers in 1351.
= Katherine Keith, daughter of Edward de Keith of Synton, and sister of Sir William de Keith, Marischal of Scotland.
David de Berclay, Mathers II, known as of "Mernys." Died c. 1411.
= A daughter of Sir William Seton.
Alexander Berclay, Mathers III. Died c. 1416.
= Helen Graeme, daughter of Gilbert Graeme of Morphie.
David Berclay, Mathers IV. Built the Kaim of Mathers.
= Elizabeth Strachan, daughter of the Laird of Thornton.
Patrick Berclay. Concerned in the murder of Sheriff Melville in 1421. Living in 1461.
John Berclay. Concerned in th murder of Sheri Melville in 1421.
George Berclay, Mathers V. Concerned in the murder of Sheriff Melville in 1421. Inherited c. 1448. Died c. 1458.
= . . . .
Alexander Barclay, Mathers VI. First charter in 1475. Gave old Mearns property to his son in 1478. Died c. 1497.
= Catherine Wishart, daughter of the Laird of Pittarrow.
David Barclay of Mearns. Died in the lifetime of his father.
= Jonet Irvine, daughter of Irvine of Drum.
Alexander Barclay, Mathers VII. Inherited from his grandfather 1497. Died c. 1520.
= Marjory Auchinleck, daughter of James Auchinleck of Glenbervie.
George Barclay, Mathers VIII. Died before 1535.
= Marjory Auchterlony, daughter of the Laird of Auchterlony and Kellie.
Mary Rait, daughter of the Laird of Halgreen.
= David Barclay, Mathers IX. Inherited 1535. Died 1560.
= Katherine Hume. Living 1564.
Mary Erskine, daughter of Sir Thomas Erskine of Brechin, Secretary to James V.
= George Barclay, Mathers X. Inherited 1560. Died 1607.
= Elizabeth Wood, of Bonnington.
John Barclay of Johnston (Pedigree VIB), Ancestor of the Barclays of Johnston and Balmakewan.
A daughter married to Fullarton.
Thomas Barclay. Died in the lifetime of his father.
= Janet Straiton, daughter of the Laird of Lauriston.
George Barclay of Bridgeton and Jackston. Ancestor of the Barclays of Bridgeton.
Walter Barclay.
John Barcla
Elizabeth Livingstone, daughter of Sir John Livingstone of Dunipace.
= David Barclay, Mathers XI. Sold Mathers in 1650. Born 1580. Died 1660.
= Margaret Keith of Benholme.
Robert Barclay.
John Barclay. Died s.p.
Alexander Barclay. Died s.p.
Colonel David Barclay.
Robert. Died s.p.
James. Died s.p.
Anne.

(See History of the Barclay Family, Part III.)

THE GRANT OF MATHERS

1351

From the original Deed at Bury Hill

The Mathers Line

ALEXANDER DE BERKELEY OF THE MEARNS

ALEXANDER DE BERKELEY, 1351, Mathers I.

Alexander de Berkeley, progenitor of the Barclays of the Mathers line, was the younger son of Andrew de Berkeley (Gartley IX), who, it will be remembered, was taken prisoner and executed by the English while fighting for Bruce in October 1322.

Alexander de Berkeley was a man of considerable property, having received as his paternal inheritance the lands in the Mearns of Kincardineshire which had been granted to his ancestor Humphrey de Berkeley by King William the Lion.

He married, about the year 1351, Katherine, daughter of Sir Edward de Keith of Synton, and had a son, David de Berclay of the "Mernys" (Mearns).

This marriage is surrounded by an interesting circle of relations. Sir Edward Keith, Marischal of Scotland, by his first wife, Isabella de Synton, had two children, Sir William de Keith and Katherine, wife of Alexander de Berkeley of the Mearns. His second wife was Christina, daughter of Sir John Menteith and his wife Ellen of Mar, who was daughter of Margery, sister of King Robert Bruce, by her husband Gartney, Earl of Mar. The issue of this second marriage was Janet Keith, who married Sir David de Berclay of Brechin (Brechin II) and was the mother of Margaret de Berclay, Lady of Brechin, who married Walter Stewart, Earl of Atholl, son of King Robert II by his second wife, Queen Euphemia.

Alexander de Berkeley's elder brother John (Gartley X), witness to the marriage deed of 1351, was, it will be remembered, stepfather to Queen Euphemia. His brother-in-law Sir William de Keith had married Margaret Fraser, heiress of the great estates of her grandfather, Sir Alexander Fraser, High Chamberlain, and husband of Mary, sister to King Robert Bruce. Sir William succeeded his father as Lord Marischal of Scotland and was three times ambassador to England. His son, John Keith, married a daughter of Robert II,

ALEXANDER DE BERKELEY, 1351, Mathers I.

and his daughter, Muriella, married a son of the same King—namely, Robert, Duke of Albany and Regent of Scotland.

These relationships serve to show us that the Barclays of this period were closely allied with the Royal House and the inner circle which surrounded the Scottish throne.

The times were troubled. King David II, who had been captured at the battle of Neville's Cross by the forces of Edward III, was a prisoner in England, and Alexander de Berkeley's nephew John (Gartley XIB) a hostage for his royal master and kinsman in the hands of the English, and on Shrove Tuesday in the year of the marriage with which we are now concerned, Sir David de Berclay, fifth Lord of Brechin (Brechin I), was murdered by the Douglas family in the streets of Aberdeen.

Sir William de Keith was the wealthiest and most influential of all the magnates of the north-east of Scotland. He acquired the lands of Dunottar in exchange for an estate in Fife, and built the first stronghold upon the cliff still surmounted by the ruins of Dunottar Castle.

He gave to his sister Katherine a noble dower of the lands of Mathers in the parish of St. Cyrus, which were part of the extensive property which had come to him through his wife, and which was henceforward to remain in the hands of the Barclay family for three centuries, and to give them their territorial designation of Mathers. Throughout that period there was a close connection, as we shall see, between the Barclays and the Keiths. The latter were hereditary sheriffs of the shire of Kincardine, and the Barclays served as deputies, discharging many of the duties of that office.

By a charter, now in the possession of the chief of the family, Sir William de Keith, Marischal of Scotland, with the consent of his wife, Margaret, granted to Alexander de Berkeley and his spouse, Katherine, sister of the said William de Keith, the lands of Wester Mathers which had come to him by his wife, Margaret, to be held by them and their heirs on payment of a pair of white spurs yearly at Christmas "at our chief dwelling house in Strathekyn." The charter is dated and sealed at Strathekyn, March 10th, 1351, and witnessed by Philip

Bishop of Brechin, William Bishop of Arbroath, David Fleming, Sir William de Ledale, John de Berkeley of Gairtoly (Gartley X), Robert de Melville, John de Straton of that Ilk, and many others. (See illustration.)

ALEXANDER DE BERKELEY, 1351, Mathers I.

The grant was confirmed by King David II at Perth on March 18th, 1353, while he was on a permitted visit to Scotland for the purpose of expediting the negotiations for his own ransom, and was witnessed by " Robert Steward, our nephew, Thomas Steward Earl of Angus, Thomas Moray Chancellor of Scotland, Robert de Erskine, Thomas de Falside, Knights, and many others."

The first witness, " Roberto Senescallo nepote nostro," sixth High Steward of Scotland, was son of Walter the Steward and Marjory, daughter of King Robert Bruce; he was Regent during the captivity of King David II and was later to succeed him on the throne of Scotland as Robert II.

The office of High Steward of the Kingdom was hereditary, and the name was gradually passing into the surname of the family who held it, and becoming common to the different branches, to one of which Thomas Steward, Earl of Angus, the second witness, belonged.

This confirmation, together with a second confirmation of the same date, but couched in rather different phraseology, is also in the archives at Bury Hill.

Bury Hill, M. 2 and 3.

DAVID DE BERCLAY

DAVID DE BERCLAY, 1353-1411, Mathers II.

David de Berclay, son of Alexander de Berkeley and Katherine Keith his wife, although he undoubtedly held the estates of Mathers, does not appear in the records "of Mathers," but as "David Berclay of Mernys" (Mearns). The next generation were the first to be styled "of Mathers."

It should be noted that the surname was now changing from "de Berkeley" to "de Berclay" or "Berclay."

Genealogical Account, p. 12.

David de Berclay of Mearns married a daughter of Sir William Seton, progenitor of the Earls of Winton, who was already connected with the Barclay family through the marriage of Margaret, daughter of Sir Walter de Berkeley (Gartley III), Chamberlain to King William the Lion, with Alexander Seton. He had one son, Alexander (Mathers III).

In addition to his estates in Kincardineshire, David de Berclay held a property at Durn in Banffshire, of which his maternal kinsmen, the Keiths, were the overlords.

Reg. Mag. Sig. 1306-1424, No. 926.

In 1407 Robert Duke of Albany confirmed a grant by Alexander of Strathekyn (Keith) of an annual rent of 5 merks from the lands of Petgarvy, in the sheriffdom of Kincardine, to David Berclay of Durn. Among the witnesses to this charter we find the name of another David Berclay, who appears as testifying several times for Robert Duke of Albany. He was of the Collairnie line (Collairnie IV) and a member of the ducal household. Cadets of the same branch, who are described as "Scutifer" and "Armiger," were also in the Duke's service.

David de Berclay of Mearns was himself also in the service of the Duke, who had, it will be remembered, married his aunt, Muriella Keith, and was at this time Governor or Regent Justiciary of Scotland north of Forth for his feeble nephew, King Robert III.

Murdach of Albany, son of Duke Robert, had been captured at the battle of Homildon in 1402, and we find David de Berclay "de Mernys" receiving payments on his behalf. From 1407 to 1409 he received from the customs of Aberdeen "for Murdach, son of our Lord Duke," his pension of 100 merks, and since he also acknowledged the receipt of £13 6s. 8d. from the Custumar, by order of the Duke for his own expenses, it would appear that he carried supplies to him in England. This service was also rendered to Murdach of Albany by members of the Comyn family.

DAVID DE BERCLAY, 1353-1411, Mathers II. Rot. Scac. Reg. Scot. IV, pp. 86, 87.

An interesting record connected with the Keith family gives us a mention of David de Berclay of Mearns, although the actual story belongs to a later date.

Collections Aberdeen and Banff, Spalding Club, Vol. iii, p. 318.

When Sir William de Keith, Lord Marischal, acquired the Crag of Dunottar in 1392 from Lindsay of the Byres he demolished the parish church upon the crag in order to strengthen and enlarge the castle, and serious trouble ensued. Sentence of excommunication was pronounced upon him in 1395 and was revoked only upon his bestowing various benefactions on the Church. Among these was the endowment of a chantry in Aberdeen Cathedral, with lands of Kyntore and Esterskene to provide the annual stipend of two chaplains.

Some forty years later the title deeds of these lands were missing, and the Bishops of St. Andrews and Aberdeen again employed the weapon of excommunication against all persons who had ever seen or read the deeds and did not straightway reveal the same. Three priests, too troubled in conscience to remain silent, appeared before an enquiry in the Cathedral of Aberdeen in 1446, to make their depositions and state what they remembered of the deeds in question, described as "one with a round seal, the other with an oblong seal." John Petkarne stated that he had seen the deeds and read them in the centre chamber over the gateway at the back of the castle of Dunottar, maybe ten or twelve years previously. William de St. Michael remembered an occasion when, at the request of the Lady Mariota, then Lady of Keith, Sir Robert Keith had ordered the deeds taken out for reading. Further questioned as to the exact date, he stated that it was about the time when the lawsuit began between the Lord of Keith and the Lord of Gordon concerning the lands of the Lady Margaret, wife of Sir William de Keith, he thought about seven years past. As to where he had seen them, he said in the chapel at

DAVID DE BERCLAY, 1353-1411, Mathers II.

Dunottar. Moreover, he averred that he had said to Sir Robert, now dead, when out hunting with him at Strathekyn, that he could not endure the threat of excommunication and must reveal what he knew about the deeds concerning the lands wherewith the chantry was endowed. Sir Robert had replied that the lands were his and had been his father's and his grandfather's before him. William Norval, the last witness, told how he had been present and heard all that passed in the mansion of Sir William Keith, Marischal of Scotland, in the Burgh of Aberdeen, before the battle of the Harlaw (July 24th, 1411), "when John Stewart of Inverury and David Berclay of Mernys insistently requested the aforesaid William de Keith to found a chantry for the priests to pray for his soul and the soul of Margaret his wife, then present. The said Sir William, at their insistence, consented to endow two chaplains with the lands of Esterskene. Then in a loud and audible voice the Lady Margaret declared that never would she consent that the endowment should be of the lands of Esterskene. Whereupon the Lord Marischal, much irate, said that never would he endow any chantry for their souls, but at the last he did consent so to do, being persuaded by the good counsel of John Stewart and David Berclay" . . .

At the conclusion of the enquiry the case for the Church was held proven.

ALEXANDER BERCLAY

Alexander Berclay, son of David de Berclay of the Mearns, married Helen Graeme, daughter of Gilbert Graeme, the first of the Graemes of Morphie, which estate was granted to him by King Robert III in 1398.

ALEXANDER BERCLAY, 1411-1416, Mathers III.

Playfair states that Alexander Berclay became possessed of the family estates in 1407, but, as we have seen by the Keith story, his father was still alive in the year of the battle of the Harlaw (1411), so that Alexander's succession must be placed at a later date.

Genealogical Account, p. 12, and Burke's Landed Gentry. British Family Antiquity, p. 230.

We have no records of him. The scarcity of charters at this time may again be accounted for by the lawless and unsettled state of the country. The young King, James I, was a prisoner in England, and Robert Duke of Albany, king in fact though not in name, was powerless to suppress the feudal anarchy which prevailed. The Duke died in 1419 and was succeeded in the Dukedom and Regency by his son Murdach, who was equally unsuccessful in curbing the turbulence of the barons, as we shall see in the history of the next holder of Mathers.

Alexander was the father of three sons, David, his heir (Mathers IV); Patrick, of whom later; and John.

DAVID BERCLAY, 1416-1448, Mathers IV.

DAVID BERCLAY

David Berclay of the Mearns and Mathers, son of Alexander Berclay (Mathers III), married Elizabeth, daughter of Strachan of Thornton in the Mearns. He had one son, George Berclay (Mathers V), who is not mentioned in the Genealogical Account.

Genealogical Account, p. 12.

It was during the time of this Lord of Mathers that John Melville of Glenbervie, Sheriff of the Mearns, was murdered by a party of barons of the shire, and numerous writers, both in song and story, have asserted that David Berclay was among them. From a record now available, however, it seems clear that it was not David but his son George who was implicated in a crime which tradition has surrounded with many gruesome details.

Robert Barclay (Urie III) must have been cognisant of so well known an event, but he makes no mention of it; neither does he include in his "Genealogy" (1740) the name of George Berclay of Mathers. Doubtless he preferred to pass over in silence both the deed and its perpetrator as reflecting discredit on his race.

Similarly, Principal Arbuthnot, a descendant of the leader in the affair, doubtless out of regard for his name, in writing his *Latin History of the Arbuthnot Family* about 1567, gives an account which reduces it into "a mere local feud and the murder done in hot blood."

He tells us that John Melville of Glenbervie, Sheriff of the Mearns, having become puffed up with pride, riches and the number of his dependants, had greatly offended his neighbours by his haughty demeanour. A "day of conference between the Sheriff and his opponents was appointed, the result of the meeting was only greater provocation . . . wherefore the Barons pursued Jhone as he was returning home and having overtane him nocht far from St. James' kirk of Garvah Hill, thai set upon him and slayis him."

Another version of the story is that certain barons of the Mearns complained to the Regent Murdach, Duke of Albany, of the high-handedness of the Sheriff, and that the Regent, already incensed against John Melville, replied in a manner which encouraged the barons to take the matter into their own hands. DAVID BERCLAY, 1416-1448, Mathers IV.

Tradition, however, has persistently maintained a very horrid description of the affair—namely, that the actual words spoken by Murdach were "Sorra gif he were sodden and supped in broo," and that the barons thereupon invited John Melville to a hunting party in the forest of Garvock, and there taking him by surprise, thrust him into a cauldron of boiling water and proceeded each to take a spoonful of the disgusting broth, under pretence of thus obeying the Regent's command.

So strong is the tradition of this ghastly cookery that Sir Walter Scott alludes to it having been actually practised upon a Sheriff of the Mearns. Border Minstrelsy, p. 405.

The scene of the murder is a small depression on the road-side over the hill to Bervie, a little to the east of Easter Tullochs Farm, which is still known as "Brownie's Kettle" or "Shirra's Pot."

Whatever the exact method may have been, the murder of so important a man as Melville of Glenbervie threatened serious consequences, but the perpetrators escaped capital punishment by claiming the ancient right of remission through kinship with Clan Macduff. This record remains to us and informs us that Hugh Arbuthnot of that Ilk was the leader and that his accomplices were George Berclay, Falconer of Halcarton, William Graham of Morphie, and his son Alexander, Gilbert Midleton and Patrick Berclay.

It is thus evident that David Berclay (Mathers IV) was not directly concerned in the crime, though, as we shall see, he did not escape the aftermath, but that his eldest son George and his brother Patrick (Mathers IVB) were guilty.

A copy of the Remission to Hugh Arbuthnot and his accomplices, written in a seventeenth-century hand, is among the manuscripts in the National Library of Scotland, and runs as follows :— No. 31, 6, 15.

LETTER OF REMISSION. SEPTEMBER 1ST, 1421

A true copy of the letter of remission granted to Hugh Arbuthnot of that Ilk anent the slaughter of Johne Malavill of Glenbervy.

"Tyll all men their present letter to comes, I Johnston Stuart,

DAVID BERCLAY, 1416-1448, Mathers IV.

of Fife, sends greting in God, witt ye, wee have resavit Hugh Arbuthnot, George Berclay (to be of Mathers), Alexander Falconer (of Halcartone or Balandrow), William the Groem or Graham (which seems to be Morphie longe before the race of this generatione, who succeeded by marrieing the heretrix, Groem or Graham of Morphie), Gilbert Midleton (this same Earle John's predecessor who wer Lairds of Kilhill and Midleton, sold by them afterwards to Halcarton Falconer in the shire of Kincardyn), Patrick Berclay (which seems to have been Boniekelly or Kirktounhill which was a cadet of Mathers, and Mathers of the Lord Brechine), Alexander of Graham (seems to have been ane sonne of Morphies and hath possest Camistoun), to the lawes of Clane Mackduff, for the deid of quhillome John the Malaville, Laird of Glenbervy, and certaine and sicker burrowise, that is to say David the Barclay of Collarnis (in Fyfe) the first broych that they ought of the lawes, David the Barclay of Leuchry, the second broych that they ought to have the lawes, (this Leuchry possiblie may be Leuchars in Fyfe now belonging to Southesk), Robert of Barclay of Touch or Towy, the third burghe that they shall fulfill the lawes as the law will. Quhairfore to all and sundrie that it effeirs, firmly we forbid on the King's halfe of Scotland, and our Lord Mackduff Duke of Albany, Earl of Fyfe and Monteith and Governor of Scotland, that the said lawes has in keeping, that no man take on hand to doe, molest, greive, or wrange the foirsaid persons in their bodies, or in their geire, because of the deid of the said Johne of Malavill and the payne that after lyes, and forfaulting of the Lawes forsaid and this present letter. In witness of the whilk this our seale to this present has putt. Att Falkland the first of September, the year of God 1421 yeirs."

[The words in parentheses are the comments of the copyist.]

Sculptured Stones of Scotland, Spalding Club, Vol. ii, p. lxix.

"From this instrument setting forth the replegiation of the accused parties to the Court of the Earl of Fife, we gather that they had been required to find securities that they would establish (1) their law-worthiness, (2) their title to the law of Clan Macduff, and (3) that they would fulfil that law as it might be declared."

The three sureties or sikerborghs were influential members of the Barclay family—namely, David Barclay of Collairnie (Collairnie IV), who had been a member of the household of Robert Duke of Albany, his brother Robert Barclay of Touch, and their uncle David Barclay of Lutherie.

This Remission was doubtless not difficult to obtain, since

the infamous Murdach of Albany was himself chief of Clan Macduff in right of his title of Earl of Fife.

DAVID BERCLAY, 1416-1448, Mathers IV.

The record does not mention the name of John Barclay (Mathers IVc), but the tradition that he and his brother Patrick actually fled to the Cross of Macduff for sanctuary receives some support from a document in the Lyon Office, which gives the names of Patrick and John as implicated in the murder.

The legendary history of the Cross of Macduff has already been related in this volume. In return for his assistance against the usurper Macbeth, in 1057, Macduff was granted special sanctuary privileges for his kinsmen by Malcolm Caenmoir.

"Skene's traditional account of the Law was that any man-slayer being within the ninth degree of kin and blood to Macduffe, sometime Earl of Fyfe, on giving 'IX ky and a colpindouch' (heifer calf) at the Cross of Macduff was free from slaughter."

Sculptured Stones of Scotland, Vol. ii, p. lxix.

The Cross stood near Lindores, in Fife, and Sir James Balfour informs us that it was destroyed by some of the "Congregation" on their way from Perth to Lindores in 1559, only the pedestal remaining.

Though escaping the extreme penalty for their crime, those concerned in it were still in grave danger of vengeance from the many friends of the Sheriff, and it was necessary for them to place themselves in strongholds capable of defence. Arbuthnot of that Ilk summoned his kinsmen and erected a castle, and David Berclay of Mathers, imperilled, we must conclude, through the guilt of his son, built in 1424 the fortalice known as the "Kaim of Mathers" on the rocky coast of Egglesgrieg, in the parish of St. Cyrus. This is described as a tower forty feet square and four stories high, perched like an eagle's eyrie on a rocky peninsula, defended by battlements on either side, and almost completely isolated from the mainland.

Tradition again steps in and tells us that David Berclay chose this impregnable site in order that he might escape the vengeance proclaimed in a vow of James I that, for his part

[Photograph by the Rev. Charles W. Barclay

THE RUINS OF THE "KAIM" OF MATHERS

Built by David Berclay (Mathers IV) in 1424

DAVID BERCLAY, 1416-1448, Mathers IV.

in the death of Melville, he should live "neither on the water nor on the land."

James returned to Scotland with his English bride in the year of the building of the "Kaim" (1424), and whether there be any truth in the foregoing legend or not, history recounts that the downfall of Murdach, Duke of Albany, followed almost immediately, and he and his two sons were found guilty of treason and executed at Stirling.

Within the last century there remained of the old "Kaim" some eight or ten feet of wall, which was used as a sheepfold, but much, even of the rock on which it stood, has now crumbled away under the attack of wind and wave, and little remains to-day to show the ancient strength of the fortress home of David Berclay of Mathers.

It would seem from the records that previous to the building of the "Kaim" the family had resided at Kirktounhill, whither they returned in later and more peaceful days.

Mr. David Macgregor Peter, in his *Baronage of Angus and Mearns*, relates the following experience: "In 1850 I was called to Mathers to examine a sculptured stone panel, found among the rubbish of the old ruin of the 'Kaim of Mathers.' This old panel, about eighteen inches by twelve (now deposited in the Stonehaven Museum), contains in bold relief the Arms of Barclay . . . Azure, a chevron between three crosses patees argent. . . The shield is leaning 'bend sinister-wise,' the dexter corner about the middle of the morion which is placed over it as a helmet, with two ostrich feathers at each side, as mantlings. Over the morion is placed for crest 'an Eagle's head regardant.' It may be observed that at that period very few of the shields were borne erect, being generally disposed 'bendwise.' From this it would seem that the above was an instance of 'complete reversal,' a mark of degradation denoting 'some ungentlemanly or disloyal act, stain or vice' on the part of the bearer. But as there is no recorded instance of any such having been actually borne this would seem 'a voluntary abatement' to indicate the Baron's repentance of the horrid deed and loyalty to the King. This old stone, though little marked by the tooth of time, when cleared of the

Baronage of Angus and Mearns, p. 21.

[Photograph by the Rev. Charles W. Barclay

THE RUINS OF THE "KAIM" OF MATHERS

Built by David Berclay (Mathers IV) in [illegible]

moss of about four hundred and twenty-eight years, is almost as entire as when first put up over the portcullised entrance of the old Baronial Tower." DAVID BERCLAY, 1416-1448, Mathers IV.

Mr. Peter's historical data in regard to the crime are erroneous, but since the foregoing incident is a personal experience we must presume it to be correct. Whether he is right in his surmise as to the "repentance" of David Berclay, as suggested by the coat of arms, may be questioned. It is possible that David, while never publicly incriminated in the murder, may have been accessory to it, but it is difficult to believe that in times so barbarous he would have taken his son's guilt so greatly to heart as to have assumed a "mark of degradation" on his coat of arms. All writers are agreed that he built the "Kaim," but it is possible that George Berclay, on succeeding his father, may have erected the sculptured stone recording repentance for his crime.

We have no other record of David Berclay (Mathers IV) nor of his brother John, but his brother Patrick, who, as we have seen, obtained remission for his share in the murder, seems in after years to have completely outlived such disgrace as succeeded it.

PATRICK BERCLAY OF BRETHERTON

Patrick Berclay was the second son of Alexander Berclay (Mathers III).

After the tragedy of 1421 above related, we do not find his name in the records until 1430, when in the month of November he is in the service of David Stewart, Master of Atholl, his Brechin kinsman, who was in England as a hostage for the ransom of King James I, as has been already recorded.

A safe conduct was issued to him on November 8th, "to travel to his Lord," and a similar permit was granted to him on February 10th in the following year. David Stewart died in the Tower of London. Only six years later his father, the Earl of Atholl, husband of Margaret de Berclay, Lady of Brechin, plotted to place young "Robin" Stewart, son of Rot. Doc. Scot. Vol. ii, pp. 271, 272.

DAVID BERCLAY, 1416-1448, Mathers IV.

David, upon the Scottish throne, a plot which culminated in the murder of King James I, and the barbarous executions of both grandfather and grandson in Edinburgh.

Reg. Episc. Brechin, Bannatyne Club, App. 36.

In 1431 Patrick Berclay witnessed as "then provost of the Burgh" a charter of King James I, signed at Montrose on June 20th.

Accounts of Gt. Chamb. Bannatyne Club, Vol. iii, p. 442.

From 1441 to 1446 he rendered accounts as Bailie of the Baronies of Glenbervie and Camnay, signed Patrick Berclay or "Patrick Berclay of Bretherton." These Baronies were adjacent to Mathers.

Reg. Episc. Brechin, Bannatyne Club, pp. 113, 115. Macfarlane's Collection, Vol. ii, pp. 268, 321.

In 1448 he appears as deputy for William de Keith, Earl Marischal, Sheriff of Kincardine, in a Court held at Invervie, in a cause concerning the teind (tithe) penny of Mearns. And as late as 1460 and 1461 we find him acting in the same capacity.

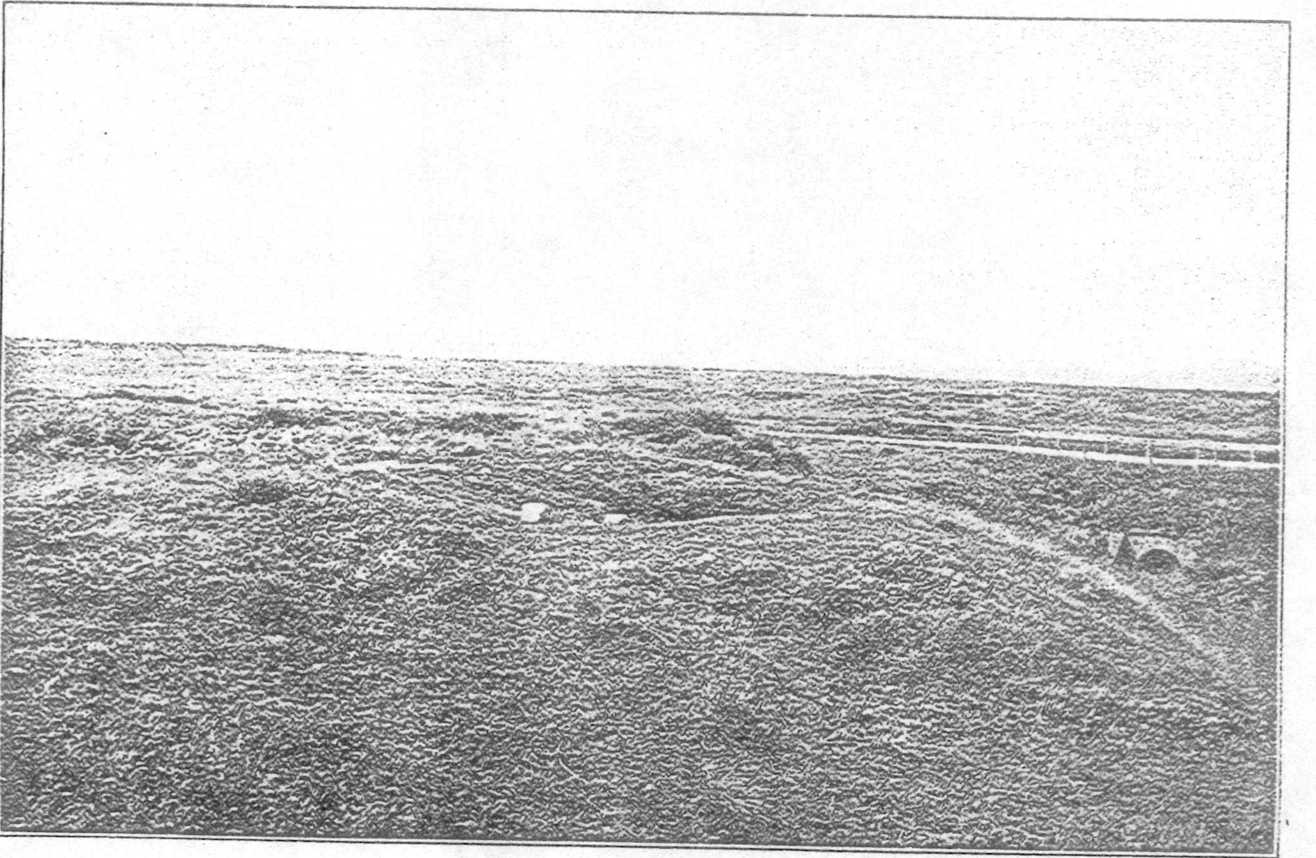

[Photograph by the Rev. Charles W. Barclay

THE SHERIFF'S POT

Forest of Garvock, Kincardineshire

GEORGE BERCLAY

George Berclay, 1448-1458, Mathers V.

George Berclay, son of David Berclay of the Mearns and Mathers (Mathers IV), was in possession of his father's estates in the year 1448. We have already related the history of his complicity in the murder of the Sheriff of the Mearns in 1421, at which time he must have been quite a young man.

In the year 1448 he witnessed as "George Berclay of Mathers" a confirmation of King James II, given at Kincardine in the Mearns, in the court of Patrick Berclay, his uncle, who was at that time Deputy Sheriff of the Shire. Among the other signatories were Andrew Ogilvy of Inchmartin, David Falconer of Halcarton, and Alexander Strachan of Thornton. It is interesting to note the recurrence of the family names of the Mearns. A Falconer of Halcarton had been, as we have seen, one of George Berclay's confederates in the crime of 1421, and his mother had been a Strachan of Thornton.

Reg. Mag. Sig. 1424-1513, No. 495.

The name of George Berclay of Mathers appears several times as Assessor in a prolonged litigation anent the teind penny of Mearns, and in 1456 he is among a long list of witnesses, which includes also "Walter Berclay of Tollie" (Towie XI), to a deed executed by Alexander Douglas, at the Court of Aberdeen on February 21st.

Collections Aberdeen and Banff, Vol. i, p. 281.

George Berclay died previous to the year 1458, and was succeeded by his son Alexander (Mathers VI).

ALEXANDER BARCLAY

ALEXANDER BARCLAY, 1475-1493, Mathers VI.

Genealog. Acct. p. 13.

Alexander Barclay of the Mearns and Mathers was the first of the family whose name is found " both by old evidents, and his own subscriptions spelled as now, viz., Barclay."

He married Catherine, daughter of Wishart of Pittarrow, and had a son David, who predeceased him. He is reputed to have been a scholar and a poet, and to have lived to a ripe old age.

Collections Aberdeen and Banff, Vol. ii, p. 585.

In 1475 " Alexander Barklay of Mathers " was witness to a charter of " Frater Patricius, Magister Domus Sancti Jherosolomitani Cruciferorum cum Stella " at Aberdeen, August 17th.

Acta Auditorum, pp. 55, 173.

Acts of Council, p. 42.

In 1476 an action was brought against him in regard to the " wrangius distraining," etc., of 17 cows and oxen, dated July 20th, and on November 9th, 1479, John Strachan of Thornton, Alexander Berclay and others were ordered by an act of Council to pay to John Chaumers certain tithes in the parish of Aberluthnot (Marykirk) pertaining to the said John by reason of a yearly pension of the " house of Sanctgermane."

About the year 1480, upon the marriage of his son David to Jonet, daughter of Irvine of Drum, Alexander of Mathers made over to him the old family property in the Mearns, reserving Mathers for his own lifetime. Robert Barclay (Urie III) states: " This marriage with Drum's daughter is vouched for by several documents in the family, viz., an antient MS. wrote A.D. 1578, entitled 'Genealogy of the Barons of the Mearns,' as also by charters upon the lands of Falside and Slains in the Mearns."

The " antient manuscript " here alluded to is mentioned by more than one writer, and although a copy made by Robert Barclay (Urie III) is still extant, the original manuscript appears to have been lost. It is well known that many old deeds and documents were found in a loft at Urie, some of which had been irretrievably damaged by the attacks of damp and mice, and this may have been among the number. The copy is endorsed by Robert Barclay (Urie III) as follows :—

"Copy of an antient manuscript being a miscellaneous collection of many curiosities which we have had for I know not how many years in our family, among other things the 'Genealogy of the Barons of the Mearns of late memory descended lineally with their spouses. In the year of God 1578.' The titles and names I have here inserted in the same order as in the book etc." ALEXANDER BARCLAY, 1475-1493, Mathers VI. Bury Hill, B.B. 14, Doc. 13.

The following verses made by a laird of Mathers are ascribed to Alexander Barclay, and the family tradition has it that they were written for his son on the occasion of his marriage. Robert Barclay states that they were given in the manuscript, "The Genealogy of the Barons of the Mearns," and he quotes them in his "Genealogical Account of the Barclays of Urie."

Gif thou desire thy house lang stand
And thy successors bruik thy land
Abive all things leif God in fear :
Intromit nought with wrangous gear :
Nor conquess nothing wrangously :
With thy neighbour keep charity.
See that thou pass not thy estate :
Obey duly thy magistrate.
Oppress not, but support the puire :
To help the common-weill take cuire.
Use no deceit : mell not with treason :
And to all men do right and reason.
Both unto word and deed be true :
All kind of wickedness eschew.
Slay no man, nor thereto consent :
Be nought cruel, but patient.
Allya ay in some guid place,
With noble, honest, godly race ;
Hate huirdome, and all vices flee ;
Be humble, haunt guide companie.
Help thy friend, and do nae wrang,
And God shall cause thy house stand lang.

On January 13th, 1482-3, Alexander Barclay received sasine on a precept from Chancery for infefting him in the lands of Slains and Fawside with the pertinents : and in August of the same year a charter from William (Keith) Earl Marischal of Scotland, and Sheriff Principal and Constable of the Shire of Mearns, confirming to him, his wife and heirs, life-rent of the
Bury Hill, M. 4.
Bury Hill, M. 5.

ALEXANDER BARCLAY, 1475-1493, Mathers VI.

British Family Antiquity, p. 231.

lands of Easter Mathers. This charter is dated from Dunottar, and in it Alexander Barclay is referred to as "our dear kinsman" (delecto consanguineo nostro), as is the case in all conveyances from the family of the Earl Marischal to the Barclays of Scotland since the marriage with Katherine Keith.

Acts of Council, p. 96.

In October 1488 an action was brought against Alexander Barclay of Mathers by one Alexander Cairale, burgess of Dundee, for "the wrangrous withholding from him of nine chalders of vitale and of £8 18s. 3d. for certain merchandise and lent money." Two years later he was the defendant in another action brought against him by Adam Auchinleck, executor of the late William Auchinleck, parson of Glenbervie, for the wrongful detention of three hundred merks for the tack of the kirk of Glenbervie, and other sums amounting to

Ibid. p. 146.

£40. Barclay of Mathers was ordered by the Lords to appear on the following March 3rd to prove payments, and this he appears to have done successfully. He was declared quit of claim for the £40, and twenty merks were deferred to the

Ibid. p. 170.

oath of Sir John Auchinleck.

Reg. Mag. Sig. 1424-1515, No. 1987.

On November 10th, 1490, Alexander Barclay was one of the witnesses to a deed relating to the property of his kinsman the late John Strachan of Thornton. Among the other signatories appear the names of Alexander Falconer of Halcarton and two Barclay cadets, George and Hugh, who must remain unidentified.

In 1493 some dispute seems to have arisen about the lands of Durn, for we find the Lords Auditors issuing a decree that

Acta Auditorum, p. 173.

> "Alexander Berclay of Mathers shall infeft James Ogilvy of Desfurd, Knight, in the lands of Durn within the sheriffdom of Banff, by charter and sasine, to be held of William Earl Marischal overlord of the same."

The decree is signed "with the said Alexander Barclay's own hand," June 19th, 1493.

For some reason, which may well have been Alexander's advanced age, this decree was not carried out until the year 1510, when we find his grandson dealing with the matter, but the record is of extreme interest as supplying additional evidence that David de Mernys (Mathers II) was identical with the so-styled David Berclay of Durn, the first holder of the lands now surrendered by his descendants.

ALEXANDER BARCLAY, 1475-1493, Mathers VI.

Though the foregoing records give us information regarding the private affairs of Alexander Barclay (Mathers VI), we find nothing to show that either he or his son took any part in the turmoil of the national affairs of the time. The friction with Edward IV of England which so nearly culminated in war, the revolt of the barons under Archibald Douglas (Bell-the-Cat), their capture of the person of King James III, and in the end his murder after the defeat at Sauchieburn, made the days in which they lived perilous enough.

DAVID BARCLAY OF THE MEARNS

Of Alexander's son David there are no records beyond the fact of his marriage with Jonet Irvine of Drum, and that they had one son, Alexander (Mathers VII), who succeeded his grandfather (Mathers VI).

Jonet was a daughter of Alexander, sixth Laird of Drum, by his second wife. After David's death she married, in 1480, John Cummyn of Culter.

Leslie's Irvine of Drum, p. 56.

ALEXANDER BARCLAY

ALEXANDER BARCLAY, 1493-1520, Mathers VII.

Alexander Barclay, son of David Barclay and Jonet Irvine, was already in possession of the property in the Mearns when, upon the death of his grandfather, Alexander (Mathers VI), he succeeded to the estates of Mathers, previous to 1497.

He married Marjory, second daughter of James Auchinleck, whose father, Sir John Auchinleck, had been his grandfather's old friend and associate. James Auchinleck was Laird of Glenbervie, having obtained a portion of the estate through his marriage with the younger daughter of John Melville, the Sheriff murdered by the barons of the Mearns in 1421. It will thus be seen that any ill-feeling between those families connected with the crime had died away.

The elder sister of Marjory Auchinleck married Sir William Douglas, second son of the famous "Bell-the-Cat," and took her portion of the lands of Glenbervie into the Douglas family.

Alexander Barclay and his wife Marjory had a son George (Mathers VIII) and a daughter Katherina, who married, first, Archibald Ramsay of Dunnone, and, secondly, George Gray.

Reg. Mag. Sig. 1513-1546, No. 1907.

In 1497 this Laird of Mathers sold the lands of Slains and Fawside, in which his grandfather had been infefted in 1482, to Walter Moncur of the Knapp. He indited with his own hand the obligation, dated at Edinburgh, March 17th, 1497–8, in which he bound himself to hold the said Walter free from liability in regard to any claim of him, or his mother, Jonet Irvine, who possessed a life-rent, the said lands having formed part of her dower. Further, in the same document he states that he has entered into a contract with Sir James Auchterlony of Auchterlony for a marriage between his daughter Marjory and his eldest son George Barclay.

Bury Hill, M. 9.

The witnesses to this holograph are William Rait, son and apparent heir to David Rait of Drumnagair, John Barclay, and Mr. William Roe, Notary Public, and others. It seems probable that John Barclay was a younger son of Alexander (Mathers VII).

Reg. Mag. Sig. 1424-1513, No. 2394.

Two notarial instruments relating to the sale of these lands of Slains and Fawside to Walter Moncur, and the charter of conveyance, which bears the seal of George Barclay, eldest son of the grantor, are also among the archives at Bury Hill.

ALEXANDER BARCLAY, 1493-1520, Mathers VII.

In 1506 we find Alexander Barclay of Mathers one of the adjudicators in an enquiry held at Rescoby, in the shire of Forfar, on May 5th, in regard to a retour of service of James, Lord Ogilvy, and in the following year his name appears in a grant from King James IV to Alexander Stratoun of Stratoun, dated at Edinburgh.

Historical MSS.Comm. Rept. vii, No. 721a.

Reg. Mag. Sig. 1424-1513, No. 3162.

In 1510 the matter of the lands of Durn is once more recorded and a precept of *clare constat* was received by Alexander Barclay from the "Lord superior of the ten pound land of Durn for infefting Alexander Ogilvy in the same."

This instrument is dated Kirktounhill, April 29th; an interesting mention of the family residence.

Robert Barclay (Urie III) states in his Genealogical Account that the original of this precept with the seal with the arms of Alexander Barclay (Mathers VII) appended was at the time of his writing in the custody of Sir James Dunbar of Durn.

On March 3rd, 1511-12, King James IV confirmed at Dunottar the charter of William Earl Marischal, Lord Keith, who granted "to his kinsman well known to the King, William Ogilvy of Stratherne Knight, and his heirs, the lands of Durn . . . etc., ..., which, said the Earl, were resigned his by his kinsman Alexander Barclay of Mathers."

Reg. Mag. Sig. 1424-1513, No. 3716, p. 803.

GEORGE BARCLAY

George Barclay, 1520-1535, Mathers VIII.

George Barclay, son of Alexander (Mathers VII), was put into possession of the family estates of Mearns and Mathers in 1520. He married, as has been noted, Marjory, daughter of Sir James Auchterlony of Auchterlony and Kellie, "a man of considerable family in the Shire of Angus," and had a son David (Mathers IX), and a daughter Margaret, who married Andrew Stratoun of Craigy.

Reg. Mag. Sig. 1546-1580, No. 194.

From the only record we find of him it is clear that he was embroiled in one of the constant feuds which rent the early years of King James V; indeed, it is only reasonable to conclude that his connection with the Douglas, through the marriage of his wife's sister, as well as the territorial association of his wife's family, must have drawn him into the incessant brawls and machinations of the faction led by the Earl of Angus.

Archibald, sixth Earl of Angus, grandson of "Bell-the Cat," whose father had been killed at Flodden, married in the same year the newly widowed Margaret Tudor, Queen Mother of Scotland.

In the ensuing years, while the Regent Albany was absent in France, the conflicts between the Earls of Angus and Arran, with their factions of Douglas and Hamilton, were unceasing; but on the return of Albany in 1525, Angus, then the subsidised agent of England, returned and seized the reins of government; and although in the following year the King, at the age of twelve years, claimed his place at the head of Parliament, he soon found himself a prisoner in the hands of Angus. The Earl issued writs for a Parliament in 1526, and for a short time his power was unlimited. We read that "nane at that tyme durst stryve with ane Douglas nor yet with ane Douglas man, for gif they did they gat the war," but two years later the King escaped and, nerved by his intense hatred of his stepfather, who had now been divorced by his mother, set to work to crush the Douglas utterly. Forfeiture was pronounced against Angus, who fled to England, and it was made treason for any of his name to come within six miles of the Royal presence.

In 1526, while the Earl was at the height of his power,

pardon under the Great Seal was granted to certain persons, and among these was George Barclay of Mathers. His name appears in a long list of men who, with Gilbert Earl of Cassillis, Lord Kennedy and a number of his kinsmen, received

GEORGE BARCLAY, 1520-1535, Mathers VIII.

"Letters of respite for the treasonable slaughter of umquhile Cornelius de Machtema, Dutchman, and for all crime and action that may follow thereupon and also for the slaughter of umquhile Martin Kennedy and Gilbert Mackilwraith, and for intercommuning with our rebellis being at the horn."

Register of the Privy Seal, Vol. i, No. 3386.

Gilbert, second Earl of Cassillis, was twice Ambassador to England. His attachment to the Queen Mother rendered him obnoxious to Angus and his lands were forfeited. He was afterwards reinstated and had a place in the Parliament of 1526, but met his death, by assassination at the hands of the Sheriff of Ayr, the following year.

G.E.C. Peerage, Vol. iii.

George Barclay (Mathers VIII) died previous to the year 1535 and was succeeded by his son David.

DAVID BARCLAY, 1535-1560, Mathers IX.

DAVID BARCLAY

David Barclay of the Mearns and Mathers was in possession of his father's estates before the year 1535. He was twice married: first to Mary Rait, daughter of Rait of Halgreen, by whom he had a son and heir George (Mathers X), and secondly to Katherine Home or Hume, by whom he had a son John, the progenitor of the Barclays of Johnston and Balmakewan, and a daughter who married Fullarton of Kinabre.

British Family Antiquity, p. 234.

The name of David Barclay of Mathers first appears in a letter addressed to Patrick, Lord Gray, Sheriff of Forfar, remitting the decree of the Lords of Council against him of deprivation of that office for a period of three years "because that David Anderson, his deput, gaif ane partial and wrangous sentence against David Barclay of Matheris . . . the impartiality and justice of the said Patrick being now proven."

Register of the Privy Seal, 1529-1542, Vol. ii, No. 1957.

This record contains no hint of the accusation upon which David Barclay received the "partial and wrangous sentence," but since it must have taken some considerable time to obtain its reversal, the consequent deprivation of Lord Gray and his subsequent remission, it follows that David Barclay, who is clearly styled as "de Matheris" at the time of the trial, must have been in possession of his property a few years before the date of this letter, which is March 1st, 1535-6.

Later in the same year David Barclay of Mathers was among those recorded as receiving "Letters of special protection" in a safe conduct granted by King James V on July 27th, 1535, to John, Lord Erskine,

> "to pas in Ingland in our ambassate and service to our dearest uncle the King of Ingland, and siclike to our dearest brother the King of France, for expedicion of errendis concernyng us as well as of our realm and lieges . . ."

Among the "personis underwritten" are

Register of the Privy Seal, 1529-1542, Vol. ii, No. 1732.

> "our cousing Alexander Lord Elphinstoun . . . Alexander Schaw of Souchy, David Barclay of Mathers . . . and all and sundry his and thir propir men, tenentis, landis, rentis . . . under our presentis quhill the said John Lord Erskines returning and hame cuming agane within our realme and 40 days thereafter."

Meanwhile King James was wreaking his hatred on the relatives of the banished Earl of Angus. One of his sisters was married to the Master of Forbes, who was executed on a dubious charge of having designed to shoot the King with a culverin as he passed through the streets of Aberdeen. Another sister, Jean or Jonet Douglas, widow of John Lord Glamis, and wife of Archibald Campbell of Skipness, was literally hunted to her death, "all men conceiving her to be innocent and but a victim to the King's hatred of her brother." This unfortunate lady was first arraigned for attempting to destroy her husband by witchcraft and poison. Jurymen were heavily fined for alienating themselves from the proceedings against her. Finally she was charged with conspiring the King's death by poison and treasonable intercommuning with the Earl of Angus. She was tried by an assize of fifteen persons headed by John Earl of Atholl, and including Gilbert Earl of Cassillis and David Barclay of Mathers, and condemned to be burnt for witchcraft. This barbarous sentence was carried out on the Castle Hill, Edinburgh, on July 17th, 1537, "among the crowd of spectators who ceased not to admire her mature yet youthful elegance and the masculine firmness of her mind." Her husband, Campbell of Skipness, was killed by falling from the Castle rock in an attempt to escape.

DAVID BARCLAY, 1535-1560, Mathers IX.

Pitcairn's Trials, Vol. i, p. 190.

The Earl of Cassillis and David Barclay of Mathers were also on the assize which pronounced upon this lady's son John, seventh Lord Glamis. He was indicted for complicity in his mother's guilt and sentenced to death, but his execution was postponed on the score of his youth. He was released later, but his estates were annexed to the Crown in 1540. He successfully instituted a summons of reduction of forfeiture in 1542, when his lands were restored to him.

Ibid. Vol. i, p. 199.

Gilbert, third Earl of Cassillis, was at this time a young man of twenty-two years, but recently returned from completing his studies in Paris. He had previously, when a lad of only thirteen at the University of St. Andrews, been compelled to sign the death warrant of Patrick Hamilton, Abbot of Ferne, who was burnt for heresy. He was taken prisoner at Solway Moss in 1542, but released two years later, pledged to the

PEDIGREE VIb.

Barclays of Johnston and Balmakewan.

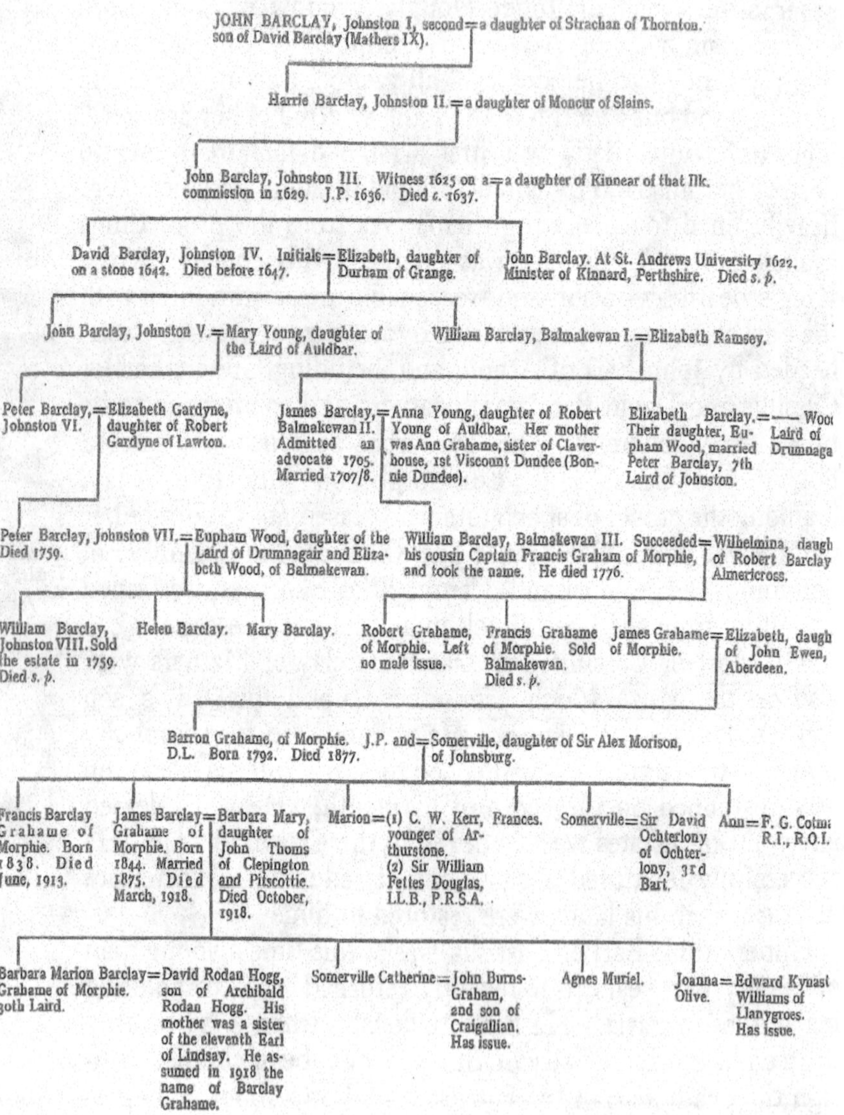
JOHN BARCLAY, Johnston I, second son of David Barclay (Mathers IX). = a daughter of Strachan of Thornton.
Harrie Barclay, Johnston II. = a daughter of Moncur of Slains.
John Barclay, Johnston III. Witness 1625 on a commission in 1629. J.P. 1636. Died c. 1637. = a daughter of Kinnear of that Ilk.
David Barclay, Johnston IV. Initials on a stone 1642. Died before 1647. = Elizabeth, daughter of Durham of Grange.
John Barclay. At St. Andrews University 1622. Minister of Kinnard, Perthshire. Died s. p.
John Barclay, Johnston V. = Mary Young, daughter of the Laird of Auldbar.
William Barclay, Balmakewan I. = Elizabeth Ramsey.
Peter Barclay, Johnston VI. = Elizabeth Gardyne, daughter of Robert Gardyne of Lawton.
James Barclay, Balmakewan II. Admitted an advocate 1705. Married 1707/8. = Anna Young, daughter of Robert Young of Auldbar. Her mother was Ann Grahame, sister of Claverhouse, 1st Viscount Dundee (Bonnie Dundee).
Elizabeth Barclay. Their daughter, Eupham Wood, married Peter Barclay, 7th Laird of Johnston. = —— Woo Laird of Drumnaga
Peter Barclay, Johnston VII. Died 1759. = Eupham Wood, daughter of the Laird of Drumnagair and Elizabeth Wood, of Balmakewan.
William Barclay, Balmakewan III. Succeeded his cousin Captain Francis Graham of Morphie, and took the name. He died 1776. = Wilhelmina, daugh of Robert Barclay Almericross.
William Barclay, Johnston VIII. Sold the estate in 1759. Died s. p.
Helen Barclay.
Mary Barclay.
Robert Grahame, of Morphie. Left no male issue.
Francis Grahame of Morphie. Sold Balmakewan. Died s. p.
James Grahame of Morphie. = Elizabeth, daugh of John Ewen, Aberdeen.
Barron Grahame, of Morphie. J.P. and D.L. Born 1792. Died 1877. = Somerville, daughter of Sir Alex Morison, of Johnsburg.
Francis Barclay Grahame of Morphie. Born 1838. Died June, 1913.
James Barclay Grahame of Morphie. Born 1844. Married 1875. Died March, 1918. = Barbara Mary, daughter of John Thoms of Clepington and Pitscottie. Died October, 1918.
Marion = (1) C. W. Kerr, younger of Arthurstone. (2) Sir William Fettes Douglas, LL.B., P.R.S.A.
Frances.
Somerville = Sir David Ochterlony of Ochterlony, 3rd Bart.
Ann = F. G. Cotm R.I., R.O.I.
Barbara Marion Barclay Grahame of Morphie. 30th Laird. = David Rodan Hogg, son of Archibald Rodan Hogg. His mother was a sister of the eleventh Earl of Lindsay. He assumed in 1918 the name of Barclay Grahame.
Somerville Catherine = John Burns-Graham, 2nd son of Craigallian. Has issue.
Agnes Muriel.
Joanna Olive. = Edward Kynast Williams of Llanygroes. Has issue.

I
B

[*Photograph by the Rev. Charles W. Barclay*

THE JOHNSTON TOMB

English interests. He was one of the four Scottish deputies to France at the time of the young Queen's marriage to the Dauphin who stood firmly against the French demands in regard to the Scottish succession. All four, it will be remembered, met their death before reaching Scotland again, three in one night, by poison at Dieppe, on November 28th, 1558.

DAVID BARCLAY, 1535-1560, Mathers IX.

Thomas Barclay of Rynd (cadet of the Collairnie line) was one of the seventeen assessors who were all amerced for not appearing when summoned to the assize in February 1532-3, when Lady Glamis was accused of using charms against her husband.

In 1539 David Barclay was a member of an assize held in the court of James Moncur, in regard to lands appertaining to Sir John Campbell of Lundy and Lady Issobella Gray, his wife. With him were Alexander Strachan of Thornton, Wishart of Pittarrow, Stratoun of Cragy, David Rait of Drumnagair and others.

Reg. Mag. Sig. 1513-1546, No. 2039.

In 1540 he acquired, by charter from Cardinal Beaton, the kirklands of Aberluthnot (Marykirk) with the mill thereof. This charter, dated April 8th, bearing the seals of the City and church of St. Andrews; the precept of sasine, as well as the Papal confirmation of the same, dated at Rome in the sixth year of the Pontificate of Paul III, October 15th, 1540, is in the possession of the chief of the family.

Bury Hill, M. 10a, No. 43.

In 1546 David Barclay exchanged a portion of his property in "Bridgetoun," with David Rait of Jackstoun, for lands in "Jackstoun" and Skadokmuir, in the parish of Egglesgrieg and the sheriffdom of Kincardine. To the confirmation of this transaction, dated Montrose, September 7th, John Barclay, younger son of David, is one of the witnesses.

Reg. Mag. Sig. 1546-1580, No. 43.

In 1553 this Laird of Mathers purchased from Andrew Stewart of Inchbreck the lands of Johnston in the Mearns and bestowed them upon his son John. The charter of William Keith, Earl Marischal, confirming the same as overlord, is dated "Deer, May 5th, 1553."

Bury Hill, BB. 13, No. 46.

Two years later he again added to his property, acquiring by purchase from Patrick, Lord Gray, the superiority of the

DAVID BARCLAY, 1535-1560, Mathers IX.

Reg. Mag. Sig. 1546-1580, No. 1020.

lands of Nether Cragy, Easter and Wester Snawtoun, Rachirhill, Ovirsett de Cragy and parts of Wester Ovir Cragy, in Kincardine. The charter is dated "Fowlis, May 13th, 1555," and was confirmed at Edinburgh in the Queen's name on January 7th following.

The name of David Barclay appears on several occasions as witness to charters under the Great Seal, and in the accounts of the Lord High Treasurer. He, like others of his line, acted as deputy to the Earl Marischal, Sheriff Principal of Kincardineshire.

He died in 1560 and was succeeded by his son George (Mathers X). His younger son John was, as has been before mentioned, the progenitor of the line of Johnston, which was later merged into that of the Barclays of Balmakewan, which is now represented by Mrs. Barclay Grahame of Morphie (see Pedigree VIB).

The name of Elizabeth Barclay, wife of John Gray, appears in a charter from the Priory of St. Andrews to John Gray, dated July 23rd, 1576. Considering the close association between the Barclays and the Grays in this generation, it seems probable that she was a daughter of David Barclay (Mathers IX), but it is nowhere so stated.

Accounts of Lord High Treasurer, Vol. xi, p. 287.

There is an interesting charter of 1564 which mentions the name of the second wife of David Barclay (Mathers IX). In it she is styled "Katrine Home relicte quondam Davidis Barclay de Matheris."

GEORGE BARCLAY

GEORGE BARCLAY, 1560-1607, Mathers X.

George Barclay of the Mearns and Mathers succeeded his father David (Mathers IX) in 1560, the year which saw the struggle between the Queen Regent, Mary of Lorraine, and the Protestant Lords, and the negotiation of the Treaty of Edinburgh, which defeated the French interest and secured the Reformed Religion.

He was twice married. His first wife was Mary Erskine, daughter of Sir Thomas Erskine of Brechin, who had been Secretary of State to King James V, and sent by him as Ambassador to France to arrange a treaty of marriage between his royal master and Magdalen, daughter of Francis I of France. By this marriage George Barclay had one son, Thomas, who married Janet Straiton of Lauriston in the Mearns, " a family eminent both for its antiquity and greatness, extinguished only in this present age." He died during the lifetime of his father, leaving two sons: David, styled in the records "the fiar" of Mathers (Mathers XI), and Robert. Genealogical Account, p. 19.

George Barclay married secondly Elizabeth Wood, of Bonnington, by whom he had three sons, George, Walter and John. To his second son, George, he granted " the lands of Bridgetoun and Jackstoun in the Mearns, which estates were not held by his descendants above two or three generations," *Ibid.* but followed the fate of Mathers, as we shall presently see. A lineal descendant of this George Barclay of Bridgeton was Sir Henry Barkly, K.C.B., G.C.M.G., who died on October 20th, 1898. To his careful research and copious notes the writers of this volume are greatly indebted.

Walter, third son of George Barclay (Mathers X), lived on the family estates, and John, the fourth son, appears in the records as " indweller in the Canongate."

In the year 1564, immediately before his second marriage, George Barclay made a contract with his stepmother, Katherine Home. A note endorsed " Taken from the Records of the Laigh Parliament House of Writes belonging to the Family of Ure in the particular Registry of Bonds " gives us this interesting information, as well as the marriage contract.

GEORGE BARCLAY, 1560-1607, Mathers X.

(1) Contract between Katherine Home relict of David Barclay of Mathers on the first part, George Barclay son and heir of the said David on the second part, and John Barclay of Johnston brother to the said George on the third part. Whereby in consideration of the said Katherine, her conjunct life-rent in the lands of Johnston, the said John obliges himself to deliver to her on the shore of Leith ten chalders victuall, two parts meal, beer. And the said George in consideration of her terce of the lands of Easter and Wester Mathers obliges himself to infeft the said Katherine in a life-rent of five chalders and a half of victuall, two part meal, third part beer, furth of the lands of Easter Mathers.

Dated 12th December and Registered the 13th 1564.

(2) Contract of Marriage betwixt the said George Barclay son and heir of the said David Barclay of Mathers and Elizabeth Wood sister-german to Patrick Wood of Bonnington whereby the said George obliges himself to cause John Barclay of Johnston his brother to renounce the said lands of Nether Weston, and the said Patrick Wood obliges himself to pay the sum of 1000 merks in the name of tocher with his said sister, which sum the said George obliges himself to employ in redeeming as many of the lands in Kirktoun of Aberluthnot as were under reversion and secure the same to the children of the marriage. Dated 11th January 1564 and Registered penult May 1567.

The second wife of George Barclay, Elizabeth Wood, is erroneously styled "Margaret" in the Genealogical Account.

Exchequer Rolls, Vol. xix, pp. 536, 557.

In the year of this marriage, 1564, George Barclay received sasine for the lands of Scaldomuir, Jackstoun, etc., in the parish of "Egilsgrieg." Also for the lands of Nether Cragy, Easter Snawtoun and Rathir Hill, all properties in Kincardineshire which had apparently lapsed to the Crown.

Reg. Mag. Sig. 1580-1593, No. 527.

In 1581 this Laird of Mathers sold to Arthur Straiton of Merton a third part of these same lands of Nether Cragy. The charter of sale was signed at Kirktounhill, the residence of the Barclays of Mathers, on 13th February, and among the witnesses were John Barclay (half-brother to the vendor) and John Fullarton of Kinnabre (husband of his half-sister). In the same year, on the 2nd of March, the confirmation is signed at "Halyruidhous."

Ibid. 1593-1608, No. 34.

In 1582 we find the name of George Barclay of Mathers heading the list of witnesses to a sale of lands in Forfar by James Rossy. It is followed by the name of Alexander Wood, brother-german to Patrick Wood of Bonnington, and Henry Barclay, son and heir-apparent of John Barclay of Johnston.

GEORGE BARCLAY, 1560-1607, Mathers X.

The next record is of considerable interest as including several branches of the family, for we find George Barclay of Mathers, George Barclay of Syde, and his son John among the witnesses to the King's confirmation on May 10th, 1588, of the sale of the lands and Barony of Carcok (Kerkow) by Sir Patrick Barclay of Towie (Towie XVII) to Alexander Campbell, Bishop of Brechin, and Helen Clephane his spouse.

Reg. Mag. Sig. 1580-1593. No. 1537.

George Barclay of Syde and Thomas Barclay of Rynd, previously mentioned, appear more than once in the records.

Unlike his kinsman George Barclay of Gartley, George Barclay of Mathers seemed to have stood apart from the tragedy surrounding the unfortunate Mary Queen of Scots, but in the year following her execution at Fotheringhay we find him acting as a surety for George (Keith) Marischal of Scotland, under " a friendly act of judgement " between him and the Earl of Huntly, dated March 6th, 1588–9.

The record in the Register of the Privy Council runs as follows :—

" All actions, feuds and debates between George Earl of Huntly and his friends on the one side and George, Earl Mairsheel and his friends on the other, having been submitted to the friendly judgement of his Majesty and the Earl of Huntly having already offered, delivered to his Majesty certaine offeris for the pairt of him his friendis and utheris specifeit, for his fulfilment of these offers, and of the decree arbitral to be pronounced by the King by 1st May next, Patrick Lord Drummond, the Master of Elphingtoun, Alexander Master of Livingstoun, James commendator Inchaffray, Sir James Cheisholme of Dundorne, Alexander Drummond of Medop, John Gordoun of Bucky, and George Drummond of Blair become surety in the King's presence for Huntly, under a penalty of 10,000 merks While

Thomas Master of Glamis, Treasurer, Robert Lord of Altrie, James Master of Lindsay, Alexander Ogilvie of Boyne, Johnne Campbell of Caddell, Alexander Straitoun of Lauristoun, Alexander Strauchane of Thornton and George Barclay of Matheris become sureties in 10,000 merks for the fulfilment of the Earl Mairshaell and his friends of whatever may be his Majesty's decree. The penalties in case of Failure to be uplifted from the said sureties and delivered to the partis observair and performair of the premises."

GEORGE BARCLAY, 1560-1607, Mathers X.

The exact cause of the enmity between the Earl of Huntly and the Earl Marischal is not stated, but it may be assumed that it had some political basis.

The next entry in the Register states :—

"It was either this day or the next that Huntly was liberated from his brief imprisonment in Edinburgh Castle, his place being taken by Lord Claud Hamilton, who had obeyed the King's summons to attend and answer for his part in the conspiracy revealed by the intercepted letters, the story which is given in Introduction XL, XLI. Huntly and Errol had been corresponding treasonably with the Spanish Court and the Duke of Parma in the Netherlands, and intercepted letters were sent by Queen Elizabeth to King James, who appears to have taken very lightly the course taken by Huntly, his cousin by marriage, one of the chief enemies of the Maitland Government. After brief imprisonment Huntly was liberated in the summer."

It will be remembered that George, fifth Earl of Huntly, the close friend of George Barclay of Gartley (Gartley XIX), in accepting the Pacification of Perth in 1572, had pledged himself to the Reformed religion, but we now find his young son, George, sixth Earl, leader, with the Earls of Errol and Angus, of the Catholic party in Scotland, and actively plotting to restore the ancient Church. Huntly was in constant correspondence with the Court of Spain, and after the defeat of the Spanish Armada in 1588 he raised the standard of rebellion in the North. King James marched against him and he and his associates were compelled to surrender. They were brought to a public trial, and repeated acts of treason were proved against them, but the King would not permit sentence to be pronounced, and after keeping them in captivity for a few months took occasion amid the rejoicing on account of his marriage to set them at liberty.

In the Introduction to the volume of the Register of the Privy Council, already quoted, the Editor gives an account of the negotiations which were in process in the summer of 1589 for a marriage between James VI and a daughter of the Royal House of Denmark.

"From a Latin letter of King James to the Danish Court, dated Aberdeen 1st August 1589, we are informed that at last a splendid embassy had been despatched to the Danish Court, led by the scholarly and wealthy George Keith, Earl Marischal of Scotland, and that this embassy having embarked at Leith in June 1589 arrived in Denmark, all difficulties had been overcome or adjusted, and on the 26th August, the Earl as representative of his Royal master, went through the ceremony of the King's marriage, at the Danish Court, with the young Princess Ann, who had been substituted for her elder sister, originally thought of, and who was only in her fifteenth year having been born 12th December 1574.... The new Queen was expected in Scotland in September.... That there might be no discord or discontent in Scotland to interfere with the universal joy on her arrival, the imprisoned Earls of the late rebellion, Huntly, Bothwell and Crawford were forgiven and liberated and Lord Maxwell was released from his longer imprisonment on sufficient caution."

GEORGE BARCLAY, 1560-1607, Mathers X.

On their way home the wedding party were delayed in Norway by storms, and the King joined his bride at Upslo, not returning to Scotland until the following spring, May 1590. It is of interest to record an underlying reason for King James's choice of a bride. Frederick II, King of Denmark, had offered to pay a large sum of money for which the Orkney and Shetland Islands had been given in pledge, and as Scotland had no wish to return the islands, the solution of the difficulty was a bride who would bring them in her dower.

Meanwhile Scotland was torn with panic lest Philip of Spain should make a second and perhaps successful attempt at invasion and bring both England and Scotland under the domination of the Pope. The Covenant for the Maintenance of the Reformed religion, which had been signed in 1581, was renewed and re-signed all through the country, and so great was the dread of the Bishops of Rome that all bishops were looked upon with increasing suspicion, and in 1592 an Act was passed by which the whole order was swept away and the Presbyterian policy established.

These days of religious conflict were full of suffering for the people, as the following tragic records in the family of Wood of Bonnington, relatives of George Barclay's second wife, serve to illustrate.

"James Wood, Fiar (son and heir) of Bonningtoune and William Wood of Latoun, accused of the breaking of the Place of Bonning-

GEORGE BARCLAY, 1560-1607, Mathers X. Pitcairn's Trials, Vol. ii, p. 340.

toune and taking away certain evidences pertening to Patrick Wood, elder of Bonningtoune, and to Lady Ufane (Euphemia) . . .

" Patrick Wood, the father, did not pursue in the case. Treated one of treason and theft. Sentenced to execution. 1st April."

Calderwood's *Church History* gives us further details.

" Upon Monday the 27th April (1601) the laird of Bonningtoune was beheaded at the Cross of Edinburgh, between six and seven in the morning, by a commission from the King directed to the sheriffs of Edinburgh . . . howbeit great intercession was made by Huntly, Errol, Hume and others. . . . He died an obstinate Papist, ever looking for pardon till the last gasp. He pretended that he suffered for the Roman Catholic Religion, but it was no point of his charge. Only the steeling of his father's evidences and writes was laid to his charge. Latoun gott remission."

In considering the terrible fate of this unhappy nephew of George Barclay (Mathers X) it is noteworthy that Patrick Wood, his father, was not pursuer in the charge of theft. When it is remembered that stealing was punishable by death, and theft by " landit men " a matter of treason, it is easy to see why a case designed to encompass a man's death often began with an accusation of stealing some possibly imaginary box or chest, when evidence of other matters could be extorted by torture. This young man was of the Roman Catholic religion, hence his condemnation and execution.

The repeated clemency of King James did not deter the Earl of Huntly and his friends from continuing to plot with Spain, and in 1592 the English secret service discovered a conspiracy in which Huntly, Errol and Angus were all involved. George Ker, a Border Catholic of position, was seized on board a ship in the Clyde, and inside the sleeves of his sailor's shirt were found certain incriminating documents, including eight blank sheets bearing the signatures of the Earls and of Sir Patrick Gordon of Auchindoun, uncle of the Earl of Huntly, and, it will be remembered, purchaser of the Barclay estates of Gartley.

The eight " Spanish Blanks," as they are called, had no other writing on them than the concluding courtesy, customary in letters addressed to royalty . . . " de votre Majestie tres humble et tres obeisant serviteur " followed by the signature.

Two were signed by Angus and Errol jointly, two by Huntly, one by Angus, one by Errol, and two (in Latin) by the three Earls and Auchindoun.

GEORGE BARCLAY, 1560-1607, Mathers X.

An explanation was elicited from Ker by torture. The arch-contriver of the plot was a Scottish Jesuit priest domiciled in Spain, who had persuaded King Philip to attempt a second invasion, relying on the Scottish Catholics instead of the English. An army was to land in Scotland thirty thousand strong, to exact vengeance for the execution of Mary Stewart and to restore the old faith.

The Earl of Angus was seized, but Huntly retreated to his own country, where Argyle was sent with full power to reduce him. The two forces met at Glenlivet in October 1594, where Huntly's two thousand defeated Argyle's swarm of Highlanders, but the Catholic party were not strong enough to follow up their advantage. King James himself advanced to Aberdeen, and destroyed Strathbogie and Slains, the castles of Huntly and Errol, but made an agreement with them by which they were permitted to depart the realm.

The persistent leniency of King James towards these Catholic earls brought him into conflict with the Kirk, who viewed his policy with deep suspicion; nevertheless, before the year 1603 James had proved his wisdom . . . the rebel earls had publicly renounced their old faith and joined the Established Church, the aggressive leaders of which were forced into obedience, and the Episcopate had been reintroduced.

Early in 1603 it was known that Elizabeth of England had not long to live, and when she expired on March 24th the English Privy Council sent to summon King James of Scotland to assume the crown of England. In less than three days' hard riding Sir Robert Carey brought the news to Holyrood, and on April 5th James left his northern kingdom, promising to revisit it every three years. He saw it but once again, though he lived for over twenty years as King of the United Kingdom.

A portrait of James I of England and VI of Scotland as he appeared to his English subjects gives us no flattering description of him.

GEORGE BARCLAY, 1560-1607, Mathers X.

"He was of middle stature, more corpulent through cloathes than in body. Yet fat enough; his cloathes ever being made large and easie, the doublets quilted for stiletto proofe, his breeches full stuffed. He was naturally a timerous disposition, which was the reason of his quilted doublets. His eyes large ever rowling after any stranger came in his prescence, in so much as many for shame have left the roome, as being out of countenance. His beard was very thin; his tongue too large for his mouth, which ever made him speake full in the mouth, and made him drinke very uncomly, as if eating his drink, which came out into the cup of each side of his mouth. His skin was as soft as Tafeta Sarsnet, which felt so because he never washt his hands only rub'd his fingers ends sleightly with the wet end of a Napkin. His legs were so very weake, that weakness made him ever leaning on other men's shoulders. His walk was ever circular. He was very temperate in his exercises and dyet, and not intemperate in his drinkings. In his Dyet Apparell and Journeys he was very constant. In his Apparell so constant as by his good will he would never change his cloathes til very ragges, his fashion never. His Dyet and Journeys were so constant that the best observing Courtier of our time was wont to say, was he asleep seven years, and then awakened he would tell where the King every day had been, and every dish he had had at his table. He was very witty and had as many ready witty jests as any man living, at which he would not smile himself, but deliver them in a grave and serious manner. In a word take him altogether and not in peeces such a King I wish this Kingdom have never any worse, on the condition, not any better; for he lived in peace, dyed in peace, and left all his Kingdomes in peaceable condition, with his own Motto, 'BEATI PACIFICI.'"

A Short History of Scotland, by Terry.

A grant made by King James a few months before leaving Scotland is of special "Barclay" interest. On September 18th, in the thirty-sixth year of his reign (1602), he granted to William Rait of Halgreen and to David Rait, his son, the lands of Kirktoun of Aberluthnot, in Kincardineshire.

This William Rait of Halgreen was evidently a near relation of the mother of George Barclay of Mathers, and the land granted adjoined the Place of Kirktounhill, then the residence of the said George Barclay. It is probable that they were the ecclesiastical lands of Aberluthnot which had been acquired by his father, David Barclay (Mathers IX), from Cardinal Beaton, Bishop of St. Andrews, in 1540.

This very long charter contains a valuable description of

boundaries, written in the Scottish vernacular, which, in addition to the information that George Barclay was occupying Kirktounhill at that date, describes the surroundings of his home. A few extracts will illustrate the nature of the boundaries.

GEORGE BARCLAY, 1560-1607, Mathers X. Reg. Mag. Sig. 1593-1608 No. 1352.

"Terras de Kirktoun de Abirluthnot, viz.:—
begynand toward the north west at ane merch stane infixit in the waid dyke standant beneth the place of Kirktounhill direct anent ane braid balk at the syde of the nyne regis . . . and discendand down that balk fra the said merch stane to the burne that divydis the lands of Balmeledie fra Kirktounhill and enterand in that burne and discendand down the samin southwart quhill it cum to the heid of the Threapaker . . . encompassand etc. . . . to the grit gray eirdfast stane, and fra thyne keipand south as the merchis lyes betwixt the landis of Balmeledie and Thornetoun on the said syde of the entering in the said burne agane quhill it cum to the eist kirkstyle of Marykirk foiranent the said burne and passand up the said dyke fra the kirkstyle quhill it cum to the commoun gait that devydis David Hamptounis fra Johne Villakis bygginys and includand the haill toftis, housis, bygginys and gairdis afoir and behind occupyit be Thomas Patril and the said David Hamptoun reservand to George Barclay of Matheris his airis and assignais ane commoun gait betwixt the said housis and kirkyard dyke to pas and repas to and fro the said burne and fra thyne northwart . . . reservand to the said William Rait and successors etc. . . . power to cast fuill and dovettis, fewall peithies and turves in the mures and myres of Eister Kirktounhill . . . also a commoun gait fra Courristock Luthermure Balmanno . . . to the Eist land endis of Corrymuir and eist thairfra quhill it cum to the grene gait that passis to the place of Kirktounhill, and with all other gaits necessary . . . and reserveand to the said George Barclay and his foirsaidis and tenentis ane commoun gait and lone to cathel and call guidis for cairt and sled fra the nether land endis of Corrymuir up the grene gait quhill it cum to the first infixit merchestane to the said George awin proper landis of Kirktounhill . . ."

Towards the end of his life George Barclay, with his three sons and his grandson, seems to have been perpetually at feud with his neighbours. The Register of the Privy Council records no fewer than ten Bonds of Caution issued between the years 1592 and 1606, that they shall be of good behaviour and not commit breaches of the peace. Their chief enemy seems to have been a Mr. William Barclay, Burgess of Montrose,

GEORGE BARCLAY, 1560-1607, Mathers X.

who also held property close to Kirktounhill, but to what branch of the family he belonged cannot be ascertained.

Records at this time are plentiful and many Barclay names appear accompanied by no territorial designation.

George Barclay died in the year 1607 and was succeeded in the estates of Mearns and Mathers by his grandson David Barclay (Mathers XI).

George Barclay (Mathers X) registered his arms, a chevron between three crosses pattee, in 1580, and in the same year his eldest son, Thomas, also registered the same arms with a bordure.

Macdonald's Armorial Seals, p. 11.

DAVID BARCLAY

DAVID BARCLAY, 1607-1660, Mathers XI.

David Barclay was born 1580. He was the son of Thomas Barclay, who died in the lifetime of his father, and Janet Straiton, his wife. He succeeded his grandfather, George Barclay (Mathers X), in 1607, and was the last of the line to hold the family estates of the Mearns and Mathers. He was twice married, his first wife being Elizabeth Livingstone, daughter of Sir John Livingstone of Dunipace, who bore him four sons, John, Alexander, David and Robert; his second wife was Margaret Keith, elder daughter of Alexander Keith of Benholme, widow of . . . Gutherie, by whom he had a son James and a daughter Anne.

The earliest record of David Barclay (Mathers XI) is found in an interesting document dated at Perth August 10th, 1604. In it he is styled "fiar" of Mathers and his brother Robert is alluded to. It is worded as follows :—

"Robert Falconer of Ballandro for George Barclay of Mathers 2000 merks, for George Barclay of Brigetoune and Walter Barclay sons of the Laird of Mathers, 1000 merks each, not to harm David Barclay, fiar of Mathers, Robert Barclay his brother, Alexander Barclay in Easter Mathers or John Barclay in Balmanno, conform to the King's letters delivered at Perth 3rd July last."

Register of the Privy Council, Vol. vii, p. 562.

Mr. James Donaldson, advocate, registered the bond,

"written by Robert Caldwell in Innerbervie, and subscribed at Ballandro, 3rd August, before William Lundy in Nether Knox, George Keith in Arbornie and Robert Falconer son of the surety. Signed writer hereof and James Neilson, notary public."

From this bond it would seem that the family of Mathers were not only at feud with their neighbours but among themselves, and that George Barclay in his old age found it necessary to protect his grandsons from their turbulent uncles.

Robert Barclay (Urie III), when writing his Genealogical Account in 1740, tells us that his great-grandfather David, eleventh laird of Mathers, was "called a very polite well-bred man, but by the easiness of his temper, and living much at Court, he brought himself into such difficulties as obliged him to sell the estates, first Mathers, after they had kept it near 300

DAVID BARCLAY, 1607-1660, Mathers XI.

years and then the old estate after they had kept it upwards of 500 years." It will be remembered that the lands in the Mearns held by his forbears had originally been bestowed upon Sir Humphrey de Berkeley (Gartley IV) by King William the Lion.

Unfortunately no records remain to us of David Barclay's visits to the Court, though he may well have been present at the coronation of King Charles I in the abbey church of Holyrood in 1633, but we have ample evidence of his financial embarrassments. These were chiefly due to obligations incurred on behalf of his father-in-law, Sir John Livingstone of Dunipace. The Livingstones were in constant difficulties and David Barclay seems not only to have assisted them but to have made himself responsible for certain of their liabilities, with the result that his own property was alienated bit by bit, until little or nothing remained to him.

David Barclay first appears as "of Mathers" in a charter signed at Dalkeith, April 3rd, 1608, and confirmed by King James VI at Edinburgh in 1610. By this document John Lord Erskine granted to his wife, Mary Stewart, lands in Forfarshire, among which are mentioned the town and lordship of Balmakelly "cum tenentibus," etc., occupied by David Barclay of Mathers. These lands were in the sheriffdom of Kincardine. The list ends with the name of Alexander Barclay "notario, writer of the charter."

Reg. Mag. Sig. 1609-1620, No. 236.

On October 26th, 1611, David Barclay signed as second of five witnesses to the presentation by John "Livingstoun" of Dunipace, patron, of Alexander Bisset to the parsonage and vicarage of Kylmoir.

Even at this early date, when he had held his heritage only some four years, his financial difficulties were becoming acute, and in consequence of the pressure of his creditors he was forced to sell the lands of Jackston and "Skaldomure," together with a portion of Easter Mathers, to Sir Robert Graham of Morphie. The King confirmed the sale of these lands by David Barclay of Mathers and George Barclay of Jackston and "Skaldomure" on September 17th, 1613, but the actual transaction appears to have taken place on April 24th, 1611.

Ibid. No. 912.

On July 28th, 1612, the lands of Sir Alexander Falconer, Kt., of Halcartoun, were erected into the free Barony of Halcartoun by Royal grant, after resignation for the purpose. The list of the lairds in Kincardineshire who resigned the lands in question is of great interest as including David Barclay "feodatarii de Matheris," and the names of many others familiar to us as having been connected with the Barclays of Mathers as far back as the murder of Melville the sheriff in 1421.

DAVID BARCLAY, 1607-1660, Mathers XI.

Reg. Mag. Sig. 1609-1620, No. 718.

David Barclay further reduced his property by sales in 1613. On December 14th of that year the King confirmed at Edinburgh the sale, with consent of George, Archbishop of St. Andrews, of "the lands of Fetterscarne and the mill thereof."

Ibid. No. 1144.

In the register of the Privy Council, December 4th, 1617, a complaint is recorded against David Barclay for assault, brought by James Ogilvie in Easter Mathers, George Ogilvie, his son, and David Watsoun and Johne Kembe, servitors of the said James Ogilvie.

"On October last while pursuers' said servitors were bringing their horses laden with waire from the seaside to the lands of Easter Mathers, David Barclay of Mathers accosted them, and not only perforce tooke them back to the seaside and coomed their craillies of the waire in the sea, bot by karge compellit theme to swear they would never thairafter lead ony waire in their said master's service.

The same day David Barclay, the defender, met the said George Ogilvie on the lands of Easter Mathers and assaulted him with a grite batoun, so that the pursuer feell to the ground as deid, and being lying on the ground, the said David Barclay with his knees and feit sua possit the said George's body that the blood comes forth at his mouth. The said George Ogilvie appearing for pursuer and no appearance by the said David Barclay, the defender, or by George Barclay of Brigetoun, David Barclay his eldest son, William Watsoun his servant, James dempster in the Temple, Mr. Andrew Wallace minister at St. Sereis (St. Cyrus) kirk, Thomas Renny, Alexander Walton, William Mylne and Johnne Salter, all servitors to the said David Barclay. The Lords order the defender and these witnesses to be denounced rebels."

Register of the Privy Council, Vol. xi, p. 274.

["David Barclay his eldest son" refers to the heir of George Barclay of Brigetoun.]

Although from the foregoing entry it is clear that David of Mathers was denounced as a rebel, he escaped the greater penalty of being "put to the horn," which might have been

DAVID BARCLAY, 1607-1660, Mathers XI.

imposed on him under the statutes of Robert III and James I. This fate overtook him later in his life, as we shall see, when he was, as we should term it, made a bankrupt. The fact that he had been found guilty of serious assault and sentence pronounced upon him seems to have been soon forgotten, for six years later, in 1623, he was made a Justice of the Peace for Kincardineshire. We find his name in a long list of appointments by the Lord Chancellor, in the Register of the Privy Council, together with the following entry :—

Register of the Privy Council, Vol. xiii, p. 348.

"At Fordoun, 20th November 1623 Justices of the Peace for Kincardineshire sign a report approving the 'ordour already taken be the ministers and elders of every parish for the intertenement of their puir.'

Signed by Alexander Falconer of Halkerton,
David Barclay of Mathers,
and many others."

Ibid. p. 833.

In 1625 David Barclay seems to have had some hope of stemming the tide of his ill-fortune, for we find him able to acquire some property. The King confirmed at Edinburgh, on December 7th, a charter of James Jaffray, merchant of the town of Aberdeen, by which, with the consent of George Johnstoun, senior, burgess of Aberdeen, and Alexander Lyall, formerly of Balmaledy, he sold to David Barclay of Mathers, his heirs and assigns, his half of the lands of Balmaledy, Balmannochie, Haltoun and Smiddiehill with the mill and the fishings, in the parish of Aberluthnot, sheriffdom of Kincardine . . . reserving to the King one penny blench, Witnesses John Barclay of Johnstoun, Alexander Jaffray burgess of Aberdeen, Mr. Alexander Jaffray his son, Mr. William Anderson, William Barclay and William Lumsdane (scriptore carta) advocate.

Reg. Mag. Sig. 1620-1633, No. 917.

It is interesting to note this first appearance of the family of Jaffray, to be later so closely associated with the Barclay family in the days of the Quakers.

An Assembly of the Barons, gentlemen and freeholders within the sheriffdom of Kincardineshire,

"anent the arming by fencible persons within the said sheriffdom,"

was held at Fordoun on November 20th, 1627, at which the Laird of Mathers was present.

"The report of the same extractit oof the Justice Court Book of the Sheriffdom of Kincardine is subscrivit as follows . . . At Fordoun Sir Robert Arbuthnot of that Ilk, Sir Alexander Falconer of Halcarton, Sir T. Burnet of Leyis, Allardes (Allardice) of that Ilk, Sir Robert Graeme of Morphie, William Douglas of Glenbervie, Sir Robert Arbuthnot, John Strachane, David Barclay of Matheris, David Rait of Halgrene, Patrick Falconer of Newtoun, David Ramsey of Balmane, John Stratton, James Allardes, John Barclay, Alexander Keith, James Arbuthnot, William Rait, Alexander Lindsay, John Douglas of Barras, J. Burnet, etc. . . ."

DAVID BARCLAY, 1607-1660, Mathers XI.

Register of the Privy Council, Ser. ii, Vol. ii, p. 559.

On January 30th, 1629, David Barclay was appointed to serve on a commission (which included Mr. Alexander Keith of Pharsdo) to apprehend Sir George Keith of Drumtogtie, who on June 26th was put to the horn at the instance of Robert Keith of Bridiestoun as Master, and William Lawson, tenant and occupier of his lands of Powburne, for failing to find caution, and appear before the Justices to answer for pursuing and invading the said Sir Robert Keith and William Lawson with hagbuts and pistols. Sir George was wounded as the result of armed affrays.

Ibid. Vol. iii, p. 26.

The following year David Barclay was one of a commission to try various persons for witchcraft, and on January 19th, 1651, he and his "lawful son" were admitted "gratis" burgesses of Glasgow. It seems probable that this record refers to Alexander, second son of David Barclay (Mathers XI), who, as we shall see, married a Glasgow lady.

Ibid. Vol. iv, p. 39.

Scot. Hist. Soc. Burgesses of Glasgow, p. 79.

By this date much of the Mathers estates had been sold to satisfy the "wadsets" or mortgages. Half the lands of Balmaledy, Balmanroche, Haltoun and Snidiehill, with the mills and fishings in the parish of Aberluthnot, had passed to Sir Robert Graham of Morphie, the sale confirmed by King Charles I at Holyrood on January 23rd, 1632, and in this year the old House or Place of Kirktounhill, which had been the family home for so many generations, was sold, with the consent of his son Alexander, to William Keith, who had married Mary Stuart, a niece of David Barclay's second wife.

Reg. Mag. Sig. 1620-1633, No. 1998.

Kirktounhill Writs.

The reason for this final sale is to be found in the following extract from the Register of the Privy Council :—

DAVID BARCLAY, 1607-1660, Mathers XI.

Register of Privy Council, Ser. ii, Vol. iv, 153.

"Supplication by Sir David Livingstone of Dunipace, John his son, and David Barclay of Mathers. . . .

Sir David and his son are very desirous to sell certain portions of their lands for the satisfaction of their creditors, and David Barclay, as cautioner for them, is ready to help so far as lies in his power, but they require to attend at Edinburgh with their advocates and procurators for this purpose, and therefore crave protection for a certain space . . ."

John Barclay, third Laird of Johnston, had acquired at one time and another many of the "wadsets" on the Mathers estates. We learn from the records that he was in charge of the management of the property and had not satisfied the family in his conduct of the business, but rather had taken advantage of the easy disposition of David of Mathers.

It is clear that David made every effort in his power to satisfy his creditors, and by his sale of all the estates he had escaped the shame of being "put to the horn," but that indignity was yet to come.

It may be of interest here to give some explanation of the "process of horning," by which the King's Court enforced its decreets.

It is first mentioned in the statute of King Robert III, where certain persons having been denounced as rebels, at the King's horn, for slaughter, all the King's subjects are strictly forbidden to assist them or intercommune with them, but, on the contrary, they are to pursue the rebels with all their might, to arrest or death. The use of the horn in this matter appears from a statute of King James I, ordaining the Sheriff to pursue murderers and raise the King's horn on them, imposing penalties upon the country in case it should not rise in support of the Sheriff on such occasions. Thus, the horn was a hunting horn; the Sheriff was to hunt like wild beasts those that put themselves outside the law. But it was not the view of our ancestors that every failure to pay one's debts involved outlawry. The early part of the Register of Deeds usually contemplates the issue not of letters of horning against a debtor but of letters to distrain him; that is, that decreets were to be enforced not against his person but against his property. But if he had undertaken by a Registered Bond not to pay a debt but to perform a certain act, then his failure was failure to obey the King; it was a sort of rebellion. In such cases consent to letters of horning was included in the clause of consent to registration, and the decreet of registration authorised in case of disobedience.

DAVID BARCLAY, 1607-1660, Mathers XI.

The result of the fact that the Church Court's "diligence" had extended to the debtor's person, while the Civil Court's "diligence" reached his property only, had thrown most of the business of the country in that department into the hands of the Church, so that the abolition of the Church Courts injuriously affected creditors. For that reason Parliament, in 1584, authorised "horning" for non-payment of money. Of course, this does not imply that a debtor "put to the horn" might be killed with impunity.

The difference between simple distraint (in Scottish called "pounding") and "horning" was, in the first place, "pounding" only authorised distraint of goods to the value of the debt; "horning" implied (until 1746) forfeiture of the whole movable estate; in the second place, when a debtor remained at the horn, letters of "caption" could afterwards be obtained for imprisonment. In 1579 Parliament had instituted a Register of Hornings to be kept in the Sheriffs' courts. One put to the horn for what was called civil rebellion was outlawed in so far that he could not sue in court, and his goods were forfeited. To render such a person liable to be seized or killed by anyone with impunity, one required to take out letters of "Fire and Sword," which was done in cases of real or alleged revolt against authority.

The Public Records of Scotland, p. 45.

The crowning ill-fortune fell upon David Barclay of Mathers in 1634, when a certain John Forbes, a zealous Covenanter, who was at that time acquiring many possessions in the shires of Kincardine and Aberdeen, put him to the horn for debt.

In 1643, being still unsatisfied, and David taking no heed, a summons was issued at the instance of John Forbes, and delivered at the Market Cross of Forfar and at his dwelling place, charging him to render his houses and enter his person within

DAVID BARCLAY, 1607-1660, Mathers XI.

ward in the castle of Blackness, the debt by that time being one thousand merks principal and interest, and three hundred merks expenses.

It would seem, however, that he did not remain long in ward at Blackness, for in the same year he was present at the marriage of his daughter Anne with David Strachan, afterwards Bishop of Brechin.

David Barclay, eleventh and last Laird of Mathers, lived until the year 1660, when he died at the house of his son, Colonel David, in Edinburgh, at the great age of eighty years.

By the sale of Kirktounhill the right of burial within the old kirk of Aberluthnot (Marykirk) had passed from the Barclays of Mathers, and Colonel David was unable to lay his father's remains with those of his ancestors, in the family vault in the east end of the kirk, where they had worshipped for so many generations.

The Barclays of Johnston, who were descended from John Barclay, the second son of an earlier David (Mathers IX), also owned a vault in the old kirk, situated in the north aisle, and upon the death of the old laird they applied to Colonel David, upon whom, as eldest surviving son, the headship of the family had devolved, for the honour of his father's burial in the Johnston tomb. Colonel David, resenting the treatment which his father had received from his more prosperous kinsman in his poverty, returned the answer: "As you have buried him in his lifetime, so I will lay him in his grave at his death." He interred his father in the church in the Canongate in Edinburgh.

The Mathers vault in Marykirk churchyard may still be distinguished by its covering of four hewn stones, each bearing the letter "B." The Johnston tomb, as it is called, lies in the churchyard outside the walls of the more modern edifice; it is covered with ivy, and having sunk into the ground is buried almost to the eaves. It bears the arms of the Barclays and contains the remains of the two branches, Johnston and Balmakewan. On each side of the coat of arms are the initials "J B" and the date 1553, which proves that it was originally erected as the resting place of the first Barclay Laird of Johnston.

Of the five sons of David Barclay, last Laird of Mathers, only two survived him.

DAVID BARCLAY, 1607-1660, Mathers XI.

Robert Barclay (Urie III), writing in 1740, stated in his *Genealogical Account of the Barclays of Urie* that both the two elder sons died young and unmarried, and repeated this statement in a letter written by him to his brother David Barclay of Cheapside, which is now in the archives at Bury Hill. The statement is also recorded on the commemoration stone fixed to the walls of the Barclay burying place at Urie. Robert Barclay, it must be remembered, was writing of two men who were his great-uncles, and his testimony clearly shows that no descendant of John or Alexander was known to him.

John Barclay, the eldest son, was born about the year 1607. He was old enough to witness a deed executed by his father in 1619. He is mentioned in many documents of the period.

In 1633 he appears as "defender" in an action by William Keith of Brubtoune, as having "transumed" a charter of the kirklands of Aberluthnot, by David Barclay of Mathers, dated January 17th, 1628. We find also reference made to a bond granted June 1628 by David Barclay of Mathers and John Barclay, "his eldest lawful son and heir apparent."

Kincardine Sasines, Vol. i, p. 109.

Acts and Decreets, Vol. cdlx, p. 311.

Unfortunately John Barclay allowed himself to become involved in his father's obligations and "diligence" was done against him. He is named in a process before the Court of Session on February 23rd, 1643. After that time he disappears from the records, and there is no evidence that he was ever married.

Ibid. Vol. dxxi, p. 168.

A claim was asserted in the *Aberdeen Journal* in 1907, on behalf of Mr. James William Barclay, M.P. for Forfarshire, whose large branch was descended from a George Barclay, born about 1660, who married in 1704 Anna, daughter of Thomas Reid, in Eslie, son of the Minister of Banchory-Ternan. The claim was based on the assumption that this George Barclay was a son of John, eldest son of David, last Laird of Mathers, and heir-male. A close consideration of the dates renders this assumption untenable. The Banchory register gives the date of George Barclay's marriage as 1704, nearly a hundred years after the birth of John, eldest of Mathers.

DAVID BARCLAY, 1607-1660, Mathers XI.

There seems no doubt that this George Barclay was one of the many cadet families which were increasing in number with each successive generation. It is on record that he was well known to Anne, the daughter of David Barclay (Mathers XI), who was then married to Douglas of Tilliwhilly. One of his descendants lived later at Fetteresso, adjacent to Urie, where he was visited by the Laird of Urie, who claimed him as a cousin.

Alexander, second son of David Barclay (Mathers), was born about 1608.

In 1631, in conjunction with his wife, Anna Ross, and others, he was pursuer against David Barclay of Mathers, his father, for six thousand merks, "paid in the first end of the tocher." As James, Archbishop of Glasgow, and Gabriel Cunningham, Provost of Glasgow, were among the Trustees to the marriage settlement, the presumption is that Anna Ross belonged to that city, in the neighbourhood of which she and her husband afterwards resided.

Acts and Decreets, Vol. cdxlii, p. 319.

Ibid. p. 262.

Mr. Fraser, in his *History of Laurencekirk*, tells us that "among the writs of Kirktounhill there is a charter of resignation by David Barclay of Mathers, with the consent of his son Alexander, dated 1632. In the Sheriff diet book at Stonehaven there is the following entry :—

> "Alexander Barclay, son of David Barclay of Mathers, dead before 1652."

Claimants have arisen from time to time stating that Alexander was father to Robert Barclay of Balmaledy, who married Catherine Erskine of Dalgetty, progenitor of the Barclays of Newtoun, in the parish of Laurencekirk, and claiming descent through him. No proof of this statement can be discovered and the present writer is of the opinion that Robert Barclay of Balmaledy was younger brother of David Barclay Mathers XI.

David, the third son of the last Laird of Mathers, was therefore eldest surviving son and heir to his father. The fourth son, Robert, became a Roman Catholic priest and was Rector of the Scots Theological College in Paris.

By his second wife, Margaret Keith, granddaughter of the fifth Earl Marischal of Scotland, David Barclay (Mathers XI) had one son, James, who was killed at the battle of Philiphaugh in 1645, while serving as a captain in his brother David's troop of horse, and a daughter Anne.

DAVID BARCLAY, 1607-1660, Mathers XI.

Anne Barclay was three times married: first to Douglas of Tilliwhilly, secondly to Robert Irvine, brother to the Laird of Drum, and thirdly, in 1649, to Mr. David Strachan, Minister of Fettescairne, who became later, on the restoration of Charles II, Bishop of Brechin. Her marriage contract of 1649 is now in the possession of the chief of the family; in it her father, David Barclay of Mathers, and her half-brother, Colonel David, appear as consenting to the marriage, the Colonel being styled "lawful son to David Barclay." It is worthy of notice that neither in Anne's marriage contract nor in that of Colonel David, two years previously, is there any mention of the other brothers in the list of witnesses. By her first husband, John Douglas, Anne had an only daughter, who married James Hogg of Biledyne, which estate their son James sold and bought the lands of Rainmoir.

Bury Hill Papers.

Ibid.

Colonel David Barclay, who succeeded his father as heir-male, purchased, after the sale of the family estates, the neighbouring property of Urie, and became the progenitor of the Barclays of Urie and Bury Hill.

He played so great a part in the stirring events in Scottish history during the later life of his father David, last Laird of Mathers, that the relation of them is left to be dealt with in the third part of this history.

Of the long line of Mathers nothing remains but the ruins of the "Kaim" and the old burial vault at Marykirk. It passed in poverty and sorrow, but the fine traditions of his race were carried on and nobly enriched by the great services rendered by Colonel David Barclay of Urie in the cause of his country and his religion.

PEDIGREE VII.

The Towie Line (*continued from page 42*)

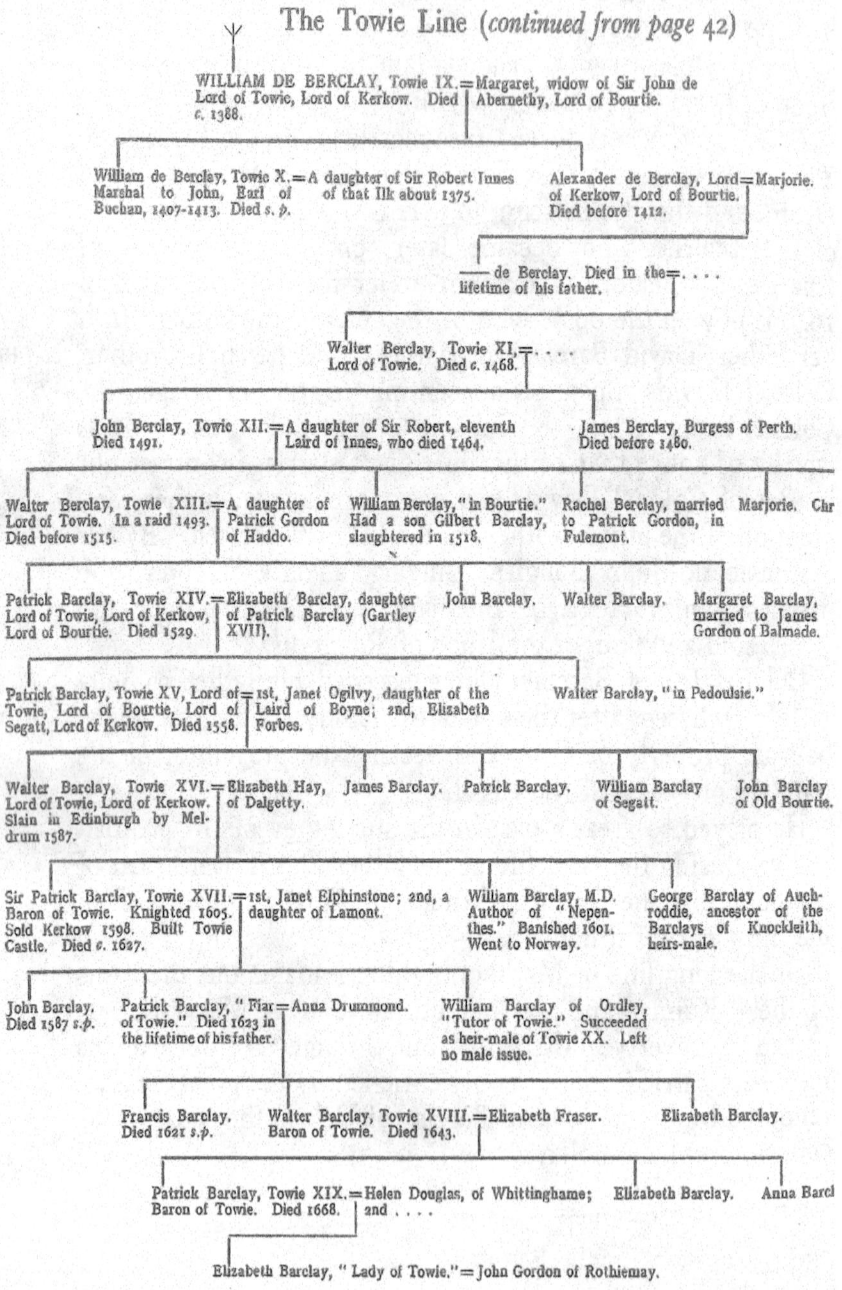

WILLIAM DE BERCLAY, Towie IX. = Margaret, widow of Sir John de Abernethy, Lord of Bourtie.
Lord of Towie, Lord of Kerkow. Died *c.* 1388.

- William de Berclay, Towie X. = A daughter of Sir Robert Innes of that Ilk about 1375. Marshal to John, Earl of Buchan, 1407-1413. Died *s. p.*
- Alexander de Berclay, Lord of Kerkow, Lord of Bourtie. Died before 1412. = Marjorie.
  - —— de Berclay. Died in the lifetime of his father. = ...
    - Walter Berclay, Towie XI. Lord of Towie. Died *c.* 1468. = ...
      - John Berclay, Towie XII. Died 1491. = A daughter of Sir Robert, eleventh Laird of Innes, who died 1464.
        - Walter Berclay, Towie XIII. Lord of Towie. In a raid 1493. Died before 1515. = A daughter of Patrick Gordon of Haddo.
          - Patrick Barclay, Towie XIV. Lord of Towie, Lord of Kerkow, Lord of Bourtie. Died 1529. = Elizabeth Barclay, daughter of Patrick Barclay (Gartley XVII).
            - Patrick Barclay, Towie XV, Lord of Towie, Lord of Bourtie, Lord of Segatt, Lord of Kerkow. Died 1558. = 1st, Janet Ogilvy, daughter of the Laird of Boyne; 2nd, Elizabeth Forbes.
              - Walter Barclay, Towie XVI. Lord of Towie, Lord of Kerkow. Slain in Edinburgh by Meldrum 1587. = Elizabeth Hay, of Dalgetty.
                - Sir Patrick Barclay, Towie XVII. Baron of Towie. Knighted 1605. Sold Kerkow 1598. Built Towie Castle. Died *c.* 1627. = 1st, Janet Elphinstone; 2nd, a daughter of Lamont.
                  - John Barclay. Died 1587 *s.p.*
                  - Patrick Barclay, "Fiar of Towie." Died 1623 in the lifetime of his father. = Anna Drummond.
                    - Francis Barclay. Died 1621 *s.p.*
                    - Walter Barclay, Towie XVIII. Baron of Towie. Died 1643. = Elizabeth Fraser.
                      - Patrick Barclay, Towie XIX. Baron of Towie. Died 1668. = Helen Douglas, of Whittinghame; 2nd . . . .
                        - Elizabeth Barclay, "Lady of Towie." = John Gordon of Rothiemay.
                      - Elizabeth Barclay.
                      - Anna Barcl
                    - Elizabeth Barclay.
                  - William Barclay of Ordley, "Tutor of Towie." Succeeded as heir-male of Towie XX. Left no male issue.
                - William Barclay, M.D. Author of "Nepenthes." Banished 1601. Went to Norway.
                - George Barclay of Auchroddie, ancestor of the Barclays of Knockleith, heirs-male.
              - James Barclay.
              - Patrick Barclay.
              - William Barclay of Segait.
              - John Barclay of Old Bourtie.
            - Walter Barclay, "in Pedoulsie."
          - John Barclay.
          - Walter Barclay.
          - Margaret Barclay, married to James Gordon of Balmade.
        - William Berclay, "in Bourtie." Had a son Gilbert Barclay, slaughtered in 1518.
        - Rachel Berclay, married to Patrick Gordon, in Fulemont.
        - Marjorie.
        - Chr
      - James Berclay, Burgess of Perth. Died before 1480.

[Photograph by the Rev. Charles W. Barclay

TOWIE-BARCLAY CASTLE

THE CASTLE OF TOWIE

Towie Castle.

It is apparent from deeds and other sources of information that the Barclays of the Towie line, until the middle of the sixteenth century at least, had their principal home at the castle of Cullen, near Auldhaven, in Banffshire. Here William Barclay (Towie XVIIB) tells us that he was born in 1570. It was shortly after this date that the family removed to the new house built at Towie, which estate had given the territorial designation to the line from the days of Sir Walter de Berkeley (Towie VIII), in the reign of Edward I of England.

It is reasonable to suppose that some house existed at Towie, probably from an early date, but it is not at all likely, for reasons which have been stated elsewhere, that any portion of the existing old castle formed part of the earlier house, notwithstanding the inscriptions built into its walls.

Of the old castle of Cullen not a vestige now remains; even the exact site is doubtful. It was probably a tower of simple construction, built for defence rather than comfort, and belonging to a type of castle not uncommon along the coasts of Kincardine, Aberdeen and Banff.

Of the earlier house at Towie, likewise, there is nothing left to show its character. From a sasine of the year 1559 it is described along with the property as "the lands of the mains of Towy with the castell and maner place of the samin." On the Procuratory of Registration by Patrick Barclay (Towie XVII), on which he received sasine of the estates in 1587, a significant change in the manner of describing the subjects is observed, viz. :—

MSS. of the late Professor Monroe, of Aberdeen.

> "all and haill the lands of Tollie with the tour, fortalice and maner place."

This change in the wording of the deeds might not mean much, but when supported by evidence derived from the building, the change in the description noticed above is of importance. It determines the probable date of the building of the castle as the latter half of the sixteenth century. One peculiarity of Towie is the ribbed cross-vaulting of the hall,

TOWIE CASTLE.

which is found in one other castle in the north-east of Scotland, at Balbegno, near Fetterscairne, the date of which is known to be 1569. The initials of Patrick Barclay and the date 1593, found at Towie, probably commemorate the completion of the building. Other features of the castle and the general plan and construction confirm the conclusion that the building belonged to the period from 1570 to 1600.

Towie as originally planned belonged to the well-known "L" type of castle, but as it exists to-day it is a rectangular block or tower, measuring some 44 feet on the west by 34 feet on the north, with the remains of the wing building on the east side 28 feet wide and curtailed to 19 feet in length. The door is placed on the north-east corner between the wings and the tower, which is 33 feet high and surrounded by a parapet. The original tower was two stories higher, and so rose considerably above the wing.

A short detailed description of the castle will give a good idea of what it must have been when complete. On entering, attention is at once directed to the ribbed cross-vault forming a small entrance hall. Behind the door is a small apartment, the door of which is some feet above the ground level, and in front is another small room, which, from its situation, may likely enough have been a store room. On the left is the inner door, strikingly low, only six and a half feet high, although it had originally been nine inches less, as the floor has evidently been lowered.

Just inside the door there is a slit in the angle commanding the entrance door and raking both walls. In the passage, on the right hand, is the door of a dark, gloomy place, with a small room off it, probably a serving room, or what would now be called the butler's pantry. Opposite this room, on the other side of the passage, is another door, and beside it a hatch, recently opened out; this was the original entrance to the lower flat of the east wing, which was the kitchen, and there are clear indications of the great fireplace or ingle. Probably the ingle became ruinous and had to be taken down.

The staircase in the south-east corner of the tower opens on the left into the upper story of the east wing, which had been a private room of the family. On the right, in the thickness of the wall, is a branch stair leading up to the hall, a large apartment 20 feet high, 30 feet long and 20 feet wide. In the south-west corner of this hall is a door leading to the back stair, going down to the pantry below. At the top of the stair is a small serving room, with a slit in the stonework to admit of communication between the servants in the hall and those outside. The dining hall had been lighted by two lofty windows on the west and one on the east. Light was also admitted through a small apartment in the thickness of the south wall, which was entered by a stair coming down from the floor above. This apartment is now called the pipers' gallery. Another small room, partly in the east wall above the lobby, and partly in the building above the passage, has a fireplace, and seems to have been the ladies' boudoir. A small withdrawing room is entered through the embrasure of the east window. On the right side of the large fireplace, in the north wall, there is a small door admitting into a dark chamber in the wall.

Towie Castle.

In the next flat, now removed, had been the bedrooms of the family, and the uppermost story of all was, most likely, one large barrack room for the men servants of the castle.

On the top of the walls was a broad walk all round, paved with large stones, resting partly on corbels projecting from the walls. On the ends of these was built a battlemented parapet, peculiar to ancient buildings. The roof had been a low pavilion, not visible from the ground, and was probably covered with divots or turf.

Around the castle was a moat, and entrance was by means of a drawbridge.

The so-called pipers' gallery is ceiled with a ribbed vaulting; on the centre boss is carved the letters IHS and the five wounds of our Saviour. The corbels, from which the ribs spring, bear each a shield with the emblems of the four Evangelists. If there was any doubt that this chamber was not the oratory or chapel of the castle it would be removed by the legend cut on the boss: "INTERSIT DOMO DOMINIS DOMO ORACIONIS" (may God be present in this house of prayer).

TOWIE CASTLE.

An altar also in the east wall and other emblems show conclusively that the chamber was designed for the celebration of the Mass before a congregation assembled in the hall. The chapel was also doubtless used for the private devotions of the household.

Towie is particularly rich in carved stonework and inscriptions, and the true reading and significance of some of the latter has proved a difficult task and given rise to many theories and speculations.

Above the doorway are the following inscriptions, which read :—

Collections Aberdeen and Banff, Spalding Club, Vol. i, p. 466.

"SIR ALEXANDER BARCLAY OF TOLLY
FOUNDATOR DECESSIT A.D. 1136."

and on the same stone :—

"In tym of Valyth al men s(eem) friendly
An friend is not knovin but in adversity, 1593."

The inscription is flanked by the initials P. B. It is reasonable to suppose that the whole of the inscription was placed where it now is by Patrick Barclay (Towie XVII) in 1593, and that the first part records his belief as to the date of Sir Alexander de Berkeley, whom he regarded as the founder of the family.

Above these two inscriptions there is a third on a scroll wound round a shaft, and to be read from below upwards :—

"SIR WALTER BARCLAY OF TOLLY MILES FOUNDIT"

On the shaft there are the figures 12 on one side, and 10 on the other. This inscription Dr. Milne thinks may have been taken from the old castle of Cullen and placed at Towie, but in any case the inscription cannot be so very old as the use of the Arabic figures was hardly known in the north of Scotland until the end of the sixteenth century.

The Barclay arms, as might be expected, occur frequently in various places, impaled in one case with arms that are at present doubtful. On the centre boss in the vaulting behind the entrance doorway there is a coat of arms showing the chevron and the three crosses patee.

On a second shield on a boss in the vaulting of the hall are the Barclay arms impaled with a coat displaying a lion rampant. Milne says that from a close personal inspection of the boss, the words "Patrick Barclay and . . . Lamont" can be read, with the figures 1 and 0. This would point to a second marriage of Sir Patrick Barclay, of which no confirmation has been found. Towie Castle.

On the second boss of the vaulting of the hall there are cut the Royal arms, with two unicorns as supporters and the inscription "arma regis."

Originally the terminations and intersections of the vaulting ribs of the hall have been ornamented with shields and masks, etc., but many of them have disappeared. The hall altogether was of unique character and much more ornate than the general run of such apartments in castles of similar date. One of the corbels on the right-hand side of the fireplace still bears the Barclay arms, and above the fireplace on the roof is the figure of a mythical beast with a long protruding tongue, which may have been intended to represent the whale of the Book of Jonah. Representations of the whale were used as emblems denoting the Resurrection.

Built into the outside wall of the castle is a stone bearing the Barclay coat of arms, which was originally on the old dove-cot. The arms are flanked by the initials "P.B." and the date 1662, and it bears a transcription of the motto of the Towie line :—

"AETHER DOE OR DIE."

Over the lintel of a door cut during the proprietorship of John Gordon and Elizabeth Barclay (Lady of Towie) there are the initials "I.G. E.B." and the date 1694.

In 1792 the tenant, Mr. Irvine, removed the turrets and battlemented parapets. He took two stories off the tower and roofed it with slate, which was out of keeping with the rest of the building. This was subsequently removed and the present roof and parapet substituted.

Within recent years the Governors of Robert Gordon's College, as proprietors of Towie-Barclay, have from time to time spent considerable sums in keeping the old castle from

TOWIE CASTLE.

further decay, and also in some measure restored the ancient features of the hall.

An illustration of the hall is given in Billings's book *Baronial Antiquities*, and also in *Castles of Aberdeenshire*.

The castle is on the Banff road midway between Fyvie and Turriff. It stood entire until 1788.

Celtic Place-names of Scotland, by Prof. W. J. Watson.

The name "Tolly" or "Tollie" is derived from "Tollaigh"="Holeplace," and the change in spelling to "Towie" is explained by the Gaelic "oll" becoming regularly "ow" in Scots.

WILLIAM DE BERCLAY I

WILLIAM DE BERCLAY, 1318-1388, Towie IX.

It is difficult to determine with any certainty the date of the birth of the first William de Berclay of Towie, but, as he was living in the year 1388, when he resigned the lands of Kerkow into the hands of King Robert II, so that they might be re-granted to his second son, Alexander, it could not have been earlier than 1318.

As his father, Sir Walter de Berkeley (Towie VIII), does not appear in the records after the year 1324, it is probable that William was a minor at the time of his inheritance of Towie and Kerkow.

He lived in the reigns of Edward II and Edward III of England, and of Robert the Bruce, David II and Robert II of Scotland. He is frequently mentioned in the documents of this period and is always referred to as "de Tolly, Lord of Kerkow."

William de Berclay also inherited from his father the moiety of the thanage of Balhelvie which had descended to Sir Walter from Sir Patrick (Towie VII).

This portion of the thanage was known as Balhelvie-Barclay as early as 1358. (Accounts of Chamberlains, Vol. i, p. 291.)

These lands do not seem to have remained in the Barclay family, as we find them possessed by the Fodringhays in the time of David II, and in 1379 they were granted by King Robert II to Sir Alexander Stewart, Lord of Badenoch. (Reg. Mag. Sig. Vol. i, Nos. 677, 678.)

Later both moieties of Balhelvie were held, as overlord, by Sir John Lyon Kt., Lord of Glamis, son-in-law of King Robert II, who made a grant to Walter Tullach. (Robertson's Index of Missing Charters.)

As we have seen, the other moiety of the thanage passed to Hugh de Berkeley, brother of Sir Walter of Kerkow (Towie VIII), from whom it descended to the family of de Bonvile, who held it for many years. It was known as Balhelvie-Bonvile.

In 1388 it was granted by John de Bonvile to Sir John Fraser, Lord of Forglen, "for a sum of money paid to me in my urgent and very serious need." The land was to be held of the Lord of Balhelvie-Barclay, and for greater security

WILLIAM DE BERCLAY, 1318-1388, Towie IX.

William de Berclay, Lord of Kerkow, and Sir Thomas Fraser, Lord of Corntoun, who had been besought to be present, appended their seals. The witnesses include Alexander de Berclay, Lord of Kerkow, and the charter was granted at Forglen on January 8th—that is to say, as we shall see later, after Kerkow had been conveyed by William de Berclay of Tolly to his son Alexander. The charter states that the rent was to be paid to Sir John de Abernethy, knight, who had received the rent due from the Fodringhays for Balhelvie-Barclay. Therefore we may presume that, at that time, the Abernethys were the overlords of the Balhelvie thanage, and that William de Berclay apparently became the overlord on his marriage with the widow of Sir John de Abernethy.

Calendar of Charters Edinburgh.

The above grant was confirmed by Sir John Lyon, Lord of Glamis, who by this time had become the overlord of the thanage, on September 29th, 1392. This confirmation recites the original grant and gives us the date.

Collections Aberdeen and Banff, Spalding Club, Vol. i, p. 289.

The original charter of confirmation of John de Bonvile's grant is to be found in the charter room at Slaines Castle. It is dated at Linlithgow, the 4th of June 1400 and the eleventh year of King Robert II.

Historical MSS. Commission, Report 5.

In the time of Sir William Fodringhay, about the year 1380, there is mention of a Sir John de Berclay of Menteith, Lord of Petmacaldore, who speaks of Sir William as "dearest father." It is not clear who this Sir John de Berclay was. He is also found granting lands in Methlak, county Aberdeen.

Reg. Episc. Aberdeen, Spalding Club, Vol. ii, p. 281.

In 1385 William de Berclay was witness to a charter of his kinsman Andrew de Berclay (Gartley XII), in which the said Andrew granted to Jonet de Berclay, his sister, widow of Sir John of Monymusk, all his lands of Melros and the mill, in the sheriffdom of Banff, in full satisfaction of any claims that she might have on the estate of their father, Sir John de Berkeley (Gartley X). He signs "William de Berclay de Tolly, dominus de Kerkow."

William de Berclay married Margaret of Abernethy, widow of Sir John of Abernethy, who had formerly held the lands of Bourtie, in the Garioch. He held them under the Earl of Mar, who obtained the Lordship through his marriage in 1326 with Christina, sister of Robert the Bruce. In 1346 Christina, in her widowhood, as Lady of the Garioch, gave a charter of the estate of Auld Bourtie with one-third of Petgrovny to .... Abernethy. On the death of his father, Sir John of Abernethy, his son by the said Margaret, inherited the Bourtie estates.

WILLIAM DE BERCLAY, 1318-1388, Towie IX. Minutes of Evidence in the Mar Case, 1875.

Margaret of Abernethy must have been the heiress of Bourtie, as her sons by Sir John of Abernethy and William de Berclay take the estates in succession. It is most likely that she was a Melgdrum, as William de Melgdrum and Sir John de Abernethy had lands in that township in 1342.

Notes by Sir Henry Barkly.

It is probable that William lived for at least two years after his resignation of the lands of Kerkow, for on May 10th, 1390, we find a William de Berclay, without territorial description, among the witnesses to a grant by Henry de Brogane of the lands of Achlowne.

Collections Aberdeen and Banff, Spalding Club, Vol. iii, p. 93.

William de Berclay and Margaret his wife had issue two sons—William, his heir to the Barony of Towie, of whom later, and Alexander, who received the lands of Kerkow.

ALEXANDER DE BERCLAY OF KERKOW

Alexander de Berclay, the younger son of William de Berclay (Towie IX), appears to have succeeded to the lands of Auld Bourtie by 1384, as we find in the Abbreviatio Registeri Magni Sigilii, Lib. vii, No. 210, MSS., General Register House, Edinburgh :—

"In the year 1384, Margaret Countess of Douglas, Lady of Mar, and of the Garioch, daughter of the deceased Donald, third of that name, Earl of Mar, gave two parts of the town of Petgrovny and the whole town of Colihill, lying in the Lordship of Bourtie (which had been granted to her for the relief of that Lordship by Alexander de Berclay, son of William de Berclay of Kerkow, and heir to the deceased John Abernethi his brother), making in the whole a ten pound land, for the endowment of a chaplain in the church of the Virgin Mary of the Garuiach, to pray for the souls of the founder, of William Earl of Douglas her deceased husband, of the deceased Thomas Earl of Mar her brother, and of James Earl of Douglas her son."

Collections Aberdeen and Banff, Spalding Club, Vol. iii, p. 416.

WILLIAM DE BERCLAY, 1318-1388, Towie IX.

The precept of sasine, in the possession of the Laird of Bourtie, contains a full description. It is issued at Kildrummy, August 20th, 1387, by John of Swinton, Lord of the same, and Margaret his wife, Countess of Douglas and Mar, and Lady of the Regality of the Garioch . . . "to our bailie," directing him to infeft Alexander de Berclay, son of William de Berclay of Kerkow, in the lands of Auld Bourtie, and a third part of Petgrovny. "Which lands of Auld Bourtie Margaret of Abernethy, *non vi aut metu* resigned in her widowhood, *in plena curia apud Enverury tanta*, and by letters of resignation in our presence in the castle of Kindrony, by staff and baton."

History of the Garioch, by Davidson, p. 64.

The descendants of Alexander de Berclay continued to hold the lands of Bourtie until 1598, when Walter Barclay (Towie XVI), with consent of his son Patrick, sold them to the family of Seton.

Ibid. p. 230.

In 1388, as has been before mentioned, there is a grant by King Robert II to Alexander de Berclay of Kerkow of the whole Barony of Kerkow, surrendered to the King by Alexander's father William for the purpose, and reserving to the said William his free tenement of the same for life, for Alexander to hold as his father William had held it. Edinburgh. May 15th, 1388.

The Red Book of Grandtully, by Sir William Fraser, Vol. i, p. 3.

In the account of the custumers of Aberdeen from March 21st, 1407, to March 21st, 1409, we find that in July 1409, by order of the Duke of Albany, there is an account of the lands of Carkow (Kerkow). And in the accounts of the same custumers from July 14th, 1410, to July 14th, 1412, there is a payment to Marjorie, wife of the late Alexander de Berclay, of her terce of her lands of Carkow. It is quite likely from these entries that Alexander de Berclay was dead before 1409, and it is clear that he did not fight in the great battle of the Harlaw in 1411.

Exchequer Rolls, Vol. iv, p. 87.

Ibid. p. 146.

Alexander de Berclay and his wife Marjorie had issue one son, whose name has not come down to us. He died in the lifetime of his father. It is possible that, as the lands of Bourtie, where he lived, were adjacent to the battlefield of the Harlaw, and that the Earl of Mar was overlord of the estate, the unnamed son of Alexander joined the forces of his Lord and laid down his life on that victorious field. He left a son, Walter Berclay (Towie XI), who inherited the lands of Auld Bourtie from his grandfather Alexander and, as we shall see later from the records, was known as "de Tolly," so that we may presume that he also inherited the Barony of Towie from his great-uncle, William de Berclay (Towie X), on that laird's death without leaving male issue.

WILLIAM DE BERCLAY, 1318-1388, Towie IX.

WILLIAM DE BERCLAY II

WILLIAM DE BERCLAY, 1388-1414, Towie X.

William de Berclay (Towie X) succeeded his father, William de Berclay (Towie IX), in the paternal estates.

It seems clear, however, that he did not inherit until he was approaching middle age, as his father must have been an old man when he resigned the lands of Kerkow in favour of his younger son Alexander in 1388.

We find in the *Records of the Innes Family* that William de Berclay married a daughter of Sir Robert Innes in 1375.

If the original record of the above marriage could be traced it would help to strengthen the contention that there were two William Berclays of Towie, father and son.

We have proof that the elder William married Margaret, the widow of Sir John de Abernethy. Mr. Thomas Innes of Learney, Garrick Pursuivant, says that the Lyon Office has no record of this Barclay-Innes marriage, but that it is mentioned in all the Innes pedigrees.

The first William died in 1388, and there is no record that his son Alexander of Kerkow was ever in possession of the Barony of Towie. This establishes the existence of an elder son who held these estates.

In the following records the younger William is called "de Tollie" only, whereas his father is always "de Tollie dominus de Kerkow." This latter estate had passed to his second son, Alexander, as we have seen.

Dr. Davidson, in his *History of the Garioch*, tells us that "the Laird of Towie" was engaged in the battle of the Harlaw on July 24th, 1411. It was fought in the Garioch, in Aberdeenshire, close to Towie, Bourtie and Gartley.

Barclays of all three branches must certainly have been among the Lowlanders who, in that small compact mass led by Alexander Stewart, Earl of Mar, kept the way against the plundering hordes of Highlanders which Donald Lord of the Isles had let loose against their lands and homes.

Many of the Lowlanders nobly laid down their lives in defence of their kith and kin, and it is beyond doubt that the Barclays must have suffered with the others. This would account for the unnamed generations that we find in both the families of Gartley and Bourtie at this period, and may be the reason for the failure of direct male issue from this William de Berclay of the Towie line.

WILLIAM DE BERCLAY, 1388-1414, Towie X.

Dr. Davidson gives us a list of names of persons of repute who were with Sir Thomas Erskine of Balhaggarty, in which he includes "Barclay de Tolly." He calls him Laird of Bourtie, but this is erroneous, as the Bourtie lands were held by Alexander de Berclay of Kerkow, the younger son of the first William of Towie.

The origin of the battle of the Harlaw was that the Duke of Albany, Regent of the Kingdom, had secured the Earldom of Ross, by Royal charter, for his own son John Stewart, Earl of Buchan; the Earldom having being resigned in his favour by Euphemia, Countess of Ross, when, without heirs of her body, she retired into a convent.

The wife of Donald, Lord of the Isles, was the rightful heiress should Euphemia die without issue.

That great chief promptly disputed the legality of the Crown and took up arms. Sweeping through Moray and Strathbogie with little opposition, he made for Aberdeen, publishing his intention of giving it to the flames. He met the defending force in the Garioch, at the Harlaw, where his Highlanders, although much greater in number, were beaten and fled to Inverness.

William de Berclay was Marischal to John Earl of Buchan from 1407 to 1412. He apparently received his salary for this office from the customs of Aberdeen. It amounted to five merks per annum. Whether the office was civil or military does not appear.

Exchequer Rolls, Vol. ii, p. 87.

A William Berclay received a pension from the fermes of Aberdeen in 1409, but for what service is unknown.

Ibid. Vol. iv, p. 87.

The names of William Berclay's sons, if any, have not been found, and it is possible that they fell, as did so many of their contemporaries, at the battle of the Harlaw.

William de Berclay (Towie X) was succeeded in the Barony of Towie by his great-nephew, Walter Berclay (Towie XI), the grandson of his brother, Alexander de Berclay of Kerkow.

WALTER BERCLAY

Walter Berclay, 1430-1468, Towie XI.

Walter Berclay was a very young child when he inherited the lands of Kerkow from his grandfather, Alexander de Berclay of Kerkow and Old Bourtie. As has been already suggested, his father, who is unnamed in the records, was likely to have been slain at the battle of the Harlaw, in 1411.

There is no mention of a Berclay de Tolly to be found between the years 1414 and 1430, which seems to point to the fact that the lands of Towie, Kerkow and Bourtie were in the possession of a minor.

The first mention of a Walter Berclay that can be found, and this does not add a territorial designation, is from an original deed, now in the archives of King's College and University, Aberdeen.

" Inquisition is made at Aberdeen in the Court of Sir Andrew Stewart Kt and sheriff locumtenens of Aberdeen on the 11th day of May 1430 by persons on oath namely . . . "

Among them is the name of " Walterum Berkelay."

Collections Aberdeen and Banff, Spalding Club, Vol. iii, p. 334.

" Which swearers said that the late Alexander de Jardyne . . . and that the said David de Bonvill was the legitimate and nearest heir to the said Alexander of the annuity derived from the Thanage of Balhelvie, held of the King in chief for homage and service."

This connection of Walter Berclay with Balhelvie strengthens the assumption that he was the Laird of Towie, although it is not so stated in the deed.

Dr. Davidson, in his *Inverury and the Earldom of the Garioch*, page 229, says :—

" The connection of the ancient House of Barclay of Tolly with the Garioch was their being possessors of the estate of Bourtie. The charters of 1346 and 1387 have been noticed. The charters of the lands of Bourtie contain the following documents in continuation. In 1441 Walter Berclay was infeft in the Bourtie lands as heir to his grandfather, Alexander (of 1387), upon a precept for William Earl of Orkney, Lord of the Regality."

Bourtie Charters.

" In 1458 the King granted a charter of the lands of Auld Bourtie and a third part of the lands of Petgroveny to Walter Berclay of Towie."

There is an original charter in the charter chest at Skene which is interesting as Walter is mentioned with his kinsman George Berclay (Mathers V). WALTER BERCLAY, 1430-1468, Towie XI.

" Decreitt vpone the breiff of richt in favores of Skene for the laundis of Ledach of Skene, Kirktoune of Skene, and Milboy and Garlogy."

A.D. 1457.

Alexander Douglas, Deputy-Sheriff of Aberdeen, on the 21st of February 1456, hears in full court the case of James de Skene of that Ilk, who brings an action, and Joneta de Keith with her father the Lord William de Keith, Earl Marischal of Scotland, for right over the above lands held of the King. George Berclay of Mathers is one of the Assessors and " Walterum Berclai " appears as one of the sureties. Collections Aberdeen and Banff, Spalding Club, Vol. i, p. 281.

Among the documents anent the claim of the family of Erskine to the Earldom of Mar, there is a transcript, under the great seal of James IV, of a process anent the service of Thomas, Lord Erskine, in the half of the Earldom of Mar, 1509. It is from the original belonging to the Lord Elphinstone, and the enquiry of 1457 is inspected and recited. The names of many prelates, magnates and free tenants are found among the witnesses and among them " Walterus Berclay de Tolly." He is also sworn and examined by himself, which shows him to have been a witness of some importance. Miscellany, Spalding Club, Vol. v, pp. 264-267.

On December 3rd, 1457, we find the name of " Walter Barkly " among the witnesses at an enquiry held at Aberdeen by William de Murray of Tilibardyn, concerning the lands of Forglen. These lands were in the Presbytery of Turreff and close to the estate of Towie. Although his territorial designation is not given, there is no doubt that " Walter Barkly " is the Laird of Towie, as he signs fifth on the list. Part of the lands of Forglen were in the possession of Roger de Berkeley (Towie V) and, as we have seen, were granted by him to the Abbey of Lindores in the thirteenth century. Collections Aberdeen and Banff, Spalding Club, p. 511.

The records quoted above strengthen the assumption that Walter Berclay, the grandson of Alexander de Berclay of Kerkow, had inherited the Barony of Towie from his great-

WALTER BERCLAY, 1430-1468, Towie XI.

uncle William (Towie X) on that laird's death without living male issue.

We do not know the name of Walter Berclay's wife, but he had certainly two sons, John Berclay (Towie XII), who succeeded him, and James, who was a Burgess of Perth. There is an entry as follows :—

" John Berclay of Tolly brother and heir of the late James Berclay, burgess of Perth, to pay to David Chaumers of Strathy, son and heir of the late John of Chaumers, £28, for which the late James was bound to the late John."

4th July, 1480.

Walter Berclay (Towie XI) died about the year 1468, and was succeeded by his eldest son, John (Towie XII).

JOHN BERCLAY

John Berclay, 1468–1491, Towie XII.

John Berclay had sasine of the lands of Towie and also of Seggatt in the year 1468. There is an entry in the Exchequer Rolls, "Libri Responsionum," as follows :—

Aberdeen 1468.
Sasine. Johannis Berclay.
to Sidget Tolly.

and again at *Perth* :—

Johannis Berclay.
to *Carock* [Kerkow].

Exchequer Rolls, Vol. ix, No. 1674.

As John Berclay of Tolly he is witness to a grant by George, second Earl of Huntly, to his beloved cousin Thomas of Gordon of the lands of Broeruddoch, signed at Banff January 24th, 1473–4. Broeruddoch is near Ferrar and the Muir of Dinnet, on Deeside.

Records of Aboyne, Spalding Club, p. 12.

From an original charter in the possession of the Spalding Club there is a precept by Lancelot Futhes for sasine of the lands of Rothie Brisbane for "nobili viro" James Innes of that Ilk, delivered at Aberdeen February 17th, 1478–9. The deed begins "Lanslotus Futhes · Wilhelmo Meldrum de Fywe · Johanni Berclay de Tolle · Patricio Gordoun de Methlek et Roberto Gordoun de Vothac, balivis meis . . . " etc.

Collections Aberdeen and Banff, Spalding Club, Vol. ii, p. 328.

John Berclay appears to have married a daughter of Sir Robert Innes, eleventh Laird of Innes, who died about 1464.

John Berclay had issue two sons and three daughters. The eldest, Walter Berclay (Towie XIII), succeeded him, and William Barclay "in Bourtie," was the father of Gilbert, who was slaughtered by James Chricton and others in the year 1518.

There is a "Letter of Slaynes" granted by Patrick Barclay (Towie XIV) and others in favour of James Chricton of Frendraught and others, his accomplices (including Alexander Leslie of Wardis and others named Guthrie, Craig, Irvine, and Allardice), for the slaughter of Gilbert Barclay, son of William Barclay in (i.e., tacksman of) Bourtie. It is

JOHN BERCLAY, 1468–1491, Towie XII. Scot. Hist. Soc. No. 62.

taken from the partial notes by John Riddell (Note Book 117) in the National Library of Scotland. The original was in the Wigton Charter Chest (now missing).

"BE IT KEND, us Patrick Barclay of Tolly, William Barclay in Bourtie, father to umquhill Gilbert Barclay, Andro Barclay, James Barclay, cousingis to umquhill the said Gilbert, James Chalmer of Torries, Alexander Chalmers, James Johnston of that Ilk, William Johnston, Alexander Innes of that Ilk, Robert Innes of Rothmakenzie, Robert of Innermarky, as Maister Principals and nearest kinsmen to the said Gilbert on his four branches on his fathers and moders sides, for us to be satisfied for amends made for the slaughter of the said Gilbert. . . ." Dated 15th September 1518.

It is obvious that the "Maister Principals" are the father and the chief of the House of Towie (Towie XIV), whilst the others are the principal relations on the three other "branches"—i.e., the descendants representing the families of the four grandparents, paternal and maternal, of the murdered man.

We know from the Innes genealogies that a daughter of Sir Robert, the eleventh Laird of Innes, married a Laird of Towie-Barclay. Sir Robert died in 1464, and his two eldest sons were Sir James Innes, twelfth of that Ilk (father of Alexander, thirteenth laird and Robert of Rothmakenzie), and Walter Innes of Innermarky (father of Robert of Innermarky and three other brothers).

Rachel, the eldest daughter of John Berclay (Towie XII), married Patrick Gordon in Fulemont, the first Gordon of Craig. On the old front of the castle of Craig there is a shield bearing quarterly the arms of Gordon, Barclay and Stewart, also the initials "P.G R.B.," which evidently refer to Patrick Gordon and Rachel Berclay.

Marjorie, the second daughter, married James King, of Bourtie. He owned the estate of Barras and obtained a new charter of part of the property on November 13th, 1490.

"Terre de Westerhous dantur Jacobo King de Bouty ejusque sposa.

XV die Novembris Anno Domini (jm cccc. XC) Jacobus King de Bourty resignauit in manibus Johannis (Comitis) de Mar et

Garioche dimid ictatem omnium terarum de Westerhous infra vicecomitatum de Aberdeen. Quiquidem dominus comes easdem dicto Jacobus Maiorie Berclay sposa sua . . . Walterus de Touy petit instrumenta. . . ."

JOHN BERCLAY, 1468–1491, Towie XII.

This charter is abridged from Notary Protocol, entitled *Register of Sasines for the Burg of Aberdene*, Vol. I.

Christian, the third daughter, married Alexander Forbes of Towie-Forbes. He lived at Little Kildrummy.

John Berclay died in 1491 and was succeeded by his eldest son, Walter Berclay (Towie XIII).

WALTER BERCLAY

WALTER BERCLAY, 1491–1515, Towie XIII.

Walter Berclay (Towie XIII) succeeded his father John Berclay (Towie XII) in the year 1491. The Spalding Club have printed the charter of enquiry, on which he got sasine of the estates. It is abridged from the original which is in their possession, and runs as follows :—

" An enquiry was made at Tullyboyauchteran Collane (Cullen) before Patrick Stewart of Lathers, Deputy Sheriff of Banff. The Jurors include William Meldrum of Fyvie, George Meldrum of Petcarre, John Gordon of Petger, Robert Meldrum in Kynbrwne, John Meldrum and many others. They say that the late John Berclay of Tolly, father of Walter Berclay, the claimant, died seized of all the lands of Cullen, in the thanage of Glendowachy, Sheriffdom of Banff. And that the said Walter is the next heir to his said father of the lands, which are now in the hands of the Earl of Buchan, the Lord of Glendowachy, through the death of the late John Berclay about three months ago." 2nd August 1491.

Collections Aberdeen and Banff, Spalding Club, Vol. ii, p. 367.

The first mention of the name of Walter Berclay is in 1481, when he is a witness to a contract of marriage between George of Meldrum son and apparent heir of William of Meldrum of Fyvie and Elizabeth of Innes, daughter of James of Innes of that Ilk and Janet Gordon. Walter signs as " Walter Berclay son and heir of John Berclay of Tolly."

Ibid. p. 328.

We find that Walter Berclay was member of an assize in an action regarding the marches between the glebe and kirkland of Aberchirder and the Barony of Aberchirder. In 1493 there was a decree following a perambulation of the aforesaid marches, by an assize, sworn on the relics of Saint Marnan, of which he was also a member.

Register of Aberdeen, Vol. ii, pp. 174, 176, 179.

On December 5th, 1492, Walter Berclay was an assessor in the dispute between Alexander Innes of that Ilk and Master Alexander Symson, vicar of Aberchirder, the Bishop of Moray and the Abbot of Arbroath.

Register Episc. Moravia, Bannatyne Club.

There is an interesting entry in the Exchequer Rolls, which gives clearly the lands that were at this time in the possession of Walter Berclay, Laird of Towie :—

"Abirdeen. Compotum Alexander Irvine de Drum."

WALTER BERCLAY, 1491–1515, Towie XIII.

"Allocation for relief of the lands of Bourtie, Sidgait and Towie, belonging to Walter Berclay, cum quibus compotum onerater anno nonagessimo tercio, . . . 10th penny owed to the Bishop of Aberdeen from five reliefs."

Exchequer Rolls, Vol. xi, p. 334.

And again in 1492:—

"Sasine for Walter Berclay to Bartley and Towie in county Aberdeen, and Carok (Kerkow) County Perth."

Ibid. Vol. x, p. 765.

On January 25th, 1493, Walter Berclay and his relative Patrick Barclay of Gartley (Gartley XVII) were "discerned by the Lords of Council to pay 100 merks to the tenants of Lord Gray at the feast of St. John the Baptist, called midsummer tocum, and another 100 merks at the later Marymas, next thereafter, in complete satisfaction for all and sundry goods, cattle, corns, sums of money, dampnage, scathis and spuilyeis committed by the said persons or any of their accomplices upon the tenancies of Leitfee, Bardmonye, etc." The raid must have been a serious one, as among those who took part in it we find the names of William Earl Marischal, Alexander Seton of Meldrum, Patrick Leslie of Balquhane, Johnston of that Ilk, Patrick Gordon of Haddo (father-in-law to Walter Berclay), Thomas Gordon of Kennarty, Walter Innes of Innermarky, Alexander Innes of that Ilk, Duncan Davidson of Auchinhamper, James King of Barras (brother-in-law of Walter Berclay), and Arthur Forbes of Raeraes.

Acts of the Lords of Council, p. 265.

In August, 1503, King James IV married Margaret Tudor, daughter of Henry VII, and we find

"A letter of Licence and Discharge to Walter Berclay of Tolly of his cummyng til owre Soverane Lordis mariage, but ony danger to be imput to him thairfore nochtwithstanding ony lettres direct hereupon."

Reg. Mag. Sig. 1503–6, No. 968.

The Spalding Club print numerous records of courts of enquiry in which this Laird of Towie was a juror between the years 1494 and 1515.

Walter Berclay (Towie XIII) married a daughter of Patrick Gordon of Haddo, and by her had issue three sons, Patrick his heir, Walter and John, who appear in the records, and one daughter, Margaret, who married James Gordon of Balmade.

PATRICK BARCLAY

PATRICK BARCLAY, 1515–1529, Towie XIV.

Patrick Barclay succeeded his father Walter Berclay (Towie XIII) on April 21st, 1515. We find among the deeds at Gordon's College, Aberdeen, the present owners of the castle and estates of Towie-Barclay, the following charter :—

"On April 21st, 1515, Alexander Bannerman of the Westertoune, sheriff depute of Aberdeenshire, issued a precept under a breve from Chancery to gif heretable stat and possession to Patrick Barclay sonne and air to umquhill Walter Barclay of Tollie, of all and haill the lands of Tollie and Sidgat with their pertinents, and also the lands of Mekil Drumquhendil, all lying in the sheriffdom of Aberdeen."

Deeds at Gordon's College.

Among the witnesses occur the names of Walter Barclay, probably his brother, and Gilbert Barclay, who, as we have seen, was murdered three years later.

Sasine was accordingly given at the same time, and we find in the Exchequer Rolls these entries :—

"*Perth*. 48 merks de relevio baronie de Carcok . . . per sasinam datam Patricio Berclay de eadem. . . .

"*Aberdene*. 50 merks de relevio terraram de Tolle et Sidgait et Mekle Drumquhendull . . . per sasinam datam Patricio Berclay de eisdem."

Exchequer Rolls, Vol. xiv, p. 569.

It was not until May 2nd, 1522, that Patrick Barclay obtained sasine on the lands of Cullen, at which date John, Earl of Buchan, issued to him the precept of sasine, as heir to his father, the late Walter Berclay of Towie.

Collections Aberdeen and Banff, Spalding Club, Vol. iii, p. 368.

The first mention found of Patrick is in the year 1503, when he and Elizabeth Barclay his wife obtained a crown charter of Auld Bourtie and a third part of Petgroveny on the resignation of his father, Walter Berclay of Towie (Towie XIII). Elizabeth Barclay was a daughter of Patrick Barclay of Gartley (Gartley XVII) and Elizabeth Arbuthnot his wife, and this grant of the lands of Bourtie was probably in the nature of a marriage settlement.

History of the Garioch, p. 229.

On June 10th, 1514, Patrick was witness to a charter by

Patrick Barclay of Gartley, his father-in-law, conveying the lands of Foulisse, in the barony of King Edward, to Sir Patrick Grantuly, rector of Glass. In the charter he is described as "Patrick son and heir of Walter Barclay of Tollie."

PATRICK BARCLAY, 1515–1529, Towie XIV.

Reg. Mag. Sig. Vol. iii, p. 17.

The issue of the marriage of Patrick Barclay (Towie XIV) and Elizabeth Barclay, his wife, was Patrick Barclay (Towie XV) and Walter "in Pedoulsie," whose descendants held these lands for some generations.

Patrick Barclay died in the year 1529, comparatively a young man. His son, Patrick Barclay (Towie XV), who succeeded him, was a minor in the hands of curators.

PATRICK BARCLAY

PATRICK BARCLAY, 1529–1558, Towie XV.

This laird was a minor at the death of his father, which occurred early in the year 1529. He had a precept of *clare constat*, dated October 2nd, 1529, from the Earl of Buchan, in which he is designated as of Towie and heir to the deceased Patrick (Towie XIV), his father, of the lands of Cullen.

Deeds at Gordon's College.

Reg. Mag. Sig. 1529–1540, Vol. ii, No. 474.

In 1530 Walter Ogilvy of Moncabo, probably his tutor, paid the reliefs of non-entry on the rest of the estates, amounting to £200.

There is a precept of Chancery, dated November 27th, 1536, which James Earl of Moray, Sheriff of Aberdeen, acting upon, gives direction to George Bisset, "mair of fees," to infeft Patrick Barclay "of Collane" (Cullen) as "son and undoubted heir to the late Patrick Barclay of Tollie in the lands of Meikle Seggatt and Mill of Seggatt, Manor lands of Tollie, lands of Towieturnot, Baldoulse, Wodtoun, Aldmyll, the half lands of the intoun of Auld Bourtie, the fourteen bovates of the lands of Meikle Drumquhendill with the mill of that same and the lands of Auchtquhrody."

Deeds at Gordon's College.

Sasine of these lands was eventually received from King James V. The Exchequer Rolls show that in 1531 the Sheriff of Aberdeen was to answer for the relief of the shadow half of the lands of Auld Bourtie, lying in the regality of the Garioch, in the sum of £7 6s. 8d. Again, in 1536, he has to answer for the sum of £66 13s. 4d. further fermes due to the King for sasine on the remainder of the above-mentioned estates. All these lands had been in the King's hands "since Martinmas last past," sasine not having been recovered, due to the King by Patrick Barclay of Cullane (Cullen). The sasine was witnessed by William and Andrew Barclay, among others.

Exchequer Rolls, Vol. xvi, pp. 543, 617.

Having entered on the family lands in Aberdeenshire and Banffshire, Patrick Barclay acquired another old family possession on June 25th, 1538, when he obtained sasine of the lands of the Barony of Carock (Kerkow), in the sheriffdom of Perth, which had been lying in the hands of the King for

[Photograph from Mrs. Blair Wilson

THE MEMORIAL TO JANET OGILVY, WIFE OF PATRICK BARCLAY (TOWIE XV) IN GAMRIE CHURCH

1547

nine years past, seven years by reason of ward, and two years by sasine not being recovered. As an indication of the size of the property at Kerkow he paid fermes amounting to £324.

PATRICK BARCLAY, 1529–1558, Towie XV.

Exchequer Rolls, Vol. xvii, p. 758.

Patrick Barclay was twice married, his first spouse being Janet Ogilvy, daughter of the Laird of Boyne. This first marriage was in 1528, while he was still under age. The King granted to Patrick Barclay, son and apparent heir of Patrick Barclay, and to Janet Ogilvy, spouse to the said Patrick "the younger," the northern halves of the lands of Drumquhendhill and those of Ardlane adjacent, in the sheriffdom of Aberdeen, extending to 20 pounds, which his father had resigned. The lands were to be held by Patrick "the younger" and Janet Ogilvy in conjunct fee, or the longest liver of them. The charter is dated at Edinburgh, September 4th, 1528, and was doubtless a marriage settlement.

Reg. Mag. Sig. Vol. iii, No. 632.

Janet Ogilvy died in 1547, and her tombstone is still extant in the east wall of the old church of Gamrie, not far from the site of the castle of Cullen. The inscription reads as follows :

> " Hic jacet honorabilis vir Patricius Barclay
> dominus de Tolly qui obiit die mensis
> anno domini millesimo quingentesimo
> et Joneta Ogilvy ejus sposa quae
> obiit sexto die mensis Januarii Anno Domini
> millesimo quingentesimo quadragesimo septimo."

Above the slab is a small niche, in which had been placed a cross or crucifix, which accounts for the following line on the upper margin of the slab :—

" Patricius Barclay S hoc me fieri fecit." (Patrick Barclay, with this sign, caused me to be made.)

During the Reformation this cross was destroyed in the general demolition of " images " recommended by John Knox. The spaces for inserting the date of Patrick's own death are left blank, either from disgust at the desecration that the tablet had received or from neglect on the part of the surviving relatives. Patrick himself, no doubt, lies in the church of Gamrie.

PATRICK BARCLAY, 1529–1558, Towie XV.

His second spouse was Elizabeth Forbes, a daughter of Alexander Forbes of Pitsligo, whom he married at the end of 1552. On January 29th, 1551–2, Queen Mary, at Edinburgh, granted a charter of confirmation to Patrick Barclay of Tollie and Elizabeth Forbes, his wife, on the lands of Auld Bourtie and Hilbrae, sheriffdom of Aberdeen, which Patrick had resigned, to hold of new infeftment by the said Patrick and Elizabeth, and the longest liver of them in conjunct fee, and the heirs lawfully begotten between them, whom failing the heirs of the said Patrick whomsoever, and this infeftment being no obstacle, the Queen promised that the nearer and lawful heirs of the said Patrick whomsoever, as soon as—after the decease of the said Patrick and Elizabeth—they should pay to the heirs procreated between the said Patrick and Elizabeth, or to their assigns being in the possession of the said lands, 800 merks on the high altar of the Cathedral Church of Aberdeen, on a notice of fifteen days, or consign them in the hands of the President (Dean) and chapter of the said church, they should have entry to the said lands. The tenor of this charter shows clearly that Patrick Barclay had a family by a previous marriage and the provision for redemption is clearly in their favour.

Reg. Mag. Sig. Vol. iv, p. 669.

This laird during his lifetime seems to have disposed of certain of the lands formerly held by the family, for on July 16th, 1532, the King confirmed a charter to Arthur Pantoun, son to Alexander Pantoun of Petmedan, by Patrick Barclay, William Innes and Mr. James Barclay, his curators, the shadow half of the lands of Intoun of Auld Bourtie, in the Regality of the Garioch.

Ibid. Vol. iii, No. 1189.

Again on January 4th, 1536–7, by a deed executed at Seggatt, he sold, for a sum of money down, the sunny half of the Intoun of Auld Bourtie, to Marjorie Barclay relict of Alexander Pantoun of Petmedan, to be held by her and her assigns whomsoever, failing Arthur Pantoun, her son. Confirmed at Edinburgh, February 8th, 1536–7.

Ibid. No. 1644.

Patrick Barclay (Towie XV) had issue by his first wife, Janet Ogilvy, two sons, Walter his heir and James.

By his second marriage with Elizabeth Forbes he had three

sons, Patrick and William, who appear in a protracted lawsuit regarding their father's estate, as we shall see later, and John, who was retoured on March 5th, 1584, in the lands of Auld Bourtie and Hilbrae, as legitimate son and nearest heir of Patrick Barclay and Elizabeth Forbes.

PATRICK BARCLAY, 1529–1558, Towie XV.

Patrick Barclay died in October 1558 and was survived by his second wife, Elizabeth Forbes. In connection with the service of Walter, as his father's heir, on January 10th, 1559, there was a protestation by her, as widow of Patrick Barclay. And on April 3rd following the jury refused to return an answer, affirmative or negative, to her claims of terce on the whole of the lands held by her late husband in Aberdeenshire. The dispute drags its way through the pages of the Diet Book, and from the process we glean that Alexander Forbes of Pitsligo appears in the action on behalf of his sister in relation to an obligation to have her infefted in the life-rent of the sunny half of the lands of Cullen, with the mill. Another protestation on the widow's behalf is made in respect of William and Patrick Barclay, pupils (wards), for the mill and multures of Meikle Seggatt claimed for the former and Woodton for the latter. These two sons were evidently the issue of the second marriage. The matters in dispute disappear from the Court Books, without any definite finding, and it is to be suspected that an amicable arrangement was arrived at.

We hear of this William Barclay (Towie XVID) again later. He took part in the battle of Corrichie, on October 28th, 1562, when Queen Mary's forces, under James Stewart, Earl of Moray, defeated George, fourth Earl of Huntly.

William Barclay's sympathies were with the Earl of Huntly and he fell into disfavour with the Queen. His name is included in a long list of Huntly's supporters in a "Precept grantit Be Queen Marie for a Remission to my Lord Huntlie and his friends for Correchie," signed at Seytoun February 26th, 1566–7. He is called "William Barclay, brother of the Lord of Tolle."

Miscellany, Spalding Club, Vol. iv, p. 164.

Patrick Barclay (Towie XV) was succeeded by his son Walter (Towie XVI).

WALTER BARCLAY

WALTER BARCLAY, 1558–1587, Towie XVI.

The original charter of the enquiry by which Walter Barclay was served heir to his father Patrick Barclay (Towie XV) is in the possession of the Spalding Club.

The enquiry was held in the court of James Dempster of Auchterless and John Duncanson, deputy sheriffs of Banff, on January 13th, 1558–9. The names of the jurors are given, including William Hay of Dalgetty, son and heir of Alexander Hay, who was brother-in-law to Walter Barclay. They swear :—

" That Walter is the legitimate and nearest heir of his said father, and that the said lands are now worth £20 per annum of Scottish money, and in time of peace would be worth fifteen pounds of the same money. That the said lands are in the hands of Christian Stewart, Countess of Buchan, as superior, held in blanch. Six silver pennies to be paid at the feast of Pentecost. The lands were in the hands of the said Countess since the death of Patrick Barclay for the space of two months and fifteen days, on account of non-entry by the said Walter."

Collections Aberdeen and Banff, Vol. ii, p. 369.

In the " Libri Responsionum " we find the sasine granted on March 4th, 1559 :—

" The Sheriff of Aberdeen has to account for £40 taxes on the lands of Mekille Siggat with the mill of Siggat and the multures, and of the lands of the mains of Towie with the castle and manor place of the same, the lands of Towy-Turnochty, Baldusy, Wodtoun, Auld Myln . . . 14 bovates of lands of Mekil Drumquhendill, the outsettis lands of Ardlane and the lands also of Auchroddie etc, being in the Queen's hands since Martinmas last, sasine not having been applied for.

" Also for £80 of reliefs of the same, owing to the King and Queen, for sasine given to Walter Barclay. At Edinburgh 4th March in the year of the reign of the King and Queen ' primo et decimo septimo.' "

Collections Aberdeen and Banff, Vol. iv, p. 580.

This deed is particularly interesting as having been executed during the short period when the Kingdoms of France and Scotland were united, under Mary of Scots and her husband Francis II of France, who had assumed the " crown matrimonial " of Scotland, on his succession to the throne of his father, in 1559. He died in the following year.

The service of the Banffshire lands was held before the sheriff of Banff, on January 15th, 1558–9, and a precept of *clare constat* was granted by Christian Stewart, Countess of Buchan, and subscribed by Walter Ogilvy of Boyne, her tutor dative, to Walter Barclay, as heir of his umquhil father, in the lands of Cullen, also dated March 4th, 1559.

WALTER BARCLAY, 1558–1587, Towie XVI.

Ross MSS. Notes.

The old family possession of Kerkow or, as it was now called, Cairock, in the sheriffdom of Perth, was confirmed by sasine, dated April 13th, 1559, and £40 was paid for the entry.

Exchequer Rolls, Vol. xix, p. 442.

Queen Mary abdicated in favour of her son King James VI in the year 1567, and on May 16th, 1568, after the defeat of her supporters by the Regent Moray at the battle of Langside, crossed the Solway. A bond acknowledging King James the Sixth their only Sovereign Lord was subscribed at Edinburgh, St. Andrews, Aberdeen and Inverness, in 1569, by Huntly, Crauford, Cassillis, and a long list, which includes Walter Barclay (Towie XVI).

Register Privy Council, Vol. i, p. 655.

Walter Barclay was surety for Sir George Barclay of Gartley (XIX), if freed from ward in Blakness, "that he would re-enter the castle if required." Signed at Banff August 30th, 1577.

Register Privy Council, Vol. ii.

Mary was executed on February 8th, 1587, and Scotland was in a very lawless state. Walter Barclay (Towie XVI) was slain in Edinburgh in 1587, by Mr. William Meldrum, of Moncoffer, brother of George Meldrum of Fyvie, and his servants. The cause of the quarrel was probably one of those private feuds which require but little provocation to lead to serious results. Some three years later peace was restored and formally embodied in "Letters of Slaynes" (or remission) signed by the members of both families. This deed is of great interest from a genealogical point of view, and it is given here in full from the original in the charter room of Duff House.

"BE IT KEND till all men, be thir present letters me Patrick Barclay of tollie elder lauchful sone to vmquhile Walter Barclay of tollie my father, dame Elizabeth Hay relict of the said vmquhile Walter, William George and Robert sones to the said Walter, William Barclay at the Myln of Seggat and John Barclay bretheren to the said vmquhile Walter, Marjorie and Lilias Barclayis dochters lauchful to the said vmquhile Walter Barclay of tollie, Thomas

WALTER BARCLAY, 1558–1587, Towie XVI.

Menzies aperand of Durne, John Keyth of Ravinscraig, Wm Windus of yat Ilk, Gideon Keyth portioner of Durne, as nearest of kyn and maist special freynds of the said vmquhile Walter Barclay, baithe of fathers syd and mothers syd for our selvis and the said Patrick Barclay, now of Tollie, eldest sone forsaid of the said vmquhile Walter, taking the burden on me for the remanet haill kin friendis allys assisteres and partakeris, men kynd and vomen kynd baithe fathers and mothers syd of the said vmquhile Walter, and all that the said patrick barclay may stope or late to have remitted and forgivein and by the tennour heir off, frelie remittis and forgivis to maister William Meldrum of Moncoffer James Achammachie his seruitor, and Williame Caldair his seruitor, all rancour of hart, deadlie feud, inemitie, hatred and malice, quhilk we or any of us haid, hes or may have or conceave against thame or any of thame in the tyme coming yhair kyn friendis, servandis, assisteres, partakeris for the said crewall slauchter of the said vmquhile Walter Barclay, comittit be the saidis personis, and throche occasione thairof with all actione, clame and questioune criminall and cruill, competent to us agains thame thairhorrow, as likewayis we be the tenour heir of remittis and forgivis all rancor of hart and malice together with all actione cruill or criminall quhil we or any of us has, haid or may haue agains the said maister William Meldrum of Moncoffer, Andrew Meldrum, of Achorteis, Alexander Innes brother to Jhone Innes of Leucharis and quhatsomever their kyn frendis, assisteries, and partakeris for the drawing and effusione of myne the said patrick barclay of tollie's bluid, and wounding and hurting of my face within the burge of Edinburghe in the month of Juin in the year of God ane thowsand fyve undreth four scoir and nyne yeirs, and sall keip and obserue the same to thame in all tymes cuming as forgetful of the said slaughter, vounding and hurting foirsaid, sua that we, our heirs and bairnies and successors nor none uthers in our hames upon our behalvis of our causing command assistance nor ratihabitioune, sall haue nor imput ony action, clame, crymes nor allegianceis agains the saidis persones nor servands, nor kyn freynds, nor yet sall follow nor parsue thame nor any of thame nor their forsaidis for the said slauchter, vounding or hurting forsaid. But sall accept thame ilk ane of thame in our harllie luif favour and kyndnes siclyk als tenderlie and fryndlie as gif the same haid never been committit and done, without grudge nor disimulatione in our harts or thoughts, and heir to we bind and obleis us under the panis periurie and infamie to ane Christiane maner and under all hiest panes quhilk we may incure baithe of the law of God and mane, and that be resoune of ane sufficent assythment maid in landis conforme to the tenour of ane contract and appointment maid betwixt me the said patrick barclay, taking the burding on me for the saidis Elizabeth Hay ladie tollie, my mother, maister William, George and Robert Barclayis, the remanent lauchful sones of the said vmquhile Walter, Marjorie and Lilias barclayis, his lauchful docteris one for is familiat and for the remanent bairnes of the said vmquhile Walter, his kyn freyndid and allys on the ane part and George Meldrum of Fyvie for himself his richt and enterest and the said maister William Meldrum of Moncoffer for himself his richt and enterest and ilk ane of thame the saids George and Mr Williame with consent of vtheris as also with consent of certain vtheris personnes mentionat therein as the tenor of the contract of the date at tollie Frendraucht and Strathbogy respectiue the twentie fourt day of July the yeir of God ane thowsand fyive hundreth four scoir and tuelf yeirs at mair lenthe proportis in faith and witnessing of the quilkis of their present lettrie of slanes subscriuit with our hands our seallis ar appendit at tollie colln (Cullen) and Aberdeen respective the thretein and fifteen dayis of October respective the yeir of God ane thowsand fyive hundreth four scoir tuelff yeirs Before their witnesses respective Robert Irvine in Aucharnne Gilbert Aquhache servitor to the ladie of Tollie elder John Urquhart of . . . tutor of Cromarty James Grant of Tillibo Patrick Copland of Idoche Alexander Hay of Dalgety James Chritoun apparand of Frendrache William Crag of Cragfintry Alexander Meldrum apparand of Fyvie.

WALTER BARCLAY, 1558–1587, Towie XVI.

Alexander Hay of Dalgetty witnes.
James Chrichtoun apperand Frendracht witness.
William Craig of Craigfintry witness.
Alexander Meldrum apperand of Fyvie.

Patrick Barclay of Tollie.
Elizabeth Hay.
Majorie barclay. with my hand.
William Winus of that Ilk.
Lilias barclay.
Robert barclay.
William barclay off . . . mill. (Seggat).
George barclay. (Auchroddie) with my hand.

Walter Barclay married Elizabeth or Elspeth Hay, daughter of Alexander Hay of Dalgetty, probably in the year 1553, as at that date there is a confirmation of a charter by Patrick Barclay (Towie XV), by which, for sums of money and other services done to him by Alexander Hay of Dalgetty, he conveys to Elizabeth alias Elspeth Hay, daughter of the said Alexander, the lands of Drumquhendill, including the Clayhills and the north side of the Intoun of Meikle Drumquhendill,

Reg. Mag. Sig. Vol. iv, No. 842.

WALTER BARCLAY, 1558–1587, Towie XVI.

Accts. of the High Treasurer, Vol. xi, p. 121.

in the parish of Ellon, sheriffdom of Aberdeen, to be held of the Queen. Dated at Tollie, August 26th, and the confirmation at Linlithgow, September 10th, 1553. This grant was probably in the nature of a marriage settlement, as we find Walter and Elizabeth consenting to dealings in these lands in 1562.

As we have seen in the "Letters of Slaynes," Walter Barclay by his marriage with Elizabeth Hay had issue a considerable family.

1. Sir Patrick Barclay (Towie XVII), his heir.
2. William Barclay (Towie XVIIB) of the mill of Seggatt was born in the year 1570. In his *Præmetia*, or first work, he refers to the scene of his birth: "For Cullen (so is the castle called in which I first touched the earth) is situated on a shore which is lashed by so vast an open sea there is on the same shore, the land of the Barclay family, a harbour, which in Scotland is called Auldhaven."

William was a man of good education, a Doctor of Physicks and graduated as M.A. He studied at Louvain, under Justus Lipsius, by whom he was highly esteemed. As will be seen later, he also practised as an advocate. William Barclay wrote two books, which attained to considerable fame, *Nepenthes*, or the virtues of tobacco, and *Callirhoe*, commonly called the Wall of Spa or the Nymph of Aberdeen. He was a writer also of Latin verse, to be found in the *Delitiatæ Poetarum*.

Miscellany of Spalding Club, Vol. i, p. 259.

William Barclay was originally educated by the Jesuits as a missionary for Scotland, but we find in Pitcairn's *Criminal Trials* the following record: "24 April 1601, William Barclay a new made advocate, brother of Sir Patrick Barclay of Tollie, was tried at Edinburgh for being present at 'twa messes whilk were said by Mr. MacWhirtie, ane Jesuit priest, within Andrew Napier's house in Edinburgh.' The crime was aggravated by perjury, he having sometime before sworn and subscribed before the presbytery of Edinburgh that he was of the religion presently professed within the realm. The culprit was declared 'infamous' and banished from the country, never to return to the same, unless by satisfaction of the Kirk he obtain our special licence to that effect." During the interval before the sentence took effect his nephew, Patrick Barclay, "fiar" of Towie, entered into a bond for his remaining quiet at Cullen with his mother. It looks as if Cullen

Pitcairn's Trials, Vol. ii, Part ii, p. 348.

Register of Privy Council, Vol. vi, p. 682.

was used as a dower house, since it is described as the home of the mother of Sir Patrick and Dr. William Barclay.

WALTER BARCLAY, 1558–1587, Towie XVI.

William Barclay is said to have died about 1630 abroad, but Dr. Milne thinks that it was later, and that the Latin inscription on his nephew's tomb, in the old church of Turriff, is his handiwork.

It is most probable that this Dr. William Barclay of the mill of Seggatt, who was banished from Scotland in 1601, is the same person who appears in Sweden at this date, whose son, Major-General William Barclay, was ennobled in 1648, and who in the list of Swedish knights is called " son of the laird of Sigot." (See Russian Barclays.)

This Dr. William Barclay must not be confused with the William Barclay of the Gartley line who was born in 1545 and was Secretary to Queen Mary of Scots, and after her downfall went to Lorraine.

3. George Barclay of Auchroddie, in New Deer (Towie XVIIc), was at one time in possession of the Royal transcript of Wyntoun's *Chronicle*, now in the British Museum. See page 261.

   After the failure of the direct male line of the Barclays of Towie in August, 1668, and the death of his nephew, William Barclay of Ordley, in 1669, without male issue, the descendants of George Barclay of Auchroddie became the heirs-male of Towie. They are dealt with under the Barclays of Knockleith.
4. Robert Barclay.
5. Walter Barclay, father of Captain William.
6. Alexander Barclay of Towie Mills.
7. Marjorie Barclay. It is possible that she married William Windus of that Ilk, whose name comes after hers in the " Letter of Slaynes."
8. Lilias, who married John Gordon of Auchindoir in 1593. Reg. Mag. Sig. Vol. iv, 1925.
9. Isobel Barclay.
10. Jean, who married Robert Innes of Innermarkie.
11. Grace Barclay.

The date of Walter Barclay's death is sometimes given as June 1589, from a wrong reading of the " Letters of Slaynes," already referred to, but it must have taken place before May 2nd, 1587, when he is mentioned as "quondam" in the precept of sasine for infefting his son Sir Patrick (Towie XVII).

SIR PATRICK BARCLAY

Sir Patrick Barclay, 1587–1627, Towie XVII.

Patrick Barclay succeeded his father Walter Barclay in 1587, on the latter's murder by William Meldrum in that year.

In the General Register House, Edinburgh, there is the charter of enquiry by which he obtained service in the following terms :—

"Patrick Barclay is nearest and lawful heir of Walter Barclay, his father in the lands of . . . Seggat, with the mill . . ., the lands of the manor of Tollie, with the tower, fortalice, and manor place, mill and multures . . . lands of Tolly Turnay, Poldoulsie, Woodtoun, Auldmylne, 14 bovates of land of Meikle Drumquhendil, with the mill, lands of the northern half of the lands of . . ., and the lands called the outsettis of the same, lands of Ardlane, lands of Auchreddie." Dated April 25th, 1587.

Aberdeenshire Retours, Special, No. 549.

Exchequer Rolls, Vol. xxi, p. 539.

Sasine was granted on the above lands, on the 30th April the same year, on the payment of £80 for relief.

He also obtained sasine on paying £40 for relief on the lands and barony of Caircok (Kerkow), sheriffdom of Perth, at Edinburgh, May 18th, 1587.

Ibid.

Aberdeenshire Retours, Special, No. 553.

On July 31st, 1588, there is a further service in lands of Craigmyln and Milnseth, with the mill, mill-lands, and astricted multures within the barony of Craigfintry.

Register Privy Council, Vol. iv, p. 376.

In 1589 Patrick Barclay was one of those who signed the Band for defence of the true religion.

The family feud with the Meldrums evidently did not cease with the death of his father, for, from the "Letters of Slaynes," not only was remission granted for Walter Barclay's death but also for the "drawing and effusione of myne, the said Patrick of Tollie's bluid and wounding and hurting of my face, within the burge of Edinburge in the month of June 1589."

On February 18th, 1589, he became cautioner for William Barclay of the Myln, Seggatt, and John Barclay, his brothers, and William Barclay of Petdoulsie, that George Meldrum of Fyvie, Mr. William Meldrum of Moncoffer, Andro Meldrum of Dunbreck, George Meldrum younger of Dunbreck, Andro

Meldrum and others shall be harmless of said persons under paine of the King's letters of law-burrows, already raised, subscribed at Turriff, February 12th, 1589–90. At the same time Alexander Hay of Dalgetty gave a bond of caution for Sir Patrick that he shall not harm any of the Meldrums above named.

SIR PATRICK BARCLAY, 1587–1627. Towie XVII.

Register Privy Council, Vol. iv, pp. 458, 459.

On March 25th a similar bond was granted by William Kirkaldy of Grange, for Mr. William Meldrum of Moncoffer, "that he should not injure Patrick Barclay of Towy, Mr. William Barclay and Mr. George Barclay his brothers, and William Barclay of Petdoulsie."

Ibid. p. 473.

It was about this date that Patrick Barclay decided on the rebuilding of "the fortalice and manor place" of Towie, As has been already mentioned, his mother, Elizabeth Hay, was living at Cullen, and Patrick with his wife and family had no doubt removed to Towie.

The expense of the building accounts for the sales of property, and we see by the records that in 1588 he sold one of the oldest family possessions, that of Kerkow or Caircock, in Perthshire, which had been held by the Barclays of Towie from the King since the days of Robert the Bruce. On May 10th the King confirmed a charter of Patrick Barclay of Towie, by which, in fulfilment of a contract, he sold to Alexander, Bishop of Brechin, and Helen Clephane, his spouse, the lands and Barony of Caircock, with grain mill, mill lands, etc. The witnesses to Patrick's charter, which is dated April 14th, 1588, include George Barclay of Mathers (Mathers X), George Barclay of Syde and Andrew Barclay servitor of the said Patrick Barclay.

Reg. Mag. Sig. Vol. v, No. 1537.

Ten years later Patrick Barclay, with the consent of his son and heir, sold to James Seton, burgess of Aberdeen, and pertainer of Barrauche, and Margaret Roland, his spouse, the town and lands of Auld Bourtie, the mill lands, and Hillbrae, in the parish of Bourtie, for the sum of 20,000 merks. Dated at Towie, August 8th, 1598.

Ibid. Vol. vi, No. 2132.

In the year 1594, and probably not unconnected with the Meldrum feud, Patrick resigned into the King's hands the whole of his lands "for new infeftment to be giffen againe

Sir Patrick Barclay, 1587-1627, Towie XVII.

of the samyne be his Majesty under the gritt seill, in due forme, to the said Patrick Barclay of Tollie and his aires-maill, quhat sumever, bering the surname and Arms of Barclay." A charter of resignation under the Great Seal, in favour of the said Patrick Barclay and his heirs-male, of the lands of Towie and others, and containing a novodamus and an erection of the lands into a Free Barony, called the Barony of Towie-Barclay, was granted, dated July 24th, 1594. It will be observed that in this charter the family property is called Towie-Barclay.

Reg. Mag. Sig. Vol. vi, p. 130.

Patrick's name occurs more than once as consenting party to the transfer or sale of lands in Aberdeenshire about this time. Many of the entries in the Great Seal Register are coupled with the name of Meldrum of Hatton, and Patrick's erstwhile enemy, Mr. William Meldrum of Moncoffer.

Sir Patrick Barclay married about the year 1578 Janet Elphinstone, second daughter of Robert, third Lord Elphinstone, and Margaret Drummond his wife, daughter and co-heiress of Sir John Drummond of Innerpeffray.

Douglas and Wood, Vol. i, p. 538.

In the charter of the sale of the estate of Auld Bourtie, in 1597, we find that Janet Elphinstone resigned at the same time her life-rent interest in these lands. She is called wife of Patrick Barclay of Towie.

From the fact that one of the bosses in the roof of the dining hall at Towie Castle still bears a shield with the arms of Barclay and Lamont, with the date 1610, it is believed that he may have been twice married.

It is to be noted that some time between the years 1601 and 1605 Patrick Barclay had been created a knight, for what service or on what occasion is not recorded, but it is quite likely that he received this honour with many other Scottish gentlemen in 1603, on the accession of King James VI to the English throne.

As has been already stated, Sir Patrick's brother George Barclay of Auchroddie was the possessor, at one time, of what is known as the Royal transcript of Wyntoun's *Chronicle*. If the reader will turn to the description of the manuscript on pages 262–263, he will note the writing upon it referring to Sir Patrick (Towie XVII). From this writing it has been erroneously asserted that Sir Patrick married the heiress of the house of Gartley, and in consequence changed the old arms of the Towie family. It is to be observed, however, that the expression is "that *hous* marit properly ane dochter of Gartly," and so far as can be learned from the deeds and other evidence of the period, Sir Patrick (Towie XVII) did not marry one of the Barclays of Gartley. Patrick Barclay (Towie XIV) married Elizabeth Barclay of Gartley, about the year 1503. There is no doubt that marriages between the two branches of the family did take place more than once, and what is more likely, for, as has been already pointed out, the two properties were but fifteen miles apart?

Sir Patrick Barclay, 1587–1627, Towie XVII.

On July 4th, 1610, there is a charter under the Great Seal proceeding on a procuratory of resignation by Sir Patrick Barclay, in favour of Patrick Barclay, his eldest son, of the whole of the lands, in a free barony of Towie-Barclay, on which the younger Patrick had sasine on December 4th of the same year.

Gordon College Deeds.

There is a retour furth of Chancery of a service before the sheriff of Banff, of Sir Patrick Barclay of Tollie, as heir to Walter Barclay his father, in the lands of Cullen "with miln, meal miln, seaport boats thereof," dated August 22nd, 1618. On October 16th following, a precept of *clare constat* was granted by James, Earl of Buchan, to Sir Patrick Barclay of Tollie as heir to Walter Barclay his father, on which sasine was taken on December 4th the same year. This proceeding was evidently taken for the purpose of confirming the transference of the property to his son Patrick, "fiar of Towie," who by procuratory of resignation had been placed in possession of these lands by his father, as implement of the contract of marriage between the "fiar" and Anna Drummond. An earlier procuratory was dated in 1600, probably in the same terms. Patrick Barclay, "fiar of Towie," died before his father.

On April 4th, 1621, Sir Patrick Barclay signed a letter of safe conduct in favour of Peter and John Barclay, sons of

Sir Patrick Barclay, 1587-1627, Towie XVII.

Andrew Barclay and his wife Maria Riddell, who, being merchants in the town of Banff, wished to settle in the town of Rostock in Livonia.

The original letter is to-day in the possession of the heirs of Baron Sass in Riga, whose wife, Auguste Julie Barclay, is a direct descendant of Peter of Rostock.

Alexander von Barclay de Tollie, in sending on January 18th, 1909, a translation from the original Latin of the letter of safe conduct, says :—

" . . . Peter remained the founder of our race. John's descendants in Norway have died out. We have very exact information about the race there from a newspaper 'Aundes Tidente,' of September 5th, 1907, where the history of that branch is related with sources of information. This article appeared on the death of the last, E Morgens Jobiessen Handstoffer V.B.D.T."

He adds :—

" William's descendants in Sweden use the same old Barclay coat of arms, only the crosses are white. He lived 1603–1675. He was raised into nobility in December 1648, and in 1664 he matriculated his Arms, and is shewn, according to our information, in the book of Swedish knights and noblemen, folio 53, No. 562."

It seems clear from the records that there were two William Barclays living in Sweden during the period 1603–1675, and that they were not nearly related to Peter and John, the elder William being a much older man. We have already seen that a William Barclay, the second son of Walter Barclay (Towie XVI), was banished from Scotland in 1601 and was supposed to have died abroad. As has been pointed out, this William was known as " of the mill of Seggatt." His name is found among the signatories to the " Letter of Slaynes," granted by his family to William Meldrum of Moncoffer, for the slaughter of his father, Walter, in 1587. He signs " William Barclay off . . . mill." It is unfortunate that the name has been obliterated in the original deed, in the charter room of Duff House, but there is little doubt that the missing word is Seggatt.

The assumption that this William is the same person as the William in Sweden is further strengthened by the following quotation from the *Nobilities of Europe*, edited by the Marquis de Ruvigny (1909):—

SIR PATRICK BARCLAY, 1587–1627, Towie XVII.

"William Barclay, Major General in the Swedish service (son of the Laird of Sigot), was ennobled in Sweden (No. 562) in 1648. Family extinct after 1706."

It seems clear that this Swedish General was the son of the banished William Barclay of the mill of Seggatt.

The letter of safe conduct is so full of interest and the wording of the time so curious that it has been decided to include it here.

"ADDRESSED to such and all Kings, Princes, temporal and spiritual, Dukes, Marquises, Earls, Archbishops, Bishops, Abbots, Priors Administrators of affairs, Marshals, Barons, Governors, Head officials, Magistrates of towns, also to each and all Admirals, Commanders of provinces, castles, bridges, camps, armies, rivers and harbours, but especially to our most dear friends, the governors, judges and magistrates of the very celebrated commercial town of Rostock, and of the renouned academy of the Dukedom of Mecklemburgh in great Germany, and to others whosoever rule either by sea or land to whose notice these writings might come.

"We Patrick Baron of Tolly, as well as we the President and Senate of the town of Banff in the Kingdom of Scotland, with him who is the surest preserver of his countrymen's perpetual health and happiness.

"Whereas it ought to be the care of those who have the chief administration of the State, that due honour should be conferred on those who are well deserving and zealous of virtue, and that those who have committed anything contrary to the laws or justice should be chastised with the appointed punishment, it has hitherto been agreed by us that we should seem to have made a provision not more partial to the one than to the other party. Thus as much as can be done either through circumstances or by means of the more mighty affairs of State. We have sedulously endeavoured and still endeavour, that whosoever from a noble race or of an illustrious exploit in other illustrious affairs have received the rights and praises handed down from their ancestors should transmit, as buildings kept in repair (unless they have departed from every trace of the uprightness of their ancestors), to as late posterity as possible, so that they also being inflamed with a thirst of praise may, by means of their own virtue, make some addition to the former, and mindful of their forefathers and setting their greatness and good renoun always

SIR PATRICK BARCLAY, 1587–1627, Towie XVII.

before their eyes, may commit no offence, but imitating their ancestors, in the same steps, may prove themselves good and faithful to all and in all things (as far as the law of God and man permit).

"Hence it came to pass that we have reasoned to furnish our beloved Peter Barclay and John Barclay, merchants and citizens under the same name of your town of Rostock, already some while since welcome among the foreigners, on account of the merit of their countrymen, either desirous of further travel, to visit more remote places, or perhaps of settling or fixing their abode elsewhere (as chance may offer to them), we have resolved, we say, to furnish them with the same marks of kindness and recommendation which seem also truly agreable with justice, that when they shall have given pattern of the race and sobriety of their countrymen, worthy to be praised abroad, we also, with certainty, truth, justice and goodness, being suppliantly entreated, may not deny them a testimony (which can be of the same avail to them among foreigners as any act of kindness). and although the things that we attest agree perfectly with ourselves, nevertheless that nothing which is accustomed to be done in like affairs, may be missed, we have taken care that Mr John Murray, minister of Gamrie, John Braker, Peter Harday, and Daniel Cruikshank, the countrymen of the said Peter and John, should be employed in this affair as important witnesses, and with all exception weightier, as their faith and trust have been well tried, and we have admitted them with the set form of oath, with spread arms and fingers turned towards heaven, and from them have collected what is very well known and understood by us, that Peter and John are legitimate full brothers, sprung from a legitimate marriage and honest parents, the father foresooth being an honest man, named Andrew Barclay, sprung from the same family as the present Baron of Tollie, and the mother, Maria, born a Miss Riddell, being equally good and chaste, these being joined by legitimate nuptials have spent their lives honestly and left behind them a living offspring zealous of the best practices of virtue.

"Wherefore we desire all of you (each having preserved his dignity) who having been examined and sworn, that you may follow the afore mentioned Peter Barclay and John Barclay with all sorts of offices of kindness, laying by yourselves good will, if you should wish to make use of our assistance at any time.

"In assurance and testimony of all and each the foregoing we have taken care that the peculiar seal of my said Baron of Tolly, as well as the said town of Banff, should be attached to these writings, signed as follows :—

"At the castle of my said Lord the Baron of Tolly, as well as at the said town of Banff, the fourth day of April in the year of our Lord 1621.

Sir Patrick Barclay, 1587–1627, Towie XVII.

Mr. John Murray, Minister of the word of God, in the church of Gamrie.
Walter Ogilvy, one of the Council.
Robert Ogilvy, one of the Council.
George Shoremead, Ordinary Clerk of the Burgh of Banff.
Sir Patrick Barclay of Tolly, knight.
Walter Ogilvy, Provost of Banff.
Mr. Alexander Craig, Bailie of Banff.
John Duncan, Bailie of Banff."

The descendants of Peter Barclay included many men of considerable note, among whom was the famous Prince Barclay de Tolly, one of Russia's greatest generals. An account of the Barclays of Rostock will be given later.

Sir Patrick Barclay and his wife, Janet Elphinstone, had issue two sons:—

1. Patrick, who is referred to as "Fiar of Towie" in numerous transactions of the period, was born about the year 1579.

He married, June 22nd, 1602, Anna Drummond, daughter of David, second Lord Drummond, and had issue two sons and one daughter. Edinburgh Reg.

He is first mentioned as witness to a bond by the Master of Elphinstone, signed September 2nd, 1595. In 1597 he was one of those who joined the Earl of Erroll in signing the bond of caution for £20,000 for the Earl of Huntly. In 1599 he acquired from John Gordon of Newton the lands and Barony of Craigfintray, with the fortalice, etc. This property he sold the following year to John Urquhart of Culbo, tutor of Cromarty. Register of Privy Council, Vol. iv, p. 633. Reg. Mag. Sig. Vol. vi, No. 1108.

In 1601 there is a re-grant by the King, for good service, in favour of Patrick Barclay, eldest lawful son of Patrick Barclay of Tolly, and his heirs-male bearing the surname and arms of Barclay, of the lands and Barony of Towie-Barclay.

In the year 1601, as has been already noted, Sir Patrick Barclay (Towie XVII) resigned the Barony in favour of Patrick, his eldest son. The latter obtained a re-grant of it, and was known as "the fiar of Towie." The father outlived the son, for in 1624 we find Walter Barclay was retoured "heir of Patrick Barclay, fiar of Towie, his father," because the fee was vested in the son.

Sir Patrick Barclay, 1587–1627, Towie XVII.

The description is almost identical with that of previous charters, with the exception of Auld Bourtie, which had been sold. All of which the said Patrick, senior, resigned in favour of the said Patrick, junior. The King anew incorporated them into the free Barony of Towie-Barclay, the free tenement being reserved in life-rent to the said Patrick, senior.

Reg. Mag. Sig. Vol. vi, No. 1209.

Reddendo rights and services due and wont, taxing ward and nonentry at 500 merks yearly, and marriage of the heir at £1000. The King's grant at Dalkeith, July 4th, 1601.

The "Fiar of Towie's" eldest son was Francis, who on the 10th August 1614 had a tack from Robert Maitland, chantor of Aberdeen and parson of Auchterless, with consent of the Dean and Chapter of Towie-Turnay (Turriff), Innerthirnie, and Over Ordley, for the lifetime of the heir succeeding to him and two nineteen years thereafter. On November 24th, 1614, he had a tack of the teind sheaves of Cullen, as the eldest son and heir of Patrick, "Fiar" of Towie. Francis died without issue October, 1622. On his tombstone, in the churchyard of Turriff, there is the following inscription :—

Deed at Gordon's College. Notes in Free Press.

> "Here rests in the hope of a happy resurection a youth of excellent promise, Francis Barclay younger of Towie, who died in the 17th year of his age Oct . . . "

Jervoise, Vol. ii, p. 222.

Walter (Towie XVIII), second son of the Fiar, inherited the estates, and of him later.

Patrick "the Fiar" had one daughter, Elizabeth, whose name occurs on more than one occasion in connection with her abduction by one John Bundane, alias Ruthven, and his accomplices. The first notice of the affair is given in a letter from the Privy Council to the Laird of Leys conveying their thanks for his services for having rescued this lady, Elizabeth Barclay "dochter to the laite laird of Towie," out of the hands of those who lured her from her mother. This letter is dated Edinburgh, 18th November 1623.

Register of Privy Council, Vol. xiii, p. 380.

In January 1624 Burnett of Leys was charged by the Privy Council to produce before them Elizabeth Barclay, "that she might give her oath what was the carriage of John Bundane, ravisher of the said Elizabeth."

Ibid. p. 421.

On February 5th following a warrant to the Justice's clerk was passed to direct "no relaxation or suspension . . . . Ruthven, son to the laird of Bundane, till he find caution for his compeirance to his tryel" for the above abduction. And on February 12th a commission was granted to Alexander, master of Forbes, and several others to search and apprehend James Barclay and several others, who were put to the horn on 21st and 23rd; proceedings at the instance of the King's advocate and Elizabeth Barclay and Anna Drummond, her mother, relict of the said Patrick and Sir Patrick Barclay Knight of Towie "gudsir to the said Elizabeth." The matter then drops and no further reference is made to it in the Register.

SIR PATRICK BARCLAY, 1587–1627, Towie XVII.

Register of Privy Council, Vol. xiii, p. 431.

Patrick Barclay (the Fiar) died in 1623 and during the lifetime of his father, Sir Patrick. His widow, Anna Drummond, afterwards married Andrew Fraser of Murtle.

In the old church of Turriff there is a mural tablet, with the Barclay and Drummond arms, the initials P B A D and the date 1636, probably the date of the erection of the monument. The inscription is as follows:—

"BARCLAVIS JACET HIC, TOVEÆ GLORIA GENTIS, SÆCVLA CVI PRISCVM QVINA DEDERE DECVS: CALCVLVS HVNC JVVENEM POST TER TRIA LVSTRA PEREMIT,
NEC MEDICÆ QVIDQVAM PROFVIT ARTIS OPVS
OSSA TEGIT TELLVS: ANIMAM CÆLESTIS ORIGO CVI FVIT,
ÆTHERIÆ LIMINA SEDIS HABENT."

[Here lies Barclay, the glory of the Towie family, to which five centuries have given old renown: calculus cut him off in his prime, after thrice three lustra (45 years),
nor were the resources of the healing art of any avail.
The earth covers his bones: his spirit, which was of celestial origin, is the tenant of a mansion beyond the skies.]

Dr. Milne is of opinion that the above inscription was written by Patrick's uncle, Mr. William Barclay, the celebrated author of *Nepenthes*.

2. William Barclay was the second son of Sir Patrick Barclay (Towie XVII). He is variously designated in the deeds of the first half of the seventeenth century as of Ordley, Pedoulsie and "tutor of Towie."

On the failure of the direct male line in 1668, William Barclay of Ordley became the heir-male of Towie. An account of him will be given later.

The exact date of Sir Patrick Barclay's death has not been ascertained, but we know that he was alive in 1624, as his

SIR PATRICK BARCLAY, 1587–1627, Towie XVII.

name occurs in the action relating to the abduction of his granddaughter Elizabeth. It is believed that he lived until 1627.

He lived in the reigns of Elizabeth and James I of England, succeeding to the lands of Towie the year of the execution of Mary Queen of Scots in Fotheringhay Castle.

He was succeeded in the Barony of Towie by his grandson, Walter Barclay (Towie XVIII).

WALTER BARCLAY

WALTER BARCLAY, 1627–1643, Towie XVIII.

Walter Barclay succeeded to the estates of Towie in the year 1623, on the death of his father, Patrick, the "fiar of Towie." It is clear that he did not inherit the barony from his grandfather until some years later.

He was retoured on a general service on April 24th, 1624, as heir of Patrick Barclay, fiar of Towie, his father, in the lands and barony of Towie-Barclay, comprehending the dominical lands of Towie, the lands of Towie-Turray, Petdoulsie, Wodtoun, and Auldmylne, lands of Meikle Seggatt, and others particularly described, which included Drumquhendill, Ardlane, Auchroddie, Wodend, and others, all united into the barony of Towie-Barclay. Aberdeenshire Retours, No. 184.

There is also a precept under the Quarter Seal for infefting him in the barony of Towie, dated October 15th, 1626. On July 16th, 1625, there was a gift under the Great Seal of a tutory of Walter Barclay, pupil, eldest son of the late Patrick Barclay, fiar of Towie, in favour of William Barclay of Ordley, only brother german to the said Patrick. Sheriff Clerk's Records, Aberdeen.

From these records it is made clear that Walter was then a minor and that his uncle, William Barclay of Ordley, was named his tutor. Deeds at Gordon's College.

Walter had a precept of *clare constat* in his favour from James, Earl of Buchan, as heir to "umquhil Patrick, fiar of Towie," of the lands of Cullen, dated July 18th, 1632. In the same year the Earl of Buchan granted a "tolerance" to Walter Barclay of Towie and Elizabeth Fraser, designated his spouse, to win peats in Hungryhills. Deeds at Gordon's College.

In 1642 Walter wadset (mortgaged) to James Forbes, in Bankhead, and Margaret Logan, his spouse, and their sons James and Arthur, the mill and mill-lands of Towie, for the sum of 3,000 merks, and also a plough land of Innerthern, for 2,000 merks, both subject to a forty days' notice, given before any term of Whit Sunday for redemption. Payment of the money to be made within the parish church of Turriff, at that part thereof where the pulpit is situate or near to the same, betwixt ten hours before noon and four hours after *Ibid.*

WALTER BARCLAY, 1627–1643, Towie XVIII.

noon. It may be noted that James Forbes also held mortgages on the Mathers estates.

In the troublous days which ensued in connection with the Civil War the Barclays of Towie seem to have sided with the Covenanting party, as we learn from the narrative of clerk Spalding in the following extract :—

"10th May 1639. Their was togidder the laird of Banff, the laird of Geicht, the young laird of Cromartie, with sum vtheris, who with lieutenant Crowder Johnstone and from the 10th Maij intendit to cum to the place of Tolly-Barclay and thair to tak out sic armes, muscates, gunis, and carrabinis, as the lairdis of Delgatie and Tollie had plunderit from the said young laird of Cromartie out of the place of Baquholly, but it hapenit the Lord Fraser and Maister Forbes to see thair coming. They manet the house of Towie cloisit the yettis and shot divers schottis fra the house heid, where ane servand of the laird of Geicht was schott, callit David Peat.

"The Barons seeing they could not haud themselfis left the hous . . . Syne rode their way . . . This was the first blood that was drawin here sen the begining of the Covenant."

Three days later we learn from the same authority that Barclay along with his Covenanting friends entered Turriff, with the view of holding that place till the meeting of the committee appointed to sit there on May 20th. The Royalists on May 13th, smarting under their defeat at Towie, took their opponents fairly by surprise, and the result was an utter rout of the Covenanters, of whom, to quote Spalding, "utheris war taken prissoneris, thair was summe hurt, summe slayne."

Spalding's Troubles, Vol. i, p. 182.

Walter Barclay appears to have got safely away from this skirmish, which was known as "The trot of Turriff," although an appointment in Aberdeen shortly afterwards was not kept by him, because the Royalists held the city, and not from any restraining cause resulting from his presence at Turriff.

All through the civil strife Walter Barclay took a most active part with the Covenanting party in the north, and as a consequence suffered considerably, the castle of Towie being plundered on more than one occasion. In 1644 Huntly took possession and placed Hugh Gordon with sixteen soldiers as a guard to hold it. Here prisoners were sent for close confinement, but the rough soldiers were not above a price, as we learn from the case of Patrick Strathanchin of Kinnardie, who had the misfortune to be confined as a prisoner in Towie Castle. "He made guyet friendschit amongst the soldiers, took the capitane, and keipit the house manfullie when the army came."

WALTER BARCLAY, 1627–1643, Towie XVIII.

Spalding's Troubles, Vol. ii, p. 426.

It is possible that Montrose, during October, 1644, while Argyll was pursuing him, stayed at Towie, as we know that he found for his troops "some vietle thair."

In 1634 Walter Barclay was appointed a Justice of the Peace for Aberdeenshire.

It has already been noted that in 1632 Walter's future spouse was Elizabeth Fraser, and the same year probably saw their marriage. This Elizabeth Fraser may have been a near relative of Lord Fraser, with whom we find Walter Barclay having intimate relations. The issue of the marriage was one son, Patrick his heir (Towie XIX), and two daughters. The eldest was Elizabeth. The younger, Anna, married George Symmers of Balzeordie, near Brechin. By her father's settlement she was entitled to a tocher of £6,666 13s. 4d. Scots, but for many years neither interest nor principal was paid, and in 1695 she and her husband raised an action in the Court of Session against Gordon of Rothiemay for the amount due. The sum was ultimately paid or security given for it by Sir George Innes of Coxtoun in circumstances to be referred to afterwards.

Walter Barclay (Towie XVIII) died in 1643 and was succeeded by his son Patrick (Towie XIX).

PATRICK BARCLAY

PATRICK BARCLAY, 1643–1668, Towie XIX.

Patrick Barclay (Towie XIX), who succeeded his father Walter in 1643, received on June 21st, 1655, "a special and general service," as heir to the lands and barony of Towie-Barclay, "comprehending the dominical lands of Towie, the lands of Towie-Turray, etc., etc. . . . all united into the Barony of Towie-Barclay"; the extent being the same as in the last retour.

Aberdeenshire Retours, No. 267.

He was a minor at the time of his inheritance, as his name appears in the list of students at King's College as late as 1665. His tutor was Mr. William Barclay of Ordley, who had acted in the same capacity at the time of the minority of Patrick's father, Walter.

Patrick lived in the reign of the ill-fated Charles I, who was executed on January 30th, 1649.

His contemporary in the Mathers line was Colonel David Barclay, the first of the Barclays of Urie, who is fully dealt with in Part III of this History, while the lands of Collairnie were in the possession of another Colonel David Barclay (Collairnie XII).

Scottish Acts of Parliament, Vol. vi, p. 434.

Both Patrick Barclay and his father had sustained "loisis and sufferings" in the Civil War. This is apparent from a representation made to Parliament in July, 1645, when an Act was passed in favour of those who had suffered "loisis for the publict." The name of Patrick Barclay of Towie occurs among those who are commended for their "well deservings for the good of the public," and for whom Parliament express themselves as "verie sensible of their sufferings and prejudices." This Act embodies a promise that the same shall be taken into consideration.

The nature of the losses referred to in the Act of Parliament is well represented in the narrative of the proceedings at Towie in March–April, 1644, as given in the "Act of Forfaulture," pronounced against John Gordon and John Logie. The indictment proceeds that "Haddo and his complices from Aberdene went to the house of Towie pertaining to . . . Barclay of Towie, and ther finding that ther was no person

PATRICK BARCLAY, 1643–1668, Towie XIX.

within the said house, you sent for Walter Grant, and from the . . . day of March or Aprile last past, or ane or other of them, and when you had commandit the said Walter to give you the armes out of the said house of Towy and when the said Walter refused to delyver the samen to you you went and caused violentlie break up the gaites of the said house and entered the samen thefteouslie did reief and steel out thereof all the armes that was therein and a certain quantity of ball pouder and match, and a silver saltpit and the heid of a silver coupe and a silver cup, all thrie overgilt and thrie hagbitts of florind." From a subsequent notice dealing with Huntly it appears that Walter Grant was also tutor to the Laird of Towie, and on this occasion suffered imprisonment at the hands of the Gordons for faithfulness to his trust. He was doubtless the same person, described as of Coullglass, who on November 10th, 1655, acquired the life-rent interest, while his brother got the fee, in the wadset of Towie Mill lands, by assignation from James Barclay, in Canterbury, parish of Fordyce.

On May 20th, 1660, Patrick Barclay had a disposition from the Earl of Dunfermline, Lord of Fyvie, of the teind sheeves and parsonage teinds of Burialdales, Cannalyne, and Woodend ; and on August 8th, 1663, he obtained from William Gray, chantor of Aberdeen, and parson of Auchterless, a confirmation of the tack granted in 1614 to Francis Barclay of the teinds of Seggatt, Towie-Turray, Innerthenie and Over Ordley.

Patrick Barclay married Helen Douglas of Whittinghame, who survived him. She married secondly (as his second spouse) Sir Patrick Ogilvie, Lord of Boyne, a Lord of Session.

By his wife, Helen, he had an only daughter, Elizabeth, Lady of Towie, of whom later.

Patrick Barclay, the last Baron of Towie, died on August 2nd, 1668. It is probably to this laird that a tombstone in the old churchyard at Turriff belongs, upon which are traces of an inscription:—

INVS . PATRICVS . BARCLA .
.AVGVSTI. II. . . .

Patrick Barclay, 1643–1668, Towie XIX.

The initials "P.B." and the date 1662, and the quaint legend, formerly on the old dove-cot at Towie,

"AETHER DOE OR DIE"

are yet a further record of this Patrick Barclay.

On Patrick's death without male issue the right of succession as heir-male of the house of Towie devolved on William Barclay of Ordley, the second son of Sir Patrick Barclay (Towie XVII).

WILLIAM BARCLAY OF ORDLEY

William Barclay of Ordley, 1668, Towie XX.

On the death of Patrick Barclay (Towie XIX) without male issue, William Barclay of Ordley, his great-uncle, became the heir-male of the Towie line. He was the second son of Sir Patrick Barclay of Towie (Towie XVII).

In 1615, at the date of his marriage, he had a charter from his father, with consent of his brother Patrick, fiar of Towie, of the lands of Ordley.

In 1624 there is a disposition in his favour of the lands of Pitdoulsie, which lands ultimately came back into the hands of the Laird of Towie. Deeds at Gordon's College.

William Barclay was twice married, his first spouse being Helen Leslie, a daughter of John, sixth Baron of Pitcaple, and relict of George Cruickshank of Tillymorgan. His second wife was Margaret Reid, who died in 1631.

He was known as "Tutor of Towie" from the fact that he was tutor during their minority to no fewer than three successive holders of the estates.

The retour of William is dated April 3rd, 1668, and runs as follows :—

> "Wilhelmus Barclay de Towie, haeres masculus Patrici Barclay de Towie, pronepotis, in terris et baronia de Towie-Barclay comprehendentibus terras domenicales de Towie etc. etc." Aberdeenshire Retours, No. 384.

The terms of service were the same as of Walter Barclay in 1624. It is stated in *Castles of Aberdeenshire*, page 154, that William held the estates in trust for Elizabeth Barclay, the daughter of Patrick.

The exact date of William's death is not known, but he was alive until after 1669, and by this date he was a very old man.

His transactions with regard to the estate will be referred to later.

The only surviving issue of his marriage was an only daughter, Elspeth, who was still unmarried in 1660, when she concurred in a deed relating to part of Ordley. Deeds at Gordon's College.

At the death of William Barclay of Ordley, without male issue, the succession, as heir-male of Towie, fell on the

WILLIAM BARCLAY of Ordley, 1668, Towie XX.

descendants of George Barclay of Auchroddie, the third son of Walter Barclay (Towie XVI). The history of these heirs-male of Towie down to the present day will be given under "the Barclays of Knockleith."

ELIZABETH BARCLAY, Lady of Towie, 1668–1711.

THE LANDS OF TOWIE AFTER 1668

It will be of interest here to give an account of the descendants of Patrick Barclay (Towie XIX), the last Baron of Towie, through the heirs-female, and of the disposal of the castle and lands to Robert Gordon's College, Aberdeen, the present possessors of the valuable family deeds, from which so much of our History has been gleaned.

Patrick Barclay by disposition, dated August 1st, 1666, the year of the great fire of London, conveyed the lands of Towie and other property to his daughter Elizabeth, and in virtue of the precept contained therein she had sasine on February 18, 1668, infefting her in the whole Barony of Towie-Barclay.

There is a long series of deeds by which William Barclay, as heir-male of his grand-nephew, was himself retoured to the last laird, and then divested himself of the lands in favour of Elizabeth Barclay. The whole transaction was completed by a charter of resignation and confirmation under the Great Seal, dated April 11th, 1668.

The succession was in favour of Elizabeth's sons, or eldest daughter or daughters, whom failing to Anna, sister of the deceased Patrick Barclay, her sons or daughters, whom all failing to William Barclay, his heirs and assigns whomsoever. There was also the provision that Elizabeth and Anna as well as their heirs-female should marry one of the name of Barclay, or at least should assume the name, and carry the arms of the house of Towie. Aunt and niece are further bound not to marry except with the special advice of Andrew Lord Fraser, Sir Alexander Abercrombie of Kirkenbog, Colonel John Fullarton of Dunwick, Francis Fraser of Kilmundie and the said William Barclay, or the major part of them living at the time, under the penalty of rendering the infeftment null and void.

Deeds at Gordon's College.

Elizabeth Barclay, sometime after 1678, married John Gordon of Rothiemay. On July 4th, 1690, she and her husband issued a procuratory resignation of the Barony of Towie, for a new infeftment in favour of themselves in liferent and their only son, Patrick, in fee. From this deed it would appear that Anna Barclay, her aunt, had no issue and that William and his daughter were both dead, no provision being made for them or their heirs. ELIZABETH BARCLAY, Lady of Towie, 1668–1711.

On June 7th, 1690, Elizabeth Barclay, Lady of Towie, and her husband, by disposition, parted with the lands of Cullen to John Gordon, younger of Nethermuir, and thus the Barclay connection with these lands, which had existed so long, was ultimately severed. Cullen two years later passed into the hands of Archibald Grant of Ballintomb, who had a second disposition from Elizabeth Barclay and her husband.

Elizabeth Barclay, " Lady of Towie " as she was designated in the deeds dealing with the Towie property, had issue by her husband, John Gordon of Rothiemay, one son Patrick, her heir, and two daughters: Elizabeth, who married Sir George Innes, Bart., of Coxtoun, and another daughter, who married James Elphinstone of Warthill.

The Lady of Towie seems to have outlived her husband and then married Francis Gordon, eighth Laird of Craig. There was no surviving issue of this marriage.

Elizabeth Barclay died before 1711.

PATRICK GORDON-BARCLAY

PATRICK GORDON-BARCLAY, 1711–1755.

Patrick Gordon, the only son of Elizabeth Barclay and John Gordon, took the name of Barclay in the terms of the deed of succession. He is usually described as " fatuous," but whatever the extent of his affliction it was not sufficient to debar him from executing deeds and the like.

In 1704 he was apparently still under tutelage, as in that year Mr. Thomas Gordon, " pedagogue to Patrick Barclay, of Towie," was appointed master of the grammar school of Elgin. Elgin Records.

On September 18th, 1711, Patrick Barclay granted a disposition of the Barony of Towie-Barclay in favour of Sir

PATRICK GORDON-BARCLAY, 1711-1755.

George Innes, the husband of his sister Elizabeth, in life-rent, and for the provision of an annuity of 1,000 merks to Elizabeth should she survive her husband. The fee of the estate was designed in favour of their eldest son and three daughters in order of age, under the former obligation to take the name and arms of Barclay. Patrick Barclay was moved to this course, the disposition says, "for certain onerous causes, weighty motives, good respects and considerations." Among the latter was the provision of a yearly sum of 500 merks, to be uplifted out of any part of the lands, and to be paid by Sir George Innes quarterly. This grant was also made under the burden of entertaining Patrick and one servant, with their horses, in the household of Sir George or in the household of any of the heirs of tailzie as they succeeded.

It is further made clear that not only had Sir George Innes met all the debts of his brother-in-law, but had also paid or made provision for the sum of 11,000 merks to George Symmers of Balzeordie, in full of the claim that had been allowed him by the Court of Session in respect of his wife's interest in the Barony of Towie, by the settlement of her father Walter Barclay (Towie XVIII).

Patrick Gordon-Barclay was still alive in 1755, when he executed a disposition of Towie, along with his grand-niece Isobel Barclay, in favour of the Earl of Findlater.

ELIZABETH INNES-BARCLAY, 1711-1715.

ELIZABETH BARCLAY, WIFE OF SIR GEORGE INNES

Elizabeth, sister to the above Patrick, was the eldest daughter of Elizabeth Barclay and her husband John Gordon. Her husband was Sir George Innes of Coxtoun, Bart., the eldest son of Sir Alexander Innes of Coxtoun, who "was esteemed by all who knew him to be one of the first gentlemen in Scotland, being a graceful person and of fine natural parts and a man of remarkable honour and undaunted courage."

Family of Innes, p. 257.

The history of the transfer of Towie, by Patrick Barclay, to Sir George Innes has already been referred to.

Elizabeth Barclay and Sir George Innes had issue one son,

Alexander, of whom afterwards, and three daughters, Jean, Elizabeth and Anne. They are mentioned in the disposition, granted in 1711, by Patrick Barclay, in the order here given, as heirs of tailzie to the lands and Barony of Towie. ELIZABETH INNES-BARCLAY, 1711–1715.

Sir George Innes died in the winter of 1715, soon after the battle of Sheriffmuir, and possibly from wounds received there. He was succeeded by his son Sir Alexander Innes-Barclay in the lands of Towie, but not in the lands of Coxtoun, which seem to have become so burdened with debt as to have fallen into the hands of the wadsetters.

SIR ALEXANDER INNES-BARCLAY

SIR ALEXANDER INNES-BARCLAY, 1715–1735.

Sir Alexander, while yet a minor, married in the early part of 1728 Helen Duff, a daughter of James Duff of Crombie, by his spouse Jean Meldrum.

A post-nuptial contract of the marriage was drawn up between the parties, and from this deed, executed at Rothiemay on April 6th, 1728, we learn that Sir Alexander got with his bride the sum of 10,000 merks, in full of all claims his wife had against her father's estates, her brother William Duff of Crombie or on the decease of her sister. On the other hand Sir Alexander undertook to infeft her in the life-rent use, in case she survived him, of the Oertoun of Segatt, comprehending Burialdales, chapel of Segatt and croft of Dykeside, the lands of Over Ordley, Kingsford and Pitdoulsie ; and also to infeft, in order of succession, the issue of their marriage in the Barony of Towie.

A curious echo of the times is to be found in the new clause, not hitherto met with, in the deeds of the estate, where it is provided " that in the case that the said Alexander Barclay shall happen at any time, during the continuance of this contract, to be attainted or convicted of the crime of High Treason, and thereby forfeit his heritable estates and fortune, then the said Helen Duff shall enter into the enjoyment of her rights as if the said Alexander were naturally dead, any law or practice to the contrair notwithstanding." The provision was introduced after the experience of 1715, and doubtless in many

SIR ALEXANDER INNES-BARCLAY, 1715–1735.

cases was successful in saving a remnant after the fateful '45. This contract of marriage was ratified by Sir Alexander at Towie, July 28th, 1729, when he had attained his majority.

Helen Duff did not long enjoy her wedded life, as she died in 1729, after the birth of her daughter.

On March 16th, 1731, Sir Alexander took as his second spouse Jean Ogilvie, a daughter of Patrick Ogilvie of Balfour in Forfarshire, who also bore him a daughter.

Sir Alexander Innes-Barclay was dead by 1735, and at his death could have been but 27 years of age. He had issue two daughters: Jean, by his first marriage, who on January 20th, 1735, was retoured on a general service; and Isobel, the issue of his second marriage.

JEAN INNES-BARCLAY

JEAN INNES-BARCLAY, 1735–1746.

Jean, who, as we have said, was retoured heir of provision to her father on January 20th, 1735, had on November 8th of the same year a corroborative and new disposition from her grand-uncle, Patrick Barclay of Towie, in which he fully conveys all his interest in the estates and also discharges all the obligations on the lands which may have fallen to him by discharge of debts and the like since the date of the granting of the deed of 1711.

Jean Barclay, while still very young, married Robert Dalrymple, doctor of medicine, but died in 1746, without issue, and was succeeded by her sister.

ISOBEL BARCLAY, WIFE OF HON. CHARLES MAITLAND

ISOBEL BARCLAY-MAITLAND, 1746–1761.

Isobel, on February 2nd, 1747, was retoured heir to her sister Jean on a special service, and had a precept from Chancery infefting her in the lands of Towie.

She was served later as heir-general to her mother, Dame Jean Ogilvie, and her aunt Anne Ogilvie, daughter of Patrick Ogilvie of Balfour.

Isobel married the Hon. Charles Maitland of Tillycoultry, second son of Charles, sixth Earl of Lauderdale.

By disposition dated January 29th and February 5th, 1755, Isobel and her husband, with Patrick Barclay, late of Towie, her grand-uncle, as consenting party, sold the Barony of Towie to James, fifth Earl of Findlater and Seafield. ISOBEL BARCLAY-MAITLAND, 1746-1761.

And so the Barony of Towie, with its lands and castle, passed away from the Towie line of the Barclay family, who had been its possessors for upwards of seven hundred years.

By her marriage with the Hon. Charles Barclay-Maitland Isobel had issue a son Charles Barclay-Maitland, a lieutenant in the 2nd Dragoon Guards. He married and his grandson Charles succeeded on September 1st, 1878, as twelfth Earl of Lauderdale. On his death in 1884, without issue, the direct line of the Barclays of Towie ceased to exist.

Isobel Barclay-Maitland died on October 23rd, 1761.

The weird of Thomas the Rhymer,

> "Towie-Barclay of the glen
> Happy to the maids
> But never to the men,"

was said to haunt the family in the death of the heir-male, who seldom survived his father; and so strong a hold had this on the faith of the people that it was the reason assigned for the sale of the estate by Mr. Barclay-Maitland in 1755.

It was then purchased, as we have said, by the Earl of Findlater for his second son, who died a few years after, when little more than of age. Of course the estate was blamed, and his Lordship of Findlater, although one of the ablest men of his day, was so far from being above the current suspicion that ever after on his journeys to and from the south, when he came upon the property at Kingsford, on the north boundary, he had the blinds of his carriage pulled down until he had passed the southern march at Blindsmill, and *vice versa*.

His son, sixth and last Earl, sold Towie in 1792 to the governors of Robert Gordon's Hospital (now College) in Aberdeen, the present proprietors, to whom we are indebted for a great deal of information that has been embodied in this history of the Towie line.

PEDIGREE VIII.

The Barclays of Knockleith (Towie Line continued)

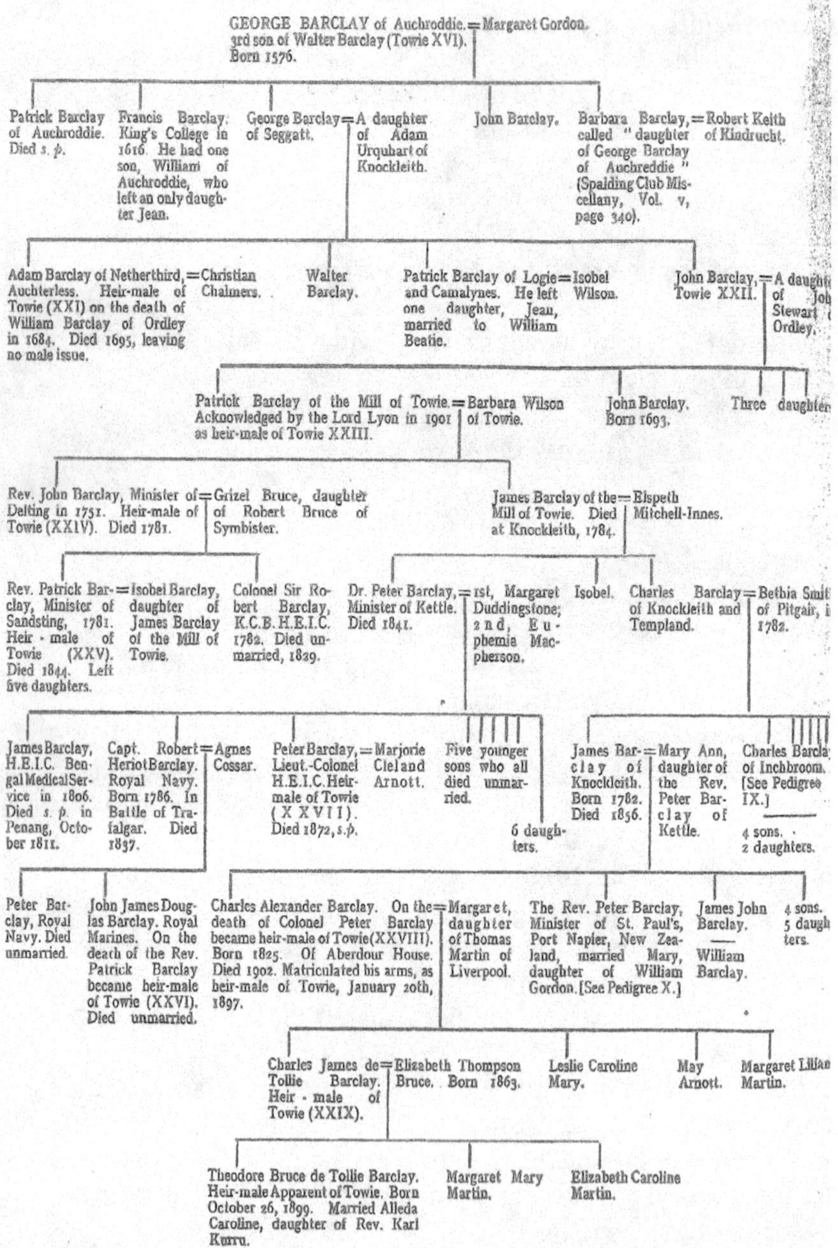
GEORGE BARCLAY of Auchroddie, 3rd son of Walter Barclay (Towie XVI). Born 1576.
= Margaret Gordon.
Patrick Barclay of Auchroddie. Died s. p.
Francis Barclay. King's College in 1616. He had one son, William of Auchroddie, who left an only daughter Jean.
George Barclay of Seggatt.
= A daughter of Adam Urquhart of Knockleith.
John Barclay.
Barbara Barclay, called "daughter of George Barclay of Auchreddie" (Spalding Club Miscellany, Vol. v, page 340).
= Robert Keith of Kindrucht.
Adam Barclay of Netherthird, Auchterless. Heir-male of Towie (XXI) on the death of William Barclay of Ordley in 1684. Died 1695, leaving no male issue.
= Christian Chalmers.
Walter Barclay.
Patrick Barclay of Logie and Camalynes. He left one daughter, Jean, married to William Beatie.
= Isobel Wilson.
John Barclay, Towie XXII.
= A daught of Joh Stewart Ordley.
Patrick Barclay of the Mill of Towie. Acknowledged by the Lord Lyon in 1901 as heir-male of Towie XXIII.
= Barbara Wilson of Towie.
John Barclay. Born 1693.
Three daughter
Rev. John Barclay, Minister of Delting in 1751. Heir-male of Towie (XXIV). Died 1781.
= Grizel Bruce, daughter of Robert Bruce of Symbister.
James Barclay of the Mill of Towie. Died at Knockleith, 1784.
= Elspeth Mitchell-Innes.
Rev. Patrick Barclay, Minister of Sandsting, 1781. Heir-male of Towie (XXV). Died 1844. Left five daughters.
= Isobel Barclay, daughter of James Barclay of the Mill of Towie.
Colonel Sir Robert Barclay, K.C.B. H.E.I.C. 1782. Died unmarried, 1829.
Dr. Peter Barclay, Minister of Kettle. Died 1841.
= 1st, Margaret Duddingstone; 2nd, Euphemia Macpherson.
Isobel.
Charles Barclay of Knockleith and Templand.
= Bethia Smit of Pitgair, i 1782.
James Barclay, H.E.I.C. Bengal Medical Service in 1806. Died s. p. in Penang, October 1811.
Capt. Robert Heriot Barclay. Royal Navy. Born 1786. In Battle of Trafalgar. Died 1837.
= Agnes Cossar.
Peter Barclay, Lieut.-Colonel H.E.I.C. Heir-male of Towie (XXVII). Died 1872, s. p.
= Marjorie Cleland Arnott.
Five younger sons who all died unmarried.
6 daughters.
James Barclay of Knockleith. Born 1782. Died 1856.
= Mary Ann, daughter of the Rev. Peter Barclay of Kettle.
Charles Barcla of Inchbroom. [See Pedigree IX.]
4 sons. 2 daughters.
Peter Barclay, Royal Navy. Died unmarried.
John James Douglas Barclay. Royal Marines. On the death of the Rev. Patrick Barclay became heir-male of Towie (XXVI). Died unmarried.
Charles Alexander Barclay. On the death of Colonel Peter Barclay became heir-male of Towie (XXVIII). Born 1825. Of Aberdour House. Died 1902. Matriculated his arms, as heir-male of Towie, January 20th, 1897.
= Margaret, daughter of Thomas Martin of Liverpool.
The Rev. Peter Barclay, Minister of St. Paul's, Port Napier, New Zealand, married Mary, daughter of William Gordon. [See Pedigree X.]
James John Barclay.
William Barclay.
4 sons. 5 daughters.
Charles James de Tollie Barclay. Heir-male of Towie (XXIX).
= Elizabeth Thompson Bruce. Born 1863.
Leslie Caroline Mary.
May Arnott.
Margaret Lilian Martin.
Theodore Bruce de Tollie Barclay. Heir-male Apparent of Towie. Born October 26, 1899. Married Alleda Caroline, daughter of Rev. Karl Kurru.
Margaret Mary Martin.
Elizabeth Caroline Martin.

GEORGE BARCLAY OF AUCHRODDIE

GEORGE BARCLAY of Auchroddie, 1576–... Towie XVIIc.

On the death of William Barclay of Ordley, second son of Sir Patrick Barclay (Towie XVII), the heir-male representation of the Towie line devolved on the descendants of George Barclay of Auchroddie, the third son of Walter Barclay (Towie XVI) and his spouse, Elizabeth Hay.

George Barclay lived at Auchroddie, in the parish of Ellon, and, as we have already mentioned, was at one time the possessor of the Royal transcript of Wyntoun's *Chronicle*.

He was born about the year 1576, and married Margaret Gordon, by whom he had issue at least four sons and a daughter.

On a careful examination of the Royal transcript of the *Orygynale Cronykill of Scotland*, by Andrew de Wyntoun, which is to be seen in the British Museum, it is proved beyond all doubt that this ancient book was in the possession of George Barclay of Auchroddie (Towie XVIIc) in the year 1604. 17 D, xx.

Andrew de Wyntoun lived between the years 1350 and 1420. He was a canon regular of St. Andrews, and Prior of St. Serf's in Lochleven in 1395. He wrote the *Chronicle* at the request of his patron, Sir John de Wemyss, whose representative, Mr. Erskine Wemyss, of Wemyss Castle, Forfarshire, possesses the oldest extant MS. of the work. The subject is the history of Scotland from the mythical period (hence the title "Originale") down to the accession of James I in 1406.

We find in the Register of St. Andrews that Andrew de Wyntoun, Prior of St. Serf's, brought an action against William Barclay (Collairnie III) for the payment of rent of the lands of Bolgy. As William refused or neglected to comply, Wyntoun brought a second action against him in the Bishop's court at St. Andrews on February 19th, 1406. Still William refused to pay, and Wyntoun was forced to bring a third action in 1411, when the Laird of Collairnie was excommunicated with bell, book and candle.

Macpherson in his preface to the 1795 edition remarks that good judges of manuscripts have pronounced that the Royal transcript belongs to the beginning of the fifteenth century, while Dr. David Laing places the date between 1460 and 1470.

GEORGE BARCLAY of Auchroddie, 1576-... Towie XVIIc.

At the end of the transcript there is a prose chronicle of ten leaves. This is not part of the manuscript as written by Wyntoun, but either the work of the transcriber or of some later hand. On the outside of one of the quairs is written in a very small hand as follows :—

"The short chronicle at the end written 1540 as appears from a date on it."

This note can be seen in the illustration. At what date it was written is impossible to say.

On the top of another of the blank folios is written "Margaret gardyne 1604 years," which is clear evidence that the Royal transcript was in the hands of George Barclay of Auchroddie at that date.

It appears to have passed from the Barclays through the hands of Sir William Innes, vicar of Banff, and of Mr. Thomas Nicholson, commissary of Aberdeen, before it was acquired by William Le Neve, in his official capacity of York Herald at the coronation of Charles I at Edinburgh in 1633. (Le Neve was York Herald in 1625, Clarenceux King of Arms 1635 and died in 1661. The MS. was then added to the Royal Library at St. James's.)

The book is made up of quairs of twenty leaves, the outer one being vellum and the others stout paper.

On the cover of one of the quairs the following lines are written, apparently by the retainers :—

"This buik does pertaine
To a richt honab^{ll} man
George barclay of Auchrody
And mony wyer propirty
Brother german is he
To Sir Patrick of Tollie
Cheiff of barclays in Scotland
And mony guid deid hes haid
in hand."

And underneath in a very small and bad hand:—

"Sir patrick barclay of Tollie
Cheiff of that name I testifie
As in his shield ye may see
Tua corsis weirs he

This buik dois pertene
To ane rycht honorall man
Georg barclay of achrody
And mony wyer properly
Brother german is he
To Sir patrik of tollie
Cheiff of barclays in scotland
And mony gud deidis hes hald
in hand

WRITING ON WYNTOUN'S CHRONICLE

(1)

Georg
Margret
Francis
Adderey

barclay
Cordonie of
barclay

M francesca

The third be resone quhy
That hous marit properly
Ane dochter of gartly
With gryt honour and dignity
Quhilk then was barclay
And was ane knycht rycht worthy
The marrag of that lady
Induit with guid qualitie
Movit her husband Toly then
Into his arms to . . .
Quhair corsis twa befoir hand
For he was . . . .
. . . . . the third to bear."

GEORGE BARCLAY of Auchroddie, 1576– . . . Towie XVIIc.

The last part is in some places so blotted as to be illegible. From the above lines it has often been concluded that Sir Patrick Barclay (Towie XVII) married the heiress of Gartley, but, as we have already pointed out when dealing with Sir Patrick, this cannot be the fact. The writing alludes to a marriage between a previous Laird of Towie (Towie XIV) and a daughter of the house of Gartley. See p. 239.

The children of George Barclay of Auchroddie do not seem to have treated this ancient volume with the reverence which was its due. We find their efforts at writing with a pen on several of the blank folios of the Royal transcript. As will be observed from the illustrations, which will repay careful study, their writings are of considerable genealogical importance, giving us the names of George's wife and certainly two of his children.

The eldest son of George Barclay and Margaret Gordon, his wife, was Patrick, who evidently died without issue, as in the year 1677 we find his great-niece Jean was served heir to Patrick Barclay of "Auchryddie," her grand-uncle.

The second son, Francis, whose name appears many times upon the blank folios of the Royal transcript, became an M.A. of King's College, Aberdeen, in the year 1616. There is another mention of him in 1636, when his mother, Margaret Gordon, raised an action against him for rent and removing. As far as can be ascertained, Francis Barclay had one son, William, who is described as "of Auchreddie" in 1654, when

GEORGE BARCLAY of Auchroddie, 1576-... Towie XVIIc.

he was a defender along with others in an action of law-burrow raised by Sir John Gordon of Haddo. In 1665 he was admitted a burgess of Aberdeen and is then described as Captain William Barclay; and in the entry of his admission it is stated that he had married a daughter of a burgess of guild. The issue of the marriage was an only daughter, Jean, who on January 12th, 1677, is described as daughter of the late William Barclay of "Auchreddie," and spouse of Alexander Sibbald, formerly of Arnage. At this date she was served heir to the estates of "Auchreddie," to her grand-uncle Patrick Barclay, as already stated. It is stated that Auchroddie was in the parish of Ellon, and the barony of Drumquhendle, held of the house of "Towy" for a penny blanch.

The third son was George Barclay, known as of Seggatt. Of him later.

The fourth son of George Barclay of Auchroddie was John. He may have died young, as the only record of him is his name on the transcript, where he signs :—

"Johnne dune with my hand at the pen led be the oder bruder [other brother]."

The last two words are almost unreadable.

His daughter Barbara married Robert Keith of Kindrucht.

GEORGE BARCLAY OF SEGGATT

GEORGE BARCLAY of Seggatt.

George Barclay of Seggatt was probably the third son of George Barclay of Auchroddie. He inherited the lands of Seggatt from his uncle William Barclay, the second son of Walter Barclay of Towie (Towie XVI).

As has been already stated, this William Barclay (Towie XVIIB) of the Mill of Seggatt was born in the year 1570, and is one of the signatories to the "Letter of Slaynes" granted by his family to George Meldrum of Montcoffer for the murder of Walter Barclay his father.

In 1897, when Charles Alexander Barclay (Towie XXVIII) matriculated his arms in the Lyon office, as heir-male of Towie, the descent given was through this George Barclay of

WRITING ON WYNTOUN'S CHRONICLE

(3)

Seggatt from Walter Barclay (Towie XVI). Charles Alexander was given the right to the arms of Towie, and the use of the supporters usually borne by the head of the family.

GEORGE BARCLAY of Seggatt.

George Barclay of Seggatt married a daughter of Adam Urquhart of Knockleith, by whom he had a large family :—

1. Adam, his heir, who became heir-male of Towie on the death of William Barclay of Ordley.
2. Walter.
3. Patrick, who in 1696 was living with his wife as tenants of Logie. He is evidently the same person who was tenant of Camalynes "of the house of Towie." His wife was Isobel Wilson, and they had one daughter married to William Beatie.
4. John, who succeeded his brother Adam as heir-male of Towie in 1695.
5. Alexander, who died in his great-nephew's house at the Mill of Towie.

George Barclay was succeeded by his eldest son, Adam Barclay.

ADAM BARCLAY

ADAM BARCLAY, 1684–1695, Heir-male of Towie XXI.

Adam Barclay became heir-male of the Towie Barclays on the death of William Barclay of Ordley. This was before July 11th, 1684.

He lived at Netherthird, Auchterless, and married Christian Chalmers, who died April 18th, 1696, and by whom he had issue :—

1. Harry, who died young and unmarried.
2. Elizabeth, who died in 1727.
3. Isobel, married to George Ellice of Knockleith. She succeeded her father in the lands of Knockleith August 12th, 1695, and died December 28th, 1727, leaving issue.

Adam Barclay died August 12th, 1695, and was succeeded as heir-male of Towie by his brother John.

JOHN BARCLAY

Heir-male of Towie XXII.

John Barclay, the fourth son of George Barclay of Seggatt, lived at Nether Ordley, at which place he and his wife were returned for taxation.

On the failure of his three elder brothers, Adam, Walter and Patrick, to leave male issue he became heir-male of the house of Towie.

John married a daughter of John Stewart of Ordley, by whom he had two sons and three daughters :—

1. Patrick Barclay, his heir, of whom later.
2. John Barclay, baptized October 22nd, 1693.

PATRICK BARCLAY

Heir-male of Towie XXIII.

Patrick Barclay is described as of the Mill of Towie.

He succeeded his father as heir-male of Towie, but at what date is unknown, as no record has been found of his father's death.

On June 19th, 1901, in a claim by his descendants, he was acknowledged by the Lyon King to have been lineally descended and heir-male of the house of Towie.

He married Barbara Wilson of Towie, and they had issue two sons and one daughter :— Heir-male of Towie XXIII.

1. The Rev. John Barclay, his heir.
2. James, whose descendants became heirs-male of Towie on the failure of his elder brother's line.
3. Margaret, married to H. Murray of Slap on January 27th, 1735. They had a large family, from whom are descended the Murray and Morrison connections.

The date of the death of Patrick Barclay of Towie Mill is unknown.

THE REV. JOHN BARCLAY

John Barclay, the eldest son of Patrick Barclay, was licensed by the Presbytery of Turriff on October 28th, 1744, as assistant to Mr. Alexander Forbes. He was ordained on November 14th of the same year. Heir-male of Towie XXIV.

He was presented to the parish of Delting by James Earl of Morton and admitted October 1751.

The Rev. John married Grizel, a daughter of Robert Bruce, third of Symbister, Zetland, on January 16th, 1755, and by her, who died in 1767, had issue :—

1. The Rev. Patrick Barclay, his heir.
2. Colonel Sir Robert Barclay, K.C.B., baptized February 27th, 1759. He entered the Honourable East India Company's service as a cadet in 1782, lieutenant August 21st, 1790, captain 1799, major 1804, lieutenant-colonel 1808, brevet-colonel 1814. He was created a K.C.B. April 7th, 1815.

   He was Adjutant-General of the Indian army commanded by the Duke of Wellington, then General Sir Arthur Wellesley, and received special mention for his conduct at the battle of Assaye in 1803.

   He seems to have remained on terms of friendship with the Iron Duke after the Indian campaign. The following letter from the Duke to Colonel Barclay is of considerable interest :

Nevada.
Nov. 5th, 1812.

My dear Barclay,

I am convinced that you will excuse me for having so long delayed to thank you for your letter of 27th August, which I received in due course, but it found me fully

Heir-male of Towie XXIV.

occupied and as you will have seen by the published accounts I have scarcely had time to write what was necessary I should write, much less a private letter.

I sincerely congratulate you upon your return to England. I conclude that you will take a look at Scotland and will then fix yourself in London. And I need not assure you how happy I shall be to see you if God should ever think my sins sufficiently punished to relieve me of my situation here.

I assure you that an allied army of Englishmen, Germans, Spaniards and Portugese, and moving and manœuvring between 60 and 70,000 of them in front of 90,000 French is no bed of roses, but thank God I have hitherto suffered no disaster or loss and I hope to continue equally successful.

Sydenham will let you know how I am. I am obliged to you for all the information you have given me upon all the various topics in your letter. We must settle somehow or other the Manilla prize money ourselves.

Believe me ever yours most sincerely,

Wellington.

I'll write to Mrs. Leese, if you will let me know when any ship will sail for the E. Indies. Have you seen her boy at my house? You should go and see Lady Wellington and my children when they will go to town.

Colonel Robert Barclay.

56 Conduit street.

Colonel Robert Barclay recorded his arms in 1816 at the Lyon office and got as an augmentation on chief or, an elephant proper, and over it the word "Assaye."

It is said that when Sir Robert gave in his coat of arms for matriculation Sir Robert Naylor said to him: "Why, Sir Robert, these cannot be your coat of arms." Sir Robert, in some surprise, said: "Why not?" "Because they are the very same arms and motto as those of the Russian Field-Marshal Prince Barclay de Tolly." "Oh," said Sir Robert, "if that is all, there is nothing wrong, for we are cubs of the same breed!"

After his retirement Sir Robert lived for some years at Montcoffer House, near Banff. He had some thought of buying the old property, but hesitated, thinking that he had not quite enough money for this.

Banffshire Journal, September 25th, 1902.

Sir Robert died, unmarried, in 1829.

3. John Barclay, M.D. (London), married Mary Duddingstone of St. Fort. They had one son and three daughters: John, died young; Mary, who married Capt. Kay and was the mother of two sons, one of whom was Sir Brooke Kay, Bart.; Grace, who died unmarried in 1872; and Elizabeth, who married the Rev. Ray Booker. Heir-male of Towie XXIV.
4. Margaret, baptized July 6th, 1756, and died in infancy.

The Rev. John Barclay, minister of Delting, Shetland, died April 18th, 1781, aged 68 years, and was succeeded, as heir-male of Towie, by his eldest son, the Rev. Patrick Barclay.

THE REV. PATRICK BARCLAY

The Rev. Patrick Barclay was baptized January 16th, 1757. He was educated at King's College and became M.A. in 1772. He was minister of Sandsting, Shetland, from 1781 to 1812. He married on April 26th, 1783, his first cousin, Isobel Barclay, daughter of James Barclay of the Mill of Towie and Knockleith. They had five daughters:— Heir-male of Towie XXV.

1. Johanna.
2. Elspeth or Isabella, who married the Rev. John Duncan, minister of Dumrossness, who lost his life in the wreck of the *Doris*, February 22nd, 1813, when returning home.
3. Elizabeth Bruce, who married Dr. Theodore Gordon, physician to the Forces. For many years he was assistant to Sir James Macgregor of the Army Medical Board. Dr. Gordon died in 1843. Mrs. Gordon died in 1885, at the advanced age of 94 years.
4. Grace, who died at the age of 20.
5. Barbara.

The Rev. Patrick Barclay demitted his charge at Sandsting on November 28th, 1812, and afterwards lived at Bowiebank, and then at Colleonard, that he might be near his brother Sir Robert. He left Shetland greatly broken by many sad bereavements, accompanied by his three orphan granddaughters (Duncan). He died at Elgin, June 12th, 1844, aged 87.

As none of the three brothers left male issue, the descent of the heir-male of Towie reverted to the descendants of James Barclay, the second son of Patrick Barclay of the Mill of Towie and Knockleith.

JAMES BARCLAY

James Barclay, the second son of Patrick Barclay of the Mill of Towie, was baptized on February 3rd, 1718. On the failure of the line of his elder brother, John, his descendants became heirs-male of the house of Towie.

He married Elspeth, a daughter of George Mitchell-Innes. They had issue four sons and four daughters :—

1. Doctor Peter Barclay of Kettle, whose descendants became heirs-male of Towie. Of him later.
2. Charles Barclay, the second son of James Barclay of the Mill of Towie. He was known as of Knockleith and Templand. On the failure of the line of his elder brother, Dr. Peter Barclay, his descendants became heirs-male of Towie.
3. George Barclay of Clyne.
4. A son who died in infancy.
5. Barbara, who married, in 1775, Alexander Smith of Pitgair.
6. Isobel, who married her first cousin, the Rev. Patrick Barclay, minister of Sandsting.
7. Anne, who married in 1785 —— Murray.
8. Jane, who married George Duncan.

Mr. James Barclay of the Mill of Towie died at Knockleith in June 1784.

THE REV. PETER BARCLAY, D.D.

The Rev. Peter Barclay, the eldest son of James Barclay of the Mill of Towie and Knockleith, was baptized June 4th, 1749. He was educated at Marischal College (1765-1769), and took his M.A. degree in 1769. He was ordained in 1778 and became minister of Kettle in Fifeshire, which he held for 63 years.

He married, March 13th, 1780, Margaret Duddingstone, daughter of James Duddingstone of St. Fort, county Fife; and, secondly, Euphemia Macpherson of Cupar, Fife.

He had a very large family, eight sons and six daughters :—

1. James, who entered the East India Company's service (Bengal Medical) September 21st, 1806. He died in Penang, Straits Settlements, October 22nd, 1811, leaving no children.

2. Captain Robert Heriot Barclay, R.N., who was born at Kettle in 1786. He entered the Royal Navy, and served as a midshipman on H.M.S. *Anson*, 44 guns, in Sir John Borlase-Warren's defeat of the French squadron, under Admiral Bompart, off the north-west coast of Ireland in 1798, and also at the capture of the French ship *Loire*, 40 guns, in the same year.

He was present at the battle of Trafalgar as a lieutenant on board H.M.S. *Swiftsure*, and performed good service in saving the lives of some of the crew of the French prize *Redoubtable*. He was subsequently in command of a detachment of boats in an attack on a French supply convoy in 1808, when he lost his left arm.

He afterwards served in the war with the United States of America, first in connection with a naval brigade, operating under Sir George Prevost, and secondly as commodore of Lake Erie, flying the broad pennant on H.M.S. *Detroit*, with which vessel he attacked a superior American squadron of ten ships, with a small flotilla of five small vessels, on September 10th, 1813. The entire British squadron was captured, he being dangerously wounded not only in his other arm, but having part of his thigh cut away. Tried by court martial, he was honourably acquitted of all blame, complimented on the gallantry of his officers and men and was promoted commander. The inhabitants of Quebec presented him with two pieces of plate, value £500. He became captain in 1824.

He married, August 11th, 1814, Agnes Cossar, of Westminster, and had two sons and four daughters: Peter, who served in the Royal Navy and died young and unmarried, and John James Douglas Barclay, who succeeded as heir-male of Towie, on the death of the Rev. Patrick Barclay in 1844. Of him later.

Captain Barclay died in Edinburgh, during the lifetime of his father, in 1837.

3. Lieut.-Colonel Peter Barclay, who succeeded his nephew as heir-male of Towie. Of him afterwards.

4. Charles Barclay, who died in Guadeloupe in 1820, unmarried.

5. The Rev. John Barclay, who was minister of Kingston in Upper Canada in 1825. He died young and unmarried.

6. William Duddingstone Barclay, joined the H.E.I.C. and died at Palaneram, September 13th, 1830, also unmarried.

7. Archibald Barclay, who was the eldest son by Doctor Barclay's second marriage, died in 1860, unmarried.
8. George Barclay, who entered the merchant marine, died young, also unmarried.

Doctor Barclay had also six daughters: Margaret, who married Robert Balingal; Elizabeth, who married Thomas Martin; Mary Anne, who married her cousin James Barclay of Knockleith; Barbara; Helen, and Robina.

The Rev. Peter Barclay, D.D., minister of Kettle, died December 13th, 1841, in his 93rd year. At the time of his death he was known as "the father of the Church of Scotland."

JOHN JAMES DOUGLAS BARCLAY

Heir-male of Towie XXVI.

John James Douglas Barclay was the second son of Captain Robert Heriot Barclay, the second son of Doctor Peter Barclay of Kettle.

He succeeded his kinsman the Rev. Patrick Barclay, minister of Sandsting, Shetland, as heir-male of Towie, June 12th, 1844.

He entered the Royal Marines as a second lieutenant, February 13th, 1842, became first lieutenant December 7th, 1846, and died unmarried June 18th, 1853.

On his death the succession as heir-male passed to his uncle.

LIEUT.-COLONEL PETER BARCLAY

Heir-male of Towie XXVII.

Lieut.-Colonel Peter Barclay, the eldest surviving son of the Rev. Peter Barclay, D.D., succeeded to the representation of the family of Towie on the death of his nephew, John James Douglas Barclay, June 18th, 1853.

He entered the H.E.I.C. as a cadet in 1802; second lieutenant, Madras Infantry, April 17th, 1803. He became major 1827, retired 1832, and afterwards received the honorary rank of lieutenant-colonel.

He married Marjorie Cleland Arnott, of Chapel, county Fife, who died in 1885.

Colonel Peter Barclay died in 1872, leaving no male issue.

On his death, being the last of the descendants of the Rev. Peter Barclay, D.D., minister of Kettle, the heir-male of the house of Towie devolved on the descendants of Charles Barclay of Knockleith and Templand, the second son of James Barclay of Towie Mill. Heir-male of Towie XXVII.

CHARLES BARCLAY

On the death of Lieut.-Colonel Peter Barclay, the third son of the Rev. Peter Barclay, D.D., minister of Kettle, without issue, and the consequent failure of that line, the heir-male of the house of Towie passed to the descendants of Charles Barclay, the second son of James Barclay of the Mill of Towie and Knockleith.

Charles Barclay was known as of Knockleith and Templand. He was baptized December 11th, 1752, and married January 22nd, 1782, to Bethia Smith of Pitgair, by whom he had six sons and two daughters :—

1. James Barclay, of whom later. His eldest son, Charles Alexander Barclay, became heir-male of Towie.
2. Alexander Barclay, who was Hon. Receiver-General of Jamaica. He was the author of *A Practical View of Slavery*, London, 1827.

   He married Miss Curran and had two sons and two daughters.

   Mr. Alexander Barclay died in Jamaica in 1864. He had no descendants.
3. Charles Barclay, tenant of Inchbroom, St. Andrews. A pedigree of his descendants is appended.
4. John Barclay was educated at Marischal College (1804–1808). He was a member of the Scottish Bar and lived at Calcots, Elgin. He was author of *Sequel to the Diversions of Purley*.

   He married, in 1816, Jessie, daughter of Patrick Haggart, and had issue. The present representative of this family is Colonel Patrick Barclay of the Grove, Elgin.
5. William Barclay, minister of Auldearn. He was educated at Marischal College (1805–1809), and took his degree.

   He married first, in 1834, Isabella, daughter of Provost Alexander Brown, Aberdeen, and secondly, in 1846, Hamilton, daughter of J. Souter of Islay. He had nine children.
6. Dr. George Barclay was educated at Marischal College, Aberdeen (1805–1809), and became M.A. and M.D. (Edinburgh) in 1812. He attained great distinction in his profession. Though only twenty-seven at the time of his

PEDIGREE IX.

The Descendants of Charles Barclay of Inchbroom

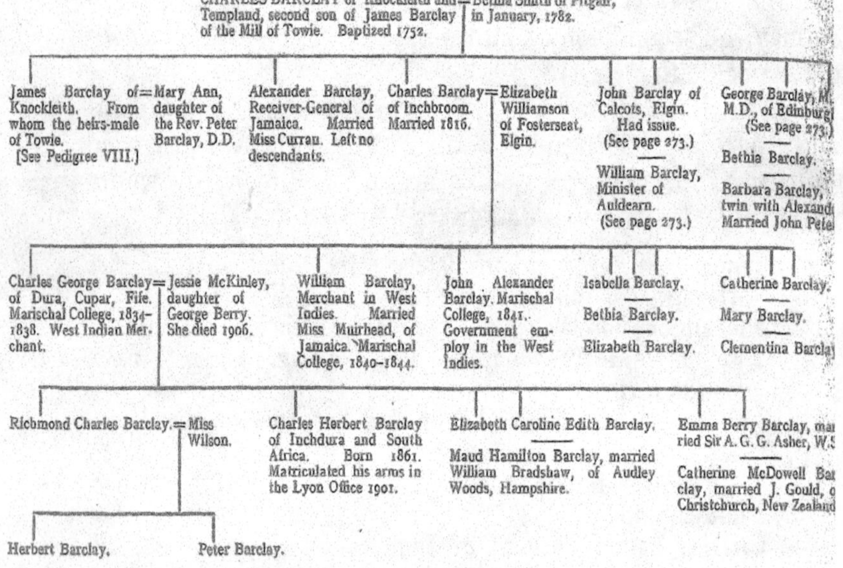

CHARLES BARCLAY of Knockleith and Templand, second son of James Barclay of the Mill of Towie. Baptized 1752.
Bethia Smith of Pitgair, in January, 1782.
James Barclay of Knockleith. From whom the heirs-male of Towie. [See Pedigree VIII.]
Mary Ann, daughter of the Rev. Peter Barclay, D.D.
Alexander Barclay, Receiver-General of Jamaica. Married Miss Curran. Left no descendants.
Charles Barclay of Inchbroom. Married 1816.
Elizabeth Williamson of Fosterseat, Elgin.
John Barclay of Calcots, Elgin. Had issue. (See page 273.)
William Barclay, Minister of Auldearn. (See page 273.)
George Barclay, M.D., of Edinburg
(See page 273.)
Bethia Barclay.
Barbara Barclay, twin with Alexand
Married John Pete
Charles George Barclay of Dura, Cupar, Fife. Marischal College, 1834–1838. West Indian Merchant.
Jessie McKinley, daughter of George Berry. She died 1906.
William Barclay, Merchant in West Indies. Married Miss Muirhead, of Jamaica. Marischal College, 1840–1844.
John Alexander Barclay. Marischal College, 1841. Government employ in the West Indies.
Isabella Barclay.
Bethia Barclay.
Elizabeth Barclay.
Catherine Barclay.
Mary Barclay.
Clementina Barcla
Richmond Charles Barclay.
Miss Wilson.
Charles Herbert Barclay of Inchdura and South Africa. Born 1861. Matriculated his arms in the Lyon Office 1901.
Elizabeth Caroline Edith Barclay.
Maud Hamilton Barclay, married William Bradshaw, of Audley Woods, Hampshire.
Emma Berry Barclay, mar
ried Sir A. G. G. Asher, W.
Catherine McDowell Bar
clay, married J. Gould,
Christchurch, New Zealand
Herbert Barclay.
Peter Barclay.

death, which occurred some months before his son George's birth, he was the recognised authority on surgery in the north of Scotland, and the first to occupy the post of Lecturer on Surgery in Aberdeen University, in 1818.

He married, in 1816, Emma, daughter of Walter Berry, merchant in Edinburgh, and died in 1819. He had two sons, Charles and George, and a daughter, Mary. The eldest son was the father of George Walter Woodfall Barclay, manager for the North British and Mercantile Insurance Company in Aberdeen, to whom we are indebted for much valuable information concerning the Towie family.

His second son, George, was educated at the ancient Grammar School at Aberdeen and was a class fellow of the late William Garden Blaikie. With Blaikie he not only divided the first Greek prize and won the coveted "silver pen," but shared the distinction of obtaining the first place on leaving Marischal College with its degree of M.A.

In 1848, before settling down as a partner in the business firm of his uncle in Leith, he took a journey to the Holy Land, a journey in those days attended by some risk.

His connection with the Royal Society of Edinburgh arose partly from his intelligent interest in science and partly from his special taste for marine zoology, which entailed much work with the microscope and the making of very delicate drawings, which injured his sight and caused the loss of one eye.

George Barclay enjoyed for over thirty years the close friendship of Dr. John Brown and other famous writers, including both Thackeray and Ruskin.

During his business connection with Leith, he was chosen as a representative of the treasury of the Harbour and Dock Commission, and was also a governor of Watt's Hospital.

In Edinburgh he was a director of the Bank of Scotland. One of his many charities was the Sick Children's Hospital, which he helped by admirable letters to the Press and with a handsome donation.

In 1850 he married his cousin, Elizabeth Berry, a woman of strong character and boundless hospitality, who predeceased him in 1896. They had issue one son, Walter Berry Barclay, and nine daughters, Elizabeth Mary, Emma Helen Constance, Alice Evelyn, married to Major Giles, Catherine Moubray, Emily Hansen, married to J. A. Grant, Ethel Maud, married to Charles Blair-Wilson, Helen Brown, and two others who died in infancy.

PEDIGREE X.

The Descendants of the Rev. Peter Barclay, 2nd son of James Barclay of Knocklei

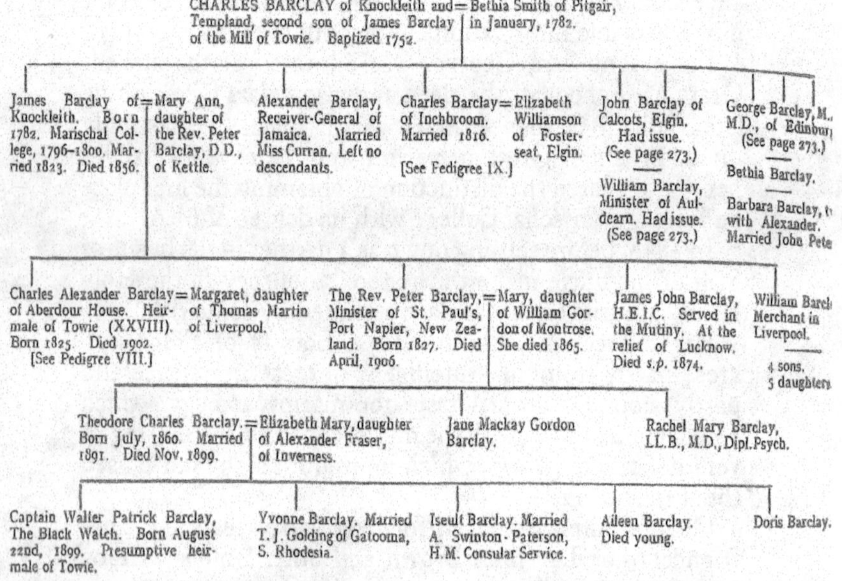

CHARLES BARCLAY of Knockleith and Templand, second son of James Barclay of the Mill of Towie. Baptized 1752. = Bethia Smith of Pitgair, in January, 1782.

James Barclay of Knockleith. Born 1782. Marischal College, 1796–1800. Married 1823. Died 1856. = Mary Ann, daughter of the Rev. Peter Barclay, D.D., of Kettle.

Alexander Barclay, Receiver-General of Jamaica. Married Miss Curran. Left no descendants.

Charles Barclay of Inchbroom. Married 1816. = Elizabeth Williamson of Fosterseat, Elgin. [See Pedigree IX.]

John Barclay of Calcots, Elgin. Had issue. (See page 273.)

William Barclay, Minister of Auldearn. Had issue. (See page 273.)

George Barclay, M., M.D., of Edinbur (See page 273.)

Bethia Barclay.

Barbara Barclay, t with Alexander. Married John Pete

Charles Alexander Barclay of Aberdour House. Heir-male of Towie (XXVIII). Born 1825. Died 1902. [See Pedigree VIII.] = Margaret, daughter of Thomas Martin of Liverpool.

The Rev. Peter Barclay, Minister of St. Paul's, Port Napier, New Zealand. Born 1827. Died April, 1906. = Mary, daughter of William Gordon of Montrose. She died 1865.

James John Barclay, H.E.I.C. Served in the Mutiny. At the relief of Lucknow. Died *s.p.* 1874.

William Barcl Merchant in Liverpool. 4 sons, 5 daughter

Theodore Charles Barclay. Born July, 1860. Married 1891. Died Nov. 1899. = Elizabeth Mary, daughter of Alexander Fraser, of Inverness.

Jane Mackay Gordon Barclay.

Rachel Mary Barclay, LL.B., M.D., Dipl.Psych.

Captain Walter Patrick Barclay, The Black Watch. Born August 22nd, 1899. Presumptive heir-male of Towie.

Yvonne Barclay. Married T. J. Golding of Gatooma, S. Rhodesia.

Iseult Barclay. Married A. Swinton-Paterson, H.M. Consular Service.

Aileen Barclay. Died young.

Doris Barclay.

Mr. George Barclay died on November 24th, 1910, in the first half of his ninety-first year.

7. Bethia, who died in infancy.
8. Barbara (twin with Alexander), married in 1812 John Peter, factor to the Earl of Kintore. Their two elder sons, the Rev. George Peter of Kemney and Mr. John Peter, compiled a very valuable pedigree of the Barclays of Towie in 1877.

Mr. Charles Barclay of Knockleith and Templand was a notable farmer and greatly improved the estates. Later, together with his eldest son James, he appears to have speculated in wheat, and at the time of the opening of the ports to foreign wheat in 1814 he became nearly ruined and was forced to sell Templand.

JAMES BARCLAY

James Barclay of Knockleith was baptized November 21st, 1782, and educated at Marischal College (1796-1800). He was a voluminous writer on historical, antiquarian and agricultural subjects. He contributed to the *Aberdeen Journal* articles numerous and varied in character.

On April 28th, 1823, he married his first cousin Mary Ann, a daughter of the Rev. Peter Barclay, D.D., minister of Kettle. By her he had the following issue :—

1. Charles Alexander Barclay, who became heir-male of Towie. Of him afterwards.
2. The Rev. Peter Barclay, licensed as a minister of the Free Church, and ordained in 1858 as minister of St. Paul's, Port Napier, New Zealand.

   He married Mary, a daughter of William Gordon of Montrose, and had one son, Theodore Charles, and two daughters.

   The Rev. Peter Barclay died in Edinburgh, April 28th, 1906, aged 78 years, and was buried at Auchterless.
3. James John, who entered the H.E.I.C. and served in the Mutiny. He was present at the relief of Lucknow and was severely wounded. Captain Barclay died in 1874, unmarried.
4. William, who became a merchant in Liverpool.

Mr. James Barclay of Knockleith had in all fourteen children. Several sons died in infancy. There were four daughters.

Mr. James Barclay died March 18th, 1856, and was succeeded by his son, Charles Alexander Barclay.

CHARLES ALEXANDER BARCLAY

Heir-male of Towie XXVIII.

Charles Alexander Barclay of Aberdour House was born October 18th, 1825, and educated at Marischal College.

On the death of his kinsman Lieut.-Colonel Peter Barclay, in 1872, he succeeded him as heir-male of the house of Towie.

For several years he was in business in Liverpool, but in 1859 he became factor to Captain Dingwall Fordyce, on the extensive estates of Brucklay and Culsh, which position he held for 43 years.

He married June 17th, 1857, Margaret, daughter of Thomas Martin of Liverpool.

On January 20th, 1897, he was declared heir-male of the ancient family of Barclay of Towie, by recognition of the Lord Lyon, and allowed the right to the old arms of the family with supporters.

By his wife, Margaret, he had the following issue :—

1. Charles James de Tollie Barclay, his heir.
2. Leslie Caroline Mary Barclay, born 1858.
3. Margaret Lilian Martin, born 1861.
4. May Arnott, born 1859, and died, unmarried, November 9th, 1912.

Mr. Charles Alexander Barclay died at Edzell, August 9th, 1902. He was succeeded as heir-male of Towie by his son.

CHARLES JAMES DE TOLLIE BARCLAY

Heir-male of Towie XXIX.

Charles James de Tollie Barclay was born December 28th, 1863. Now living in California.

He married October 12th, 1897, Elizabeth Thompson Bruce, daughter of the Rev. Thomas Bruce, of Rhynie, Aberdeenshire, and has issue :—

1. Theodore Bruce de Tollie Barclay, born October 26th, 1899.
2. Margaret Mary Martin Barclay.
3. Elizabeth Caroline Martin Barclay.

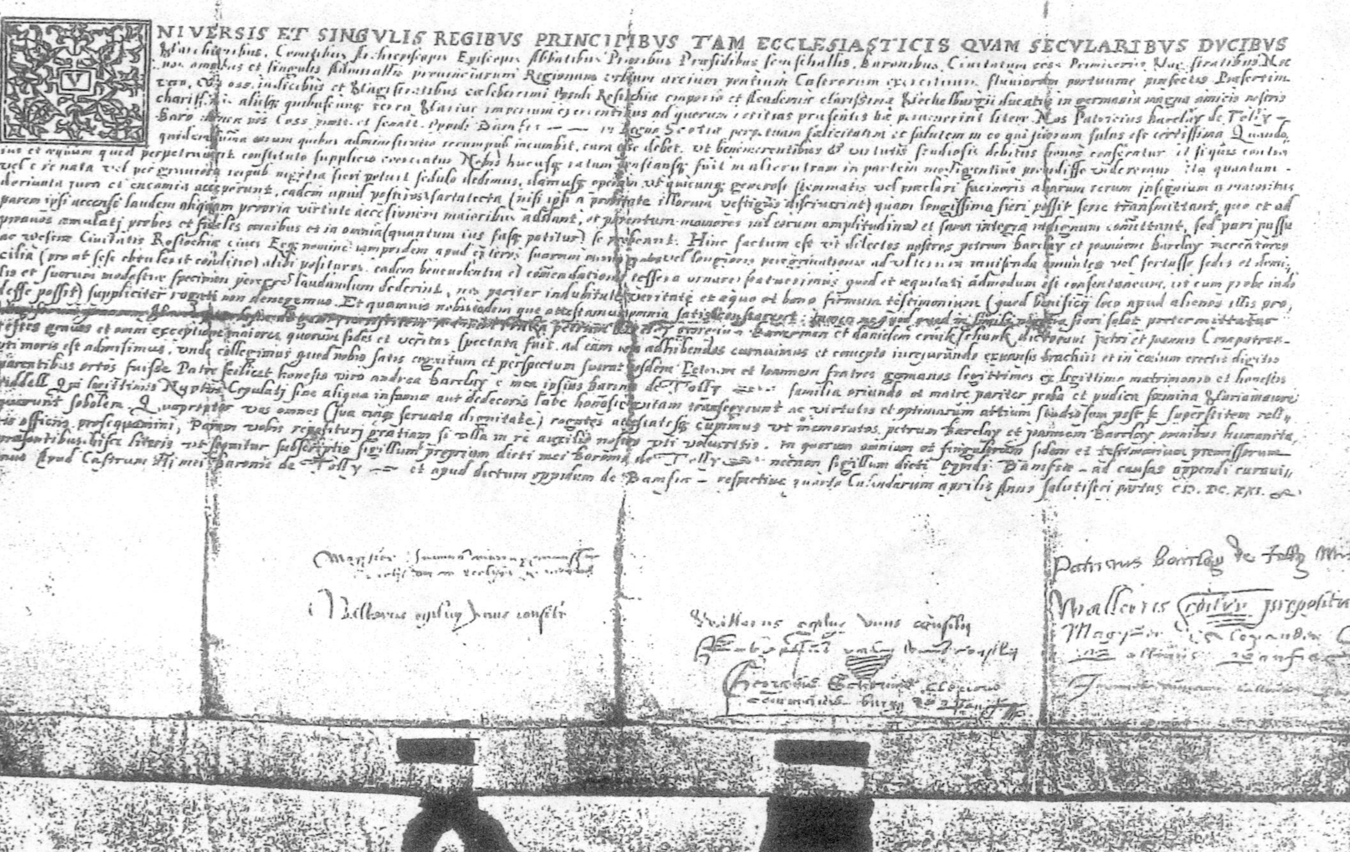

UNIVERSIS ET SINGULIS REGIBUS PRINCIPIBUS TAM ECCLESIASTICIS QUAM SECULARIBUS DUCIBUS Marchionibus, Comitibus Archiepiscopis Episcopis Abbatibus Prioribus Praesidibus Senescallis, Baronibus, Civitatum coss Primicerii [illegible] stratibus Nec non omnibus et singulis Admirallis provinciarum Regionum [illegible] arcium pontium Caeterorum exercituum fluviorum portuumque praefectis Praesertim vero [illegible] oss. iudicibus et Magistratibus celeberrimi oppidi Rostochiae emporio et Academia clarissima Meckelburgii ducatus in germania magna amicis nostris charissimis aliisque quibuscunque vero [illegible] imperium exercentibus ad quorum notitiam praesentes hae pervenerint literae. Nos Patricius barclay de Tolly Baro [illegible] Coss. [illegible] et senatu oppidi Bamfis in Regno Scotiae perpetuam felicitatem et salutem in eo qui verorum salus est certissima Quando quidem [illegible] quibus administratio reipub. incumbit, cura esse debet. ut benemerentibus et virtutis studiosis debitus honos conservetur et siquis contra ius et aequum quod perpetraverit constituto supplicio coerceatur Nobis hucusque ratum constansque fuit in alterutram in partem negligentiae [illegible] videremur ita quantum vel e re nata vel per gravioris reipub. negotia fieri potuit sedulo dedimus, damusque operam ut quicunque generosi stemmatis vel praeclari facinoris aliarum rerum insignium a maioribus derivata iura et encomia acceperunt, eadem apud posteros sarta tecta (nisi ipsi a probitate illorum vestigiis discrucerint) quam longissima fieri possit serie transmittant, quo et ad parem ipsi accensi laudem aliquam propria virtute accessionem maioribus addant, et parentum manores vel eorum amplitudinem et famam integram [illegible] conservant, sed pari passu pravos aemulati probes et fideles omnibus et in omnia (quantum ius fasque patitur) se praebeant. Hinc factum est ut dilectos nostros petrum barclay et joannem barclay mercatores ac vestrae Civitatis Rostochiae cives [illegible] nomine iampridem apud exteros [illegible] longioris peregrinationis ad ulteriora [illegible] vel fortasse sedis et domicilia (prout sese obtulerit conditio) alibi posituros. eadem benevolentia et commendationis tessera ornare statueremus quod et aequitati admodum est consentaneum, ut cum probe inde sio et suorum modestiae specimen [illegible] laudandum dederint, nos pariter indubitatae veritatis ex aequo et bono firmum testimonium (quod beneficii loco apud alienos illis pro desse possit) suppliciter rogati non denegemus. Et quamvis nobis eadem quae attestamur omnia satis constarent: [illegible] ne quid quod in similibus [illegible] fieri solet praetermittatur [illegible] petrum barclay [illegible] et danielem cruikschank [illegible] petri et joannis [illegible] testes graves et omni exceptione maiores quorum fides et veritas spectata fuit. ad eam [illegible] adhibendas [illegible] et concepto iureiurando expansis brachiis et in caelum erectis digitis uti moris est admisimus. unde collegimus quod nobis satis cognitum et perspectum fuerat eosdem Petrum et Ioannem fratres germanos legitimos ex legitimo matrimonio et honestis parentibus ortos fuisse Patre scilicet honesto viro andrea barclay e mea ipsius barone de Tolly [illegible] familia oriundo et matre pariter proba et pudica foemina [illegible] riddell Qui legitimis Nuptiis Copulati sine aliqua infamiae aut dedecoris labe honestam vitam transegerunt ac virtutis et optimarum artium studiosam post se superstitem reliquerunt sobolem. Quapropter vos omnes (sua cuique servata dignitate) rogatos atque obsecratos cupimus ut memoratos petrum barclay et joannem barclay omnibus humanitatis officiis prosequamini, Parem vobis repositur gratiam si ulla in re auxilio nostro uti volueritis. In quorum omnium et singulorum fidem et testimonium praemissorum praesentibus hisce literis ut sequitur subscriptis sigillum proprium dicti mei Baronis de Tolly nec non sigillum dicti oppidi Bamfiae ad causas appendi curavimus Apud Castrum [illegible] mei Baronis de Tolly et apud dictum oppidum de Bamfia respective quarto Calendarum aprilis Anno salutiferi partus CIↃ.IↃC.XXI.

Magister [illegible]

Willelmus ogilvy [illegible] consul

Willelmus ogilvy [illegible]

[illegible]

[illegible]

Patricius barclay de Tolly Miles

[illegible]

[illegible]

[illegible]

THE RUSSIAN BARCLAYS DE TOLLY

In the year 1621, as we have seen, Sir Patrick Barclay, Baron of Towie (Towie XVII), signed a letter of safe conduct in favour of Peter and John Barclay, "merchants in the town of Banff," who were desirous of settling in the town of Rostock in Livonia. It is stated in the letter that it was "very well known . . . that Peter and John are legitimate full brothers, sprung from a legitimate marriage and honest parents, the father forsooth being an honest man, named Andrew Barclay, sprung from the same family as the present Baron of Tollie, and the mother, Maria, born a Miss Riddell, being equally good and chaste, these . . . have spent their lives honestly and left behind them a living offspring zealous of the best practices of virtue." RUSSIAN BARCLAYS.

The original letter of safe conduct, with the seals still attached, is in existence in Riga in the possession of the heirs of Baron Edward Sass, whose wife was a Barclay directly descended from the same Rostock branch of the Barclays of Towie. It is written in Latin and is a most curious and interesting document. A translation has already been given in this Part, on pages 241–243.

From the above it is clear that Peter and John went to Rostock in Livonia in 1621, and that they were sons of Andrew Barclay and his wife Maria Riddell, who were both dead at this date. We know also from the letter that they were of the Towie line. RUSSIAN BARCLAYS. Peter I.

Peter and John Barclay duly arrived in Rostock in the year 1621, and became silk merchants in that city.

Peter became the founder of the branch that is usually called the Russian Barclays, the most notable of whom was Field-Marshal Michael Andrew, Prince Barclay de Tolly.

John moved to Norway, where he founded a branch of the family which became extinct in the year 1907.

From the records in Rostock we find that both Peter and John became burghers in that city.

Peter married Angela von Vöhrden, daughter of Johann von Vöhrden of Rostock, which is clearly proved by the

PEDIGREE XI.

The Russian Barclays de Tolly

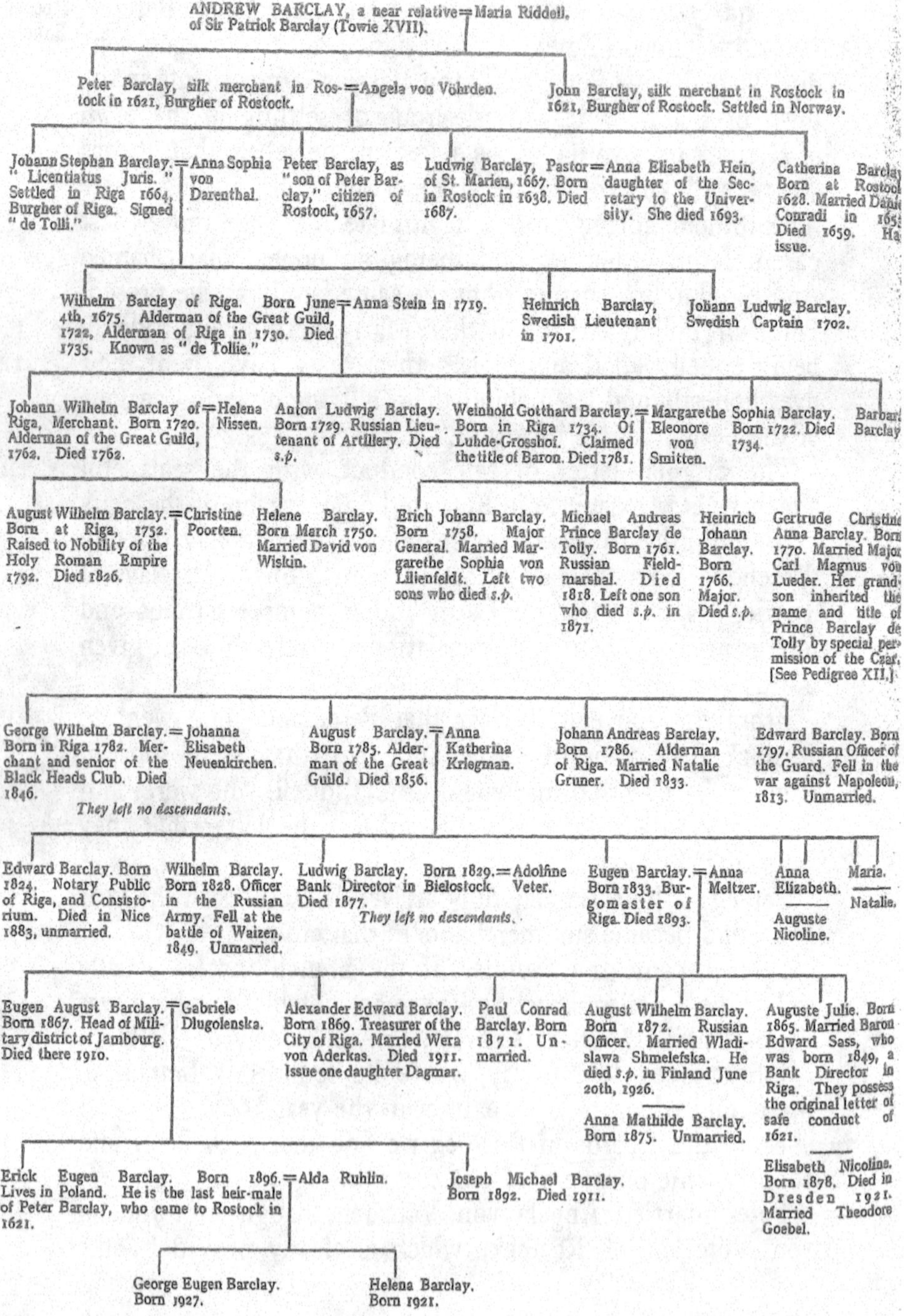

ANDREW BARCLAY, a near relative of Sir Patrick Barclay (Towie XVII). = Maria Riddell.

Peter Barclay, silk merchant in Rostock in 1621, Burgher of Rostock. = Angela von Vöhrden.

John Barclay, silk merchant in Rostock in 1621, Burgher of Rostock. Settled in Norway.

Johann Stephan Barclay. "Licentiatus Juris." Settled in Riga 1664, Burgher of Riga. Signed "de Tolli." = Anna Sophia von Darenthal.

Peter Barclay, as "son of Peter Barclay," citizen of Rostock, 1657.

Ludwig Barclay, Pastor of St. Marien, 1667. Born in Rostock in 1638. Died 1687. = Anna Elisabeth Hein, daughter of the Secretary to the University. She died 1693.

Catherina Barclay. Born at Rostock 1628. Married Daniel Conradi in 1655. Died 1659. Had issue.

Wilhelm Barclay of Riga. Born June 4th, 1675. Alderman of the Great Guild, 1722, Alderman of Riga in 1730. Died 1735. Known as "de Tollie." = Anna Stein in 1719.

Heinrich Barclay, Swedish Lieutenant in 1701.

Johann Ludwig Barclay. Swedish Captain 1702.

Johann Wilhelm Barclay of Riga, Merchant. Born 1720. Alderman of the Great Guild, 1762. Died 1762. = Helena Nissen.

Anton Ludwig Barclay. Born 1729. Russian Lieutenant of Artillery. Died *s.p.*

Weinhold Gotthard Barclay. Born in Riga 1734. Of Luhde-Grosshof. Claimed the title of Baron. Died 1781. = Margarethe Eleonore von Smitten.

Sophia Barclay. Born 1722. Died 1734.

Barbara Barclay.

August Wilhelm Barclay. Born at Riga, 1752. Raised to Nobility of the Holy Roman Empire 1792. Died 1826. = Christine Poorten.

Helene Barclay. Born March 1750. Married David von Wiskin.

Erich Johann Barclay. Born 1758. Major General. Married Margarethe Sophia von Lilienfeldt. Left two sons who died *s.p.*

Michael Andreas Prince Barclay de Tolly. Born 1761. Russian Field-marshal. Died 1818. Left one son who died *s.p.* in 1871.

Heinrich Johann Barclay. Born 1766. Major. Died *s.p.*

Gertrude Christine Anna Barclay. Born 1770. Married Major Carl Magnus von Lueder. Her grandson inherited the name and title of Prince Barclay de Tolly by special permission of the Czar. [See Pedigree XII.]

George Wilhelm Barclay. Born in Riga 1782. Merchant and senior of the Black Heads Club. Died 1846. = Johanna Elisabeth Neuenkirchen.
They left no descendants.

August Barclay. Born 1785. Alderman of the Great Guild. Died 1856. = Anna Katherina Kriegman.

Johann Andreas Barclay. Born 1786. Alderman of Riga. Married Natalie Gruner. Died 1833.

Edward Barclay. Born 1797. Russian Officer of the Guard. Fell in the war against Napoleon, 1813. Unmarried.

Edward Barclay. Born 1824. Notary Public of Riga, and Consistorium. Died in Nice 1883, unmarried.

Wilhelm Barclay. Born 1828. Officer in the Russian Army. Fell at the battle of Waizen, 1849. Unmarried.

Ludwig Barclay. Born 1829. Bank Director in Bielostock. Died 1877. = Adolfine Veter.
They left no descendants.

Eugen Barclay. Born 1833. Burgomaster of Riga. Died 1893. = Anna Meltzer.

Anna Elizabeth.

Auguste Nicoline.

Maria.

Natalie.

Eugen August Barclay. Born 1867. Head of Military district of Jambourg. Died there 1910. = Gabriele Dlugolenska.

Alexander Edward Barclay. Born 1869. Treasurer of the City of Riga. Married Wera von Aderkas. Died 1911. Issue one daughter Dagmar.

Paul Conrad Barclay. Born 1871. Unmarried.

August Wilhelm Barclay. Born 1872. Russian Officer. Married Wladislawa Shmelefska. He died *s.p.* in Finland June 20th, 1926.

Anna Mathilde Barclay. Born 1875. Unmarried.

Auguste Julie. Born 1865. Married Baron Edward Sass, who was born 1849, a Bank Director in Riga. They possess the original letter of safe conduct of 1621.

Elisabeth Nicoline. Born 1878. Died in Dresden 1921. Married Theodore Goebel.

Erick Eugen Barclay. Born 1896. Lives in Poland. He is the last heir-male of Peter Barclay, who came to Rostock in 1621. = Alda Ruhlin.

Joseph Michael Barclay. Born 1892. Died 1911.

George Eugen Barclay. Born 1927.

Helena Barclay. Born 1921.

funeral sermon of his daughter Catherina Conradi, a copy of which is still in existence. RUSSIAN BARCLAYS. Peter I.

Peter Barclay and his wife Angela had several children, of whom the following are known to us :—

1. Johann Stephan Barclay, of whom later. He signed "Johann Barclay de Tolli."
2. Peter Barclay, who as "Peter, son of Peter Barclay," became a citizen of Rostock in the year 1657.
3. Ludwig Barclay, who was born in Rostock in 1638, and is clearly recorded there as son of the merchant Peter Barclay and of Angela von Vöhrden of Rostock.

   He became a deacon in 1667 and archdeacon in 1670, and was Pastor of St. Marien's until his death.

   He married Anna Elisabeth Hein, daughter of the secretary to the University of Rostock.

   Elisabeth Barclay, *née* Hein, died in 1693 and was buried on March 21st.

   Ludwig Barclay died in 1687 and left two daughters.

   This is from the book *Das Etwas von gelehrten Rostocker Sachen* (Something about learned Rostock matters), Volume I, 1737, page 634, and Volume IV, page 405.
4. Catherina Barclay, born at Rostock June 14th, 1628. In 1653 she married Daniel Conradi, Doctor of Law.

   She died August 6th, 1659. The exhortation given by the Rector of the University of Rostock, Johannes Georgius Dorscheus, Professor of Theology, is still preserved in the Town Hall archives in Rostock among the Barclay documents. It is of considerable genealogical interest and runs as follows :—

   "Given at the funeral service of the most noble and most excellent matron CATHARINA BARCLAY, the wife of the most distinguished in legal matters and causes, etc., Dr. DANIEL CONRADI, who died piously in the Lord Jesus on the sixth day of August in the year of Christ 1659, which the most sorrowful husband to-day at one o'clock, in the afternoon, tenth August, prepares in the church of St. Mary. . . ."

   As will be seen later, Catherina Conradi died in childbirth, and the Rector draws a parallel between her death and that of Rachel, wife of the Patriarch Jacob, followed by much comfort and advice to the bereaved husband.

   He continues : "Let us according to received practices go back to the birthplace and origin of the pious matron

RUSSIAN BARCLAYS. Peter I.

recently deceased. It is our duty to record those recollections which have been communicated to us.

"She first saw the light in this town of Rostock, in the parish of the Virgin Mary, in the year of our Lord one thousand six hundred and twenty-eight, on the 14th of June, that is thirty and one years ago. It was in the first terribly sorrowful years when Germany had embraced in those parts the pure Gospel of Jesus Christ. . . . Our Dame grew up under the discipline and example of her father's most prosperous family. . . . Moreover she persevered with exquisite industry in those things that were an ornament to her sex. She owed all these things to the piety and industry of her most noble and honourable parents, who now a blissful eternity embraces. As her parent she had the most noble and prudent man PETER BARCLAY, a most honourable citizen amongst us. He was born in Scotland, of the ancient and most illustrious family, the Barons of Barclay. She had a most noble mother, the matron Angela von Vöhrden.

"She married Doctor Daniel Conradi in 1653, and she delighted her husband with two sons, of whom the elder passed away to better things. After him another and a little daughter.

"On sixth August, on the birth of a little son, set free by Him who gave the happiness to give birth, to heaven immediately she was called to her nobler part."

Previous to the arrival of Peter and John Barclay there was living in the town of Rostock another family of Barclay, of whom mention is made in the records of that city. They were certainly of Scottish origin, and it is possible that their residence there had some connection with the migration of Peter and John.

The Rostock Town Hall archives speak of a Paul Barchley who was citizen there and died in 1591. His widow Catherina, with her sons, Heinrich, Paul and Joachim, transferred the brewery in the Altstadt (Old town) to another son, Steffen, on September 11th, 1591. Steffen's widow Tilsche Schmiedes, on December 31st, 1603, had the said brewery transferred, with the consent of her brothers-in-law, as a wedding gift to her subsequent husband, Johann Mass, later a Senator. On January 18th, 1620, her sons handed over their interest in the brewery to their stepfather, Johann Mass. Steffen appears from the baptismal register at the church of St. Jacobi to have had seven children, of whom Johann Heinrich became a citizen of Lübeck in 1727 and his descendants are to be found in Hamburg and in London.

RUSSIAN BARCLAYS. Peter I.

For most of the early history of the Barclays of Livonia we are indebted to Herr Oberst Lieutenant Max von Falkenhayn, Provincial Adviser to the Mecklenburg Head Office of "Records of Families of Lower Saxony," who has made most careful researches among the records at Rostock and elsewhere.

JOHANN STEPHAN BARCLAY

RUSSIAN BARCLAYS. Johann Stephan II.

Johann Stephan Barclay was the eldest son of Peter Barclay and succeeded him as heir of the line of the Barclays of Rostock.

He became "Licentiatus Juris," and then settled in Riga, where he was admitted to the Bar in 1664. He became a burgher of Riga in August of the same year. We find him fiscal of the city of Riga on May 20th, 1663, and signing "Johann Barclay de Tolli." On August 12th, 1678, he used the title "dominus."

Johann Stephan married Anna Sophia von Darenthal, daughter of Stephan Darenthal, lawyer of Riga. They had issue three sons:—

1. Heinrich Barclay, Swedish lieutenant in 1701.
2. Johann Ludwig, Swedish captain 1702.
3. Wilhelm Barclay, succeeded him.

WILHELM BARCLAY

RUSSIAN BARCLAYS. Wilhelm III.

Wilhelm Barclay was born June 4th, 1675. On November 5th, 1719, he was accepted as apprentice-merchant burgher of the city of Riga, and on February 5th, 1722, as an alderman of the Great Guild. On September 27th, 1730, he was appointed Alderman of the city of Riga.

William Barclay bought the estates of Luggenois and Tolkenhoff in the parish of Loudon in Livonia.

Russian Barclays. Wilhelm III.

He died May 4th, 1735, and at the time of his death he was Quartermaster of the city of Riga. He was known as "Wilhelm Barclay de Tollie."

He married Anna Stein on September 3rd, 1719, daughter of Anton Stein, Alderman of the Great Guild. She was the widow of Claus Eggero, also Alderman of the Great Guild.

Wilhelm Barclay's coat of arms, with inscription, hangs in the church of St. Peter in Riga.

By his wife Anna he had issue five children :—

1. Johann Wilhelm Barclay, born 1720, of whom later.
2. Sophia Barclay, born 1722, died 1734.
3. Barbara Elisabeth Barclay, born 1724, married Michael Fabian.
4. Anton Ludwig Barclay, born 1729, Russian lieutenant of artillery. Died unmarried.
5. Weinhold Gotthard Barclay, born in Riga, April 25th, 1734, who was the father of Field-Marshal Prince Barclay de Tolly.

It is not necessary to give any further details of the descendants of the direct male line of the Barclays of Livonia, as they will be found fully described in Pedigree XI, which shows six generations from Johann Wilhelm Barclay (IV), the eldest son of Wilhelm Barclay of Riga and his wife Anna Stein. The family is now settled in Poland and is represented to-day by Erick Eugen Barclay, who was born in 1896. He married Alda Ruhlin. They have issue one son, George Eugen Barclay, born 1927, and a daughter, Helena, born in 1921.

The only Barclays of the Livonian line living to-day, so far as can be traced, are Erick Eugen Barclay and his family, together with his uncle Paul Conrad Barclay and his aunt Anna Mathilde Barclay.

WEINHOLD GOTTHARD BARCLAY

Russian Barclays. Weinhold Gotthard IVc.

Weinhold Gotthard Barclay was the third son of Wilhelm Barclay. He was born April 25th, 1734, in Riga. At one time he was a lieutenant in the Russian army.

He was leaseholder of the estate of Luhde-Grosshof.

In December, 1753, Weinhold Gotthard Barclay notified the Livonian Body of Knights that he and his brother, First Lieutenant Anton Ludwig Barclay (IVB), would henceforth make use of the baronial title which was their right. They founded this on a document dated April 4th, 1621, of which they enclosed a copy, and requested to be received into the Livonian Body of Knights.

RUSSIAN BARCLAYS. Weinhold Gotthard IVC.

It is evident that the document referred to was the letter of safe conduct given to Peter and John by Sir Patrick Barclay (Towie XVII) and the Town Council of Banff when they left that city for Rostock in 1621.

Weinhold Gotthard married Margarethe Eleonore von Smitten, heiress of the estates of Buckhoff, in Livonia. She was the daughter of Erich Johann von Smitten, Swedish captain, and died May 13th, 1771.

Weinhold Gotthard died at Luhde-Grosshof, April 30th, 1781, and by his wife Margarethe left issue three sons and one daughter :—

1. Erich Johann, born 1758. He is mentioned in the church register as " Baron Barclay de Tollie."

   He was a Russian major-general and was blinded in 1819.

   He married Margarethe Sophia von Lilienfeldt, by whom he had two sons : Andreas Otto Heinrich Barclay, who was born July 3rd, 1788, and who became a Finnish baron and also an ambassador ; and George, who died young. Andreas Otto married —— von der Hoven, and died in Dresden in 1851. We have not been able to trace that he had any descendants, and as no son of his inherited the title of Prince Barclay de Tolly, on the death of Prince Ernst Magnus, his cousin, he probably died without issue.
2. Michael Andreas, Prince Barclay de Tolly, born December 16th, 1761, in Luhde-Grosshof in Livonia. An account of his life will be given later.
3. Heinrich Johann Barclay, born July 30th, 1766. He became a major in the Russian army and died unmarried.
4. Gertrude Christine Anna Barclay, born January 6th, 1770.

   She married Major Carl Magnus von Lueder, leaseholder of Kollist.

   On the death of her nephew, Ernst Magnus Prince

RUSSIAN BARCLAYS. Weinhold Gotthard IVc.

Barclay de Tolly, the only son of her brother the Field-Marshal, without male issue, the Czar, Alexander II, on June 7th, 1872, transferred the name and title of "Prince Barclay de Tolly" to her grandson, Alexander Magnus Friedrich von Weymarn. A pedigree of this family will be given later (Pedigree XII).

FIELD-MARSHAL PRINCE BARCLAY DE TOLLY

RUSSIAN BARCLAYS. Michael Andreas. Vth generation.

Michael Andreas, Prince Barclay de Tolly, the second son of Weinhold Gotthard Barclay, was born at Luhde-Grosshof, in Livonia, December 16th, 1761.

He entered the Russian army when he was a very young man, and is said to have commenced his military career as a sergeant of cuirassiers. In 1788-89 he served against the Turks and in the Polish war. He fought in Sweden in 1790, and again in Poland in 1792 and 1794. He became colonel in 1798 and major-general in 1799. In the year 1806 we find him in command of one of the divisions of the Russian army sent to the assistance of Prussia against the French. Here he highly distinguished himself, when in command of Benningsen's advance guard, defeating the French in the bloody battles of Wagram and Eylau, in the latter of which he had his horse shot under him and was severely wounded, losing an arm. This disabled him from taking the field again during the remainder of the disastrous campaign. This being the first time that the French had received a check for a very long period, General Barclay became a great favourite with the Czar Alexander, who made him lieutenant-general.

In 1808 he commanded against the Swedes in Finland, and in 1809, by a rapid and daring march over the frozen Gulf of Bothnia, he surprised and seized Umea.

In 1810 he was made Minister of War, and retained the post until 1813.

In 1812 Barclay was given command of the armies operating against Napoleon. There was very great opposition to a Scottish commander-in-chief by the old Russian nobility, but his advice was taken on all occasions.

FIELD-MARSHAL MICHAEL ANDREAS,
PRINCE BARCLAY DE TOLLY

From the portrait by George Dar in the Winter Palace at Petrograd

His plan of campaign, as is well known, was to drive off the cattle, burn the corn, remove the people and leave the country desolate through which the French troops were to pass, and to avoid compromising the safety of the empire to the issue of a pitched battle. He assured the Czar that if he would allow him to follow this mode of warfare, he would answer with his head for giving a good account of the apparently irresistible army which Napoleon had brought against him. In pursuance of this plan thus laid down he allowed the army to pass the Vistula without opposition, retreating slowly before them in good order until he came to Smolensk.

RUSSIAN BARCLAYS. Michael Andreas. Vth generation.

The position here being strong, the city considered by the Russians as a holy city, and, above all, it being important to gain time, he made a stand, compelling the French to lose time in concentrating their army and bringing up their artillery to attack a strongly fortified position. After a day's hard fighting and an enormous loss of life to the assailants, he repulsed them at every point.

But it was no part of Barclay's plan to decide the fate of the Russian Empire there ; he continued his retreat next day, to the great disappointment of the Russian nobility, who wished the post maintained to the last extremity, and it was in vain for the commander-in-chief to argue that the flanking divisions of the French army were advancing to turn them and would soon be in his rear and frustrate his plan.

So high did the discussions run that the Czar found it necessary to supersede him and give Kutusoff, an aboriginal Russian, the command. He continued the retreat to Borodino, where he fought a bloody and disastrous battle, at which Michael Barclay was present in a subordinate position, but left the army soon afterwards. Alexander, who had never lost confidence in him, rewarded him with the Order of Maria Theresa, and he was created a Count of the Holy Roman Empire, having practically broken the great army of Napoleon, which never recovered from the tragic retreat from Moscow. In 1813 he was re-employed in the field, and took part in the campaign in Germany. After the battle of Bautzen he was

PEDIGREE XII.

The Descent of Prince Barclay de Tolly-Weymarn

GERTRUDE CHRISTINE ANNA BARCLAY, daughter of Weinhold Gotthard Barclay, sister of first Prince Barclay. Born November 6th, 1770. Died March 21st, 1865. = Major Carl Magnus von Lueder, leaseholder of Kollist. Born 1775. Died January 4th, 1857.

Christine Auguste von Lueder, Lady-in-Waiting to the Empress. She was the adopted daughter of her uncle Prince Barclay de Tolly, and was with him when he died, 1818. Born June 9th, 1803. Died in St. Petersburg, October 30th, 1888. = Peter William von Weymarn, General Adjutant, Chief of Staff of the Guards. Born January 14th, 1793. Died May 10th, 1846.

Alexander Magnus Friedrich, Prince Barclay de Tolly-Weymarn Born December 22nd, 1824. Died May 8th, 1905, in Dresden. On June 7th, 1872, he assumed by Imperial permission the name and title of Prince Barclay de Tolly. In 1888 he left Russia, for religious reasons, and went to Dresden. = Baroness Maria von Zeddeler, Lady-in-Waiting to the Empress of Russia. Born January 25th, 1825. Died December 19th, 1868. Daughter of General Louis von Zeddeler.

Constantine von Weymarn. 1829–1881. Married (1) Constance von Helfreich; (2) Nelly von Baranon. Had issue.

William von Weymarn. 1832–1913. Married (1) Augusta Ahrens; (2) Maria Weymarn. Had issue.

Marie Eva von Weym
Born June 2nd, 1842.
in Dresden October
1919. Married Baron F
rich Alexander Emil
Hoyningen Huene.

Nicolas von Weymarn. Born March 30th, 1853. Died June 10th, 1867.

Louis von Weymarn. Born January 21st, 1859, in St. Petersburg. Died December 16th, 1903. = Catherina Czernisheff, a Russian. She died in Paris in 1926.

Alexandrine Olga Augusta von Weymarn (Ada). Born July 4th, 1854. = Alexis von k
senstjerna, Li
Colonel on Ge
Staff.

Nicolas Prince Barclay de Tolly-Weymarn. Born 1892. A Russian officer. Fled to Harbin after the Revolution.

Catharina von Weymarn. Born 1887. Married — Sishkoff, a Russian. Living at Richmond, Surrey.

Mira von Weymarn. Born 1888. Married Count Armfelt, Nobility of Finland. Living in New York.

reinstated as commander-in-chief of the Russian forces, and in this capacity he served at Dresden, Kulm and Leipzig. He took part in the invasion of France in 1814, and at Paris received the baton of a field-marshal. In 1815 he was again commander-in-chief of the Russian army which invaded France, and was made a prince at the close of the war. He then returned to St. Petersburg, where the Emperor gave him a most distinguished reception, and appointed a great review to be held in the honour of Michael, Prince Barclay de Tolly.

RUSSIAN BARCLAYS. Michael Andreas. Vth generation.

Encyclopædia Britannica, Vol. iii. p. 395.

King George III made him a G.C.B., and he came to London to receive it. It is stated that when in London he called upon Colonel Robert Barclay (Towie XXVB) and told him in course of conversation that he was perfectly acquainted with his descent from the Barclays of Towie in Scotland, but that was the extent of his knowledge. The Prince excused himself further by remarking "that having entered the army very early in life, he had had little leisure since to perfect his education, which he regretted to say had been very far from complete, or to acquire that knowledge of foreign countries or his remote ancestors which otherwise he would have had pleasure in investigating. He should take care that his son should not have that to complain of." At that time the castle and land of Towie were for sale, and he was desired to purchase it, but he felt that as all his interests were in Russia he could not entertain the idea.

Michael Andreas, Prince Barclay de Tolly, married Helene von Smitten, who was, no doubt, his cousin, as his father, Weinhold Barclay, had married a lady of the same name. They had issue an only son, Ernst Magnus.

By 1818 Prince Barclay's health was shattered, and he undertook a voyage and a journey to see what change would do for him, and he died near Insterburg, in Prussia, May 25th, 1818. He treated his niece, Christine von Lueder, his sister Gertrude's child, as his adopted daughter; she accompanied him on his last journey and was with him when he died.

Universal Dictionary of Biography.

He was succeeded by his son, Ernst Magnus Barclay.

RUSSIAN BARCLAYS.

ERNST MAGNUS BARCLAY

Ernst Magnus, second Prince Barclay de Tolly, was born July 10th, 1798. He was the owner of the estate of Stolben in Livonia, which had been given to his father by the Czar Alexander I.

He was a colonel in the Russian army and a wing adjutant. He was also A.D.C. to the Czar Nicholas I.

He married, first, Baroness von Campenhausen, and, secondly, Alexandrine von Cramer, but left no issue.

He died in Mitau, October 31st, 1871. The name and title Prince Barclay de Tolly was extended by an Imperial ukase of December 1859 at his request to the husband of his aunt Gertrude Christine Anna von Lueder, with the right to transmit it to her descendants of either sex.

After his death the Czar Alexander II, on June 7th, 1872, transferred the title and name of " Prince Barclay de Tolly " to his cousin, Alexander Magnus Friedrich von Weymarn. (See Pedigree XII.)

COLLAIRNIE TOWER

Reproduced from "Castles and Mansions in Fife and Kinross," by A. H. Millar, F.S.A.Scot.

The Collairnie Line

THE CASTLE OF COLLAIRNIE

The following account is taken from *The Castles and Mansions of Fife and Kinross*, by A. H. Millar, F.S.A. COLLAIRNIE CASTLE.

The Tower of Collairnie is in the parish of Dunbog, and stands about seven miles north-west of Cupar.

Its situation forbids the supposition that its original builders intended it as a place of great strength, for it stands on a level plateau close beside the main road, presenting none of those difficulties of access which are essential to the formation of an impregnable fortress.

Though the existing remains appear to belong to a peaceful period, there is proof of the existence of a castle in this locality in the fourteenth century. No baron in these early times would have erected his principal fortalice in the situation occupied by Collairnie Tower, and it is evident, therefore, that the original building was not the chief seat of the family whose name is associated with the Tower for nearly five centuries. An examination of the documents connected with the history of the Barclays of Collairnie confirms this supposition, as we shall have occasion to show.

The present appearance of Collairnie Tower is not very dignified. The only remaining portion of what has evidently been a very extensive castle is the square keep or tower, which once formed the main entrance to the building. The courtyard and the quadrangular structure which surrounded it have disappeared, and their places have been usurped by a series of barns and byres, which are much more useful than ornamental. The picturesque corner turrets and quaint dormer windows have been reduced to meanness or abolished entirely. Utility has further commanded that the decorated halls, within which many historical personages have been entertained, should be reserved in these days as a storehouse for agricultural implements and a refuge for discarded tools. Yet there are still remaining some few traces of the departed glory of Collairnie

COLLAIRNIE CASTLE.

to be detected by careful examination, both in its external and internal arrangements.

The estate of Collairnie has borne that name from a very early period. It appears in the Registrum Vetus Aberbrothoc under date 1249 and in a very peculiar relationship. When the Abbey of St. Thomas the Martyr was founded at Arbroath the parish of Dunbog had been placed under its spiritual supervision, and the teind sheaves from the farms in this parish were treated as a proprietary interest even in the seventeenth century. The entry in the register is in a taxation, showing what sums were due to the monks of Arbroath from the numerous vicarages under their charge, and it records that the vicar of Dunbog (Dunbuig) has all the altarages and whatsoever pertained to the monastery of Arbroath, and paid twenty shillings to the Episcopate. The names of the towns in Dunbog parish at this time were "Culerny, Johnstoun and Balmadid," but no clue is given to the names of the proprietors, nor do we find any family associated with the estate for a hundred years later.

The first name linked with Collairnie is that of Barclay.

The tower had originally consisted of a square structure with corner turrets and augmented by a similar building of equal height at right angles to the main wall. One of the corners of the latter building is rounded off, and contains the circular staircase by which the upper floors are reached. The principal doorway, which is in the large tower, has been of a highly ornate description. The embrasure of the door has been enriched with heavy mouldings, these being contained within an embattled blocking course that impinges on the flat surface of the wall. On the lintel above the door an inscription has been carved, the letters D. B. and M. W., with the date 1581, being still visible. Immediately above the lintel a triangular sculptured stone has been inserted at a much later date. It is apparently the pediment from one of the dormer windows, and bears the initials and the date H. B. 1602, with the armorial bearings of the Balfours. An ornamental rope-moulding stands out in high relief from the wall about fourteen feet from the ground, and has apparently run around the double tower, forming a very effective decoration. COLLAIRNIE CASTLE.

Close beside the main door a peculiar shot-hole has been inserted, which deserves some notice. It is carved in the form of a quatrefoil, the four leaves being so arranged that a musket could be directed to right or left, and either upward or downward.

The ground plan of the tower is difficult to understand at first sight in consequence of the alterations which it has undergone. On entering the main door nothing is visible save three vaulted apartments which probably formed the kitchen and offices. No access is now visible to the staircase from this portion of the tower, though doubtless some aperture by which it was reached has been recently built up. The doorway at the base of the staircase, now the only access thereto, was not in the original plan. The staircase itself has been built in a very superior manner, the masonry showing that it was erected in an age of culture, and could not be a part of a very early castle. From its appearance one might judge that it was not earlier than the date 1581 over the doorway. Some parts of the castle, however, clearly belong to the beginning of the sixteenth century.

The principal room on the first floor has been the banqueting chamber or dining hall. It was lighted by two windows on the east and west sides, but these have been partially bricked up, portions of the leaded casements still remaining. A large fireplace has extended over a considerable portion of the south wall, but has been afterwards reduced in size.

The roof is not plastered, but is formed by the open joists and the under side of the planks that serve for the floor of the flat above. A very interesting style of decoration has been adopted here. The lower surface of each joist is painted in distemper colour, with a succession of interlaced scroll designs that are wrought in with great ingenuity. On the sides of each joist long sentences in black-letter have been painted. One of these quaint compositions is as follows :—

" FLEE YE COMPENY OF A LIER BUT THOU MUST KEEP COMPENY WT HIM. BEWAR THAT IN NA WAYS THOU TRW HIM."

COLLAIRNIE CASTLE.

The monograms D.B. and H.B., which are introduced throughout the decoration, show that the work has been executed for David Barclay (Collairnie XI), who succeeded to the estates in 1587, and his wife Helen Balfour, whose arms and initials are now over the door. The most interesting portion of this room, however, is the embellishment of the flooring boards between the joists. As the beams run north and south, they make what may be regarded as a series of panels about twelve inches wide. Within the space thus formed are the armorial bearings of all the leading families with which the Barclays had been connected before the time of David Barclay (Collairnie XI), and painted in their true heraldic colours, the names and titles of many of the families being still legible. In this room alone there are no fewer than twenty-seven coats of arms fully blazoned, whilst in the bedchamber over this dining-room a similar method of decoration has been adopted, and there are twenty-nine different shields painted in it, thus making fifty-six arms in all. In many cases these are barely decipherable, the floor in the upper room especially having been torn up and destroyed in several parts.

This bedroom was probably the guest-chamber. The newelled stair by which it is reached has been finished with dressed stone, and gives tokens of some attempts at architectural luxury. The chamber is not very spacious, but the landscape seen from any of the windows is very beautiful. There can be little doubt that this was the room that Queen Mary occupied when she visited Collairnie in January 1564/5. It is now used as a seed store.

The castle had originally consisted of five flats, but the roof has been altered and the greater part of the corner turrets cut away. All the dormer windows by which the attic flat was lighted are entirely removed, and only the open rafters are visible.

It is impossible to tell from the existing remains what precise form the other parts of the castle took. On the extreme north the gable wall shows signs of having had an extension in that direction, but the place has been so seriously damaged that no intelligible theory can be founded upon these marks.

It is only safe to say generally that the keep, which probably stands on the site of the older castle, was surrounded by a walled courtyard, constructed to afford accommodation for menials and for the stables. COLLAIRNIE CASTLE.

The place was abandoned as a residence when the last of the direct line of the Barclays of Collairnie sold it in 1790, and it has since been transformed almost beyond recognition.

PEDIGREE XIII.

The Collairnie Line

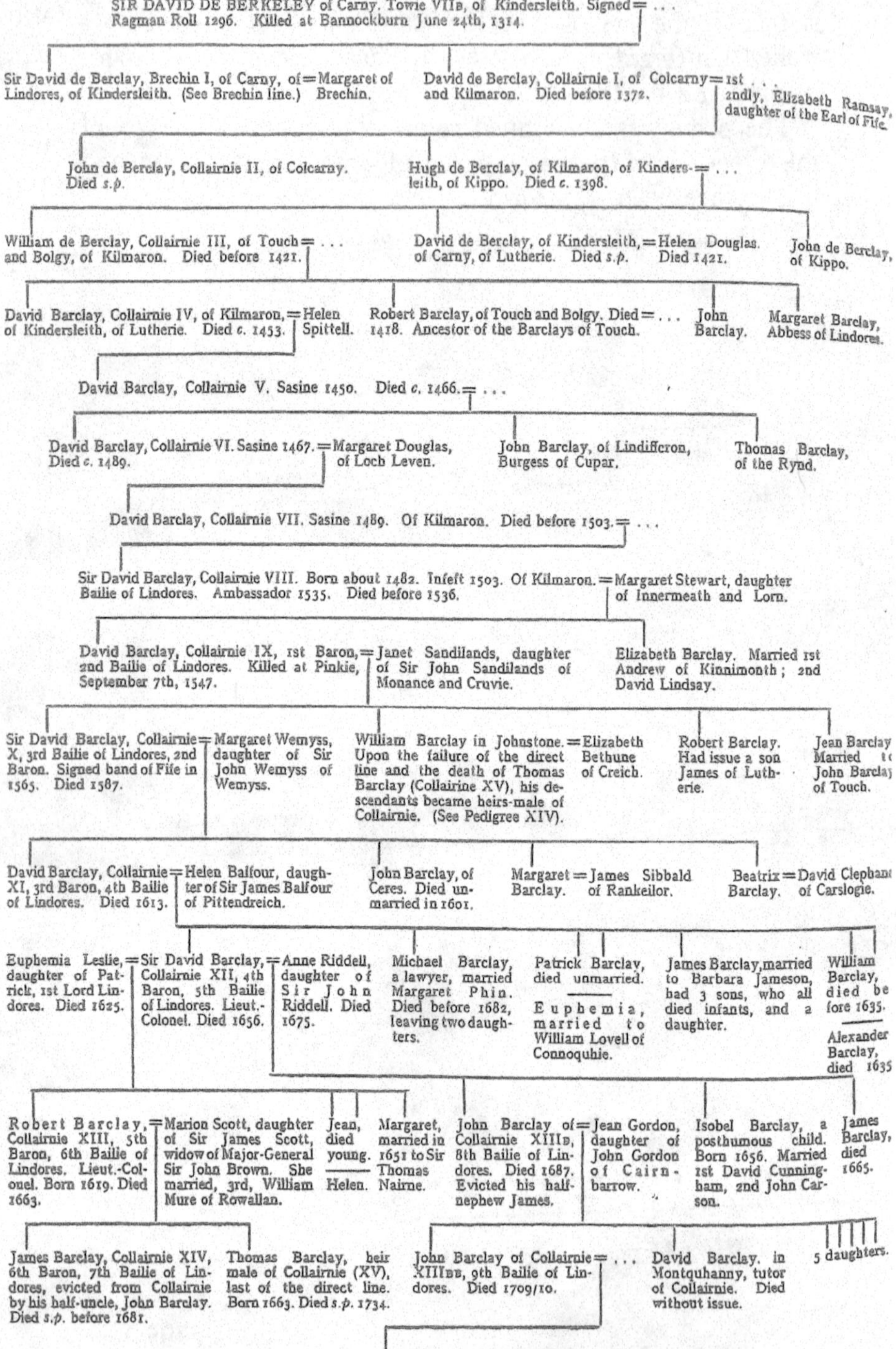

SIR DAVID DE BERKELEY of Carny. Towie VIIB, of Kindersleith. Signed Ragman Roll 1296. Killed at Bannockburn June 24th, 1314. = . . .
Sir David de Berclay, Brechin I, of Carny, of Lindores, of Kindersleith. (See Brechin line.) = Margaret of Brechin.
David de Berclay, Collairnie I, of Colcarny and Kilmaron. Died before 1372. = 1st . . . 2ndly, Elizabeth Ramsay, daughter of the Earl of Fife.
John de Berclay, Collairnie II, of Colcarny. Died s.p.
Hugh de Berclay, of Kilmaron, of Kindersleith, of Kippo. Died c. 1398. = . . .
William de Berclay, Collairnie III, of Touch and Bolgy, of Kilmaron. Died before 1421. = . . .
David de Berclay, of Kindersleith, of Carny, of Lutherie. Died s.p. = Helen Douglas. Died 1421.
John de Berclay, of Kippo.
David Barclay, Collairnie IV, of Kilmaron, of Kindersleith, of Lutherie. Died c. 1453. = Helen Spittell.
Robert Barclay, of Touch and Bolgy. Died 1418. Ancestor of the Barclays of Touch. = . . .
John Barclay.
Margaret Barclay, Abbess of Lindores.
David Barclay, Collairnie V. Sasine 1450. Died c. 1466. = . . .
David Barclay, Collairnie VI. Sasine 1467. Died c. 1489. = Margaret Douglas, of Loch Leven.
John Barclay, of Lindifferon, Burgess of Cupar.
Thomas Barclay, of the Rynd.
David Barclay, Collairnie VII. Sasine 1489. Of Kilmaron. Died before 1503. = . . .
Sir David Barclay, Collairnie VIII. Born about 1482. Infeft 1503. Of Kilmaron. Bailie of Lindores. Ambassador 1535. Died before 1536. = Margaret Stewart, daughter of Innermeath and Lorn.
David Barclay, Collairnie IX, 1st Baron, 2nd Bailie of Lindores. Killed at Pinkie, September 7th, 1547. = Janet Sandilands, daughter of Sir John Sandilands of Monance and Cruvie.
Elizabeth Barclay. Married 1st Andrew of Kinnimonth; 2nd David Lindsay.
Sir David Barclay, Collairnie X, 3rd Bailie of Lindores, 2nd Baron. Signed band of Fife in 1565. Died 1587. = Margaret Wemyss, daughter of Sir John Wemyss of Wemyss.
William Barclay in Johnstone. Upon the failure of the direct line and the death of Thomas Barclay (Collairine XV), his descendants became heirs-male of Collairnie. (See Pedigree XIV). = Elizabeth Bethune of Creich.
Robert Barclay. Had issue a son James of Lutherie.
Jean Barclay Married to John Barclay of Touch.
David Barclay, Collairnie XI, 3rd Baron, 4th Bailie of Lindores. Died 1613. = Helen Balfour, daughter of Sir James Balfour of Pittendreich.
John Barclay, of Ceres. Died unmarried in 1601.
Margaret Barclay. = James Sibbald of Rankeilor.
Beatrix Barclay. = David Clephane of Carslogie.
Euphemia Leslie, daughter of Patrick, 1st Lord Lindores. Died 1625. = Sir David Barclay, Collairnie XII, 4th Baron, 5th Bailie of Lindores. Lieut.-Colonel. Died 1656. = Anne Riddell, daughter of Sir John Riddell. Died 1675.
Michael Barclay, a lawyer, married Margaret Phin. Died before 1682, leaving two daughters.
Patrick Barclay, died unmarried.
Euphemia, married to William Lovell of Connoquhie.
James Barclay, married to Barbara Jameson, had 3 sons, who all died infants, and a daughter.
William Barclay, died before 1635.
Alexander Barclay, died 1635
Robert Barclay, Collairnie XIII, 5th Baron, 6th Bailie of Lindores. Lieut.-Colonel. Born 1619. Died 1663. = Marion Scott, daughter of Sir James Scott, widow of Major-General Sir John Brown. She married, 3rd, William Mure of Rowallan.
Jean, died young.
Helen.
Margaret, married in 1651 to Sir Thomas Nairne.
John Barclay of Collairnie XIIID, 8th Bailie of Lindores. Died 1687. Evicted his half-nephew James. = Jean Gordon, daughter of John Gordon of Cairnbarrow.
Isobel Barclay, a posthumous child. Born 1656. Married 1st David Cunningham, 2nd John Carson.
James Barclay, died 1665.
James Barclay, Collairnie XIV, 6th Baron, 7th Bailie of Lindores, evicted from Collairnie by his half-uncle, John Barclay. Died s.p. before 1681.
Thomas Barclay, heir male of Collairnie (XV), last of the direct line. Born 1663. Died s.p. 1734.
John Barclay of Collairnie XIIIDD, 9th Bailie of Lindores. Died 1709/10. = . . .
David Barclay, in Montquhanny, tutor of Collairnie. Died without issue.
5 daughters.
Antonia Barclay, Lady of Collairnie = Henry Steuart.

DAVID DE BERCLAY

DAVID DE BERCLAY, 1350–1372, Collairnie I.

The progenitor of the Collairnie line was Sir David de Berkeley of Carny (Towie VIIB), the second son of Sir Hugh de Berkeley, Justiciar of the Lothians (Towie VI). A full account of Sir David of Carny has been given in the Brechin line, and, as we have already seen, he had issue two sons, both of whom bore the name of David. This was not unusual in these early days. The elder became Sir David de Berclay of Brechin, and the second David de Berclay received from his father the lands of Colcarny and became the founder of the Collairnie line.

David de Berclay of Colcarny and Kilmaron (Collairnie I) does not appear to have received the honour of knighthood. He is first found as a witness to a charter of Duncan, Earl of Fife, in the year 1350:—

"Appropriation to the Abbot and Canons of Londers (Lindores).

"Grant by Duncan, Earl of Fife, to the Monastery of St. Mary and St. Andrew of the church of Auchtermuchti, in the diocese of St. Andrews, 16th March 1350."

Witnesses include "William Bishop of St. Andrews, Robert Steward of Scotland Guardian of the Realm, Thomas Steward Earl of Angus, David de Lindesey, David de Wemys, and Thomas de Flawford, Knights, Master Walter Rector of Erlol Canon of Glasgow, . . . Lawrence de Wimmeston, Norman de Lascely, John Melevil, David de Barkelay, Henry de Swynton, John the Earls clerk and many others."

Cal. Pap. Reg. Vol. iii, p. 539

The grant was made in fulfilment of a vow when the Earl was taken prisoner by the English at the battle of Durham.

David de Berclay of Colcarny and Kilmaron was twice married. The name of his first wife has not come down to us, but he married secondly, in 1358, Elizabeth Ramsay, daughter of Sir William Ramsay of Colluthie, who in right of his second marriage with Isabella became Earl of Fife. An extract from the Papal Registers giving her father's petition for special dispensation for the alliance will be found on page 77.

David de Berclay had two sons: John, who succeeded him, and Hugh, to whom were granted the lands of Kilmaron.

DAVID DE BERCLAY, 1350–1372, Collairnie I.

About the year 1353 Sir David de Berclay, Lord of Brechin (Brechin II), granted to his cousin Hugh, " son of our uncle David " (Collairnie I), the upper and lower vill of Kindersleith, for a rent of one pair of gilt spurs yearly to be paid at " our Manor of Lindores " (see page 88).

Macfarlane's Collections, Vol. ii, pp. 456, 462. Collairnie Charters.

In 1372 Hugh de Berclay of Kilmaron got a charter from Andrew de Leslie in his favour, for the yearly payment of twenty-four merks of good sterling money, out of his lands and Barony of Ballinbreich, Fife.

Hugh de Berclay appears to have held Kippo as well, and as Lord of Kippo surrendered to the King lands at Estirfossach in the abthanery of Dulle, in Perthshire, on October 24th, 1370, afterwards granted to Donald Macnayre by King David.

Reg. Mag. Sig. 1306–1424, p. 125, No. 355.

Among the witnesses in one of the Wemyss charters we find the name of Hugh de Berclay of Kippo :—

" Charter by Robert Steward, Earl of Fife and Menteith, later Duke of Albany and Guardian of the Realm, granting to John de Wemys the lands of Tulibric, in the sheriffdom of Fife. Among the witnesses is ' Hugone Berclai of Kippo, and also Sir William Ramsay of Coluthie.' "

Memorials of Wemyss, Vol. ii, p. 17.

The date of the death of Hugh de Berclay is not known, but he left three sons : William (Collairnie III), who succeeded him in the lands of Kilmaron ; David, who inherited the estates of Kindersleith; and John, to whom he granted the lands of Kippo. John was the ancestor of the Barclays of Kippo, which branch became extinct in the year 1498, on the marriage of Margaret Barclay, the heiress of Kippo and Arngask, to Sir Andrew de Murray. There is a female effigy in the courtyard of Balvaird Castle which is thought to be that of Dame Margaret.

The second son, David, of Lutherie and Kindersleith, obtained from his father a grant of the lands of Kindersleith, and was also proprietor of the adjoining lands of Lutherie, in the parish of Creich.

He is frequently mentioned during the Regency of Robert, Duke of Albany, as " Armiger " and " Scutifer."

In company with his brothers William and John, he witnessed many charters for the Duke, which leads us to conclude that they were all three of the Duke's household.

He was also a witness to several charters, which are to be found in the Exchequer Rolls, one of the most important being dated at Dunfermline, May 1413, granting the Barony of Stewarton, etc., to John, Earl of Buchan, and Elizabeth his wife, daughter of Archibald, 4th Earl of Douglas.

DAVID DE BERCLAY, 1350–1372, Collairnie I.

Collairnie Charters.

In 1421 he, with his nephews David Barclay (Collairnie IV) and Robert Barclay of Touch, were, as we have seen, cautioners for George Barclay, heir-apparent of Mathers, and his two uncles, Patrick and John, who had claimed sanctuary at Macduff's Cross after being concerned in the murder of Sir John Melville, the Sheriff of the Mearns.

David married Helen de Douglas, but they had no issue, for on July 28th, 1425, he resigned his lands of Kindersleith and Lutherie in favour of his nephew David Barclay (Collairnie IV).

Collairnie Charters.

On July 8th, 1839, when digging a grave within the old church of Creich, a few inches under the pavement was discovered a tombstone, on the top of which are carved two figures, one of a man in a complete coat of mail, and the other of a lady in a long embroidered robe. Upon two shields are emblazoned the arms of Barclay and Douglas. This stone was found lying partly within, and partly without, a niche on which are the Barclay arms. On the outer edge of the stone, which is bevelled, is the following inscription in old English characters :—

"Hic jacet David Berclay de Luthrie dominus de Carny qui obiit die mensis anno domini MCCCC ."

The line immediately below this inscription reads :—

"Hic jacet Helena de Douglas uxor predicti qui obit XXIX die mensis Januarii anno domini MCCCCXXI."

Statistical Account of Scotland, Vol. ix.

This stone had evidently been erected by David de Berclay in memory of his wife, which accounts for the date of his own death being left blank, his heirs having neglected to record it.

Lady Helen de Douglas, commemorated on the tombstone, seems to have been a daughter of Douglas of Cavers, as Sir William Douglas of Cavers, Kt., came into possession of a portion of Lutherie shortly after her decease.

David de Berclay, 1350–1372, Collairnie I.

The burying place of the Barclays of Collairnie for generations was in the Old Kirk and Kirkyard of Creich. Over a niche, in the wall of the church, evidently intended for an altar tomb, the arms of the Barclays of Collairnie are carved, and it is probablé that the earliest members of this family are buried in that place.

David de Berclay (Collairnie I) died about the year 1372 and was succeeded by his eldest son, John de Berclay (Collairnie II).

JOHN DE BERCLAY

JOHN DE BERCLAY, 1372–1398, Collairnie II.

John de Berclay of Colcarny succeeded his father, David de Berclay (Collairnie I), about the year 1372, but he was put into possession of the estate of Colcarny two years previously, as is seen by the following Crown charter :—

"Grant to John de Berclay, son of David de Berclay, of all that part of Colcarny, county Kynros, which belonged to David his father and was surrendered by him." Perth. David II, 41st year. Reg. Mag. Sig. 1306–1424, p. 126.

At an earlier date, 1369, John de Berclay had replaced his father David de Berclay as "Collector of Contributions" of the seven shires, for which he received the handsome salary of 4s. 6d. per annum. Exchequer Rolls, Vol. ii, p. 335.

No further records of John de Berclay can be found, and it seems certain that he died without issue, as the next holder of the estate of Collairnie was William Berclay, who had inherited the lands of Kilmaron from his father, Hugh de Berclay (Collairnie IIB), and appears to have received the lands of Collairnie from his uncle, John de Berclay (Collairnie II), on his death without issue.

WILLIAM BERCLAY

William Berclay, 1390–1418, Collairnie III.

William Berclay of Collairnie, Kilmaron, Touch and Bolgy, was born about the year 1350. He succeeded his father in the lands of Kilmaron, and inherited from his uncle, John de Berclay of Colcarny (Collairnie II), the estates which were henceforward known as the lands of Collairnie.

William Berclay's name appears third among the jurors at an inquisition taken at Glenducky on July 5th, 1390, which is quoted in the confirmation by King Robert III of the charter of Sir Norman de Lesly, Kt., of Balnabreck, dealing with the lands of Balmadyside and Petachop.

Reg. Mag. Sig. 1306–1424, Vol. i, p. 208, No. 37

In the same year William Berclay received by charter from King Robert the lands of Touch and Bolgy, previously held by William . . . . (the surname is unfortunately obliterated).

Ibid. Appendix II, No. 1760.

The lands of "Bolgyn, son of Torfyny," were granted by Macbeth, King of Scotland, and his wife Queen Gruoch (1040–1057) to the hermits of St. Serf's Island in Lochleven. Afterwards these lands were granted to the Monastery of Dunfermline by Malcolm III. The Abbey of Dunfermline received from Bolgyn half a merk annually, the right to which John Abbot of Dunfermline (*ob.* A.D. 1251) surrendered to the Priory of St. Andrews. While Dunfermline had right to half a merk from Bolgyn, the Priory of St. Serf's had right to "twenty meli of chese" and one pig, at Martinmas, from the same land.

Register of Dunfermline, Nos. 1, 2.

When William Berclay of Collairnie became possessed of the land of Bolgy he refused or neglected to pay this rent. The matter became the subject of prolonged litigation. The famous Andrew Wyntoun, author of *The Cronykill of Scotland*, was then prior of the Monastery of Lochleven, and in fulfilment of his office he brought an action against the Laird of Collairnie in the court of the Bishop of St. Andrews claiming payment of this contribution. Bishop Walter Traill, before whom this action was brought on March 27th, 1395, gave judgment against William for his contumacy in not appearing to defend himself, and decreed that, because of the hardness of his heart, he should be solemnly excommunicated from the Church, "by the sounding of the bells, by the lighting and extinguishing of candles and by public denunciation." This sentence does not seem to have had much effect, as we find that on February 19th, 1406, Wyntoun again applied to the bishop's successor, and the laird was subjected to the penalty of the major excommunication. Even these terrors did not bring him into subjection, for Wyntoun summoned him once more before the bishop, in 1411, complaining that he was then five years in arrears, and was due "ten chalders of wheat, twenty swine and forty shillings." Unfortunately we cannot tell how this curious dispute terminated. In these records William Berclay is referred to as both Lord of Collairnie and Lord of Touch.

WILLIAM BERCLAY, 1390–1418, Collairnie III.

Register of St. Andrews, pp. 6–21.

As has been already mentioned, William Berclay, together with his brothers David Berclay of Lutherie and John Berclay, afterwards of Kippo, were members of the household of Robert, Duke of Albany. They are witnesses to many charters for the Duke, sometimes together and sometimes separately, as "scutifer" or "armiger." It is of value to quote the following deed :—

> "Charter by Robert, Duke of Albany, Earl of Fife and Menteith, and Governor of Scotland, confirming to John Melville of Rait a grant to him by William Scot of Balweny. Witnessed by carissimo nepote nostro Roberto Senescallo de Fyfe, carissimo filio nostro Johanne Senescalli domino Buchane, Ricardo Commyne milite, Domino Andrea Hamit secretario nostro rectore de Lystoun, David Berclay, Johnne Wricht and William Berclay scutiferis nostris et aliis," 3rd August, 1411.

The Melvilles and Leslies, Vol. ii, p. 18.

"Scutifer" or "armiger" was a rank in which the holder, if horsed, was entitled to the same allowances as a knight. Service as "scutifer" in the Royal household continued to be given by Barclays of the Kippo line.

John Wright, witness to the above charter, was the same person who received, together with Alexander Berclay (Gartley XIII), a pension as co-heirs of Richard son of Randolphi.

Living at the same date as William Berclay of Collairnie was another William Berclay (Towie X), who was marshal to John, Earl of Buchan, son of Robert, Duke of Albany, by his second

WILLIAM BERCLAY, 1390–1418, Collairnie III.

marriage, with Muriella daughter of Sir William Keith, the father-in-law of Alexander de Berclay (Mathers I). It is very difficult to distinguish between these two William Berclays.

Collairnie Charters.

The name of the wife of William Berclay (Collairnie III) has not been found, but they had issue three sons and a daughter, Margaret, who became Abbess of Lindores.

The eldest son, David (Collairnie IV), succeeded his father in the lands of Collairnie and Kilmaron, of whom later. The second son, Robert, was granted the lands of Touch and Bolgy and was ancestor of that branch of the Barclay family which became extinct at the end of the seventeenth century. The youngest son, John, is mentioned in the deed of sasine in favour of his nephew, David Berclay of Collairnie (Collairnie V), dated October 22nd, 1450.

Ibid.

William Berclay (Collairnie III) died before 1421, in which year his son David (Collairnie IV) was in possession of the estates.

DAVID BARCLAY

David Barclay, 1418–1450, Collairnie IV.

David Barclay of Collairnie, Kilmaron, Kindersleith and Lutherie, succeeded his father, William Berclay (Collairnie III), about the year 1418. He was the first of no fewer than nine successive holders of the Collairnie estates all of whom bore the name of David.

He married Helen Spittell, daughter and heiress of John Spittell of Kinnimonth and his wife, Dornagild Stirling, who appears to have received as her marriage settlement the baronies of Crambeth and Cleish, in Kinross, and the lands of Kinnimonth in the parish of Kinglassie, county Fife, for in the year 1415 David Barclay obtained a charter of these baronies and lands on the resignation of the said John Spittell and Dornagild Stirling.

Reg. Mag. Sig. 1306–1424, Appendix II, No. 1973.

In 1421, as has been already recorded, he was one of the sureties, together with his uncle, David Berclay of Lutherie, and his brother, Robert Barclay of Touch, for three members of the Mathers line who had claimed the sanctuary of the cross of Macduff after the murder of the Sheriff of the Mearns.

On February 10th, 1423, he received from John Pitblado of that Ilk a charter of the lands of Kilmaron. These lands were formerly held by his grandfather, Hugh de Berclay, at whose death they had passed to David's father, William Berclay (Collairnie III).

Collairnie Charters.

On July 28th, 1425, David Barclay obtained an instrument of sasine in his favour, on the resignation of his uncle David, of the lands of Lutherie and Kindersleith.

David Barclay (Collairnie IV) died about the year 1453, having resigned the estates into the hands of his son David (Collairnie V) in 1450.

DAVID BARCLAY

David Barclay, 1450–1466, Collairnie V.

David Barclay, the fifth Laird of Collairnie, lived in the reigns of James II and James III of Scotland and Henry VI and Edward IV of England. It was during the time of his occupation of the family estates that Scotland was plunged into civil war. Neither of the two kings was able to control the turbulent nobles and both were unpopular. The English kings were continually plotting with first one party and then with the other. James II was killed by the bursting of a cannon when besieging the English in the castle of Roxburgh in 1460. His son James III was murdered when fleeing from the disastrous defeat at Sauchieburn in 1488.

With the country in this disturbed condition it is easy to realise that there are but few records concerning the doings of David Barclay (Collairnie V) to help the genealogist.

On October 22nd, 1450, he obtained sasine, as son and heir of his father David on the latter's resignation. In this sasine are mentioned John Barclay and Margaret Barclay, Abbess of Lindores, presumed to be his uncle and aunt. The name of his grandfather, William Barclay (Collairnie III), is also referred to in the deed.

Collairnie Charters.

There is another deed of sasine among the Collairnie Charters, dated September 17th, 1454, of the lands of Carskerdo, in the parish of Ceres, county Fife.

Nisbet in his *Heraldry* tells us that in 1457 David Barclay was one of the assessors in a perambulation between Easter and Wester Kinghorn.

Register of Dunfermline, p. 346.

We do not know the name of the wife of this David Barclay, but he had issue three sons. His eldest son, David, succeeded him as the sixth Laird of Collairnie. His second son, John Barclay, was defender in an action before the Lords Auditors, February 19th, 1483, and is there described as "brother to David Barclay of Collairnie." From him are supposed to have descended the Barclays of Blair Crambeth, Kinross, from whom sprang the Barclays of Keavil. The third and youngest son of David Barclay (Collairnie V) was Thomas Barclay "of the Rynd," mentioned in a decreet by

Acts of the Lords Auditors, 1466–1494, p. 130.

Ibid. p. 204.

the Lords Auditors on December 15th, 1494, as brother german to the deceased David Barclay of Collairnie.

DAVID BARCLAY, 1450–1466, Collairnie V.

The Barclays of the Rynd held the lands until 1640, when with the lands of Innergelly and Ardit they were sold to Sir James Lumsdane of Airdrie.

One of this family, William Barclay of the Rynd, was Captain and Keeper of the King's Palace of Falkland and Seneschal and Chamberlain of the Stewartry of Fife. He was killed at the battle of Pinkie in 1547.

David Barclay (Collairnie V) died about the year 1466.

DAVID BARCLAY

DAVID BARCLAY, 1466–1489, Collairnie VI.

This David Barclay succeeded his father, David Barclay (Collairnie V), in the year 1466. On February 6th, 1467, he obtained a precept of *clare constat* from the Earl of Rothes, "as eldest son and heir of the late David Barclay (Collairnie V), who was eldest son and heir of David Barclay (Collairnie IV), of a twelfth part of Collairnie," and in 1468 he again got sasine for further property and annual rents, as is seen by the following charter :—

Collairnie Charters.

Exchequer Rolls, Vol. xi, p. 674.

"Sas David Barclay t. Kinslevis, Freland, Bin, Kynnard, Forth Ramsay, Kynnimonth, Bordland, and annual rent of Middle Cleish, Nevigston, Colston, etc."

On June 13th, 1477, he obtained a charter in his favour on the resignation of John Barclay, Burgess of Cupar, of the lands of Lindifferon, Fife.

Collairnie Charters.

On August 3rd, 1481, David Barclay sold to John Blackburn an annual rent of two and a half merks from the lands of Ottertoun, in the sheriffdom of Fife, held by him from the King, the witnesses being John Barclay his brother, David Barclay of Touch, David Barclay his brother, and John Urvel Notary Public.

Reg. Mag. Sig. 1424–1513, No. 1488.

On February 18th, 1483, an action was brought by Arthur Ferny of that Ilk against Thomas Simson, sheriff of Fife, David Barclay of Collairnie and others for having wrongly issued a brief of inquest.

Acts of the Lords Auditors, 1466–1494, p. 128.

In 1484, on May 19th, David Barclay is again before the Lords Auditors in an action brought by Thomas Grandison against James of "Petblatho," John his son and heir, David Barclay of Collairnie and others for wrongfully "rasing and taking" £50 from the lands of "Petblatho." The Lords give a decision in which David is made to pay £18.

Acts of the Lords Auditors, 1466–1494, p. 139.

David Barclay (Collairnie VI) married Margaret, daughter of Douglas of Lochleven, ancestor of the Earls of Morton. He died about the year 1489 and was succeeded by his son David Barclay (Collairnie VII).

DAVID BARCLAY

David Barclay, 1489–1503, Collairnie VII.

David Barclay, the seventh Laird of Collairnie, held the estates for only fourteen years.

On May 15th, 1489, he obtained an instrument of sasine as "eldest son and heir of David Barclay of Collairnie and Margaret Douglas his spouse" of the lands of Carskerdo. Collairnie Charters.

There are also among the Collairnie deeds further charters, dated August 10th, 1490, and October 10th, 1494, granting to him other estates in Fife.

David Barclay (Collairnie VII) has sasine in 1494, as follows:—

"Sasin for David Barclay t. Kinslevis, Freland, Landifron, Carskerdo, Nevyngston and Medil Cleish, etc." Exchequer Rolls, Vol. x, p. 769.

It will be remembered that the lands of Kilmaron had been the property of the Barclays of Collairnie ever since the days of David de Berclay (Collairnie I). They appear to have been held under the overlordship of the Lairds of Pitblado. During the time of this David Barclay (Collairnie VII) with whom we are now concerned, these lands were the cause of much dispute and continual litigation. A certain Matthew White claimed that by heritage he was entitled to occupy a twelfth part of Kilmaron and to receive the "tak" of the same. The matter dragged on through the years 1492, 1493 and 1494, when the Lords Auditors decided that Matthew White was correct in making this claim, that Peter of Pitblado was to infeft him in this twelfth part of the said lands, and to defend him against any claim that David Barclay of Collairnie might make. The Lords also decreed that David Barclay was to resign the said part of the lands of Kilmaron. These actions are of considerable interest, showing that the Barclays of Collairnie were still in possession of the lands of Kilmaron at this date. Acts of the Lords Auditors, 1478–1496, pp. 319, 355, 360, etc.

There are two more entries in the Acts of the Lords Auditors concerning this David Barclay, and on July 1st, 1494, he is found as a witness to an acquittance by Alexander Ramsay of Dalwidsy. Hist MSS. Comm. Earl of Home, p. 90.

The name of David Barclay's wife has not been recovered, but he had issue a son, Sir David Barclay (Collairnie VIII), who succeeded him. He died before the year 1503.

SIR DAVID BARCLAY

Sir David Barclay, 1503–1536, Collairnie VIII.

Sir David Barclay was born about 1482, and at the time of his father's death he was not yet of age.

Previous to his time there had been some dispute between the Lairds of Collairnie and their superiors, the Lords of Balnabreich, afterwards Earls of Rothes. In consequence of this feud, George, Earl of Rothes, refused to infeft David Barclay (Collaïrnie VIII) when he came of age in 1503. The young laird, however, had by some means gained the ear of King James IV, who issued a special Royal precept, on July 10th, 1503, to the sheriff of Fife, ordering that Barclay should at once be put into possession of his paternal estates.

Collairnie Charters. Exchequer Rolls, Vol. xii, p. 713.

The Royal favour was further continued, for in 1510 he obtained a charter of the lands of Collairnie directly from the King, as these lands had fallen to the Crown, in consequence of George, Earl of Rothes, having alienated the greater portion without the King's consent.

Reg. Mag. Sig. 1424–1513, No. 3524.

In 1506, on May 18th, he resigned the lands of Kilmaron for new infeftment.

Collairnie Charters.

Together with Henry Pitcarne, David bought the lands of Forthar-Ramsay, in Fife, which they resigned into the King's hands, for infeftment and incorporation into a free Barony, in favour of the said Henry Pitcarne. Dated at Edinburgh February 14th, 1510-11.

Reg. Mag. Sig. 1424–1513, No. 3541.

In an action between David Balfour of Lalethime and Marion, his spouse, and Jonete Ramsay, relict of George Balfour, in the year 1516, David Barclay is cautioner to the sheriff for the said Jonete and her "bairnys": and during the year 1517 his name appears on inquisitions, together with his kinsmen, Thomas Barclay of the Rynd and David Barclay of Touch.

Sheriff Court Book of Fife, 1515–1522, pp. 41, 48.

The battle of Flodden Field had taken place on September 9th, 1513, when King James IV, with twelve of his earls and thirteen of his barons, was slain. On the accession of James V the country was in a very disturbed state. The French and English parties were continually plotting against each other. King Henry VIII of England was meddling in the affairs of Scotland, and at one time wished to marry his daughter Mary to the Scottish King.

SIR DAVID BARCLAY, 1503–1536, Collairnie VIII.

Henry Orme, who was Abbot of Lindores (1502–1523), appears to have taken some precaution with regard to the safety of the abbey and the monks serving there. David Barclay was appointed bailie, and, as we shall see in a later grant, his duties were of an onerous character. On May 4th, 1516, we find him entering a "protestation of privilege." His son, David Barclay (Collairnie IX), was appointed, by Abbot John Philp, to succeed him in the year 1536, at which date the appointment was made hereditary.

Sheriff Court Book of Fife, 1515–1522, p. 142.

In 1517 David Barclay was one of a jury who settled a valuation of Fife, in a court held by Patrick, 4th Lord Lindsay of the Byres, sheriff depute of Fife.

On September 2, 1521, he obtained a precept of sasine in his favour, and of Margaret Stewart his spouse, of the lands of Carskerdo.

Collairnie Charters.

It is not known at what date or for what service David Barclay (Collairnie VIII) received the honour of knighthood.

On October 25th, 1525, there is an obligation by Peter Pitblado of that Ilk and David Pitblado fiar thereof, by which they renounce in Sir David Barclay's favour all inversions of the lands of Kingask, and the same day there is a contract between Sir David and the above Peter and David by which Sir David renounced twelve merks of the annual rent that he has out of the lands of Pitblado, and for which renunciation the said Peter and David renounce in his favour five twelfth parts of the lands of Kilmaron, which he, the said Sir David Barclay, "has now in blench."

Collairnie Charters.

In the *History and Chronicles of Scotland*, by Robert Lindsay of Pitscottie, we read of an embassy to England in the time of King James V, dated 1533. The chronicler describes :—

"how ane ambassadour came out of Ingland, called Lord William, how the King promisit to pass to Ingland to the King therof, how the wicket bischopis of Scotland wid nocht tholl the King to pass thair. For the bischopis concedit in thair myndis that gif King Harrie mett with our King of Scotland that he wid cause him to

SIR DAVID BARCLAY, 1503–1536, Collairnie VIII.

cast doune the abbayis of Scotland lykeas he had done in Ingland. . . . Therefor they hidit and a force sent under the King's brother, the Earl of Murray Scotland divided into four parts and every man constrained to keep in his own quarters. The King was constrainit to send ane ambassadour to Ingland, namit the bischope of Aberdene, with him three ancient knightis to wit Schir William Scot of Balwiril, Schir David Barklay of Collernie, Schir Alexander Stewart of Gartlies. Thes ambassadours passit with the commissioun and promiseid that he sould meit the King of Ingland in York."

Then follows a description of the King of England's preparations :—

"of all things necessary for their Royall estait, of the King of Scotland's cuming and for his owne honour and magnificence of his realme, and nobilitie thereof, for I haird say thair was never sic provisioun nor preparation made for no tryumphe nor meeting that ever was nather within the realme of Scotland nor in Ingland since they first inhabit. But in the end the King of Scotland mockid the King of Ingland, the ambassadours forsaid passit into Ingland with a secret writing in the King's own hand to present to the King of Ingland sealed and not to be broken, and were well received in London, and presented the writing for the King's own consideration, and passed to their lodging and made merry. But on the morne they were sent for to the castell like other ambassadours there, and found the matter laid before the council, whereat they were very angry, took the King by the hand and led him away to the window to a table and expostulated with him for putting a secret matter before his council. The King warned the bischope and told him to warn the King of the danger of these secret methods. The bischope remained in Ingland a quarter of a year and returned and told the King of the King of Ingland's feeling for the Lord of Angus and the Lord of Douglas. Wherefor these men fell under suspicion with the King of Scotland especially of all Douglas."

History and Chronicles of Scotland, Vol. i, p. 342.

On July 27th, 1535, King James V granted letters of protection to William (Stewart), Bishop of Aberdeen, with his kinsmen, friends and servants, among whom was Sir David Barclay of Cullerny and his son, in all a great company, "to pas in our ambassate and service to the maist Cristin King [Francis the First—but no mention of France or his name], for treting of oure mariage and uther matters concerning us and the common weile of our realme."

Reg. Sec. Sig. Vol. ii, Nos. 1740, 1745.

The name of Sir David Barclay (Collairnie VIII) does not occur after this embassy, and it is possible that he did not return.

SIR DAVID BARCLAY, 1503-1536, Collairnie VIII.

He married, as already noted, Margaret Stewart, daughter of Thomas, Lord Innermeath and Lorn, and had issue one son, David (Collairnie IX), who succeeded him, and one daughter, Elizabeth, who married first Andrew of Kinnimonth, by contract of him on the one part and David Barclay of Collairnie of the other, dated April 25th, 1540. Andrew died about the year 1545, and Elizabeth Barclay married secondly David Lindsay of Piotstown, whom she divorced.

Macfarlane's Collections, Vol. ii, pp. 539, 548.

Liber Officiales of St. Andrews, Abbotsford Club.

DAVID BARCLAY

DAVID BARCLAY, 1536–1547, Collairnie IX.

David Barclay, first Baron of Collairnie, succeeded his father, Sir David Barclay (Collairnie VIII), early in the year 1536.

He married, in 1523, Janet Sandilands, daughter of Sir John Sandilands of Monance and Cruvie, by Catherine his wife, daughter of Sir William Scott of Balweane. Sir David settled upon his daughter-in-law the lands of Kinnimonth as her wedding gift. The charter was confirmed (technically) by Queen Mary in 1547, shortly before Janet's husband, David Barclay, was killed at the battle of Pinkie.

Collairnie Charters.

David Barclay (Collairnie IX) obtained a retour of special service, dated at Cupar, March 7th, 1536, as son and heir of Sir David Barclay, Kt.

There is a curious document relating to this Laird of Collairnie still extant among the charters connected with the estate. It is dated January 14th, 1536, and declares "that David Barclay of Collairnie accept from John Abbot of Lindores [John Philp, 1532–1566] and the monks thereof the office of the bailiary of the monastery there, and obliged himself to be bailie to them, and their keeper, defender and protector, to hold their courts and do Law and Justice to 'outmen and inmen' as oft as necessary, and to keep their freedom and borrow their men if any be attached or arrested to any other Lord's Court." For this arduous duty his remuneration was set down at ten merks of fee yearly.

Exchequer Rolls, Vol. xvii, p. 758.

On April 30th, 1537, we find in the "Libri Responsionum" that David Barclay was owing to the King for sasine on the lands of Collairnie, Lumbenny, Carskerdo, Lindiffron, Kinnimonth, Bin and for several annual rents, including Middle Creich.

All these places have been mentioned as being held by the Lairds of Collairnie in previous generations.

King James V confirmed to David Barclay and to Jonete Sandilands, his wife, in conjunct infeftment, five pounds worth of land at the ancient estate of Carskerdo, county Fife, and incorporating at the same time the lands of

Collairnie with the fortalice, Easter and Wester Kindersleith, free lands of Lindiffron, three parts of Kinnimonth, half of Bin and Kynnard, Lumbenny, and Lutherie, into the Free Barony of Collairnie, of which he granted him exemption from wardship so far as the dwelling and demain were concerned. The rights of David Barclay, his heirs and assigns, to an annual rent of 18 merks from the lands of Kilmaron, county Fife, which John Seton had sold to William Hunter, are also expressly reserved in the charter of confirmation, dated May 29th, 1540.

DAVID BARCLAY, 1536–1547, Collairnie IX.

Reg. Mag. Sig. Vol. iii, No. 2149.

Queen Mary, at Stirling, June 26th, 1545, with the consent of her Privy Council, grants the lands of Kinnimonth, in the Barony of Collairnie, which David Barclay resigned, to Elizabeth Leslie, daughter of George, Earl of Rothes, in her virginity, in life rent.

James V died on December 14th, 1542, of grief, it is said, at the disaster of Solway Moss, combined with disappointment that his hopes of an heir had been destroyed by the birth of his daughter Mary.

During the first five years of Queen Mary's reign Scotland was subjected to no fewer than three invasions by the English: first by order of Henry VIII, and later by the Duke of Somerset, Protector of King Edward VI. At the third invasion the Scottish Regent, James, Earl of Arran, mustered a large force to resist the English. The two hosts faced each other on opposite banks of the Esk and the Scots were defeated with great slaughter at the battle of Pinkie, on September 10th, 1547.

Among those who fell on that day was David Barclay, first Baron of Collairnie (Collairnie IX).

By his wife, Janet Sandilands, he left issue three sons and one daughter.

He was succeeded by his eldest son David (Collairnie X), of whom later. William Barclay in Johnstone (XB) was styled "second son." He married Elizabeth Bethune of Creich. On the failure of the direct male line of Collairnie, by the death of Thomas Barclay (Collairnie XV) in 1734, the descendants of William Barclay in Johnstone claimed to

DAVID BARCLAY, 1536–1547, Collairnie IX.

be heirs-male of Collairnie. A pedigree of this line will be given later. Robert Barclay, the third son of David Barclay, had issue a son, James Barclay, who in the year 1610 acquired from David Barclay, the then Laird of Collairnie, a portion of the lands of Lutherie, where the family remained for some generations. Jean Barclay, the daughter of David Barclay (Collairnie IX) married in 1564 John Barclay of Touch, and had issue.

SIR DAVID BARCLAY

Sir David Barclay, 1547–1587, Collairnie X.

Sir David Barclay, second Baron of Collairnie, was only barely of age when he inherited the estates on his father being slain at the battle of Pinkie on September 10th, 1547.

Before that date he had been contracted to marry the Lady Elizabeth Leslie, fourth daughter of George, fourth Earl of Rothes, who, as we have seen, had received a grant of part of the lands of Kinnimonth in the contract of marriage. This grant was confirmed at Stirling, June 26th, 1545. However, David refused the alliance, and in 1557 she was the wife of Patrick Crichton, younger of Lugton.

Reg. Mag. Sig. Vol. iii, No. 3125.

Scots Peerage.

Sir David married Margaret Wemyss, eldest daughter of Sir John Wemyss of Wemyss, ancestor of the Earls of Wemyss and March, by Margaret his first wife, a daughter of Sir Adam Otterburn of Redhall, Lord Advocate to James V. The marriage contract is dated November 27th, 1555.

Douglas's Peerage.

Wemyss Memorials, Vol. ii, p. 182.

On October 22nd, 1548, he obtained a retour of special service, under the Act of Parliament granting this favour to the sons of those who fell at Pinkiecleuch, and received the lands and Barony of Collairnie.

Collairnie Charters.

In the "Libri Responsionum," under date November 8th, 1549, the Sheriff of Fife has to account for £273 6s. 8d. for sasine from the Barony of Collairnie, from the lands of Collairnie with the Tower and buildings, Carskerdo, Easter and Wester Kindersleith, Freland, Lindiffron, three-fifths of Kinnimonth, half of Bin and Kynnard, one-seventh of Lumbenny with the mill and other holdings within the barony, and for certain annual rents. Also a further £136 13s. 4d. for reliefs owing to the Queen, for sasine from Sir David Barclay, reserving free the lands of Carskerdo to Janet Sandilands, widow of the late David Barclay (Collairnie IX), in life rent, excepting the before-mentioned three-fifths of Kinnimonth, which are in the hands of Elizabeth Leslie, "ratione sue allegati vitatio reditus earundem."

Exchequer Rolls, Vol. xviii, p. 486.

On July 21st, 1553, there is an act of ratification by Justiciar General, Alexander, Earl of Argyle, approving of the charter of the erection of the Barony of Collairnie in 1540.

Collairnie Charters.

SIR DAVID BARCLAY, 1547–1587, Collairnie X.

Collairnie Charters.

On February 20th, 1563, Sir David obtained a charter from John (Philp) Abbot of Lindores, in favour of himself and the heirs-male of his body, of the heritable office of the bailiary of the lands, baronies and other property belonging to the monastery of Lindores and also of the Barony of Ecclesmagirdle, in Strathearn, county Perth.

Reg. Mag. Sig.

In 1564, on May 8th, he obtained a charter under the Great Seal of Queen Mary of the lands of Kilmaron in the Barony of Pitblado.

The lot of Sir David Barclay (Collairnie X) was cast in very critical times. The widowed Queen of France returned to Scotland to rule over her country, as Queen Mary, during his tenure, and he had to decide between supporting her or aiding the Lords of the Congregation, who strove to dethrone her. His decision in her favour was possibly confirmed when she honoured the Tower of Collairnie with her presence in January, 1564-5. This was the period of her memorable residence in St. Andrews, during which time her first interview with Darnley on Scottish soil took place. She sailed from the Forth to the Tay, landed at Balmerino, then rode to Collairnie, and thence to St. Andrews, where she spent a week.

The time of her residence at Collairnie is proved by the fact that whilst there she signed a charter under the Great Seal, which is dated January 24th, 1564-1565. As she left Edinburgh on January 23rd, and was at Collairnie on the 24th, and did not arrive at St. Andrews until the 28th, she probably spent three days within the ancient Tower, attended by the four faithful "Maries," on her way to meet the lover whose fate was to be so cruelly linked with her own.

It is not wonderful to find that Sir David Barclay (Collairnie X) was an ardent adherent of his Queen.

Register of Privy Council, Vol. i, p. 367.

On September 12th, 1565, he signed "The band in Fyffe . . . that we and ilk ane of us sall trewlie serve the King and Queen's Mayesties and their Lieutenant."

Queen Mary was married on July 29th, 1565, to her cousin, Henry Stewart, Lord Darnley. He was the son of the Earl of

Sir David Barclay, 1547-1587, Collairnie X.

Lennox by his wife Margaret Douglas, and was therefore the grandson of Margaret Tudor, and was received as first prince of the blood at the English Court. They were married with the rites of the Romish Church. Moray refused his consent to the marriage, and he and some of the lay lords took up arms. They entered the town of Edinburgh, but were fired at from the castle, and retreated to Dumfries. There they issued a declaration that their religion was in danger. Queen Mary and her husband seem to have made preparations for their safety in case of further action by the Protestant party, and we find in the register of the Privy Council an interesting record, dated at Strongbow, November 18th, 1565, in which "David Drury of that Ilk, David Barclay of Cullerny (Collairnie X), Michaell Balfour of Burly, John Anstruther of that Ilk and Maister Alexander Sym, advocat procurator speciale, be Sir William Scott of Balweny, Kt., appear personally before the Lords of secrit Council with their band and letters."

By these Sir William Scott, Kt., of Balweny, and these other signatories (Sir David Barclay, signing simply as "Cullerny") are "bundin and oblist as cautioners and souerties for William Douglas, of Lochleven, that the house and place of Lochleven shall be reddie and patent at their Majesties commandment with all munitions and altailyerie [artillery] being within the samyn, quhilkis pertenit to James Erl of Moray . . . upon 24 hours warning, and that nane of their Majesties rebellis . . . sal be suppleit or intertenit in the said place in menetyme under pine of 5000 merks." The original charter is signed "MARY R."

Register of Privy Council, Vol. i, p. 397.

On May 26th, 1567, Sir David Barclay obtained a charter under the Great Seal of Queen Mary, confirming to him the office of Heritable Bailie of Lindores, "which had been held by his father and grandfather," and increasing the fee to £100 Scots per annum. The Barclays of Collairnie continued to hold the office until 1748, when heritable jurisdiction was abolished.

Darnley was murdered at Kirk o' Field on February 9th, 1567, and three months later, on May 15th, Mary married

Sir David Barclay, 1547–1587, Collairnie X.

James Hepburn, Earl of Bothwell, who had been openly accused of the murder.

These events produced increasing discontent, which would have ended in civil war, but the Queen surrendered to William Kirkcaldy of Grange at Carberry Hill on June 15th the same year. She was taken first to Edinburgh and then to Lochleven, where shortly afterwards she signed the demission of the Government to her son, and desired that Moray should be the first regent.

On the escape of Mary from Lochleven Castle Sir David Barclay was one of those who entered the Association at Hamilton on May 8th, 1568, to adhere to her against her rebellious subjects. It is interesting to recall here that Sir George Barclay (Gartley XIX) was at this time a member of the Queen's household, and is mentioned in a document relating to the Association.

Pitcairn's Criminal Trials, p. 60.

Sir David took part in the disastrous battle of Langside, on May 13th of the same year, when the hopes of Mary's followers were crushed, and three days afterwards she crossed the Solway and threw herself upon the mercy of Elizabeth.

For some years after the battle of Langside those who took part in it received harsh treatment from the Regent and the other rulers of the young King's court, and we find many entries in the records to this effect.

Ibid.

In 1578 Sir David is custodian of one of the Border rievers called Ringan Armstrong, who had been captured in a foray and sent to Collairnie Tower as prisoner, Sir David being held responsible for his production to the Privy Council under a penalty of 2,000 merks. Apparently he remained a prisoner in the tower for nearly two years, so tedious was the process of criminal law in those days.

Register of Privy Council, Vol. iii, p. 307.

In 1580 Sir David Barclay again becomes cautioner for Sir William Douglas of Lochleven, afterwards Earl of Morton, in a bond for £20,000 that he would exile himself from Scotland until permitted to return.

Douglas does not seem to have remained long in exile, for in 1584 we find David again his cautioner with several others in a sum of £10,000 that he shall not harm David Borswell nor any of his family.

SIR DAVID BARCLAY, 1547–1587, Collairnie X.

On November 14th, 1583, David obtained from Patrick, Archbishop of St. Andrews, a tack of the teinds of Kilmaron and other lands in his favour and of Master David Barclay, his eldest son and heir apparent, and John Barclay, his second son.

Collairnie Charters.

Sir David Barclay and his wife Margaret Wemyss rebuilt a portion of the Tower of Collairnie, and inscribed their initials over the doorway.

They had issue two sons, David and John, and two daughters, Margaret and Beatrix. The eldest son, David (Collairnie XI), succeeded to the estates. The second son, John, died unmarried in 1601. On November 10th of that year David Barclay of Collairnie was served heir to his brother John in an annual rent of three chalders victual furth of the town and lands of Ceres. John Barclay of Touch, and David Barclay of Strowie, were jurors at the inquest. Margaret married James Sibbald, of Rankeilor; and Beatrix, David Clephane of Carslogie. Sir David died August 9th, 1587.

Fife Records.

DAVID BARCLAY

DAVID BARCLAY, 1587–1613, Collairnie XI.

David Barclay, who became Laird of Collairnie on the death of his father, Sir David (Collairnie X), in 1587, had been educated at the University of St. Andrews, and took his degree as Master of Arts.

He was married at an early age to Helen Balfour, youngest daughter of the famous Sir James Balfour of Pittendreich, Lord President of the Court of Session, and this union brought him into contact with some of the most eminent politicians of the time. His wife's brother was Michael, first Lord Balfour of Burleigh.

Douglas's Peerage.

David Barclay (Collairnie XI) was infeft in the lands and Barony of Collairnie on January 29th, 1587–8, confirmed to instruments of sasine proceeding upon a "*precept furth of Chancery*."

Collairnie Charters.

On September 16th, 1590, he obtained a tack of the teinds of Easter and Wester Kindersleith, and on April 16th, 1613, from David Murray, Lord Scone, a tack of the lands of Easter Lumbenny.

Ibid.

He proved to be one of the most turbulent of the Fife lairds of his time. We find his name on many entries in the Register of the Privy Council. At Edinburgh on November 10th, 1592 :—

"Caution by Mr. David Barclay of Cullerny as principal and Mr Patrik Balfour as surety for him in £2000 that he shall behave loyally and answer when required upon."

Register of Privy Council, Vol. v, p. 20.

And in the same register :—

"Caution in £2000 by . . . Wemyss of Bolgy for Barclay of Cullerny that he shall pass benorth the water of Tay by 22nd inst and keep ward betwixt the said water and the Spey till he be freed."

Ibid. p. 141.

"Stirling 9th May 1592.

"Caution in £2000 by Sir John Wemyss apparent of that Ilk for Mr. David Barclay that on being freed of his ward betwixt the waters of North Esk and of Tay, he shall appear befor the council on six days warning, and shall not reset nor intercommune with the Earl of Bothwell or his associates in time coming."

Ibid. p. 144.

"Edinburgh 28th July 1593. DAVID BARCLAY, 1587–1613, Collairnie XI.

"Band of caution in 2000 merks by Mr David Barclay of Cullerny as principal and David Wemyss of that Ilk as surety for him not to harm John Barclay brother to the said Mr David Barclay. Among the witnesses is Robert Barclay, 'father-brother to the said Mr David Barclay.'" *Ibid.* p. 598.

At this time there seems to have been a feud between the two brothers, as at the same date there is a similar band that John Barclay should not harm his brother David.

Other bands of the same nature are among the entries in the register, and again David seeks protection, together with his brother John and his "father-brother" Robert.

The following incident will show the disturbed state of the country at this time:—

"Complaint by Sir Thomas Hammiltoun of Bynnie for his Majestie's interest and by David Barclay of Cullerny heritable proprietor of one half of the lands of Glashlie that on 26th May 1609 David Bowman baillie and others of Falkland to the number of eight score men armed with weapons including hagbuts and pistolets came to the said David Barclay's lands, demolished the fold dykes built by him within his marches, threatened his servitors, discharged a great number of hagbuts and pistolets, whereby the oxen ploughing were so afraid that they ran away athorte the feilds and brik the haill pleughis and pleugh graith.

"Parties appear. Defendants plead the day was appointed by magistrates of Falkland for a wapinschawing. Ordained that they did wrong in mustering without the town and going about with unlawful arms and that they abstain from such behaviour." Register of Privy Council, Vol. viii, p. 334.

A wapinschaw in ancient Scottish usage was a periodical gathering of the people within various areas for the purpose of seeing that each man was armed in accordance with his rank, and ready to take the field when required.

It was owing to the refined taste of David and his wife that the internal decorations of Collairnie Tower were executed, and their monograms are wrought into the designs. A careful examination of these heraldic paintings shows that the following important families have been represented there. In many cases labels with the printed names in black-letter are still intact, but not a few have suffered from the destructive hands of inappreciative owners.

DAVID BARCLAY, 1587–1613, Collairnie XI.

The dining-hall contains the arms of Ramsay of Colluthie, Wyntoun of that Ilk, Sandilands of St. Monance quartered with Douglas, Traill of Blego, Lairmont of Dairsie, Melville of Cairny, Monypenny of Pitmillie, Moncrief of that Ilk, Halket of Pitfirren, Henderson of Fordell, Inglis of Tarvitt, Kinnaird in the Carse, Forret of Garden, Fernie of that Ilk, Colville of Cleish, Bethune of Balfour, Bethune of Creich, Melville of Balgarvie, Balfour of Corston, Balfour of that Ilk, Balfour of Burleigh, Balfour of Denmyln, Barclay of Collairnie, Barclay of Touch, Barclay of Towie, Barclay of Mathers.

In the guest-chamber the roof is more dilapidated than in the dining-hall beneath it, and there is more difficulty in deciphering the heraldic blazonings. Many portions of the roof have been torn away, and at some period the arms have been repainted by an inexpert person who did not understand the primary importance of colouring in heraldry, as many of the arms show incorrect heraldic colouring through the substitution of wrong tints for those borne by the various families.

The arms still remaining in a fair state of preservation are those of Scott of Abbotshall, Melville of Raith, Stewart of Rosyth, Sibbald of Balgony, Scott of Balweary, Wardlaw of Pitreavie, Murray of Gledoich, Durward of Lundin, Colville of Easter Wemyss, Lundy of Lundyn, Strang of Balcaskie, Lundin of Balgonie, Ramsay of Crackeston, Lundy of that Ilk, Kincraigy of that Ilk, Dishington of Ardross, Toures of Innerleith, Anstruther of that Ilk, Pitblado of that Ilk, Seaton of Pitmeddon, Lord Innermeith, Stewart of Mynto.

Six of the heraldic pictures are so disfigured by breakages in the roof, and so imperfect in consequence of the colours having been altered, that they have not been deciphered, but from the above list it will be seen that the decoration of this room, as designed by the Laird of Collairnie, contained representations of the armorial bearings of many of the principal Fifeshire families.

The arms on the sculptured stones above the doorway

were those borne by Helen Balfour, the Lady of Collairnie, and it is therefore probable that she was responsible for the decorations of this tower in conjunction with the second Sir David Lindsay of Mount, and her own kinsman Sir James Balfour of Denmyln, who were both Lords Lyon King-of-Arms. DAVID BARCLAY, 1587-1613, Collairnie XI.

David Barclay did not adhere so faithfully to the fortunes of the Stewarts as his father. He was concerned in the raid of Holyrood, when Francis, Earl of Bothwell, sought to obtain control of King James VI, and he fell under the displeasure of his Royal master. We have already seen that, in 1592, he was bound over "to behave himself loyally," and that later he was for a time banished from Fife, and only obtained a relaxation of his sentence provided that he would not "reset" the fugitive Earl of Bothwell.

From his will, dated May 1st, 1613, we find that David had by his wife, Helen Balfour, the following issue :—

1. Sir David Barclay, who succeeded him as Collairnie XII.
2. Michael, a lawyer, who married Margaret Phin, daughter of David Phin of Whitehill. He died before 1682, leaving issue two daughters : Margaret, married in 1664 to David, brother to Lord Colville of Culross ; Anna, who married Sir George Wishart, Bt. Douglas's Peerage. Fife Records.
3. Patrick, died unmarried.
4. James, who on December 23rd, 1635, was served heir to his "immediate younger brother," Alexander. Retours of Service.

   (N.B.—William had died before Alexander.)

   In 1648 he was fined £50 for assault to the effusion of blood, on James Clephane in Cupar. Fife Records.

   On December 17th, 1661, there is a band by George Duddingstone of Kilduncan and Mr. James Barclay, brother german to the Right Hon. Sir David Barclay of Collairnie (Collairnie XII), "for love and favour they bear to James Barclay, Burgess of Cupar, and Margaret Killoch, his spouse," for a certain quantity of victual.

   James married Barbara Jameson, and had issue :

   (1) David, who died at Cupar, November 24th, 1654. Cupar Parish Reg.

   (2) Margaret, baptised December 4th, 1654, and married Hugh Scot 1680. Fife Records.

   (3) John, baptised July 12th, 1657, died at Cupar, March 8th, 1659. Cupar Parish Reg.

DAVID BARCLAY, 1587–1613, Collairnie XI.

(4) James, baptised August 2nd, 1661, buried at Cupar February 28th, 1664.

5. William, died unmarried before 1635.
6. Alexander, died unmarried 1635. His elder brother James was served heir to him.
7. Euphemia, who married William Lovell of Connoquhie.

From the Collairnie charters it is evident that the death of David Barclay (Collairnie XI) took place on August 8th, 1613.

SIR DAVID BARCLAY

Sir David Barclay, 1613-1656, Collairnie XII.

Sir David Barclay (Collairnie XII), who succeeded his father, David (Collairnie XI), on August 8th, 1613, was the ninth laird in succession to bear the name of David. The oft-repeated Christian name has caused much difficulty to the genealogist, and accounts for many erroneous statements in previous writings.

He was knighted by King Charles I, when that monarch visited Scotland in 1633, and survived to see the King dethroned and beheaded, and his son exiled from the land of his fathers.

Douglas's Peerage.

Sir David married first, in 1618, Euphemia Leslie, fifth and youngest daughter of Patrick, first Lord Lindores, by his wife Lady Jane Stewart, daughter of Robert, second Earl of Orkney. By her, who died December 10th, 1625, he had issue one son and three daughters. Sir David married secondly Anne Riddell, only child of Sir John Riddell of Riddell, Bt., by Jean his second wife, a daughter of Sir James Anstruther of Anstruther in Fife, and by her he had issue two sons and two daughters.

Douglas's Baronage.

There is an entry in the register of the Privy Council, dated at Edinburgh, November 14th, 1614, showing that Sir David was a minor at the time of his inheritance.

> "Dispensation to the Sheriff of Fyfe in favour of David Barclay, now of Collairnie, who in spite of his minority is to be served heir to his late father, Mr. David Barclay, of Collairnie, in his lands, some of which are held by the Crown."

On June 29th, 1614, David obtained a charter of confirmation from James Marquis of Hamilton of the twelfth part of the lands of Collairnie and others, and on January 3rd, 1616, he was served heir to his father in the barony of Collairnie, comprehending the lands of Collairnie, lands of Carskerdo, the lands of Easter and Wester Kinsleith, Freeland and Lindifferon, three fifth parts of the lands of Kinnimonth, half of the lands of Bin and Kinnaird, and seven parts of the lands of Lumbenny, with the mill thereof, all united in the barony of Collairnie, also in the

Collairnie Charters.

Inquisition Retour, Fife, Abb. i, No. 256.

Sir David Barclay, 1613–1656, Collairnie XII.

five twelfth parts of the lands of Kilmaron, in the barony of Pitblado.

On December 18th, 1617, he obtained from Patrick, Lord Lindores, a precept of *clare constat* of the heritable Bailiary of the Abbacy of Lindores and others, as heir of Sir David Barclay of Collairnie (Collairnie X), his grandfather.

Collairnie Charters.

On February 5th, 1618, he obtained a discharge and assignation of the whole barony of Pitblado in his favour, comprehending the lands of Pitblado, Kilmaron, Pitlurg, Hilton, Boghall and Foulcausey, from James Pitblado, eldest son and heir of the deceased Alexander Pitblado, sometime of that Ilk.

On August 2nd, 1621, he obtained a charter under the Great Seal of King James VI of the lands of Luthrie, Glaslie, Kinnimonth, etc.

The following charters are of considerable interest in helping to prove the previous holders of the Collairnie estates. On April 28th, 1630, Sir David Barclay (Collairnie XII) was served heir to Sir David Barclay (Collairnie VIII) " abavi sui," that is, the Sir David who died in 1536. At the same time he was served heir to David Barclay (Collairnie IV) " intavi sui proavi inter ipsum et quondam Helenam Spittel suam sposam legitime procreat," which David died about 1450.

Fife Records.

On June 2nd, 1630, there is a protest at the instance of Robert Colvile of Cleish against the above services of David Barclay (Collairnie IV) having acquired through his wife, Helen Spittell, the Barony of Cleish.

Inquisition Retours, Abbrev. ii, Nos. 1622, 1623.

On February 4th, 1634, Sir David Barclay, as " heritable bailie of the Regality of Lindores," is " complainer " in an action before the Privy Council against Mr. David Orme, minister at Newburgh, " for having locked and made fast the doors of St. Katherine's chapel of Newburgh, on April 13th, 1632, and debarred the complainer from entering, as had been the constant practice of himself and his predecessors to hold his court there." Repeating of the same conduct, on October 8th the same year, when Michael

Barclay, the complainer's deputy, was holding the same court. (Michael Barclay was Sir David's brother.)

SIR DAVID BARCLAY, 1613–1656, Collairnie XII.

The minister produced a letter from the brethren of the Presbytery of Cupar, ordering him "to use all good means for keeping the kirk of Newburgh for the service of God," and he said "that in the case of any seeking to act contrary to the order of the kirk and Acts of Parliament he could lock the kirk door." The Lords therefore upheld the defender.

Register of Privy Council, Series ii, Vol. v, p. 196.

The laird was appointed a Justice of the Peace in the year 1634.

Ibid. p. 384.

Sir David Barclay (Collairnie XII) lived in a most momentous period of Scottish and English history. He became owner of the estates twelve years before the accession of Charles I. He and his son, Robert, afterwards Collairnie XIII, both took an active part in the civil wars, and both signed the Covenant. It is probable that Sir David fought in the army of the Estates against the Royalist rising in Scotland under the Marquess of Montrose, in 1645, as later we find him mentioned in the records as Colonel Sir David.

He must not be confused with Colonel David Barclay (Urie I), son of the last laird of Mathers, a well-known leader in the civil war, who is constantly mentioned. A full account of Colonel David Barclay (Urie I) will be found in Part III of this History.

The execution of Charles I took place in January 1649. The Estates always denied that they had in any way participated in the affair, and at once received his son in Scotland, where he was duly crowned, at Scone, as King Charles II.

As a consequence Cromwell marched to the north and defeated the Scots at the battle of Dunbar, on September 3rd, 1650. While Cromwell was engaged in subduing the north, the Scottish army invaded England, and reached Worcester, where Cromwell overtook them and finally defeated them. This was the end of the civil war; Charles's cause was lost, and after many adventures he escaped to France.

Sir David joined the army of the Estates in the year 1644,

Sir David Barclay, 1613–1656, Collairnie XII.

and among the Acts of the "Committees of warr in the shires" there is the following entry :—

Acts of Parliament (Scots), Vol. vi (i), p. 54.

"The Estates of this Kingdome. . . ." Reciting "that this Kingdome be put partly into a posture of defence. . . . They have nominate and appoyntit to be Colonells of horse and foote, within the several sheriffdoms. . . ."

For "the sheriffdom of Fyffe and Kinroch" (30 lines of names) including Sir David Barclay of Collairnie.

"On July 24th, 1644, appoynting the committees of warr in the several shires and divisions of the Kingdom. Shire of Fyffe and Kinroch" includes Sir David Barclay of Collairnie.

Ibid. p. 202.

The laird of Collairnie was also appointed again in 1646.

In the year 1647 Sir David Barclay, as bailie of the Regality of Lindores, had to obtain dispensation from the Estates for himself and his deputies to hold their courts, notwithstanding the Parliament. He was granted the necessary warrant.

Ibid. p. 662.

On page 378 in a book called *The Army of the Covenant*, by Charles Sandford Terry, there is an interesting description of a pay sheet :—

"Accompt of Sir Adam Hepburne, from 14th December 1645.

Total for Rutmaister Sir David Barclay of Colerny, his trouppe	£1735 : 0 : 0.
To 13 trouppers	100 : 16 : 0.
more „ 4 „	7 : 4 : 0.
„ „ 6 „	36 : 2 : 0.
To Leutenant Horne, Cornet Clephane, quarter Term for themselves and 18 trouppers	£254 : 5 : 0.

On February 15th, 1649, under "The Act for putting the Kingdom into a posture of defence," again we find in the list of persons to be Colonels of horse and foot, for the "presbiterie of Coupar," the name of the laird of Collairnie. This time the entry is "the lairds of Collerney elder and younger."

Ibid. (2), p. 186.

Among the estates brought before the commission for re-valuation in the sheriffdoms, on May 8th, 1649, are included those of Collairnie.

Ibid. p. 243.

Sir David Barclay witnessed the pacification of Scotland by General Monk, the settlement of the country under the Parliament and the re-establishment of episcopacy, and the Union with England in 1651. He died four years before the

Restoration of Charles II. The laird appears to have fallen into disfavour through his resistance to the imposition of episcopacy by the Parliament, but he did not survive to suffer the rigorous punishment meted out to such offenders.

Sir David Barclay, 1613–1656, Collairnie XII.

The penalty which should have been inflicted upon him fell upon his unfortunate widow. That lady was Dame Anne Riddell, whose name was prominently in the history of the suffering Kirk of Scotland in her day. On July 16th, 1674, the Lady of Collairnie was denounced as a rebel at the market cross of Cupar, " for not compearing to answer the Privy Council for the charge brought against her for keeping and being present at house and field conventicles and for inviting and countenancing ' outed ' ministers in their invasion and intrusion upon the kirks and pulpits of Forglen, Balmerinoch, Colessy and Auchtermuchty, with Walsh and others in her company, in April, May and June, 1674." This denunciation did not cure Lady Collairnie of her contumacy, for in September of the same year she was once more declared a rebel, and an attempt was made to inflict upon her the fine that should have been exacted from her deceased husband. She does not seem to have survived this persecution, and her eldest son, John, managed to retain the property, which otherwise would have been confiscated.

By his first wife Euphemia Leslie, Sir David had four children: Robert, who succeeded him as Collairnie XIII; Jean, who died young and unmarried; Helen, of whom we have no further record; and Margaret, who married, in 1651, Sir Thomas Nairne of Sandfurd in Fife.

The laird married secondly Anne Riddell, who, as has been already stated, survived him. By her he had issue two sons: John, who evicted from Collairnie his half-nephew James, of whom later; and James, who died whilst a student at Edinburgh College and was buried at Cupar May 8th, 1665. He also had two daughters: Jean, of whom nothing is known; and Isobel, a posthumous child, born August, 1656, married first David Cunningham, merchant in Edinburgh, secondly Mr. John Carson, minister of Abdie in Fife. She died in 1724.

Sir David Barclay (Collairnie XII) died June 28th, 1656.

ROBERT BARCLAY, 1656–1663, Collairnie XIII.

ROBERT BARCLAY

Robert Barclay succeeded his father Sir David, on June 28th, 1656, and died in 1663.

He was born about the year 1619, and, as has been stated, after fighting for the Estates against Montrose's Royalist rising, on the murder of Charles I, he joined the Scottish rebellion and, with his father, was deeply involved.

The first mention of him is on February 15th, 1649, when at the age of thirty he is appointed under "The Act for putting the Kingdom into a posture of defence" to be a colonel of horse or foot for the Presbytery of Cupar. In this record he and his father are styled "lairds of Collairnie elder and younger."

He must not be confused with the other Robert Barclay appearing at this time, who was Robert Barclay of Pierston, Provost of Irvine and Commissioner to Parliament.

In May 1654—that is, in the lifetime of his father—he was included in Oliver Cromwell's Act of Grace and Pardon and was fined £1,000 sterling.

Retours of Service.

On September 2nd, 1656, Robert Barclay was served heir to his father Sir David in the barony of Collairnie and that of Pitblado and the lands of Kilmaron, Hilton and Boghall.

His debts were enormous and the property heavily mortgaged, the sum amounting to 43,000 merks. These financial embarrassments compelled him to part with some of the outlying lands, and it was at this time that he sold Carskerdo, which had been in possession of the family for nearly 500 years.

It is not improbable that the 43,000 merks, afterwards owed by Robert's son James to his half-uncle John, had originally been sums advanced by John's mother Anne Riddell to help her stepson Robert when he had difficulties with Cromwell. Anne was no doubt an heiress, as her grandfather, Sir James Anstruther, was a rich man and she was her mother's only child.

Robert Barclay married, in 1654, Marion, one of the daughters and co-heiresses of Sir James Scott of Rossie, in

Fife. She was the widow of Major-General Sir John Brown of Fordell, in Perthshire and in the parish of Arngask. Sir John was defeated and killed fighting against Cromwell at the battle of Inverkeithing, July 20th, 1651. Cromwell then marched on Perth and halted at Arngask to bury the dead general with full military honours. By his wife, Marion Scott, Sir John Brown left an only daughter, Antonia, married in 1667 to Alexander Dunlop of Dunlop, Ayrshire. They sold the estate of Fordell in 1669. Antonia was half-sister to the evicted James and his brother Thomas.

ROBERT BARCLAY, 1656–1663, Collairnie XIII.

James, the elder of Robert Barclay's two sons, succeeded him as Laird of Collairnie, but was evicted from the barony by his half-uncle John in 1672 and died previous to the year 1681. The second son, Thomas, succeeded his brother James as heir-male of Collairnie.

Robert Barclay (Collairnie XIII) died at Edinburgh, and was buried, in the night time, at Collairnie, February 14th, 1663. His death occurred but two years after the Restoration of Charles II, but that monarch did little for the sufferers in the Royal cause.

Marion Scott outlived her husband and married thirdly, in 1667, William Mure of Rowallan, Ayrshire.

JAMES BARCLAY

James Barclay, 1663–1681, Collairnie XIV.

James Barclay, who succeeded his father Robert on February 14th, 1663, was a very young boy when he came into possession of the estates. He could not have been more than eight years of age, as his father married in the year 1654.

He received a precept of *clare constat* from Lord Crawford Lindsay and his elder son, Lord Lindsay, dated March 1st, 1672. This was for certain lands in which his grandfather Sir David (Collairnie XII) had been infeft by Lord Crawford Lindsay, as security for a loan of 18,000 merks, made on October 5th, 1651.

James Barclay (Collairnie XIV) did not hold the castle and estates for many years, for when he was about seventeen he was turned out by his half-uncle, John Barclay.

As has been already stated, James's father Robert had left the property heavily mortgaged and burdened his son with a legacy of many debts. John Barclay gradually acquired all the mortgages, amounting to 43,000 merks, besides sheriff's fees, and foreclosed, evicting his nephew. He obtained a decreet against the young man on May 7th, 1672, and three months later a charter of appraisement, under the Great Seal of Charles II, by which in addition to the Barony of Collairnie he also acquired the office of Heritable Bailie of the Regality of Lindores.

James was living in the year 1678, and died before September 20th, 1681, leaving no issue.

THOMAS BARCLAY

Thomas Barclay, 1663–1734, Collairnie XV.

On the death of James Barclay, the last of the direct line to hold the Barony of Collairnie, the descent fell on his brother, Thomas, as heir-male.

Thomas, the second son of Robert Barclay (Collairnie XIII) and his wife Marion Scott, was born in 1663, the year of his father's death. His name appears in the previously mentioned Decreet of Appraisement by which his brother James was evicted from the barony in 1672.

THOMAS BARCLAY, 1663–1734, Collairnie XV.

In 1667, when he was but four years old, his mother married, for the third time, William Mure of Rowallan in Ayrshire, and took Thomas, the child of her late husband, to her new home.

By William Mure she had an only daughter, Jean Mure of Rowallan, who married first William Fairlie, younger of Bruntsfield, and secondly, as his second spouse, contracted at Edinburgh, June 16th, 1695, David, first Earl of Glasgow, and by him had issue.

On March 9th, 1682, there was a case before the Lords of Council and Sessions at the instance of his uncle, John Barclay, now of Collairnie, and his cousin and tutor John Leslie, fourth Lord Lindores, against Dame Marion Scott, Lady Rowallan (his mother), complaining that she had taken her son away to Ayrshire and was not educating him in a suitable manner, and stating that the Collairnie family "was of known loyalty and upon all occasions gave obedience to the Royal commands and adhered in the most difficult times to the Royal interest." They also stated that "he was being bred up in a family of fanatical and disloyal principles, not being permitted to visit or be acquainted with his nearest relations and friends, and denied all manner of education suitable to his quality . . . nor being sent to College. He had moreover been influenced to choose curators altogether strangers to his family, of known disaffected and disloyal principles."

It seemed, in John Barclay's judgment, that in these circumstances a supporter would be lost to his Majesty's interest, unless a remedy were provided.

It is so far creditable to a government which has a good many sins to its charge that when the case came before the Duke of York and the Privy Council, on John Barclay's petition, and both sides had been heard—namely, the uncle on the one side, and Lady Rowallan with the three curators, Montgomery younger of Skelmorley, the laird of Dunlop and Mr. John Stirling of Irvine, on the other—they decided that the young Barclay was of age to act and choose curators for himself, and that the defenders were not bound to produce him in court, thus frankly consenting that the young man

Chambers's Domestic Annals, p. 436.

THOMAS BARCLAY, 1663–1734, Collairnie XV.

should rest in the danger of being perverted from the loyalty of his family. (Register of the Privy Council.)

In 1708, after the death of his uncle John, Thomas Barclay (Collairnie XV) attempted to recover possession of the family estates.

He served himself nearest lawful heir-male of the late Robert Barclay (Collairnie XIII), his father, and also of the late Sir David Barclay (Collairnie XII), his grandfather. Both services dated October 23rd and recorded at Cupar February 9th, 1709. Thomas Barclay was at this date about 44 years of age. His claim was not successful, and, as we shall see, the property passed to his cousin Antonia.

There is no further record to be found of Thomas Barclay, and he seems to have become a person of little importance.

Cupar Parish Register.

He was buried at Cupar on December 19th, 1734. At his death without male issue the heir-male of the house of Collairnie devolved on John Barclay of Hiltarvet (see Pedigree XIV), a descendant of William Barclay in Johnstone, the second son of David Barclay (Collairnie IX), the first Baron of Collairnie, and husband of Janet Sandilands.

The heir-male of the Collairnie line to-day is Hugh Arthur Barclay, son of the late David Hay Barclay.

THE REV. THOMAS BARCLAY OF ALBANY

REV. THOMAS BARCLAY of Albany.

Some writers have confused Thomas Barclay (Collairnie XV) with a certain Thomas Barclay who matriculated at St. Salvator's College, St. Andrews, at about this time, and have presumed that Thomas (Collairnie XV) was sent to that College as the result of the complaint of his lack of education.

Barclays of New York, by Moffat, p. 42.

"Thomas Barclay, M.A., of St. Salvator's" was ordained, under that description, as deacon and priest successively, in May 1707, by Henry Compton, Bishop of London. On May 31st of the same year he signed the Act of Uniformity, and was then appointed chaplain to the garrison at Fort Orange, Albany, N.Y. He landed in Boston in November, 1707, and was later appointed missionary to the Mohawk Indians.

The Rev. Thomas Barclay was appointed missionary to the Indians' by the Society for the Propagation of the Gospel, and among their records are many of his letters, giving accounts of his work and of the building of the church of St. Peter at Albany. In a letter dated at Albany, April 17th, 1713, he writes as follows :—

REV. THOMAS BARCLAY of Albany.

"Please give my humble services to Mr Hodges, the Society's treasurer, and acquaint him that I continue My Brother Henry Barclay and his Spouse my Attorneys, as also that I heartily thank him for the punctuall payment of my Salary."

This mention of a brother Henry may at some future time afford a clue to the origin of the Rev. Thomas Barclay, minister of Albany, but the present compiler has been unable to trace his parentage.

A letter from his wife, Anna Dorothea Drauyer, dated at Albany, May 22nd, 1722, shows that the closing years of the Rev. Thomas Barclay's life were darkened by a mental affliction, so grave as to render necessary actual physical restraint. In July 1724 there is a further letter from Mrs. Barclay saying that her husband was "continuing in the same deplorable condition" and asking for assistance, as the family were starving.

The Rev. Thomas Barclay was living in 1725, but appears to have died shortly after that date. His descendants became a notable family in America, and at the time of the War of Independence remained loyal to the English throne. The family carry the arms of the Pierston Barclays to-day.

Dr. de Lancy Hethcote Barclay, of Baltimore (d. 1900), who made many researches in both Scotland and England, without feeling at all committed to the point of view, was inclined somewhat to the belief that the Rev. Thomas was possibly, if not probably, of the Pierston family.

Mr. R. Burnham Moffat, in his valuable book *The Barclays of New York: Who they are and who they are not; And some other Barclays*, published 1904, has dealt fully with the descendants of the Rev. Thomas Barclay of Albany.

The Lands of Collairnie after 1672

JOHN BARCLAY of Collairnie, 1672–1687. John Barclay of Collairnie, eldest son of Sir David Barclay (Collairnie XII), by his second wife, Anne Riddell, became the possessor of the Barony of Collairnie and the office of Bailie of Lindores in 1672.

As has been already stated, Robert (Collairnie XIII), owing to financial embarrassments, had been obliged to raise heavy mortgages on the family estates. John Barclay had acquired these mortgages, which may have been originally held by his mother, Anne Riddell, who was the only child of Sir John Riddell and his wife, a daughter of Sir James Anstruther, and was probably wealthy.

We have seen under James Barclay (Collairnie XIV) that John Barclay, having obtained a Decreet of Appraisement, evicted his half-nephew from the Barony in 1672.

John Barclay married Jean Gordon, a daughter of John Gordon of Cairnbarrow, Aberdeenshire, the marriage contract dated May 8th, 1669 (her mother was Euphemia Barclay). By her John Barclay had two sons and five daughters. His eldest son, John, succeeded him, of whom later. His second son, David, who was born in 1678, was probably twin with John. He was known as "in Montquhanny" and was tutor of Collairnie during the minority of his niece, Antonia, the heiress of Collairnie. He married and died without male issue.

Collairnie Evidences.

John Barclay had also five daughters, Christian, Anna, Helen, Jean and Isobel. He died in 1687, and was succeeded in the Barony of Collairnie and the office of Bailie of Lindores by his eldest son,

JOHN BARCLAY,

who on June 19th, 1702, obtained a "precept furth of Chancery," following upon a retour of special service in his favour, as son and heir of the deceased John Barclay, his father. He also got a Charter of Resignation and Novodamus, under the Great Seal of Queen Anne, of the lands and Barony of

Collairnie and the office of the Bailie of Lindores, on a process of resignation of Sir David Barclay, his grandfather (Collairnie XII), and also upon two adjudications against Thomas Barclay of Collairnie, surviving heir-apparent of the deceased Robert Barclay of Collairnie his father, and brother and heir-apparent of the deceased James Barclay (Collairnie XIV). Which charter was dated at Windsor Castle, October 1st, 1704, and recorded at Cupar, December 14th, 1707.

Reg. Mag. Sig. L. 82, No. 154.

By this charter John Barclay was declared the rightful heir, and the Barony of Collairnie was reconstituted by a new erection. In this charter the succession was declared to be "heirs whomsoever"; consequently when John Barclay died, leaving an only daughter, Antonia, she became sole heiress of the estate, to the exclusion of her cousin Thomas and his descendants.

ANTONIA BARCLAY

ANTONIA STEUART-BARCLAY, Lady of Collairnie, 1709–1780.

Antonia Barclay, Lady of Collairnie, was a very young child when she succeeded her father in the estate of Collairnie. She was served heir to him in the Bailiary of the Abbacy of Lindores, January 9th, and in the lands and Barony of Collairnie, February 21st, 1710–11.

Antonia married in 1717 Henry Steuart, second son of Sir James Steuart of Goodtrees, county Lanark, Lord Advocate of Scotland, and nephew of Sir Thomas Steuart, Bart., of Coltness, Lanarkshire, and Provost of Edinburgh. He was born in 1697 and was under age at the time of his marriage.

Henry Steuart assumed the additional surname and the arms (not matriculated). He became a member of the Scottish Bar.

In 1747 Antonia Steuart-Barclay received the sum of £215, as compensation for the abolition of the office of Bailie of Lindores, which the Barclays of Collairnie had held for over two hundred years.

She and her husband had issue, with other children who died young :—

1. James Steuart-Barclay, their heir.

2. William Steuart-Barclay, who succeeded his brother.
3. Antonia, married in 1744 John Leslie of Lumquhat, an officer in Gardiner's Dragoons.
4. Margaret, married in 1754 James Steuart of Allanton.

JAMES STEUART-BARCLAY of Collairnie, 1780.

JAMES STEUART-BARCLAY

James Steuart-Barclay of Collairnie succeeded to the estates February 10th, 1780, and died unmarried.

WILLIAM STEUART-BARCLAY, 1780–1783.

WILLIAM STEUART-BARCLAY

William Steuart-Barclay of Collairnie, who succeeded his brother James in 1780, held the Barony for only three years, and died in 1783, aged forty-seven.

He married first, in 1756, Euphemia Angus and by her had an only daughter Elizabeth, who married Arthur Robertson, M.D., of Antigua.

By his second wife, Elizabeth Hay, daughter of Peter Hay of Leys, he had with other issue:

SIR HENRY STEUART-BARCLAY of Collairnie, 1783–1851.

SIR HENRY STEUART-BARCLAY,

who was born in 1765 and succeeded his father in 1783. He was an ensign in the Jamaican Regiment of Foot, March 18th, 1782; lieutenant 50th Foot (Royal West Kent Regiment), April 1st, 1783; transferred to the 29th Foot (Worcestershire Regiment), October 15th, 1788. He was afterwards a captain in the Perthshire Militia.

In 1790 Sir Henry sold Collairnie, Kilmaron, Hilton and Pitblado, to Francis Balfour, M.D., of Fernie, county Fife, and the estates of Collairnie passed from the Barclay family, who had held them for over 450 years.

The Scottish Barclays p. 71.

Sir Henry Steuart-Barclay succeeded his kinsman, the eighth Baronet of Coltness, on August 12th, 1839. He died without issue in 1851.

The Barclays of Wavertree Lodge

In Burke's *Landed Gentry* (1865 edition), under the heading "The Barclays of Wavertree Lodge," there appears the lineage of a cadet branch who claim descent from the Barclays of Collairnie.

Their progenitor was a George Barclay of Collairnie, said to have been born in the year 1679. No other mention of a George Barclay has been found either in the *Collairnie Evidences* or the records of the time.

George Barclay married first Grace Clayton, of Goosnargh, county Lancaster, and secondly Alice Rigbye of the same place, by whom he had issue Thomas, who succeeded him, and other children. He died in 1724.

His son Thomas married Dorothy, daughter of Robert Thomson of Kilham, county York, by whom he had issue one surviving son, George Barclay of Burford Lodge, Surrey, who sat as M.P. for Bridport, and died June 19th, 1819. George married July 13th, 1782, Rebecca Brockhurst, and by her had three sons. The eldest, Thomas Brockhurst Barclay of Wavertree Lodge, Lancaster, married Sarah Peters, daughter of Henry Peters of Betchworth Castle, and died without issue. The second son, George Perks Barclay of Burford Lodge, was born in 1784 and married in 1810 Maria, daughter of Henry Boulton of Givons Grove. He had issue two sons, who both died unmarried, and four daughters: Maria, married in 1842 to Richard Fuller of The Rookery, Dorking; Rebecca, married in 1843 to George James Barnard Hankey of Fetcham Park, Leatherhead; and Juliana and Emily, who lived in the village of Westcott, near Dorking, and both died unmarried.

PEDIGREE XIV.

Heirs Male of Collairnie

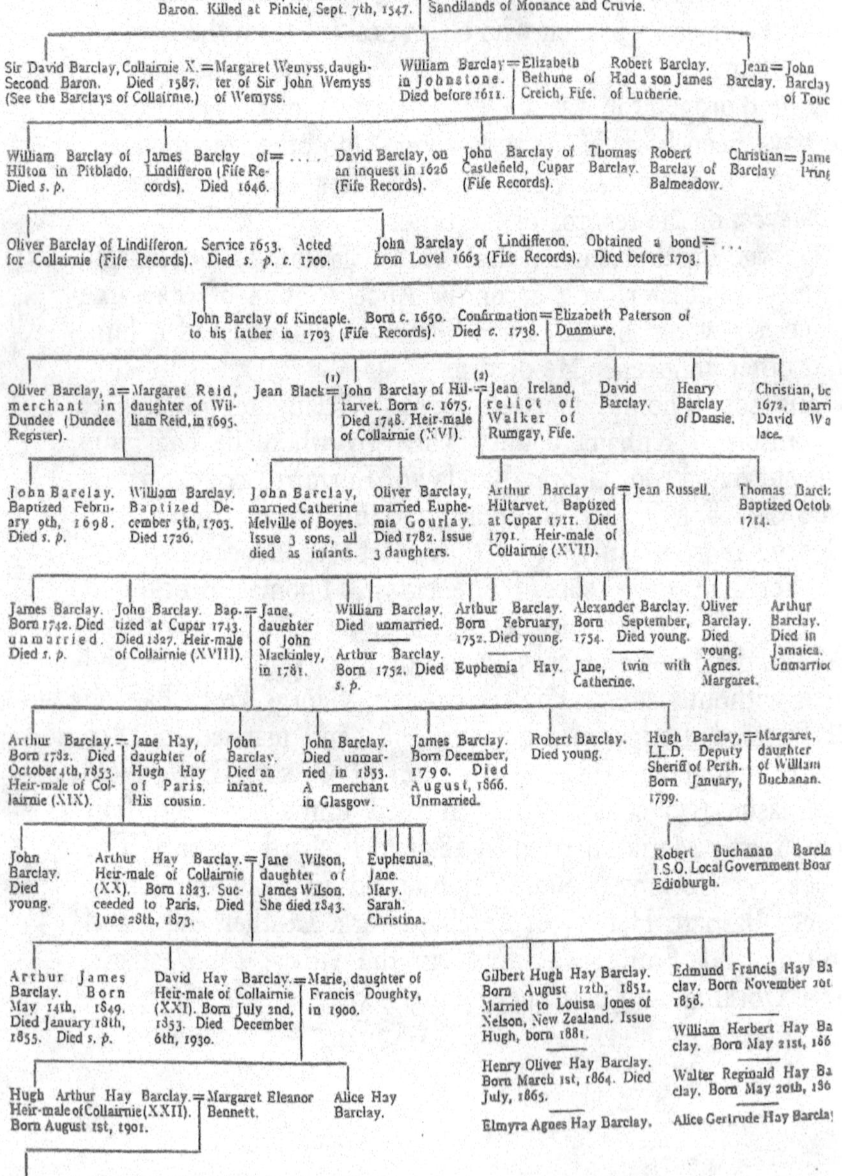

DAVID BARCLAY, Collairnie IX. First Baron. Killed at Pinkie, Sept. 7th, 1547. = Janet Sandilands, daughter of Sir John Sandilands of Monance and Cruvie.
Sir David Barclay, Collairnie X. Second Baron. Died 1587. (See the Barclays of Collairnie.) = Margaret Wemyss, daughter of Sir John Wemyss of Wemyss.
William Barclay in Johnstone. Died before 1611. = Elizabeth Bethune of Creich, Fife.
Robert Barclay. Had a son James of Lutherie.
Jean Barclay. = John Barclay of Touc
William Barclay of Hilton in Pitblado. Died s. p.
James Barclay of Lindifferon (Fife Records). Died 1646. = ...
David Barclay, on an inquest in 1626 (Fife Records).
John Barclay of Castlefield, Cupar (Fife Records).
Thomas Barclay.
Robert Barclay of Balmeadow.
Christian Barclay = James Pring
Oliver Barclay of Lindifferon. Service 1653. Acted for Collairnie (Fife Records). Died s. p. c. 1700.
John Barclay of Lindifferon. Obtained a bond from Lovel 1663 (Fife Records). Died before 1703. = . . .
John Barclay of Kincaple. Born c. 1650. Confirmation to his father in 1703 (Fife Records). Died c. 1738. = Elizabeth Paterson of Dunmure.
Oliver Barclay, merchant in Dundee (Dundee Register). = Margaret Reid, daughter of William Reid, in 1695.
Jean Black = (1) John Barclay of Hiltarvet. Born c. 1675. Died 1748. Heir-male of Collairnie (XVI). = (2) Jean Ireland, relict of Walker of Rumgay, Fife.
David Barclay.
Henry Barclay of Dansie.
Christian, born 1672, married David Wallace.
John Barclay. Baptized February 9th, 1698. Died s. p.
William Barclay. Baptized December 5th, 1703. Died 1726.
John Barclay, married Catherine Melville of Boyes. Issue 3 sons, all died as infants.
Oliver Barclay, married Euphemia Gourlay. Died 1782. Issue 3 daughters.
Arthur Barclay of Hiltarvet. Baptized at Cupar 1711. Died 1791. Heir-male of Collairnie (XVII). = Jean Russell.
Thomas Barcl: Baptized Octob 1714.
James Barclay. Born 1742. Died unmarried. Died s. p.
John Barclay. Baptized at Cupar 1743. Died 1827. Heir-male of Collairnie (XVIII). = Jane, daughter of John Mackinley, in 1781.
William Barclay. Died unmarried.
Arthur Barclay. Born 1752. Died s. p.
Arthur Barclay. Born February, 1752. Died young.
Euphemia Hay.
Alexander Barclay. Born September, 1754. Died young.
Jane, twin with Catherine.
Oliver Barclay. Died young.
Agnes.
Margaret.
Arthur Barclay. Died in Jamaica. Unmarried.
Arthur Barclay. Born 1782. Died October 4th, 1853. Heir-male of Collairnie (XIX). = Jane Hay, daughter of Hugh Hay of Paris. His cousin.
John Barclay. Died an infant.
John Barclay. Died unmarried in 1853. A merchant in Glasgow.
James Barclay. Born December, 1790. Died August, 1866. Unmarried.
Robert Barclay. Died young.
Hugh Barclay, LL.D. Deputy Sheriff of Perth. Born January, 1799. = Margaret, daughter of William Buchanan.
John Barclay. Died young.
Arthur Hay Barclay. Heir-male of Collairnie (XX). Born 1823. Succeeded to Paris. Died June 28th, 1873. = Jane Wilson, daughter of James Wilson. She died 1843.
Euphemia.
Jane.
Mary.
Sarah.
Christina.
Robert Buchanan Barcla I.S.O. Local Government Boar Edinburgh.
Arthur James Barclay. Born May 14th, 1849. Died January 18th, 1855. Died s. p.
David Hay Barclay. Heir-male of Collairnie (XXI). Born July 2nd, 1853. Died December 6th, 1930. = Marie, daughter of Francis Doughty, in 1900.
Gilbert Hugh Hay Barclay. Born August 12th, 1851. Married to Louisa Jones of Nelson, New Zealand. Issue Hugh, born 1881.
Henry Oliver Hay Barclay. Born March 1st, 1864. Died July, 1865.
Elmyra Agnes Hay Barclay.
Edmund Francis Hay Barclay. Born November 20t 1858.
William Herbert Hay Barclay. Born May 21st, 186
Walter Reginald Hay Barclay. Born May 20th, 186
Alice Gertrude Hay Barcla
Hugh Arthur Hay Barclay. Heir-male of Collairnie (XXII). Born August 1st, 1901. = Margaret Eleanor Bennett.
Alice Hay Barclay.
David Arthur Hay Barclay. Born December 7th, 1931.

The Barclays of the West Country

The first Barclay to appear in the records of the West of Scotland is Richard de Berkeley, styled "Dominus de Ardrossan." He is mentioned once, by Timothy Pont, in his *History of the Cuninghame* (1604–1608), as witnessing a charter of Sir Richard de Morville, Lord of Cuninghame, in 1140, granting land to the monks of Kilvining. There is good reason for assuming that he was a younger son of John de Berchlai (Towie I). ARDROSSAN

All subsequent Lords of Ardrossan are styled of that place, without family surname. In 1148 we find Fergus de Ardrossan, in 1266 Brice de Ardrossan, in 1296 Godfrey de Ardrossan, swore fealty to Edward I and subscribed the Ragman Roll. The Lords de Ardrossan continued to hold the castle until the year 1357, when, another Godfrey de Ardrossan having died without male issue, the estate was carried by the marriage of the heir-female to Sir Hugh Eglintoun of that Ilk.

There is no evidence whatever to show that the Lords of Ardrossan, subsequent to Richard de Berkeley, in 1140, were of the Berkeley family, and we may conclude that he had no issue, or that he was only temporarily in command of Ardrossan.

The Barclays of Kilbirnie and Crawford-John have been erroneously assumed to be descendants of Richard de Berkeley of Ardrossan, but it seems clear that the founder of their line was Walter de Berkeley, son of Roger de Berkeley (Towie V), who with his brother Sir Hugh de Berkeley, Justiciar of Lothian, signed a treaty with the Welsh, as has already been related. KILBIRNIE.

Tradition in the Towie Line has always held that Sir Walter settled in the west of Scotland and married the co-heiress of Crawford-John and Kilbirnie, and that he was known as "of Ayrshire." Scottish Barclays, p. 109.

Sir Walter is supposed to have died in 1286.

The second Lord of Kilbirnie and Crawford-John was JOHN DE BERKELEY, so styled in a charter dated June 11th, 1309, which is printed in the *Red Book of Menteith*.

PEDIGREE XV.

Kilbirnie, Ladyland and Pierston Lines

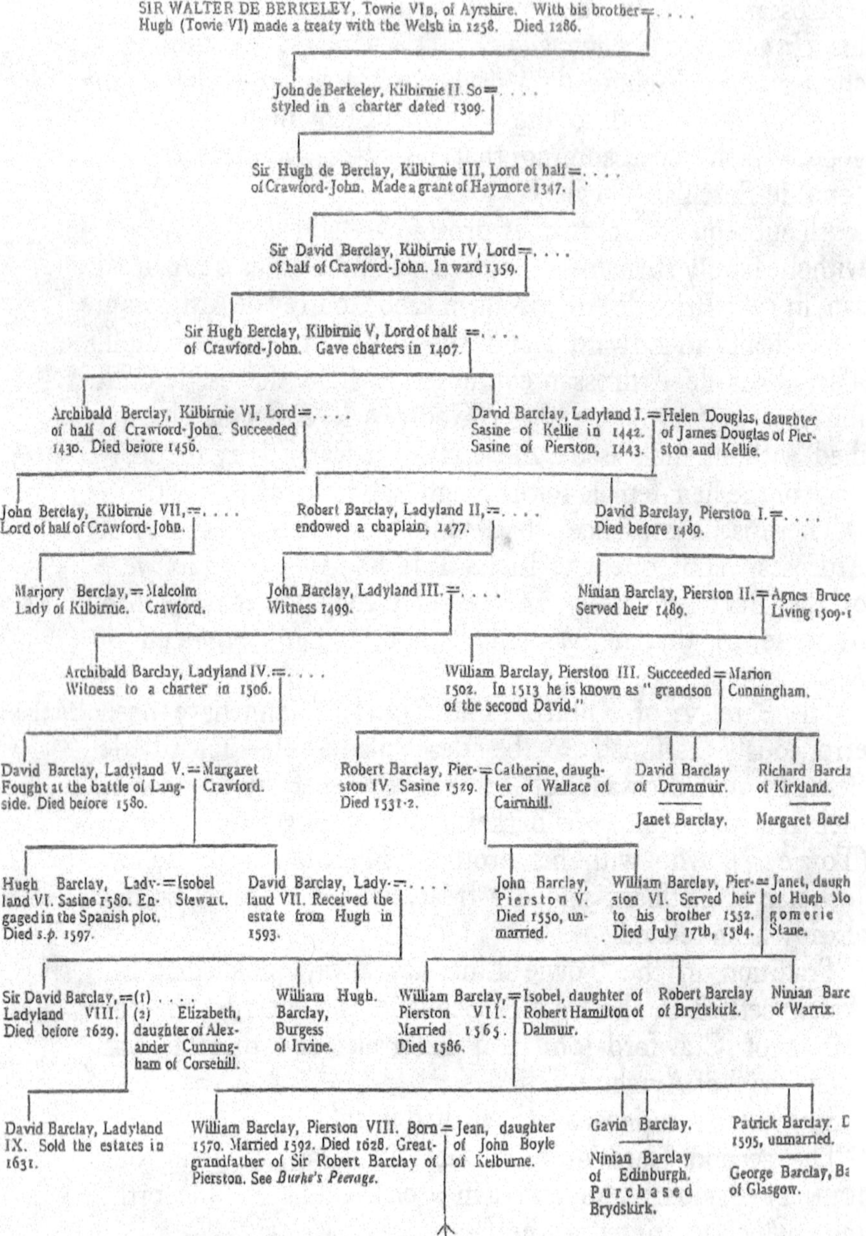
SIR WALTER DE BERKELEY, Towie VIB, of Ayrshire. With his brother Hugh (Towie VI) made a treaty with the Welsh in 1258. Died 1286. = ...
John de Berkeley, Kilbirnie II. So styled in a charter dated 1309. = ...
Sir Hugh de Berclay, Kilbirnie III, Lord of half of Crawford-John. Made a grant of Haymore 1347. = ...
Sir David Berclay, Kilbirnie IV, Lord of half of Crawford-John. In ward 1359. = ...
Sir Hugh Berclay, Kilbirnie V, Lord of half of Crawford-John. Gave charters in 1407. = ...
Archibald Berclay, Kilbirnie VI, Lord of half of Crawford-John. Succeeded 1430. Died before 1456. = ...
David Barclay, Ladyland I. Sasine of Kellie in 1442. Sasine of Pierston, 1443. = Helen Douglas, daughter of James Douglas of Pierston and Kellie.
John Berclay, Kilbirnie VII, Lord of half of Crawford-John. = ...
Robert Barclay, Ladyland II, endowed a chaplain, 1477. = ...
David Barclay, Pierston I. Died before 1489. = ...
Marjory Berclay, Lady of Kilbirnie. = Malcolm Crawford.
John Barclay, Ladyland III. Witness 1499. = ...
Ninian Barclay, Pierston II. Served heir 1489. = Agnes Bruce Living 1509-1
Archibald Barclay, Ladyland IV. Witness to a charter in 1506. = ...
William Barclay, Pierston III. Succeeded 1502. In 1513 he is known as "grandson of the second David." = Marion Cunningham.
David Barclay, Ladyland V. Fought at the battle of Langside. Died before 1580. = Margaret Crawford.
Robert Barclay, Pierston IV. Sasine 1529. Died 1531-2. = Catherine, daughter of Wallace of Cairnhill.
David Barclay of Drummuir.
Janet Barclay.
Richard Barcla of Kirkland.
Margaret Barcl
Hugh Barclay, Ladyland VI. Sasine 1580. Engaged in the Spanish plot. Died s.p. 1597. = Isobel Stewart.
David Barclay, Ladyland VII. Received the estate from Hugh in 1593. = ...
John Barclay, Pierston V. Died 1550, unmarried.
William Barclay, Pierston VI. Served heir to his brother 1552. Died July 17th, 1584. = Janet, daugh of Hugh Mo gomerie Stane.
Sir David Barclay, Ladyland VIII. Died before 1629. = (1) . . . . (2) Elizabeth, daughter of Alexander Cunningham of Corsehill.
William Barclay, Burgess of Irvine.
Hugh.
William Barclay, Pierston VII. Married 1565. Died 1586. = Isobel, daughter of Robert Hamilton of Dalmuir.
Robert Barclay of Brydskirk.
Ninian Barc of Warrix.
David Barclay, Ladyland IX. Sold the estates in 1631.
William Barclay, Pierston VIII. Born 1570. Married 1592. Died 1628. Great-grandfather of Sir Robert Barclay of Pierston. See Burke's Peerage. = Jean, daughter of John Boyle of Kelburne.
Gavin Barclay.
Ninian Barclay of Edinburgh. Purchased Brydskirk.
Patrick Barclay. D 1595, unmarried.
George Barclay, Ba of Glasgow.

Sir Hugh de Berclay (Kilbirnie III), Lord of Kilbirnie and Crawford-John, who on February 26th, 1347-8, made a grant of his lands of Haymore to his vassal John Mackmoran for services rendered and to be rendered to him. Haymore (Haymuir) was a farm in the parish of Stewarton, and part of the Barony of Bonshaw in Ayrshire. KILBIRNIE. Pont's Cuninghame, p. 102.

Sir David Berclay (Kilbirnie IV) of Kilbirnie and half Crawford-John appears to have inherited the estates as a youth, as we find in the Exchequer Rolls that he was in ward in the year 1359.

Sir Hugh Berclay (Kilbirnie V) was the next owner of the estates of Kilbirnie and Crawford-John; he was the father of two sons. About the year 1407 he granted to his eldest son, Archibald, a charter of half all his lands of "Ledilandis de Kylbyny, in the Barony of Cuninghame, Sheriffdom of Are, viz.:—Langlandis, Welhirst, Milnside, half of Resslezet and Auchinhuffe." And by another charter he granted to his son David the other half of the lands of "Ledilandis, viz.: Estircathus, Closingarthe, Hutehirst, Gatehirst, Thyrnelehill and half of Resslezet." These charters have no date, but appear to have been granted at the same time, as they are both attested at Kilbirnie by the same witnesses. They were confirmed by King James I, at Edinburgh, March 25th, 1430. Pont's Cuninghame, p. 308. Ladyland Charter Chest.

Sir Hugh appears to have died about the year 1430, leaving two sons. He was succeeded by his eldest son, Archibald (Kilbirnie VI). David, his second son (Ladyland I), assumed that territorial designation, and of him later.

Archibald Berclay (Kilbirnie VI) inherited the estates from his father about the year 1430. He lived in the reigns of James II and James III, and, as has been already pointed out when writing the history of other branches of the family, it was at this time that the country was plunged into civil war. Nobles were warring against each other, and but few charters were drawn and witnessed, and we have no records of Archibald.

He died in or before the year 1456.

John Berclay (Kilbirnie VII) succeeded his father,

KILBIRNIE. Archibald, about the year 1456. In that year he was fined by the Sheriff of Lanark, Lord Hamilton, on September 30th. The entry in the Exchequer Rolls is as follows :—

Exchequer Rolls, Vol. vi, p. 162.

"Amerciament of John Berclay of Kilbirnie for his lands which he holds of our Lord the King in Crawford-John."

Acta Auditorum, p. 32.

On May 16th, 1474, John Berclay and George Montgomery fought an unsuccessful action against John Stewart of Buchan before the Lords Auditors.

John Berclay died before 1481 and was succeeded in the estates of Kilbirnie and Crawford-John by his only child, Marjory.

Exchequer Rolls, Vol. ix, p. 68.

MARJORY BERCLAY (Kilbirnie VIII) had sasine as heir to her father, John Berclay, in the year 1481.

Reg. Mag. Sig., 1424–1513, No. 2490.

She married, in 1470, Malcolm Crawford of Greenock, a descendant of the family who originally owned Crawford-John. They had issue, and on April 24th, 1499, the Lady of Kilbirnie resigned her lands to their eldest son, Malcolm Crawford. The charter of resignation was witnessed by John Berclay (Ladyland III).

The Barclays of Kilbirnie thus ceased to exist. The family of Crawford are now represented as heirs-of-line by that of Shaw-Stewart, Barons of Greenock and Blackhall.

The old castle of Kilbirnie was built by the Barclays during the first half of the fourteenth century, prior to the general introduction of firearms, as is shown by the absence of gun ports. It was unfortunately destroyed by fire in the year 1757. The old tower still stands, an imposing structure, 41 ft. long by 32 ft. broad. The walls are 7 ft. thick.

The Barclays of Ladyland

The old house on the estate of Ladyland, in the parish of Kilbirnie, spoken of by Timothy Pont as "ane strong Tower" seems to have been built for defensive purposes. It was pulled down in 1815, but a portion still remains which is 6 ft. thick. LADYLAND.

DAVID BARCLAY (Ladyland I) was the second son of Sir Hugh Berclay (Kilbirnie V), who granted to his younger son, David, the estate of Ladyland in the year 1407.

David Barclay was known as "of Ladyland."

He married Helen Douglas, the youngest daughter of James Douglas of Pierston, Ayrshire, and Baron of Kellie, Forfarshire. She was co-portioner with her sisters: Agnes, who married John Blair of Adamton, and Margaret, who married Archibald Crawford of Auchinames.

David Barclay had sasine of a portion of Kellie in 1442, and half the lands of Pierston in 1443. Exchequer Rolls, Vol. ix, p. 657.

Agnes Blair, Archibald Crawford and David Barclay resigned their lands and Barony of Kellie to William Ochterlony, confirmed by Crown charter signed at Stirling, November 4th, 1443.

Pont tells us that David Barclay was witness to a Crown charter in 1451–2. We know that he was living in the year 1456, when his second son was styled "Master and Patron of Pierston," as will be shown later.

David and his wife Helen Douglas had two sons, the eldest of whom, Robert, succeeded to the estates of Ladyland, while the younger, David, received the lands of Pierston (see that line).

ROBERT BARCLAY (Ladyland II) succeeded his father in the estate of Ladyland. He is mentioned in the *Muniments of Irvine*, Vol. i, as endower of a chaplaincy in the church of Irvine, on August 18th, 1477.

JOHN BARCLAY (Ladyland III) succeeded his father, Robert, before the year 1499, for on April 24th of that year, as has been already stated, he was one of the witnesses to a charter of resignation by Marjory Barclay, Lady of Kilbirnie, in favour of her eldest son. The list of witnesses is interesting and includes Thomas Crawford and James Crawford "filiis naturalibus dicte Marjorie," John Barclay of Ladyland and David Barclay in Boghouse.

ARCHIBALD BARCLAY (Ladyland IV) appears in a charter dated December 18th, 1506, by which John Lord Sempill granted the lands of Kilbrachen in Renfrewshire for chaplaincies in the College of Lochkynneoth, diocese of Glasgow. The witnesses include Robert Crawford of Kilbirnie, Florimund Sempill, Archibald Barclay and others.

Reg. Mag. Sig., 1424–1513, No. 3020.

Among the Laing Charters, dated November 10th, 1537, there is an instrument of sasine, proceeding on a precept from King James V, dated November 8th, for infefting John Fullarton as nearest and lawful heir of his father, the late John Fullarton of Corsby, in the lands of Troon, with fishings, the lands of Fullarton with fishings from Troon inclusive to the mouth, and those of the water of Irvine from the mouth, etc., and other lands, taking security for £253 13s. 4d. of the fermes of the said lands. The witnesses include David Blair of Adamton, Archibald Barclay and George More, presbyter of Glasgow diocese, "by apostolic authority notary public."

Laing Charters, p. iii.

In neither of these charters is Archibald Barclay designated as of Ladyland, but the dates and the names of his co-witnesses Robert Crawford and David Blair make it safe to assume that he was the Laird of Ladyland.

DAVID BARCLAY (Ladyland V) was one of a jury of eleven in the trial of Patrick Houston of that Ilk and others for invading Andrew Hamilton of Cockno within the burgh of Dumbarton, on March 18th, 1564.

Pitcairn's Trials, Vol. i, p. 450.

With several other noblemen and gentlemen of Ayrshire, he joined the standard of Mary Queen of Scots at Hamilton in Lanarkshire and fought in the battle of Langside, May 13th, 1568, when her cause was lost and she fled to England. Apparently in consequence of this, on May 24th, 1568, he was charged to give up Ladyland House as a seditious person, "an enemy to the King's Majestie and common weal of Scotland."

Montgomeries of Eglinton, Vol. ii, p. 192.

Register of Privy Council, Vol. i, p. 625.

In 1576 he seems to have had a feud with his kinsman Malcolm Crawford of Kilbirnie, as we find in the Register of the Privy Council that bonds were given that they should both be of good behaviour.

LADYLAND.

Register of Privy Council, Vol. ii, p. 548.

He married Margaret Crawford, and by her, who was alive on April 24th, 1593, he had issue two sons: Hugh, who succeeded him, and David, who on the death of his brother without male issue inherited the estate of Ladyland. He had also a daughter Isobel, who married, as his second wife, Hugh Crawford of Kilbirnie.

HUGH BARCLAY (Ladyland VI) had sasine as heir to his father, David, in 1580. Early in life he "imbibed Popish principles" and was obliged to leave the country. In 1587 he returned, and in a list of "Certaine Grievers" of the Kirk of Scotland given into His Majesty on February 20th of that year he is included among those who "pollute the land with idolatrie." It was said of him that he was "lately come out of Flanders, an apostate, reasoning against the truth and blaspheming."

He was deeply involved in the "Spanish plot," an account of which has already been given in this History, and was mentioned in Kerr's confession as "Hugh Barclay of Ladyland." He was imprisoned in Edinburgh, but shortly released. He then came under suspicion of having treasonable correspondence with the Jesuits and was committed a prisoner to Glasgow Castle, but escaped and fled to Spain. He returned to Scotland with a party of his friends, and took possession of the Rock of Ailsa, using it as a temporary station for forces which the King of Spain was to send. One night he met a party of his enemies on the shore, and to avoid the disgrace of capture he rushed into the sea and was drowned.

In happier days this Laird of Ladyland had associates of a different class. He was a friend of Montgomerie, the author of *The Cherry and the Slae*. Two sonnets written by him addressed to Montgomerie have been preserved.

He married Isobel Stewart, who was probably of the family of Stewart of Fairlie Crevoche, in the parish of Stewarton,

LADYLAND. county Ayr. Isobel Lady of Ladyland appears in the will of John Barclay, "in Kilbirnie," in July, 1618. Hugh died without issue in 1597.

DAVID BARCLAY (Ladyland VII) succeeded his brother Hugh, who had executed a conveyance of his estate on April 24th, 1593, in favour of David and his heirs-male, and on their failure to the nearest heir-male of entail of Hugh, to be held of himself, with a reservation of a life-rent out of them to his mother, Margaret Crawford, and to Isobel Stewart, his own spouse. This disposition was confirmed May 7th, 1593.

Pont's Cuninghame, p. 310.

Reg. Mag. Sig.

The name of David's wife is not known, but he had issue three sons: Sir David, who succeeded him; William, a burgess of Irvine, who in 1619 with his spouse was infeft in a certain tenement in that burgh; and Hugh, who was witness to a sasine in 1616 and again in 1619. David died before the year 1606.

Scottish Barclays, p. 112.

SIR DAVID BARCLAY (Ladyland VIII) was served heir to his father David in the 20 merk land of old extent of Ladyland and Auchenhuiff on March 25th, 1606. The honour of knighthood was conferred on him by James VI.

In 1617 he gave a sum of money on loan to Hugh, fifth Lord Sempill. He was probably identical with the Sir David Barclay who was, on August 25th, 1625, summoned to Court concerning his mission to Spain.

Sir David seems to have married twice. His second wife was Elizabeth Cunningham, daughter of Alexander Cunningham of Corsehill, county Ayr, and relict of John Crawford, younger of Crawford-land.

By his first marriage he had issue an only son, David, who succeeded him.

Scottish Barclays, p. 112.

Sir David died before October 15th, 1629.

DAVID BARCLAY (Ladyland IX) was served heir to his father in the estates of Ladyland and Auchenhuiff on October 15th, 1629.

His father had become cautioner for a debt in 1621 which had never been paid, and in 1631 he was, as his heir, forced to pay this, with costs, by the order of the Lords of Session.

It was at the instigation of John Blair of Cloberhill, in the parish of Stewarton, who in the same year was infeft in the estate of Ladyland. LADYLAND.

The estate was sold in 1669 to Captain William Hamilton, son of James Hamilton of Arcoch, from whose family it passed in 1710.

Whether David Barclay, the last Laird of Ladyland, married or left any issue is unknown, and who is the heir-male or heir-of-line to-day it is impossible to discover, but that some members of the family continued to reside in the parish of Kilbirnie up to the middle of the eighteenth century seems certain. Scottish Barclays, p. 112.

The Barclays of Canal Bank, who are descended from Robert Barclay "in Kilbirnie" and his wife Elizabeth Sheddon, and the Barclays of Abbey Mills, Paisley, descended from John Barclay "in the parish of Kilbirnie," are stated to have been of the Ladyland stock. These families have been fully dealt with by Captain Leslie Barclay in his *History of the Scottish Barclays*.

The Barclays of Pierston

PIERSTON.

David Barclay (Pierston I) was the second son of David Barclay (Ladyland I), who had sasine of the lands of Pierston, as heir to his father-in-law, James Douglas, in 1443.

The first mention of him is in a charter dated July 16th, 1456, when he exchanged "the Browylands with the pertinents lying within the ancient village of Pierston" for the lands of Caprieston, the property of Robert Cunningham of Cunninghamhead, county Ayr, the transaction being "in pure excambie." In this deed he is styled "Master and Patron of Pierston."

Scottish Barclays, p. 51.

In another charter dated November 18th, 1461–2, he is called Lord of Pierston.

David Barclay died in the year 1489.

Ninian Barclay (Pierston II) succeeded his father, David Barclay (Pierston I), in the year 1489. He was retoured heir to his father in the £10 lands of Pierston, and in ten bolls of meal from the lands of Bourtreehill, etc., April 24th, 1489.

He married Agnes Bruce (styled Agnes Bruce, Lady of Pierston), and by her, who was living in January, 1509–10, he had a son William Barclay (Pierston III).

Ninian Barclay died before the 10th July, 1501.

William Barclay (Pierston III) was retoured heir to his father, April 11th, 1502, and had sasine of Pierston, the lands of Bourtreehill, Bertanholm, Bogside and Borrowmill, in the parish of Irvine in 1502–3.

Exchequer Rolls, Vol. xii, p. 712.

On November 24th, 1509, he is witness to a grant by John Crawford to Robert of Cunninghamhead and Margaret Mure, his wife, of the lands of Mydle.

Reg. Mag. Sig. 1424–1513, No. 2484.

He was also witness to a Crown charter, dated July 10th, 1510.

Scottish Barclays, p. 86.

In the *Protocol Book of Gavin Ross* (1512–1524) there is an Instrument from Robert Cunningham of Cunninghamhead, which states as follows: "Not withstanding that William Barclay of Pierston freely resigned the lands of Caprieston, which the late Ninian Barclay and William himself held in security in the hands of the said Robert, as superior by staff and baton from himself, he binds himself anew to infeft William Barclay in full form and grant a new charter and sasine." PIERSTON. Scot. Rec. Soc. No. 32.

He also appears in a precept signed March 6th, 1515–16, and in a letter disposing of some property at Pierston to one Adam Boyd, April 5th, 1527. He was a witness to a proclamation at the Cross of the burgh of Ayr, January 2nd, 1519. He is again a witness in the Tolbooth of Ayr for David Blair, son and heir apparent of the late John Blair of Adamton, "a noble young man, true heir of Adamton, and heir portioner of Pierston, proving his age." *Ibid.* No. 362.

He appears twice as an arbitrator in the year 1527. And in the Accounts of the Lords Auditors for the same year he is given credit for a sum of £13 6s. 8d. received from him, due on the lands sold to Adam Boyd. *Ibid.* Nos. 578, 770.

William Barclay married Marion Cunningham, and by her he had issue three sons and two daughters. His eldest son, Robert, succeeded him. David, his second son, was known as of Drummuir, and his third son, Richard, of Kirkland. His two daughters, Janet and Margaret, are both mentioned in the will of their nephew William (Pierston VI). The laird died before April 20th, 1529.

ROBERT BARCLAY (Pierston IV) had sasine as heir of his father on April 20th, 1529, done in the Tolbooth of Ayr, April 6th, 1529. Scot. Rec. Soc. Gavin Ross, No. 981.

He had a charter of his father, in favour of himself and his spouse, of the lands of Law, on the estate of Pierston, September 15th, 1518.

He married Catherine Wallace, daughter of Wallace of Cairnhill. The laird held the estates for only a very short period and died before February 21st, 1531–2, leaving issue two sons and one daughter. His eldest son John succeeded him in the estate of Pierston and his young son, William, succeeded his brother, who died without issue.

JOHN BARCLAY (Pierston V) succeeded his father, Robert, before February 21st, 1531–2. He was a minor, and on attaining lawful age he had sasine on November 7th, 1539.

PIERSTON.

In 1530 Robert Tempiltoun of Tourlandis became cautioner for Lawrence Crawford of Kilbirnie in 600 merks "that John Barclay shall be safe from bodily injury in terms of letter from the King."

Scot. Rec. Soc. Protocol Book of Gavin, No. 1077.

In 1548 he was at law with his brother William. The laird died without issue between Whitsunday and Martinmas 1550, and was succeeded by his brother.

WILLIAM BARCLAY (Pierston VI) had sasine, as heir to his brother John, January 23rd, 1551–2, the lands having been in non-entry for a year and a term.

Exchequer Rolls, Vol. xviii, p. 509.

He is described in a deed dated at Lanark, December 10th, 1550, as "William Barclay, brother german to the late John Barclay of Pierston."

He married Janet Montgomerie, daughter of Hugh Montgomerie of Stane, county Ayr, elder surviving son of the Honourable William Montgomerie of Stane (second son of Hugh, first Earl of Eglinton, and his wife, Helen Campbell, daughter of Colin, first Earl of Argyle).

By his wife, Janet, William Barclay had three sons and one daughter: William, who succeeded him in the lands of Pierston, and is often mentioned as "fiar" of that estate; Robert, who succeeded to Brydskirk, and had a son David, who sold that estate; and Ninian, who inherited Warrix and was in the possession of these lands in 1587. The lands of Warrix remained in the hands of this branch of the Barclays of Pierston until the year 1777, when Charlotte Barclay of Warrix married, as his second wife, George Colquhoun of Tilliquhoun, county Dumbarton.

William Barclay (Pierston VI) had, as has been already stated, a daughter Margaret, who died in her father's lifetime before 1578. She married Alexander Cunningham of Toir.

Scottish Barclays, p. 88.

William Barclay (Pierston VI) was witness to a surety by Hugh, third Earl of Eglinton, and George Buchanan of that Ilk, for the Earl of Menteith "appearing before the Privy Council when required and keeping good rule," dated at Holyrood, February 16th, 1577-8.

He died July 17th, 1584.

WILLIAM BARCLAY (Pierston VII) first appears in the year 1564 in the accounts of the Lord High Treasurer, in an entry as follows:— PIERSTON.

"£40 in settlement of a charter of confirmation of the £10 lands, formerly extending from Pierston and Righouse with the tower, fortalice and mill and multures, lying within the sheriffdom of Ayr, granted to William Barclay, son and apparent heir of William Barclay of Pierston, and his heirs and assigns." Accounts of Lord High Treasurer, Vol. xi, p. 273.

There is a Bond of Manrent by William Barclay, "fiar of Pierston," to Hugh, third Earl of Eglinton; it is dated August 29th, 1577, and is signed "William Barclay, younger of Pierston." Memorials of Montgomeries of Eglinton, Vol. ii, p. 216.

In the Register of the Privy Council of King James VI, we find an entry dated March 9th, 1574-5, showing that William Barclay "fiar of Pierston" obtained a decreet charging Margaret Cunynghame, relict of "umquhile Maister David Barclay" of Drummuir, and William Lyn her spouse, to "flit and remove themselves, servands, subtenentis, guids etc. from the 46s. land of Drummuir in the parish of Pierston.". He had been infefted in these lands in 1564. Register of Privy Council, Vol. ii, p. 438.

He succeeded his father on July 17th, 1584. On February 27th, 1584-5, he had a precept for infefting him in the Temple-lands of Pierston.

He married Isobel Hamilton (contract dated May 10th, 1565), daughter of Robert Hamilton of Dalmuir, by whom he had issue five sons and one daughter. His eldest son, William, succeeded him. Gavin became a burgess of Irvine and died in 1604. Patrick, who died in June, 1595, apparently unmarried, is mentioned as "son lawful to late William Barclay of Pierston" in 1606 in the Commisariat of Glasgow (1547-1800). George, a merchant and bailie of Glasgow, acted as executor to his brother Patrick, and also to his sister-in-law Jean Boyle, Lady of Pierston, of whom later. His will was confirmed at Glasgow March 21st, 1654-5. Ninian was apprenticed to John Somervell of Edinburgh, February 26th, 1600-1, and became a merchant and bailie of that burgh. He purchased the estate of Brydskirk from his cousin David Barclay, as before mentioned. His will was confirmed at Edinburgh, May 16th, 1629.

PIERSTON.

William Barclay (Pierston VII) died June 26th, 1586, and was succeeded by his eldest son.

Exchequer Rolls, Vol. xxii, p. 461.

Pont's Cuninghame, p. 348.

WILLIAM BARCLAY (Pierston VIII) was evidently born in 1570, as on attaining lawful age he had sasine, "as heir to his father, December 13th, 1591, the lands having been in the King's hands for five and a half years by reason of ward." He had previously received precept of infefting him in the lands of Drummuir in October, 1586.

On December 19th, 1589, he was charged before the Lord Chancellor, Sir John Maitland of Thirlstane, for assisting William Cunningham of Tourlands, put to the horn for not surrendering Cunninghamhead to the above Chancellor. The entry is as follows :—

Register of Privy Council, Vol. iv, p. 446.

"William Barclay of Pierston, Lawrence Lin of Bourtriehill etc. . . . to the number of eight Score persons all bodin in weirlike manner with jakkit, lang gunnis and pistollettis, they have collected mails and duties tenents and repaired to Cunninghamhead kept by the Chancellor's servands and shot and discharged their said gunnis and pistollettis at the windows thereof."

Scottish Barclays, p. 90.

He had a Crown charter in favour of himself and his spouse of the £2 6s. lands of old extent of Law, on the estate of Pierston, dated June 17th, 1592. On March 30th, 1605, he was served tutor to his niece, Jean Barclay, daughter of the late Master Gavin Barclay, his brother, and on March 8th, 1609, he was retoured heir-general to William Barclay (abavi), his great-grandfather's father (Pierston III).

Pont's Cuninghame, p. 348.

Reg. Privy Council, Vol. v, p. 703.

He appears in a bond, dated 1598, as principal, together with John Crawford of Kilbirnie, David Barclay of Ladyland and many others.

Ibid. Vol. vi, p. 745.

On August 31st, 1602, he is cautioner for Robert Barclay, his uncle, for 500 merks . . . Bonds subscribed at Irving before Ninian Barclay, Provost of Irving, Lawrence Lyn, and Mr. Gavin Barclay.

William Barclay (Pierston VIII) married May 24th, 1592, Jean Boyle, eldest daughter of John Boyle of Kelburne (ancestor of the Earls of Glasgow), by his spouse Marion Crawford, second daughter of Hugh Crawford of Kilbirnie.

Her maternal grandmother was Isobel Barclay, daughter of David Barclay (Ladyland V). PIERSTON.

By Jean Boyle, Lady Pierston, who died in July, 1631, he had with other issue a son Robert (Pierston IX).

On June 25th, 1627, the King confirmed a charter of William Barclay of Pierston, being the marriage settlement of his son Robert. The witnesses included George Barclay, merchant and citizen of Glasgow. Reg. Mag. Sig. 1620–1633, No. 1093.

William Barclay (Pierston VIII) died August, 1628. He was the great-grandfather of Sir Robert Barclay of Pierston, who was created a baronet of Nova Scotia, October 22nd, 1668.

The remaining generations of the Barclays of Pierston to the fourteenth baronet, the present holder of the title, Sir Colville Herbert Sanford Barclay, Bart., of Pierston, co. Ayr, born May 7th, 1913, have been set forth in *Burke's Peerage*. The history of the family has been ably dealt with by Captain Leslie Barclay in his *History of the Scottish Barclays*.

www.ingramcontent.com/pod-product-compliance
Lightning Source LLC
Chambersburg PA
CBHW071351290326
41932CB00045B/1420

* 9 7 8 1 5 8 5 4 9 8 5 8 1 *